Principles of
Irish Human Rights Law

Principles of Irish Human Rights Law

By
Dr Elaine Dewhurst
BCL, PhD
Dr Noelle Higgins
BA, HDipEd, MA, LLM, PhD
Los Watkins
BA, LLB, PGDip, LLM

CLARUS
PRESS

Published by
Clarus Press Ltd,
Griffith Campus,
South Circular Road,
Dublin 8.

Typeset by
Datapage International Limited,
18 Docklands Innovation Park,
East Wall Road,
Dublin 3.

Printed by
CPI Group (UK) Ltd,
Croydon,
CR0 4YY,
UK.

ISBN
978-1-905536-50-4

Do mo thuismitheoirí, Paddy agus Kathleen:
Noelle Higgins

To my husband, John Cotter and to my parents, Margaret and Peter:
Elaine Dewhurst

To my son, Chris:
Los Watkins

FOREWORD

The concept of rights is by no means new and has constantly evolved throughout the ages. Rights have been intricately tied to religions, customs and laws throughout history. One of the first references to individual rights protecting people from arbitrary persecution and punishment dates back approximately 4000 years. In ancient Greece the concept of natural rights began to develop and was continued in the laws of ancient Rome. In ancient Ireland the Brehon Law was progressive in many ways, recognising divorce, gender equality and showed concern for the environment. However what we understand by human rights today is quite different to the natural rights of the past.

Human rights, as we understand them, are a relatively modern concept developed in the 20th Century largely in response to the aftermath of World War II. As John F. Kennedy said, "The rights of every man are diminished when the rights of one man are threatened." In the intervening years the study, practice and implementation of human rights have become an increasingly important consideration for all lawyers, advocates and policy makers.

Much has been written about the development of the rights enumerated and unenumerated in the Irish Constitution in the Irish courts and more written about the impact of the European Convention of Human Rights since its incorporation into domestic law in 2003. Relatively little has been written thus far as to how the Charter of Fundamental Rights enshrined in European law since December 2009 in the Treaty of Lisbon will impact on the protection and development of human rights in this country. This textbook uniquely compares the modern principles of Irish human rights law through these sources; nationally, regionally and internationally.

Aimed at students of human rights law this book is an excellent introduction to the subject, providing a helpful definition of terms and history of how human rights have developed. The analysis and examination of the sources of these rights and the authors' consideration of the principles emerging through jurisprudence under each of the key rights identified is balanced, insightful and will no doubt provide an excellent starting point for any student interested in this subject. In each of the chapters devoted to examining the key rights the authors carefully explore the principles developed by the relevant courts, and clearly signal the similarities of approach, identify differences and highlight areas where law reform might be considered. They remind us too that with rights come important duties and obligations.

This comparison of the local, regional and international systems and principles will no doubt prove to be a most useful tool not just for the students for whom this book is primarily intended but will prove to be of great interest to practitioners and anyone interested in this developing area of law.

I congratulate the authors on this important and insightful publication.

Colin Daly
Judge of the District Court
24 September 2012

PREFACE

This book provides a unique overview and insight into the three levels of human rights protection in Ireland (national protection, regional protection and international protection) through a rights-based analysis of the relevant legal principles. This book was inspired by a desire to clarify the law relating to human rights by consolidating the increasing jurisprudence on human rights in Ireland which was emanating, and which continues to emanate, from the Irish courts, the European Court of Human Rights, the European Court of Justice and the UN treaty bodies. In an effort to consolidate and succinctly analyse these legal principles, each chapter begins with an investigation of the constitutional protection under Irish law, the protection afforded under the European Convention on Human Rights and under the Charter of Fundamental Rights and finally a brief analysis of the protection of the right at an international level. For ease of reference, and to ensure consistency, each section of the chapter examines the nature of the human right in question, considers what amounts to an interference with the right and outlines acceptable justifications for such interferences, as well as considering the impact of the doctrine of proportionality. This book aims to provide not only a succinct examination of the legal principles, but also insightful comment on the current legal framework and recommendations for reform. It is hoped that this book will be of use and practical benefit to students, academics, legal practitioners, researchers and members of the public.While the authors have taken every effort to ensure the accuracy of this book, any errors that remain are the sole responsibility of the authors.

Elaine Dewhurst

Noelle Higgins

Los Watkins

14 September 2012

ACKNOWLEDGEMENT

There were many people involved in making this book possible and the authors would like to thank everyone who contributed in any small way to this publication.

In particular, the authors would like to thank Mr David McCartney of Clarus Press for his commitment, energy, and enthusiasm in making this publication a reality. This book would not have been possible without his dedication and hard work. Special thanks must also be given to Ms Amina Adanan for her expert research assistance and for her good humour and persistence throughout.

The authors would also like to thank the Office of the Vice President for Research and Innovation of Dublin City University for the Publication Assistance Fund which made the funding of the research assistant possible. We would also like to thank our colleagues, the administration staff and the librarians at the institutions of Dublin City University, and the Max Planck Institute for Social Law and Social Policy for their unfailing support throughout this process.

Elaine Dewhurst would like to thank her husband and her family for supporting her throughout the entire process. She would also like to thank all her colleagues at DCU and at the Max Planck Institute for being so patient and encouraging.

In particular, she would like to thank Dr Brenda Daly, Dr Noel McGrath and Mr Mark Coen for their constant good humour and friendship.

Ba mhaith le Noelle Higgins buíochas croíúil a ghabháil lena muintir agus lena dlúthchairde áille. Ba mhaith léi freisin buíochas a ghabháil lena hiar-chomhoibrithe agus a cairde i DCU, Dr Yvonne Daly agus Dr Michael Doherty. Ní bheidh a léithéid arís ann!

Los Watkins would like to give his heartfelt thanks to all those who have supported, helped and encouraged him.

TABLE OF CONTENTS

TABLE OF CASES

TABLE OF LEGISLATION

Primary Legislation

Secondary Legislation

UN Resolutions

EU Directives, Framework Decisions and Regulations

Other Jurisdictions

CHAPTER 1
Introduction

Introduction

The principles of Irish Human Rights law derive from three distinct areas of law: national, regional, and international law. In the national context, human rights are protected by the Irish Constitution (particularly, but not exclusively, Arts 40–44) and by legislation (in particular, the European Convention on Human Rights Act 2003 (ECHR)). At a regional level, human rights are protected by two distinct bodies: the Council of Europe (in particular, the European Convention on Human Rights) and the European Union (in particular, the Charter of Fundamental Rights (CFR)). At an international level, human rights are protected by the international instruments developed, in particular, by the United Nations. This book will examine the fundamental human rights in turn and will analyse the protection of the right under national, regional, and international law. **[1–01]**

However, before this examination and analysis begins, it is important to consider what we mean by the term "human rights", where these rights derive from, and how human rights are protected at a national, regional and international level.

A. What are "Human Rights" and Where Do They Come From?

In order to consider the subject of "human rights", which are often misquoted and misunderstood, it is necessary to understand the background to this concept. Human rights are a relatively modern concept; for most of documented history there was little sympathy with or support for them, as the right then belonged to the most powerful (usually militarily) person or group in a specific area. **[1–02]**

The Definition and Characteristics of Human Rights

The most common definition of human rights is that formulated by the United Nations Office of the High Commissioner for Human Rights, which defines "human rights" as: **[1–03]**

> "... basic rights and freedoms that all people are entitled to regardless of nationality, sex, national or ethnic origin, race, religion, language, or other status".

There are certain generally agreed features of human rights, which may be grouped into six sections:

(1) People have rights simply because they are human - therefore they have the right to lead a dignified and human life, and the right to work towards achieving this for all people. These rights cannot be earned, nor are they lost for bad behaviour.
(2) Human rights are universal - they take no account of race, sex, colour or other status.
(3) Human rights treat all people as equal—this follows the idea that "all human beings are born free and equal in rights and dignity"[1] and are therefore deserving of the same opportunities and treatment, whilst simultaneously respecting their different cultures and traditions, political persuasion, sexuality, social origin, status, etc. Governments must therefore work to create the same opportunities for all the people in their country and this may involve extra work to make those opportunities the same for certain sections in society, e.g. women, children, people with disabilities or racial minorities.
(4) These rights belong primarily, but not exclusively, to individuals—this means that they are concerned with the relationship between an individual and the State. Consequently, it is for the government of a State to create a society where each individual can enjoy and freely exercise his or her rights to the full, although sometimes the opposition forces or political parties also have a responsibility to uphold human rights in their actions.
(5) Human rights encompass the fundamental principles of humanity—many rights are absolute and therefore cannot be overridden under any circumstances. Examples of rights of this type are the right to life, freedom from slavery and freedom from torture. Other rights are not absolute and may have certain, specific limits placed upon them.
(6) The promotion and protection of human rights is not limited to national boundaries but rather stipulates certain ideals that apply the world over. The law which enables Human Rights holds States accountable for meeting legally binding and agreed conditions which seek to ensure the requisite promotion, protection and respect of Human Rights.

Types of Human Rights

[1–04] There are three main types of human rights:

(1) Civil and political rights: These rights are often referred to as "first generation rights" and are designed to protect individuals against State interference. Examples of civil and political rights include the right to life, equality and liberty. These rights are generally recognised in all human rights instruments.
(2) Economic, social and cultural rights: These rights are often referred to as "second generation rights" and often require State action to ensure their protection. Examples of economic, social and cultural rights include the right to

[1] Universal Declaration of Human Rights, Art 1.

an adequate standard of living, to education, housing and health care. These rights are not always recognised in human rights instruments. So for example, the ECHR, while protecting some economic, social and cultural rights such as education, does not protect the majority of economic, social and cultural rights.

(3) Group rights: These are often referred to as "third generation rights" and involve the rights of a group to seek self- determination and protection. These are not generally recognised in traditional human rights instruments or in domestic law, but are becoming increasingly prevalent at an international level, for example, the UN Convention on the Rights of Migrant Workers and Members of Their Families.

Discussion has taken place in recent years on a possible fourth generation of rights, rights which are for the good of all humankind, rather than just for the good of an individual or a group. Such rights relate, in particular, to new developments in biotechnology[2] and how advancements in this area can be used for the good of all humankind.[3]

The Historical Development of Human Rights

However, it is not enough to simply state that these rights exist and are agreed upon, there must also be some legitimacy of origin. Early European charters supporting the idea of certain freedoms were the *Magna Carta Libertatum*[4] of 1215, the *Union of Utrecht* in 1579[5] (Netherlands), and the *UK Bill of Rights* in 1689.[6] However, these charters all had the characteristic of specifying certain freedoms that one could claim if one held a particular status and were not all-encompassing, but rather, were conferred upon an individual, or an individual's position in society. Over the next few centuries, however, the idea of liberty gradually separated from that of status and came to be viewed as a right pertaining to all human beings. **[1–05]**

This was mirrored by the Aristotelian concept of "natural law", proposed by Aquinas and Grotius in the 13th and 17th centuries respectively, which theory suggests that there is an essential connection between law and morality. This view is frequently summarised by the maxim: an unjust law is not a true law, a point tragically

---

[2] See, for example, the Council of Europe Convention for the Protection of Human Rights and Dignity of the Human Being with regard to the Application of Biology and Medicine 1997.

[3] See F Falcón y Tella, *Challenges for Human Rights* (Martinus Nijhoff, The Netherlands, 2007), p 66.

[4] Although this, in modern terms, is very limited in scope, and certainly was not conceived of as pertaining to human rights generally, it is important as it recognises that there should be limitations on the power of the King, (i.e. the State), putting forward the concept of the Rule of Law, that government should be according to law and not the, often, arbitrary dictates of the ruler. It should also be noted that various amended versions of the charter came into being subsequently.

[5] Bringing together States with a degree of religious tolerance without recourse to the pre-existing monarchy.

[6] Which set down limits on the power of the Monarch, together with asserting the rights of Parliament and rules for allowing for freedom of speech in Parliament. It is one of the basic constitutional documents in the UK for limiting and defining the powers of the Monarch in comparison to those of the people, through an elected Parliament.

demonstrated by the anti-Semitic racial purity laws of Nazi Germany—these laws were passed through the legally elected government of the day and were considered perfectly legitimate in that State.

[1–06] The next major development was the Age of Enlightenment and Reason—a time when human rights concepts were widely developed. This was seen particularly in the work of John Locke (1632–1704),[7] who developed the idea of natural rights, and of Jean Jacques Rousseau (1712–1778) who developed Locke's work and expounded the idea of a "social contract" whereby the individual surrendered some of his natural rights to the State machinery in return for State protection and State assistance in the protection of property.

[1–07] This was also the time when the British colonies in North America strove for independence and drew up their own Declaration of Independence in 1776, based on the idea of universal equality, and the existence of certain inalienable rights. The legitimacy of these rights was stated as:

> "We hold these truths to be self-evident, that all men are created equal, that they are endowed by their Creator with certain inalienable Rights, that among these are Life, Liberty and the pursuit of Happiness. That to secure these rights, Governments are instituted among Men, deriving their just powers from the consent of the governed."

The drafters of this document therefore considered that their legitimacy came initially from God, and that they were then part of the "social contract" with the State. Also, in comparison to modern charters and conventions, it was defined by its time in that it was another century in America before women enjoyed rights equal to those of men, whilst the continued issue of slavery is too well known to require further exposition.

[1–08] This documentation was eventually incorporated into the American Bill of Rights, which is a part of the country's Constitution. Following the 1789 revolution, France, with the intellectual lead of Locke and Paine (1737–1809) taken up by Montesquieu (1689–1755) and Rousseau, adopted the Declaration of the Rights of Man (and of the Citizen) in 1789. However, by this time, and reflecting the secularism of the revolution, the emphasis of legitimacy had turned from God to the State:

> "The principle of any sovereignty resides essentially in the Nation. No body, no individual can exert authority which does not emanate expressly from it".[8]

[1–09] The rights protected in the 18th and 19th centuries can be termed as "classic" or "first generation rights", relating to the freedom of the individual and, were incorporated in many national constitutions created at this time, along with other roles for governments in the fields of employment, education, health and welfare—today these

---

[7] Locke theorised that people of the State have a right to that property which is the product of their labours, and that government should not have the right to remove that property, in taxation, for example, without the consent of the people being governed. It was an idea which was taken on by the American people in the phrase "no taxation without representation".

[8] Art III.

are defined as social rights.[9] Following the First World War, there was an attempt at international co-operative law with the establishment of the League of Nations. Although this was primarily an attempt to remove further threats of global warfare through discussion and arbitration, together with related treaties, other issues addressed were workers' labour conditions, the treatment of native inhabitants in the widespread colonial Empires of the day, human and drug trafficking, the arms trade, global health, prisoners of war, and the protection of minorities in Europe. Sadly, the rise of Fascism through the decade of the 1930s proved the League to have no realistic power of sanction, and when its bluff was repeatedly called, it was patently inadequate in response. Nevertheless, it should be seen in context as a significant milestone on the road towards international co-operation in terms of human rights, and the lessons learnt were incorporated in its successor, the post-war United Nations (UN).

The widespread reaction to the atrocities of the Second World War period can be said to mark the start of the current "era of human rights", for they ended the view that it was up to the individual State to determine how to treat its citizens. This led to the UN's[10] initial task after the War of formulating an up-to-date catalogue of human rights and freedoms to be incorporated into international law. In 1946, the UN Commission on Human Rights was established and less than two years later it had drafted the Universal Declaration of Human Rights (UDHR) which was adopted by the UN General Assembly in Paris in 1948. Subsequently, membership of the UN was made conditional on endorsement of the UDHR, thereby, in theory, increasing the sphere in which human rights operated. The preamble now stated that legitimacy derived not from God or from the State, but rather from the very fact of being human: **[1–10]**

> "Whereas recognition of the inherent dignity and of the equal and inalienable rights of all members of the human family is the foundation of freedom, justice and peace in the world . . ."

The ECHR provisions were, in many aspects, more detailed than those of the UDHR. However, the UDHR was eventually supplemented by two more detailed covenants: the International Covenant on Civil and Political Rights (ICCPR) and the International Covenant on Economic, Social and Cultural Rights (ICESCR).[11] The ICCPR does provide greater protection than the ECHR in respect of certain rights, such as non-discrimination, a fair trial and treatment while in detention; also, the ECHR mainly confined itself to the protection of civil and political rights. Yet the diverse ideologies and traditions of the UN Member States delayed the twin covenants coming into force until 1976. **[1–11]**

---

9 Ironically, rather than the classic rights being seen as internationally important, it was the social rights which were first embodied in international regulations. For example, the International Labour Organisation (ILO) was founded in 1919 and was the originator of various labour regulations.

10 The UN had 50 members in 1945; it now has approaching 200 members. Art 1 of the United Nations Charter of 1945 seeks among its purposes "to achieve international co-operation . . . in promoting and encouraging respect for human rights and for fundamental freedoms for all".

11 Together with the First and Second Optional Protocols to the ICCPR, these five documents comprise the International Bill of Human Rights (IBHR).

B. The Protection of Human Rights in Ireland

[1–12] The protection of human rights in Ireland can be divided into three specific spheres: national, regional, and international law.

Protection of Human Rights in the National Context

[1–13] At a national level, human rights are protected by the Irish Constitution and international instruments which have been incorporated into Irish law, e.g. ECHR which was incorporated by ECHR Act 2003.

The Irish Constitution

[1–14] Articles 40–44 of the Irish Constitution expressly protect a variety of rights including the right to life, liberty and freedom of religion. The drafters of the Constitution did not attach huge importance to these provisions but "in practice they have been the basis of many very significant decisions, and are invoked with steadily increasing frequency".[12] The Constitution has also given life to certain latent or unenumerated rights arising out of the wording of Art 40.3 which states that "[t]he State guarantees in its laws to respect, and, as far as practicable, by its laws to defend and vindicate the personal rights of the citizen"[13] and:

> " ... [t]he State shall, in particular, by its laws protect as best it may from unjust attack and, in the case of injustice done, vindicate the life, person, good name, and property rights of every citizen".[14]

Thus the courts have recognised that the Constitution protects, *inter alia*, the right to bodily integrity, to travel, to earn a livelihood, to legal aid, to individual privacy and marital privacy, to litigate and have access to the courts, to justice and fair procedures, to travel, to marry and procreate, to communicate and to freedom from torture and from inhuman or degrading treatment or punishment. While this recognition of latent rights has had many positive results, it has been criticised as creating a:

> " ... certain blurring of definition, a certain bursting of conceptual banks, rather as though legal rivers finding their confluence in the estuary of liberty and justice, had their courses confused by flooding further upstream, leaving a somewhat trackless delta for the constitutional geographer".[15]

This book will set out the nature and extent of most of these enumerated and unenumerated rights under the Irish Constitution. However, it is important to consider some preliminary matters in relation to the application of the Constitution, the *locus standi* required to take a human rights claim and the impact of an assessment that a measure or action is contrary to the Constitution.

---

12 GW Hogan, and GF Whyte, *JM Kelly: The Irish Constitution* (4th ed, Butterworths, Dublin 2003), p 1245.

13 Art 40.3.1°, Irish Constitution 1937.

14 Art 40.3.2°, Irish Constitution 1937.

15 GW Hogan, and GF Whyte, *supra* n 12, p 1413.

Application of the Constitutional Rights

A fundamental question arising in many cases is whether the particular constitutional right is capable of being relied upon by a particular individual. One of the most interesting debates in Irish constitutional law is that relating to whether the constitutional rights protected in Arts 40–44 apply to citizens or whether they are equally applicable to non-citizens. While this may seem obvious, the provisions of the Constitution are particularly confusing as certain rights refer specifically to the citizen. For example, Art 40.4.1° provides that "no citizen" shall be deprived of his liberty save in accordance with law, while others have no reference to citizenship. This distinction between citizens and non-citizens has given rise to some case law. **[1–15]**

Early decisions of the courts essentially denied rights to non-citizens where the rights that the non-citizens relied upon were expressly addressed to citizens. In the case of *The State (Nicolaou) v An Bord Uchtála,*[16] it was held in the High Court that non-citizens could not invoke Art 40 as it referred expressly to "citizens" as defined in Art 9 of the Constitution,[17] although the Supreme Court reserved the consideration of this question for another and more appropriate case.[18] However, more recent decisions would appear to suggest that non-citizens are entitled to rely on the provisions of the Constitution, even if they expressly refer to non-citizens. In the case of *Northants Co Council v ABF*[19] it was held that as natural law applies to all human persons, be they citizens of this State or not, the non-citizen involved was entitled to rely on Art 41. Similarly in *Finn v Attorney General*[20] it was held that these constitutional rights derive not from one's citizenship but from their nature as a human being. The State does not create these rights; it recognises them and promises to protect them.[21] While the general view would appear to be that "non-nationals will, in practice, be able to invoke the Constitution for most purposes",[22] there is still some doubt cast over those provisions that have not yet been challenged by non-nationals. **[1–16]**

Another interesting question is whether legal persons, such as companies, can rely on the provisions of the Irish Constitution. The answer to this question would appear to depend on the nature of the right being claimed. For example, it has been held in relation to the equality guarantee in Art 40.1 that it is confined by its terms and references to the "citizen" and "person" and therefore not applicable to legal persons.[23] Similarly, Arts 40 and 43 have been confined to the protection of human persons.[24] However, Art 44.2.3°, is not so confined and therefore could be relied upon by legal persons.[25] Equally, in relation to property rights, which are in a different **[1–17]**

---

16 [1966] IR 567 (*per* Henchy J).
17 *ibid* at 616–617 (*per* Henchy J).
18 *ibid* at 645 (per Walsh J).
19 [1982] ILRM 164.
20 [1983] IR 154.
21 *ibid* at 159–160 (*per* Barrington J).
22 J Casey, *Constitutional Law in Ireland* (3rd ed, Round Hall Sweet and Maxwell, Dublin, 2000) at p 448
23 *Quinn's Supermarket Ltd v Attorney General* [1972] IR 1.
24 *PMPS Ltd and Moore v Attorney General* [1983] IR 339.
25 See the decision of the Supreme Court in *Quinn's Supermarket Ltd v Attorney General* [1972] IR 1.

category to more personal rights, legal entities have been held to be protected by the provisions of the Constitution.[26] Where the rights are confined by their terminology to "citizens" or "persons" the courts have often circumvented the problem by seeking a "person" who could be legitimately held to be affected for the purposes of the case. So, for example, in *PMPS Ltd and Moore v Attorney General*[27] the High Court held that although the corporate entity could not rely on Arts 40 or 43, a shareholder could claim that his constitutional rights had been violated.

Balancing Constitutional Rights

[1–18] Cases before the courts will often involve the difficult question of balancing conflicting constitutional values. Initially, the Irish courts took the view that the role of the courts in such cases was to balance or harmonise the rights in question. A useful example of this is the case of *Quinn's Supermarket Ltd v Attorney General* [28] in which a regulation which exempted kosher butcher shops from closing hour regulations was challenged by the plaintiff who was not a kosher butcher. In this case, the Supreme Court had to grapple with a conflict between the right of the Jewish community to practice their religion and the right of non-Jewish shop owners not to be discriminated against on grounds of religion. The Supreme Court held that the most appropriate and correct approach in such cases was to balance/harmonise the rights in question and, on the facts of the case, held that the right to non-discrimination could be justifiably interfered with for the purposes of ensuring the free profession of religion, as long as the measure implementing this balance was not disproportionate in that regard. On the facts, the measure, which exempted kosher butcher shops from the entire regulation on closing hours, was disproportionate as it went further than was necessary to protect the right to free profession of religion.

[1–19] An alternative approach can be identified in the case of *People (DPP) v Shaw*[29] involving a conflict, in tragic circumstances, between the right to liberty and the right to life. In this case, the Gardaí had held a suspect for questioning beyond the legal time limit in the hope of gaining information on the whereabouts of two missing women whose lives may have been in danger. The Supreme Court held that where there is a conflict between two rights, the one that ranks higher prevails and, in the circumstances of this case, the right to life outranked the right to liberty. However, in the case of *Attorney General v X*[30] there is evidence of a reversion to the harmonious balancing approach. In that case, involving a balancing act between the right to life of the mother and the right of the mother to travel and the right to life of the foetus, the Supreme Court held that courts, in making determinations in cases where a conflict between rights arises, should in all cases first attempt to harmonise the rights. Only in cases where this balancing is not possible, should a hierarchy of rights be established.[31]

---

[26] *Iarnród Éireann v Ireland* [1996] 3 IR 321.
[27] *supra* n 24.
[28] [1972] IR 1.
[29] [1982] IR 1.
[30] [1992] 1 IR 1.
[31] For an excellent explanation of this concept, please refer to O Doyle, *Constitutional Law: Texts, Cases and Materials* (Clarus Press, Dublin, 2008).

Remedies for Breach of Constitutional Rights

While the Constitution does not set out the remedies that might be available to a plaintiff who manages to establish a breach of a constitutional right, it has been held that damages might be awarded in some cases.[32] However, of wider consequence is the possibility of obtaining a declaration of unconstitutionality which is an official statement that some section of legislation or some regulation, for example, is unconstitutional. This will have immediate effects not just for the individual litigant but also for the public at large. **[1–20]**

An illuminating example is the case of *A v Governor of Arbour Hill Prison*[33]. Mr A pleaded guilty to the unlawful carnal knowledge of a girl under the age of consent contrary to s 1(1) of the Criminal Law Act 1935 and was sentenced to three years in prison. In another case, heard almost two years later, s 1(1) was found to be unconstitutional[34] as it precluded a defence being raised by a person charged with an offence under the section to the effect that he had reasonable grounds for believing that the girl in question was over the age of consent to sexual intercourse. Mr A sought release from prison under Art 40.4.1° of the Constitution on the grounds that the section under which he had been convicted was unconstitutional. The High Court ordered his release and the respondents appealed to the Supreme Court. **[1–21]**

Doyle identifies that the central issue arising from this case relates to when declarations of constitutionality take effect.[35] The general rule would appear to be that in the case of provisions of pre-1937 Statutes, the impugned provision would be considered void from the date of the enactment of the Constitution, and provisions of post-1937 Statutes are considered void *ab initio*.

However, the Supreme Court held in the A case that not every action taken on foot of a void statute is invalid.[36] In a criminal prosecution where the State relies in good faith on a statute in force at the time and the accused does not seek to impugn the bringing or conduct of the prosecution, on any grounds that may in law be open to him, including the constitutionality of the statute, then the final decision in the case must be deemed to be and to remain lawful notwithstanding any subsequent ruling that the statute, or a provision of it, is unconstitutional. There may be exceptional cases where this general rule will not be applicable for reasons related to some fundamental unfairness amounting to a denial of justice. However, in general the conviction will remain lawful despite the unconstitutionality of the provision. **[1–22]**

The European Convention on Human Rights Act 2003

The European Convention on Human Rights Act 2003 incorporates the ECHR (see below) into Irish law.[37] The history of incorporation is a chequered one and calls for **[1–23]**

---

[32] See for example the case of *Kennedy v Ireland* [1987] IR 587.

[33] [2006] IESC 45.

[34] *CC v Ireland & Ors* [2006] IESC 33.

[35] O Doyle, *supra* n 31 at p 446.

[36] See the cases of *State (Byrne) v Frawley* [1978] IR 326 and *McDonnell v Ireland* [1998] 1 IR 134.

[37] For a detailed assessment of the Act: see F de Londras and C Kelly, *European Convention on Human Rights Act: Operation, Impact and Analysis* (Thomson Reuters, Dublin, 2010).

the incorporation of the ECHR dating back to 1975 can be identified.[38] However, there was a hesitancy to incorporate the ECHR into Irish law due to the fact that many people believed that the Irish constitutional protection of human rights was in fact sufficient and that the incorporation would be considered to be an encroachment on sovereignty.[39] The eventual incorporation of the ECHR was achieved mainly for the purposes of ensuring equivalency of rights between Northern Ireland and the Republic of Ireland which was required under the Good Friday Agreement 1998[40] which was largely for "symbolic and political reasons"[41] because the ECHR was viewed as a "politically neutral template for sensitive cross border dealings".[42] Despite many recommendations from the Irish Human Rights Commission,[43] the Irish Government chose to incorporate the Convention at a sub-constitutional level which was met with the criticism of being a "minimalist" approach to human rights protection.[44] However, the European Convention on Human Rights Act 2003 has generated a vast amount of human rights litigation in Ireland and could be considered the single greatest achievement relating to human rights in recent times.

Organs of State and the ECHR

[1–24] The Act asserts a general obligation on all "organs of State" that they must perform their duties in a manner compatible with the convention.[45] Anyone who suffers injury, loss or damage as a result of such a body's failure is entitled to damages. Section 1 defines an organ of State as a tribunal or any other body (other than the President or the Oireachtas or either House of the Oireachtas or a Committee of either such House or a Joint Committee of both such Houses or a court) which is established by law or through which any of the legislative, executive or judicial powers of the State are exercised.

---

38 It was Fianna Fáil who originally called for incorporation of the Convention in 1975 and this was also recommended by the Constitutional Review Group in 1996. See F de Londras and C Kelly, *supra* n 37 at p 6.

39 See D O'Donnell, "A Comparison of Article 6 of the European Convention on Human Rights and the Due Process Requirements of the Constitution of Ireland" (2004) 4(2) JSIJ 27 at p 48; R Murphy and S Wills "The European Convention on Human Rights Bill 2001" (2001) 6(9) BR 541; F de Londras and C Kelly, *supra* n 37 at p 7.

40 C Ó Cinnéide, "The European Convention on Human Rights and the Irish Constitutional System of Rights Protection: Complementary or Divergent?" in O Doyle *et al*, eds *The Irish Constitution: Governance and Values*, (Thomson Round Hall, Dublin, 2008) at p 530; F de Londras and C Kelly, *supra* n 37 at p 8.

41 See F de Londras and C Kelly *supra* n 37 at p 9.

42 See G Hogan, "The Belfast Agreement and the Future Incorporation of the European Convention of Human Rights in the Republic of Ireland" (1999) 4(4) BR 205 at p 210; see F de Londras and C Kelly, *supra* n 37, p 9.

43 Constitutional Review Group Report of May 1996 at p 193. See F de Londras and C Kelly, *supra* n 37 at p 10.

44 Irish Human Rights Commission, *Submission on the European Convention on Human Rights Bill to the Joint Oireachtas Committee on Justice, Equality, Defence and Women's Rights* (June 2002) at p 7. See also F de Londras and C Kelly, *supra* n 37 at p 11.

45 s 3, European Convention on Human Rights Act 2003.

The Courts and the ECHR

The courts must take judicial notice of the provisions of the ECHR and of any declaration, decision, advisory opinion or judgment of the ECtHR, any decision or opinion of the European Commission of Human Rights and any decision of the Committee of Ministers, on any question in respect of which these bodies have jurisdiction.[46] The courts are also under an obligation, when interpreting and applying the provisions of the ECHR to take due account of the principles laid down by those declarations, decisions, advisory opinions, opinions and judgments.[47] **[1–25]**

A Finding of Incompatibility with the ECHR

The ECHR Act 2003 makes provision for two specific remedies in the case of a finding of incompatibility: a declaration of incompatibility and damages. **[1–26]**

Section 5 of the Act grants to the High and Supreme Court the power to make a declaration that a statutory provision or common law rule is incompatible with the Convention.[48] Such a declaration does not render the law in question invalid, and does not impact on the continuing operation or enforcement of the statutory provision or rule.[49] Nor does it prevent a party to the proceedings from making submissions or representations in any proceedings before the ECtHR.[50] The significance of the declaration rather lies in the impact that this decision has on the business of Government. The Taoiseach is obliged to lay any such declaration before both the Dáil and Seanad Éireann within 21 days.[51] However, the obligation ends there. An illuminating example of this is the situation in relation to gender recognition in Ireland. Despite a declaration of incompatibility being issued in the case of *Foy v An t-Ard Chláraithóir*[52] to the effect that the failure of Irish law to provide for a system of gender recognition for transsexual individuals was incompatible with Art 8 of the ECHR, no legislation remedying this situation has been developed. The Gender Recognition Advisory Group was formed in 2010 (three years after the declaration was made) and reported in 2011.[53] However, to date there has still been no legislative developments in this area of law.

The Act requires that a number of criteria be meet before damages can be awarded in a given case. First, there must be a declaration of incompatibility made in respect of the particular case.[54] Secondly, the party to the proceedings concerned must make an application in writing to the Attorney General for compensation in respect of an injury or loss or damage suffered by him or her as a result of the incompatibility.[55] Finally, the Government must consider, at their discretion, to make an *ex gratia* payment of **[1–27]**

46 s 4, European Convention on Human Rights Act 2003.
47 *ibid.*
48 s 5(1), European Convention on Human Rights Act 2003.
49 s 5(2)(a), European Convention on Human Rights Act 2003.
50 s 5(2)(b), European Convention on Human Rights Act 2003.
51 s 5(3), European Convention on Human Rights Act 2003.
52 [2007] IEHC 470.
53 See Report of the Gender Recognition Advisory Group available at http://www.welfare.ie/EN/Policy/Legislation/Documents/gragreportjune11.pdf (last accessed 29 July 2012).
54 s 5(4)(a), European Convention on Human Rights Act 2003.
55 s 5(4)(b), European Convention on Human Rights Act 2003.

compensation.[56] If the party can show that all these conditions are met, then the Government can request an advisor appointed by them to advise as to the amount of compensation (if any) that should be paid and may make such payment. However, payment is entirely at the discretion of the Government.

Protection of Human Rights in the Regional Context

[1–28] At a regional level, there is protection for human rights by two distinct organisations: the Council of Europe and the European Union. Each of these bodies has their own human rights treaties and enforcement mechanisms.

The Council of Europe and the European Convention on Human Rights (ECHR)

[1–29] The Council of Europe was established in 1949 and adopted the ECHR in 1950. The ECHR protects a variety of civil and political rights and a limited number of economic social and cultural rights. Section II of the Convention sets out a system for application and enforcement. Three institutions were entrusted with this responsibility:

(1) the European Commission of Human Rights (set up in 1954);
(2) the European Court of Human Rights (ECtHR) (set up in 1959, newly constituted in 1998); and
(3) the Committee of Ministers of the Council of Europe, being composed of the ministers for foreign affairs of the Member States.

The Committee of Ministers of the Council of Europe has the responsibility of supervising the execution of the Court's judgments. Up until 1998, the Commission determined the admissibility of applications. However, with a growing backlog of cases and dissatisfaction at other complexities in procedure, the system for application and enforcement was radically overhauled by Protocol 11, which came into force in November 1998. Under the new procedure, all decisions on the admissibility and the merits of an application are decided by the ECtHR, a newly constituted, single, full-time court.

[1–30] The ECtHR is composed of a number of judges equal to the number of Member States of the Council of Europe. There is no restriction on the number of judges of the same nationality, and judges are elected by the Parliamentary Assembly of the Council of Europe for a term of six years, sitting in their individual capacity and without representing any State. Judges sit on the Court in Committees (of three), in Chambers (of seven) and in the Grand Chamber (of 17).

Application of the ECHR

[1–31] Any contracting State (State application) or individual claiming to be a victim of a violation of the Convention (individual application) may lodge their complaint directly with the ECtHR. However, before this can be done, any domestic remedies that are available must be exhausted (Art 35). Only where there is no further court of appeal or where an appeal is certain to fail (e.g. strong domestic precedents against the applicant)

---

56 s 5(4)(c), European Convention on Human Rights Act 2003.

may an individual lodge an application. This application must be registered at the ECtHR's registry within six months of the final decision of the highest court having jurisdiction within the domestic legal system.[57]

After a preliminary examination by an appointed judge rapporteur, the admissibility of an individual application will be decided either by a Committee or directly by a Chamber. Individual applications which are not declared inadmissible by Committees, along with those that are referred directly to a Chamber by the rapporteur, and State applications, are examined by a Chamber. Chambers determine both admissibility[58] and merits. However, a Chamber may, at any time, relinquish jurisdiction in favour of the Grand Chamber, either where there is a serious question of interpretation of the ECHR or where there is a risk of departing from existing case law. All final judgments of the ECtHR are binding on the respondent States concerned. **[1–32]**

Limitations on the Rights in the ECHR

There will almost always be a tension between the expression of different rights, for example, between the right to express oneself freely and the right not to have, for example, the free dissemination of racist material. This balancing of the rights and liberties must be reconciled through each individual case, and is usually made more evident in the use of Arts 8–11, where the rights are "qualified". This means that each individually stated positive right is qualified by restrictions which may be placed upon it by the State, although these restrictions are, themselves, not without qualification, since they must be "necessary in a democratic society" for listed public interest purposes. **[1–33]**

In addition, restrictions must be "in accordance with the law" or "prescribed by law". This latter concept might have caused a certain amount of trouble in the English text version, since these two phrases are not, on the face of it, identical in meaning; the former could have the meaning of simply being unlawful, the latter, that there was some form of legal authorisation required. However, this was settled by the case of *Malone v UK*,[59] where the two were ruled to be interpreted and read as being identical. In essence, the phrase means that the State must have a legal reason for its action; whether this is set down in domestic, international or community law does not matter, provided that the rule or reason purports to give an authority for the interference with the rights of the citizen. There are also cases where the rule came from more than one legal order or from delegated legislation. The ECtHR has taken a generous view of the scope of delegated law, in all of its considerations, from the rules of a professional organisation to case law. In reality, of course, any form of delegated law making will have checks and balances built in with regard to its use, which will act to deal with any form of arbitrariness or to the body acting *ultra vires*. **[1–34]**

---

[57] A case may be terminated by a friendly settlement between the parties at any stage of the proceedings.

[58] Criteria for admissibility: It must not be a matter ruled on and investigated previously. It must relate to a right protected by the Convention. There must be no relevant derogations or reservations by the State concerned. It must relate to an organisation for which a Member State has responsibility. It must not be such as to represent an attack on another's rights (Art 17). It must be plausible, genuine and based on good evidence of violation.

[59] *Malone v UK* (1985) 7 EHRR 14.

[1–35] This is not to say that a valid rule may not be challenged. In *Silver v UK*,[60] the ECtHR ruled that, when a legal rule had a discretionary element, then the limits of the discretion must be apparent and verifiable. This was taken up by the Court in the case of *Kruslin v France*,[61] which concerned the secret taping of telephone conversations, and for which the French law was provided in their Code of Criminal Procedure. However, the ECtHR did not agree that this law was sufficiently transparent, since it did not allow for sufficient supervision or checks, in that the identity of those being "tapped" were not revealed, and that there was no time limit imposed on the process, and that it did not, therefore, suffice to be considered as valid "law".

[1–36] This need for precision can be seen as rather adaptable, particularly, as we shall see later, in the context of the margin of appreciation, mostly because the Convention has to be seen as a living instrument, changing pace with society. This leads to the proposition that a degree of anticipation and, indeed, foresight is required. This was stated openly in the *Sunday Times* case,[62] in answer to the applicant's argument that the House of Lords, in their judgment, had put forward an entirely novel concept which could not have reasonably been anticipated:

> " ... the applicants were able to foresee, to a degree that was reasonable in the circumstances, a risk that publication of the draft article might fall foul of the principle."

[1–37] An interesting example of where this need for foresight might be required is the case of *Open Door Counselling and Dublin Well Woman Centre v Ireland*,[63] concerning the contentious domestic issue of abortion within Ireland. The applicants had been issued with an injunction, forbidding them from giving information about abortions which might be undertaken outside Ireland. The Court stated that, taking into account the high threshold of protection of the unborn provided under Irish law generally, the possibility that action might be taken against the applicants must have been reasonably foreseeable.

The ECtHR found that this was, indeed an unjustified interference with the right of expression under Art 10, since the law in this area clearly had to be expressed with "particular precision" but that it was foreseeable that the Irish courts would act against the applicants, since the matter was clearly seen as of some considerable importance within Irish society, who had "... profound moral values concerning the nature of life, which were reflected in the stance of the majority of the Irish people". In terms of the legitimacy of the aim it was held that this was, in fact, quite legitimate, since it concerned "... the protection of morals of which the protection, in Ireland, of the right to life of the unborn is one aspect."

[1–38] Another case of uncertainty[64] concerned the English magistrate's power of an order to someone to be 'bound over' to keep the peace, in this instance, with the Latin phrase of *contra bonos mores*, roughly translatable as "an order to behave oneself". Since those

---

60 *Silver v UK* (1983) 5 EHRR 347.
61 *Kruslin v France* (1989) No 11801/85.
62 (1979) 2 EHRR 245
63 *Open Door Counselling and Dublin Well Woman Centre v Ireland* (1992) No 14234/88.
64 *Hashman and Harrop v United Kingdom* (2000) 30 EHRR 241.

being bound over did not, or indeed, could not, know with precision what was or was not allowed, the ruling was overturned for imprecision.

In cases of dispute, the situation is then that the ECtHR is called upon to consider whether the State has acted disproportionately, thereby getting the balance wrong. In *R (Daly) v Secretary of State for the Home Department*[65] a case concerning a prisoner and Art 8, a test of proportionality was reiterated which has been followed in many cases since then. In essence, the court must ask if:

(1) the legislative objective is sufficiently important to justify limiting a fundamental right;
(2) the measures designed to meet the legislative objective are rationally connected to it;
(3) the means used to impair the right or freedom are no more than is necessary to accomplish the objective.

This was also addressed by Lord Phillips, PSC, in the extradition case of *Norris v United States (No 2),*[66] when he considered that:

> "The critical issue in this case is whether this interference is ' . . . necessary in a democratic society . . . for the prevention of disorder or crime'. Resolving this issue involves a test of proportionality. The interference must fulfil a 'pressing social need'. It must also be proportionate to the 'legitimate aim' relied upon to justify the interference."

As a general rule, disproportionality may be found to have occurred where there is little or no purpose to the interference with the individual by the State. For instance, in the case of *Weber v Switzerland,*[67] the concern with balancing freedom of expression with that of protecting confidential information was disproportionate when the confidential information was available elsewhere. **[1–39]**

The State must also prove its case adequately, so that when, in *Kokkinakis v Greece,*[68] the freedom to proselytise was being challenged on the grounds of "improper means", and the State failed to offer evidence as to the impropriety, then the interference with the applicant's rights under Art 9 was held as unnecessary.

If the action of the State is unlikely to have the required effect, this will incline the ECtHR against the State, so that in the case of *Campbell v UK,*[69] the opening of a prisoner's mail to guard against official EC mail being forged was held to be improbable, and disproportionate to the right of the prisoner to have private correspondence. However, the Court did suggest that a narrower rule might suffice, where reasonable suspicion rather than a blanket ruling might lead to letters being inspected in the presence of the prisoner legitimately. **[1–40]**

---

65 *R (Daly) v Secretary of State for the Home Department* (2001) UKHL 26.
66 *Norris v United States* (No 2) [2010] UKSC 9.
67 *Weber v Switzerland* (1990) No 11034/84.
68 *Kokkinakis v Greece* (1994) 17 EHRR 397.
69 *Campbell and Cosens v UK* (1982) 4 EHRR 293.

The Margin of Appreciation

[1–41] Another doctrine that plays an important part for the Court in interpretation of the Convention is the "margin of appreciation". In basic terms it means that the State is given a certain measure of discretion when it takes an action in the area of a Convention right, since an individual Member State might have different attitudes than their neighbours. This makes for a situation where a degree of flexibility is required, hence the need for a margin of appreciation. This doctrine enables the ECtHR to consistently interpret rights without riding roughshod over national and cultural differences, although there is an argument that it actually dilutes the protection of rights. The basis of the doctrine is that the ECtHR (and it is this court, not the domestic courts, which use the concept) determines the core content of any given right but also allows each Member State a margin of appreciation within which it must operate.

For example, one State with liberal social values might allow publication of a sex manual whereas another, more conservative State, may wish to ban it. Both may be operating within their margins of appreciation and so not infringing any citizen's freedoms.

[1–42] To some extent the doctrine pays deference to the expertise of the national authorities. As an example, in *Handyside,*[70] a book that had been published elsewhere in Europe was banned by the UK for promoting promiscuity in children. The ECtHR deferred to the State authority's assessment of the moral dangers and found no violation of Art 10(1) (freedom of expression), holding that the State restriction fell within Art 10(2) (permissible State restrictions to the freedom). However, the ECtHR also stated "that this did not give the contracting States an unlimited power of appreciation". While a certain margin of appreciation will be granted, therefore, any action by the State must still be proportionate.

The Interpretive Approach of the ECtHR

[1–43] The ECtHR has always emphasised the "object and purpose" of the ECHR (a teleological approach) rather than taking a "literalistic" approach, accomplished through the principle of proportionality. The jurisprudence of the Convention is centred on a need to find a balance between the demands of society, or its members, and the fundamental rights of the individual. In weighing such a balance, proportionality requires that a measured and justifiable approach be adopted by the ECtHR when assessing the cases before it. In essence, any restrictions that a State places on the rights of the individual "must be proportionate to the legitimate aim pursued".[71]

The Brighton Declaration

It has become clear that the ECtHR has an increasingly large backlog of cases, presently estimated at over 150,000, and this has led to moves towards reducing this backlog. The reform process began in 2010 with the Interlaken (Switzerland) and Izmir (Turkey) declarations, and led to a Council of Europe conference in Brighton (UK) on 19-20 April 2012. This resulted in agreement by the Council of Europe of the Brighton

---

[70] (1979–80) 1 EHRR 737.

[71] *Handyside v UK* (1979–80) 1 EHRR 737.

Declaration, which is intended to modify and improve the way the ECtHR operates, and which is due to be ratified by all 47 states by 2013.

The Brighton Declaration will amend the European Convention, in order to give more prominence to the principles of subsidiarity and the margin of appreciation, thereby allowing national courts more latitude in the interpretation of Convention rights. In addition, "repetitive" cases - where an alleged violation of the Convention has already been considered in a similar previous case, will be removed earlier in the system than at present, though this process is still unclear in detail.

Further, an amendment will tighten the ECHR's admissibility criteria, so that more "trivial" cases can be rejected, though, again, there is little detail on how this will be decided. Finally, applicants will have only four months (rather than the current six) in order to bring a case before the ECtHR, once they have exhausted all actions in the national courts, and it confirms the ultimate authority of the ECtHR in interpretation of the Convention.

The European Union and the Charter of Fundamental Rights (CFR)

The adoption of the CFR is a reflection of the increasing importance attached to human rights issues within the EU in recent years, and indeed there has been a marked increase in the number of human rights issues arising in cases before the Court of Justice of the European Union (CJEU) (formerly the European Court of Justice (ECJ)). The CFR consolidates the range of civil, political and economic, social and cultural rights applicable to EU citizens and residents. Chalmers, Davies and Monti comment that: **[1–44]**

> " ... the Charter incorporates a wider array of rights and freedoms possibly than any other human rights treaty.... It can be seen as ambitious and nuanced ... in what it considers humans need for a good life".[72]

The Charter was drafted[73] by a European Convention, which included representatives from Member State parliaments, the Commission and the European Parliament, with civil society organisations and other EU institutions also being granted observer status. The Draft Charter was proclaimed by the European Parliament, Commission and Council of Ministers in December 2000. The instrument did not have full legal effect, however, until the Treaty of Lisbon entered into force in December 2009. The mandate given by the European Council to the European Convention was to consolidate and highlight the EU's existing obligations to respect fundamental rights.[74] In explaining the rationale for drafting the CFR the Council stated: **[1–45]**

---

[72] D Chalmers, G Davies and G Monti *European Union Law: Cases and Materials* (Cambridge University Press, Cambridge, 2010), p 239.

[73] See G de Búrca, "The Drafting of the EU Charter of Fundamental Eights" (2000) 25 ELR 331.

[74] Conclusions of the Cologne European Council, June 1999, para 44, available at: http://www.consilium.europa.eu/ueDocs/cms_Data/docs/pressData/en/ec/kolnen.htm, last accessed 27 July 2012. This paragraph states: "The European Council takes the view that, at the present stage of development of the European Union, the fundamental rights applicable at Union level should be consolidated in a Charter and thereby made more evident."

> "Protection of fundamental rights is a founding principle of the Union and an indispensable prerequisite for her legitimacy. The obligation of the Union to respect fundamental rights has been confirmed and defined by the jurisprudence of the European Court of Justice. There appears to be a need, at the present stage of the Union's development, to establish a Charter of fundamental rights in order to make their overriding importance and relevance more visible to the Union's citizens."[75]

[1–46] The CFR thus highlights various rights which are cornerstones of the EU. The instrument is divided into six sections: dignity, freedoms, equality, solidarity, citizens' rights and justice. The rights enshrined in the CFR have various identifiable bases, the main ones being the rights recognised by the ECHR, the Social Charter of the Council of Europe, the constitutional traditions of the EU Member States, the Community Charter of Fundamental Social Rights of Workers and other international conventions.[76] These rights had been recognised by the CJEU and in various EU instruments in various ways for many years before the adoption of the CFR. It was not the intention of the Council that new rights, beyond those already recognised by, and applicable to, the EU institutions and Member States, be created; rather it was the intention to reaffirm and consolidate these rights. However, it should be noted that the CFR does not align exactly with previous human rights instruments which were recognised by EU law. Craig and de Búrca comment that

> "overall the Charter could perhaps best be described as a creative distillation of the rights in the various European and international agreements and national constitutions on which the ECJ had for some years already drawn."[77]

Application of the CFR

[1–47] It is important to note that the CFR applies only to EU institutions and to EU Member States and institutions when they are implementing EU law. Article 51 states:

> "The provisions of this Charter are addressed to the institutions, bodies, offices and agencies of the Union ... and to the Member States only when they are implementing Union law."

Given the context of the CFR as an instrument of the EU, a number of non-traditional, commercially-focused rights are included, including the freedom to conduct a business.[78] Some of the other fundamental rights included in the instrument, such as the right to life, may seem a little out of place in the context of the EU, given the limited ability of the EU institutions, or of Member States when implementing EU law to violate a person's right to life, however, the increasing competencies of the EU may encroach on these fundamental rights to a certain extent.[79]

---

[75] Conclusions of the Cologne European Council, June 1999, Annex IV, available at: http://www.consilium.europa.eu/ueDocs/cms_Data/docs/pressData/en/ec/kolnen.htm, last accessed 27 July 2012.

[76] *ibid.*

[77] P Craig and G de Búrca, *EU Law: Text, Cases and Materials* (5th ed, Oxford University Press, Oxford, 2011) p 395.

[78] This right is recognised in Art 16 CFR, which states that "The freedom to conduct a business in accordance with Community law and national laws and practices" is recognised.

[79] P Craig and G de Búrca, *supra* n 77, pp 395–6.

The Interpretation of the CFR

The CJEU / ECJ has relied on the ECHR and referred to ECtHR case law for many years,[80] and Arts 52(3) and 53 of the CFR clarify the nature of the relationship between the CFR and the ECHR.[81] Article 52(3) states: [1–48]

> "In so far as this Charter contains rights which correspond to rights guaranteed by the Convention for the Protection of Human Rights and Fundamental Freedoms, the meaning and scope of those rights shall be the same as those laid down by the said Convention. This provision shall not prevent Union law providing more extensive protection."

Article 53 then clarifies the relationship of the CFR with other international instruments, and states:

> "Nothing in this Charter shall be interpreted as restricting or adversely affecting human rights and fundamental freedoms as recognised, in their respective fields of application, by Union law and international law and by international agreements to which the Union, the Community or all the Member States are party, including the European Convention for the Protection of Human Rights and Fundamental Freedoms, and by the Member States' constitutions."

The Lisbon Treaty's amendment to Art 6(2) of the Treaty on European Union (TEU) states that the EU "shall" accede to ECHR. Protocol 14 to the ECHR[82] amended Art 59(2) of the Convention, allowing for the accession of the EU to the Convention. The future accession by the EU to the ECHR would further formalise the relationship between the CFR and ECHR and the CJEU and the ECtHR.

International Protection of Human Rights

The Primary Treaties and their Obligations

The status of international legal instruments under Irish law is dealt with in Art 29.6 of the Irish Constitution which states: [1–49]

> "No international agreement shall be part of the domestic law of the State save as may be determined by the Oireachtas."

Therefore, the impact of international human rights instruments on the State and individuals within the State will depend on whether the instrument has been

---

[80] See Discussion document of the ECJ on certain aspects of the accession of the EU to the ECHR, Luxembourg, 5 May 2010. See also S Douglas Scott, "A Tale of Two Courts: Luxembourg, Strasbourg and the Growing European Human Rights Acquis" (2006) 43 CMLR 629.

[81] G Harpaz, "The European Court of Justice and its Relationship with the European Court of Human Rights" (2009) 46 CMLR 105 and P Lemmens "The Relationship between the Charter of Fundamental Rights of the EU and the ECHR: Substantive Aspects" (2001) 8 MJ 49.

[82] Protocol No. 14 to the Convention for the Protection of Human Rights and Fundamental Freedoms, amending the control system of the Convention, Strasbourg, 13 May 2004.

incorporated into domestic law or not. If the State has ratified an instrument but not incorporated it into domestic law, then while it is binding on the State, it is not directly enforceable in Irish courts. Ireland has ratified a number of international instruments, the most important and influential of these being human rights instruments of the United Nations (UN). Currently, there are nine basic human rights treaties in the UN system, and a number of optional protocols.

[1–50] The nine basic human rights instruments are:

- International Covenant on Civil and Political Rights (ICCPR) 1966, International Covenant on Economic, Social and Cultural Rights (ICESCR) 1966;
- International Convention on the Elimination of All Forms of Racial Discrimination (CERD) 1965;
- Convention on the Elimination of All Forms of Discrimination against Women (CEDAW) 1979;
- Conventional against Torture and Other Cruel, Inhuman or Degrading Treatment or Punishment (CAT) 1984;
- Convention on the Rights of the Child (CRC) 1989;
- International Convention on the Protection of the Rights of All Migrant Workers and Members of their Families (CMW) 1990;
- International Convention of the Protection of All Persons from Enforced Disappearance (CED) 2006;
- Convention on the Rights of Persons with Disabilities (CRPD) 2006.

Ireland has ratified the first six of these treaties and has also signed, but not yet ratified, the conventions dealing with disability and enforced disappearances. The ratification of these international instruments requires the State to report on its human rights activities to UN treaty bodies. The State's reporting record is good but the Irish government has often been very late with its reporting obligations.[83] Ireland has incorporated the CAT into domestic law by means of Criminal Justice (United Nations Convention Against Torture) Act 2000,[84] but has not incorporated the other instruments to date.

General Review of Government Obligations

[1–51] The government now also has an obligation to submit a report on its human rights activities every four years to the UN Human Rights Council, under a relatively new

[83] For example, the government was six years late submitting its first report on the CAT and still has not published its second report which was due in 2007, and has also been a number of years late in submitting reports on other conventions.

[84] Ireland signed the Optional Protocol to the UN Convention in 2007 (Optional Protocol to the Convention against Torture and other Cruel, Inhuman or Degrading Treatment or Punishment, adopted on 18 December 2002 at the 57th session of the General Assembly of the United Nations by resolution A/RES/57/199, but has not yet ratified it.The objective of the Protocol is "to establish a system of regular visits undertaken by independent international and national bodies to places where people are deprived of their liberty, in order to prevent torture and other cruel, inhuman or degrading treatment or punishment" (Art 1).

procedure, the Universal Periodic Review (UPR) mechanism.[85] The Human Rights Council was created on 15 March 2006,[86] with a mandate to:

> " . . . undertake a universal periodic review, based on objective and reliable information, of the fulfilment by each State of its human rights obligations and commitments in a manner which ensures universality of coverage and equal treatment with respect to all States".[87]

The mechanism by which this was to be undertaken was cemented in UN Council Resolution A/HRC/RES/5/1.

The UPR is a type of peer review where all members of the UN are required to report on human rights laws and practices in their state every four years. The review is conducted by the UPR Working Group which consists of all 47 Members of the Human Rights Council. In addition to the State report the UN compiles its own report on each State and stakeholders in every State are also invited to submit a report. All other members of the UN can question, in writing and orally, and make recommendations on, other States' human rights activities.[88] An outcome report is then adopted during a plenary session of the Human Rights Council and this report includes questions, comments and recommendations to the State under review. Finally, a follow-up to the review is conducted during the next review of the SUR. The review process began in 2008 and 48 States are reviewed every year and Ireland made its first report in 2011. **[1–52]**

Complaint Mechanisms

Under the UN human rights system, there is also an optional individual complaints mechanism attached to most treaties, whereby an individual may make a complaint to the respective treaty body, alleging that rights under the treaty have been violated by their government. Six of the human rights treaty bodies, the Human Rights Committee, the Committee on the Elimination of Racial Discrimination, the Committee on the Elimination of Discrimination Against Women, the Committee Against Torture, the Committee on the Rights of Persons with Disabilities and the Committee on Enforced Disappearance can currently hear complaints relating to their respective treaties. The Optional Protocol to the ICESCR which allows for the creation of a complaints mechanism in relation to that treaty was adopted in 2008 but is not yet in force. The Optional Protocol to the CRC which allows for a similar complaints mechanism was adopted in 2011 but has not entered into force yet either. Article 77 of the Migrant Workers Convention establishes a complaints mechanism which will come into force when ten States Parties have made a declaration recognising the Committee's competence to deal with complaints. **[1–53]**

---

[85] For a discussion of the Universal Periodic Review mechanism, see G Sweeney and Y Saito, "An NGO Assessment of the New Mechanisms of the UN Human Rights Council" (2009) 9 HRLRev 210 and A M Abebe, "Of Shaming and Bargaining: African States and the Universal Periodic Review of the United Nations Human Rights Council"(2009) 9 HRLRev 1.

[86] UNGA Res 60/251.

[87] *ibid.*

[88] See E Dewhurst and N Higgins, "Human Rights:Ireland and the United Nations" in *Irish Foreign Policy* (B Tonra *et al* eds, Gill and Macmillan, Dublin, 2012), Chapter 13.

[1–54] To date, only five complaints have been lodged against the Irish government for failing to uphold the rights enshrined in these international instruments, (*Holland*,[89] *Kavanagh* (No 1),[90] *Kavanagh (No 2)*,[91] *Ó Colchúin*,[92] *O'Neill* and *Quinn*[93]) all under the civil and political rights convention (ICCPR) with only two of these being found to be admissible (*Kavanagh (No 1)* and *O'Neill* and *Quinn*). Of the two admissible decisions only one violation has ever been found against Ireland by the UN Human Rights Committee. This was the case of *Kavanagh (No 1)* in which Mr Kavanagh claimed that the State had violated his rights under Arts 14 and 26 of the ICCPR which include a right to a fair trial and equality of arms. Mr Kavanagh complained that these rights had been violated when the Director of Public Prosecutions ordered that he should be tried before the Special Criminal Court "which did not afford him a jury trial and the right to examine witnesses at a preliminary stage".[94] The author complained that he had:

> " ... been seriously disadvantaged compared to other persons accused of similar or equal criminal offences, who unlike him were tried by ordinary courts and therefore could avail themselves of a wider range of possible safeguards".[95]

The Committee held that the Irish State was in violation of Art 26 of the ICCPR and held that the State was both "under an obligation to provide the author with an effective remedy" and:

> " ... to ensure that similar violations do not occur in the future: it should ensure that persons are not tried before the Special Criminal Court unless reasonable and objective criteria for the decision are provided".[96]

The Irish government responded to this finding by making a financial payment to the complainant and by compiling a report on proposed reform of the Special Criminal Court,[97] illustrating the State's willingness to take on board the findings of international human rights bodies.

Conclusion

[1–55] There is significant protection for human rights in Ireland including protection at a national, regional and international level. While enforcement of the rights protected at a national level before the Irish courts system is of the most effective remedial value, other human rights complaints mechanisms also exist, although certain mechanisms (such as recourse to the ECtHR) are certainly more utilised than others.

[1–56] This book will highlight in each chapter the protection of a given fundamental human right under national, regional, and international law. Each chapter will begin with an

---

89 *Holland v Ireland* (593/1994).
90 *Kavanagh v Ireland* (819/1998).
91 *Kavanagh v Ireland* (1114/2002).
92 *Ó Colchúin v Ireland* (1038/2001)
93 *O'Neill v Quinn v Ireland* (1314/2004).
94 *Kavanagh v Ireland* (819/1998) at para 10.1.
95 *ibid* at para 4.1.
96 *ibid* at para 12.
97 CCPR A/57/40, Vol. I, 2002.

analysis of the constitutional position of the right, its nature and scope and will examine any potential interference with that right and how these might be legitimated in certain circumstances. This will be followed by an analysis of the same right under the ECHR, examining once again the nature and scope of the right and the potential legitimate justification for interfering with the right. The chapter will then proceed to the CFR and follow the same line of analysis. In this way, the reader will be able to make suitable comparisons between the different levels of protection and to identify the most effective enforcement mechanism in the case at hand. Finally, the chapter will identify the protection of the right under international human rights instruments and other regional instruments.

CHAPTER 2
The Right to Equality

Introduction

The principle of equality and non-discrimination permeates all international human rights treaties, regional agreements and national constitutions and in many ways is the cornerstone of human rights law. Generally this right is characterised by the Aristotelian concept that equals should be treated equally and unequals unequally. However, this does not mean that in every case where there is some form of difference in treatment that this is contrary to the guarantee of equality. Most human rights instruments recognise that in some cases, direct discrimination, and in all cases, indirect discrimination, can be justified in certain circumstances by reference to some legitimate aim which is proportionate. This chapter will outline the protection under the Irish Constitution, European Convention on Human Rights (ECHR) and European Union (EU) law and will identify the areas where qualification of the principle of equality is permitted. **[2–01]**

A. Irish Constitutional Protection

Article 40.1: **[2–02]**

> "All citizens shall, as human persons, be held equal before the law. This shall not mean that the State shall not in its enactments have due regard to differences of capacity, physical and moral, and of social function".

The right to equality in the Irish Constitution is based on the central ideal that Ireland is a democratic State as provided for in Art 5 of the Constitution[1] and "a democratic State denotes one in which all citizens have equal rights".[2] Despite the centrality and importance of this concept, Art 40.1 has been described as probably the "most difficult and elusive concept contained in the Constitution".[3]

[2–03] Equality, in the Irish constitutional context, is essentially a negative right (although there have been statements to the effect that this is a positive proposition),[4] forbidding the State from discriminating against its citizens in conducting its legislative and administrative functions. This negative construction has meant that Art 40.1 has rarely been the sole invalidating factor of statutory provisions[5] and the courts have shown a tendency to ground invalidity in other constitutional articles.[6] Casey, in his analysis, concludes that the courts "show a marked reluctance to apply Article 40.1"[7] and instead prefer to rely on other constitutional articles or "invoke the unenumerated rights doctrine under Art 40.3",[8] perhaps because Art 40.3 offers more scope for expansion or due to the fact that the courts do not want to give the impression that they "are acting as 'super-legislatures'—imposing their own policy preferences on the public".[9] However, Doyle, Hogan and Whyte all argue that this trend of reluctance appears to be abating[10] and that there appears to be evidence that Art 40.1 may become, in future years, "a more useful constitutional guarantee for litigants", due to the fact that the "current generation of judges—accustomed to applying non-discrimination guarantees of European Community law, as well as domestic legislation ... may be more prepared to develop some of the potential of this constitutional provision".[11]

1. Nature of the Right

[2–04] Article 40.1 does not require the State to treat all persons equally. On the contrary, sometimes it is necessary to introduce legislation to assist a particular class of persons. As noted by the Supreme Court in *Re Article 26 and Part V of the Planning and Development Bill 1999,*[12] to interpret Art 40.1 so as to treat all people equally, "far

[1] *An Blascaod Mór Teoranta v Commissioners of Public Works (No 3)* [2000] 1 IR 6 at 19 (*per* Barrington J).

[2] *O'Donovan v Attorney Gerneral* [1961) IR 114 at 137 (*per* Budd J). For some comparative assessments of the right to equality with other constitutions see: FX Beytagh, "Equality Under the Irish and American Constitutions: A comparative analysis" (1983) 18(2) IJ 219.

[3] *Brennan v Attorney General* [1983] ILRM 449.

[4] See in *Re A Ward of Court* [1996] 2 IR 73 at 159 (*per* Denham J). However, there have never been any cases asserting the right in a positive fashion.

[5] Hogan and Whyte note that the law is underdeveloped (GW Hogan and GF Whyte, *JM Kelly: The Irish Constitution* (4th ed, Butterworths, Dublin, 2003) at p 1324.

[6] J Casey, *Constitutional Law in Ireland* (3rd ed, Round Hall Sweet & Maxwell, Dublin, 2000) at p 451. O Doyle, *Constitutional Law: Texts, Cases and Materials* (Clarus Press, Dublin, 2008) at p 61.

[7] *ibid* p 451.

[8] J Casey, *supra* n 6 at p 451.

[9] *ibid.*

[10] GW Hogan and GF Whyte, *supra* n 5 at p 1325.

[11] O Doyle, *supra* n 6 at p 61.

[12] [2000] 3 IR 321.

from promoting equality, such an approach would simply result in greater inequality in our society".[13] The exact scope of the protection guaranteed under Art 40.1 has been delimited by the courts in a number of interesting cases and the following principles can be gleaned from the constitutional guarantee and the jurisprudence.

To Whom Does Art 40.1 Apply?

All "human persons" are entitled to the benefit of Art 40.1. This means that there are certain necessary exclusions from Art 40.1. First, it has been determined that non-human persons are not entitled to benefit from the guarantee of equality in Art 40.1. An example of this is the case of *Macauley v Minister for Posts and Telegraphs.*[14] In this case, the applicant argued that the rule which required the *fiat* of the Attorney General before a Minister could be sued infringed the constitutional guarantee of equality as no other person required the *fiat* of the Attorney General before they could be sued. In holding that the Minister in this context was a corporation sole and not a human person, Kenny J did not think "that the necessity ... to get the *fiat*" was an infringement of the constitutional guarantee. **[2–05]**

Secondly, the provision does not apply to business or corporations of any sort. In *Quinn's Supermarket Ltd v Attorney General,*[15] a supermarket was prosecuted for being in contravention of an Order made in 1948 under s 25 of the Shops (Hours of Trading) Act 1938 which declared that it was unlawful for the proprietor of a meat shop in a certain trading area to open or keep the shop open at certain times. The Order of 1948 exempted the proprietors of meat shops in which only kosher meat was sold from these regulations. Walsh J in the Supreme Court held that the equality provision is: **[2–06]**

> " ... not a guarantee of absolute equality for all citizens in all circumstances but it is a guarantee of equality as human persons and (as the Irish text of the Constitution makes quite clear) is a guarantee related to their dignity as human beings and a guarantee against any inequalities grounded upon an assumption, or indeed a belief, that some individual or individuals or classes of individuals, by reason of their human attributes or their ethnic or racial, social or religious background, are to be treated as the inferior or superior of other individuals in the community".[16]

Walsh J held that therefore the provisions of Art 40.1 guarantees equality to human persons for what they are in themselves as opposed to any trade or activities they may be involved in and that "under no possible construction of the Constitution could a body corporate or any entity but a human being" be considered to be a human person for the purposes of Art 40.1.[17] The fact that a legal entity cannot be a subject of the equality guarantee has been reiterated by the Supreme Court in *Abbey Films v Attorney General*[18] and appears to be firmly established in the constitutional jurisprudence.

[13] *ibid* at 357. See also *Dokie v DPP* [2010] IEHC 110.

[14] [1966] IR 345.

[15] *Quinn's Supermarket Ltd v Attorney General* [1972] 1 IR 1.

[16] *ibid* at 13 and 14.

[17] *ibid* at 14.

[18] [1981] IR 158 at 172 (*per* Kenny J).

[2–07] Thirdly, even if the claimant is a human person, a claim can only be made if the claim relates to the "essential attributes of the human person", a criterion that has "greatly emasculated the guarantee of equality".[19] There appear to be two diverging interpretations of the essential attributes doctrine; a contextual approach and a basis approach. The contextual approach espouses the idea that it is important to consider the context of the case. If the context is linked to some essential attribute of the human person then the claim will be considered. For example, in *Quinn's Supermarket Ltd v Attorney General*, as the context of the dispute was linked to the individual's trade or business this was not considered to be an essential attribute of a human person and as such did not fall within the scope of the guarantee. Walsh J referred to the concept of human persons as:

> " ... merely intended to illustrate the view that this guarantee refers to human beings for what they are in themselves rather than to any lawful activities, trades or pursuits which they may engage in or follow".[20]

However, Hogan and Whyte argue that:

> " ... if rights such as the right to work, to earn a livelihood, choose and follow a profession or career are natural personal rights, they are such because the ordinary conditions of the world, in which the human personality has to exist, impose necessities on that personality to which working, earning a livelihood, following a career etc are a response, the same can be said, with only a very slight expansion of these rights, of engaging in business, acquiring property ... and negotiation ancillary trading and working conditions".[21]

[2–08] Despite the clarity of this argument by Hogan and Whyte, the courts have reaffirmed this contextual approach in many cases.[22] There has been some evidence of judicial disquiet with this approach. For example in *Brennan v Attorney General*,[23] Barrington J commented that Art 40.1 is concerned with human beings in society displaying a move away from the human personality in context doctrine. However, on appeal to the Supreme Court, O'Higgins CJ restated and reaffirmed the restrictive doctrine. A move has been made in recent years to a "basis approach". In *Re Article 26 and the Employment Equality Bill 1996*,[24] counsel challenged the Bill on the grounds that

[19] GW Hogan and GF Whyte, *supra* n 5 at p 1342; See O Doyle, "The Human Personality Doctrine in Constitutional Equality Law" (2001) 9 ISLR 101; See also G Whyte "A Comment on the Constitutional Review Group's Proposals on Equality" in R Byrne and W Duncan (Irish Centre for European Law, Dublin, 1997) at pp 100–104; and J O'Dowd "The Principles of Equality in Irish Constitutional and Administrative Law" (1999) 11 ERPL 769 at pp 808–823.

[20] [1972] 1 IR 1 at 14.

[21] GW Hogan and GF Whyte, *supra* n 5 at p 1343.

[22] However, this been reiterated time and time again See *Murtagh Properties v Cleary* [1972] IR 330; *de Búrca and Anderson v Attorney General* [1976] IR 38; and *Murphy v Attorney General* [1982] IR 241.

[23] *supra* n 3.

[24] (1997) 4 BHRC 91.

certain provisions discriminated on grounds of age. The Supreme Court went into great detail in assessing the proportionality of the measure in the employment context, a fact "not usually seen as a an essential attribute of human personality" and Hogan and Whyte view this as the court now seeing:

> "Article 40.1 as having a much wider field of application than previously thought, covering any context in which discrimination or classification may have been based on the essential attribute of the human person."[25]

So what constitutes an essential attribute of the human person? In *Quinn's Supermarket Ltd v Attorney General*, Walsh J referred to "ethnic or racial, social or religious background"[26] attributes while accepting that this list was incomplete. In *Re Article 26 and the Employment Equality Bill 1996* the Supreme Court indicated that classifications based on sex, race, language, religious or political opinions were presumptively proscribed by Art 40.1.[27] In *Redmond v Minister for the Environment*[28] all classifications adversely affecting the dignity of the individual were considered to be essential attributes of the human person.[29] Classifications based on wealth, pregnancy, language, nationality or which inhibit or impede the exercise of constitutional rights might also be considered to be essential attributes of the human person.[30]

Given the confusion surrounding the human personality doctrine, it is not surprisingly then that the Constitutional Review Group recommended that the words "as human persons" should be deleted from Art 40.1.[31] However, an extension of the guarantee to legal persons or collective bodies was not recommended.

What is a Law and Who is the Addressee for the Purposes of Article 40.1?

The equality guarantee applies to all laws (common law[32] and statutory law) but not international agreements.[33] It also includes the process of enacting the law, the application of the law and the administration of the law.[34] In the case of *East Donegal Co-op Limited v Attorney General*,[35] the court had to consider the Livestock Marts Act 1967 which provided that marts could only take place with a licence from the Minister for Agriculture. In the High Court, O'Keeffe P held that the Act could be operated in such a manner as to differentiate between citizens in an arbitrary manner. In the [2–09]

[25] GW Hogan and GF Whyte, *supra* n 5 at p 1345.
[26] *Quinn's Supermarket Ltd v Attorney General, supra* n 15 at 14.
[27] *Re Article 26 and the Employment Equality Bill 1996, supra* n 24 at 107.
[28] [2001] 4 IR 61.
[29] *Per* Herbert J Dignity was also used as the qualifying criterion in *Criminal Assets Bureau v PS* [2004] IEHC 351.
[30] GW Hogan and GF Whyte, *supra* n 5 at p 1350.
[31] Constitution Review Group, *Report of the Constitution Review Group* (Stationery Office, Dublin, 1996) at p 198.
[32] See for example the case of *State (DPP) v Walsh* [1982] IR 412. Where it was held that the common law defence of marital coercion was available to a wife in certain circumstances.
[33] *McGimpsey v Ireland* [1990] 1 IR 110.
[34] GW Hogan and GF Whyte, *supra* n 5 at p 1326.
[35] [1970] IR 317.

Supreme Court, this argument was rejected because it was held that the Minister must carry out his discretion in a manner compatible with the constitutional guarantees and solely to further the objects of the Act and that the Minister would have to show rational justification for attaching different conditions to two licences in a given area providing evidence that the guarantee applies to administrative acts as well as the enactment and application of the law.

[2–10] Naturally, the legislature is open to scrutiny for legislative acts and administration. However, the equality provision is aimed at all organs of government including the executive and the judiciary. An example of the executive branch of Government being held to scrutiny by the judiciary in relation to Art 40.1 is the case of *McKenna v An Taoiseach No 2*[36] where the Supreme Court held that the use of public money by the executive in support of a particular outcome in a constitutional referendum was unconstitutional. Denham J held that the right to equality "includes the concept that in the democratic process, including referenda, neither side of an issue will be favoured, treated unequally by the Government".[37] Naturally it also binds the judiciary. In the case of *The People (Attorney General) v O'Driscoll*[38] the defendant alleged that they had been discriminated against in a criminal trial because they were members of the travelling community. The complaint made was that the judge in some way permitted the fact that the applicants were members of the travelling community to creep into the evidence or to colour the case in a way which had caused them to be the objects of discrimination at the trial.[39] Walsh J noted that if such a position were established "the conviction would be quashed without hesitation".[40] However no such disclosure was made. Henchy J has stated that Art 40.1 requires that "people who appear before the Courts in essentially the same circumstances should be dealt with in essentially the same manner".[41]

The Problem of Under-Inclusive Classifications

[2–11] Some difficulties have emerged in equality cases where legislation which provides for a certain right for a group of individuals but does not apply this right to another set of individuals (under-inclusive). An example of such a law would be a law that provides that widows but not widowers are entitled to a specific benefit. In such cases, an argument has arisen in the courts as to what remedy would be effective in a particular case and this has largely depended on the type of law under consideration. Where a common law rule is under-inclusive, the courts have appeared content to extend the law to cover the previously excluded group. So in the case of *McKinley v Minister for Defence*,[42] a common law rule that provided that the tort of loss of consortium could only be claimed by husbands and not wives was extended so as to allow wives to

36 [1995] 2 IR 10.
37 *ibid* at p 52. See also GW Hogan and GF Whyte, *supra* n 5 at p 1332.
38 [1972] 1 Frewen 351. See also GW Hogan and GF Whyte, *supra* n 5 at p 1332.
39 *The People (Attorney General) v O'Driscoll* [1972] 1 Frewen 351 at 353.
40 *supra* n 38 p 353. See GW Hogan and GF Whyte, *supra* n 5 at p 1336.
41 *The State (Keegan) v Stardust Compensation Tribunal* [1986] IR 642 at 658.
42 [1992] 2 IR 333.

recover for loss of consortium. However, where an under-inclusive classification arises in a statutory context the courts are not so content to extend the law for fear of being accused of judicial law making.

Where the court refuses to extend the rule, the only other option is to strike the rule down as incompatible with the Constitution, something the courts have also been reluctant to do as this would leave the included class of persons with no right and the excluded class of person with no right. For example in the case of *Somjee v Minister for Justice*[43] which involved a statutory provision which allowed female non-nationals who married Irish males to have citizenship but non-national males who married Irish females had to wait for a period of two years before being allowed to apply for citizenship. In this case the court held that the rule was not invalid and even if it was "a declaration of incompatibility" would not have given any redress to the plaintiff. The court did not consider extending the legislation as this was the role of the legislature and not the courts. Interestingly, in a more recent case *G v District Judge Murphy and Ors*,[44] there appears to be an attempt made to circumvent this under-inclusive classification problem. In this case a person who had been charged with an indictable offence and had mental capacity could plead guilty before the District Court but those who did not have this capacity, but were later found to do so, were not able to avail of this mechanism. Hogan J, in the High Court, did not strike down the legislation or extend the legislation—merely he granted a declaration that in the event that the applicant was found fit to plead in the Circuit Court and subsequently pleaded guilty, if a sentence of more than the equivalent District Court sentence was imposed this would be in breach of the plaintiff's right to equality under Art 40.1. **[2–12]**

Who has the Burden of Proof?

In all cases, due to the presumption of constitutionality of legislation, the plaintiff has the burden of proving that the particular statutory provision in question is unconstitutional. However, there has been some discussion in the equality cases that there may be certain circumstances in which the burden may shift to the defendant to prove that an inequality is in fact justified under the Constitution. **[2–13]**

A good example is the case of *Gallagher v Minister for Finance*[45] in which the court had to consider whether certain employees who were exempted from the pension levy were being treated unequally to other employees who were not. In dealing with the issue of burden of proof, the High Court had to consider whether the burden of proof rested on the plaintiff or whether there was a shift from the plaintiff to the defendant once the unequal treatment had been established. The court quoted with approval the *dictum* of McMahon J in *Haire v Minister for Health and Children*[46] to the effect that "the normal rule is well established that Acts passed by the Oireachtas are entitled to the **[2–14]**

[43] [1981] ILRM 324.
[44] [2011] IEHC 445.
[45] [2010] 10 JIC 0803.
[46] [2010] 2 IR 615.

presumption of constitutionality until the contrary is proved".[47] In quoting from the decision in *JD* v *Residential Institutions Redress Board*[48] he held that:

> " ... any person wishing to challenge the compatibility of a provision of an Act of the Oireachtas with the Constitution must overcome and rebut the fundamental principle of the presumption of constitutionality which operates in favour of the impugned provision".[49]

However, there are some judicial decisions which propose that where the discrimination is based on one of the very essential attributes of human personality such as sex or race, then it would appear that the burden of proof shifts to the State to defend the classification. However, where the difference in treatment is not so clear, the courts leave the burden of proof with the plaintiff. In *Haire v Minister for Health and Children*,[50] there was a suggestion that in some cases, where discrimination as such is based on sex, race language or religious or political opinion "that the onus of proof may shift and the State may be obliged to justify the legislation in the first instance".[51] In any case, the general feeling arising from the courts' decisions is that the burden of proof on a plaintiff in equality cases is very high.

What Constitutes an Interference with the Right?

[2–15] It is unclear whether Art 40.1 prohibits both direct and indirect discrimination and, in furtherance of some clarity in the area, the Constitutional Review Group[52] has recommended that there be explicit reference in the Article to both direct and indirect discrimination so as to put the question beyond doubt.

What is clear is that there must be some difference in treatment which amounts to an interference with Art 40.1. A good example of this is the case of *Dillane v Ireland*[53] where a provision of the District Court Rules prohibited the District Court Judge from awarding costs against a "member of the Garda Síochána acting in discharge of his duties as a police officer".[54] The court held that there was a difference in treatment in this case because the District Justice may grant "costs or witnesses' expenses to an accused if the person who prosecuted him is not a member of the Garda Siochana" but not if he is. Similarly in the case of *G v District Judge Murphy and Ors*,[55] the High Court had to consider a case in which the legislation provided that a person charged with an indictable offence and whose mental capacity was not in doubt could avail themselves of a guilty plea before the District Court but no such mechanism was in place for persons whose capacity was in doubt but who was later found fit to plead. In

---

47 *ibid* at 659.
48 [2009] IESC 59.
49 *Haire v Minister for Health and Children, supra* n 46 at 659. See also *Re Article 26 and the Employment Equality Bill 1996, supra* n 24 at 357 (*per* Keane CJ); and *Brennan v Attorney General, supra* n 3 at 480 (*per* Barrington J).
50 *supra* n 46.
51 *Haire v Minister for Health and Children, supra* n 46 at 659
52 *supra* n 31.
53 [1980] ILRM 167.
54 *ibid at* 167.
55 *supra* n 44.

this case, the High Court found a "plain inequality of treatment with potentially far-reaching consequences".[56]

Establishing a difference in treatment necessarily requires the use of a comparator. For example, in *Breathnach v Ireland*,[57] the right of a prisoner to vote involved a comparison with other prisoners and as no other prisoners had a right to vote: [2–16]

> " . . . consequently there is no inequality as between prisoners. The inequality as between a free person and a person lawfully in prison arises as a matter of law. It is a consequence of lawful custody that certain rights of the prisoner are curtailed, lawfully. Many constitutional rights are suspended as a result of the lawful deprivation of liberty. It is a consequence of a lawful order not an arbitrary decision".[58]

This comparative approach is also evident in the case of *JW v JW*,[59] where Blayney J made a comparison between husbands and wives and married and unmarried women in considering the common law rule on domicile and whether a married woman had an independent domicile from that of her husband. Blayney J held that:

> " . . . if the rule were still in force a married woman would not be held equal before the law. She would be in a position of inequality firstly by comparison with her husband, and secondly by comparison with women who are not married".[60]

The rule would also treat unequally the married woman by comparison with a woman who is not married. It would continue to attribute an independent domicile to the latter whereas the former, simply by virtue of her marriage, would cease to have an independent domicile.[61] Interestingly, Blayney J also looked not only at the theoretical inequality in the rule but also at the practical inequalities that might arise. [2–17]

> "For example, on her death, the law to be applied in the administration of her movable estate would be that of the domicile of her husband, so that if he had left her and established a domicile in a foreign country where she had never been, it would nonetheless be the law of that country which would apply. This obviously might cause considerable hardship to her estate. In addition, domicile is an important factor in giving a court jurisdiction in matrimonial matters and in this regard also a married woman could be prejudiced by not having an independent domicile".[62]

In the case of *Foy*,[63] McKechnie J, once again drew a simple comparison between transgender persons:

> "What difference of treatment there is, it should be pointed out, does not apply within male to female transsexuals as a group, or within female to male transsexuals as a group.

---

[56] *ibid* at para 31
[57] [2001] 3 IR 230.
[58] *ibid* at 249 (*per* Denham J).
[59] [1993] 2 IR 477.
[60] *ibid* at 499 (*per* Blayney J).
[61] *supra* n 58 at 499 (*per* Blaney J).
[62] *ibid.*
[63] [2002] IEHC 116

> In either of these groups if the post-surgical transsexual was to seek the same rectification as the applicant does, the Register General would respond in precisely the same way. Therefore I do not believe there is any breach of this article."[64]

[2–18] Another good example of the application of the comparator is that of *de Búrca v Attorney General*[65] where the Supreme Court had to consider whether a law[66] which excluded citizens who were not ratepayers from the lists of jurors and exempted women from jury service was "invidious" within the meaning of Art 40.1. The Supreme Court held that both the exclusion of citizens who were not ratepayers and the exemption of women did, in fact, amount to invidious discrimination. In relation to the issue of sex discrimination, Walsh J made a simple comparison between the treatment of men and women and concluded that the different treatment of women in this context was:

> " ... undisguisedly discriminatory on the ground of sex only. It would not be competent for the Oireachtas to legislate on the basis that women, by reason only of their sex, are physically or morally incapable of serving and acting as jurors. The statutory provision does not seek to make any distinction between the different functions that women may fulfil and it does not seek to justify the discrimination on the basis of any social function. It simply lumps together half of the members of the adult population, most of whom have only one thing in common, namely, their sex. In my view, it is not open to the State to discriminate in its enactments between the persons who are subject to its laws solely upon the ground of the sex of those persons. If a reference is to be made to the sex of a person, then the purpose of the law that makes such a discrimination should be to deal with some physical or moral capacity or social function that is related exclusively or very largely to that sex only".[67]

2. Legitimate Justifications for Interference with the Right

[2–19] Even where there is evidence of disparate treatment, there may be a legitimate justification for the difference in treatment which will save the offending difference in treatment from falling foul of the constitutional guarantee of equality. Where a difference in treatment has been found by the court, such differences may in fact be legitimate as long as they are related to a difference in capacity—physical or moral—or a difference in social function (second sentence in Art 40.1) or serve a particular constitutional value. However, the courts have also held that the rule must also satisfy a proportionality test defined as a "legitimate legislative purpose ... it must be relevant to that purpose, and that each class must be treated fairly".[68] This test has been expanded upon in recent years and the most cited formulation is now that of Costello J to the effect that the measure must:

> "(a) be rationally connected to the objective and not be arbitrary, unfair or based on irrational considerations; (b) impair the right as little as possible, and (c) be such that their effects on rights are proportional to the objective".[69]

---

64 *ibid* at para 174.
65 *de Búrca v Attorney General, supra* n 22.
66 s 3, Juries Act 1927.
67 *de Burca v Attorney General, supra* n 22 at 71.
68 *Brennan v Attorney General, supra* n 3 at 480 (*per* Barrington J).
69 *Heaney v Ireland* [1994] 3 IR 593 at 607, *per* Costello J in his landmark judgment.

Social Function

This has been one of the most utilised legitimate aims examined by the courts in the Irish context. One of the key cases in which the courts have found that a difference in social function justified a difference in treatment is the case of *Dillane v Ireland*[70] where the court found that the "desirability that members of the Garda Síochána should be encouraged to discharge their police duties assiduously by being given immunity from liability for costs or witnesses' expenses in the District Court" justified a discrimination which meant that costs could not be awarded against a Garda Síochána who was acting in the course of his duties.[71] Similarly, in *Landers v Attorney General*[72] the Supreme Court held that the provisions of the Prevention of Cruelty to Children Act 1904 which prevented a child from giving singing performances on licensed premises at night were not in contravention of Art 40.1 as there was a social function in ensuing protection for children. **[2–20]**

Other differences in social function which might justify a difference in treatment include the function of marriage. In *Murphy and Murphy v Attorney General*[73] it was argued that the taxation system treated married couples more unfavourably than unmarried couples. Kenny J held that the: **[2–21]**

> " . . . social function of married couples living together is such as to justify the legislature in treating them differently from single persons for income tax purposes . . . This particular unfavourable tax treatment of married couples living together, set against the many favourable discriminations made by the law in favour of married couples, does not, in the opinion of the Court, constitute an unequal treatment forbidden by Article 40, s. 1, particularly having regard to the vital roles under the Constitution of married couples as parents, or potential parents, and as heads of a family".[74]

Physical Capacity

One of the earliest cases in Irish equality law is also a case related to the difference in treatment of a person of different physical and social capacity (in this case a mental illness). In *re Philip Clarke*,[75] the applicant claimed that the provisions of the Mental Treatment Act 1945, were in breach of Art 40.1. However, the Supreme Court held that the person had a different capacity due to "mental infirmity" and the legislation was intended to ensure the "care and custody" of such persons for the "safety and well-being of the public generally".[76] In a very different context, difference in capacity has been a justifying ground for laws which require proficiency in the Irish language **[2–22]**

---

[70] *supra* n 53.

[71] *Dillane v Ireland, supra* n 53 at 499; See also the case of *Brohoon v Ireland* [2011] IEHC 74. where the court approved the decision in *Dillane v Ireland.*

[72] [1997] 3 IR 347.

[73] [1982] IR 241.

[74] *ibid* at 284.

[75] [1950] IR 235.

[76] *ibid* at 247 (*per* O'Byrne J).

as long as such proficiency is relevant to the discharge of the duties of the office.[77] A difference in capacity was also a justifying factor in the case of prisoners and non-prisoners and the right to vote.[78]

Moral Capacity/Social Function

[2–23] Moral capacity is often cited alongside social function by the courts in justifying differences in treatment and, as such, it could be argued that the two are often inextricably linked. In the case of *State (Nicolaou) v An Bord Uchtala*[79] the applicant took a case against the State alleging that the Adoption Act 1952 was inconsistent with Art 40.1 as it prevented the natural father from having a role in consenting to, or refusing, the adoption of a non-marital child, whereas the natural mother had such rights. The Supreme Court held that unmarried fathers did not have a moral capacity or a social function in relation to the child based on the fact that it was "rare for a natural father to take any interest in his offspring"[80] and therefore the difference in treatment between unmarried mothers and unmarried fathers could be justified. However, this reasoning has been criticised by Barrington J in *WO'R v EH*[81] where he held that as the father was a loving and caring parent to treat him in the same category as other unmarried fathers who were not so loving and caring was "treating equally persons who were in different situations, and amounted to unfair discrimination".[82] In *MacMathuna v Ireland*[83] the plaintiffs claimed that a rule that allowed an unmarried mother to get a tax-free allowance of £2,000 which was not available to married couples was contrary to Art 40.1. Carroll J held that:

> " . . . position of a single parent is different to the position of two parents living together. The parent on his or her own has a more difficult task in bringing the children up singlehandedly because two parents living together can give each other mutual support and assistance. I have no doubt that the role of a single parent is more difficult than that of two parents and that in giving a tax-free allowance to a single parent, the Oireachtas recognised that and attempted to alleviate it".[84]

[2–24] Similarly the differences in moral capacity and social function between legitimate and illegitimate children were highlighted in *State (M) v AG*[85] in a case where the Adoption Act 1952 was challenged on the grounds that it allowed a passport to be issued to a legitimate child to go and live with its father's family abroad but not in the case of an illegitimate child. The High Court held that there is a:

> " . . . difference of moral capacity and social function [between a legitimate and illegitimate child] at least in the context of the removal of the child out of the State.

---

77 *O'Shiel v Minister for Education* [1999] 2 IR 321.
78 *Breathnach v Ireland, supra* n 57.
79 [1966] IR 567.
80 *ibid* at 641 (*per* Walsh J).
81 [1996] 2 IR 248.
82 *ibid* at 280.
83 [1989] 1 IR 504.
84 *ibid* at 511 (*per* Carroll J).
85 [1979] IR 73.

> A legitimate child is part of a family unit; the rights and, in a sense, the duties of the family being specifically provided for in the Constitution. In the generality of cases, the illegitimate child has not the benefit of being a member of a family unit ... further, in my view there is much weight in the submissions to the effect that, in the generality of cases, the mother of an illegitimate child may be subjected to strains, stresses and pressures arising from the economic and social conditions which fully justify the Legislature in making special provisions with regard to the welfare of an illegitimate child".[86]

Differences in social function and moral capacity have also been held to exist between men and women. In *Norris v Attorney General*,[87] O'Higgins CJ held that the legislature would be perfectly entitled to "have regard to the difference between the sexes and to treat sexual conduct or gross indecency between males as requiring prohibition because of the social problem which it creates, while at the same time looking at sexual conduct between females as being not only different but as posing no such social problem".[88]

Barrington J addressed the matter of differences in social and moral capacity in *Brennan & Ors v The Attorney General*[89] where he stated that: **[2–25]**

> " ... to legislate is to discriminate. The legislature in its efforts to redress the inequalities of life or for other legitimate purposes may have to classify the citizens into adults and children, employers and workers, teachers and pupils and so on. Pringle J stated in *O'Brien* v *Manufacturing Engineering Company Limited* [1973] IR 334 that such division of the citizens into different classes was envisaged by the second sentence of Art. 40.1".[90]

He then added:

> "Therefore it would appear that there is no unfair discrimination provided every person in the same class is treated in the same way. No doubt this is true, but it might be prudent to express, what is perhaps implied in it, that the classification must be for a legitimate legislative purpose, that it must be relevant to that purpose, and that each class must be treated fairly".[91]

Distinctions on the Basis of Other Constitutional Values

In *O'Brien v Stoutt*,[92] there is some indication that justifications can be made on the basis of other constitutional articles and that: **[2–26]**

> " ... if legislation can be justified under one or more Articles of the Constitution, when read with all the others, it cannot be held to be unjust within the meaning of any Article".[93]

---

86 *ibid* at 78 (*per* Finlay P).
87 [1984] IR 36.
88 *ibid* at 59.
89 *Brennan v Attorney General, supra* n 3 at 480.
90 *ibid.*
91 *ibid.*
92 [1984] 1 IR 316.
93 *ibid* at 335 (*per* Walsh J).

Doyle[94] notes that in *O'Brien v Stoutt*[95] the Supreme Court upheld the constitutionality of ss 67 and 69 of the Succession Act 1965 having regard to the constitutional guarantees relating to the family or legitimate public policy objectives. Another example is the case of *Dennehy v Minister for Social Welfare*[96] where the plaintiff was a married man with two children who had been deserted by his wife. He applied for benefit as a deserted spouse under the Social Welfare (Consolidation) Act 1981 but his claim was refused as the benefit only applied to deserted wives. If he had been a woman he would have qualified. The court held that having regard to Art 41.2 it was not unreasonable, unjust or arbitrary for the Oireachtas to protect deserted wives who were mothers having dependent children residing with them or to recognise that mothers having dependent children residing with them or who had had to care for children would have lost out in the labour market and so were likely to need protection. This reliance on other constitutional articles was also a key feature of *Re Article 26 and the Illegal Immigrants Trafficking Bill 1999*[97] where the Supreme Court rejected challenges to certain immigration decisions which had to be taken in an unusually short period of time, in order to serve the:

> " ... legitimate public policy objective of seeking to bring about at an early stage legal certainly as regards the administrative decisions in question. It also facilitates the better administration and functions of the system of dealing with applicants for asylum or refugee status".[98]

3. Proportionality

[2–27] In *Dillane v Ireland*[99] the court accepted that in order for a difference in treatment to be justified it must not be:

> " ... arbitrary or capricious or otherwise not unreasonably capable, when objectively viewed in the light of the social function involved, of supporting the selection or classification complained of".[100]

In examining a difference in treatment the court will apply a standard of invidious discrimination.[101] The courts seem to be unhappy with this concept and Kenny J has described it as "more likely to mislead than to help".[102] The Irish Constitution and Art 40.1 forbid discrimination which is "arbitrary, unreasonable or unjust".[103] Therefore, the constitutional provision of equality provides that some forms of discrimination are justifiable as long as such discriminatory treatment does not amount to arbitrary, unjust or unreasonable treatment, an Aristotelian concept of treating "equals equally,

94 O Doyle, *supra* n 6 at pp 321–323.
95 *supra* n 92.
96 [1984] IEHC 27.
97 [2000] 2 IR 360.
98 *ibid* at 403.
99 *supra* n 53.
100 *supra* n 53, at 169. See also *Brohoon v Ireland* [2011] IEHC 74.
101 GW Hogan and GF Whyte, *supra* n 5 at p 1353.
102 *Murphy and Murphy v Attorney General, supra* at n 73 at 286.
103 J Casey, *supra* n 6 at p 452, quoting from *O'Brien v Stoutt* [1984] IR 316 at 355.

and unequals unequally".[104] Other concepts used to define unreasonableness include "invidious",[105] "capricious",[106] or "unjust". While this may seem like a perfectly simple test, Casey notes that "this test is notoriously difficult to apply".[107]

A useful example is the case of *Prendergast v The Higher Education Authority, the Minister for Education and Science, Ireland the Attorney General*[108] where the court had to consider whether there was a breach of the equality guarantee where an Irish student could not apply and pay for a place at a University that was designated for non-EU nationals. The High Court, in applying the proportionality test held that: **[2–28]**

> " ... once the Oireachtas strikes a reasonable balance in the resolution of that question, the courts must not interfere even though they might have balanced the result differently".[109]

In this case:

> " ... the access to State subsidised education at primary degree level by European citizens should be unrelated to any ability by the student, or his or her parents, to gain such a place by paying economic fees, at the expense of another student who does not have that ability".[110]

In the case of *Loftus v Attorney General*,[111] the Supreme Court had to consider the validity of the provisions of Electoral Act 1963, s 13 which provided, in effect, that political parties which on that date were represented in the Dáil were given automatic registration in accordance with s 13, while all other political parties had to apply for registration and had to comply with the statutory provisions in order to succeed. The court looked at the difference between existing and new parties and concluded that no discrimination could be found because: **[2–29]**

> "The very fact of being represented in the Dáil satisfied, in respect of each such party, the statutory requirements that the party be genuinely political and that it be organised to contest elections. To require existing parties, not then represented, or newly-formed parties to apply and to satisfy these requirements in the manner laid down in the section is a treatment of such parties in a manner which, although necessarily different, is not invidious and unfair."[112]

In the case of *Dokie v Director of Public Prosecutions at the Suit of Garda Thomas Moreley*,[113] the applicant challenged a law which required non-nationals to carry identity documents as such a law was a disproportionate interference with the equality

---

[104] *de Búrca and Anderson v Attorney General, supra* at n 22 at 68.

[105] *O'Brien v Stoutt, supra* n 91 at 355; See also *O'Brien v Keogh* [1972] IR 144 and *O'Brien v Manufacturing Engineering Company Limited* [1973] IR 334 at 364 (*per* Walsh J).

[106] *Dillane v Attorney General, supra* n 53 at 169.

[107] J Casey, *supra* n 6 at p 453.

[108] [2008] IEHC 257.

[109] *ibid* at para 74.

[110] *supra* n 108 at para 74.

[111] [1979] IR 221.

[112] *ibid* at 242–243 (*per* O'Higgins CJ).

[113] [2010] IEHC 110.

provisions in the Constitution as Irish nationals were not required to carry any identification. Kearns J held that the law was not disproportionate as the State had a public interest in having suitably strict measures to deal with undocumented entrants in the State.

4. Relevant Irish Legislation Protecting the Right to Equality

[2–30] At a statutory level, there is a great deal of legislation protecting individuals against both direct and indirect discrimination in both employment and in the provision of goods and services. In the employment context, the Employment Equality Act 1998 (as amended by the Equality Act 2004) protects against both direct and indirect discrimination in the employment context on nine distinct grounds: gender, marital status, family status, sexual orientation, religion, age, disability, race and membership of the travelling community.[114] Outside the employment context, the Equal Status Act 2000 (as amended by the Equality Act 2004) protects against discrimination in the provision of goods and services to the members of the public on the same nine grounds.

B. Protection under the European Convention on Human Rights

[2–31] Article 14:

> "The enjoyment of the rights and freedoms set forth in this Convention shall be secured without discrimination on any ground such as sex, race, colour, language, religion, political or other opinion, national or social origin, association with a national minority, property, birth or other status."

Protocol 12, Art 1 (not yet ratified by Ireland):

> "1. The enjoyment of any right set forth by law shall be secured without discrimination on any ground such as sex, race, colour, language, religion, political or other opinion, national or social origin, association with a national minority, property, birth or other status.
>
> 2. No one shall be discriminated against by any public authority on any ground such as those mentioned in paragraph 1."

1. Nature of the Right

[2–32] Unlike other discrimination provisions in other constitutional and international documents, Art 14 does not provide for a standalone provision on equality. This means that if a person wants to make a claim relating to Art 14, they have to hang this claim on another right as set out in the Convention. For example, if an unmarried father wanted to claim that he was treated differently to a married father, he would have to claim that his right to family life (as protected by Art 8) was being interfered with in a discriminatory manner (as protected by Art 14). In this respect, Art 14 has been described as a "parasitic provision"[115] which merely "complements"[116]

---

[114] s 6.

[115] D Harris, *et al*, *Law of the European Convention on Human Rights* (2nd ed, Oxford University Press, Oxford, 2009) at p 548.

[116] *EB v France* (Application No 43546/02) at para 47.

other provisions of the ECHR. Protocol 12 fills this gap by providing for a standalone non-discrimination clause. However, this has not been ratified by many States, leaving Art 14 as the most important non-discrimination clause in the Convention in the Irish context.

A good case example, illustrating the most important principles of Art 14, is the *Belgian Linguistics* case.[117] In this case, the applicants sought a declaration that certain provisions of the Belgian Linguistics legislation relating to education were not in conformity with Arts 8 and 14, and Protocol 1, Art 2 of the Convention. The applicants, of Belgian nationality and French speaking, wanted to have their children educated in French. However, they lived in Dutch-speaking regions where education was conducted in Dutch. In relation to Art 14, the ECtHR took the opportunity to clarify some important aspects of Art 14. The Court reiterated that Art 14 "has no independent existence"[118] but it is to be interpreted as "though the latter formed an integral part of each of the Arts laying down rights and freedoms".[119] In relation to the test to be applied in Art 14 cases, the court held that Art 14 does not forbid every difference in treatment and that the "principle of equality of treatment is violated if the distinction has no objective and reasonable justification".[120] It: **[2–33]**

> " ... must not only pursue a legitimate aim: Article 14 is likewise violated when it is clearly established that there is no reasonable relationship of proportionality between the means employed and the aim sought to be realised".[121]

In this case, the court held that there was a violation of Art 14 in conjunction with Protocol 1, Art 2 because it prevented certain children, solely on the basis of the residence of their parents, from having access to the French-language schools.

One important question which has arisen is that if a claim is made under, for example Art 8 and 14, but no breach of the main article is found, (in this case Art 8), can a breach of Art 14 be found independent of this other article of the Convention? If Art 14 is raised in conjunction with another Article, yet no breach of that other Article is found, the ECtHR can still hold that a breach of Art 14 has occurred.[122] However, where a separate breach of another Article is found, the ECtHR may decide not to consider the Art 14 argument unless "a clear inequality of treatment is a fundamental aspect of the case".[123] It has repeatedly been held that Art 14 of the Convention is pertinent if "the subject matter of the disadvantage ... constitutes one of the modalities of the exercise of a right guaranteed ... ", or if the contested measures are "linked to the exercise of a right guaranteed ... ".[124] Therefore, for Art 14 to be **[2–34]**

---

117 Application Nos 1474/62; 1677/62; 1691/62; 1769/63; 1994/63; 2126/64.

118 *ibid* at para 9. See, among many other authorities, *Sahin v Germany* (Application No 30943/96) at para 85.

119 *ibid.*

120 *ibid* at para 10.

121 *ibid.*

122 *Belgian Linguistics, supra* n 117; *Sommerfeld v Germany* (Application No 31871/96).

123 *Aziz v Cyprus* (Application No 69949/01); *Airey v Ireland* (Application No 6289/73); *Dudgeon v United Kingdom* (Application No 7525/76); and *Chassagnou v France* (Applications Nos 25088/94, 28331/95 and 28443/95).

124 *Petrovic v Austria* (Application No 156/1996/775/976) at para 28.

applicable, it is enough for the facts of the case to fall within the ambit of one or more of the provisions of the Convention.[125]

Although the application of Art 14 does not presuppose a breach of another Article of the Convention, it has been held that "there can be no room for its application unless the facts at issue fall within the ambit of one or more of them".[126] The prohibition of discrimination enshrined in Art 14 extends beyond the enjoyment of the rights and freedoms, "to those additional rights, falling within the general scope of any Convention Article, for which the State has voluntarily decided to provide".[127] This principle has now become well entrenched in the court's case-law.[128] In the case of *EB v France*,[129] the applicant challenged the French adoption law which discriminated against her on the grounds of her sexual orientation. The court held that even though Art 8 did not guarantee the right to adopt,[130] where the State goes beyond its obligations under Art 8 in creating such a right, "it cannot, in the application of that right, take discriminatory measures within the meaning of Article 14".[131]

What Constitutes an Interference with the Right?

[2–35] The court has established in its case law that only differences in treatment based on an identifiable characteristics, or "status", are capable of amounting to discrimination within the meaning of Art 14.[132] Article 14 lists a number of prohibited grounds of discrimination including, sex, race, colour, language, religion, political or other opinion, national or social origin, association with a national minority, property, birth or other status. The reference to other status would suggest that the list is non-exhaustive and the court has held that other grounds such as age, sexual orientation, marital status, illegitimacy, status as a trade union member, military status, conscientious objection, professional status and imprisonment, are protected by Art 14.[133] The court has reiterated that all differences "having as their basis or reason a personal characteristic by which persons or groups of persons are distinguishable from each other"[134] are covered by Art 14. However, similar to the Irish position, this has caused some confusion. For example, financial status is not generally considered to

[125] *Thlimmenos v Greece* (Application No 34369/97) at para 40; *EB v France, supra* n 116 pargraphs 47–48; and *Fretté v France* (Application No 36515/97) at para 31.

[126] *Konstantin Markin v Russia* (Application No 30078/06) at para 124; *Abdulaziz, Cabales and Balkandali v United Kingdom* (Application Nos 9214/80; 9473/81; 9474/81) at para 71; *Karlheinz Schmidt v Germany* (Application No 13580/88) at para 22; and *Petrovic v Austria, supra* n 123 at para 22.

[127] *Munoz Diaz v Spain* (Application No 49151/07) at para 42.

[128] *Konstantin Markin v Russia, supra* n 125 at para. 124. See, among many other authorities, *EB v France, supra* n 115 at paras 47–48. *Belgian Linguistics Case, supra* n 117 at para 9; *Abdulaziz, Cabales and Balkandali v United Kingdom, supra* n 125 at para 78; and *Stec and Others v the United Kingdom* (Application Nos 65731/01 and 65900/01) at para 40.

[129] *supra* n 116.

[130] *Fretté v France, supra* n 124 at para 32; *EB v France, supra* n 115 at para 41.

[131] *supra* n 116 at para 49.

[132] *O'Donoghue and Others v United Kingdom* (Application No 34848/07) at para 101; *Kjeldsen, Busk Madsen and Pedersen v Denmark* (Application No 5095/71; 5920/72; 5926/72) at para 56.

[133] D Harris, *et al*, *supra* n 115 at p 584.

[134] *Kjeldsen, Busk Madsen and Pedersen v Denmark, supra* n 132 at para 56.

be a personal characteristic but a person's profession (e.g. a fisherman)[135] is so considered.

The guarantee in Art 14 covers instances of both direct and indirect discrimination. The court has defined indirect discrimination as a "general policy or measure that has disproportionately prejudicial effects on a particular group"[136] and has stated that this may result from a "de facto situation".

The court has held that not every difference in treatment will amount to a violation of Art 14. It must be established that other persons in an analogous or relevantly similar situation enjoy preferential treatment and that this distinction is discriminatory.[137] This is essentially the comparator test which exists under the Irish Constitution. In the case of *Ünal Tekeli v Turkey*[138] the court had to consider whether a law that obligated women to change their maiden name on marriage was contrary to Art 8 in conjunction with Art 14. The court held, in relation to the application of Art 14, that it was so discriminatory as "undoubtedly a 'difference in treatment' on grounds of sex between persons in an analogous situation"[139] In other words, the notion of discrimination includes general cases where a person or group is treated, without proper justification, less favourably than another.[140] Article 14 does not "prohibit distinctions in treatment which are founded on an objective assessment of essentially different factual circumstances".[141] There is also an obligation on States to treat differently persons whose situations are significantly different. For example in *Thlimmenos v Greece*,[142] the applicant, a Jehovah's witness, was not appointed to the Greek Institute of Chartered Accountants on the grounds that he had a prior conviction for insubordination for failing to wear a military uniform which stemmed from the exercise of his religious beliefs. The Grand Chamber held that in certain circumstances the right not to be discriminated against could also be violated "when States without an objective and reasonable justification fail to treat differently persons whose situations are significantly different".[143] Harris notes that if the State had treated him differently then there would have been no violation of Art 9 or 14 in the circumstances.[144] **[2–36]**

---

135 *Alatulkkila and Others v Finland* (Application No 33538/96).

136 *DH and Others v Czech Republic* (Application No 57325/00) at para 175—*Hugh Jordan v United Kingdom* (Application No 24746/94) at para 154; *Zarb Adami v Malta* (Application No 17209/02) at para 76; D Harris, *et al*, *supra* n 115 at p 580.

137 *Ünal Tekeli v Turkey*, (Application No 29865/96) at para 49. See, for example, *National & Provincial Building Society, Leeds Permanent Building Society and Yorkshire Building Society v United Kingdom*, judgment of 23 October 1997, *Reports of Judgments and Decisions* 1997-VII at para 88.

138 *ibid.*

139 *ibid* at para 55. See *Schuler-Zgraggen v Switzerland*, (Application No 14518/89) at para 67.

140 *ibid* at para 51. See *Abdulaziz, Cabales and Balkandali v the United Kingdom, supra* n 126 at para 82.

141 See, among other authorities, *GMB and KM v Switzerland* (Application No 36797/97).

142 *supra* n 125.

143 *supra* n 125 at para 44.

144 D Harris, *et al*, *supra* n 115 at p 584.

2. Legitimate Justifications for Interference with the Right

[2–37] Under the Convention, differential treatment on some identifiable ground will constitute a breach of Art 14 unless "it has no objective and reasonable justification; in other words, if it does not pursue a legitimate aim".[145]

If the State does not claim any justifications, then "other than in exceptional circumstances",[146] the applicant will have proved his/her claim of discrimination. Where the State does put forward certain justifications, it "must be given a rational basis and an evidential foundation".[147] Some examples of legitimate aims proffered by governments include, the development of linguistic unity of two large language regions,[148] the protection of the labour market and public order,[149] or the protection of national security, public safety, the economic wellbeing of the country and the rights and freedoms of others.[150] Normally, the court gives a lot of leeway to the State in its legitimate objective unless evidence is brought forward to deny the justification. It is in this context that the margin of appreciation given to states becomes most relevant.[151] "The scope of the margin of appreciation will vary according to the circumstances, the subject matter and its background"[152] but the final decision as to the observance of the Convention's requirements rests with the Court.

> "Since the Convention is first and foremost a system for the protection of human rights, the Court must have regard to the changing conditions in Contracting States and respond, for example, to any emerging consensus as to the standards to be achieved".[153]

Proportionality

[2–38] The State must also show that the law is proportionate and in this regard the court must look at whether the measure strikes "a fair balance between the protection of the interests of the community and respect for the rights and freedoms safeguarded by the Convention".[154] While this question is not easily answered, there are some general principles which have emerged from the case law of the court.

145 *Konstantin Markin v Russia, supra* n 126 at para 125; *Stec and Others v the United Kingdom, supra* n 127 at para 51.

146 D Harris, *et al, supra* n 115 at p 586.

147 *ibid* at p 587.

148 *Belgian Linguistics, supra* n 117 at para 40.

149 *Barthold v Germany* A 94 (1985) 7 EHRR 163 para 78 and 81 PC.

150 *Sidabras and Dziautas v Lithuania* (Applications Nos 55480/00 and 59330/00) at para 55.

151 *Konstantin Markin v Russia, supra* n 125 at para 126; see *Gaygusuz v Austria* (Application no 17371/90) at para 42.

152 *Konstantin Markin v Russia, supra* n 125 at para 126; see *Rasmussen v Denmark* (Application No 8777/79) at para and *Inze v Austria* (Application no 8695/79) at para 41.

153 *Konstantin Markin v Russia, supra* n 125 at para 126; See *Weller v Hungary* (Application No 44399/05) at para 28; *Stec and Others v the United Kingdom, supra* n 127 at paras 63–64; *Ünal Tekeli, supra* n 136 at para 54; and, *mutatis mutandis, Stafford v the United Kingdom* (2002) 35 EHRR 32 at para 68.

154 *Belgian Linguistics, supra* n 117 at para 7.

Discretion on Grounds of Social and Economic Policy

First and in general, the court grants a very wide discretion to States where issues of economic or social policy are involved. The case of *Burden* v *United Kingdom*[155] involved two sisters who had lived together all their lives in a house that they inherited from their parents. The applicants submitted that the value of their jointly-owned property had increased to the point that each sister's one-half share was worth more than the current exemption threshold for inheritance tax, and that the survivor might have to sell the house in order to pay the tax, whereas if they were a married couple living together this would not be the case. In relation to the proportionality of the measure, the ECtHR held that: **[2–39]**

> " ... any system of taxation, to be workable, has to use broad categorisations to distinguish between different groups of tax payers. The implementation of any such scheme must, inevitably, create marginal situations and individual cases of apparent hardship or injustice, and it is primarily for the State to decide how best to strike the balance between raising revenue and pursuing social objectives ... In the circumstances of the case, the Court finds that the United Kingdom cannot be said to have exceeded the wide margin of appreciation afforded to it and that the difference of treatment for the purposes of the grant of inheritance tax exemptions was reasonably and objectively justified for the purposes of Article 14 of the Convention."[156]

Comparative Standards in Member States

Secondly, the court will examine comparative standards in Member States and where there is a marked deviance, the court is more likely to find that the actions of the State are disproportionate. In *Konstantin Markin v Russia*,[157] the court had to consider a difference in treatment between servicemen and servicewomen in relation to parental leave. The court held that the argument advanced by the State, that the special social role of women in the raising of children justified the measure and observed "the gradual evolution of society towards a more equal sharing between men and women of responsibilities for the upbringing of their children".[158] It referred, in particular to the case of *Petrovic v Austria*[159] in which it held that a distinction on the basis of sex with respect to parental leave allowances, which had existed in Austria in the 1980s, was not in violation of Art 14 taken in conjunction with Art 8. The court held that at the time the court had taken into account "the great disparity at the material time between the legal systems of the Contracting States in the sphere of parental benefits".[160] The court went on to hold that times had changed and that the **[2–40]**

> "relevant international and comparative-law material demonstrates that the evolution of society—which began in the 1980s as acknowledged in the *Petrovic* case—has since significantly advanced. It shows that in a majority of European countries, including in Russia itself, the legislation now provides that parental leave may be taken by civilian men and women, while the countries limiting the parental leave entitlement to women are in a

155 Application No 13378/05.
156 *ibid* at paras 60–61.
157 *Konstantin Markin v Russia, supra* n 126.
158 *ibid* at para 139.
159 *supra* n 124.
160 *Petrovic v Austria, supra* n 124 at para 139.

> small minority. Even more important for the present case is the fact that in a significant number of the Member States both servicemen and servicewomen are also entitled to parental leave. It follows from the above that contemporary European societies have moved towards a more equal sharing between men and women of responsibility for the upbringing of their children and that men's caring role has gained recognition. The court cannot overlook the widespread and consistently developing views and associated legal changes to the domestic laws of Contracting States concerning this issue".[161]

The More Limited the Rule, the More Limited the Interference

[2–41] Thirdly, where the rule is specific to a Member State, Harris has argued that "the more limited in scope the alleged differential treatment is the easier it is for it to be outweighed by 'lighter' public interest considerations".[162] A good example of this is the case of *Cha'are Shalom Ve Tsedek v France*,[163] in which the applicant argued that the refusal of the French authorities to give the approval necessary for it to authorise its own ritual slaughterers, in accordance with the religious prescriptions of its members, infringed in a discriminatory way their right to manifest their religion through observance of the rites of the Jewish religion. The court in examining the proportionality of the measure, held that as the measure had "limited effect" and was "limited in scope",[164] it was not disproportionate.

Less Intrusive/More Proportionate Measures

[2–42] Fourthly, while the court does examine whether less intrusive or more proportionate measures exist, Harris comments that:

> " ... the court frequently asserts that it is not its function to substitute itself for the national decision-maker, if the applicant can identify an alternative this will not be decisive evidence that the state has acted excessively".[165]

It would appear that the margin of appreciation afforded to States extends to choosing between various alternatives.[166]

Specific Categories of Discrimination: Specific Treatment

[2–43] Finally, in relation to certain specific categories of differential treatment the court has been known to apply a much more intensive scrutiny of legitimate justifications and will require "weighty reasons" before it will find that a measure is justifiable. This statement has been made in relation to race and ethnicity, sex, nationality, sexual orientation, religion, and the illegitimate birth status of an individual.[167] Harris also argues that race and religion are also contained in this category and it might well be that such treatment applies specifically to those grounds listed in Art 14.

[161] *ibid* at para 140; See *mutatis mutandis, Smith and Grady v United Kingdom* (Applications Nos 33985/96 and 33986/96) at para 104.
[162] D Harris, *et al, supra* n 115 at p 589.
[163] Application no 27417/95.
[164] *Cha'are Shalom Ve Tsedek v France, supra* n 163 at para 87.
[165] D Harris, *et al, supra* n 115 at p 589.
[166] *Rasmussen v Denmark, supra* n 152 at para 41.
[167] D Harris, *et al, supra* n 115 at p 590.

The grounds that have been defined as "suspect" will now be defined more clearly. Discrimination on the grounds of race, ethnic or national origin has been described as a "particular invidious kind of discrimination...(that) in view of its perilous consequences, requires from the authorities special vigilance and a vigorous reaction".[168] In the case of *Timishev v Russia*[169] the ECtHR held that

> "ethnicity and race are related and overlapping concepts. Whereas the notion of race is rooted in the idea of biological classification of human beings into subspecies according to morphological features such as skin colour or facial characteristics, ethnicity has its origin in the idea of societal groups marked by common nationality, tribal affiliation, religious faith, shared language, or cultural and traditional origins and backgrounds".

Protocol 12

Protocol 12 Article 1—General prohibition of discrimination. **[2–44]**

(1) The enjoyment of any right set forth by law shall be secured without discrimination on any ground such as sex, race, colour, language, religion, political or other opinion, national or social origin, association with a national minority, property, birth or other status.
(2) No one shall be discriminated against by any public authority on any ground such as those mentioned in paragraph 1.

The Protocol was adopted in November 2000, and came into force in April 2005, having had the necessary ten State ratification, and as of writing (2012) has a total, from 47 Council of Europe members, of 19 member States and 18 signatory States.

Protocol 12 prohibits discrimination in relation to 'enjoyment of any right set forth by law' and has, therefore, a potentially greater application than Art 14, which relates only to the rights guaranteed by the ECHR. The main addition of Protocol 12 to the jurisprudence of Art 14 is that it is not seen as having the same 'parasitic' nature in relation to the substantive rights of the ECHR, but this seems to have led to some caution on the part of States when considering ratification, and, hence, there is very little Protocol 12 jurisprudence.

The grounds of discrimination remain the same, which, since the list is non-exhaustive, means that the Court can keep options open for any possible additions to discrimination in the future, in line with the 'living instrument' aims of the Convention. Likewise, the concept of positive discrimination by a State on reasonable and objective grounds can be justified, as under the existing Art 14. This is also seen in the Explanatory Report, which states categorically that Protocol 12:

> " ... is to embody a negative obligation for the Parties: the obligation not to discriminate against individuals."[170]

---

[168] *DH v Czech Republic* [2007] ECHR 57325/00 at para 176.
[169] *Timishev v Russia* (2005) 44 EHRR 776 at para 55.
[170] Protocol No 12 to the Convention for the Protection of Human Rights and Fundamental Freedoms (ETS No 177), Explanatory Report, para 22, Available at: http://conventions.coe.int /Treaty/en/Reports/Html/177.htm.

Adding that Protocol 12 is certainly not:

> " . . . intended to impose a general positive obligation on the Parties to take measures to prevent or remedy all instances of discrimination in relations between private persons."[171]

However, the Explanatory Report also makes clear that this may differ where the State has input into the regulation of relations between individuals, such as "...for example, arbitrary denial of access to work, access to restaurants, or to services which private persons may make available to the public such as medical care or utilities such as water and electricity."[172]

In the case of *Sejdić and Finci v Bosnia and Herzegovina*,[173] so far the only case brought under Protocol 12, the ECtHR stated that Protocol 12 should be seen as introducing a general prohibition of discrimination, and affirmed that it intended to follow the same lines of reasoning that it had applied in Article 14 cases.

The applicants in this case, who were of Jewish and Roma origin, complained that they were unable to stand in elections. The background to this case was that as part of a peace settlement to bring an end to the conflict of the 1990s, a power-sharing agreement was put in place between the three main ethnic groups. This included that any candidate standing for election had to declare an affiliation to either the Bosnian, Serb or Croat community. The applicants refused to do so and alleged discrimination on the basis of race and ethnicity.

Repeating its explanation of the relationship between race and ethnicity, the ECtHR conflated ethnic and racial discrimination, emphasising the interplay between ethnicity and religion, and finally finding that, despite the terms of the peace agreement, there was insufficient justification for the discrimination suffered by the applicants.

It is important to consider equality claims in light of other Articles of the Convention and where overlaps occur to consider potential claims based on this overlap. A useful illustration is a claim of discrimination on the grounds of ethnicity. Discrimination on the grounds of race, ethnic or national origin has been defined as a "particular invidious kind of discrimination. . .(that) in view of its perilous consequences, requires from the authorities special vigilance and a vigorous reaction".[174] In the case of *Timishev v Russia*[175] the ECtHR held that "ethnicity and race are related and overlapping concepts. Whereas the notion of race is rooted in the idea of biological classification of human beings into subspecies according to morphological features such as skin colour or facial characteristics, ethnicity has its origin in the idea of societal groups marked by common nationality, tribal affiliation, religious faith, shared

[171] Protocol No 12 to the Convention for the Protection of Human Rights and Fundamental Freedoms (ETS No 177), Explanatory Report, para 24. Available at: http://conventions.coe.int /Treaty/en/Reports/Html/177.htm.

[172] Protocol No 12 to the Convention for the Protection of Human Rights and Fundamental Freedoms (ETS No 177), Explanatory Report, para 28. Available at: http://conventions.coe.int /Treaty/en/Reports/Html/177.htm.

[173] *Sejdić and Finci v Bosnia and Herzegovina* (27996/06, 34836/06) 22 December 2009.

[174] *DH v Czech Republic* [2007] ECHR 57325/00 at para 176.

[175] *Timishev v Russia* (2005) 44 EHRR 776 at para 55.

language, or cultural and traditional origins and backgrounds".[176] What is interesting in this regard is the holistic approach, which the Court seems to be moving toward, of considering ethnicity together with race and also religious faith. In this regard, it is worth considering the link between Art 9 and Art 14 and Protocol 12. Where there is a discrimination on grounds of ethnicity, this may fall within Protocol 12 (where this is applicable) or it may well fall within Art 14 in conjunction with Art 9. In developing a case based on ethnic discrimination then, an applicant may therefore wish to consider, not only a claim based on racial or ethnic discrimination, but also a case based on Art 9.

C. CFR

Article 21 CFR: **[2–45]**

> "1. Any discrimination based on any ground such as sex, race, colour, ethnic or social origin, genetic features, language, religion or belief, political or any other opinion, membership of a national minority, property, birth, disability, age or sexual orientation shall be prohibited.
>
> 2. Within the scope of application of the Treaty establishing the European Community and of the Treaty on European Union, and without prejudice to the special provisions of those Treaties, any discrimination on grounds of nationality shall be prohibited."

One of the first notable features of Art 21 is that it includes much wider grounds of discrimination than are covered expressly by the ECHR and extends to a wider range of economic, social and cultural rights. There has been a lot of emphasis on non-discrimination law in the EU since its inception and this review seeks to provide a very brief overview of the myriad of protections that are available under EU Law.[177]

The Treaty on the Functioning of the European Union (TFEU) provides in Art 19 that without:

> " ... prejudice to the other provisions of the Treaties and within the limits of the powers conferred by them upon the Union, the Council, acting unanimously in accordance with a special legislative procedure and after obtaining the consent of the European Parliament, may take appropriate action to combat discrimination based on sex, racial or ethnic origin, religion or belief, disability, age or sexual orientation."

This treaty provision is supplemented by a wide variety of Directives with varying scope and provisions. This chapter seeks to outline, based on grounds of discrimination, the protections currently available in EU Law.

---

[176] *ibid* at para 55.

[177] M Dawson, E Muir and M Claes, "Enforcing the EU's Rights Revolution: The Case of Equality" (2012) 3 EHRLR 276; J Cameron, "What You Can Do with Rights" (2012) 2 EHRLR 147; S Spencer and J Pobjoy, "Equality for All? The Relationship Between Immigration Status and the Allocation of Rights in the United Kingdom" (2012) 2 EHRLR 160; T Papadoupolous, "Criticising the horizontal direct effect of the EU general principle of equality" (2001) 4 EHRLR 437.

1. Gender

[2–46] Gender equality has been a key aspect of EU policy since 1975 and continues to be a cornerstone of the development of EU social policy. Employment was the first area to receive significant attention under the EU anti-discrimination agenda. Equal pay between men and women is protected by the Equal Pay Directive of 1975[178] and provides for the elimination of gender discrimination in all aspects of pay during employment. An extension of gender equality to other aspects of employment law was facilitated by the Equal Treatment Directive of 1976[179] which seeks to eliminate sex discrimination (both direct and indirect or by reference to marital or family status) in access to employment, training, working conditions, promotion or dismissal. Similar protections, in relation to pregnancy and motherhood, were extended to self-employed women in 1986.[180] In 1992, in order to improve and harmonise protections for pregnant workers across the EU, the Pregnant Workers Directive was introduced[181] and this was followed by further efforts to encourage family friendly procedures such as parental leave 1996.[182] Finally, in an effort to extend and harmonise the protections against sex discrimination in employment, the Equal Treatment in Employment Directive was introduced in 2002 to define certain concepts such as harassment and to develop equality bodies to support, monitor and promote equal treatment in the workplace.[183] These Directives were all complemented by the Burden of Proof Directive which required Member States to amend the burden of proof to allow for greater equity between the parties in sex discrimination cases.[184] The extension of the concept of gender discrimination to other areas outside of the employment sphere did not occur until 2004 with the introduction of the Goods and Services Directive[185]

---

[178] Council Directive 75/117/EEC of 10 February 1975 on the approximation of the laws of the Member States relating to the application of the principle of equal pay for men and women, *Official Journal* L 045, 19 February 1975 pp 19–20.

[179] Council Directive 76/207/EEC of 9 February 1976 on the implementation of the principle of equal treatment for men and women as regards access to employment, vocational training and promotion, and working conditions, *Official Journal* L 039, 14 February 1976 pp 40–42.

[180] Council Directive 86/613/EEC of 11 December 1986 on the application of the principle of equal treatment between men and women engaged in an activity, including agriculture, in a self-employed capacity, and on the protection of self-employed women during pregnancy and motherhood, *Official Journal* L 359, 19 December 1986 pp 56–58.

[181] Council Directive 92/85/EEC of 19 October 1992 on the introduction of measures to encourage improvements in the safety and health at work of pregnant workers and workers who have recently given birth or are breastfeeding (tenth individual Directive within the meaning of Article 16 (1) of Directive 89/391/EEC), *Official Journal* L 348, 28 November 1992 pp 1–8.

[182] Council Directive 96/34/EC of 3 June 1996 on the framework agreement on parental leave concluded by UNICE, CEEP and the ETUC, *Official Journal* L 145, 19 June 1996 pp 4–9.

[183] Directive 2002/73/EC of the European Parliament and of the Council of 23 September 2002 amending Council Directive 76/207/EEC on the implementation of the principle of equal treatment for men and women as regards access to employment, vocational training and promotion, and working conditions (Text with EEA relevance), *Official Journal* L 269, 05 October 2002 pp 15–20.

[184] Council Directive 97/80/EC of 15 December 1997 on the burden of proof in cases of discrimination based on sex, *Official Journal* L 014, 20 January 1998 pp6–8.

[185] Council Directive 2004/113/EC of 13 December 2004 implementing the principle of equal treatment between men and women in the access to and supply of goods and services, *Official Journal* L 373, 21 December 2004 pp 37–43.

which applies the principle of equal treatment to goods and services available in the public sphere but not to education. Finally in 2006, the Recast Directive on Equal Treatment in Employment and Occupation enhanced the coherence of the law relating to gender discrimination in the workplace.[186]

2. Other Forms of Discrimination

It was not until 2000, that the EU developed specific legislation in relation to protection against discrimination in the employment context, and in the case of race, both within and outside the employment context. Within the employment context, everyone is protected against discrimination by virtue of the Employment Equality Directive 2000.[187] The purpose of the Directive is to "lay down a general framework for combating discrimination on the grounds of religion or belief, disability, age or sexual orientation as regards employment and occupation" and to protect workers against both direct and indirect discrimination in this context. Special provisions are made in relation to age discrimination including allowing employers to discriminate on the grounds of age where there are general occupational requirements (Art 4) or where the difference in treatment is: [2–47]

> " ... objectively and reasonably justified by a legitimate aim, including legitimate employment policy, labour market and vocational training objectives, and if the means of achieving that aim are appropriate and necessary" (Art 6).

This is in stark contrast to the other provisions of the Directive in which only indirect discrimination can be justified by reference to an "objectively justified ... legitimate aim and the means of achieving that aim are appropriate and necessary". Special provisions are also made in relation to disability including reasonable accommodation measures for the purposes of enabling: [2–48]

> " ... a person with a disability to have access to, participate in, or advance in employment, or to undergo training, unless such measures would impose a disproportionate burden on the employer" (Art 5).

Outside of the employment context, racial equality is also protected by virtue of the Racial Equality Directive.[188] The Directive prohibits both direct and indirect discrimination and applies to a wider variety of goods and services than the Gender Equality Directive applies to including health and social care and education.

---

[186] Directive 2006/54/EC of the European Parliament and of the Council of 5 July 2006 on the implementation of the principle of equal opportunities and equal treatment of men and women in matters of employment and occupation (recast), *Official Journal* L 204, 26 July 2006 pp 23–36.

[187] Council Directive 2000/78/EC of 27 November 2000 establishing a general framework for equal treatment in employment and occupation, *Official Journal* L 303, 02 December 2000 pp 16–22.

[188] Council Directive 2000/43/EC of 29 June 2000 implementing the principle of equal treatment between persons irrespective of racial or ethnic origin, *Official Journal* L 180, 19 July 2000, pp 22–26.

Nature of the Right

[2–49] Discrimination on the grounds of sex, racial or ethnic origin, religion or belief, disability, age or sexual orientation are all prohibited in the employment context by a variety of directives (outlined above). Gender and race discrimination are also prohibited in the context of public goods and services, although the Race Equality Directive would appear to have a wider scope than the Gender Equality Directives. For example, racial equality in the provision of education is protected in the Race Equality Directive but not in the context of gender or any other form of discriminatory grounds.

Interference with the Right

[2–50] All of the Directives prohibit both direct and indirect discrimination. Direct discrimination is generally defined[189] as having occurred where one person is treated less favourably than another is, has been or would be treated in a comparable situation, on any of the grounds and indirect discrimination is defined as an apparently neutral provision, criterion or practice would put persons at a particular disadvantage compared with other persons unless: that provision, criterion or practice is objectively justified by a legitimate aim and the means of achieving that aim are appropriate and necessary. Therefore, there can be no defence for direct discrimination but this is not the case in relation to indirect discrimination.

[2–51] Indirect discrimination, by its very nature, is very difficult to prove but there are certain aspects of it that require clarification. First, it is important that there is an apparently neutral rule or provision. Secondly, it must place that protected group of individuals at a particular disadvantage. Normally statistical evidence of disadvantage would be required to prove that such disadvantage exists. The case of *Schonheit*[190] is a good example of this. In that case, there was a rule which provided that part-time workers had their pensions calculated on a different rate to full time workers. While the neutral rule applied to all part-time workers, as most the part-time workers were women, the European Court of Justice (CJEU) held that this placed women at a particular disadvantage in relation to their pension entitlements.

Legitimate Justification for Interference with the Right

[2–52] In the context of indirect discrimination, all the Directives provide the defence of a legitimate aim, which is proportionate to the aim sought to be achieved, in order to justify a difference in treatment. It should be noted that "this is not, strictly speaking, a defence to discrimination as such but rather a justification of differential treatment, which will prevent a finding of discrimination being made. However, in substance, if not in form, the courts treat issues of justifications as defences to discrimination".[191] A good example of this is the case of *Bilka-Kaufhaus GmbH v Weber Von Hartz*[192] in

---

[189] Joined Cases C–4/02 and C–5/02 *Hilde Schönheit v Stadt Frankfurt am Main* and *Silvia Becker v Land Hessen.*

[190] Case C–4/02 *Hilde Schönheit v Stadt Frankfurt am Main.*

[191] European Union Fundamental Rights Agency Handbook on Anti-Discrimination Law at p 44 http://fra.europa.eu/fraWebsite/attachments/182601_FRA_CASE_LAW_HANDBOOK_ENpdf, last accessed 27 July 2012.

[192] Case C–170/84 *Bilka-Kaufhaus GmbH v Karin Weber von Hartz.*

which part-time workers were excluded from the occupational pension scheme. As most of the part-time workers in Bilka–Kaufhaus were women, it was argued that this was indirect discrimination against women. The CJEU held that the:

> " ... measures chosen by Bilka correspond to a real need on the part of the undertaking, are appropriate with a view to achieving the objectives pursued, and are necessary to that end".[193]

The argument of Bilka was that it wanted to incentivise full-time work as part-time workers were inflexible and made it difficult for Bilka to maintain adequate staffing at peak times such as Saturdays and evenings. The CJEU considered that this was a legitimate aim within the context of the Directive. The case law of the CJEU would suggest that broader social and employment policy goals with fiscal implications are more likely to be considered legitimate whereas more specific management goals based on the economic resources of an undertaking would not be so well-received. Naturally, the CJEU must also consider whether an aim is proportionate, that is that the aim is necessary and that there are no other more proportionate ways in which the aim could be achieved.

D. International and Regional Laws

The right to equality and non-discrimination is a cornerstone of other human rights regimes, both internationally and nationally. The basis of the universal human rights system is set out in Art 1 of the Universal Declaration of Human Rights (UDHR) which states that all people are born "free and equal in dignity and rights". Therefore, all people should access, and benefit from, all human rights equally. Consequently, Art 2 of the UDHR states: [2–53]

> "Everyone is entitled to all the rights and freedoms set forth in this Declaration, without distinction of any kind, such as race, colour, sex, language, religion, political or other opinion, national or social origin, property, birth or other status."

The list of bases on which distinction is prohibited under this provision is not exhaustive, thus allowing the provision to be interpreted in light of an evolving society. The right to equality is also protected at an international level in Art 2 and Art 3 of the International Covenant on Civil and Political Rights, Art 2 and Art 3 of the International Covenant on Social, Economic and Cultural Rights, Art 1 of the UN Convention on the Elimination of All Forms of Racial Discrimination, Art 1 of the UN Convention on the Elimination of All Forms of Discrimination against Women, Art 5 of the UN Convention on the Rights of People with Disabilities and Article 2 of the Convention on the Rights of the Child. At a regional level, the right to equality is protected by Art 1 and Art 24 of the American Convention on Human Rights, Art 2 of the African Charter on Human and Peoples' Rights and Art 3 of the Arab Charter on Human Rights.

Conclusion

Equality is the cornerstone of all human rights and is the basis upon which all other human rights rely. From this analysis, it is clear that certain classifications receive [2–54]

193 *ibid* at para 36.

protection at a national, regional and international level, including sex, race, religion, disability, sexual orientation and age. However, this list is not conclusive and all national, regional and international texts provide scope for the recognition of other classifications by using terms such as "other status". In relation to the scope of the rights, it is clear that the national and regional protections limit the scope of the application of the equality guarantee to certain key areas. In the context of national law, the restriction takes the form of a judicial determination that the issue complained of is linked in some way to the "essential attributes" of the individual, an issue that has limited the application of the guarantee to such things as employment. While there is extensive protection available in the form of legislation (Employment Equality Acts 1998–2004, Equal Status Act 2000), it is unfortunate that the equality guarantee has been limited in this uncertain way. Similarly, in the ECHR context, the equality guarantee is limited to the exercise of the rights guaranteed within the Convention, which are all civil and political rights with the exception of education. At an EU level, the situation is even more restrictive with only gender and race discrimination being protected outside the employment context.

[2–55] Similar treatment of the right to equality is provided across all legal systems. All national and regional protections require the identification of a difference in treatment and all systems appear to protect, although not expressly, both direct and indirect discrimination. In relation to defences, the Irish approach would appear to be the most complicated as some link has to be made to the second part of Art 40.1 which refers in rather archaic language to differences in capacity and function as being legitimate justifications for differences in treatment. Only EU law expressly provides that there can be no legitimate justification for direct discrimination. All of the systems apply a proportionality test which appears to be fairly consistently applied.

CHAPTER 3
The Right to Life

Introduction

The most basic of all rights is the right to life. Nowak states that it "is often characterized as the supreme or most fundamental of all human rights, since without an effective guarantee of this right, all other rights of the human being would be devoid of meaning".[1] Unsurprisingly, this right is protected by various international and legal provisions and is also protected as a fundamental right under the Irish Constitution. The constitutional provision and the prohibition on abortion in Ireland have been the source of much legal and academic debate in both Ireland and in the European Court of Human Rights (ECtHR). This chapter examines the Irish Constitution's protection of the right to life and then discusses the right to life under the European Convention on Human Rights (ECHR) and under the Charter of Fundamental Rights (CFR). The chapter concludes with a brief study of the right to life under international and regional human rights instruments. **[3–01]**

A. Irish Constitution

Article 40.3: **[3–02]**

> "1° The State guarantees in its laws to respect, and, as far as practicable, by its laws to defend and vindicate the personal rights of the citizen.
>
> 2° The State shall, in particular, by its laws protect as best it may from unjust attack and, in the case of injustice done, vindicate the life, person, good name, and property rights of every citizen.

[1] M Nowak, "Article 6: The Right to Liberty and Security" in *Commentary of the Charter of the Fundamental Rights of the EU*, June 2006 p 30, available at: http://infoportal.fra.europa.eu/InfoPortal/infobaseShowContent.do?btnCat_182&btnCountryBread_169, last accessed 21 June 2012.

> 3° The State acknowledges the right to life of the unborn and, with due regard to the equal right to life of the mother, guarantees in its laws to respect, and, as far as practicable, by its laws to defend and vindicate that right.
>
> This subsection shall not limit freedom to travel between the State and another state.
>
> This subsection shall not limit freedom to obtain or make available, in the State, subject to such conditions as may be laid down by law, information relating to services lawfully available in another state."

[3–03] Article 40.3.2° places an obligation on the State to vindicate the life of every citizen. This right has rarely been litigated in Irish courts. This is perhaps unsurprising, given the fact that the State does not, generally, interfere with the right to life of citizens and is constitutionally obliged to vindicate the right. Article 40.3.3° equally protects the right to life of a mother and the right to life of the unborn child. The latter provision was inserted into the Constitution in 1983 following a referendum. The question of how to adequately balance the right to life of the unborn with the right to life of the mother is very complex. Unfortunately, the Irish Government has yet to enact legislation which elucidates the law in this area. The recent ECtHR decision in the case of *A, B and C v Ireland*[2] has increased the pressure on the Government to regulate the provision of termination of pregnancy services in the State, but legislation in this area is still lacking.[3]

1. Nature of the Right

[3–04] The multifaceted nature of the right to life was highlighted in the case of *G v An Bord Uchtála* where Walsh J stated that "the right to life necessarily implies the right to be born, the right to preserve and defend (and to have preserved and defended) that life, and the right to maintain that life at a proper human standard in matters of food, clothing and habitation".[4]

When does Life Begin?

[3–05] Whilst Art 40.3 seeks to vindicate the right to life of Irish citizens, and the right to life of the unborn, it does not address the question of when life begins. This question was,

---

[2] *A, B and C v Ireland* (2011) 53 EHRR 13.

[3] For a more detailed consideration of this case see the contributions of C Staunton, "As easy as A, B and C: will A, B and C v. Ireland be Ireland's wake-up call for abortion rights?" (2011) 18(2) *European Journal of Health Law* 205; B Daly, "'Braxton Hick's' or the birth of a new era? Tracing the development of Ireland's abortion laws in respect of European Court of Human Rights Jurisprudence" (2011) 18(4) *European Journal of Health Law* 375; S Calt, "A, B & C v Ireland: 'Europe's Roe v Wade?'" (2010) 14(3) *Lewis and Clark Law Review* 1189; S Donnelly, "A, B & C v Ireland: will the European Court of Human Rights address Ireland's restrictive abortion laws?" (2010) 16(1) *Medico-Legal Journal of Ireland* 16; S Krishnan, "What's the consensus: the Grand Chamber's decision on abortion in A, B and C v Ireland" (2011) *European Human Rights Law Review* 200; S McGuinness, "Commentary: A, B, and C leads to D (for delegation!): A, B and C v. Ireland 25579/05 [2010] ECHR 2032" (2011) 19(3) *Medical Law Review* 476; P Ronchi, "A B and C v Ireland Europe's Roe v Wade still has to wait" (2011) 127 (Jul) *Law Quarterly Review* 365; J Schweppe, "Taking Responsibility for the 'Abortion Issue': Some Thoughts on Legislative Reform in the Aftermath of A, B and C" (2011) 14(2) *Irish Journal of Family Law* 50.

[4] *G v An Bord Uchtála* [1980] IR 32 at 69.

however, recently addressed in the case of *Roche v Roche*.[5] The case centred on a married couple who subsequently separated and disagreed on what was to happen to three frozen embryos which were the result of *in vitro* fertilisation (IVF) treatment. Six viable embryos were created, with three being implanted into the mother, and three being frozen. The couple had a daughter who was a result of the IVF treatment. The appellant, the wife, wished to have the remaining eggs implanted with the hope of becoming pregnant but the husband refused to give consent to allow this and argued for a right not to reproduce. The appellant claimed that the frozen embryos were "unborn",[6] thus falling within the scope of protection of Art 40.3.3°. In the High Court, McGovern J stated:

> "The Courts have never, thus far, considered whether the word 'unborn' in Article 40.3.3° includes embryos in vitro ... There has been no evidence adduced to establish that it was ever in the mind of the people voting in the Eight Amendment to the Constitution that 'unborn' meant anything other than a foetus or child within the womb. To infer that it was in the mind of the people that 'unborn' included embryos outside the womb or embryos in vitro would be to completely ignore the circumstances in which the amendment giving rise to Article 40.3.3° arose".[7]

McGovern J then stated that embryos outside the womb have a very precarious existence and that while embryos *in vitro* deserve special respect, they are not "unborn" in the context of the Irish Constitution and it was up to the legislature to decide the issue.

On appeal, the Supreme Court decided the case with reference to the contract between the appellant and the respondent, finding against the appellant. In relation to the status of the "unborn" under Art 38, the Supreme Court upheld the decision of the High Court and held that the frozen embryos did not fall within the meaning of "unborn" for constitutional purposes. Thus, under the Irish Constitution the protection of the unborn begins once implantation occurs. The decision in this case places pressure on the legislature to enact legislation to deal with issues concerning assisted human reproduction and human embryonic stem cell research.[8] **[3–06]**

The Right to Die a Natural Death[9]

The Irish courts inferred a "right to die a natural death" from the right to life provisions of the Constitution in the case of *Re a Ward of Court (No 2)*.[10] This case concerned the right of a woman who had been in a near persistent vegetative state for over 20 years, following a minor gynecological procedure, to have medical treatment withdrawn and to die a natural death. The woman required fulltime nursing care and was incontinent and spastic. She could not speak, communicate, or swallow. She was fed through a nasogastric tube until 1992 but this seemed to cause her some distress and was replaced by a gastrostomy tube. Because her lungs and heart functioned **[3–07]**

---

5 *Roche v Roche* [2010] 2 IR 321.

6 In relation to the personhood of the foetus under Irish law, see N Cox, "Foetal Personhood in Perspective" in *The Unborn Child, Article 40.3.3° and Abortion in Ireland* (J Schweppe ed, Liffey Press, Dublin, 2008), pp 89–112.

7 *Roche v Roche* [2010] 2 IR 321 at 338.

8 See F Gough, "Ireland and the Frozen Embryo: A Slight Thawing?" (2010) 18(2) Med L Rev 239.

9 See D Feenan, "Death, Dying and the Law" (1996) 14 ILT 90.

10 *Re a Ward of Court (No 2)* [1996] 2 IR 79.

properly, she could have continued to live for many years with the aid of the feeding tube.

[3–08] In the High Court it was held that it was in the best interests of the ward that the feeding be discontinued and that she be allowed to die naturally. The test applied by the court in determining the issue was whether it was in the best interests of the ward that her life should be prolonged by the continuation of the abnormal, artificial means of nourishment, or, whether the medical treatment should be withdrawn. The case was appealed to the Supreme Court, with four judges upholding the High Court decision.

[3–09] The Supreme Court held that the nature of the right to life and its importance imposed a strong presumption in favour of taking all steps capable of preserving it, save in exceptional circumstances. However, the court also held that the treatment being afforded to the ward by means of a gastrostomy tube surgically inserted into her stomach was intrusive and an interference with the ward's bodily integrity. The Supreme Court upheld the test employed by the High Court. Hamilton CJ stated:

> "As the process of dying is part, and an ultimate, inevitable consequence, of life, the right to life necessarily implies the right to have nature take its course and to die a natural death and, unless the individual concerned so wishes, not to have life artificially maintained by the provision of nourishment by abnormal artificial means, which have no curative effect and which is intended merely to prolong life. This right, as so defined, does not include the right to have life terminated or death accelerated and is confined to the natural process of dying. No person has the right to terminate or to have terminated his or her life, or to accelerate or have accelerated his or her death".[11]

O'Flaherty J focused on the issue of natural death, stating "this case is not about terminating a life but only to allow nature to take its course".[12]

Euthanasia and Assisted Suicide[13]

[3–10] It is clear from the discussion in *Re a Ward of Court (No 2)* that Irish law does not infer a right to have one's life terminated or death accelerated; rather the right to die is simply a right to die a natural death and not to be kept alive by artificial means.[14] O'Flaherty J clearly distinguished the case of *Re a Ward of Court (No 2)* from situations of euthanasia, stating "[t]his case is not about euthanasia; euthanasia in the strict and proper sense relates to the termination of life by a positive act".[15] He then stated: "We are concerned here only with allowing nature to take its course and for the ward to die with dignity. We are not thereby going down any slippery slope or stepping into any abyss".[16]

[3–11] Section 2 of the Criminal Law (Suicide) Act 1993 (the 1993 Act) prohibits assisted suicide in Ireland. It prohibits the aiding, abetting, counselling or procuring the suicide

---

[11] *ibid* at 124.
[12] *ibid* at 131.
[13] See Irish Council for Bioethics, *Your Body, Your Death, Your Choice?*, available at: http://www.bioethics.ie/uploads/docs/Euthanasia.pdf, last accessed 21 June 2012.
[14] See *Re a Ward of Court (No 2)* [1996] 2 IR 79 at 124.
[15] *ibid* at 130.
[16] *ibid* at 131.

of another, which carry a 14-year prison sentence. However, any person who aids in this process is liable to be charged under the 1993 Act. To date, there have been no prosecutions under this legislation, but the possibility remains that if an individual were to assist in the suicide of another, then he or she could be prosecuted.[17] Given that UK law regarding assisted suicide is similar to Ireland's, recent UK cases are relevant, especially the case of *Purdy*.[18] Ms Purdy was diagnosed with primary progressive multiple sclerosis, which is incurable, in 1995. She now requires the use of an electric wheelchair and has lost the ability to perform many basic tasks. She has difficulty swallowing and has choking fits when she drinks. Her condition will continue to deteriorate. She wishes, at some point, to end her life by means of an assisted suicide in Switzerland, a State in which assisted suicide is legal. However, similar to the Irish 1993 Act, s 2(1) of the Suicide Act 1961 (the 1961 Act) in the UK prohibits a person from aiding the suicide of another. Ms Purdy's husband is willing to assist her suicide but the couple wanted clarification on the prosecution policy of the Director of Public Prosecutions (DPP) with regard to offences committed under the 1961 Act. The DPP refused to publish details of the prosecution policy and this was judicially reviewed in 2008. It was argued for Ms Purdy that, given the serious consequences for her husband if he assisted her suicide (up to 14 years in prison), the law should provide her with clarity on the prosecution issue so that she and her husband could regulate their conduct accordingly. The Court of Appeal described this situation as "an impossible dilemma"[19] but did not find in her favour, stating that her right to personal autonomy did not include the right to decide where and when to die. The Court of Appeal said that the failure to publish a crime-specific policy regarding assisted suicide did not invalidate s 2(1) of the 1961 Act. The case was appealed to the House of Lords following the ECtHR's decision in *Pretty v UK*,[20] discussed below. The House of Lords said the 1961 Act interfered with Ms Purdy's right to respect for her private life and that she had the right to determine how to die. The DPP was required to prepare a policy identifying the factors his office would take into account when deciding to prosecute assisted suicide offences.[21]

The Right to Life of the Unborn and Abortion

When the Supreme Court identified an unenumerated right to marital privacy in *McGee v AG*,[22] some began to fear the position in the United States, where the right to **[3–12]**

---

[17] Irish authorities had sought the extradition of an American man who had admitted assisting in the suicide of an Irish woman in Dublin in 2002. US authorities decided not to extradite. There have been reports of Gardaí intervening to stop people from travelling to Dignitas, a euthanasia clinic in Switzerland. See P Duncan, "Group Seeks Law Change on Assisted Suicide", *The Irish Times*, 13 April 2012.

[18] *R (on the application of Purdy) v DPP* [2009] UKHL 44. See K Greasley, "R(Purdy) v DPP and the Case for Wilful Blindness" (2010) 30(2) OJLS 301.

[19] *R (Purdy) v DPP* [2009] EWCA Civ 92; [2009] All ER(D) 197 (Feb) at para 9.

[20] (2002) 35 EHRR 1.

[21] This policy was published in 2010 - *Policy for Prosecutors in Respect of Cases of Encouraging or Assisting Suicide*, available at: http://www.cps.gov.uk/publications/prosecution/assisted_suicide_policy.html, last accessed 21 June 2012.

[22] *McGee v AG* [1974] IR 284.

privacy had been successfully raised to invalidate legislation which criminalised abortion[23] in the case of *Roe v Wade*,[24] would also happen in Ireland. This fear led to a campaign to ensure legal protection for the unborn child. This eventually culminated in a referendum in 1983 and the subsequent passing of the Eighth Amendment of the Constitution Act 1983 which inserted the first part of Art 40.3.3° into the Constitution. This has proven to be a controversial inclusion and led to the instigation of a number of cases before Irish courts and the ECtHR.

[3–13] In the case of *AG (SPUC (Ireland) Ltd) v Open Door Counselling Ltd*[25] the plaintiffs sought an injunction prohibiting Open Door Counselling from assisting women in Ireland to procure an abortion and from providing advice on abortion. This was granted by the High Court and Open Door Counselling appealed to the Supreme Court. In the Supreme Court Finlay CJ stated:

> "If it is established to the satisfaction of the Court that the admitted activities of the defendants constitute an assistance to pregnant women within the jurisdiction to go out of the jurisdiction for the purpose of having an abortion, then that is an activity which directly threatens the right to life of the unborn, not only in a single case but in all cases of women who are assisted by those activities to have an abortion.
>
> If, therefore, the jurisdiction of the courts is invoked by a party who has a *bona fide* concern and interest for the protection of the constitutionally guaranteed right to life of the unborn, the courts, as the judicial organ of government of the State, would be failing in their duty as far as practicable to vindicate and defend the right if they were to refuse relief upon the grounds that no particular pregnant woman who might be affected by the making of an order was represented before the court".[26]

[3–14] The defendants claimed that the Constitution contained an unenumerated right to receive and impart information, which in this case included information on abortion services abroad. This argument was, however, rejected by the court, with Finlay CJ stating:

> "The performing of an abortion on a pregnant woman terminates the unborn life which she is carrying. Within the terms of Article 40, s. 3, sub-s. 3 it is a direct destruction of the constitutionally guaranteed right to life of that unborn child.
>
> It must follow from this that there could not be an implied and unenumerated constitutional right to information about the availability of a service of abortion outside the State which, if availed of, would have the direct consequence of destroying the expressly guaranteed constitutional right to life of the unborn ... no right could constitutionally arise to obtain information the purpose of the obtaining of which was to defeat the constitutional right to life of the unborn child".[27]

---

[23] See J Casey, *Constitutional Law in Ireland* (3rd ed, Round Hall Sweet & Maxwell, Dublin, 2000), p 434.

[24] *Roe v Wade* (1973) 410 US 113.

[25] *AG (SPUC (Ireland) Ltd) v Open Door Counselling Ltd* [1988] IR 593.

[26] *ibid* at 623.

[27] *ibid* at 625.

The Supreme Court injunction stated:

> "And it is ordered that the defendants and each of them, their servants or agents, be perpetually restrained from assisting pregnant women within the jurisdiction to travel abroad to obtain abortions by referral to a clinic, by the making for them of travel arrangements, or by informing them of the identity and location of and method of communication with a specified clinic or clinics or otherwise".[28]

The defendants subsequently claimed a breach of the ECHR in the case of *Open Door Counselling and Dublin Well Woman v Ireland*,[29] where the ECtHR found a violation of Art 10.

In the case of *SPUC (Ireland) Ltd v Grogan (No 1)*,[30] the plaintiffs sought to restrain a number of student bodies from publishing welfare guides which included information on abortion services in England, claiming a breach of Art 40.3.3°. In the High Court, Carroll J found that an issue of European Communities (EC) law arose as to whether a right to receive and disseminate information on abortion existed under EC law, and referred the matter to the then European Court of Justice (ECJ), without granting the interlocutory injunction sought. The plaintiffs then appealed to the Supreme Court which held that the injunction should be granted. Finlay CJ stated: [3–15]

> " … where an injunction is sought to protect a constitutional right, the only matter which could properly be capable of being weighed in a balance against the granting of such protection would be another competing constitutional right. I am satisfied that in the instant case where the right sought to be protected is that of a life, there can be no question of a possible or putative right which might exist in European law as a corollary of a right to travel so as to avail of services, counterbalancing as a matter of convenience the necessity for an interlocutory injunction".[31]

The ECJ held that abortion was a service for the purposes of the EC Treaty and that a commercial agent of an abortion clinic in another Member State could legitimately distribute information on that service in Ireland.

The seminal abortion case in Ireland is the case of *AG v X*,[32] which led to the insertion of Art 40.3.3° into the Constitution. This case involved an application to prohibit a 14-year-old girl, who was pregnant as a result of unlawful carnal knowledge, from travelling to the UK for an abortion. The girl's parents had informed the Gardaí that the girl had been raped and also of their intention to bring her to the UK for an abortion. They inquired if evidence resulting from scientific tests carried out on the foetus, which may have led to the identification of the father, would be admissible in court. The Gardaí consulted with the DPP and the information was then communicated to the Office of the Attorney General. The Attorney General then obtained an interim injunction restraining the girl from travelling to the UK for an abortion. X and her family were already in the UK at this time but returned to Ireland to contest the [3–16]

---

[28] *ibid* at 627.

[29] *Open Door Counselling and Dublin Well Woman v Ireland* (1992) 15 EHRR 244.

[30] *SPUC (Ireland) Ltd v Grogan (No 1)* [1989] IR 753.

[31] *ibid* at 765.

[32] *AG v X* [1992] 1 IR 1.

injunction. Evidence from a clinical psychologist was heard which stated that there was a real and substantial risk that the girl would commit suicide if forced to continue with the pregnancy. However, in the High Court Costello J granted a permanent injunction, prohibiting her from travelling to the UK for the purpose of obtaining an abortion, stating that the risk to the life of the girl was less than the certainty that the life of the unborn would be terminated if the injunction was not made. The case was appealed to the Supreme Court, which reversed the High Court's decision, holding, by a majority, that there was a real and substantial threat to the life of the mother. Therefore, the termination of the pregnancy was legal. Finlay CJ stated:

> "I ... conclude that the proper test to be applied is that if it is established as a matter of probability that there is a real and substantial risk to the life, as distinct from the health, of the mother, which can only be avoided by the termination of her pregnancy, such termination is permissible, having regard to the true interpretation of Article 40.3.3°".[33]

It is clear from this case that abortion is permissible under Irish law in very limited circumstances only, i.e. where there is a real and substantial risk to the life of the mother which can only be avoided by the termination of the pregnancy.

[3–17] The decision in *X* was very controversial,[34] to both pro-life and pro-choice organisations. The pro-life campaigners were disappointed that an Irish court had allowed a woman to obtain an abortion, albeit in very limited circumstances, and the pro-choice campaigners were concerned about the court's comments regarding the prospect of women being restrained from travelling abroad to obtain an abortion.[35]

[3–18] In the aftermath of *X* the law in relation to access to information on abortion services was in need of amendment because, as Casey comments, "if a woman could lawfully seek an abortion abroad – even if only in limited circumstances – it would be curious of she could not obtain information enabling her to seek one".[36] Two referenda on the issue of abortion were held, one in 1992 and a second in 2002, but the Irish public rejected any change to the substantive right to life issue. In 1992, however, constitutional amendments were passed which allowed for the provision of information and the right to travel. These amendments expanded Art 40.3.3° to include the sentences:

> "This subsection shall not limit freedom to travel[37] between the State and another state. This subsection shall not limit freedom to obtain or make available, in the State, subject

---

[33] *ibid* at 54.

[34] See N Cox, "Judicial Activism, Constitutional Interpretation and the Problem of Abortion: *Roe v Wade* (1973) and *X v AG* (1992)" in *Leading Cases of the Twentieth Century* (Eoin O'Dell ed, Round Hall Sweet & Maxwell, Dublin, 2000), p 253.

[35] See J Casey, *supra* n 23, p 437.

[36] J Casey, *supra* n 23, p 438.

[37] It should be noted that an unenumerated right to travel also exists under the Irish Constitution. A right to travel within the State was interpreted as a personal right of every citizen by Kenny J in *Ryan v AG* [1965] IR 294 at 313, and this right to travel was developed in *State (M) v AG* [1979] IR 73 to include the right to travel outside of Ireland and the right to obtain a passport for such travel.

> to such conditions as may be laid down by law, information relating to services lawfully available in another state."

Following on from the enactment of the Fourteenth Amendment of the Constitution Act 1992, the Oireachtas drafted the Regulation of Information (Services outside the State for Termination of Pregnancies) Bill 1995.[38] The President referred this Bill to the Supreme Court under Art 26 with the court upholding the constitutionality of the Bill.[39] In *Re Article 26 and the Regulation of Information (Services outside the State for Termination of Pregnancies) Bill 1995*,[40] Hamilton CJ commented: **[3–19]**

> "If the purpose of the travel or the securing of information is to procure an unlawful abortion, then it would be unlawful having regard to the provisions of Article 40, s. 3, sub-s. 3 of the Constitution, but if the purpose was the procurement of a permitted or lawful abortion, i.e. one that complies with the test laid down in *The Attorney General v. X.* [1992] 1 I.R. 1, then neither the travel nor the giving or obtaining of information with regard thereto would be unlawful".[41]

The case of *A and B v Eastern Health Board*[42] considered a situation similar to the *X* case. The case concerned a girl who was pregnant as a result of an alleged rape and was in local authority care. However, in this case the girl's parents wanted to prevent the Health Board from arranging for her to have an abortion outside the jurisdiction. There was a risk that the girl would commit suicide if she was forced to continue with her pregnancy. Geoghegan J held that the evidence on the psychiatric state of the girl substantiated the risk of suicide and that, therefore, the girl could legally travel to procure an abortion. **[3–20]**

Geoghegan J highlighted the need for legislation in this area, stating:

> " . . . I think it highly undesirable for the courts to develop a jurisprudence under which questions of disputed rights to have a termination of pregnancy can only be determined by plenary action in the High Court. The High Court undoubtedly has a function in granting injunctions to prevent unlawful terminations taking place and it may in certain circumstances properly entertain an action brought for declarations and consequential orders if somebody is being physically prevented without just cause from having a termination. But it would be wrong to turn the High Court into some kind of licensing authority for abortions".[43]

---

[38] s 4 of the Regulation of Information (Services outside the State for Termination of Pregnancies) Act 1995 prohibits public advertisements for abortion services; s 5 prohibits information providers from promoting the termination of pregnancy; and s 6 deals with the prohibition on financial link between the information givers.

[39] *In re Article 26 and the Regulation of Information (Services outside the State for Termination of Pregnancies) Bill 1995* [1995] 1 IR 1.

[40] *ibid.*

[41] *ibid* at 34–35.

[42] *A and B v Eastern Health Board* [1998] 1 IR 464.

[43] *ibid.*

[3–21] The Constitutional Review Group's 1996 report found that Irish law on abortion was inadequate.[44] The report highlighted a number of gaps in the legal framework concerning abortion. One of the main issues highlighted by the group was the fact that there was no formal procedure for certifying that a real and substantial risk to the life of the mother existed. The lack of legislation with regard to abortion has been criticised by various United Nations and Council of Europe bodies,[45] which have all recommended that Ireland take steps to enact legislation in this area. These issues were all highlighted in the case of *A, B and C v Ireland* before the ECtHR in 2010,[46] where the court held that Ireland had breached Art 8 of the ECHR (right to private life) by failing to properly implement Art 40.3.3°. As a result of this judgment, Ireland is under an obligation to enact legislation regulating the area of abortion.[47]

Death Penalty

[3–22] The Irish Constitution was amended to prohibit the imposition of the death penalty following a referendum in 2001. Article 15.5.2° now states:

> "The Oireachtas shall not enact any law providing for the imposition of the death penalty."

Various other constitutional provisions had to be amended to come in line with this amendment.[48]

2. Legitimate Justifications for Interference with the Right

[3–23] It was held in the case of *Re a Ward of Court (withholding medical treatment) (No 2)* that although the State had an interest in preserving life, this interest was not absolute. The Supreme Court held that despite the fact that the right to life ranked first in the hierarchy of personal rights, it might nevertheless be subject to the citizen's right of autonomy, self-determination, privacy or dignity, when exercised by a competent citizen or on his or her behalf. However, as Hamilton CJ stated: "The nature of the

---

[44] *Report of the Constitution Review Group* (Stationery Office, Dublin, 1996), pp 273–279.

[45] These critiques are summarised in *A, B and C v Ireland* (2011) 53 EHRR 13.

[46] *A, B and C v Ireland* (2011) 53 EHRR 13.

[47] The Irish Government made a commitment to review its current abortion regime and to implement the *A, B and C* decision in its recent Universal Periodic Review before the UN Human Rights Council. In its State report to the Council, it says: "In December 2010, the European Court of Human Rights judgment in the A, B and C v Ireland case found that there was an absence of accessible and effective procedures to enable Ms C establish whether she had a right to a termination under Irish law and this represented a violation of her human rights. Ireland is committed to ensuring that the judgment in this case is implemented expeditiously. In response to the Court judgment, the Government will establish an expert group, drawing on appropriate medical and legal expertise, with a view to making recommendations to Government on how this matter should be properly addressed" (at 79). This Expert Group was established in January 2012 and is due to make recommendations on the Irish abortion framework to the Government in 2012. A Private Member's Bill, proposed by Clare Daly TD (former Socialist Party now United Left Alliance), which sought to regulate limited access to abortion services, was rejected by the Oireachtas in April 2012.

[48] Art 28.3.3°, Art 13.6 and Art 40.4.

right to life and its importance imposes a strong presumption in favour of taking all steps capable of preserving it, save in exceptional circumstances".[49]

The discussion on abortion above illustrates that the right to life of the unborn must also be balanced with the right to life of the mother.

B. ECHR

Article 2 – Right to life: **[3–24]**

> "1. Everyone's right to life shall be protected by law. No one shall be deprived of his life intentionally save in the execution of a sentence of a court following his conviction of a crime for which this penalty is provided by law.
> 2. Deprivation of life shall not be regarded as inflicted in contravention of this article when it results from the use of force which is no more than absolutely necessary:
> a. in defence of any person from unlawful violence;
> b. in order to effect a lawful arrest or to prevent the escape of a person lawfully detained;
> c. in action lawfully taken for the purpose of quelling a riot or insurrection."

1. Nature of the Right

The right to life is a non-derogable right. Whilst it took quite some time for a case concerning this right to come before the ECtHR, it has since been litigated quite frequently before the court, which has allowed for significant analysis of the nature of the right.[50] The ECtHR first dealt with the right to life in the case of *McCann v United Kingdom*,[51] where it was stated: **[3–25]**

> " ... as a provision which not only safeguards the right to life but sets out the circumstances when the deprivation of life may be justified, Article 2 ranks as one of the most fundamental provisions in the Convention".[52]

Jacobs, White and Ovey comment that since the *McCann* case "an increasingly rich and diverse case-law has developed".[53] They continue that from this case law:

> "[I]t emerges that a Contracting Party's obligation to safeguard life consists of three main aspects: the duty to refrain, by its agents, from unlawful killing; the duty to investigate suspicious deaths; and, in certain circumstances, a positive obligation to take steps to prevent the avoidable loss of life".[54]

---

[49] *Re a Ward of Court (No 2)* [1996] 2 IR 79 at 123.
[50] See Council of Europe, *Table of Violations 1959–2011*, available at: http://www.echr.coe.int/ECHR/EN/Header/Reports+and+Statistics/Statistics/Statistical+data/, last accessed 21 June 2012.
[51] *McCann v United Kingdom* (1995) 21 EHRR 97.
[52] *ibid* at 97.
[53] R White and C Ovey, *Jacobs, White and Ovey: The European Convention on Human Rights* (5th ed, Oxford University Press, Oxford, 2010), p 143.
[54] *ibid.*

Article 2 is wide-ranging in scope and covers, in its main areas, deliberate ill-treatment by the State, a failure to protect individuals from others, a failure to protect individuals in custody from themselves, decisions about beginning of life and rights of the unborn, end-of-life medical care and capital punishment.

Intentional Killing by the State

[3–26] Under Art 2, contracting States are prohibited from deliberate unjustified killing through its agents. This was the main issue in the *McCann* case which was taken by the relatives of three members of the Provisional IRA who had been killed by British security forces in Gibraltar. The British soldiers had been informed that Irish Republicans had planted a car bomb in a busy area and were carrying a detonator. The UK claimed that the actions were justified as they fell within the parameters of Art 2(2)(a) and that the killings were necessary to protect civilians from the bomb attack. The ECtHR interpreted the phrase "absolutely necessary" in Art 2(2) as meaning that the force used had to be in proportion to the achievement of one of the aims set out in Art 2(a), (b) and (c). This meant that an honest belief that the use of force was necessary was insufficient for it to be deemed legal; this belief also had to be based on reasonable grounds with reference to available information.[55] Taken together with other courses of action,[56] the ECtHR therefore concluded that the use of lethal force was not necessary in these circumstances and that the United Kingdom had breached Art 2.

[3–27] The *McCann* case can be contrasted with the case of *Ramsahai v The Netherlands.*[57] Ramsahai had stolen a scooter from its owner at gunpoint. He later drew his gun on two police officers. One of the officers shot at him and hit him in the neck and Ramsahai died at the scene. The incident was investigated by both the public prosecutor for the police area to which the officers belonged and also by the State Criminal Investigation Department. The actions of the police officers were found to be legitimate, a decision which was challenged by Ramsahai's family, who complained of an Art 2 breach. However, the Grand Chamber of the ECtHR found that the use of force by the police was no more than was absolutely necessary.

[3–28] It should be noted that death does not have to occur for Art 2 to apply. In *Makaratzis v Greece*[58] the applicant had driven through a red light and was chased by a number of police vehicles. When the applicant failed to stop police officers shot at his car and he was hit several times. The ECtHR held that because he could easily have been killed by the police officers' bullets, Art 2 applied. The intention to kill was not shown, but the use of force was seen as "potentially lethal"[59] and disproportionate.

[55] The bomb and single press detonator were given as solid intelligence to those on the ground, whereas the reality was that their superiors had made assumptions. The car bomb did exist, but had a timing device. The fault was therefore found to be with the control of the mission.

[56] The main factors were the control and intelligence issues, but there was also the point made that the Provisional IRA members could have been arrested at an earlier point as they entered Gibraltar.

[57] *Ramsahai v The Netherlands* (2008) 46 EHRR 983.

[58] *Makaratzis v Greece* (2005) 41 EHRR 1092.

[59] *ibid* at para 52.

Jacobs, White and Ovey comment that "[w]here an individual is known to have been taken into custody and subsequently disappears or is found dead ... it is logical that a heavy burden should fall on the State to establish an innocent explanation".[60] In the case of *Salman v Turkey*[61] the State was unable to provide such an innocent explanation for the death of Mr Salman. The applicant's husband was arrested in 1992 on suspicion of aiding and abetting Kurdish rebels. He was taken to the hospital 24 hours later where he was declared dead on arrival. An autopsy did not reveal the cause of death but disclosed a broken sternum and other marks and bruises on his body. The case was referred to the Forensic Institute in Istanbul whose report concluded that the applicant died as a result of a heart attack. The heart attack was caused by the effect of the arrest on a pre-existing heart condition. The applicant had photographs taken of her husband's corpse which showed that her husband had marks on the soles of his feet. The ECtHR stated that there is a heavy burden on a contracting State to provide a satisfactory explanation for the death of a person in custody. Since, in this case, Turkey was unable to adequately explain how the applicant's husband had received his injuries, and also since the evidence did not support the Forensic Institute's conclusion that the applicant's husband had died of a heart attack, the ECtHR found that Turkey had breached Art 2. **[3–29]**

Article 2 can apply even in the absence of a body. In the case of *Timurtaş v Turkey*[62] the applicant claimed that his son had disappeared after he had been taken into custody by Turkish authorities in August 1993. The public prosecutor had failed to investigate the father's complaint because there was some evidence that the son was a member of a Kurdish rebel organisation and also because the father was not able to substantiate his claims. Turkey denied that the applicant's son had ever been detained and produced custody records which contained no reference to the son's detention. While the applicant was unable to find any eyewitnesses as to his son's detention, he had a photocopy of what he claimed was an army post-operational report which recorded his son's arrest. Turkey disputed the authenticity of this document and claimed that the reference number corresponded to a different case but did not produce the other document for security reasons. Whilst the ECtHR acknowledged the danger of relying on a photocopy, it found that Turkey's response to the document was inadequate. This led the ECtHR to infer the validity of the document. The ECtHR then went on to find that even in the absence of a body, Art 2 could potentially apply depending on the circumstances of the case. Given the fact, in this case, that the applicant's son had been arrested over six years previously and that the State had been unable to satisfactorily explain what happened to him, the ECtHR concluded that there had been a breach of Art 2. **[3–30]**

The Obligation to Protect Life

The ECtHR found in *LCB v United Kingdom*[63] that Art 2(1) includes a positive obligation on the part of the State to protect the lives of those in its jurisdiction. The **[3–31]**

---

[60] R White and C Ovey, *supra* n 53, p 147.

[61] *Salman v Turkey* (2002) 34 EHRR 425.

[62] *Timurtaş v Turkey* (2000-VI) 33 EHRR 121.

[63] *LCB v United Kingdom* (1998) 27 EHRR 212.

extent of this obligation was discussed in the case of *Őneryildiz v Turkey*[64] where the Grand Chamber of the ECtHR held " ... that this obligation must be construed as applying in the context of any activity, whether public or not, in which the right to life may be at stake".[65]

[3–32] This obligation requires contracting States to implement frameworks which deter unlawful killing.[66] In *Kiliç* Turkey was found to be in breach of Art 2 where the applicant claimed that his bother had been assassinated by security force members. While a legal and administrative framework which sought to protect life was in place in the form of police and a court system, this framework was inadequate as it was seriously undermined by the emergency rule measures which were in place at the time in the south-east region of Turkey.

[3–33] The ECtHR clarified the obligation further in the *Kontrová* case.[67] It stated:

> "The Court reiterates that the first sentence of Article 2(1) enjoins the State not only to refrain from the intentional and unlawful taking of life, but also to take appropriate steps to safeguard the lives of those within its jurisdiction ... This involves a primary duty on the State to secure the right to life by putting in place effective criminal-law provisions to deter the commission of offences against the person backed up by law-enforcement machinery for the prevention, suppression and punishment of such provisions. It also extends in appropriate circumstances to a positive obligation on the authorities to take preventive operational measures to protect an individual whose life is at risk from the criminal acts of another individual ...
>
> Bearing in mind the difficulties in policing modern societies, the unpredictability of human conduct and the operational choices which must be made in terms of priorities and resources, the scope of the positive obligation must be interpreted in a way which does not impose an impossible or disproportionate burden on the authorities. Not every claimed risk to life, therefore, can entail for the authorities a Convention requirement to take operational measures to prevent that risk from materialising. For a positive obligation to arise, it must be established that the authorities knew or ought to have known at the time of the existence of a real and immediate risk to the life of an identified individual from the criminal acts of a third party and that they failed to take measures within the scope of their powers which, judged reasonably, might have been expected to avoid that risk".[68]

Jacobs, White and Ovey comment that:

> "[W]here the risk to life arises from an inherently dangerous, but basically lawful, activity, such as, for example, military tests, or the operation of a factory involving toxic emissions, or of a large waste disposal site, there is a duty on the Contracting Party to provide an effective system of regulation, supervision and control, providing for the identification and correction of any dangerous shortcomings".[69]

---

64 *Őneryildiz v Turkey* (2005) 41 EHRR 325.
65 *ibid* at para 93.
66 *Kiliç v Turkey* (2001) 33 EHRR 1357.
67 *Kontrová v Slovakia* (No 7510/04), 31 May 2007, ECHR 2007-VI.
68 *ibid* at paras 49–50.
69 R White and C Ovey, *supra* n 53, p 155.

This may require a contracting State to provide adequate information to those in danger of the risk.[70] This positive obligation also arises in cases of natural disasters.[71]

The Duty to Investigate Deaths

The duty to investigate suspicious deaths is a corollary of the prohibition of arbitrary killing by State agents.[72] The ECtHR clarified the elements of an effective investigation in the case of *Ramsahai.*[73] First, the investigation must be adequate, i.e. "it must be capable of leading to the identification and punishment of those responsible".[74] Secondly, it is necessary for the people in charge of, and carrying out, the investigation to be independent from those involved in the event.[75] The ECtHR went on to state that "[w]hat is at stake here is nothing less than public confidence in the state's monopoly on the use of force".[76] [3–34]

The effectiveness of an investigation was addressed in the case of *Kaya v Turkey*[77] where the applicant's brother was found dead with bullet holes in his body near to his village. Turkey claimed that the dead man was a terrorist and had been killed during an incident with security forces. A basic post-mortem examination was carried out before the body was handed over for burial. The public prosecutor accepted the statements of the security forces and did not interview witnesses or undertake any forensic tests. The European Commission of Human Rights (the Commission) and the ECtHR were unable to clearly establish the facts of the incident and were unable to find that the State was responsible for the killing of the applicant's brother. However, the ECtHR nevertheless found a breach of Art 2 because the investigation into the death of the applicant's brother was ineffective. [3–35]

Euthanasia and Assisted Suicide

In the case of *Pretty v United Kingdom*[78] the applicant suffered from a motor-neuron disease which was untreatable. Her muscles were becoming weaker, she was paralysed from the neck down and had to be fed through a tube. Her intellect, however, remained unimpaired. She was aware that her life expectancy was limited and the final stages of the disease were expected to be undignified, which she did not want to experience. She wanted her husband to help her commit suicide without a risk that he would be prosecuted for helping her. The ECtHR held that Art 2 concerned obligations [3–36]

---

70 *Öneryildiz v Turkey* (2005) 41 EHRR 325, ECHR 2004-XII.

71 See *Budayeva v Russia* (Nos 15339/02, 21166/02, 20058/02, 11673/02 and 15343/02), 20 March 2008.

72 *McCann v United Kingdom* (1996) 21 EHRR 97 at para 161: "The obligation to protect the right to life under this provision, read in conjunction with the State's general duty under Article 1 of the Convention to 'secure to everyone within their jurisdiction the rights and freedoms defined in [the] Convention', requires by implication that there should be some form of effective official investigation when individuals have been killed as a result of the use of force by, *inter alios*, agents of the State."

73 *Ramsahai v The Netherlands* (2008) 46 EHRR 983, ECHR 2007-nyr.

74 *ibid* at para 324.

75 *ibid* at para 325.

76 *ibid* at para 325.

77 *Kaya v Turkey* (1999) 28 EHRR 1.

78 *Pretty v United Kingdom* (2002) 35 EHRR 1.

in respect of protection of life and did not deal with issues of quality of life or self-determination. Because assisted suicide is legal in some contracting States, the applicant argued that a failure to acknowledge that a right to die existed under the ECHR would place contracting States which do allow assisted suicide in breach of the ECHR. The ECtHR did not deal with this issue in the abstract and stated that even if a contracting State which permitted assisted suicide was found to be in breach of the ECHR, this would be a very different proposition to the applicant's argument that the UK would be in breach of Art 2 of the ECHR if it did not permit assisted suicide.

The Right to Life of the Unborn and Abortion

[3–37] Article 2 does not clarify when life begins.[79] Initially, the Strasbourg institutions were reluctant to deal with the compatibility of domestic laws on abortion across the contracting States with Art 2 of the ECHR in the abstract.[80] The Commission acknowledged in the case of *X v United Kingdom*[81] a "divergence of thinking on the question of where life begins"[82] and stated that "while some believe that it starts already with conception, others tend to focus upon the moment of nidation, upon the point that the foetus becomes 'viable', or upon live birth".[83] The Commission ruled out the existence of an absolute right to life of the foetus but did not decide whether Art 2 protected the foetus at all or if the right to life of the foetus existed, but with certain limitations. It stated:

> "The 'life' of the foetus is intimately connected with, and it cannot be regarded in isolation of, the life of the pregnant woman. If Art 2 were held to cover the foetus and its protection under this Article were, in the absence of any express limitation, seen as absolute, an abortion would have to be considered as prohibited even where the continuance of the pregnancy would involve a serious risk to the life of the pregnant woman. This would mean that the 'unborn life' of the foetus would be regarded as being of a higher value than the life of the pregnant woman".[84]

[3–38] The issue of abortion was also dealt with in the case of *H v Norway*[85] which concerned a non-medical abortion which was carried out on a woman against the wishes of the putative father. The Commission stated that Art 2 obligated contracting States to refrain from taking a person's life intentionally and also to take appropriate steps to safeguard life. While the Commission did not feel it was necessary to decide whether a foetus was protected by Art 2, it did not exclude the possibility that "in certain circumstances this may be the case notwithstanding that there is in the Contracting Parties a considerable divergence of views on whether or to what extent Article 2 protects the unborn life".[86] The Commission went on to comment that as abortion was

---

[79] See C Zampas and J Gher, "Abortion as a human right: international and regional standards" (2008) 8 HRL Rev 249.
[80] *X v Norway* (No 867/60), decision of 29 May 1961, (1961) 6 CD 34 and *X v Austria* (No 7045/75), decision of 10 December 1976, (1976) 7 DR 87.
[81] *X v United Kingdom* (No 8416/79), decision of 13 May 1980, (1980) 19 DR 244.
[82] *ibid* at para 12.
[83] *ibid* at para 12.
[84] *ibid* at para 19.
[85] *H v Norway* (No 17004/90), decision of 19 May 1992, (1992) 73 DR 155.
[86] *ibid.*

such a sensitive issue, contracting States must be allowed to have discretion and a margin of appreciation must be applied. In *H* the mother had the abortion in line with Norwegian law and therefore there was no breach of Art 2.

The right to life of the foetus was considered in the case of *Vo v France*.[87] The issue in this case was whether harming a foetus could be treated as a criminal offence in light of Art 2. In this case two women of the same family name were in the same hospital, one of whom was six months pregnant and was in hospital for a check-up and the other had requested her intra-uterine device to be removed. Hospital staff confused the two patients and due to the doctor's negligence the applicant suffered a miscarriage. She had been precluded from initiating criminal proceedings against the doctor in France, as under domestic law a foetus could not be the victim of unintentional homicide. The ECtHR sidelined the main issue of the right to life of the foetus, observing: **[3–39]**

> "At European level ... there is no consensus on the nature and status of the embryo and/or foetus ... although they are beginning to receive some protection in the light of scientific progress and the potential consequences of research into genetic engineering, medically assisted procreation or embryo experimentation. At best, it may be regarded as common ground between States that the embryo/foetus belongs to the human race. The potentiality of that being and its capacity to become a person — enjoying protection under the civil law, moreover, in many States, such as France, in the context of inheritance and gifts ... require protection in the name of human dignity, without making it a 'person' with the 'right to life' for the purposes of Art 2".[88]

The ECtHR held that it was impossible to answer in the abstract whether the unborn child is a person for the purposes of Art 2 of the ECHR. The ECtHR considered that it was unnecessary to examine if the situation in *Vo* came within the remit of Art 2 because, even if Art 2 applied, French domestic law already had a criminal offence of unintentionally causing injury to the mother and also allowed for the initiation of civil proceedings.

Recently, significant decisions with regard to abortion have been made with reference to Art 8, the right to a private life. In the *Tysiac* case,[89] for example, the ECtHR held that Poland had breached the applicant's right to a private life by failing to ensure effective access to a legal abortion through a review and appeals mechanism for medical decisions regarding abortion.[90] **[3–40]**

---

87 *Vo v France* (2005) 40 EHRR 259.

88 *ibid* at para 84.

89 *Tysiac v Poland* (No 5410/03), (Sect 4), ECHR 2007-I.

90 In this case, the applicant was partially blind and the continuation of her pregnancy led to the worsening of her sight. In order for the applicant to obtain a legal abortion in Poland two medical experts were required to sign an abortion authorisation document. Despite the fact that the applicant had received numerous medical opinions stating that her sight would deteriorate if the pregnancy continued, doctors were reluctant to sign the authorisation. Polish law did not have an appeals mechanism which would have allowed the applicant to appeal a decision of a doctor who refused to sign the authorisation. By the time she got the authorisation it was too late to obtain an abortion. Once she had the baby her eyesight deteriorated. The ECtHR awarded the applicant €25,000 for pain and suffering and a further €14,000 for legal fees.

[3–41] The recent case of *A, B and C v Ireland*[91] once again revisited the Irish law on abortion. All three applicants had to travel to the UK for abortions and claimed that because of the unclear abortion regime in Ireland,[92] their rights under Arts 2, 3, 8 and 14 of the ECHR has been violated. Reaffirming the *Tysiac* decision, the ECtHR, in deciding in favour of the third applicant with regard to a breach of Art 8, held that any contracting State which permits abortion must implement a "legislative or regulatory regime providing an accessible and effective procedure" by which women can understand clearly if they can legally have an abortion in that State. The important issue from Ireland's perspective is that the Government must now review and amend its abortion framework with a view to implementing a clear regime.[93] McGuinness, however, comments that this decision "will disappoint anyone who hoped that the . . . Court . . . was 'champing at the bit' to enshrine a Convention right to abortion, as one thing that is resoundingly clear in the wake of this case is that the ECHR *does not* confer a right to abortion".[94]

Death Penalty

[3–42] Article 2 of the ECHR retains the possibility for contracting States to impose the death penalty. Protocol 6 to the ECHR sought to remedy this situation by abolishing the death penalty, except in times of war. Article 2 of this instrument states that:

> "[A] State may make provision in its law for the death penalty in respect of acts committed in time of war or of imminent threat of war; such penalty shall be applied only in the instances laid down in the law and in accordance with its provisions. The State shall communicate to the Secretary General of the Council of Europe the relevant provisions of that law."

---

91 *A, B and C v Ireland* (2011) 53 EHRR 13.

92 "A" had become pregnant unintentionally, believing that her partner was infertile. She was unemployed, quite poor, was addicted to alcohol and was unmarried. She already had four children, all of whom were in foster care, and one of whom was disabled. She borrowed €650 from a money lender to pay for travel and a private clinic in the UK. When she came home she began bleeding profusely, was taken to hospital for a dilation and curettage and suffered pain, nausea and bleeding for weeks thereafter but did not seek further medical advice. "B" became pregnant after her "morning after pill" failed. She had been advised by two doctors that she was at risk of an ectopic pregnancy, although this did not happen. Two weeks after returning home from the UK where she had her pregnancy terminated she began to start passing blood clots, and sought follow-up care in a clinic in Dublin, rather than attending an ordinary doctor because she was uncertain of the law regulating abortion in Ireland. "C" had been undergoing chemotherapy for cancer for three years. She had wanted children, but her doctor had indicated that a foetus could be harmed during chemotherapy treatment. She alleged that she received insufficient information on the issue of the possible effect of the treatment on the foetus due to the uncertainty concerning the regulation of abortion in the State. Because she was unsure of the impact of the chemotherapy on the foetus she went to the UK for a surgical abortion. The abortion was incompletely performed and she suffered prolonged bleeding and infection. She claimed that her doctor in Ireland failed to refer to her pregnancy in subsequent visits despite the fact that she was visibly no longer pregnant.

93 See discussion on *A, B and C v Ireland* in section on Irish constitutional law above.

94 S McGuinness, "A, B and C Leads to D (for delegation!)" (2011) 19(3) Med L Rev 476. See also P Ronchi, "A, B and C v Ireland. Europe's Roe v Wade still has to wait" (2011) 127(Jul) LQR 365.

Protocol 13 then prohibited the imposition of the death penalty at all times. Article 1 states: "The death penalty shall be abolished. No one shall be condemned to such penalty or executed."

Under Art 2 of Protocol 13, no derogations from that Protocol are allowed and Art 3 prohibits the making of reservations to the instrument. States Parties to the Protocols may violate the instruments if they extradite an accused to a State which imposes the death penalty.[95] The case of *Soering v UK*[96] established that certain conditions on death row in the United States amounted, in the particular circumstances of that case, to a violation of Art 3 of the ECHR. However, the ECtHR did not find that the implementation of capital punishment amounted to inhuman punishment. In *Öcalan v Turkey*, however, the ECtHR stated that "it can be said that capital punishment in peacetime has come to be regarded as an unacceptable, if not inhuman, form of punishment which is no longer permissible under Article 2".[97] **[3–43]**

Extraterritoriality

The extent of this jurisdiction is just one of a number of areas where Art 2 has been relevant in recent litigation in the UK, but has significance for any contracting State with troops outside its own territory, particularly with the widespread use of "peace-keeping" forces. **[3–44]**

The deaths in Iraq of a number of civilians at the hands of the British Army led to the important case of *R (Al-Skeini) v Secretary of State for Defence.*[98] The concept of extraterritoriality came initially from *Loizidou v Turkey*, where the ECtHR stated that jurisdiction over State servants " ... was not restricted to the national territory"[99] of the State in question. It was also held in the case of *Drozd and Janousek*[100] that the responsibility of Contracting Parties can be involved because of acts of their authorities, whether performed within or outside national boundaries, which produce effects outside their own territory.

Following the controversial ECtHR decision in *Bankovic v Belgium*,[101] the court ruled[102] that the ECHR applied only where troops had effective operational control of a territory. This meant civilians killed by British soldiers in street battles in Basra (rather than in military custody) were not entitled to protection under the Human Rights Act 1998, which incorporated the ECHR into domestic UK law. This principle has been extended, in the domestic courts, by *R (Smith) v Secretary of State for Defence*,[103] to cases of deaths of British soldiers on active overseas service. Unless they

---

95 See *Nivette v France* (No 44190/98), decision of 3 July 2001, ECHR 2001-VII and *Bader and Kanbor v Sweden* (2008) 46 EHRR 197.

96 *Soering v United Kingdom* (1989) 11 EHRR 439.

97 *Öcalan v Turkey* (2005) 41 EHRR 45.

98 *R (Al-Skeini) v Secretary of State for Defence* [2007] UKHL 26.

99 *Loizidou v Turkey* (1995) 20 EHRR 99.

100 *Drozd and Janousek v France and* Spain (1992) 14 EHRR 745 at para 99

101 *Bankovic v Belgium* (2007) 44 EHRR SE5. The ECtHR ruled the application as inadmissible.

102 *Al-Skeini and others* v *Secretary of State for Defence* (2007) UKHL 26. And see *Al-Skeini v United Kingdom* (2011) No. 55721/07

103 *R (Smith) v Secretary of State for Defence* (2010) UKSC 29.

are on a military base, British troops will not be under the UK jurisdiction and hence not afforded the protection of the Human Rights Act 1998 and of the State obligations flowing from Art 2 of the ECHR.

2. Legitimate Justifications for Interference with the Right

[3–45] Article 2(2) sets out a number of legitimate justifications for interference with the right. This states:

> "Deprivation of life shall not be regarded as inflicted in contravention of this Article when it results from the use of force which is no more than absolutely necessary:
> a. in defence of any person from unlawful violence;
> b. in order to effect a lawful arrest or to prevent the escape of a person lawfully detained;
> c. in action lawfully taken for the purpose of quelling a riot or insurrection."

It should be noted that the list provided in Art 2(2) is exhaustive and quite restrictive.

Self-Defence or Defence of Another

[3–46] The use of force in self-defence must be "absolutely necessary". This is seen in the case of *McCann,*[104] discussed above, where the ECtHR held that the shooting dead of three members of the Provisional IRA was deemed not to be "absolutely necessary" to protect civilians from a bomb they were planting, as the British authorities could have arrested them before they planted the bomb.

To Effect an Arrest or Prevent an Escape

[3–47] The limitations on this restriction are seen in the case of *Nachova v Bulgaria*[105] where the ECtHR held that "potentially deadly force cannot be considered absolutely necessary where it is known that the person to be arrested poses no threat to life or limb and is not suspected of having committed a violent offence".[106] The ECtHR then went on to state that this is so even though "a failure to use lethal force may result in the opportunity to arrest the fugitive being lost".[107] The applicants in this case were known to be unarmed and not dangerous but the police shot them when they refused to obey a police warning to stop or be fired on. They had run away to avoid arrest regarding an offence of unauthorised absence from work. The ECtHR found that Art 2 had been breached.

To Quell a Riot or Insurrection

[3–48] This element of Art 2 was discussed in *Stewart v UK.*[108] In this case the ECtHR held that there was no obligation to retreat when quelling a riot. The use of force to quell the riot must, of course, be absolutely necessary for that purpose. The proportionality

104 *McCann v UK* (1995) 21 EHRR 97.
105 *Nachova v Bulgaria* (2005) 42 EHRR 933.
106 *ibid* at para 95.
107 *ibid* at para 107.
108 *Stewart v UK* (No 10044/82), (1984) 39 DR 162.

requirement attaches not only to those who carry out the use of force but also to those who plan the use of force. In *Ergi v Turkey*[109] an innocent teenager was caught in the crossfire when security forces ambushed a group of terrorists. The ECtHR found a breach of Art 2 as the operation had not been planned in such a way as to minimise the loss of civilian life.

C. CFR

Article 2: [3–49]

> "1. Everyone has the right to life.
> 2. No one shall be condemned to the death penalty, or executed."

The first paragraph of Art 2 of the CFR corresponds with the first sentence of Art 2(1) of the ECHR. The second paragraph corresponds with Protocol 6 to the ECHR dealing with the death penalty. The CFR provisions have the same meaning and scope as the ECHR provisions in line with Art 52(3) of the CFR.[110] Since the adoption of the CFR, Protocol 13 to the ECHR, which completely abolishes the death penalty, has been adopted. Nowak comments that as a number of Council of Europe and EU States have ratified Protocol 13, and that as:

> "[a]rticle 52(3) of the Charter is to be interpreted as a dynamic clause, one may conclude that Article 2(2) of the Charter corresponds to Article 2 ECHR as amended by both Protocols 6 and 13. In other words, the prohibition of the death penalty is absolute for EU member States and applies both in times of war and of peace".[111]

Council Regulation (EC) No 1236/2005[112] relates to trade in certain goods which could, potentially, be used for the purposes of capital punishment or torture. It prohibits[113] the importation and exportation of goods that have no other practical purpose than for implementing the death penalty or for torture.[114] The right to life has not been considered before the ECJ. The ECJ has, however, clarified that there are no [3–50]

---

109 *Ergi v Turkey* (1998) 32 EHRR 388.

110 See Explanations of the Praesidium of the Convention which drafted the Charter of Fundamental Rights of the European Union, available at: http://infoportal.fra.europa.eu/InfoPortal/infobaseShowContent.do?btnCat_182&btnCountryBread_169, last accessed 21 June 2012.

111 M Nowak, "Article 2: The Right to Life" in *Commentary of the Charter of Fundamental Rights of the European Union,* p 32, available at: http://infoportal.fra.europa.eu/InfoPortal/infobaseShowContent.do?btnCat_182&btnCountryBread_169, last accessed 21 June 2012.

112 Council Regulation (EC) No 1236/2005 of 27 June 2005 concerning trade in certain goods which could be used for capital punishment, torture or other cruel, inhuman or degrading treatment or punishment [2005] OJ L200/1.

113 *ibid.*

114 This Regulation has been amended by other EU legislation (see http://eur-lex.europa.eu/Notice.do?val=405732:cs&lang=en&list=423544:cs,405732:cs,&pos=2&page=1&nbl=2&pgs=10&hwords =), including Commission Regulation (EC) No 675/2008 of 16 July 2008 amending Council Regulation (EC) No 1236/2005 concerning trade in certain goods which could be used for capital punishment, torture or other cruel, inhuman or degrading treatment or punishment [2008] OJ L189/14.

restrictions on the right to life.[115] The opinion of Advocate General Bot in the recent case of *Federal Republic of Germany v Y and Z*[116] reiterates the central importance of the right to life. Advocate General Bot held that there are certain rights which are 'absolute' or 'inalienable' and "no limitation can be provided for, even in cases of exceptional public danger".[117] This included the right to life.

D. International and Regional Laws

[3–51] Predictably, the right to life is protected in numerous international and regional legal instruments. The Universal Declaration on Human Rights states that "Everyone has the right to life, liberty and security of the person".[118] The right to life is also reaffirmed in the International Covenant on Civil and Political Rights (ICCPR) and the International Covenant on Economic, Social and Cultural Rights, both of 1966. Article 6 of the ICCPR seeks to protect the right to life and to clarify when the death penalty can be imposed in States Parties which have retained this method of punishment:

> "1. Every human being has the inherent right to life. This right shall be protected by law. No one shall be arbitrarily deprived of his life.
> 2. In countries which have not abolished the death penalty, sentence of death may be imposed only for the most serious crimes in accordance with the law in force at the time of the commission of the crime and not contrary to the provisions of the present Covenant and to the Convention on the Prevention and Punishment of the Crime of Genocide. This penalty can only be carried out pursuant to a final judgement rendered by a competent court.
> 3. When deprivation of life constitutes the crime of genocide, it is understood that nothing in this article shall authorize any State Party to the present Covenant to derogate in any way from any obligation assumed under the provisions of the Convention on the Prevention and Punishment of the Crime of Genocide.
> 4. Anyone sentenced to death shall have the right to seek pardon or commutation of the sentence. Amnesty, pardon or commutation of the sentence of death may be granted in all cases.
> 5. Sentence of death shall not be imposed for crimes committed by persons below eighteen years of age and shall not be carried out on pregnant women.
> 6. Nothing in this article shall be invoked to delay or to prevent the abolition of capital punishment by any State Party to the present Covenant."

Many international and regional instruments remain silent on important aspects of the right to life, such as the question of when life begins and the legality of abortion. The American Convention on Human Rights, however, provides that the right to life must be protected "in general, from the moment of conception".[119] The right to life is also

---

[115] Case C-112/00, *Schmidberger* v *Republik Österreich* at para 80.
[116] Joined cases C-71/11 and C-99/11, *Federal Republic of Germany v Y and Z*.
[117] Joined cases C-71/11 and C-99/11, *Federal Republic of Germany v Y and Z*, opinion of AG Bot at para 65.
[118] Universal Declaration of Human Rights 1948, Art 3.
[119] Art 4 of the American Convention on Human Rights.

protected under Art 4 of the African Charter of Human and Peoples' Rights[120] and Art 5 of the Arab Charter of Human Rights.[121]

Conclusion

The right to life is the most fundamental of all rights and enjoys wide protection. The right encompasses a number of complex issues, including abortion, euthanasia and the imposition of the death penalty. In Ireland, the general right to life has received very little attention, when compared with the right to life of the unborn, which has been the source of significant jurisprudence. It is clear that legislation is urgently needed to clarify this area of Irish law. While the ECtHR has accepted that contracting States can apply a wide margin of appreciation with regard to the right to life and abortion, the force of the ECtHR has been felt in the recent *A, B and C* case. It is clear that Irish law on euthanasia and assisted suicide is also in need of clarification, and Ireland may look to recent developments in the UK and before the ECtHR for guidance on this issue. **[3–52]**

[120] Art 4 states: "Human beings are inviolable. Every human being shall be entitled to respect for his life and the integrity of his person. No one may be arbitrarily deprived of this right."

[121] Art 5 states: "1. Every human being has the inherent right to life. 2. This right shall be protected by law. No one shall be arbitrarily deprived of his life."

CHAPTER 4
The Right to Liberty and Security

Introduction

The right to liberty and security is one of the oldest human rights to find protection in domestic legal systems, being protected in England by the *Magna Carta Libertatum* of 1215. In later years, liberty was one of the cornerstones of the French Declaration on the Rights of Man and of the Citizen 1789. It is now seen in all legal systems as a vital component of the rule of law and a hallmark of democratic societies, although the right can be limited in a number of circumstances. This chapter discusses the constitutional protection of liberty, followed by an analysis of how the right is protected under the European Convention on Human Rights (ECHR), the Charter of Fundamental Rights (CFR), and regional and international law. **[4–01]**

A. Irish Constitution

Article 40.4:

> "1° No citizen shall be deprived of his personal liberty save in accordance with law."

There are two main aspects to the right to liberty under the Constitution. The first is the basic guarantee that a person shall not be deprived of his or her liberty except when such detention is in accordance with law, which is enshrined in Art 40.4.1°. The second aspect allows for a basic *habeas corpus* procedure which enables the High Court to inquire into, and indeed, end an illegal detention (Art 40.4.2°, 40.4.3°, and 40.4.4°). **[4–02]**

1. The Nature of the Right

Article 40.4.1° is a succinct provision. Doyle states that an issue arises regarding the nature of this provision and whether it is a "purely procedural guarantee, permitting all restrictions of liberty that have been authorised by law, or whether it posits a substantive guarantee of liberty that, *prima facie* at least, cannot be restricted by **[4–03]** laws".[1] The issue of the nature of the provision was discussed in *State (Burke) v Lennon*[2] when a prisoner challenged the legality of his detention under s 55 of the Offences Against the State Act 1939, which permitted internment without trial. The legislation allowed the Minister for Justice to issue a warrant for detention in circumstances where a person's activities interfered with the preservation of peace, order and security of the State. The court deemed the power of the Minister to be in breach of the Constitution and opted for the broader interpretation of Art 40.4.1°, finding that it was not merely a procedural guarantee, but rather a provision which could be "tested against a constitutionally endorsed notion of liberty".[3] Thus, the court found that it could test detentions authorised by law "against the substantive concept of personal liberty endorsed by the Constitution".[4] Gavan Duffy J stated:

> "In my opinion, the saving words in the declaration that 'No citizen shall be deprived of his liberty save in accordance with law' cannot be used to validate an enactment conflicting with the constitutional guarantees... The Constitution, with its most impressive Preamble, is the Charter of the Irish people and I will not whittle it away. There is nothing novel in the solemn recognition of the right to personal freedom as an essential basis of the social structure of a society of free men. In my opinion, the Constitution intended, while making all proper provisions for times of emergency, to secure his personal freedom to the citizen as truly as did Magna Carta in England . . . In my opinion, the right to personal liberty and the other principles which we are accustomed to summarise as the rule of law were most deliberately enshrined in a national Constitution, drawn up with the utmost care for a free people, and the power to intern on suspicion or without trial is fundamentally inconsistent with the rule of law, and with the rule of law as expressed in terms of our Constitution".[5]

[4–04] Quite soon after this case, the constitutionality of the Offences Against the State (Amendment) Bill 1940 was tested by the Supreme Court. The Bill included very similar provisions to those that had been found to be unconstitutional by Gavan Duffy J in the case of Lennon. The Supreme Court, however, upheld the constitutionality of the Bill, with Sullivan CJ stating:

> "The phrase 'in accordance with law' is used in several Articles of the Constitution, and we are of opinion that it means in accordance with the law as it exists at the time when the

---

[1] O Doyle, *Constitutional Law: Text, Cases and Materials* (Clarus Press, Dublin, 2008), p 167.

[2] *State (Burke) v Lennon* [1940] IR 36.

[3] O Doyle, *supra* n 1, p 170. This interpretation is at odds with the interpretation of the equivalent provision under the 1922 Constitution, Art 6 of which stated: "The liberty of the person is inviolable, and no person shall be deprived of his liberty save in accordance with law." In relation to the interpretation of the phrase "save in accordance with law" in the context of this provision, see *State (Ryan) v Lennon* [1935] IR 170 at 229 where Fitzgibbon J states: "In Article 6 it is declared that 'the liberty of the person is inviolable,' but that is not a law of universal application, for the Article proceeds: 'and no person shall be deprived of his liberty *except in accordance with law*'. The law may, therefore, make provisions in accordance with which a person may be deprived of his liberty. It is for the Legislature to prescribe those provisions, and for the Courts to enforce them, and even if, under Amendment No. 17, a person has been deprived of his liberty by the mere caprice of an Executive Minister . . . or the unfounded suspicion . . . of any member of the Garda Síochána . . . it would be 'in accordance with law' and the prisoner would have no redress."

[4] O Doyle, *supra* n 1, p 179.

[5] *State (Burke) v Lennon* [1940] IR 136 at 155–156.

> particular Article is invoked and sought to be applied. In this Article, it means the law as it exists at the time when the legality of the detention arises for determination. A person in custody is detained in accordance with law if he is detained in accordance with the provisions of a statute duly passed by the Oireachtas; subject always to the qualification that such provisions are not repugnant to the Constitution or to any provision thereof. Accordingly, in our opinion, this Article cannot be relied upon for the purpose of establishing the proposition that the Bill is repugnant to the Constitution - such repugnancy must be established by reference to some other provision of the Constitution".[6]

This early case decided that Art 40.4.1° was procedural only in nature and did not offer any substantive rights to Irish citizens. However, in later cases there seemed to be a move away from such an interpretation. *In Re Philip Clarke*[7] the nature of Art 40.4.1° arose in the context of the deprivation of liberty of a person detained under the Mental Treatment Act 1945. Mr Clarke challenged his detention under s 165(1) of this Act, which empowered a member of the Gardaí to take a person believed to be of unsound mind into custody if he or she held a belief that detention was necessary for the safety of the person him or herself and/or for the safety of the public. In its decision, the Supreme Court went beyond a purely procedural interpretation of Art 40.4.1 in upholding the constitutionality of the provision, justified by reference to the need to protect a person who is mentally ill.

In *People (Attorney General) v O'Callaghan*[8] the Supreme Court set out a number of constitutional criteria which must be fulfilled before bail could be refused. In relation to the issue of Art 40.4.1° and the right to liberty, Walsh J stated: **[4–05]**

> "In this country it would be quite contrary to the concept of personal liberty enshrined in the Constitution that any person should be punished in respect of any matter upon which he has not been convicted or that in any circumstances he should be deprived of his liberty upon only the belief that he will commit offences if left at liberty, save in the most extraordinary circumstances carefully spelled out by the Oireachtas and then only to secure the preservation of public peace and order or the public safety and the preservation of the State in a time of national emergency or in some situation akin to that".[9]

According to Doyle, "[f]ollowing this decision, the State ceased to rely on the procedural interpretation of Article 40.4.1 to defend legislative restrictions of liberty".[10]

Where a person believes that he or she is being unlawfully detained Article 40.4.2° allows for a review of this detention. This provision states:

> "Upon complaint being made by or on behalf of any person to the High Court or any judge thereof alleging that such person is being unlawfully detained, the High Court and any and every judge thereof to whom such complaint is made shall forthwith enquire into the said complaint and may order the person in whose custody such person is detained to

6 *Re Article 26 and the Offences Against the State (Amendment) Bill 1940* [1940] IR 470 at 482.
7 *Re Philip Clarke* [1950] IR 235.
8 [1966] IR 501.
9 *ibid* at 516.
10 O Doyle, *supra* n 1, p 172.

> produce the body of such person before the High Court on a named day and to certify in writing the grounds of his detention, and the High Court shall, upon the body of such person being produced before that Court and after giving the person in whose custody he is detained an opportunity of justifying the detention, order the release of such person from such detention unless satisfied that he is being detained in accordance with the law."

One of the most important cases on the right to liberty in recent years is the case of *McCann v Judges of Monaghan District Court & Ors*[11] which concerned the case of a woman, Mrs McCann, who owned over €18,000 to a credit union. As she was unable to pay this debt, eventually, an order under s 6 of the Enforcement of Court Orders Act 1940 was made without her being present in court. This order provided that Mrs McCann should be arrested and detained in prison for one month or until such time as she repaid the debt. In relation to the right to liberty, Mrs McCann asserted that s 6 provided for no mechanism for ensuring the attendance of the debtor in Court and also submitted that, in the application of the proportionality test, the Court should assess whether the term of imprisonment imposed in this case was proportionate to the sum due to the Credit Union.

In considering whether s 6 also violated the right to personal liberty guaranteed by Art 40.4.1°, it was acknowledged that in s 6 the Oireachtas had implicitly recognised that a debtor should not be imprisoned if the failure to pay the debt is due to inability to pay. The problem, however, was that the combination of the statutory enforcement of debt process which culminates in s 6 and the formulation of s 6 by the Oireachtas was not structured in a manner and did not contain safeguards, such as the implementation of the debtor's constitutional right to fair procedures, so as to ensure that a debtor who is unable to pay the debt is not imprisoned. The core question for the court was whether s 6 constituted a disproportionate interference with the right to liberty. The High Court held that while having in place an effective statutory scheme for enforcement of contractual obligations, including the payment of debt, is unquestionably a reasonable and legitimate objective in the interests of the common good in a democratic society, the means by which effectiveness is achieved may reasonably necessitate affording a creditor a remedy which entitles him or her to seek to have a debtor imprisoned, but such means will constitute an infringement of the debtor's right to personal liberty guaranteed by Art 40.4.1° unless they pass the proportionality test.

The High Court held that the application of elements of the proportionality test to s 6 illustrates that it is a disproportionate interference with the constitutionally protected right to liberty for the following reasons:

> "(a) The objective of imprisoning a debtor for failure to comply with an instalment order is to procure the discharge of the arrears of instalments. A statutory procedure under which a debtor who is unable to discharge the arrears is imprisoned because of the absence therein of procedures, including procedures which give effect to the debtor's right to fair procedures under the Constitution, which ensure that the Judge ascertains that the debtor is unable to discharge the arrears, cannot be said to be rationally connected with

---

[11] [2010] ILRM 17.

> the objective. Such a procedure is arbitrary, unfair and not based on rational considerations. It is an unreasonable and unnecessary interference with the debtor's right to personal liberty.
>
> (b) In circumstances in which a debtor has some resources to meet the debt, a statutory scheme which does not require the creditor to seek redress by attaching those resources, does not impair the debtor's right to liberty as little as possible. Similarly, the failure to impose on the creditor pursuing an application for an order for arrest and imprisonment the obligation to go through an Order 46B type process, including personal service of an order with the penal endorsement, does not impair the debtor's right to liberty as little as possible. The rationale of the ECtHR in the *Saadi* case, that the detention of an individual is such a serious measure that it is justified only as a last resort where less severe measures have been considered and found to be insufficient to safeguard the individual or public interest, is equally applicable in considering the right to liberty guaranteed by the Constitution"[12].

Laffoy J held that the restrictions on the right to liberty in s 6 goes beyond what is permitted by the Constitution and is invalid.

This provision provides a *habeas corpus* procedure enabling the High Court to end an illegal detention swiftly. It is important to note, however, that the Irish courts have "been slow to hold that every and any illegality in the process leading to detention renders the detention itself illegal".[13] In *State (McDonagh) v Frawley* O'Higgins CJ stated that an illegal detention did not necessarily require that the detainee be released just because of the illegality. Rather, the nature of the illegality must be considered. Release from detention was required when the illegality resulted in a "default of such fundamental requirements that the detention may be said to be wanting in due process of law".[14] Similarly, in the case of *State (McKeever) v Governor of Mountjoy Prison*, Ó Dálaigh CJ stated that the nature of the illegality or irregularity must be such that it "would invalidate any essential step in the procedures leading to detention".[15] **[4–06]**

Legality of Detention Powers

Irish courts have been hesitant to find legislatively-authorised detentions unconstitutional. The issue of legality of detention was considered in the case of *DPP (Stratford) v Fagan*[16] which dealt with s 109 of the Road Traffic Act 1961 which requires a driver to stop if requested to do so by a member of the Gardaí. Garda Stratford stopped the defendant, smelt his breath, breathalysed him and then charged him with the offence of drinking while under the influence of alcohol, which was contrary to s 49 of that Act. The Supreme Court held that such a detention was legal, with Blayney J commenting that members of the Gardaí have a common law duty to prevent crime and the stopping of a car and the subsequent detention in the present case was, therefore, warranted. **[4–07]**

---

[12] *McCann v Judges of Monaghan District Court & Ors* (2010) ILRM 17 (*per* Laffoy J).
[13] *ibid*, pp 172–173.
[14] *State (McDonagh) v Frawley* [1978] IR 131 at 136.
[15] *State (McKeever) v Governor of Mountjoy Prison*, Unreported, Supreme Court, 19 December 1966.
[16] *DPP (Stratford) v Fagan* [1994] 3 IR 265.

[4–08] Detention under mental health legislation[17] was considered in the case of *Re Philip Clarke*,[18] as mentioned above. In this case the Supreme Court upheld the validity of the detention powers provision of the Mental Treatment Act 1945[19] which allowed a Garda to detain a person of unsound mind in a Garda station for his or her own safety or for the safety of the public. The Act provided that once a person of unsound mind had been detained in a Garda station a medical officer could make a recommendation for the person to be moved to, and further detained in, a mental hospital. In *Clarke* the applicant challenged the absence of the possibility of judicial intervention between the arrest of the person of unsound mind and his or her detention. However, the court stated in relation to s 6 of the Act:

> "The impugned legislation is of a paternal character, clearly intended for the care and custody of persons suspected to be suffering from mental infirmity and for the safety and well-being of the public generally. The existence of mental infirmity is too widespread to be overlooked, and was, no doubt, present to the minds of the draughtsmen when it was proclaimed in Article 40,1 of the Constitution that, though all citizens, as human beings are to be held equal before the law, the State may, nevertheless, in its enactments, have due regard to differences of capacity, physical and moral, and of social function. We do not see how the common good would be promoted or the dignity and freedom of the individual assured by allowing persons, alleged to be suffering from such infirmity, to remain at large to the possible danger of themselves and others.
>
> The section is carefully drafted so as to ensure that the person, alleged to be of unsound mind, shall be brought before, and examined by, responsible medical officers with the least possible delay. This seems to us to satisfy every reasonable requirement, and we have not been satisfied, and do not consider that the Constitution requires, that there should be a judicial inquiry or determination before such a person can be placed and detained in a mental hospital".[20]

The courts clearly took a paternalistic attitude with regard to people with mental illness in this case.

Preventive Detention

[4–09] The issue of bail in the context of the legality of preventive detention was discussed in the case of *People (Attorney General) v O'Callaghan*,[21] mentioned earlier. Mr O'Callaghan was charged with a number of criminal offences and sought bail which was opposed by the Attorney General. The decision in the High Court enumerated a number of factors which could be taken into consideration by a judge on a bail application. One of these factors was the likelihood that the individual would commit further offences while on bail. This issue was considered in the Supreme Court, where the nature of the Irish constitutional protection of the right to liberty was discussed by Walsh J, who stated:

---

[17] See M Keys, "Challenging the Lawfulness of Psychiatric Detention under Habeas Corpus in Ireland" (2004) 24 DULJ 26.

[18] *Re Philip Clarke* [1950] IR 235.

[19] s 6 of the Mental Treatment Act 1945.

[20] *Re Philip Clarke* [1950] IR 235 at 247–248.

[21] [1966] IR 501.

> " . . . the likelihood of the commission of further offences while on bail, is a matter which is in my view quite inadmissible. This is a form of preventative justice which has no place in our legal system and is quite alien to the true purposes of bail. It is true that in recent years a number of decisions in England on the question of bail appear to have admitted this concept of preventative justice being applied by the refusal of bail. It has also been stated in English cases that a professional criminal, knowing he is guilty and the probability of conviction, may be tempted to commit some more offences before imprisonment in the belief that it will probably make little difference to his ultimate sentence having regard to his record and the meanwhile may offer some present profit.
>
> In this country it would be quite contrary to the concept of personal liberty enshrined in the Constitution that any person should be punished in respect of any matter upon which he has not been convicted or that in any circumstances he should be deprived of his liberty upon only the belief that he will commit offences if left at liberty, save in the most extraordinary circumstances carefully spelled out by the Oireachtas and then only to secure the preservation of public peace and order or the public safety and the preservation of the State in a time of national emergency or in some situation akin to that".[22]

This decision was approved in *Ryan v DPP.*[23] However, the Constitution was amended in 1996 to insert Article 40.4.6° which makes provision for the refusal of bail by a court to a person charged with a serious offence where it is reasonably considered necessary to prevent the commission of a serious offence by that person. More detailed statutory consideration was given to this issue in the Bail Act 1997, in particular, s 2. Section 2 provides that where an application for bail is made by a person charged with a serious offence, a court may refuse the application if the court is satisfied that such refusal is reasonably considered necessary to prevent the commission of a serious offence by that person. Section 2(2) sets out the factors that the court shall take into account in making this determination:

(*a*) the nature and degree of seriousness of the offence with which the accused person is charged and the sentence likely to be imposed on conviction,
(*b*) the nature and degree of seriousness of the offence apprehended and the sentence likely to be imposed on conviction,
(*c*) the nature and strength of the evidence in support of the charge,
(*d*) any conviction of the accused person for an offence committed while he or she was on bail,
(*e*) any previous convictions of the accused person including any conviction the subject of an appeal (which has neither been determined nor withdrawn) to a court,
(*f*) any other offence in respect of which the accused person is charged and is awaiting trial, and, where it has taken account of one or more of the foregoing, it may also take into account the fact that the accused person is addicted to a controlled drug within the meaning of the Misuse of Drugs Act 1977.

Section 2(3) provides that in determining whether the refusal of an application for bail is reasonably considered necessary to prevent the commission of a serious offence by a

[22] *People (Attorney General) v O'Callaghan* [1966] IR 501 at 516–517.
[23] [1989] IR 399.

person, it shall not be necessary for a court to be satisfied that the commission of a specific offence by that person is apprehended.

This should be contrasted with the case of *Gregory v Windle*[24] where the system of binding over a person to keep the peace was deemed to be constitutional. Here the court stated that the courts' power to bind a person to keep the peace and/or to be of good behaviour for a specified period of time "is a beneficial and necessary jurisdiction, which, if exercised prudently and with discretion, does not give rise to any conflict with the constitutional guarantee of personal liberty".[25]

Treatment During Detention

[4–10] The treatment of a prisoner during detention has two important aspects; first, the consequences of treatment in detention, and second, the respect of the rights of prisoners/detainees.

Can a Legal Detention become Illegal?

[4–11] The Irish courts have, on occasion, had to deal with the question of whether a detention which was originally legal can become illegal as a result of the treatment of the detainee. In *State (McDonagh) v Frawley*[26] a prisoner who had been sentenced to two years' imprisonment and was detained in accordance with law, complained that he had not received adequate medical attention for backache while in detention. The court, however, held that the detention could not be considered to be illegal just because the detainee was not receiving the same kind of treatment for backache which he may have received if he was not detained.

[4–12] This case should be compared with the case of *State (C) v Frawley*[27] where a prisoner who was suffering from a sociopathic disorder, which led him on many occasions to attempt dangerous escapes from prison, had been subjected to a very strict detention. The Prison Governor had generally kept him in solitary confinement and he was often handcuffed for his own protection. While it was accepted that the prisoner would have been more appropriately detained in a psychiatric unit suitable to deal with his condition, at the time there was no facility in the State suitable for his detention. Finlay P considered whether his detention, which was in accordance with law, was still lawful in such circumstances. He stated:

> "The question which has given me the most trouble in this case is whether the conditions under which the prosecutor has been and is detained in prison constitute a failure to protect him from torture or from inhuman and degrading treatment and punishment – thus making his detention unlawful. Notwithstanding the harshness of the privations which he has undergone and, to a lesser extent, continues to suffer, I have finally come to the conclusion that those conditions do not constitute such failure.

---

[24] [1994] 3 IR 613

[25] *ibid* at 622.

[26] [1978] IR 131.

[27] [1976] IR 365.

> I am quite satisfied that the purpose and intention of the restrictions and privations surrounding the prosecutor's detention are neither punitive nor malicious... I must construe the entire concept of torture, inhuman and degrading treatment and punishment as being not only evil in its consequences but evil in its purpose as well. It is most commonly inspired by revenge, retaliation, the creation of fear or improper interrogation. It is to me inconceivable to associate it with the necessary discharge of a duty to prevent self-injury or self-destruction".[28]

Despite a number of cases on this issue, the Irish courts have yet to identify an instance where treatment during detention renders an originally lawful detention unlawful.[29]

Rights of Prisoners[30]

The seminal case regarding the protection of prisoners' rights is the case of *Murray v Ireland.*[31] This case concerned a married couple who were serving life sentences for the murder of a Garda. The court had to consider the nature and extent of the prisoners' rights as they asserted that their right to a family life was being breached by the denial of conjugal visits. The court stated: **[4–13]**

---

[28] *ibid* at 374.

[29] See decision in *Re Article 26 and the Emergency Powers Bill 1976* [1977] IR 159, which assessed the legality of a Bill which provided members of An Garda Síochána with extensive arrest powers: " ... a person detained under section 2 of the bill may not only question the legality of his detention if there has been non-compliance with the express requirements of section 2, but may also rely on provisions of the Constitution for the purpose of construing that section and of testing the legality of what has been done in purported operation of it" (at 173). In relation to this, Doyle states: "It is difficult to ascertain how extreme the circumstances of detention must be in order for a prisoner's detention to be deemed illegal. It may be that there was no reality to the Supreme Court's suggestion in the *Emergency Powers Bill Reference* that the conditions of detention could render such detention illegal. The Court's statement may instead have been an *obiter dictum* intended to lessen the blow of upholding such draconian legislation." O Doyle, *supra* n 1, p 175.
See also the cases of *Cahill v Gov of the Curragh Military Detention Barracks* [1980] ILRM 191 where soaking a prisoner with water was not considered to be a breach as the prisoner had deliberately soiled his cell; *State (Comerford) v Gov of Mountjoy* [1981] ILRM 86 where the prisoner (on remand) was transferred in contravention of the prison rules to the part of prison reserved for convicted prisoners as it was considered that he was involved in an escape plot. This was not enough to render the detention unlawful; *State (Murray) v Gov of Limerick Prison* unreported, High Court, 23 August 1978 where the right to receive and send letters and have visits was removed as part of a punishment, this was not enough to make the detention unlawful; *State (Tyndall) v Gov of Mountjoy* [1985] IR 550 where the transfer to the special AIDS unit of the prison was not considered unlawful as it was done in the best interests of the prisoner and was not considered a punishment.

[30] See R Byrne, "Habeas Corpus and Conditions of Confinement in Prison" (1979) 14 IJ 109. See also C Hamilton and U Kilkelly, "Human Rights in Irish Prisons" (2008) 8(2) JSIJ 58. The condition of Irish prisons has been highlighted in numerous reports to UN and regional human rights bodies. See the Draft Report of the Working Group on the Universal Periodic Review on Ireland's submission to the Human Rights Council (2011) A/HRC/WG.6/12/L, where numerous States recommended that Ireland take measures to improve prison conditions within the State – see, for example, paras 105.33 – 205.48.

[31] [1985] IR 532.

> "When the State lawfully exercises its power to deprive a citizen of his constitutional right to liberty many consequences result, including the deprivation of liberty to exercise many other constitutionally protected rights, which prisoners must accept ...
>
> I do not think that the plaintiffs' claim, that they be permitted to leave prison from time to time to exercise their right to beget children, is a valid one as it is clearly incompatible with the restriction on their liberty, which is constitutionally permitted by their imprisonment. What remains then to consider is the claim to exercise this right in prison and the practical consequences involved in it. For if the plaintiffs' right to beget children cannot now be exercised without putting unreasonable demands on the prison service, the restriction on its exercise cannot be constitutionally invalid as it is a reasonable consequence of the lawful exercise of the power of the State to imprison them".[32]

The decision was upheld on appeal, with McCarthy J stating:

> "The unenumerated right to procreate children, like all unenumerated rights, must be given a rational meaning. It may be lost temporarily as a result of any form of detention, arrest or imprisonment for a criminal offence; detention for a contempt of court; detention pursuant to mental treatment procedures. The suspension or abeyance of the right does not depend upon practical considerations but because of the nature of a constitutional right. If a person is deprived of liberty in accordance with law, then that person loses, for instance, the express right to vote (Article 16); the person loses the non-expressed or unenumerated right to travel, to earn a livelihood, the right to be let alone, to give some examples".[33]

[4–14] In the case of *Breathnach v Ireland*[34] the Supreme Court held that a prisoner's right to vote, as enshrined in Art 16.1.2° of the Constitution, was not infringed, by reason of his detention. The court held that the State was not under an obligation to provide facilities to enable prisoners to exercise their right to vote as this right "remains in suspension or abeyance during the period of ... imprisonment".[35] Denham J stated that:

> "[t]he applicant has no absolute right to vote under the Constitution. As a consequence of lawful custody many of his constitutional rights are suspended. The lack of facilities to enable the applicant vote is not an arbitrary or unreasonable situation ... If a person is lawfully deprived of their liberty and is in prison then that person loses certain constitutional rights including the right to vote. That does not exclude the legislature from deciding in the future to legislate for a scheme whereby prisoners could vote".[36]

In *Holland v Governor of Portlaoise Prison* the court summarised a number of conditions concerning limitations on prisoners' rights. McKechnie J stated:

> "1. that when serving a prison sentence, lawfully imposed, a prisoner must suffer a diminution or compromise on the exercise of certain constitutional rights;
> 2. the rights so affected, the 'affected rights' for the duration of the sentence, are in the first instance his right to liberty and secondly certain other rights (i) which are affected by the loss of this rights and (ii) which are consequential on the convicted prisoner having to serve his sentence in a place of detention, namely a prison;

---

32 *ibid* at 542.
33 [1991] ILRM 465 at 477.
34 [2001] 3 IR 230.
35 *ibid* at 239 per Keane CJ.
36 *ibid* at 249.

3. these 'affected rights' are not, in my view, capable of exhaustive definition but will depend on the circumstances of each case;
4. to be lawful, any limitation, either complete or partial, on the exercise of the 'affected rights' must have as their objective:
(i) the incarceration of the prisoner so as to serve his sentence; and
(ii) the maintenance of security, discipline and good order within the prison; these being the basis of the justification advanced in this case;
5. the objective underpinning the restriction must be of such significance or value in a democratic society so as to warrant the position of overriding a right which is constitutionally based;
6. the interference on restriction:
(i) must be rationally connected to the said objective and must not be arbitrary, unfair or based on irrational considerations;
(ii) must be necessary or essential in order to achieve the legitimate aim to which it is addressed;
(iii) must be not more extensive than the minimum required to achieve its intended aim; and
(iv) must otherwise be proportionate to that objective".[37]

The case concerned a prisoner's claim that a blanket ban policy on communication with the media imposed on prisoners infringed his right to communication. The court found that such a complete ban was not justified.

One of the most important rights of a prisoner in detention is the right to access a legal advisor. It has been held by the Court of Criminal Appeal in the case of *DPP v Doyle*[38] that a person in detention has a right of "reasonable access" to a legal advisor. A refusal, on request for reasonable access, may render a detention unlawful. What constitutes "reasonable access" has been outlined in subsequent case law. Therefore, it has been held that access to legal advisors should occur in private and out of the hearing of the police.[39] The right of access to a legal advisor was confirmed by the Supreme Court in *DPP v Healy*[40] where it was held that such a right has the vital function of ensuring awareness of rights in the first instance and the opportunity to seek independent advice which would be appropriate in order to permit him to reach a truly free decision as to his attitude to interrogation or to the making of any statement.

2. Legitimate Justifications for Interference with the Right

Many of the cases discussed above, which help to illuminate the nature of the right to liberty, also identify when the right can be legitimately limited. The right to liberty can be restricted for many reasons, which are not set out explicitly in the Constitution but which are in accordance with law. **[4–15]**

Arrest and Detention

At common law a Garda can arrest a person, in the absence of a warrant, if he or she reasonably suspects that person of having committed a crime. A number of statutes also authorise arrest without warrant, e.g. the Road Traffic Act 1961, discussed above **[4–16]**

[37] *Holland v Governor of Portlaoise Prison* [2004] 2 IR 573 at 600.
[38] Unreported, Court of Criminal Appeal,16 November 1976.
[39] *State (Harrington) v Garvey,* unreported, High Court, 14 December 1976.
[40] [1990] 2 IR 110.

in the case of *DPP (Stratford) v Fagan*.[41] Generally such an arrest is for a limited purpose and this purpose must be clarified to the person arrested. In *Re Ó Laighléis*, Maguire CJ stated:

> "We accept it as settled law that in the case of an arrest without the production of a warrant the arrest will not be lawful unless the person being arrested is told why he is being arrested or unless he otherwise knows ... Arrest must be for a lawful purpose; and since no one is obliged to submit to an unlawful arrest the citizen has a right before acquiescing in his arrest to know why he is being arrested".[42]

Legislation now provides that a person who has been arrested must be brought before a District Court judge as soon as practicable.[43]

Under s 39 of the Offences Against the State Act 1939, Gardaí are given wide powers to stop, search, question and arrest an individual who is suspected of having committed an offence under that Act.[44] The constitutionality of this provision was questioned in the case of *People (DPP) v Quilligan (No 3)*[45] as it was claimed that it infringed an individual's right to liberty, but this was rejected by the Supreme Court. Similar broad powers are given to Gardaí with regard to investigation of drug trafficking.[46]

The Criminal Justice Act 1984 also empowers Gardaí to detain certain persons for questioning.[47] Section 50 of the Criminal Justice Act 2007 also confers significant detention powers on Gardaí, in the absence of a warrant, in relation to individuals suspected of specified offences, including murder involving firearms or explosives and offences Under the Non-Fatal Offences against the Person Act 1997.

Imprisonment Following Conviction

[4–17] The deprivation of liberty by means of imprisonment following conviction and sentencing are, logically, an acceptable restriction on the right to liberty. Even if some defect attaches to the detention, this does not necessarily mean that the interference with the right to liberty is unacceptable. In *State (McDonagh) v Frawley*, O'Higgins CJ stated:

> "The stipulation in Article 40, s.4, subs. 1 of the Constitution that a citizen may not be deprived of his liberty save 'in accordance with law' does not mean that a convicted person must be released on habeas corpus merely because some defect or illegality attaches to his detention. The phrase means that there must be such a default of fundamental requirements that the detention may be said to be wanting in due process of law".[48]

---

[41] [1994] 3 IR 265.
[42] *Re Ó Laighléis* [1970] IR 93.
[43] s 15 of the Criminal Justice Act 1951, as substituted by s 26 of the Criminal Justice Act 1984 and s 50 Criminal Justice Act 2007.
[44] See also Offences Against the State (Amendment) Act 1998.
[45] [1993] 2 IR 305.
[46] Criminal Justice (Drug Trafficking) Act 1996.
[47] See J Casey, *Constitutional Law in Ireland* (3rd ed, Round Hall Sweet & Maxwell, Dublin, 2000), pp 492–495.
[48] *State (McDonagh) v Frawley* [1978] IR 131 at 136–137.

The deprivation of liberty following a finding of contempt of court is also a legitimate restriction on the right.[49]

Mental Health

It is clear that the Irish courts have taken a rather paternalistic attitude to people with mental illnesses and have been willing to restrict their right to liberty under mental health legislation[50] for their own good and for the good of society. This is clearly seen in the case of *Re Philip Clarke*,[51] discussed above. Under s 12 of the Mental Health Act 2001 a member of the Gardaí who has reasonable grounds for believing that a person is suffering from a mental disorder, and because of this disorder is likely to cause serious harm to himself or herself or others, can take that person into custody. Gardaí also have the authority to enter any premises, by force, if necessary, if they believe that a person suffering from a mental illness is there. In *Croke v Smith (No 2)*[52] the Supreme Court held that a person held under the Mental Treatment Acts could test the legality of his or her detention under Art 40.4.2° of the Constitution. **[4–18]**

B. ECHR

Article 5: **[4–19]**

> "1. Everyone has the right to liberty and security of person. No one shall be deprived of his liberty save in the following cases and in accordance with a procedure prescribed by law:
>
> (a) the lawful detention of a person after conviction by a competent court;
> (b) the lawful arrest or detention of a person for noncompliance with the lawful order of a court or in order to secure the fulfilment of any obligation prescribed by law;
> (c) the lawful arrest or detention of a person effected for the purpose of bringing him before the competent legal authority on reasonable suspicion of having committed an offence or when it is reasonably considered necessary to prevent his committing an offence or fleeing after having done so;
> (d) the detention of a minor by lawful order for the purpose of educational supervision or his lawful detention for the purpose of bringing him before the competent legal authority;
> (e) the lawful detention of persons for the prevention of the spreading of infectious diseases, of persons of unsound mind, alcoholics or drug addicts or vagrants;
> (f) the lawful arrest or detention of a person to prevent his effecting an unauthorised entry into the country or of a person against whom action is being taken with a view to deportation or extradition.
>
> 2. Everyone who is arrested shall be informed promptly, in a language which he understands, of the reasons for his arrest and of any charge against him.
> 3. Everyone arrested or detained in accordance with the provisions of paragraph 1 (c) of this Article shall be brought promptly before a judge or other officer authorised by law to exercise judicial power and shall be entitled to trial within a reasonable time or to release pending trial. Release may be conditioned by guarantees to appear for trial.

---

49 See J Casey, *supra* n 47, pp 484–486.
50 Mental Treatment Act 1945.
51 [1950] IR 235.
52 [1988] 1 IR 101.

> 4. Everyone who is deprived of his liberty by arrest or detention shall be entitled to take proceedings by which the lawfulness of his detention shall be decided speedily by a court and his release ordered if the detention is not lawful.
> 5. Everyone who has been the victim of arrest or detention in contravention of the provisions of this Article shall have an enforceable right to compensation."

1. Nature of the Right

[4–20] Article 5 seeks to guarantee the liberty of the person and also provides a number of guarantees against arbitrary arrest and detention. Nowak comments that the reference to arrest and detention in Art 5 "illustrates that the term 'personal liberty' is quite narrow and must not be confused with the general notion of freedom or liberty".[53] The European Court of Human Rights (ECtHR) has often highlighted the fundamental nature of the protection afforded by Art 5. In *Bazorkina v Russia*[54] the ECtHR stated:

> "The Court stresses the fundamental importance of the guarantees contained in Article 5 for securing the right of individuals in a democracy to be free from arbitrary detention at the hands of the authorities. It has stressed in that connection that any deprivation of liberty must not only have been effected in conformity with the substantive and procedural rules of national law but must equally be in keeping with the very purpose of Article 5, namely to protect the individual from arbitrary detention. In order to minimise the risks of arbitrary detention, Article 5 provides a corpus of substantive rights intended to ensure that the act of deprivation of liberty be amenable to independent judicial scrutiny and secures the accountability of the authorities for that measure".[55]

While Art 5 refers to the right to liberty and security of the person, the ECtHR has indicated that the main focus of the provision is the deprivation of liberty.[56] In cases concerning the disappearance of prisoners, however, the ECtHR often uses the term "liberty and security of the person".[57]

[4–21] Although the Article itself is relatively lengthy, the aim of the right may be succinctly encapsulated by the comment in *Engel v Netherlands*[58] as being to ensure that " . . . no one should be dispossessed of their liberty in an arbitrary fashion." Plainly, as part of this concept, State powers must be used with both fairness and proportionality and should be compatible with existing case law.

Article 5(1)(a) – (f) give the legal bases for detention, while Art 5(3) requires the rapid court appearance of the accused, thereby limiting the amount of time a person may be held without charge. Art 5(4) gives the arrestee the right to challenge the lawfulness of his or her detention, and have this determined speedily. Even in the case of a wanted

---

[53] M Nowak, "Article 6: The Right to Liberty and Security" in *Commentary of the Charter of the Fundamental Rights of the EU*, June 2006 p 67, available at: http://infoportal.fra.europa.eu/InfoPortal/infobaseShowContent.do?btnCat_182&btnCountryBread_169, last accessed 21 June 2012.

[54] *Bazorkina v Russia* (2008) 46 EHRR 15.

[55] *ibid* at para 146.

[56] *Bozano v France* (1987) 9 EHRR 297.

[57] See R White and C Ovey, *Jacobs, White and Ovey: The European Convention on Human Rights* (5th ed, Oxford University Press, Oxford, 2010), p 210.

[58] *Engel v Netherlands* (1979–80) EHRR 647 at para 58.

man giving himself up,[59] and thereby voluntarily surrendering his liberty, the ECHR will still oversee and protect his rights in custody.

Article 5(2) ensures that a person is aware of the reasoning behind his or her deprivation of liberty, either to effect a denial or to commence habeas corpus proceedings, and this should be in plain, intelligible language which he or she understands. This last requirement may be complied with if the questioning subsequent to arrest is in an intelligible language.[60] **[4–22]**

The question of what may constitute promptness is an interesting one, and it seems that the basic grounds being given for the arrest will suffice initially, but that the time limit may be extended for all the relevant information to be given, this being up to some seven hours in the case of *Fox, Campbell and Hartley v UK*.[61]

Article 5(3) relates to prompt appearance of the accused before a judicial body,[62] and to the granting of bail.[63]

Deprivation of Liberty

Article 5(1) makes it clear that an arrest must be "in accordance with a procedure prescribed by law", i.e. it must be lawful. "Lawful" may be judged either according to national law or according to the principle of legality so often stated by the ECtHR, and indeed, a procedure may be found lawful under national law but unlawful under the ECtHR, the determining factor appearing to be the precision of the national law and its implementation.[64] There is both an objective element (actual confinement in a restricted space for a period of time) and a subjective element (the detained person must not have consented to the deprivation/loss of liberty).[65] **[4–23]**

When deciding if a case falls within Art 5, the ECtHR takes a number of factors into consideration, including the duration and effects of the confinement. In *Guzzardi v Italy*[66] the ECtHR had to examine the legality of a detention order in the light of Art 5. The applicant had been issued with a residence order, requiring him to live on a small island near Sardinia for sixteen months. He was ordered to stay within two-and-a-half square kilometres of the island, which contained a village inhabited by men who were subject to similar residence orders. Whilst his wife and child could have stayed with **[4–24]**

---

59 *De Wilde, Ooms and Versyp v Belgium* (1979–80) 1 EHRR 373.

60 *Delcourt v Belgium* (1979–80) 1 EHRR 355.

61 (1990) 13 EHRR 157. 10 days is too long: *Van der Leer v Netherlands* (1990) 12 EHRR 567.

62 *Brogan v UK* (1989) 11 EHRR 117.

63 See *Caballero v UK* (2000) 30 EHRR 643 where the discretion of the national court as to the granting of bail had been removed by legislation, the Criminal Justice and Public Order Act 1994, s 25, which was contrary to Art 5(3). This was accepted by the UK and bail may now be given under the Crime and Disorder Act 1998 in specific situations involving "exceptional circumstances". *Letellier v France* (1992) 14 EHRR 83 suggests that bail may not be refused even if there is a suggestion of absconding or witness intimidation, where the time in custody is unreasonably lengthy.

64 Contrast the case of *Steel v UK* (1999) 28 EHRR 603 with *Hashman and Harrup v UK* (2000) 30 EHRR 241.

65 *Storck v Germany* (2006) 43 EHRR 96, ECHR 2005-V at para 74.

66 (1981) 3 EHRR 333.

him, his accommodation was dilapidated and unsuitable for a family. The applicant was subject to a curfew and was required to report twice a day to the police. The police also restricted his visitors and use of the telephone. The ECtHR found that such detention violated Art 5.

[4–25] In *HL v United Kingdom*[67] an autistic man who could not speak and had self-harmed in the past was admitted to hospital without his consent. He was admitted as an informal patient and did not resist admittance, and subsequently remained in the hospital for a period of three months. At the end of this period he was compulsorily detained following a court case. The man then complained about this three-month detention to the ECtHR under Art 5. The ECtHR acknowledged that the applicant could have left the hospital and never complained of his detention but held that this was not an adequate reason to find that the detention was legal. Rather, the ECtHR focused on the fact that the doctors treating the applicant had a high level of control over him. The nature of this control was such that the applicant could not have, in fact, left the hospital if he wished. If he had made an attempt to leave, evidence showed that the doctors would have compulsorily detained him. Therefore, the ECtHR found that there had been a violation of Art 5.

Arbitrariness

[4–26] Detention must not be arbitrary. Even if a detention is lawful under domestic law, a breach of Art 5 will still occur if the detention is arbitrary. This may be characterised by the comment of Lord Hope in the case of *R. v Governor of Brockhill Prison, Ex p Evans (No 2)*, as being " ... resorted to in bad faith or was not proportionate".[68] See also the cases of *Weeks v UK*[69] and *Stafford v UK*.[70]

Positive Obligations

[4–27] Jacobs, White and Ovey state that the "development of positive obligations under Article 5 has lagged somewhat behind its development under other articles of the Convention, most notably Articles 2, 3, and 8".[71] They go on to state that the judgment in *Storck v Germany*[72] has remedied this situation somewhat. The applicant complained about her detention in a lock ward in a psychiatric clinic which lasted for almost two years. When she attempted to escape the police assisted in her return to the clinic. In relation to Art 5, the ECtHR stated:

> "Article 5(1), first sentence ... must ... be considered as laying down a positive obligation on the State to protect the liberty of its citizens. Any conclusion to the effect that this was not the case would not only be inconsistent with the Court's case-law, notably under Articles 2, 3 and 8 of the Convention. It would, moreover, leave a sizeable gap in the protection from arbitrary detention which would be inconsistent with the importance of personal liberty in a democratic society. The State is, therefore, obliged to take measures

---

[67] (2005) 40 EHRR 761.

[68] [2000] 4 All ER 15.

[69] *Weeks v UK* (1988) 10 EHRR 293.

[70] *Stafford v UK* (2002) 35 EHRR 32.

[71] R White and C Ovey, *supra* n 57, p 213.

[72] *Storck v Germany* (App 61603/00), 16 June 2005 (2006) 43 EHRR 96, ECHR 2005-V.

> providing effective protection of vulnerable persons, including reasonable steps to prevent the deprivation of liberty of which the authorities have or ought to have knowledge".[73]

Knowledge of Reason for Detention

Article 5 provides that a person deprived of his or her liberty should be informed of the reason for his or her detention. Article 5(2) states: **[4–28]**

> "Everyone who is arrested shall be informed promptly, in a language which he understands, of the reasons for his arrest and of any charge against him."

Article 5(2) can be compared with Art 6(3)(a) which provides that anyone charged with a criminal offence must be informed promptly, and in a language in which he or she understands, of the nature and cause of the charge.

In *Murray v United Kingdom*[74] the ECtHR considered the issue of the content and the promptness of notification and held that whether these were sufficient depended on the circumstances of each individual case. The ECtHR has found that, on occasion, the circumstances of the arrest fulfil the notification element of Art 5. In *Dikme v Turkey*[75] the applicant was arrested immediately after it was discovered that he had supplied false identification documents to the police. The ECtHR found that even if the police had not provided the applicant with reasons for his arrest, there was no breach of Art 5(2) given the circumstances of the case. **[4–29]**

The Lawfulness of the Deprivation of Liberty

Under Art 5, a deprivation of liberty must be carried out "in accordance with a procedure prescribed by law", i.e. in accordance with provisions of substantive and procedural national law. Non-compliance with national law can constitute a breach of Art 5,[76] however, "a mere procedural defect, as distinct from a more serious irregularity, in national law will not be sufficient to constitute a failure to follow national law".[77] **[4–30]**

In order for a deprivation of liberty not to fall foul of Art 5, it is not enough that it be carried out in accordance with national law; the national law in question must have some important characteristics, e.g. it must contain clear rules in relation to when a State can deprive an individual of his or her liberty and it must also clearly state the procedures which should be followed.[78] In *Baranowski v Poland*[79] the ECtHR found that there was an absence of clear rules on detention in Polish national law.

---

73 *ibid* at para 102.

74 28 October 1994, Series A No 300-A (1995) 19 EHRR 193.

75 App 20869/92, 11 July 2000, ECHR 2000-VIII.

76 See, for example, *Benham v United Kingdom* (1996) 22 EHRR 293.

77 R White and C Ovey, *supra* n 57, p 216. See *Mooren v Germany* (2010) 50 EHRR 23 at paras 72–98.

78 See *Steel v United Kingdom* (1998) 28 EHRR 603.

79 No 28358/95, 28 March 2000, ECHR 2000-III.

Reviewing the Legality of Detention

[4–31] Article 5(4) permits a review of the legality of detention. This provision states:

> "Everyone who is deprived of his liberty by arrest or detention shall be entitled to take proceedings by which the lawfulness of his detention shall be decided speedily by a court and his release ordered if the detention is not lawful."

The "court" mentioned in this provision does not have to be a "Court of law of the classic kind integrated within the standard judicial machinery of the country",[80] but must be independent of the parties to the case and of the executive. The ECtHR considered the nature and scope of the review provided for in Art 5(4) in the case of *E v Norway*[81] where it stated:

> "Article 5(4) does not guarantee a right to judicial review of such a scope as to empower the court on all aspects of the case, including questions of pure expediency, to substitute its own discretion for that of the decision-making authority. The review should, however, be wide enough to bear on those conditions which are essential for the 'lawful' detention of a person according to Article 5(1)".[82]

[4–32] Article 5(4) states that "the lawfulness of detention shall be decided speedily". The temporal aspect of this provision is analysed on a case-by-case basis. In *Rehbock v Slovenia*,[83] for example, a delay of three weeks in completing a simple bail application was deemed to be too long, whereas longer periods might be acceptable in more difficult and complex cases, "but, given the importance of the right to liberty, there is still a pressing obligation on the authorities to deal quickly with such applications for release".[84] Protocol 4 to the ECHR prohibits the deprivation of liberty for reasons of debt.[85] The case of *McCann v Judges of Monahan District Court*[86] involves an interesting discussion of this Protocol in the Irish context.

2. Legitimate Justifications for Interference with the Right

[4–33] Derogations from this provision are still allowed under Art 15.[87] In addition, Art 5(1) sets out the conditions under which a person may be lawfully deprived of his or her liberty.

Permitted Grounds of Detention

Pre-Trial Detention

[4–34] Article 5(1)(c) allows for detention in circumstances of arrest and also for pre-trial detention. The provision states:

---

80 *Weeks v United Kingdom* (1988) 10 EHRR 293 at para 61.

81 *E v Norway*, 29 August 1990 (1990) 17 EHRR 20.

82 *ibid* at para 50.

83 *Rehbock v Slovenia* (No 29462/95) 28 November 2000, ECHR 2000-XII.

84 R White and C Ovey, *supra* n 57, p 239.

85 Art 1 states: "No one shall be deprived of his liberty merely on the ground of inability to fulfil a contractual obligation."

86 (2010) ILRM 17.

87 See *A v United Kingdom* (2009) 49 EHRR 29.

> "... the lawful arrest or detention of a person effected for the purpose of bringing him before the competent legal authority on reasonable suspicion of having committed an offence or when it is reasonably considered necessary to prevent his committing an offence or fleeing after having done so."

This provision must be read in light of Art 5(3), which states:

> "Everyone arrested or detained in accordance with the provisions of paragraph (1)(c) of this article shall be brought promptly before a judge or other officer authorised by law to exercise judicial power and shall be entitled to trial within a reasonable time or to release pending trial. Release may be conditioned by guarantees to appear for trial."

The issue of promptness has given rise to a number of cases, although the ECtHR has not placed a temporal limit on the acceptable length of preliminary detention, and has dealt with the issue on a case-by-case basis. In *Brogan v United Kingdom*[88] the applicants had been detained under a special law which allowed the Secretary of State for Northern Ireland to extend periods of detention in certain circumstances. The applicants were held for periods of time ranging from four days, six hours to six days and sixteen hours before all were released without charge. The ECtHR referred to the Northern Ireland conflict and how this impacted on the need for extended powers of detention, but even taking this into consideration, the ECtHR held that these detentions constituted breaches of Art 5(3). The decision led the UK government to file a derogation from Art 5(3) under Art 15 of the ECHR as a result of an emergency threatening the life of the nation. The validity of this derogation was accepted in the *Brannigan and McBride* case.[89] **[4–35]**

Even when a contracting State derogates from Art 5(3), the ECtHR has the power of review, as was highlighted in *Aksoy v Turkey.*[90] The applicant was arrested on suspicion of involvement in a terrorist group, the PKK. He was detained, under emergency legislation, *incommunicado* for two weeks. Turkey had filed a derogation under Art 15 of the ECHR due to an emergency threatening the life of the nation. While the ECtHR accepted that an emergency of this kind existed, it decided that 14 days was too long to detain a suspect without any access to a lawyer or a doctor or without any kind of judicial supervision. **[4–36]**

The issue of the "other officer authorised by law to exercise judicial power" has been discussed in a number of cases. In *Schiesser v Switzerland*[91] the ECtHR highlighted that such an officer must be independent of the parties to the case. In *Huber v Switzerland*[92] it was held that a District Attorney who had been involved in the prosecution of the applicant did not qualify for the role of officer under Art 5(3).

---

88 *Brogan v United Kingdom* (1989) 11 EHRR 117.
89 *Brannigan and McBride v United Kingdom* (1994) 17 EHRR 539.
90 1996 (1997) 23 EHRR 553.
91 4 December 1979, Series A No 34 (1979–80) 2 EHRR 417.
92 *Huber v Switzerland* (No 12794/87), 23 October 1990, Series A No 188.

Detention after Conviction

[4–37] Under Art 5(1)(a), detention following a conviction by a competent court is lawful. Article 5(1)(a) does not give the ECtHR the power to consider the legality of convictions before national courts.

A "competent court" in the context of Art 5(1)(a) is one that "must have the power under national law to order the detention in question" and to satisfy Art 5(1)(a); the court "must possess a judicial character and follow a fair procedure".[93] These issues were addressed in the *Ilaşcu* case.[94] In this case the applicants had been convicted and sentenced by the Supreme Court of the Moldovan Republic of Transdniestria, which is a break-away region of Moldova. The region has not been recognised as a State. The ECtHR then had to consider whether this court was a "competent court" for the purposes of Art 5(1)(a). The ECtHR stated that even though Transdniestria was not recognised under international law, this did not preclude its Supreme Court from being a competent court if it was part of a judicial system which operated on a constitutional and legal basis and reflected a judicial tradition which was compatible with the ECHR so that the Convention rights could be guaranteed to the inhabitants of the region. In the ECtHR's opinion, however, the Transdniestrian Supreme Court did not form part of such a judicial system. Therefore, the convictions and the subsequent periods of detention at issue in the case were not considered to be lawful detention in accordance with a procedure prescribed by law.

Failure to Comply with an Obligation Prescribed by Law

[4–38] Article 5(1)(b) provides for the deprivation of liberty following "the lawful arrest or detention of a person for non-compliance with the lawful order of a court or in order to secure the fulfilment of any obligation prescribed by law."

[4–39] There are two elements to this provision, i.e. first, lawful detention for non-compliance with a lawful order of a court, and secondly, lawful detention in order to secure fulfilment of obligations prescribed by law. With regard to lawful detention for non-compliance with a lawful order, this relates to situations including imprisonment for failure to pay a fine,[95] failure in complying with a summons[96] or failure in complying with custody and maintenance orders.[97] With regard to detention in order to fulfil obligations prescribed by law, the ECtHR has stated that detention must always be in proportion to the aim pursued. In *Vasileva*,[98] the applicant was arrested following a quarrel with a bus inspector concerning whether she had a valid bus ticket. The 65-year-old woman was then detained in police custody for over 24 hours when she would not provide her name and address to the police as was required under Danish law. As soon as she provided her details the police released her. The ECtHR accepted that the applicant's detention had been in order to fulfil obligations prescribed by law, however

[93] R White and C Ovey, *supra* n 57, p 225. See *De Wilde, Ooms and Versyp v Belgium* (1979–80) 1 EHRR 373 at para 78.

[94] *Ilaşcu v Moldova and Russia* (2005) 40 EHRR 1040, ECHR 2004-VII.

[95] See *Tyrell v United Kingdom* (No 28188/95), 4 September 1996.

[96] See *GK v Austria* (No 32206/96), 16 October 1996.

[97] See *Santa Cruz Ruiz v United Kingdom* (No 26109/95), 22 October 1997.

[98] *Vasileva v Denmark* (No 52792/99) 25 September 2003, (2005) 40 EHRR 681.

the ECtHR then went on to consider if the detention was in proportion to the aim pursued. The ECtHR considered the nature of the obligation which arose under Danish law, including its object and purpose, the characteristics of the person in detention and the length of detention. The ECtHR concluded that the detention was not in proportion to the aim pursued.

Detention of Minors

Article 5(1)(d) allows for "the detention of a minor by lawful order for the purpose of educational supervision or his lawful detention for the purpose of bringing him before the competent legal authority." [4–40]

This provision allows for the detention of minors in two circumstances. The first concerns compulsory attendance at school. Orders for the purpose of educational supervision can be made by a court or an administrative authority.[99] The second allows minors to be taken before an authority which can order their detention. The age at which majority is attained has not been established definitively in the Council of Europe and varies between Member States.[100] This issue was discussed in the case of *Koniarska v United Kingdom*[101] where the ECtHR decided that the applicant was a minor until the age of 18 and that she could be detained for educational supervision up until that age under Art 5(1)(d), despite the fact that school-leaving age in the UK was 16. [4–41]

Detention of Members of Vulnerable Groups

Article 5(1)(e) permits the lawful detention of members of a number of vulnerable groups, i.e. persons of unsound mind, alcoholics, drug addicts and vagrants. The provision also permits the lawful detention of persons for the prevention of the spreading of infectious diseases.[102] The purpose of this provision is "social protection".[103] The provision does not require that the detention be imposed by a court and detention may be ordered by an administrative authority, but such an order is subject to judicial control under Art 5(4). [4–42]

Vagrancy

There have been very few recent cases in relation to vagrancy, given the relative wealth of the Council of Europe region and: [4–43]

> "as standards evolve in Europe it appears increasingly repugnant forcibly to detain people merely because they are homeless. It is difficult to imagine many such cases where the

---

[99] Orders made by administrative authorities can be subject to review under Art 5(4).

[100] The Council of Europe adopted a resolution which recommended that Member States reduce the age of majority from 21 to 18 in principle – Resolution CM(72) 29 of the Committee of Ministers of the Council of Europe.

[101] *Koniarska v United Kingdom* (No 33670/96), 12 October 2000.

[102] The provision permits "the lawful detention of persons for the prevention of the spreading of infectious diseases, of persons of unsound mind, alcoholics or drug addicts or vagrants."

[103] R White and C Ovey, *supra* n 57, p 229.

detention would not in reality be prompted by some other aspect of the vagrant's conduct or condition, such as criminal offending, addiction, or mental illness".[104]

Mental Illness

[4–44] The most important case concerning the detention of people with mental illness is *Winterwerp v Netherlands*[105] where the ECtHR set out three procedural tests which must be satisfied in order for the detention to be valid. First, objective medical evidence must be provided to determine the presence of an "unsound mind". Secondly, the mental illness must make the person a danger to him- or herself or others. Thirdly, the detention of the person of unsound mind must be justified on a continuing basis. In *Aerts v Belgium*[106] the ECtHR added to these three tests by stating that the place where a person of unsound mind is detained must be suitable, i.e. it must be a hospital or clinic, rather than a prison which does not provide treatment for the detainee.

[4–45] In *Johnson v United Kingdom*[107] the ECtHR dealt with the issue of release from detention on mental illness grounds. The applicant had been suffering from mental illness and had been validly detained. Even though his condition improved and medical evidence proved this, authorities still felt that he was not ready to live on his own and ordered that he resided in a hostel under supervision when he was discharged from hospital. However, a suitable place was unavailable and his release from hospital was delayed for four years when he was finally unconditionally released. The applicant claimed that Art 5(1)(e) was breached and that he should have been unconditionally released at the time of his review. The ECtHR stated that even when medical evidence shows that an individual is no longer suffering from mental illness, release from detention is not automatic. The ECtHR highlighted that the decision of the authorities to make his release conditional on a stay in a hostel had not been unreasonable. It stated that an assessment of mental illness was not an exact science. However, it was the responsibility of the authorities to then find suitable accommodation. The delay of four years, combined with the lack of procedural safeguards (there was no process for the applicant to petition the authorities in between his annual reviews) had led to a breach of Art 5(1)(e).

Alcoholics

[4–46] In *Witold Litwa v Poland*[108] the ECtHR considered the meaning of "alcoholic". The applicant was a partially-blind pensioner. He was taken by the police to a sobering-up centre after he had caused a commotion at the post office, claiming his post box had been opened and emptied. At the centre a doctor had certified him as being moderately intoxicated and he had been detained at the centre for six-and-a-half hours. The ECtHR noted that normally the word "alcoholic" connotes a person who is addicted to alcohol. The ECtHR looked at the Vienna Convention on the Law of Treaties which states that it is necessary to look at the object and purpose of a treaty in interpreting it. The ECtHR then

---

104 *ibid*, p 230. See *De Wilde, Ooms and Versyp v Belgium* 1 EHRR 373. These cases are known collectively as the "vagrancy cases".

105 *Winterwerp v Netherlands* (1979–80) 2 EHRR 387.

106 *Aerts v Belgium* (1999) 29 EHRR 50.

107 *Johnson v United Kingdom* (No 22520/93), 24 October 1997 (1997) 27 EHRR 296, ECHR 1997-VII.

108 *Witold Litwa v Poland* (No 26629/95), 4 April 2000 (2001) 33 EHRR 1267, ECHR 2000-III.

stated that the object and purpose of the provision would be defeated if "alcoholic" was given this limited interpretation, as the aim of Art 5(1)(e) was the protection of society and protection of the safety of the detained person and others. The ECtHR also looked to the *travaux préparatoires* of the ECHR which included a reference to "drunkenness" and did not just focus on alcoholism. The ECtHR, therefore, found that the applicant's detention fell within the ambit of Art 5(1). However, the ECtHR found that the provision had been violated because the applicant had not behaved in such a way as to constitute a threat to himself or others. The ECtHR found that the detention was unnecessary in his case.

Infectious Diseases

The ECtHR applied similar principles as it had in *Witold Litwa* to cases of detention of people with infectious diseases. In *Enhorn v Sweden*[109] the applicant was HIV positive and the domestic court made a compulsory order that he be detained in hospital in isolation for a period of almost seven years. He had been deprived of his liberty for 18 months. The applicant had been issued with various instructions by the county medical examiner which aimed at preventing the disease, including a requirement to inform sexual partners of the infection and to inform medical practitioners. The instructions also required him to abstain from drinking so much that his judgement would be impaired as others could be placed at risk of being infected by him. The applicant had complied in the main with the medical officer's instructions. However, he refused to voluntarily see a psychiatrist. The Swedish courts ordered that he be detained because they claimed there was reasonable cause to believe that he would not comply with the instructions. The ECtHR stated that the test for lawfulness of detention of a person for the purpose of preventing the spreading of infectious disease was whether the spreading of the disease was dangerous to public health or safety and whether the detention of the person was a last resort and less severe restrictions had been insufficient. The ECtHR held that the detention in this case was in breach of the ECHR. [4–47]

Deportation or Extradition

Article 5(1)(f) provides for "the lawful arrest or detention of a person to prevent his effecting an unauthorised entry into the country or of a person against whom action is being taken with a view to deportation or extradition." This provision contains two elements; the first concerns unauthorised entry into a State and the second concerns detention prior to deportation or extradition. [4–48]

The first of these elements was considered by the ECtHR in *Saadi v United Kingdom*,[110] where the Grand Chamber stated:

> "To avoid being branded as arbitrary . . . such detention must be carried out in good faith; it must be closely connected to the purpose of preventing unauthorised entry of the person to the country; the place and conditions of detention should be appropriate, bearing in mind that 'the measure is applicable not to those who have committed criminal offences but to aliens who, often fearing for their lives, have fled from their own country' . . . and the length of the detention should not exceed that reasonably required for the purpose pursued".[111]

---

109 *Enhorn v Sweden* (2005) 41 EHRR 633.

110 *Saadi v United Kingdom* (2008) 47 EHRR 17.

111 *ibid* at 74.

[4–49] With regard to the issue of detention for the purpose of deportation or extradition, it is important to note that there is no requirement on States to show that the detention was reasonably considered necessary for the purpose of preventing the detainee from absconding or from committing a crime. This is in contrast to individuals who are detained under Art 5(1), paragraphs (b), (c) and (e).[112] Another important aspect to Art 5(1)(f) is that so long as the detention is lawful, the decision to deport or extradite is in line with domestic or ECHR law, and will not be examined by the ECtHR.[113]

The only way that an applicant can establish a breach of Art 5(1)(f) is to establish that some period of the detention was not for the purpose of deportation or extradition.

The Right to Compensation

[4–50] The right to compensation for illegal detention is dealt with in Art 5(5). This provision states:

> "Everyone who has been the victim of arrest or detention in contravention of the provisions of this article shall have an enforceable right to compensation."

It follows that any breach of Art 5 which is established by either the ECtHR Court or by national courts will give rise to a breach of Art 5(5) if there is no enforceable right to compensation under national law. This provision is unusual because the ECHR already contains an Article which provides for compensation by requiring an effective remedy for all violations of the ECHR in Art 13. The right to liberty is the only ECHR right which contains such a clause in relation to specific compensation. Very few cases make a claim under Art 5(5); however, in a number of cases concerning Northern Ireland,[114] the ECtHR found a breach of Art 5(5) as no provision of domestic law provided for compensation in the case of arrest and prolonged detention of the applicants under terrorism legislation.

C. CFR

[4–51] Article 6:

> "Everyone has the right to liberty and security of person."

The rights in Art 6 of the CFR correspond with the rights protected by Art 5 of the ECHR, and in line with Art 52(3) of the CFR, they have the same meaning and scope.[115] It should be noted that although Art 6 of the CFR does not include specific limitations, the limitations contained in Art 5 of the ECHR can apply.

---

112 See *Chahal v United Kingdom* (No 22414/93), 15 November 1996 (1997) 23 EHRR 413, ECHR 1996-V.

113 See *Chahal v United Kingdom* (No 22414/93), 15 November 1996 (1997) 23 EHRR 413, ECHR 1996-V at para 112.

114 See *Fox, Campbell and Hartley v United Kingdom* (1991) EHRR 157 and *Brogan v United Kingdom* (1989) 11 EHRR 117.

115 See Explanations of the Praesidium of the Convention which drafted the Charter of Fundamental Rights of the European Union, available at: http://infoportal.fra.europa.eu/InfoPortal/infobaseShowContent.do?btnCat_182&btnCountryBread_169, last accessed 21 June 2012.

Given that the provisions of the CFR are directed at the institutions of the EU, and the Member States when implementing EU law, many of the rights contained therein, including the right to liberty, seem unlikely to play much of a role in case law or legislation (although there is an obligation on the Union institutions and Member States to promote rights (Art 51)). The right to liberty, for example, when one considers the limits of EU competence, seems most likely to feature in case law relating to the Area of Freedom, Security and Justice (Part III, Title V of the Treaty on the Functioning of the European Union (TFEU)). **[4–52]**

Article 67 TFEU (ex Art 61 TEC and ex Art 29 TEU) states:

> "1. The Union shall constitute an area of freedom, security and justice with respect for fundamental rights and the different legal systems and traditions of the Member States.
> 2. It shall ensure the absence of internal border controls for persons and shall frame a common policy on asylum, immigration and external border control, based on solidarity between Member States, which is fair towards third-country nationals. For the purpose of this Title, stateless persons shall be treated as third-country nationals.
> 3. The Union shall endeavour to ensure a high level of security through measures to prevent and combat crime, racism and xenophobia, and through measures for coordination and cooperation between police and judicial authorities and other competent authorities, as well as through the mutual recognition of judgments in criminal matters and, if necessary, through the approximation of criminal laws.
> 4. The Union shall facilitate access to justice, in particular through the principle of mutual recognition of judicial and extrajudicial decisions in civil matters."

Member States must respect Art 6 of the CFR when co-operating on penal issues, including the determination of minimum rules for defining penal infractions.[116] Regarding issues of arrest and detention within the EU, the European Arrest Warrant system[117] must be noted.[118]

D. International and Regional Laws

As mentioned earlier, the right to liberty was one of the first human rights recognised in a human rights document, being recognised in the *Magnta Carta* and later becoming a cornerstone of the French Declaration of the Rights of Man. Today, the right to liberty is widely protected by laws at regional and international levels. In international human rights law the issue of slavery,[119] which was "the first human rights issue to **[4–53]**

[116] In this regard, see Proposal for a Council framework Decision on certain procedural rights in criminal proceedings throughout the European Union, 2004/0113/CNS.

[117] 2002/584/JHA: Council Framework Decision of 13 June 2002 on the European arrest warrant and the surrender procedures between Member States—Statements made by certain Member States on the adoption of the Framework Decision, [2002] OJ L190/1.

[118] See J Wouters and F Naert, *Of Arrest Warrants, Terrorist Offences and Extradition Deals: An Appraisal of the EU's Main Criminal Law Measures against Terrorism after '11 September'*, (2004) Institute for International Law, KU Leuven. https://www.law.kuleuven.be/iir/nl/onderzoek/wp/WP56e.pdf, last accessed 21 June 2012.

[119] See The Convention to Suppress the Slave Trade and Slavery 1926 known as the Slavery Convention, sponsored by the League of Nations, and the UN Supplementary Convention on the Abolition of Slavery, the Slave Trade, and Institutions and Practices Similar to Slavery of 1953.

awaken broad international concern"[120] can fall under provisions dealing with the right to liberty.[121]

Article 3 of the Universal Declaration of Human Rights states that everyone "has the right to life, liberty and security of person." Other UN instruments including the International Covenant on Civil and Political Rights (ICCPR) also protect the person's right to liberty. The ICCPR provides a general protection of the right to liberty in Art 9(1)[122] before proceeding to deal with issues such as the timely provision of information regarding reasons for arrest, timely trials and the right to compensation.[123] At a regional level, the right to liberty is also protected by Art 7 of the American Convention on Human Rights,[124] Art 6 of the African Charter

[120] R Smith, *Textbook on International Human Rights Law,* (5th ed, Oxford University Press, Oxford, 2012), p 248.

[121] Nowak defines slavery as "the most extreme expression of the power human beings possess over their fellow human beings, representing the most direct attack on the essence of the human personality and dignity". M Nowak, "Civil and Political Rights" in *Human Rights: Concepts and Standards* (J Symonides ed, Ashgate, Aldershot, 2000), p 69 at p 80.

[122] Art 9 states: "1. Everyone has the right to liberty and security of person. No one shall be subjected to arbitrary arrest or detention. No one shall be deprived of his liberty except on such grounds and in accordance with such procedure as are established by law.

2. Anyone who is arrested shall be informed, at the time of arrest, of the reasons for his arrest and shall be promptly informed of any charges against him.

3. Anyone arrested or detained on a criminal charge shall be brought promptly before a judge or other officer authorized by law to exercise judicial power and shall be entitled to trial within a reasonable time or to release. It shall not be the general rule that persons awaiting trial shall be detained in custody, but release may be subject to guarantees to appear for trial, at any other stage of the judicial proceedings, and, should occasion arise, for execution of the judgement.

4. Anyone who is deprived of his liberty by arrest or detention shall be entitled to take proceedings before a court, in order that that court may decide without delay on the lawfulness of his detention and order his release if the detention is not lawful.

5. Anyone who has been the victim of unlawful arrest or detention shall have an enforceable right to compensation."

[123] In relation to the issue of security under Art 9, see decision of the Human Rights Committee in the case of *Delgado Paéz v Colombia*, Communication No 195/1985, 23 August 1990 (CCPR/C/39/D/195/1985).

[124] Art 7 states: "1. Every person has the right to personal liberty and security.

2. No one shall be deprived of his physical liberty except for the reasons and under the conditions established beforehand by the constitution of the State Party concerned or by a law established pursuant thereto.

3. No one shall be subject to arbitrary arrest or imprisonment.

4. Anyone who is detained shall be informed of the reasons for his detention and shall be promptly notified of the charge or charges against him.

5. Any person detained shall be brought promptly before a judge or other officer authorized by law to exercise judicial power and shall be entitled to trial within a reasonable time or to be released without prejudice to the continuation of the proceedings. His release may be subject to guarantees to assure his appearance for trial.

6. Anyone who is deprived of his liberty shall be entitled to recourse to a competent court, in order that the court may decide without delay on the lawfulness of his arrest or detention and order his release if the arrest or detention is unlawful. In States Parties whose laws provide that anyone who believes himself to be threatened with deprivation of his liberty is entitled to recourse to a

of Human and Peoples' Rights[125] and Art 14 of the Arab Charter on Human Rights.[126]

The issue of arbitrary arrest and detention is also dealt with in the UN International Convention for the Protection of All Persons from Enforced Disappearance.[127]

Conclusion

The right to liberty is protected by the Constitution, the ECHR and the CFR, as well as by various other regional and international instruments. The constitutional protection has been developed through substantial case law over the years which has clarified the nature of the right as a substantive, rather than just a procedural, protection. The case law has also clarified the limitations on the right to liberty under the Constitution, including in cases of, for example, the safety of the individual whose liberty has been interfered with, as well as for the safety of the general population. The ECHR formulation of the right to liberty is quite similar to the Constitution in its basic form but the ECHR also provides an exhaustive list of cases of lawful arrest and detention, which lead to legal deprivations of liberty. While the constitutional protection of the right to liberty has been interpreted by the Irish courts to reflect a general right to liberty as enshrined in the *Magna Carta*,[128] the ECHR position is **[4–54]**

competent court in order that it may decide on the lawfulness of such threat, this remedy may not be restricted or abolished. The interested party or another person in his behalf is entitled to seek these remedies.

7. No one shall be detained for debt. This principle shall not limit the orders of a competent judicial authority issued for nonfulfillment of duties of support."

[125] Art 6 states: "Every individual shall have the right to liberty and to the security of his person. No one may be deprived of his freedom except for reasons and conditions previously laid down by law. In particular, no one may be arbitrarily arrested or detained."

[126] Art 14 states: "1. Everyone has the right to liberty and security of person. No one shall be subjected to arbitrary arrest, search or detention without a legal warrant.

2. No one shall be deprived of his liberty except on such grounds and in such circumstances as are determined by law and in accordance with such procedure as is established thereby.

3. Anyone who is arrested shall be informed, at the time of arrest, in a language that he understands, of the reasons for his arrest and shall be promptly informed of any charges against him. He shall be entitled to contact his family members.

4. Anyone who is deprived of his liberty by arrest or detention shall have the right to request a medical examination and must be informed of that right.

5. Anyone arrested or detained on a criminal charge shall be brought promptly before a judge or other officer authorized by law to exercise judicial power and shall be entitled to trial within a reasonable time or to release. His release may be subject to guarantees to appear for trial. Pre-trial detention shall in no case be the general rule.

6. Anyone who is deprived of his liberty by arrest or detention shall be entitled to petition a competent court in order that it may decide without delay on the lawfulness of his arrest or detention and order his release if the arrest or detention is unlawful.

7. Anyone who has been the victim of arbitrary or unlawful arrest or detention shall be entitled to compensation."

[127] The Convention entered in force in 2010 and has 31 States Parties.

[128] *State (Burke) v Lennon* [1940] IR 136 at 155–156.

somewhat different, and focuses on arbitrary arrest and detention.[129] However, the interpretation of the right by Irish Courts has, at times, been paternalistic,[130] especially in relation to the detention of people suffering from mental illness.

[129] M Nowak, *supra* n 53, p 67.
[130] O Doyle, *supra* n 1, p 184.

CHAPTER 5
Right to Integrity of the Person and the Right to Freedom from Torture, Cruel, Inhuman or Degrading Treatment and Punishment

Introduction

The rights to bodily integrity and freedom from torture are connected and inter- **[5–01]** related. Torture is an ancient activity with a very broad scope[1] and the prohibition on torture is a *jus cogens* norm which is binding on all States. Smith comments that "[t]orture is a serious violation of the physical and mental integrity of the person".[2] In some instances, therefore, the right to bodily integrity can be subsumed under the broader right to freedom from torture. However, the right to bodily integrity can also stand independently in relation to certain issues, especially those concerned with healthcare law. Both rights have been deemed to be unenumerated rights, protected by the Constitution of Ireland. The nature and scope of these rights is discussed in the first section of this chapter. However, at a regional and international level, the right to bodily integrity is generally[3] not specifically enumerated but has been interpreted to fall under the remit of the right to freedom from torture and cruel, inhuman or degrading treatment or punishment, in addition to the right to security of the person, the right to privacy and the right to health. The way in which the rights to bodily

[1] See R Smith, *Textbook on International Human Rights* (5th ed, Oxford University Press, Oxford, 2012), Chapter 14.
[2] *ibid,* p 233.
[3] An exception to this is Art 4 of the African (Banjul) Charter on Human and Peoples' Rights, adopted 27 June 1981, OAU Doc. CAB/LEG/67/3 rev. 5 which states: "Human beings are inviolable. Every human being shall be entitled to respect for his life and the integrity of his person. No one may be arbitrarily deprived of this right".

integrity and freedom from torture are interpreted under the European Convention on Human Rights (ECHR), the Charter of Fundamental Rights (CFR) and international instruments will be discussed following the discussion on Irish constitutional law.

A. Irish Constitution

[5–02] Article 40.3.1°:

> "The State guarantees in its laws to respect, and, as far as practicable, by its laws to defend and vindicate the personal rights of the citizen."

Article 40.3.2°:

> "The State shall, in particular, by its laws protect as best it may from unjust attack and, in the case of injustice done, vindicate the life, person, good name, and property rights of every citizen."

1. Nature of the Rights

The Right to Bodily Integrity

[5–03] The Supreme Court held that the Constitution protected the right to bodily integrity in the case of *Ryan v Attorney General.*[4] The plaintiff argued that the planned fluoridation of the public water supply would infringe her right to bodily integrity and that of her children. While the Court did not define the term 'bodily integrity', Kenny J stated:

> "I understand the right to bodily integrity to mean that no mutilation of the body or any of its members may be carried out on any citizen under the authority of the law except for the good of the whole body and that no process which is or may, as a matter of probability, be dangerous or harmful to the life or health of the citizen or any of them may be imposed (in the sense of being made compulsory) by an Act of the Oireachtas."[5]

[5–04] The Court did, however, go on to link the right to bodily integrity with health issues, stating that the State had "... the duty of protecting the citizens from dangers to health in a manner not incompatible or inconsistent with the rights of those citizens as human persons".[6] However, the Court did not expand the right to bodily integrity to include a right to a level of healthcare. In the case of *Re a Ward of Court (No 2)*[7] the right to bodily integrity was once again linked with health issues when the Court held that no one may be compelled to undergo a medical procedure or treatment, even if the result of this was death. However, in the case of *JS v CS (orse CT)*[8] it was held that subjection to a psychiatric evaluation did not amount to a violation of the right to bodily integrity.

---

[4] [1965] IR 294.

[5] *ibid* at 313–14.

[6] *ibid* at 348.

[7] [1996] 2 IR 79. In relation to enforced medical procedures, see TA Cooney, "Sterilisation and the Mentally Handicapped" (1989) 11 DULJ 56; and M Donnelly, "Non-Consensual Sterilisation of Mentally Disabled People" (1997) XXXII Ir Jur 297.

[8] [1997] 2 IR 506.

The right to bodily integrity was also discussed in the case of *AD v Ireland*.[9] The plaintiff was the victim of rape, buggery and assault in May 1988 and she had sustained very serious injuries, which continued to afflict her. She was unable to claim compensation for pain and suffering caused by the injuries as a result of changes to the *ex gratia* criminal injuries compensation scheme which had come into effect in 1986. She claimed that the State, by excluding compensation for pain and suffering under the compensation scheme, had failed to protect her right to bodily integrity as far as practicable. The defendants claimed that the State had done sufficient to protect the plaintiff's right to bodily integrity by "seeking to prevent crime, punishing wrongdoers and by providing a civil remedy against a wrongdoer"[10] and that, therefore, compensation was not required. The defendants also claimed that to oblige the State to pay compensation for personal injuries received due to a criminal act would be to make the State an insurer.[11] The Court held that the plaintiff had not established that a right to compensation for her injuries arose from Art 40.3 and found that the issue of compensation was a matter of policy for the Oireachtas. **[5–05]**

Freedom from Torture, Inhuman or Degrading Treatment and Punishment

In *State (C) v Frawley*[12] it was held that the Constitution includes the unenumerated right to freedom from torture and inhuman or degrading treatment and punishment. However, the Court did not attempt to define the various elements of this right. The applicant in this case had objected to the conditions of the prison in which he was detained. As a result of previous attempts to flee the prison and his tendency to swallow metal objects due to his sociopathic personality disturbance, the prison authorities had often kept the applicant in solitary confinement and had handcuffed him. He was also deprived of ordinary supplies including cutlery, a sprung bed and a radio. His treatment involved sedation and custodial care only, because his behaviour prevented effective therapy. There was no suitable facility in the State in which prisoners with such psychiatric difficulties could be detained but expert medical evidence illustrated that only dedicated long term psychiatric treatment would benefit the patient. Counsel for the prosecutor argued, firstly, that the right to bodily integrity required the State to protect the health of the prisoner as far as reasonably possible and secondly that freedom from torture or inhuman or degrading treatment, was also an unenumerated right, which had been violated in this case. In putting forward the second argument, counsel for the prosecutor referred to the freedom from torture, inhuman and degrading treatment which was enshrined in Art 3 of the ECHR.[13] Finlay P referred to Kenny J's discussion in *Ryan* on unenumerated rights[14] which flowed from the Christian and democratic nature of the State and stated that one of **[5–06]**

---

[9] [1994] 1 IR 369.

[10] *ibid* at 369.

[11] *ibid* at 373.

[12] [1976] IR 365.

[13] *ibid* at 371.

[14] See *Ryan v AG* [1965] IR 294, at 312–314. See the examination of the "Christian and democratic nature of the State" by Finaly P in *State (M) v Attorney General* [1979] IR 73 at 80–81.

these personal rights was freedom from torture and inhuman and degrading treatment. He stated:

> "If the unspecified personal rights guaranteed by Article 40 follow in part or in whole from the Christian and democratic nature of the State, it is surely beyond argument that they include freedom from torture, and from inhuman or degrading treatment and punishment. Such a conclusion would appear to me to be inescapable even if there had never been a European Convention on Human Rights, or if Ireland had never been a party to it."[15]

[5–07] However, this right had not been violated in this case due to the lack of an evil purpose. Finlay P stated:

> "I must construe the entire concept of torture, inhuman or degrading treatment and punishment as being not only evil in its consequences but evil in its purpose as well. It is most commonly inspired by revenge, retaliation, the creation of fear or improper interrogation. It is to me inconceivable to associate it with the necessary discharge of a duty to prevent self-injury or self-destruction."[16]

In *Murray v Ireland*[17] Costello J referred to the right not to be tortured as one of the unenumerated rights under Art 40.3.1° of the Constitution and in the case of *HMW v Ireland (No 2)*[18] Costello J stated that this was an absolute right which was incapable of being abridged.

Criminal Justice (United Nations Against Torture Act) 2000: Definition of Torture

[5–08] While both the right to bodily integrity and the right to freedom from torture had been identified as unenumerated rights in the Constitution, the nature of the rights was clarified to a certain extent with the incorporation of certain sections of the United Nations Convention Against Torture and Other Cruel, Inhuman or Degrading Treatment or Punishment 1984[19] into Irish law by means of the Criminal Justice (United Nations Convention Against Torture) Act 2000.[20] This is one of the very few international human rights treaties which have been incorporated into Irish domestic law.

---

15 *State (C) v Frawley* [1976] IR 365 at 374.

16 *ibid.*

17 [1985] IR 532.

18 [1997] 2 IR 141.

19 Convention against Torture and Other Cruel, Inhuman or Degrading Treatment or Punishment, adopted and opened for signature, ratification and accession by General Assembly resolution 39/46 of 10 December 1984.

20 Ireland signed the Optional Protocol to the UN Convention in 2007 (Optional Protocol to the Convention against Torture and other Cruel, Inhuman or Degrading Treatment or Punishment, adopted on 18 December 2002 at the fifty-seventh session of the General Assembly of the United Nations by resolution A/RES/57/199, but has not yet ratified it. The objective of the Protocol is "to establish a system of regular visits undertaken by independent international and national bodies to places where people are deprived of their liberty, in order to prevent torture and other cruel, inhuman or degrading treatment or punishment" (Art 1).

Section 1 of the 2000 Act defines torture as:

> "an act or omission by which severe pain or suffering, whether physical or mental, is intentionally inflicted on a person—
>
> (a) for such purposes as—
>
> (i) obtaining from that person, or from another person, information or a confession,[21]
>
> (ii) punishing that person for an act which the person concerned or a third person has committed or is suspected of having committed, or
>
> (iii) intimidating or coercing that person or a third person,
>
> or
>
> (b) for any reason that is based on any form of discrimination."

Torture does not include "any such act that arises solely from, or is inherent in or incidental to, lawful sanctions".[22] Neither the UN Convention nor the Irish legislation define "cruel, inhuman or degrading treatment". It is clear that some instances of violations of the right to bodily integrity could fall within the ambit of this definition. The Irish legislation also introduces offences with regard to the carrying out of an act of torture by a public official.[23] It also provides for a sentence of life imprisonment on conviction for carrying out an act of torture.[24] **[5–09]**

As a result of ratification of the United Nations Convention Against Torture, Ireland is under an obligation to submit a State report every four years to the United Nations Committee Against Torture, documenting the ways in which the State has given direct effect to the provisions of the Convention.[25] These reports, along with the 'shadow reports' prepared by non-governmental organisations[26] and the Concluding **[5–10]**

---

[21] Regarding the distinction between torture and enhanced interrogation, see M Hunter, M McDonnell, LF Nordgren and G Loewenstein, "Torture in the Eyes of the Beholder: The Psychological Difficulty of Defining Torture in Law and Policy", (2011) 44 VJIL. 87.

[22] Criminal Justice (United Nations Convention against Torture) Act 2000, s 1.

[23] *ibid,* s 2.

[24] *ibid,* s 3.

[25] This obligation arises under Art 19 of the UN Convention against Torture and Other Cruel, Inhuman or Degrading Treatment or Punishment, adopted and opened for signature, ratification and accession by General Assembly resolution 39/46 of 10 December 1984. Ireland's initial report was due in 2003, but was not submitted until 2009. See Ireland's Initial Report to the Committee Against Torture CAT/C/IRL/1, available at: http://www2.ohchr.org/english/bodies/cat/cats46.htm, last accessed 21 July 2012.

[26] Under the United Nations treaty-monitoring system, in addition to State reports, stakeholders often submit 'shadow reports' on the UN treaties. These reports outline the NGO / civil society view of how the State has incorporated international law obligations into domestic law. See, for example, *Joint Shadow Report to the First Periodic Review of Ireland under the United Nations Convention against Torture and Other Cruel, Inhuman or Degrading Treatment of Punishment,* compiled by the Irish Council for Civil Liberties and the Irish Penal Reform Trust, April 2011, available at: http://www2.ohchr.org/english/bodies/cat/cats46.htm, last accessed 21 July 2012.

Observations[27] provided by the Committee Against Torture in response are helpful in clarifying the nature of the rights to bodily integrity and freedom from torture.

Ireland has also ratified the European Convention for the Prevention of Torture and Inhuman or Degrading Treatment or Punishment[28] and, of course, the ECHR which deals with torture in Art 3, discussed below.

Activities which Fall under the Definition of Torture and Cruel, Inhuman or Degrading Treatment or Punishment / Bodily Integrity

Conditions of Detention

[5–11] Claims of breaches of the right to bodily integrity have, on occasion, been made by prisoners in relation to conditions under which they are detained, as was seen in the case of *Frawley* discussed above.[29] In addition, in the cases of *State (Richardson) v Governor Mountjoy Prison*[30] and *State (Comerford) v Governor Mountjoy Prison*[31] the Courts held that if conditions in places of detention, including prisons, amount to a health hazard for prisoners, the High Court can order their improvement. In *State (Richardson) v Governor Mountjoy Prison,* Barrington J found that prison authorities had violated the right to bodily integrity with regard to the requirement on prisoners to slop out their cells which could lead to human faeces ending up in the sinks which prisoners used for washing themselves.[32] Prison conditions, especially the issue of slopping out, have been highlighted in various non-governmental reports on Ireland's compliance with international law.[33] They have also been highlighted by the United Nations Committee Against Torture[34] and the

[27] The Committee Against Torture's Concluding Observations of Ireland's 1st periodic report, CAT/C/IRL/CO/1, are available at: http://www2.ohchr.org/english/bodies/cat/cats46.htm, last accessed 21 July 2012.

[28] European Convention for the Prevention of Torture and Inhuman or Degrading Treatment or Punishment, adopted 1987, CETS No. 126.

[29] *State (C) v Frawley* [1976] IR 365.

[30] [1980] ILRM 82.

[31] [1981] ILRM 86.

[32] See also *Byrne v Governor of Castlerea Prison* [2007] 3 IR 451. In relation to conditions of detention which could amount to breaches of the right to bodily integrity and the right to freedom from torture, see *Joint Shadow Report to the First Periodic Review of Ireland under the United Nations Convention against Torture and Other Cruel, Inhuman or Degrading Treatment or Punishment*, compiled by the Irish Council for Civil Liberties and the Irish Penal Reform Trust, April 2011, Chapter 5, available at: http://www2.ohchr.org/english/bodies/cat/cats46.htm, last accessed 21 July 2012.

[33] See, for example, Amnesty International, *Ireland: Briefing to the UN Committee Against Torture*, April 2011, *Joint Shadow Report to the First Periodic Review of Ireland under the United Nations Convention against Torture and Other Cruel, Inhuman or Degrading Treatment of Punishment*, compiled by the Irish Council for Civil Liberties and the Irish Penal Reform Trust, April 2011, available at: http://www2.ohchr.org/english/bodies/cat/cats46.htm, last accessed 21 July 2012.

[34] The Committee Against Torture's Concluding Observations of Ireland's 1st periodic report, CAT/C/IRL/CO/1, available at: http://www2.ohchr.org/english/bodies/cat/cats46.htm, last accessed 21 July 2012.

European Committee for the Prevention of Torture and Inhuman or Degrading Treatment.[35]

Corporal Punishment

Instances of corporal punishment have been deemed to be cruel, inhuman and degrading treatment or punishment by the European Court of Human Rights (ECtHR), as will be discussed later,[36] however, there is no full legislative prohibition on corporal punishment in Irish law. While s 24 of the Non-Fatal Offences against the Person Act 1997 prohibits the use of corporal punishment by teachers,[37] the prohibition does not extend to actions of parents or actions of those in charge of care settings. The Children Act 1908 allowed parents to use "reasonable and moderate chastisement" when disciplining children but this provision was repealed by the Children Act 2001. However, this defence still exists at common law and its removal requires the introduction of new legislation.[38] In 2004 the Council of Europe's European Committee of Social Rights ruled, in response to a complaint brought by the World Organisation Against Torture,[39] that the common law defence of reasonable chastisement is in violation of Art 17 of the Revised European Social Charter[40] which deals with the right of children and young people to social, legal and economic protection.[41] A change in legislation is currently being considered by the Government.[42] **[5–12]**

Female Genital Mutilation[43]

The Special Rapporteur on torture and other cruel, inhuman or degrading treatment or punishment has stated that female genital mutilation may amount to torture **[5–13]**

[35] See the Committee's report on Ireland at http://www.cpt.coe.int/en/states/irl.htm. last accessed 21 July 2012.

[36] See *Tyrer v United Kingdom*, 25 April 1978, Series A No 26, (1979–80) 2 EHRR 1 at 33 and *Campbell and Cosans v United Kingdom*, 25 February 1982, Series A No 48, (1982) 4 EHRR 293 at 26.

[37] With regard to this provision, see Law Reform Commission, *Report on Non-Fatal Offences against the Person*, (LRC 45–1994), p 284.

[38] See Department of Health and Children, *Parenting Styles and Discipline: Parents' and Children's Perspectives*, Summary Report, The National Children's Strategy Research Series, (2009).

[39] http://www.omct.org.

[40] European Social Charter, CETS No. 163, adopted 1961, revised 1996.

[41] Complaint No 18/2003.

[42] See P Cullen, "Ban on Parents Smacking Children Considered", *The Irish Times*, 28 December 2011, available at: http://www.irishtimes.com/newspaper/frontpage/2011/1228/1224309553679.html.

[43] See *Ireland's National Plan of Action to Address Female Genital Mutilation* (2008), which was developed by a number of non-governmental organisations, including Amnesty International Ireland, AKiDwA, Children's Rights Alliance, etc. The Plan is available at: www.akidwa.ie/FGM%20Plan%20of%20Action%20Report.pdf, last accessed 21 July 2012.

under Art 2 of the UN Convention Against Torture "if States fail to act with due diligence".[44] The Children's Rights Alliance estimate that there are currently 2,500 women living in Ireland who have undergone the procedure.[45]

[5–14] The issue of female genital mutilation has come before the Irish courts in a number of cases with regard to asylum seekers seeking refugee status as a result of fear of being returned to a State where they may be forced to undergo a female genital mutilation procedure.[46] For example, in the case of *Meadows v Minister for Justice Equality and Law Reform*[47] the applicant was a Nigerian national who was seeking asylum in Ireland on the basis that she would be subjected to female genital mutilation if she was returned to Nigeria. However, the Refugee Applications Commissioner recommended that she would not be granted refugee status. While a member of the Appeals Chamber stated that "female genital mutilation is an abhorrent practice and amounts to a form of torture"[48] the Chamber considered that the applicant had failed to prove that she would be subjected to such a procedure if she was returned home and the decision not to grant her refugee status was confirmed. The applicant then sought leave from the Minister to stay in Ireland on humanitarian grounds, arguing that female genital mutilation amounted to torture or inhuman and degrading treatment and that if the State returned her to Nigeria it would be in breach of Art 1 of the UN Convention against Torture and Art 3 of the ECHR, both of which had been incorporated into domestic law.[49] The Minister did not address the material in the applicant's submission concerning the incidence of female genital mutilation in Nigeria and rejected her application, finding that there was no violation of the Refugee Act 1996. The High Court refused the applicant leave to appeal for judicial review, applying the standard of review for reasonableness formulated in *O'Keeffe v An Bord Pleanála*[50] (i.e. that an administrative decision can only be set aside for unreasonableness if it is fundamentally at variance with reason and common sense). The High Court found that in this context the Minister's decision was not unreasonable, however, the Court did grant the applicant leave to appeal this decision to the Supreme Court. The Supreme Court held that in assessing the reasonableness of administrative decisions which affect fundamental rights, the courts can consider the proportionality of the decision.[51] When taking the issue of proportionality into consideration, the Court found that the

---

[44] M Nowak, *Report of the Special Rapporteur on torture and other cruel, inhuman or degrading treatment or punishment*, (A/HRC/7/3 of 15 January 2008), p 13.

[45] See http://www.childrensrights.ie/resources/ireland%E2%80%99s-national-plan-action-address-female-genital-mutilation-%E2%80%93-one-year-launch, last accessed 21 July 2012.

[46] See, for example, *G.E. v Refugee Appeals Tribunal* [2006] 2 IR 11, *Agbonlahor v Minister for Justice* [2007] 4 IR 309, *AN v Minister for Justice* [2008] 2 IR 48, *PPA v Refugee Appeals Tribunal* [2007] 4 IR 94, *BO v Minister for Justice* [2006] 3 IR 218, *FN v Minister for Justice* [2009] 1 IR 88.

[47] [2010] IESC 3.

[48] *ibid.*

[49] These obligations were incorporated into Irish law by s 3 of the European Convention on Human Rights Act 2003 and s 5 of the Refugee Act 1996.

[50] *O'Keeffe v An Bord Pleanála* [1993] 1 IR 39.

[51] While this decision was made in the context of asylum cases, it is potentially important for all administrative decisions on cases with a fundamental rights focus.

Minister's failure to provide reasons for his decision rendered it unreasonable. Leave to seek judicial review was granted and the matter was remitted to the High Court.

The issue of female genital mutilation is now dealt with under the Criminal Justice (Female Genital Mutilation) Act 2012. Section 1 of this Act defines female genital mutilation as: "any act the purpose of which, or the effect of which, is the excision, infibulation or other mutilation of the whole or any part of the labia majora, labia minora, prepuce of the clitoris, clitoris or vagina of a girl or woman". The Act seeks to prohibit this practice in Ireland and to prohibit the removal of any person from Ireland for the purpose of any of these procedures outside the State. The penalty for those found guilty under the Act is a fine and/or imprisonment for up to 14 years.

Rendition Flights

A number of complaints have been made by various non-governmental organisations[52] **[5–15]** and the Irish Human Rights Commission[53] in recent years concerning the use of Shannon airport as a transit point by aircraft involved in the US rendition programme. As de Londras comments:

> "There is no suggestion that Ireland is torturing detainees on behalf of the United States. In fact, even the most hardened anti-war activist would quite readily admit that such a scenario of direct involvement by Ireland is outside the realm of reasonable contemplation."[54]

The issue is that the State allows aircraft which are involved in rendition to stopover and refuel in Shannon airport, which makes Ireland complicit in breaches of the right to freedom from torture and the prohibition on refoulement. Reports from both the Council of Europe and the European Union dealing with the issue of rendition refer to these stopover flights.[55] However, in response to a report by the Irish Human Rights Commission on the issue of the use of Shannon airport in the extraordinary rendition context, the then Minister for Foreign Affairs, Dermot Ahern, TD stated: "It is very important to recall that at no stage has any evidence ever emerged, or even a specific allegation made, that any person has ever been subject to extraordinary rendition through Ireland".[56] Successive Irish governments have emphasised that they have received

---

[52] See Amnesty International, *Ireland: Briefing to the UN Committee Against Torture*, April 2011, Chapter 3.

[53] See Irish Human Rights Commission, *'Extraordinary Rendition': A Review of Ireland's Human Rights Obligations.*

[54] F de Londras, "Ireland's Potential Liability for Extraordinary Renditions through Shannon Airport", (2007) 25(7) ILT 106.

[55] Parliamentary Assembly, Committee on Legal Affairs, *Secret detentions and illegal transfers of detainees involving Council of Europe member states: second report*, Doc. 11302 rev. 11 June 2007 and Temporary Committee on the alleged use of European countries by the CIA for the transportation and illegal detention of prisoners, *Report on the alleged use of European countries by the CIA for the transportation and illegal detention of prisoners (2006/2200(INI))*, A6-9999/2007, last accessed 21 July 2012.

[56] Statement by the former Minister for Foreign Affairs, Dermot Ahern, TD, in response to the Irish Human Rights Commission's Report on Extraordinary Rendition, 11 December 2007, available at: http://www.dfa.ie/home/index.aspx?id =37641. The Irish Human Rights Commission's report, *'Extraordinary Rendition': A Review of Ireland's Human Rights Obligations*, is available at: www.ihrc.ie/download/pdf/ihrc_rendition_report_final.pdf, last accessed 21 July 2012.

diplomatic assurances[57] from the United States that rendition has not been carried out through Shannon airport.[58] It is unclear if such diplomatic assurances are sufficient to eschew international legal liability if flights involved in extraordinary rendition have indeed been allowed to stopover and refuel in Shannon. In a 2008 report, the then Council of Europe's Commissioner for Human Rights, Thomas Hammarberg, recommended that the Government "... review the current inspection and monitoring arrangements in Ireland with a view to ensuring that effective and independent investigations are carried out into any serious allegation of extraordinary rendition".[59] The Irish Government responded that it was "... confident that under international law, it is fully entitled to rely on the categoric and absolute assurances secured from the United States Government that they have not engaged in extraordinary rendition through Ireland".[60] The State Report to the UN Committee Against Torture in 2009 states that

> "[w]here complaints of alleged unlawful activity concerning the use of Irish airports have been made to the Garda Síochána, investigations have ensued and, where appropriate, files have been submitted to the Director of Public Prosecutions. In the very small number of cases investigated, no further action was found to be warranted, owing to a lack of evidence of any unlawful activity".[61]

The Government also established a Cabinet Committee on Aspects of International Human Rights in 2008, whose mandate includes an examination of the current legal framework in this context.

Clerical Abuse

[5–16] A number of recent reports (the Ferns,[62] Ryan,[63] Murphy[64] and Cloyne[65] Reports) into abuse of children by the clergy have documented the abuse of children in residential institutions run by religious orders on behalf of the State. According to an Amnesty

---

[57] See *Dáil Debates,* 21 February 2012, Column 65.

[58] See *Joint Shadow Report to the First Periodic Review of Ireland under the United Nations Convention against Torture and Other Cruel, Inhuman or Degrading Treatment or Punishment*, compiled by the Irish Council for Civil Liberties and the Irish Penal Reform Trust, April 2011, Chapter 3, available at: http://www2.ohchr.org/english/bodies/cat/cats46.htm, last accessed 21 July 2012.

[59] Recommendation 32, *Report by the Commissioner for Human Rights Mr Thomas Hammarberg on Ireland 26–30 November 2007,* (CoE, Strasbourg, 2008).

[60] *ibid,* Irish Government's response to the Commissioner's Recommendation No 34.

[61] Ireland's State Report, CAT/C/IRL/1, (2009), p 57, available at: http://www2.ohchr.org/english/bodies/cat/cats46.htm, last accessed 21 July 2012.

[62] *The Ferns Report,* presented to the Minister for Health and Children October 2005, (Government Publications, Dublin, 2005).

[63] *Commission to Inquire into Child Abuse, Report, Vols I-V,* (Government Publications, Dublin, 2009).

[64] *Commission of Investigation, Report into the Catholic Archdiocese of Dublin,* July 2009, (Government Publications, Dublin, 2009).

[65] *Commission of Investigation, Report into the Catholic Diocese of Cloyne,* (Government Publications, Dublin, 2010).

International Report, the treatment documented in these reports "... can be categorised as torture, and cruel, inhuman and degrading treatment under human rights law".[66] The UN Committee Against Torture recommended to Ireland to implement the recommendations of the Ryan Report, as a matter of some urgency.[67]

2. Legitimate Justifications for Interference with the Right

The Right to Bodily Integrity

Interference with the right to bodily integrity was justified in the case of *Minister for Justice, Equality and Law Reform v SMR*.[68] The case concerned an Irish national who was arrested under a European Arrest Warrant[69] issued by the UK in 2005 in connection with three offences of indecent assault on his granddaughter in 2000 and 2001. He was in poor health, suffering from acute coronary disease, and claimed that stress which could be caused by his surrender would exacerbate his health problems and violate his right to bodily integrity. The Supreme Court held that the mere possibility that stress associated with the surrender of an applicant under a European arrest warrant[70] could precipitate acute coronary disease was not sufficient for a court to prohibit a trial. Something much more definite by way of threat to life was required. Finnegan J stated: "The court, I am satisfied, must balance the risk to the health of the respondent directly related to his surrender on the one hand and the obligations of the State under the Framework Decision".[71] [5–17]

Interference with the right to bodily integrity has also been discussed in cases regarding blood transfusions.[72] For example, in the case of *Fitzpatrick v FK*[73] the defendant was given a blood transfusion against her wishes in the Coombe Hospital and the High Court found that her constitutional rights were not infringed. The defendant, a foreign national from the Democratic Republic of the Congo, had given birth in the Coombe Hospital. After the birth she suffered a massive haemorrhage and when the hospital staff began to prepare a blood transfusion procedure for her they became aware that [5–18]

---

[66] Amnesty International Report, written by C Holohan, *In Plain Sight*, (2011), p 37.

[67] Ireland's State Report, CAT/C/IRL/1, (2009), p 6, available at: http://www2.ohchr.org/english/bodies/cat/cats46.htm. last accessed 21 July 2012.

[68] [2008] 2 IR 242.

[69] In Ireland the European Arrest Warrant Act 2003 (as amended) regulates arrangements for surrender between Ireland and other Member States of the EU. s 37 of the Act provides that a person will not be surrendered if this surrender would be incompatible with the State's obligations under the ECHR and its protocols.

[70] This is in line with Framework Decision 2002/584/JHA on the European Arrest Warrant and the surrender procedures between Member States [2002] OJ L190/1. In relation to the European Arrest Warrant, see J Spencer, "The European Arrest Warrant" (2003) 6 CYELS 201 and J Wouters and F Naert, "Of Attest Warrants, Terrorist Offences and Extradition Deals: An Appraisal of the EU's Main Criminal Law Measures Against Terrorism after 11 September"' (2004) 41 CMLRev 911.

[71] *Minister for Justice, Equality and Law Reform v SMR* [2008] 2 IR 242 at 242–243.

[72] With regard to the issue of blood transfusion in the United Kingdom, see *In Re (O) (a minor) (Medical Treatment)* [1993] 2 FLR 149. See also C Bridge, "Religious Beliefs and Teenage Refusal of Medical Treatment", (1999), 62(4) MLR, pp 585–594.

[73] [2008] 2 IR 7.

she would refuse the transfusion because she was a Jehovah's Witness. The hospital staff stabilised her but there was a risk to her life if she began to bleed again. The staff had communicated with the defendant through an interpreter and believed that she had not made a fully informed refusal of treatment. Based on communication with the defendant they also believed that if the defendant died her child would be abandoned, as they had been informed that the child's father was not in the State. The Master of the Hospital applied to the High Court for an *ex parte* order authorising the hospital to proceed with the transfusion. The Court held that although the defendant was competent, it could override her decision to refuse treatment on the grounds that the welfare of her child, who was newly born in the State with no other parent, was paramount. The Court felt that it was in the interests of the child that the wishes of his mother, which could result in her death, should be overridden. The hospital authorities then sought an injunction, similar to the *ex parte* order issued by the High Court, a declaration that the hospital was, in fact, entitled to apply to the Court for the injunction sought by virtue of the Constitution and a declaration that the defendant's rights under Art 44.2 of the Constitution had to yield to Art 40.3.1°, Art 40.3.2°, Art 41 and Art 42.5 of the Constitution in order to safeguard the constitutional rights of the defendant's child. The defendant brought a counterclaim which sought a declaration that her constitutional rights under Arts 40.3.1° and 40.3.2° of the Constitution were violated by the issuance of the *ex parte* order. The High Court focused on the issue of capacity and held that the defendant did not have the capacity to refuse the blood transfusion, holding that "... there was a presumption that an adult patient had the cognitive ability to make a decision to refuse medical treatment, but that presumption could be rebutted"[74] and had been in this case. The Court refused the injunctive relief sought by the plaintiffs as it was no longer necessary but granted a declaration that the plaintiffs had acted lawfully in administering the blood transfusion in line with the *ex parte* order. The Court also dismissed the defendant's counterclaim.[75]

The Right to Freedom from Torture and Cruel, Inhuman or Degrading Treatment and Punishment

[5–19] The right to freedom from torture is a *jus cogens* norm which cannot be limited by any State. In relation to the nature of Irish constitutional rights, Costello J stated in the case of *W v Ireland (No 2)*:

> "The rights guaranteed under the Constitution are not absolute rights (with the exception of an implied right not to be tortured which must be regarded as an absolute right never to be abridged) and their exercise and enjoyment may be, and frequently are, limited by reason of the exigencies of the common good."[76]

---

[74] *Fitzpatrick v FK* [2008] 2 IR 7 at 8.

[75] In relation to blood transfusions of minors see K Doran, "Blood Transfusions and Consent from Parents", IMT, 27 March 2009, available at: http://www.imt.ie/opinion/guests/2009/03/blood-transfusions-and-consent-from-parents.html. For a recent case regarding blood transfusions and Jehovah's Witnesses, which focuses on the issue of religious autonomy, see *In Re Baby AB* [2011] 1 JIC 1201.

[76] *W v Ireland (No 2)* [1997] 2 IR 141.

In the case of *People (AG) v O'Brien*,[77] which was decided even before the right to freedom from torture was found to be an unenumerated right in *Frawley*, Kingsmill Moore J stated *obiter* that to consider using evidence extracted or discovered by gross personal violence would "involve the State in moral defilement".[78] It is clear, therefore, that not only is torture prohibited but that any evidence obtained through the use of torture is inadmissible in court.

B. ECHR

Article 3 of the ECHR: **[5–20]**

> "No one shall be subjected to torture or to inhuman or degrading treatment or punishment."

1. Nature of the Right

Given the events which precipitated the drafting of the ECHR, particularly the Holocaust, it is unsurprising that Art 3 was drafted as one of the few articles under the ECHR from which derogation is not possible. This has meant that the litigation concerning this provision has concentrated on defining the individual elements of torture, inhuman or degrading treatment or punishment. The ECtHR has taken a 'living instrument' approach to the definition of the various elements of Art 3 and it is important, therefore, to consider the timing and judgment of the cases when applying them. It is by no means certain that, were some of the early cases heard today, the same decision would be reached. It is clear that the margins where the treatment complained of moves from degrading to inhuman to torture have shifted through the years, becoming less and less tolerant of the degree of ill-treatment complained of. A very high standard of proof is needed before the Court will make a finding of a breach of Art 3 because of the stigma attached to such as finding,[79] so in *Ireland v United Kingdom,*[80] the ECtHR stated that the burden of proof was "beyond a reasonable doubt", a high burden not usually seen in civil matters. **[5–21]**

Article 3 Threshold

The threshold for the application of Art 3 was discussed in the case of *Ireland v United Kingdom*.[81] It was held in this case that in order for Art 3 to apply the alleged conduct must "attain a minimum level of severity".[82] The Court commented in the case of *Jalloh v Germany*[83] that the assessment of this severity is relative and stated that "it depends on all the circumstances of the case, such as the duration of the treatment, **[5–22]**

---

77 [1965] IR 142.

78 *ibid* at 150.

79 R White and C Ovey, *Jacobs, White and Ovey: The European Convention on Human Rights* (5th ed, Oxford University Press, Oxford, 2010), p 177.

80 18 January 1978, Series A No 25, (1979–80) 2 EHRR 25, at 161. In relation to this issue, see R Wolfrum, "The Taking and Assessment of Evidence by the European Court of Human Rights" in *Human Rights, Democracy and the Rule of Law, Liber amicorum Luzius Wildhaber,* (S Breitenmoser and others ed, Baden-Baden, Nomos, 2007), p 915.

81 *Ireland v United Kingdom* (1979–80) 2 EHRR 25.

82 *ibid* at 162. See also *Tyrer v United Kingdom* (1979–80) 2 EHRR 1 at para 30.

83 *Jalloh v Germany* (2007) 44 EHRR 667.

its physical and mental effects and, in some case, the sex, age and state of health of the victim ...".[84] According to Jacobs, Ovey and White the Court:

> "now subjects allegations of violations of Art 3 to a particularly thorough scrutiny even if there has been domestic proceedings and investigations into the allegations. The enquiries in the national legal order must themselves be very thorough, and represent a genuine attempt to find out what happened and who may be responsible for any reprehensible conduct".[85]

[5–23] The Court, however, commented in the case of *Selmouni v France*[86] (discussed below) that conduct which did not constitute inhuman or degrading treatment in early judgments of the Court could be found to constitute torture in future cases because the Convention is a living instrument. Jacobs, White and Ovey comment:

> "[p]resumably, it would follow that conduct which previously had not attained the threshold for categorization as inhuman or degrading treatment might be so categorized in the future."[87]

Definition of Torture

[5–24] The term torture is not defined in the ECHR. However, a number of instruments adopted after the ECHR define torture. The 1975 UN Declaration defines torture as "an aggravated and deliberate form of cruel, inhuman and degrading treatment or punishment".[88]

The first Strasbourg case where torture[89] was held to have occurred was the *Greek* case.[90] This was a Commission case and was confirmed by the Committee of Ministers, which was the procedure at the time. Political detainees had been subjected to torture and ill treatment, contrary to Art 3. It is an important case in that it enumerated the principle that the State was responsible for the actions of its agents, whether authorised or not, if these could be reasonably assumed.

[5–25] The case of *Ireland v United Kingdom*[91] was the first inter-State complaint to come before the Court. The case concerned a complaint made by Ireland that individuals held in custody in Northern Ireland had been subjected to treatment which fell within

---

84 *ibid* at 67.

85 R White and C Ovey, *supra* n 79, p 147.

86 *Selmouni v France* (2000) 29 EHRR 403.

87 R White and C Ovey, *supra* n 79, p 168.

88 Declaration on the Protection of All Persons from Being Subjected to Torture and Other Cruel, Inhuman or Degrading Treatment or Punishment, adopted by General Assembly resolution 3452 (XXX) of 9 December 1975.

89 The *Greek* case defined Torture as: "inhuman treatment, which has a purpose, such as the obtaining of information or confessions, or the infliction of punishment, and it is generally an aggravated form of inhuman treatment"; Inhuman Treatment as "deliberately causes severe suffering, mental or physical"; Degrading Treatment as: "if it grossly humiliates (him) before others or drives (him) to act against (his) will or conscience.": 12YB (the *Greek* case) 1 at 504 (1969) Com Rep; CM Res DH (70) 1.

90 12YB (the *Greek* case) 1 at 504 (1969) Com Rep; CM Res DH (70) 1.

91 *Ireland v United Kingdom*, (1979–80) 2 EHRR 25.

the remit of Art 3. In particular, interrogation activities which involved the "five techniques" of covering the detained persons' head with hoods, making them stand against a wall for long periods with their limbs outstretched (stress positions), subjection to loud noise, deprivation of sleep and inadequate diet by British security forces. The Commission's report of 1976 concluded that these five techniques amounted to torture for the purposes of the Convention. However, the ECtHR decided that the techniques did not amount to torture because the intensity of the suffering was insufficient, but did constitute inhuman and degrading treatment.

The judgment in the case of *Ireland v United Kingdom* attempted to clarify the terms of Art 3: **[5–26]**

> "... it was the intention that the Convention with its distinction between torture and inhuman treatment should by the first of these terms attach a special stigma to deliberate inhuman treatment causing very serious and cruel suffering."[92]

The Court went on to enumerate a number of factors which must be taken into account when determining the existence of inhuman treatment, as opposed to torture. These are: the duration of the treatment, its physical or mental effect, in addition to the sex, age and state of health of the victim.[93]

Since this case, the ECtHR has been more willing to make findings of torture and as Jacobs, White and Ovey comment:

> "It is almost certain that if similar facts to those in *Ireland v United Kingdom* came before the Strasbourg Court, it would have no hesitation in categorizing the interrogation techniques as torture."[94]

The first case in which the ECtHR itself, as opposed to the Commission, found that a Contracting Party had committed torture is the case of *Askoy v Turkey*.[95] In this case the applicant was stripped, his arms were tied behind his back and he was hung up and suspended by his arms. The Court commented: **[5–27]**

> "In order to determine whether any particular form of ill-treatment should be qualified as torture, the Court must have regard to the distinction drawn in Article 3 between this notion and that of inhuman or degrading treatment. As it has remarked before, this distinction would appear to have been embodied in the Convention to allow the special stigma of 'torture' to attach only to deliberate inhuman treatment causing very serious and cruel suffering."[96]

The evolution of the definition of torture by the Court can be seen in a succession of cases since *Askoy*. The first of these was *Aydin v Turkey*[97] where a young girl was blindfolded, beaten, paraded naked and hosed down with a fire hose by Turkish security forces, finally being raped by an unidentified person. The ECtHR held that the "...

---

[92] *ibid* at 167.
[93] *ibid* at 162.
[94] R White and C Ovey, *supra* n 79, p 172.
[95] *Askoy v Turkey* (1997) 23 EHRR 553.
[96] *ibid* at 63.
[97] (1997) 25 EHRR 251.

accumulation of acts, of physical and mental violence inflicted on the applicant and the especially cruel act of rape",[98] taken together, gave rise to the infliction of torture. However, it is instructive that the rape alone would have been held by the Court to have been sufficiently serious to amount to a violation of Art 3, torture.

[5–28] The threshold of torture was further expanded in the case of *Selmouni v France*[99] and which should be compared with the facts of *Ireland v UK* discussed above in order to show the progression of the 'living instrument' doctrine from 1978 to 1999. In *Selmouni* the applicant claimed that he was assaulted, had his hair pulled, was verbally abused, urinated over and threatened with the use of a blow lamp and the insertion of a truncheon into his anus by the police (the last two remained threats only). The severity of the treatment may, by comparison with *Aydin*, seem slight, but the Court unanimously in Grand Chamber held that the succession of maltreatment must be seen cumulatively and could, therefore, be classified, without reserve, as torture.[100]

The force-feeding of a prisoner in the absence of a definite medical necessity was held to constitute torture in the case of *Nevmerzhitsky v Ukraine.*[101]

Definition of Inhuman Treatment and Degrading Treatment or Punishment

[5–29] The Court does not always differentiate between inhuman and degrading treatment.[102] The elements of inhuman and degrading treatment were dealt with in the case of *T and V v United Kingdom*, where the Court stated:

> "Treatment has been held by the Court to be 'inhuman' because, inter alia, it was premeditated, was applied for hours at a stretch and caused either actual bodily injury or intense physical and mental suffering, and also 'degrading' because it was such as to arouse in its victims feelings of fear, anguish and inferiority capable of humiliating and debasing them. In order for a punishment or treatment associated with it to be 'inhuman' or 'degrading', the suffering or humiliation involved must in any event go beyond that inevitable element of suffering or humiliation connected with a given form of legitimate treatment or punishment. The question whether the purpose of the treatment was to humiliate or debase the victim is a further factor to be taken into account but the absence of any such purpose cannot conclusively rule out a finding of a violation of Article 3."[103]

---

98 *ibid* at 86.

99 (1999) 29 EHRR 403.

100 See the section on international prohibition on torture below, particularly the UN Convention on Torture.

101 *Nevmerzhitsky v Ukraine* (No 54825/00), 5 April 2005, ECHR 2005-II.

102 See the case of *II v Bulgaria* (No 44082/98), 9 June 2005, where the Court defined as "inhuman and degrading treatment" the detention of a person for a period of three months in a cell without natural light or ventilation, in poor sanitary conditions without being allowed to leave the cell.

103 *T and V v United Kingdom* (Nos 24888/94 and 24724/94), 16 December 1999 [GC], (2000) 30 EHRR 121, ECHR 1999-IX, at 71.

On occasion, the ECtHR does however, differentiate the concept of inhuman from degrading.

Inhuman Treatment

Inhuman treatment is where the severity of the treatment is sufficient to violate Art 3 and amounts to more than degrading treatment, but has not sufficient severity to amount to torture.[104] It should "cause either actual bodily harm or intense physical or mental suffering".[105] A threat of torture may in and of itself constitute inhuman treatment[106] and certainly mental suffering has been found sufficient cause for an Art 3 action.[107] The ECtHR will usually consider assaults by State agents to be sufficient case for inhuman treatment to be proven and will tend to be persuaded by evidence of assaults such as bruises, which would result from actions more severe than basic restraint.[108] Regarding the *Ribitsch* case,[109] Jacobs, White and Ovey comment that this "might be regarded as the first of the modern cases on physical assault while in police custody, since it couples the failure of the authorities to provide an explanation for the applicant's injuries with its finding of a violation of Article 3".[110] The applicant had sustained numerous injuries while in custody and the State had not provided satisfactory evidence that the injuries were caused at any time but during custody. The Court found that the applicant had been subjected to treatment constituting inhuman and degrading treatment. [5–30]

In the case of *Tomasi v France*[111] the medical reports attesting to a large amount of bruising following Mr Tomasi's release from police custody were found to be sufficient to evidence inhuman treatment. [5–31]

---

[104] In the *Greek* case, the European Commission of Human Rights pointed out that: "The notion of inhuman treatment covers at least such treatment as deliberately causes severe suffering, mental or physical, which in the particular situation is unjustifiable ... Treatment or punishment of an individual may be said to be degrading if it grossly humiliates him before others or drives him to act against his will or conscience.": 12YB (the *Greek* case) 1 at 504 (1969) Com Rep; CM Res DH (70) 1.

[105] *Kudla v Poland* (2000) 35 EHRR 198 at para 92.

[106] *Campell and Cosans v UK* A 48 1982.

[107] *Selcuk and Asker v Turkey* (1996) 26 EHRR 477.

[108] *Ribitsch v Austria* (1995) 21 EHRR 573. The Court stated: "Any recourse to physical force which has not been made strictly necessary by his own conduct ... is in principle an infringement" of Art 3 (at para 38).

[109] *Ribitsch v Austria*, 4 December 1995, Series A No 336, (1996) 21 EHRR 573.

[110] R White and C Ovey, *supra* n 79, p 186.

[111] (1992) 15 EHRR 1. The applicant had been ill-treated while he was detained in custody for two days. The police had kicked, slapped and punched him. He was required to stand for long periods of time with his hands handcuffed behind his head. He was stripped, deprived of food and threatened with a firearm. The State did not provide an adequate explanation for the injuries inflicted on the applicant but claimed that the injuries did not reach the threshold level of Art 3.

Detention in solitary confinement can, depending on the circumstances, also amount to inhuman treatment.[112] A failure to provide medical attention to a sick prisoner could also amount to an Art 3 violation.[113]

Degrading Treatment

[5–32] The definition of degrading treatment comes from the case of *Kudla v Poland* as treatment which "... is such as to arouse in the victims feelings of fear, anguish and inferiority capable of humiliating and debasing them".[114] Alternatively, treatment is degrading if it "humiliates or debases and individual showing a lack of respect for, or diminishing, his or her human dignity or arouses feelings of fear, anguish or inferiority capable of breaking an individual's moral and physical resistance".[115] It is clear that there need be no intention of humiliation or debasement for a finding of degrading treatment. In the case of *Price v UK*[116] the applicant was a four-limb deficient thalidomide victim who, for contempt of court, had been detained overnight in a cold police cell and then for three and a half days in an inadequate prison where male staff had to lift her on and off the toilet. She complained of a breach of Art 3. The ECtHR held that Art 3 had been breached. Ms Price was awarded £4,500 compensation.

[5–33] The ECtHR has increasingly found that the conditions in detention will be degrading, rather than inhuman, although, of course, this will always depend on the seriousness of the case.[117] The Court will consider if any force used was reasonable in the circumstances of the case.[118]

In *Poltoratskiiy*[119] the Court stated that detention conditions must be in line with respect for human dignity and highlighted the importance of ensuring the health and well-being of the detained person.[120]

[5–34] In *Kalashnikov v Russia*[121] the lack of ventilation, privacy and infestation of vermin in the cell, from which the applicant contracted skin and fungal infections, combined with the five year detention on remand, amounted to degrading treatment. Regardless of the

---

112 *Van der Ven v The Netherlands* (No 50901/99), 4 February 2003, (2004) 38 EHRR 967, ECHR 2003-II, at 51. See however, the case of *Ramirez Sanchez v France* (No 59450/00), 4 July 2006 [GC], (2007) 45 EHRR 1099, ECHR 2006-IX where solitary confinement was deemed to be permissible, since compliance with the European Prison Rules 2006 is likely to comply with Art 3.

113 *Mouisel v France* (No 67263/01), 14 November 2002, (2004) 38 EHRR 735, ECHR 2002-IX, at 40.

114 (2000) 35 EHH 198 at para 92.

115 *Pretty v UK* (2002) 35 EHRR 1 at para. 52.

116 (2001) 34 EHRR 1285.

117 In *Keenan v UK*, the suicide in custody of a mentally-ill prisoner was found to breach Art 3, since there had been insufficient monitoring and psychiatric assessment, and the prisoner had been inappropriately detained in segregation in a punishment block – *Keenan v UK* (2001) 33 EHRR 38.

118 See *Rainen v Finland* (No 20972/92), 16 December 1997, (1998) 26 EHRR 563, ECHR 1997-VIII, at 52–59.

119 *Poltoratskiiy v Ukraine* (No 38812/97), 29 April 2003, ECHR 2003-V.

120 *ibid* at 132.

121 (2002) 36 EHRR 587.

State's defence that the conditions were no worse than conditions in any other Russian detention facility, the ECtHR found that this was not an argument it would accept, since European standards applied to all States Parties irrespective of economic or domestic circumstances.

In the case of *Peers v Greece*[122] the applicant complained of the conditions in which he was detained. His cell had no ventilation and no window and he had to use the toilet facilities in the presence of another. The Court held that this diminished his human dignity and constituted degrading treatment.

In *Van der Ven v Netherlands*[123] the ECtHR considered that even though the applicant was a dangerous individual with a need for high security detention, the regime of personal and cell searches were not proportionate given the existing rigid circumstances of their confinement. **[5–35]**

Strip searches in the absence of any real security concerns can also constitute degrading treatment and a breach of Art 3.[124]

In the case of *Tyrer v United Kingdom*, the Court found that birching as a method of punishment for a juvenile who had been convicted of a crime was degrading, but not inhuman punishment.[125]

Punishment and Treatment

The Court does not always distinguish between punishment and treatment and "[p]unishment and treatment are often not subject to separate analysis, since in many cases punishment must involve treatment".[126] **[5–36]**

Obligations on Contracting Parties

The ECtHR expounded on the obligations on contracting parties arising from Art 3 in the *Moldovan* case.[127] It stated: **[5–37]**

> "The obligation of the High Contracting Parties under Article 1 of the Convention to secure to everyone within their jurisdiction the rights and freedoms defined in the Convention, taken together with Article 3, requires States to take measures designed to ensure that individuals within their jurisdiction are not subjected to ill-treatment, including ill-treatment administered by private individuals."[128]

Jacobs, White and Ovey comment that the obligations on contracting States arising from Art 3 involve two elements, i.e. the contracting States must have deterrent measures in place and the contracting States must undertake effective investigations into allegations

122 *Peers v Greece* (No 28524/95), 19 April 2001, (2001) 33 EHRR 1192, ECHR 2001-III.
123 (2003) ECHR 62.
124 *Iwańczuk v Poland* (App 25196/94) 15 November 2001, (2004) 38 EHRR 148. See also *Wainwright v UK* (2007) 44 EHRR 40.
125 *Tyrer v United Kingdom* (1979–80) 2 EHRR 1.
126 R White and C Ovey, *supra* n 79, p 174.
127 *Moldovan and others v Romania* (Nos 41138/98 and 64320/01), 12 July 2005, (2007) 44 EHRR 302, ECHR 2005-VII.
128 *ibid* at para 98.

of ill-treatment.[129] The *Okkali* case[130] deals with the first of these elements. In this case a 12 year old boy was beaten by police. The ECtHR found that the respondent State had breached Art 3 as the criminal law system was not rigorous and therefore did not have a deterrent effect. The second requirement has given rise to significant case law. The ECtHR has stated that for an investigation to be effective, it must be thorough, expedient and independent[131] and be able to lead to the identification of perpetrators. In the case of *Sevtap Veznedaroglu v Turkey*[132] the ECtHR stated:

> "[T]he Court reiterates that, where an individual raises an arguable claim that he has been seriously ill-treated by the police or other such agents of the State unlawfully and in breach of Article 3, that provision, read in conjunction with the State's general duty under Article 1 of the Convention to 'secure to everyone within their jurisdiction the rights and freedoms defined in ... [the] Convention' requires by implication that there should be an effective official investigation capable of leading to the identification and punishment of those responsible ... If this were not the case, the general legal prohibition of torture and inhuman and degrading treatment and punishment, despite its fundamental importance, would be ineffective in practice and it would be possible in some cases for agents of the State to abuse the rights of those within their control with virtual impunity."[133]

Extraterritorial Effect

[5–38] Article 3 can have extraterritorial effect in certain circumstances. An interesting case which dealt with the issue of extraterritorial effect to a certain extent is the case of *Soering v United Kingdom.*[134] This case concerned a possible deportation to the US, to a State which allows the death penalty to be imposed. People waiting to be put to death can be waiting on death row for many years. This "death row phenomenon" was regarded by the ECtHR as inhuman punishment. Therefore, any State that would deport a person who could be subjected to this punishment would be in violation of the Convention. In this case the ECtHR clarified that it was not seeking to assess the behaviour of non-contracting parties to the Convention.[135]

In *Chahal*[136] the UK was precluded from deporting a Sikh, who was a separatist, back to India. ECtHR stated that if the applicant was returned there would be a real risk that he would be mistreated by some employees of the Punjab Police force.

[5–39] In *HLR v France*[137] the ECtHR allowed the deportation of a convicted drug trafficker who had given information to authorities on other traffickers back to Colombia, despite his claim that drug traffickers would seek revenge on him. The ECtHR

---

129 See Jacobs, White and Ovey, *The European Convention on Human Rights*, (5th ed OUP, Oxford, 2010), p 176.

130 *Okkali v Turkey* (No 52067/99), 17 October 2006, ECHR 2006-XII.

131 *Akkoç v Turkey* (Nos 22947/93 and 22948/93), 10 October 2000, (2002) 34 EHRR 1173, ECHR 2000-X, at para 118.

132 *Sevtap Veznedaroglu v Turkey* (App 32357/96), 11 April 2000, (2001) 33 EHRR 1412.

133 *ibid* at para 32.

134 *Soering v United Kingdom*, 7 July 1989, Series A No 161, (1989) 11 EHRR 439.

135 *ibid*, at para 91.

136 *Chahal v United Kingdom* (App 22414/93) 15 November 1996, (1997) 23 EHRR 413, ECHR 1996-V.

137 *HLR v France* (No 24573/94), 29 April 1997, (1998) 26 EHRR 29, ECHR 1997-III.

accepted that Art 3 could apply extraterritorially in respect of ill treatment by private parties but in the instant case the ECtHR felt that the risk of such treatment was not serious enough.

A very unusual broadening of Art 3 was undertaken by the ECtHR in the case of *D v United Kingdom*.[138] The applicant was from St Kitts and had been arrested in Gatwick airport and was found to be in possession of a large quantity of drugs. He was imprisoned in the UK and while he was serving his prison sentence it was discovered that he was suffering from AIDS. On completion of his sentence he was subject to deportation back to St Kitts. He claimed that he would be unable to access proper medical care in St Kitts if he was deported, arguing that the medical system in St Kitts was inadequate and that therefore deportation would be in breach of Art 3. Unlike previous cases regarding the extraterritorial application of Art 3, this case did not concern the risk of ill treatment by a State or private actors, rather it concerned the risk inherent in the St Kitts medical system. In the judgment the ECtHR highlighted the fundamental nature of the protection offered by Art 3. The ECtHR also highlighted the "very exceptional circumstances"[139] of the case and decided that deportation would amount to inhuman treatment under Art 3. **[5–40]**

The issues which arose in *D* were further clarified in the case of *N*.[140] Here the ECtHR stated that, normally, deportation of an individual suffering from AIDS would not constitute a breach of Art 3, even if there is a difference in the quality of treatment between the country of origin and the deporting State. Jacobs, White and Ovey stated that "[i]t would seem that only the removal of a person who was actually on the point of death. As in the *D* case, or possibly a pregnant woman whose child could be saved by anti-retroviral medication during pregnancy and immediately after birth, would give rise to a violation of Article 3".[141] The ECtHR clarified in *N* that individuals suffering from other physical or mental illnesses would likely be dealt with in the same way. **[5–41]**

In assessing whether an individual would be at risk if deported the ECtHR can take a number of factors into consideration, including assurances from the receiving State[142] and reports of non-governmental organisations.[143]

---

[138] *D v United Kingdom* (No 30240/96), 2 May 1997 (1997) 24 EHRR 423, ECHR 1997-III.

[139] *ibid*, at para 54.

[140] *N v United Kingdom* (No 26565/05), 27 May 2008, ECHR 2008-nyr.

[141] R White and C Ovey, *supra* n 79, p 180.

[142] See *Olaechea Cahuas v Spain* (App 24668/03), 10 August 2006, (2009) 48 EHRR 572, ECHR 2006-X where Peru provided assurances that the applicant would not be sentenced to death or life imprisonment.

[143] See *Saadi v Italy* (No 37201/06), 28 February 2008 [GC], (2009) 49 EHRR 730, ECHR 2008-nyr at para 138 where an NGO report was taken into consideration by the Court. See also *Mamatkulov and Askarov v Turkey* (Nos 46827/99 and 46951/99), 4 February 2005 [GC], (2005) 41 EHRR 494, ECHR 2005-I where the Court stated that a NGO report constituted a description of the general situation in a State and did not support the specific claim made by the applicant.

Disappearances

[5–42] Article 3 has been deemed to apply to situations of disappearances. In the case of *Kurt*,[144] an application on behalf of a mother in respect of her disappeared son, the ECtHR concluded that there was a breach of Art 3 as the mother had suffered apprehension and worry over a long period of time leading to severe mental distress. As the authorities had not given consideration to her requests for information about her son, the ECtHR concluded that the State had breached Art 3.

[5–43] The factors which will be taken into consideration by the Court when assessing whether a family member can be considered as a victim of ill treatment contrary to Art 3 were discussed in the case of *Çakici*.[145] The Court stated that in determining whether a family member will benefit from Art 3:

> "... will depend on the existence of special factors which gives the suffering of the applicant a dimension and character distinct from the emotional distress which may be regarded as inevitably caused to relatives of a victim of a serious human rights violation. Relevant elements will include the proximity of the family tie (in that context, a certain weight will attach to the parent-child bond), the extent to which the family member witnessed the events in question, the involvement of the family member in attempts to obtain information about the disappeared person and the way in which the authorities responded to those enquiries. The Court would further emphasise that the essence of such a violation does not so much lie in the fact of the 'disappearance' of the family member but rather concerns the authorities' reactions and attitudes to the situation when it is brought to their attention. It is especially in respect of the latter that a relative may claim directly to be a victim of the authorities' conduct."[146]

Destruction of Property and Possessions

[5–44] The ECtHR has held that destruction of property and possessions can constitute a breach of Art 3. In *Bilgin v Turkey*[147] the respondent State was found to have breached Art 3 when security forces intentionally destroyed the applicant's property and possessions. The ECtHR found that this constituted inhuman treatment as the security forces had undertaken their operations with disregard for the safety of the applicant.

Corporal Punishment

[5–45] In the *Tyrer* case,[148] the ECtHR held that the use of birching as a penalty for a juvenile constituted degrading treatment and a breach of Art 3. The case concerned a police constable who birched a 15-year-old boy as a penalty for assaulting another pupil at his school. In concluding that Art 3 had been breached, the ECtHR stated that the birching was an assault on the boy's dignity and on his physical integrity. The ECtHR went on to comment that the birching may also have adverse psychological effects on the boy[149] and stated that if punishment constituted degrading treatment then the nature of the punishment, in addition to the manner and method of the execution of

---

144 *Kurt v Turkey* (No 24276/94), 25 May 1998, (1999) 27 EHRR 373, ECHR 1998-III.
145 *Çakici v Turkey* (No 23657/94), 8 July 1999 [GC], (2001) 31 EHRR 5, ECHR 1999-IV.
146 *ibid* at para 98. See also *Selcuk and Asker v Turkey* (1996) EHRR 477.
147 *Bilgin v Turkey* (No 23819/94), 16 November 2000, (2003) 35 EHRR 879.
148 *Tyrer v United Kingdom* (1979–80) 2 EHRR 1.
149 *ibid* at para 33.

the punishment, should be considered.[150] The ECtHR said the Convention is a living instrument which must be interpreted in the light of present-day conditions although such a punishment might once have been acceptable, changing views on penal policy generally made it no longer so, and his claim should succeed.

In the cases of *Campbell* and *Cosans*[151] the corporal punishment in question was the striking of the hand with a leather strap (a tawse). In one case, the school would not assure the applicant that her son would not be subjected to corporal punishment. In the other case, the applicant's son refused to accept the punishment and was suspended from school. While the ECtHR did not find a violation of Art, 3 as neither boy had undergone the punishment, it stated that "provided it is sufficiently real and immediate, a mere threat of conduct prohibited by Article 3 may itself be in conflict with the provision".[152] [5–46]

In the case of *Costello-Roberts v UK*[153] the ECtHR found that the punishment of a boy in a UK private school (he had been whacked three times with a soft-soled shoe on his clothed buttocks) did not reach the level of severity to breach Art 3. It should be noted, however, that this judgment was by five votes to four, and the ECtHR emphasised that it did not wish to be taken as approving in any way school corporal punishment, and that the treatment of the boy was at, or near, the borderline. [5–47]

The case of *A v UK*[154] was the first case concerning parental corporal punishment to be considered by the ECtHR. A stepfather beat his nine-year-old stepson with a garden cane and was subsequently acquitted by the domestic court on a charge of assault occasioning actual bodily harm (the 'lawful correction' defence). The ECtHR held that there had been a breach of Art 3 as the UK had not adequately protected the rights of the child. The prosecution of the stepfather in a UK court had thus failed on the grounds that the punishment was 'reasonable chastisement', but the ECtHR unanimously found that the punishment violated Art 3 of the Convention. [5–48]

Rendition

The Parliamentary Assembly of the Council of Europe began an investigation in 2005 into allegations about the existence of CIA detention centres in Council of Europe Member States. The investigation was instigated under Art 52 of the ECHR which allows the Secretary-General of the Council of Europe to request: [5–49]

> "any High Contracting party [. . .to] furnish an explanation of the manner in which its internal law ensures the effective implementation of any of the provisions of this Convention."

[150] *ibid* at para 30.

[151] *Campbell and Cosans v United Kingdom*, 25 February 1982, Series A No 48, (1982) 4 EHRR 293.

[152] *ibid* at para 26.

[153] (1983) 19 EHRR 112.

[154] (1999) 27 EHRR 611.

The Swiss Senator, Dick Marty, was appointed as Rapporteur, and the report was completed in June 2007.[155] The report highlights the extent of the transfer of detainees through Council of Europe States and underlines the international legal obligations of the States with regard to the right to freedom from torture.[156]

2. Legitimate Justifications for Interference with the Right

[5–50] As stated above, the protection from torture is an absolute right and a derogation from Art 3 is not permitted even in time of war or public emergency. The absolute nature of the prohibition on torture was discussed by the ECtHR in *Chahal v United Kingdom*[157]:

> "Article 3 enshrines one of the most fundamental values of democratic society. The Court is well aware of the immense difficulties faced by States in modern times in protecting their communities from terrorist violence. However, even in these circumstances, the Convention prohibits in absolute terms torture or inhuman or degrading treatment or punishment, irrespective of the victim's conduct."[158]

The nature of Art 3 was highlighted again in the case of *Saadi v Italy*[159] where the Court stated:

> "As the prohibition of torture and inhuman and degrading treatment or punishment is absolute, irrespective of the victim's conduct ... the nature of the offence allegedly committed by the applicant is therefore irrelevant for the purposes of Article 3..."[160]

C. CFR

[5–51] Article 3:

> "(1) Everyone has the right to respect for his or her physical and mental integrity.
> (2) In the fields of medicine and biology, the following must be respected in particular:
> – the free and informed consent of the person concerned, according to the procedures laid down by law,
> – the prohibition of eugenic practices, in particular those aiming at the selection of persons,
> – the prohibition on making the human body and its parts as such a source of financial gain,
> – the prohibition of the reproductive cloning of human beings."

---

155 Parliamentary Assembly, Committee on Legal Affairs, *Secret detentions and illegal transfers of detainees involving Council of Europe member states: second report*, Doc. 11302 rev,11 June 2007.

156 The Parliamentary Assembly has also passed a number of resolutions with regard to extraordinary rendition, e.g. Recommendation 1507 (2006), Recommendation 1754 (2006), Recommendation 1562 (2007), Recommendation 1801 (2007).

157 *Chahal v United Kingdom* (No 22414/93), 15 November 1996, (1997) 23 EHRR 413, ECHR 1996-V.

158 *ibid* at 80.

159 *Saadi v Italy* (No 37201/06), 28 February 2008 [GC], (2009) 49 EHRR 730, ECHR 2008-nyr.

160 *ibid* at 127.

Article 4:

> "No one shall be subjected to torture or to inhuman or degrading treatment or punishment."

Article 3 CFR merely reaffirms principles previously included in the Council of Europe Convention on Human Rights and Biomedicine[161] and various initiatives with regard to bioethics have been made by the EU institutions, e.g. European Parliament and Council Directives with regard to organ donation, procurement and distribution.[162]

Article 4 of the CFR has the same wording as Art 3 of the ECHR and therefore, by virtue of Art 52(3) of the Charter, has the same meaning and the same scope as the ECHR Article.[163]

In addition, various other EU documents relate to the prohibition on torture, for example, Council Regulation (EC) No 1236/2005.[164] This Regulation concerns inhuman or degrading treatment or punishment and prohibits[165] the import and export of goods that have no other practical purpose than for implementing the death penalty or for torture.[166] [5–52]

The European Parliament and Council Decision No 779/2007/EC[167] established a programme to be implemented between 2007 and 2013 to prevent and combat violence against children, young people and women and to protect people and groups at risk (Daphne III programme) while is related to the prohibition on inhuman or degrading treatment.

---

161 Convention for the protection of Human Rights and Dignity of the Human Being with regard to the Application of Biology and Medicine, CETS No 64, adopted 1997.

162 See, for example, Directive 2004/23/EC of the European Parliament and of the Council on setting standards of quality and safety for the donation, procurement, testing, processing, preservation, storage and distribution of human tissues and cells [2004] OJL 102/48, and Commission Directive 2006/17/EC of 8 February 2006 implementing Directive 2004/23/EC of the European Parliament and of the Council as regards certain technical requirements for the donation, procurement and testing of human tissues and cells [2004] OJL 38/40.

163 Explanation of the Praesidium of the Convention which drafted the charter – available at: http://infoportal.fra.europa.eu/infoPortal/infobaseShowContent.do?btnCat_321&btnCountryBread_169, last accessed 21 July 2012.

164 Council Regulation (EC) No 1236/2005 of 27 June 2005 concerning trade in certain goods which could be used for capital punishment, torture or other cruel, inhuman or degrading treatment or punishment, [2005] OJL 200/1.

165 *ibid.*

166 This Regulation was amended by Commission Regulation (EC) No 675/2008: Commission Regulation (EC) No 675/2008 of 16 July 2008 amending Council Regulation (EC) No 1236/2005 concerning trade in certain goods which could be used for capital punishment, torture or other cruel, inhuman or degrading treatment or punishment.

167 Decision No 779/2007/EC of the European Parliament and of the Council of 20 June 2007 establishing for the period 2007–2013 a specific programme to prevent and combat violence against children, young people and women and to protect victims and groups at risk (Daphne III programme) as part of the General Programme of Fundamental Rights and Justice.

[5–53] European institutions have addressed the issue of extraordinary rendition in a number of ways. The Parliament established the Temporary Committee on the alleged use of European countries by the CIA for the transportation and illegal detention of prisoners in 2006. The Committee issued its *Report on the alleged use of European countries by the CIA for the transportation and illegal detention of prisoners*[168] in 2007, which reviews the practice of EU States, including Ireland,[169] with regard to rendition. The Parliament has also adopted a number of resolutions with regard to rendition, e.g., European Parliament resolution on the alleged use of European countries by the CIA for the transportation and illegal detention of prisoners.[170]

D. International and Regional Laws

[5–54] The right to bodily integrity is not specifically recognised under the International Covenant on Civil and Political Rights (ICCPR), International Covenant on Economic, Social and Cultural Rights (ICESCR), or under the ECHR. However, it has been interpreted as being part of the right to security of the person (ICCPR Art 9, ECHR Art 5), the right to freedom from torture and cruel, inhuman, and degrading treatment (ICCPR 7, ECHR 3), the right to privacy (ICCPR Art 17, ECHR Art 8), and the right to the highest attainable standard of health (ICESCR Art 12, ESC Art 11).

The right to bodily integrity is, however, specifically protected in the human rights instruments of the African Union. Article 4 of the African Charter on Human and Peoples' Rights states:

> "Human beings are inviolable. Every human being shall be entitled to respect for his life and the integrity of his person. No one may be arbitrarily deprived of this right."

In addition, Art 4(1) of the Protocol to the African Charter on Human and Peoples' Rights on the Rights of Women in Africa states:

> "Every woman shall be entitled to respect for her life and the integrity and security of her person."

The United Nations General Assembly's Declaration on Torture 1975 states:

> "Torture constitutes an aggravated and deliberate form of cruel, inhuman and degrading treatment or punishment."[171]

[5–55] The right to freedom from torture is protected under the ICCPR (Art 7). The Convention on the Rights of the Child also seeks to protect the child from all forms of

---

[168] *Report on the alleged use of European countries by the on the alleged use of European countries by the CIA for the transportation and illegal detention of prisoners (2006/2200(INI))*, A6-9999/2007.

[169] *ibid*, at 122.

[170] European Parliament resolution on the alleged use of European countries by the CIA for the transportation and illegal detention of prisoners (2006/2200(INI)).

[171] UNGA Res. 3452 (XXX) of 9 December, Declaration on the protection of all persons from being subjected to torture and other cruel, inhuman or degrading treatment or punishment, Art 1.

physical or mental violence (Art 19). As already mentioned, the United Nations Convention Against Torture and Other Cruel, Inhuman or Degrading Treatment or Punishment 1984[172] offers protection against torture. An Optional Protocol to the Convention was adopted in 2002,[173] which set up a Subcommittee on Prevention of Torture and Other Cruel, Inhuman or Degrading Treatment or Punishment of the Committee against Torture, which has the mandate to visit places of detention on the territory of States Parties "with a view to strengthening, if necessary, the protection of these persons against torture and other cruel, inhuman or degrading treatment or punishment".[174]

The European Convention for the Prevention of Torture and Inhuman and Degrading Treatment[175] instituted under the Council of Europe system, also created a body with the power to visit places of detention in States Parties. The Committee does not have any judicial powers but writes reports on the Contracting States' adherence to the Convention and makes recommendations to the States concerned. The Commission and the ECtHR have taken reports of the Committee into consideration in some of its decisions in the past, e.g., in *Aerts v Belgium*.[176] **[5–56]**

Article 5 of the European Convention on Human Rights and Biomedicine[177] states: **[5–57]**
"An intervention in the health field may only be carried out after the person concerned has given free and informed consent to it". Similarly, the UN Special Rapporteur on Torture and Other Cruel, Inhuman or Degrading Treatment or Punishment has stated:

> "... [w]hereas a fully justified medical treatment may lead to severe pain or suffering, medical treatments of an intrusive and irreversible nature, when they lack a therapeutic purpose, or aim at correcting or alleviating a disability, may constitute torture and ill-treatment if enforced or administered without the free and informed consent of the person concerned."[178]

---

[172] Convention against Torture and Other Cruel, Inhuman or Degrading Treatment or Punishment, adopted and opened for signature, ratification and accession by General Assembly resolution 39/46 of 10 December 1984 entered into force on 26 June 1987.

[173] Optional Protocol to the Convention against Torture and other Cruel, Inhuman or Degrading Treatment or Punishment, adopted on 18 December 2002 at the fifty-seventh session of the General Assembly of the United Nations by resolution A/RES/57/199, entered into force on 22 June 2006.

[174] Art 4, Optional Protocol to the Convention against Torture and other Cruel, Inhuman or Degrading Treatment or Punishment, adopted on 18 December 2002 at the fifty-seventh session of the General Assembly of the United Nations by resolution A/RES/57/199, entered into force on 22 June 2006.

[175] European Convention for the Prevention of Torture and Inhuman and Degrading Treatment 1989, ETS 126, and Protocols 1 and 2, ETS 151 and 152.

[176] *Aerts v Belgium* (No 25357/94), 30 July 1998 (2000) 29 EHRR 50, ECHR 1998-V.

[177] Convention for the Protection of Human Rights and Dignity of the Human Being with regard to the Application of Biology and Medicine, CETS No 64, adopted 1997.

[178] Interim report of the UN Special Rapporteur on Torture and Other Cruel, Inhuman or Degrading Treatment of Punishment, UN Doc A/63/175 (28 July 2008), p 11.

Conclusion

[5–58] It is clear that Ireland's obligations with regard to the right to bodily integrity and the right to freedom from torture are onerous. Given the *jus cogens* nature of the prohibition on torture, no State activity which impinges in any way on the right to freedom from torture can be tolerated. It is unusual that such important and basic rights are not enumerated in the Irish Constitution, and indeed, Ireland has been criticised for the lack of an explicit prohibition on torture and cruel, inhuman or degrading treatment or punishment in the basic law of the State.[179] Ireland's law has been influenced by the incorporation of the UN Torture Convention into domestic law, in addition to Art 3 of the ECHR, with regard to torture in a number of ways, including the definition of torture. However, there are still a number of gaps in the domestic law with regard to the right to bodily integrity and the right to freedom from torture, including an absence of legislation prohibiting all forms of corporal punishment.

[179] See Ireland's Initial Report to the Committee Against Torture CAT/C/IRL/1, pp 59–60, available at: http://www2.ohchr.org/english/bodies/cat/cats46.htm, last accessed 21 July 2012.

CHAPTER 6
The Right to Fair Trial and Fair Procedures

Introduction

The right to a fair trial and the right to fair procedures in decision making are prerequisites of all legal systems which purport to be founded on, and seek to promote, the rule of law. The protection of these rights is vital to ensure that other human rights can be protected and subjected to the rule of law. These rights have been enshrined in various international human rights documents, generally under "equality before the law" headings. They are also protected by Irish constitutional law, the European Convention on Human Rights (ECHR) and the Charter of Fundamental Rights (CFR) in various ways. This chapter discusses the protection of the right to a fair trial found in Art 38.1 of the Irish Constitution and then analyses how the right to fair procedures has been held to fall within the protective parameters of Art 40.3.1° as an unenumerated right. The chapter then focuses on the protection granted to these rights under Art 6 of the ECHR and under the CFR before concluding with a brief discussion of the protection of these rights under the international human rights law regime. **[6–01]**

A. Irish Constitution

Article 40.3.1°: **[6–02]**

> "The State guarantees in its laws to respect, and, as far as practicable, by its laws to defend and vindicate the personal rights of the citizen."

Article 38.1:

> "No person shall be tried on any criminal charge save in due course of law."

The way in which the right to a fair trial and the right to fair procedures are protected by the Irish Constitution is slightly unusual. Article 38.1 seeks to ensure fairness in criminal trials only, while the issue of fair procedures, including decision making in civil cases, has been found to fall within Art 40.3.1° as an unenumerated right. It took some time (until the 1970s) for the Irish courts to broaden out the protection of the right to a fair trial in criminal cases to a more general guarantee of fairness in decision-making procedures. This chapter begins with an analysis of the right to a fair trial under Art 38 before discussing how the broader right to fair procedures has evolved through the years in the jurisprudence of the Irish courts. It should be noted that the right of access to the courts is dealt with separately in Art 34 of the Irish Constitution,[1] rather than as part of the main provision on fair trials. See also the discussion on the right of access to the courts under the ECHR section below.

1. Nature of the Right

The Right to a Fair Trial

To Whom does the Right Apply?

[6–03] The protection of Art 38.1 can only be enjoyed by an individual who has been charged, in due course of law, with a criminal charge. With regard to the "criminal charge" element of Art 38.1, Doyle states:

> "In the vast majority of cases, it will be uncontentious whether a legal provision creates a criminal offence or not. In the contentious cases, it appears that the courts assess whether a provision creates an offence by ascertaining whether the provision (and provisions related to it) contains a number of features that are generally shared by provisions which are uncontroversially accepted to be criminal in character. Once a provision is deemed to be criminal in character, the protections afforded to the accused person dramatically increase as Art. 38.1 comes into play".[2]

"In Due Course of Law"[3]

[6–04] The meaning of "in due course of law" is not clarified in the Constitution. However, the courts have interpreted this phrase in an expansive manner in various cases. This is clear from the case of *Heaney v Ireland*[4] where Costello J discussed the nature and scope of Art 38.1:

> "It is an Article couched in peremptory language and has been construed as a constitutional guarantee that criminal trials will be conducted in accordance with basic concepts of justice. Those basic principles may be of ancient origin and part of the long established principles of the common law, or they may be of more recent origin and

---

[1] Art 34 states: "Justice shall be administered in courts established by law by judges appointed in the manner provided by this Constitution, and, save in such special and limited cases as may be prescribed by law, shall be administered in public." See *Macauley v Minister for Posts and Telegraphs* [1966] IR 345 and *Tuohy v Courtney* [1994] 2 IR 1. Regarding the right of access to the court system under Art 6 of the ECHR, see *Airey v Ireland* (1979) 2 EHRR 305, discussed below.

[2] O Doyle, *Constitutional Law: Text, Cases and Materials* (Clarus Press, Dublin, 2008), p 20.

[3] It should be noted that various evidential issues attach to the right to a fair trial, e.g. the admissibility of illegally and unconstitutionally obtained evidence, but a discussion on these issues is outside the remit of this chapter. For a discussion on these issues, see J Casey, *Constitutional Law in Ireland* (3rd ed, Round Hall Sweet & Maxwell, Dublin, 2000), pp 530–535.

[4] *Heaney v Ireland* [1994] 3 IR 593.

> widely accepted in other jurisdictions and recognised in international conventions as a basic requirement of a fair trial. Thus, the principle that an accused is entitled to the presumption of innocence, that an accused cannot be tried for an offence unknown to the law, or charged a second time with the same offence, the principle that an accused must know the case he has to meet and that evidence illegally obtained will generally be inadmissible at his trial, are all principles which are so basic to the concept of a fair trial that they obtain constitutional protection from this Article".[5]

Costello J went on to discuss the interpretations given to the right to a fair trial in regional (ECHR) and international instruments (the International Covenant on Civil and Political Rights (ICCPR)) and under the common law. Subsequent cases have included a fairly comprehensive analysis of the right, with reference to common law, natural law, and regional and international interpretations and conceptions of a fair trial. The Irish courts have duly found that the right to a fair trial encompasses various ancillary rights which fall under Art 38.1 of the Constitution. **[6–05]**

Presumption of Innocence

At common law, an individual was presumed innocent until found guilty and this has been reiterated on numerous occasions by the Irish courts.[6] In the case of *Hardy v Ireland* Hederman J held that this presumption also emanated from the Constitution, stating that the requirement of a trial in due course of law: **[6–06]**

> "protects the presumption of innocence; it requires that the prosecution should prove its case beyond all reasonable doubt; but it does not prohibit that, in the course of the case, once certain facts are established, inferences may not be drawn from those facts and I include in that the entitlement to do this even by way of documentary evidence".[7]

This was reiterated in the case of *O'Leary v AG* where the plaintiff had been convicted in the Special Criminal Court of possession of a number of incriminating documents, contrary to s 12 of the Offences Against the State Act 1939. These incriminating documents were 27 copies of a poster stating "IRA calls the shots". Section 27 of this Act states: **[6–07]**

> "On the trial of a person charged with the offence of being a member of an unlawful organisation, proof to the satisfaction of the court that an incriminating document relating to the said organisation was found on such person or in his possession or on lands or in premises owned or occupied by him or under his control shall, without more, be evidence until the contrary is proved that such person was a member of the said organisation at the time alleged in the said charge."

Mr O'Leary claimed that this provision interfered with the presumption of innocence, highlighting that the phrase "until the contrary is proved" imposed a burden to prove that he was not an IRA member. However, this argument was rejected by the court which held that possession of incriminating documents amounted to documentary evidence rather than proof of an offence. The fact that Mr O'Leary possessed these

[5] *Heaney v Ireland* [1994] 3 IR 593 at 605.

[6] See, for example, *People (AG) v McMahon* [1946] IR 267 and *People (AG) v O'Callaghan* [1966] IR 501.

[7] *Hardy v Ireland* [1994] 2 IR 550 at 564–565.

documents could be examined at the trial. The court therefore held that the presumption of innocence was not offset by means of s 27 of the Offences Against the State Act 1939. Regarding the presumption, O'Flaherty J stated:

> " ... the presumption of innocence in a criminal trial is implicit in the requirement of Article 38, s. 1 of the Constitution that no person shall be tried on any criminal charge save in due course of law".[8]

Vague and Indefinite Laws

[6–08] Legislative provisions which create criminal offences will only be valid if they are not vague and/or indefinite. In *King v AG* the Supreme Court considered provisions of the Vagrancy Act 1824 concerning the offence of "loitering with intent" to be vague and indefinite and they were struck down. The provisions applied to every "suspected person or reputed thief" who had been proved to have been loitering in various public places "with intent to commit a felony". Henchy J stated:

> " ... the ingredients of the offence and the mode by which its commission may be proved are so arbitrary, so vague, so difficult to rebut, so related to rumour or ill-repute or past conduct, so ambiguous in failing to distinguish between apparent and real behaviour of a criminal nature ... so out of keeping with the basic concept inherent in our legal system that a man may walk abroad in the secure knowledge that he will not be singled out from his fellow-citizens and branded and punished as a criminal unless it has been established beyond reasonable doubt that he has deviated from a clearly prescribed standard of conduct, and generally so singularly at variance with both the explicit and implicit characteristics and limitations of the criminal law as to the onus of proof and mode of proof, that it is not so much a question of ruling unconstitutional the type of offence we are now considering as identifying the particular constitutional provisions with which such an offence is at variance".[9]

Kenny J stated that the language of the imputed provisions was so uncertain that they could not form the foundation of a criminal charge. He referred to Art 38.1, stating that if the ingredients of an offence were vague and uncertain, a trial which was carried out based on those ingredients was not in due course of law.

The Right to Legal Representation

[6–09] In the case of *State (Healy) v Donoghue*[10] the Supreme Court held that Art 38.1 included a right of the accused to legal representation. The case centred on the Criminal Justice (Legal Aid) Act 1962 which allowed for criminal legal aid in certain circumstances. The entitlement to such aid arises where the insufficient means of the accused and the gravity of the charge or exceptional circumstances render it essential in the interests of justice that legal aid be allowed. Legal aid will only be granted on an application made by a solicitor or barrister. Mr Healy, who had limited education, was charged with breaking and entering and pleaded guilty. He was subsequently sentenced to three months' imprisonment. He was not informed of his right to apply for legal aid and he was unrepresented. He was later charged with other offences with a co-accused

---

[8] *O'Leary v AG* [1995] 1 IR 254 at 263.
[9] *King v AG* [1981] IR 233 at 257.
[10] [1976] IR 325.

and they both applied for, and were granted, legal aid. They were both convicted and given a six-month sentence. The Supreme Court held that neither of the convictions could stand. Henchy J stated:

> "A person who has been convicted and deprived of his liberty as a result of a prosecution which, because of his poverty, he has had to bear without legal aid has reason to complain that he has been meted out less than his constitutional due. This is particularly true if the absence of legal aid is compounded by factors such as a grave or complex charge; or ignorance, illiteracy, immaturity or other conditions rendering the accused incompetent to cope properly with the prosecution; or an inability, because of detentional restraint, to find and produce witnesses; or simply the fumbling incompetence that may occur when an accused is precipitated into the public glare and alien complexity of courtroom procedures, and is confronted with the might of a prosecution backed by the State. As the law stands, a legal-aid certificate is the shield provided against such an unjust attack".[11]

The court did not clarify the level or extent of the legal representation which accrues under Art 38.1. This issue was, however, clarified to a certain extent in the case of *Carmody v Minister for Justice, Equality and Law Reform* where Mr Carmody questioned the equality of arms principle. He had been charged with certain offences under the Disease of Animals Act 1966, as amended, and was being prosecuted by the Minister for Agriculture. The Minster almost always retained the services of a barrister for such cases but under s 2 of the Criminal Justice (Legal Aid) Act 1962, a defendant can only be granted legal aid in respect of a solicitor. In the High Court, Laffoy J held that this did not create an inequality of arms which breached the constitutional right to legal representation, stating: **[6–10]**

> "The fact that there may, in terms of lawyers, be a numerical imbalance or a divergence of legal qualification between the prosecution team and the defence team does not disadvantage the accused person to the extent that his guarantee to a fair trial is imperilled unless the lawyer defending him cannot do so effectively. In my view it has not been shown that such is the case".[12]

Mr Carmody appealed[13] to the Supreme Court, which held that the principle of equality of arms did not require parity of representation, rather, it merely implied that neither party to a criminal trial should be procedurally disadvantaged. In deciding whether there were particular issues of the case as regards gravity, complexity or other exceptional circumstances which required the grant of legal aid for counsel, however, a court was entitled to consider the fact that the State was represented by both solicitor and counsel. While the Supreme Court ultimately upheld the constitutionality of the legislation, it held that the appellant could not be tried until he was afforded an opportunity to apply for legal aid to include solicitor and counsel. **[6–11]**

The constitutional right to legal representation is not very expansive with regard to the pre-trial stages of a case. In the case of *People (DPP) v Healy*[14] it was held that a right to reasonable access to legal representation applies to people in custody. Any **[6–12]**

---

[11] *ibid* at 354.

[12] *Carmody v Minister for Justice* [2005] 2 ILRM 1

[13] *Carmody v Minister for Justice* [2010] 1 IR 635.

[14] *People (DPP) v Healy* [1990] 2 IR 73.

interference with this right can render the detention illegal. However, there is no obligation to inform the detainee of this right.[15] The meaning of "reasonable access" to a solicitor has not been clearly defined in Irish law. In *Lavery*[16] the right was given a very narrow meaning and the court found that it did not encompass a right to have a solicitor present while being questioned. In *O'Brien*[17] the accused was arrested and detained in Pearse Street Garda Station. He asked for a solicitor but did not know the name of any. The Gardaí then requested a particular solicitor based on the outskirts of Dublin who was unable to come to the Garda station for a number of hours. While he was waiting for the solicitor to arrive Mr O'Brien made several inculpatory statements. When the solicitor arrived he consulted with him for approximately half-an-hour. When the solicitor left, Mr O'Brien once again made a number of inculpatory comments when interviewed by the Gardaí. It was held in the Circuit Court that Mr O'Brien's right to reasonable access to a solicitor had been breached because the Gardaí must have known that there would be a delay before the solicitor arrived, given his geographic base. Therefore, the statements admitted prior to the solicitor's arrival were inadmissible. The court then held that statements made after Mr O'Brien's consultation with his solicitor could be admitted in evidence. Mr O'Brien appealed his conviction, but the appeal was rejected by the Supreme Court which found no causative link between the breach of Mr O'Brien's rights and the evidence obtained.[18]

The Right to Silence[19]

[6–13] The right to silence has evolved from the common law privilege against self-incrimination. The right entitles suspects to refrain from answering questions from, and providing information to, the prosecution which may be to the benefit of the prosecution. The nature of this common law right was discussed in *Re National Irish Bank Ltd*, where Shanley J stated:

> " ... it should be said that the privilege against self-incrimination has always encapsulated a right in the individual to refuse to answer a question or produce a document when to do so would in the opinion of a court tend to expose such an individual to a real risk of criminal prosecution or penalty".[20]

There has been some disagreement as to which constitutional provision relates to the right to silence. In the case of *Heaney v Ireland*[21] the High Court held that the right to

---

[15] *People (DPP) v Madden* [1977] IR 336.

[16] *Lavery v Member in Charge, Carrickmacross Garda Station* [1999] 2 IR 390. See also *People (DPP) v Buck* [2002] 2 IR 268.

[17] *People (DPP) v O'Brien* [2005] 2 IR 206.

[18] See Y Daly, "Does the Buck Stop Here: An Examination of the Right to Pre-Trial Legal Advice in the Light of *O'Brien v DPP*" (2006) 28 DULJ 345.

[19] See generally, D McGrath, "The Right to Silence" in *Annual Review of Irish Law 1996* (R Byrne and W Binchy eds, Thomson Round Hall, Dublin, 1997), p 329; Y Daly, "Is Silence Golden? The Legislative and Judicial Treatment of Pre-Trial Silence in Ireland" (2009) 16(1) DULJ 31; G Hogan, "The Right to Silence after National Irish Banks and Finnerty" (1999) 21 DULJ 176.

[20] *Re National Irish Bank Ltd* [1999] 3 IR 145 at 153.

[21] *Heaney v Ireland* [1996] 1 IR 580.

silence fell under the protection of the right to a fair trial. However, the Supreme Court held that the right to silence was protected under the freedom of expression provision in Art 40.6.1° of the Constitution. O'Flaherty J stated that "[t]he right to freedom of expression necessarily implies the right to remain silent".[22] *Heaney* was subsequently appealed to the European Court of Human Rights (ECtHR)[23] which agreed with the High Court's determination that the right to silence formed part of the right to a fair trial. In *Re National Irish Bank Ltd*[24] the Supreme Court also accepted that the protection of the right to silence falls under Art 38.1.[25]

The right to silence protection under Irish law is quite weak compared to similar protections in other legal systems and the Irish courts have shown little enthusiasm for the right.[26] Illustrative of this is the case of *Heaney* in which O'Flaherty J intimated that only a guilty person would benefit from utilising the right to silence, stating that "the innocent person has nothing to fear from giving an account of his or her movements..."[27] However, in more recent cases the Irish Courts seem to have been influenced by the approach taken by the ECtHR with regard to the right to silence[28] and have strengthened the right to silence protection. In *Dunnes Stores Ireland Co Ltd v Ryan*, for example, s 19(6) of the Companies Act 1990 was struck down because it provided that any answers given to the Minister under the Act were admissible in court, therefore overriding the right to silence. Also, in *People (DPP) v Finnerty*[30] the Supreme Court quashed a rape conviction on the ground that the prosecution had cross-examined the accused with regard to why he had remained silent when questioned in Garda custody. [6–14]

The Constitution of the Court

Criminal trials must be heard by a judge appointed by the Constitution. The case law on this issue does not conclude whether this right flows from Art 38.1 of the Constitution or elsewhere. A number of interesting cases on this point concern the same issue, i.e. the continuation of Mahon J in his office as District Judge after reaching the age of 65, the statutory retirement age for District Justices.[31] While an extension to his tenure was possible on a year-to-year basis, the procedural criteria with regard to this extension had not been fulfilled. In the cases of *Shelly v District Justice Mahon*[32] and *Glavin v Governor Training Unit, Mountjoy Prison*[33] it was held that [6–15]

---

[22] *ibid* at 589.

[23] *Heaney v Ireland* (2001) 33 EHRR 334.

[24] *Re National Irish Bank Ltd* [1999] 3 IR 145.

[25] See also *People (DPP) v Finnerty* [1999] 4 IR 364.

[26] See D McGrath, *supra* n 19, p 329.

[27] *Heaney v Ireland* [1996] 1 IR 580 at 590.

[28] Doyle comments that "developments in the jurisprudence of the European Court of Human Rights appear to have been a factor in the Irish courts significantly strengthening the level of protection provided by the Irish Constitution."—O Doyle, *supra* n 2, p 36.

[30] [1999] 4 IR 364.

[31] The Courts (No 2) Act 1988 was subsequently enacted to provide for a retrospective extension of such terms of office.

[32] *Shelly v District Justice Mahon* [1990] 1 IR 36.

[33] *Glavin v Governor Training Unit, Mountjoy Prison* [1991] 2 IR 421.

decisions made by Mahon J were invalid on the basis that the court was not properly constituted and therefore Art 38.1 was breached.[34]

Expeditious Nature of the Trial

[6–16] It was held by the Supreme Court in the case of *State (O'Connell) v Judge Fawsitt*[35] that Art 38.1 requires that a trial should be carried out with reasonable expedition. The courts have considered many cases concerning delays in bringing sexual abuse cases where it has been held that delays may be justified due to the nature of crimes and the effect on the victims.[36] In *D v DPP* Finlay CJ stated:

> "The court asked to prohibit the trial of a person on such offences, even after a very long time, might well be satisfied and justified in reaching a conclusion that the extent to which the applicant had contributed to the delay in the revealing of the offences and their subsequent reporting to the prosecution authorities meant that as a matter of justice he should not be entitled to the order".[37]

In *B v DPP* Denham J proposed a test which should be applied with regard to the expeditiousness of a trial, stating that:

> "[t]he test is whether there is a real risk that the applicant, by reason of the delay, would not obtain a fair trial, that the trial would be unfair as a consequence of the delay. The test must be applied in the light of the circumstances of the case and the law".[38]

[6–17] The nature and requirements of sexual abuse cases were again discussed in *SH v DPP* where Murray CJ reformulated Denham J's test as:

> "The test is whether there is a real or serious risk that the applicant, by reason of the delay, would not obtain a fair trial, or that a trial would be unfair as a consequence of the delay. The test is to be applied in light of the circumstances of the case".[39]

The issue of delays in prosecution in non-sexual abuse cases was discussed in *MacFarlane v DPP*.[40] The applicant was charged with false imprisonment 15 years after the alleged offence took place. The court held that the delay in prosecution did not *per se* prohibit the trial and that the applicant must prove that he had been prejudiced in some way as a result of the delay.

[6–18] In the recent case of *Cunningham v President of the Circuit Court*[41] the applicant, who had been charged in 2003 with poisoning offences alleged to have occurred on various dates in 1977, 1991 and 1992, arising out of the administration of contaminated blood products, sought an order prohibiting the continuation of her trial. She claimed that

---

[34] See also the case of *McCarthy v Commissioner of An Garda Síochána* [1993] 1 IR 489.

[35] *State (O'Connell) v Judge Fawsitt* [1986] ILRM 639.

[36] See S Ring, "Beyond the Reach of Justice? Complainant Delay in Historic Child Sexual Abuse cases and the Right to a Fair Trial" (2009) 9 (2) JSIJ 162.

[37] *D v DPP* [1994] 1 IR 374 at 380.

[38] *B v DPP* [1997] 3 IR 140 at 196.

[39] *SH v DPP* [2006] 3 IR 575 at 620.

[40] [2007] 1 IR 134.

[41] [2010] 1 IR 18.

the delay in trying her case had prejudiced her right to a fair trial, and that such a delay was of a type where prejudice could be inferred. It was held by McKechnie J in the High Court, in refusing the relief sought, that, when determining whether a criminal trial should be prohibited on grounds of delay, it was necessary for a court to adopt the following procedure: (i) the court should determine whether specific prejudice had resulted from the delay, and where there was such prejudice, the trial should be prohibited; (ii) where no specific prejudice had occurred the court should determine whether the right of an accused to an expeditious trial had been violated, and where there was no such violation the trial should proceed; and (iii) where the right to an expeditious trial had been violated, the court should engage in a balancing process between the right of an accused to be protected from the stress and anxiety caused by unnecessary and inordinate delay and the public interest in having the prosecution of serious charges brought to a conclusion.

Publicity[42]

Irish courts have, on a number of occasions, considered whether publicity surrounding a trial could impact on the right to a fair trial. In *D v DPP*[43] the accused claimed that his trial on a rape charge should be prohibited. He had been tried twice previously but both trials ended in mistrials. After the second trial a national newspaper published an interview with the complainant, although neither the accused nor the complainant were identified. It was possible, however, to link the interview with the trial that had just ended. Six months later the third trial was scheduled. The High Court held that the trial should be prohibited, but the Supreme Court disagreed and allowed the trial to proceed. The Supreme Court held that a trial should be prohibited if there was a real and serious risk of unfairness, but such risk did not exist in the present case. The court highlighted the fact that the interview in the paper was published six months previously, the interview was published in only one paper and the parties had not been identified.[44] **[6–19]**

In the recent case of *DPP v Dumbrell and Dumbrell*[45] the applicants were convicted of murder and sentenced to life imprisonment in the Central Criminal Court. The applicants applied for leave to appeal against conviction, arguing that the verdict was unsafe. They argued that the trial judge erred both in law and in fact in failing to discharge the jury during the trial where the possibility existed of the jury being biased against the accused as a result of adverse publicity emanating from a lecture delivered by the trial judge while the trial was ongoing. The lecture had been well-publicised and had been circulated to the Press. The Court of Criminal Appeal held that the trial judge underestimated the possible impact of the publication and publicisation of the lecture on the jury and the trial, that a reasonable person would have a reasonable apprehension that jurors would be influenced by the contents of the lecture and, therefore, that the applicants did not receive a fair trial. Irish courts have also chosen **[6–20]**

---

42 See G Browne, "Pre–trial publicity, prejudice, and the right to a fair trial" (1994) 4(1) ICLJ 113 and (1994) 4(2) ICLJ 141.

43 *D v DPP* [1994] 2 IR 564.

44 See also the case of *Z v DPP* [1994] 2 IR 476 and *Magee v O'Dea* [1994] 1 IR 500.

45 [2010] IECCA 84.

the option of postponing trials to allow publicity surrounding a trial to die down before proceeding, e.g. *DPP v Haugh*.[46]

The Right to Cross-Examine

[6–21] The Irish courts have not discussed the right to cross-examine in too much depth, unlike the ECtHR. In the case of *Re Haughey* it was determined that the right to a fair trial encompassed the right of an accused to cross-examine any person giving evidence against him. Recent cases have also discussed the issue of evidence via video link and its impact on the right to cross-examine.[47]

Jury Trial

[6–22] Article 38.5 of the Constitution provides that no person shall be tried on any criminal charge without a jury, expect in situations of minor offences and in cases before special courts, military courts, all of which are dealt with in Art 38.2, Art 38.3 and Art 38.4.

The Irish courts debated the meaning of "minor" offences for the purposes of Art 38 in the cases of *Melling v Ó Mathghamhna*[48] and *Conroy v AG*.[49] With regard to the issue of "special courts", Art 38.3 of the Constitution states:

> "1° Special courts may be established by law for the trial of offences in cases where it may be determined in accordance with such law that the ordinary courts are inadequate to secure the effective administration of justice, and the preservation of public peace and order.
> 2° The constitution, powers, jurisdiction and procedure of such special courts shall be prescribed by law."

In Ireland, the Special Criminal Court was set up to deal with offences under the Offences Against the State Act 1939 and other offences. The non-jury nature of this court has been persistently criticised by various observers[50] and has been reviewed by the Human Rights Committee, the treaty-monitoring body of the ICCPR. In the case of *Kavanagh v Ireland*[51] Mr Kavanagh claimed that the State had violated his rights under Arts 14 and 26 of the ICCPR which include a right to a fair trial and equality of arms. Mr Kavanagh complained that these rights had been violated when the DPP ordered that he should be tried before the Special Criminal Court. The author complained that he had been disadvantaged when compared to other persons who were tried for similar offences before ordinary courts and who could, therefore, avail themselves of a wider range of possible safeguards. The Committee held that the Irish State was in violation of Art 26 of the ICCPR and stated that in order to preclude similar future violations, it should ensure that no-one is tried before the Special Criminal Court unless reasonable and objective criteria for the decision are provided.

---

46 *DPP v Haugh (No 2)* [2001] 1 IR 162.

47 See also the case of *Donnelly v DPP* [1998] 1 IR 321; *DO'D v DPP* [2009] IEHC 559 and *DPP v O'Brien* [2010] IECCA 103 regarding the giving of evidence by video link.

48 [1962] IR 1.

49 [1965] IR 411.

50 Compilation prepared by the Office of the High Commissioner for Human Rights on Ireland for the Universal Periodic Review 2011, A/HRC/WG.6/12/IRL/2 at 36.

51 *Kavanagh v Ireland*, Communication No 819/1998, 4 April 2001, CCPR/C/71/D/819/1998.

The Irish Government responded to this finding by making a financial payment to the complainant and by compiling a report on proposed reform of the Special Criminal Court.[52] In Ireland's 2011 Universal Periodic Review Report, the Government stated:

> "The Government is satisfied that there is a continuing need for this Court to deal with a limited range of offences arising from terrorism and organised crime. This need is kept under continuing review".[53]

Mens Rea Requirements

In *Re Article 26 and the Employment Equality Bill 1996* the Supreme Court held that ss 15 and 16 of that Bill, which imposed vicarious liability on employers for acts of employees which infringed s 14 of the Bill regarding unlawful discrimination and victimisation, subject to the defence that the employer took reasonably practicable steps to prevent breaches of s 14, breached the right to a fair trial. **[6–23]**

> "The Court concludes that to render an employer liable to potentially severe criminal sanctions in circumstances which are so unjust, irrational and inappropriate would make any purported trial of such a person not one held in due course of law and, therefore, contrary to Article 38.1 of the Constitution and also repugnant to the provisions of Article 40.1 of the Constitution".[54]

According to Doyle, "[t]his case appeared to suggest a general principle that, outside the domain of regulatory offences, it was constitutionally impermissible to provide for criminal offences that had no *mens rea* element".[55] This principle was accepted in *C v Ireland (No 2)*.[56]

Nullum Crimen Sine Lege

The *nullum crimen sine lege* principle must be considered with regard to limitations on the right to a fair trial. The principle, that no crime can be committed without a violation of a law as it existed at the time, is a basic requirement of the rule of law and is also addressed in Art 7 of the ECHR. In Ireland, this right is actually protected, not under Art 38.1, but under Art 15.5.1° of the Constitution which states that the "Oireachtas shall not declare acts to be infringements of the law which were not so at the date of their commission." There has been very little case law on this provision but in the case of *Magee v Culligan*[57] it was held that this provision applies to civil law as well as criminal law. **[6–24]**

Non Bis In Idem

The *non bis in idem*, or "double jeopardy" principle is recognised at common law. This prohibits a person who has been acquitted of an offence to be tried for the same **[6–25]**

---

[52] CCPR A/57/40, Vol I, 2002.

[53] Ireland's National Universal Periodic Review Report 2011, submitted to the Human Rights Council of the United Nations, A/HRC/WG.6/12/IRL/1.

[54] *Re Article 26 and the Employment Equality Bill 1996* [1996] 2 IR 321 at 374.

[55] O Doyle, *supra* n 2, p 54.

[56] [2006] IESC 33.

[57] [1992] 1 IR 233.

offence. However, in Ireland an acquittal on a criminal charge does not preclude a disciplinary investigation arising out of the same facts.[58] Part 3 of the Criminal Procedure Act 2010 sets out a number of exceptions to the rule against double jeopardy in order to allow a person who has been acquitted of an offence to be re-tried in circumstances where "new and compelling evidence" emerges or where the acquittal is tainted due, for example, to corruption or intimidation of witnesses or jurors or perjury.

The Right to Fair Procedures

[6–26] In addition to the right to a fair trial with regard to criminal offences, Irish law also guarantees the right to fair procedures in decision making generally. This protection existed at common law[59] but has since been recognised as an unenumerated right under Art 40.3 of the Constitution. This was accepted in *Garvey v Ireland* where O'Higgins CJ stated:

> "The Constitution incorporates into our laws and their administration the requirements of natural justice, and by Article 40, s. 3, there is guaranteed to every citizen whose rights may be affected by decisions taken by others the right to fair and just procedures. This means that under the Constitution powers cannot be exercised unjustly or unfairly. This applies as well to the Government as to any other authority within the State to which is given the power to take action which may infringe on the rights of others".[60]

The court applied the fair procedures principle to s 6(2) of the Police Forces Amalgamation Act 1925, which empowered the Government to remove the Garda Commissioner from office at any time. Such powers were deemed to be in breach of the fair procedures principle. Griffin J stated:

> "Article 40, s.3 of the Constitution ... has been held by this Court to be a guarantee of fair procedures, and statutes which permit decisions to be taken which may affect the rights or fortunes of individual citizens should be construed as providing for fair procedures. The rules of natural justice are only the rules of fair play and fair procedures put into practice. In my opinion, where a person's livelihood and that of his family are concerned, a failure to tell him the reason why he is being removed from his office, and to give him a reasonable opportunity of meeting whatever charges, allegations, or suggestions are being made against him, constitute a breach of the obligation to proceed fairly".[61]

[6–27] The constitutional recognition of the right to fair procedures requires that this right be read into all statutory provisions or else all provisions which require decisions to be made as a result of unfair procedures are deemed invalid.

[58] See *McGrath v Commissioner of An Garda Síochána* [1991] 1 IR 69.
[59] See, for example, *Maunsell v Minister for Education* [1940] IR 213; *State (Horgan) v Exported Live Stock Insurance Board* [1943] IR 581; *Foley v Irish Land Commission* [1952] IR 118; *Re Estate of Roscrea Meat Products Ltd* [1958] IR 47.
[60] *Garvey v Ireland* [1981] IR 75 at 97.
[61] *ibid* at 108.

In the case of *Re Haughey* the issue of the right to legal representation as an aspect of the right to fair procedures was considered. Ó Dálaigh J stated:

> " . . . in proceedings before any tribunal where a party is on risk of having his good name, or his person or property, or any of his personal rights jeopardised, the proceedings may be correctly classified as proceedings which may affect his rights, and in compliance with the Constitution of the State, either by its enactments or through the Courts, must outlaw any procedures which will restrict or prevent the party concerned from vindicating these rights".[62]

In this regard, the cases of *Gallagher v Revenue Commissioners (No 1) and (No 2)*[63] held that the denial of legal representation in the case of an oral disciplinary hearing on serious charges, which could have resulted in dismissal, was a breach of the right to fair procedures.

2. Legitimate Justifications for Interference with the Right

Neither the right to a fair trial nor the right to fair procedures is an absolute right. **[6–28]** While the Constitution does not clarify under which conditions and for what purposes the rights can be interfered with, they must, clearly, be balanced with, and may have to yield to, the rights of others, or indeed, to countervailing factors, a number of which are considered below.

The Right to a Fair Trial

In *Heaney v Ireland*[64] it was held that limiting the right to silence, as in s 52 of the **[6–29]** Offences Against the State Act 1939, was a legitimate interference and was no more than was necessary in the circumstances. In this case the plaintiffs claimed that s 52 of the Offences Against the State Act 1939 was invalid as it infringed their right to silence. Section 52 states:

> "(1) Whenever a person is detained in custody under the provisions in that behalf contained in Part IV of this Act, any member of the Garda Síochána may demand of such person, at any time while he is so detained, a full account of such person's movements and actions during any specified period and all information in his possession in relation to the commission or intended commission by another person of any offence under any section or sub-section of this Act or any scheduled offence.
> (2) If any person, of whom any such account or information as is mentioned in the foregoing sub-section of this section is demanded under that sub-section by a member of the Garda Síochána, fails or refuses to give to such member such account or any such information or gives to such member any account or information which is false or misleading, he shall be guilty of an offence under this section and shall be liable on summary conviction thereof to imprisonment for a term not exceeding six months."

---

[62] *Re Haughey* [1971] IR 217 at 264.
[63] *Gallagher v Revenue Commissioners (No 1)* [1991] 2 IR 370, *Gallagher v Revenue Commissioners (No 2)* [1995] 1 IR 55.
[64] [1996] 1 IR 580.

[6–30] Both of the plaintiffs were required under this provision to answer questions about their activities over the previous number of days, but both refused to do so and were convicted under this section, and were sentenced to six months imprisonment. O'Flaherty J stated:

> "On the one hand, constitutional rights must be construed in such a way as to give life and reality to what is being guaranteed. On the other hand, the interest of the State in maintaining public order must be respected and protected. We must, therefore, ask ourselves whether the restriction which s. 52 places on the right to silence is any greater than is necessary having regard to the disorder against which the State is attempting to protect the public".[65]

He then stated that "the State is entitled to encroach on the right of the citizen to remain silent in pursuit of its entitlement to maintain public peace and order",[66] so long as the principle of proportionality is applied.

[6–31] In *Re National Irish Bank*[67] the Supreme Court held that the right to silence was not absolute but could in certain circumstances give way to the requirements of the common good, so long as the means used to curtail the right were proportionate to the public object to be achieved. The proportionality test should centre on whether the restriction placed on the right to silence by statute was any greater than was necessary to enable the State to fulfil its obligations under the Constitution.[68]

The Right to Fair Procedures

[6–32] The case of *Cassidy v Minister for Industry and Commerce* highlighted that issues of reasonableness and practicality may require a limitation on the right to fair procedures. In this case the right to fair procedures (although the right is not mentioned by name, rather, the term "natural justice" was utilised) was deemed not to apply to the legislative process, in this case the making of regulations under statutory authority by a Minister. McMahon J stated:

> "I am not satisfied that the exercise of a legislative power by the Minister in making the order can be subject to the concept of Constitutional or natural justice which is so frequently applicable where a decision-making function is exercised".[69]

The right to fair procedures may also be limited in times of emergency, where a decision is required quickly for the good of society, to protect the public interest or to prevent harm.[70]

---

65 *ibid* at 589–590.
66 *ibid* at 590.
67 *Re National Irish Bank Ltd* [1999] 3 IR 145.
68 *ibid* at 146. See also *People (Attorney General) v Gilbert* [1973] IR 383; *Rock v Ireland* [1997] 3 IR 484; *People v McGowan* [1979] IR 45.
69 *Cassidy v Minister for Industry and Commerce* [1978] IR 297 at 304.
70 See *O'Callaghan v Commissioners of Public Works* [1985] ILRM 364. However, see the case of *DK v Crowley* [2002] 2 IR 744.

B. ECHR

Article 6: [6–33]

> "1. In the determination of his civil rights and obligations or of any criminal charge against him, everyone is entitled to a fair and public hearing within a reasonable time by an independent and impartial tribunal established by law. Judgment shall be pronounced publicly but the press and public may be excluded from all or part of the trial in the interests of morals, public order or national security in a democratic society, where the interests of juveniles or the protection of the private life of the parties so require, or to the extent strictly necessary in the opinion of the court in special circumstances where publicity would prejudice the interests of justice.
> 2. Everyone charged with a criminal offence shall be presumed innocent until proved guilty according to law.
> 3. Everyone charged with a criminal offence has the following minimum rights:
> (a) to be informed promptly, in a language which he understands and in detail, of the nature and cause of the accusation against him;
> (b) to have adequate time and facilities for the preparation of his defence;
> (c) to defend himself in person or through legal assistance of his own choosing or, if he has not sufficient means to pay for legal assistance, to be given it free when the interests of justice so require;
> (d) to examine or have examined witnesses against him and to obtain the attendance and examination of witnesses on his behalf under the same conditions as witnesses against him;
> (e) to have the free assistance of an interpreter if he cannot understand or speak the language used in court."

1. Nature of the Right

Article 6 is the most frequently invoked provision of the ECHR.[71] Although the ECtHR has no jurisdiction to reopen cases that have been decided by national courts, it does have the power to adjudicate on whether the proceedings were fair and fulfilled the requirements of the ECHR. The ECtHR has called this the "fourth instance" doctrine,[72] as the ECtHR is not a third or fourth instance court of appeal from a decision of a national court, meaning that there had already been a first hearing in a national court, a second in a national appeal court, and a third in a supreme (or constitutional) court. The Commission, initially, and then the ECtHR, have always interpreted Art 6 broadly, on the grounds that it is of fundamental importance to democratic accountability. [6–34]

In the case of *Delcourt v Belgium*, the ECtHR stated that: [6–35]

> "In a democratic society within the meaning of the Convention, the right to a fair administration of justice holds such a prominent place that a restrictive interpretation of Article 6 (1) would not correspond to the aim and the purpose of that provision."[73]

---

[71] Council of Europe, *Table of Violations 1959–2011*, available at: http://www.echr.coe.int/ECHR/EN/Header/Reports+and+Statistics/Statistics/Statistical+data/, last accessed 21 June 2012.

[72] Interlaken Conference Declaration Action Plan, Point 9, available at: http://www.coe.int/t/dghl/monitoring/execution/themes/interlaken/index_EN.asp, last accessed 21 June 2012.

[73] *Delcourt v Belgium*, (1970) No 2689/65, para 25.

Article 6(1) applies to both civil[74] and criminal proceedings. Article 6(2) and Art 6(3) deal with criminal offences, but may have an application in some civil proceedings in terms of the guarantees they offer, for instance, the "equality of arms".[75]

It should be noted that, although Art 6 appears to be concerned with the right to a fair trial, the guarantees contained within the Article will also apply to an individual who has been formally charged with a criminal offence, or, in civil cases, may apply to the administrative stages that precede the initiation of judicial proceedings. In addition, Art 6 may also be engaged post-judgment, for instance, in prison whilst serving a sentence (see below for details). In addition, the proceedings must involve a dispute of some kind.[76]

Access to the Courts

[6–36] Even though the right of access to a court as such is not explicitly stated in Art 6, it was defined, at least as regards civil cases, by the case of *Golder v United Kingdom.*[77] The ECtHR focussed on the "object and purpose" of the ECHR and its underlying principle of the rule of law, concluding that the right of access to a court was implicitly guaranteed:

> "In civil matters one can scarcely conceive of the rule of law without there being a possibility of having access to the courts ... It would be inconceivable, in the opinion of the Court, that Article 6(1) should describe in detail the procedural guarantees afforded to parties in a pending lawsuit and should not first protect that which alone makes it in fact possible to benefit from such guarantees, that is, access to a court. The fair, public and expeditious characteristics of judicial proceedings are of no value at all if there are no judicial proceedings".[78]

[74] Rights and obligations of private persons in their relations *inter se* are always considered as civil rights and obligations, so, legal relations between persons, in, for example, contract law, commercial law, tort, family law, employment law and the law of property are always seen as civil. However, where a case involves the relationship between an individual and the State, the area is more problematic, and the ECtHR has recognised a number of such rights and obligations as being civil. These mostly concern the area of property law, and, within that area, usually where there may be direct consequences for the right of ownership or some effect on the use or the enjoyment of property. In these cases, there will be an assumption of a right to a fair hearing.

[75] *Dombo Beheer v Netherlands* (1994) 18 EHRR 213 and *Lobo Machado v Portugal* (1997) 23 EHRR 79.

[76] See and contrast the cases of *Benthem v Netherlands* No 8848/80, judgment of 23 October 1985 with *Anne-Marie Andersson v Sweden* No 20022/92, judgment of 27 August 1997

[77] *Golder v United Kingdom* (1979–80) 1 EHRR 524. The applicant was serving a sentence in a prison and a serious disturbance broke out. One of the police officers accused the applicant of assault and the applicant wished to bring a defamation claim against him. The Prison Rules, however, precluded him from bringing such proceedings.

[78] *ibid* at paras 34 and 35.

The right of access to a court is invoked by everyone who is a party to a dispute over "civil rights or obligations",[79] but is also applicable, arguably primarily, in criminal cases,[80] and even within administrative law.[81]

In addition, the ECtHR has made it clear that access to a court is not an absolute right; in the *Golder* judgment it acknowledged that "implied" limitations on the right of access exist.[82] Having said this, the ECtHR respects contracting States' margins of appreciation, provided that any limitation does not affect the essence of the right itself. As with the usual margin of appreciation *dictum*, any imposed limitations must be justified and proportionate: **[6–37]**

> "Certainly, the right of access to the courts is not absolute but may be subject to limitations; these are permitted by implication since the right of access 'by its very nature calls for regulation by the State, regulation which may vary in time and in place according to the needs and resources of the community and of the individuals' . . . In laying down such regulation, the Contracting States enjoy a certain margin of appreciation. Whilst the final decision as to observance of the Convention's requirements rests with the Court, it is no part of the Court's function to substitute for the assessment of the national authorities any other assessment of what might be the best policy in this field".[83]

However, it must be noted that this right is limited and States can impose restrictions on it as long as these pursue a legitimate aim and are not so wide-ranging that they destroy the essence of the right.[84] The right of access to the court must be real,[85] and applies only in relation to rights protected by national law so that Art 6(1) cannot be invoked to challenge aspects of substantive domestic law.

In *Markovic*[86] the applicants were relatives of people from Serbia and Montenegro who had been killed in the NATO bombing of Belgrade. They had taken a case in Italy because Italy had provided the air bases which facilitated the bombings. The Italian Court of Cassation stated that it did not have jurisdiction to deal with the claim. The applicants then brought a case before the ECtHR, claiming a breach of Art 6. The ECtHR stated: **[6–38]**

> "Where . . . the superior national courts have analysed in a comprehensive and convincing manner the precise nature of the impugned restriction, on the basis of the relevant Convention case-law and principles drawn therefrom, this Court would need strong reasons to differ from the conclusion reached by those courts by substituting its own views for those of the national courts on the question of interpretation of domestic law . . .

---

[79] *Fayed v United Kingdom* (1994) 18 EHRR 393
[80] *Deweer v Belgium* (1980) (Series A-35).
[81] However, the relevant section of administrative law must fall within the scope of either of the concepts of "civil rights and obligations" or "criminal charge" in their autonomous meanings, and is, therefore, little used in practice. See *De Geouffre de la Pradell v France* (1992) (Series A-253-B) at para 34 and *Schmautzer v Austria* (1995) (Series A-328-A).
[82] *Golder v United Kingdom* (1979–80) 1 EHRR 524 at para 3.
[83] *Ashingdane v United Kingdom* (1985) 7 EHRR 258 at para 57.
[84] *Ashingdane v United Kingdom* (1985) 7 EHRR 258 and *Markovic v Italy* (2007) 44 EHRR 1045.
[85] The parties must be able to participate effectively in the proceedings: *International Transport Roth GmbH v Secretary of State for the Home Department* [2002] EWCA Civ 158.
[86] *Markovic v Italy* (2007) 44 EHRR 1045.

> and by finding, contrary to their view, that there was arguably a right recognised by domestic law".[87]

The ECtHR then concluded that there was no breach of Art 6 as the inherent right to a fair trial does not extend to determining claims for damages which domestic law classifies as "political acts" which are not justiciable before the domestic court.

[6–39] Access to a court system may also concern the need for legal representation, and where this is mandatory, then denial of representation will be considered a violation of Art 6(1), since access to court is thereby being prevented.[88] The right of access to a court must, therefore, be seen as one where it must not only be accessible in theory, but also effective in practice.[89] In the case of *Aerts* the ECtHR discussed this issue:

> "It was not for the Legal Aid Board to assess the proposed appeal's prospects of success; it was for the Court of Cassation to determine the issue. By refusing the application on the ground that the appeal did not at that time appear to be well-founded, the Legal Aid Board impaired the very essence of Mr Aert's right to a tribunal".[90]

Whilst a complete denial of any possibility of bringing an action will normally breach Art 6, restrictions to court access by certain categories of applicant, have been found acceptable. For instance, access for minors,[91] persons of unsound mind,[92] and vexatious litigants[93] may find restrictions legitimately placed on their access for obvious reasons. In the *Canea Catholic Church* case, the applicant was denied the right to an action because a domestic court had ruled that the church did not have a legal personality under national law.[94]

Time limitation for court action was discussed in *Stubbings v United Kingdom*, where it was considered a matter for the State and within the margin of appreciation, though, naturally, this is subject to the usual *caveat* of proportionality.[95]

Civil Rights and Obligations

[6–40] The ECtHR first interpreted the term "civil rights and obligations" in *Ringeisen v Austria*.[96] The applicant applied for approval of the transfer of land to him by a private

---

87 *ibid* at para 94.

88 *Aerts v Belgium* (2000) 29 EHRR 50 at para 60.

89 *Airey v Ireland* (1979) 2 EHRR 305. The ECtHR held that contracting States must provide legal aid if the costs of initiating a claim are so much so as to preclude access to the domestic court.

90 *Aerts v Belgium* (2000) 29 EHRR 50 at para 60.

91 *M v United Kingdom*, No 12040/86, (1987) 52 DR 269.

92 *Winterwerp v Netherlands* (1979) 2 EHRR 387.

93 *H v United Kingdom*, No 11559/85, (1985) 45 DR 281 The applicant needed judicial permission to bring a case because he was subject to a "vexatious litigant's order".

94 *Canea Catholic Church v Greece* (1997) 27 EHRR 521.

95 *Stubbings v United Kingdom* (1996) 23 EHRR 213. See also, e.g. *Miragall Escolano v Spain* (1998) 34 EHRR 658 and *Tricard v France* (2001) 37 EHRR 388.

96 *Ringeisen v Austria* 1 EHRR 455.

person. He claimed that the appeal decision by the Regional Real Property Transactions Commission against a decision made by the District Commission was biased, and not decided by an impartial tribunal, as required by Art 6(1). The Commission stated that Art 6(1) did not apply to this situation because the provision only applied to disputes between private individuals and not to situations involving a public authority. The ECtHR, however, decided that Art 6(1) was applicable. It stated:

> "For Article 6, paragraph (1), to be applicable to a case ('contestation') it is not necessary that both parties to the proceedings should be private persons, which is the view of the majority of the Commission and of the Government. The wording of Article 6, paragraph (1), is far wider; the French expression 'contestations sur (des) droits et obligations de caractère civil' covers all proceedings the result of which is decisive for private rights and obligations. The English text, 'determination of ... civil rights and obligations', confirms this interpretation".[97]

Even though in *Ringeisen* the ECtHR found that Art 6(1) applied, the ECtHR decided that this provision had not been breached as the ECtHR did not find that the Regional Real Property Transactions Commission had been biased. **[6–41]**

Jacobs, White and Ovey comment that after the *Ringeisen* decision "the Strasbourg Court has adopted an increasingly liberal interpretation of the concept of civil rights and obligations".[98] This trend was evident in the case of *König v Germany*[99] where Art 6(1) was deemed to be applicable in a dispute involving a decision by an authority whose function included acting in the interests of public health.

Cases concerning issues such as planning and the environment,[100] taking children into care,[101] applications for release from detention in a psychiatric wing of a prison,[102] amongst others,[103] have all been deemed to fall within the purview of Art 6(1). Cases regarding tax liability will, however, not fall within its ambit.[104]

Jacobs, White and Ovey comment "it can be seen that the expression 'civil rights and obligations' has come to encompass many areas which are frequently regarded by national systems as part of public or administrative law".[105] However, the ECtHR has illustrated some inconsistency in its approach to Art 6(1). Some of the decisions which concern the areas of what actually falls within the ambit of Art 6(1) and what does not are confusing.[106] Article 6(1) recognises five separate guaranteed rights, namely, the right of access to the courts, the right to a fair hearing, the right to a public hearing, the **[6–42]**

---

[97] *ibid* at para 94.
[98] R White and C Ovey, *Jacobs, White and Ovey: The European Convention on Human Rights* (5th ed, Oxford University Press, Oxford, 2010), p 249.
[99] *König v Germany* (1979–80) 2 EHRR 170.
[100] *Mats Jacobsson v Sweden* (1991) 13 EHRR 79.
[101] *McMichael v United Kingdom*, (1995) 20 EHRR 205.
[102] *Aerts v Belgium*, (2000) 29 EHRR 50.
[103] R White and C Ovey, *supra* n 98, pp 250–251.
[104] See *Charalambos v France*, No 49210/99, Decision of 8 February 2000.
[105] R White and C Ovey, *supra* n 98, p 253.
[106] *ibid*, p 253.

right to a judgment within a reasonable time and, finally, the right to an independent and impartial tribunal.

"Criminal Charge"

[6–43] The ECtHR has defined the concept of "criminal charge" for the purposes of the ECHR. In *Engel v Netherlands*[107] the ECtHR set out three factors which must be taken into consideration when determining a "criminal charge": 1. the domestic classification of the proceedings; 2. the essential nature of the offence; and 3. the nature of the penalty that could be imposed, giving due regard to any loss of liberty. With regard to the classification of the proceedings under domestic law, once an activity is classed as criminal under domestic law, Art 6 will be triggered, even if the issue is relatively trivial.

[6–44] The *Engel* factors were endorsed in *Ezeh and Connors v United Kingdom.*[108] In that case the applicants were serving sentences for rape and during their prison terms both had infringed the Prison Rules. The Governor of the Prison tried both applicants and sentenced them to additional time in custody.[109] The applicants had no legal representation during these proceedings. The ECtHR applied the *Engel* criteria to the case. In its consideration of the position of the proceedings under domestic law, the ECtHR noted that, although the disciplinary Prison Rules applied only to inmates, they corresponded to domestic criminal law offences, and could therefore be seen as analogous to them. Regarding the nature and the severity of the offence the ECtHR held that the offences were "criminal" for the purposes of Art 6. As there was normally a right of remission under domestic law, the additional time served of 40 days for Ezeh and seven for Connors equated to a new deprivation of liberty, since the prisoners' sentences were effectively extended. The respondent State argued that, in order to maintain discipline in prisons, prison governors required an amount of flexibility allowing them to impose punishment of loss of remission; even if the proceedings might not necessarily comply with Art 6, they could be seen as proportionate and necessary. The ECtHR, nevertheless, decided that there was a breach of Art 6 as other sanctions were open to the prison governor which would allow him to maintain discipline.

[6–45] Article 6(1) applies all the way throughout the criminal process, from the time a person is charged, right up to possible appeal and sentencing.[110] It does not, however, apply to proceedings which take place after conviction and sentencing, e.g. applications for a review of sentence after a domestic decision has become *res judicata*,[111] or applications

---

[107] (1979–80) EHRR 647.

[108] (2004) 39 EHRR 1.

[109] One of the applicants had threatened to kill a probation officer and was sentenced to 40 extra days in custody and the other had collided with a prison officer during exercise and was sentenced to seven additional days.

[110] See *Eckle v Federal Republic of Germany* (1983). 5 EHRR 1 at paras 76–77 and *Phillips v United Kingdom*, No 41087/98, 5 September 2001, ECHR 2001-VII. See also *T v United Kingdom*, No 24724/94 and *V v United Kingdom*, (2000) 30 EHRR 121.

[111] *X v Austria*, No 1237/61, Decision of 5 March 1962 (1962) 5 YCHR 96 at 102.

for provisional release pending trial,[112] etc.[113] The ECtHR has defined a "charge" for the purpose of this provision as "the official notification given to an individual by the competent authority of an allegation that he has committed a criminal offence".[114] The ECtHR also stated in *Foti* that a charge can, "in some instances take the form of measures which carry the implication of such an allegation and which likewise substantially affect the situation of the suspect".[115]

The application of Art 6(1) was considered in the case of *Delcourt*[116] where the respondent State claimed that Art 6 did not apply to decisions of the Belgian Court of Cassation since that court did not assess the merits of a case. However, the ECtHR decided that even though the Belgian court only had the power to confirm or quash a decision and did not have the power to reverse a decision or to replace it, it was still involved in "determining" a criminal charge. **[6–46]**

Public Hearing and Pronouncement

There may be seen to be two aspects to this; that the hearing should take place in public, and that, by implication, it should have an oral element, and not depend solely on writing. This reference to "public" should be taken to include the Press,[117] whose informative role is more fully explored within the materials on Art 10. **[6–47]**

In the various contracting States, there are, of course, differences as to court systems, but they fall into only two categories as regards Art 6—those instantly recognisable as a "classic" court, spending all its time hearing criminal or civil cases, and others. The latter is the more problematic, as it is necessary to consider tribunals, administrative or quasi-judicial entities, such as professional disciplinary bodies.[118] These may well qualify as either civil or criminal for the purposes of Art 6, and therefore if the decisions, perhaps affecting a person's right to practice a profession, are "... subject to review by a judicial body that has full jurisdiction",[119] then any failure of public hearing may be remedied under Art 6.

However, Art 6(1) also lists exhaustive grounds on which it is justifiable to restrict access to court proceedings, and it is clear that this gives a considerable margin of appreciation to States in this matter. For instance, the ECtHR has stated that prison disciplinary hearings can be held in private in the case of *Campbell and Fell v United Kingdom*.[120] Here, the ECtHR declared that there were significant public order and **[6–48]**

---

[112] *Neumeister v Austria*, No 1936/63, 27 June 1968, Series A No 8 (1979–80) 1 EHRR 91.

[113] For example, Art 6(1) does not apply to an application for release on probation or parole (*X v Austria*, No 606/59, 19 September 1961 (1961) 4 *Yearbook* 340). It does not apply to applications for a retrial (*Fischer v Austria*, No 27569/02, Decision of 6 May 2003); or to proceedings after a decision that the applicant was unfit to plead (*Antoine v United Kingdom*, No 62960/00, Decision of 13 May 2003).

[114] *Eckle v Germany*, (1983) 5 EHRR 1 at para 73.

[115] *Foti v Italy*, 5 EHRR 313 at para 52.

[116] *Delcourt v Belgium*, (1979–80) 1 EHRR 355.

[117] See *Axen v Federal Republic of Germany* (1984) 6 EHRR 195

[118] See the section on "Independent and Impartial Tribunal" *infra*.

[119] *Riepan v Austria*, No 35115/97, judgment of 14 November 2000.

[120] (1984) 7 EHRR 165.

security issues which would be involved if these proceedings were conducted in public, thereby imposing a disproportionate burden on the State.

It should also be noted that, although a complete lack of publicity cannot be justified, professional disciplinary proceedings may be held in private depending on the circumstances. In this instance, some factors that should be taken into account when deciding if a public hearing is necessary include consideration for professional confidentiality and the private lives of clients or patients.[121]

[6–49] In the case of *B and P v United Kingdom,*[122] the ECtHR found no violation of a fair trial when hearings were held *in camera* concerning child custody proceedings. The judge had discretion to allow a public hearing, and had exercised that discretion in the interests of the child. Here the ECtHR found that the judgment and reasoning were available to interested parties, thereby satisfying, to some degree, the public aspect of the hearing.

[6–50] The pronouncing of judgment is, likewise, subject to interpretation by the ECtHR. It is clear that the phrase "pronounced publicly" does not necessarily mean that the judgment has always to be read out in court. In the case of *Pretto v Italy*[123] the ECtHR declared that it:

> "... considers that in each case the form of publicity to be given to the 'judgment' under the domestic law of the respondent state must be assessed in the light of the special features of the proceedings in question and by reference to the object and purpose of Article 6 (1)".[124]

So depositing the judgment in the court registry, which made the full text of the judgment available to everyone, was, in this case, sufficient to satisfy the requirement of being "pronounced publicly". The essence of the right is that the judgment is available, suggesting that it does not have to be thrust under the nose of the public, but must not be unduly hidden or difficult to access. This can also be seen in the case of *Sutter v Switzerland*[125] where the ECtHR held that public delivery of a decision of a military court appeal was not necessary, as public access to that decision was available by obtaining a copy of the judgment from the court registry and by its subsequent publication in an official collection of case law.

[6–51] In *Axen v Federal Republic of Germany*[126] the ECtHR found that public oral delivery of a judgment of the Supreme Court was unnecessary given that the judgments of the lower courts had been pronounced publicly.

However, in the cases of *Werner v Austria*[127] and *Szucs v Austria,*[128] judgment was not given in public either by the courts of first instance or the courts of appeal, nor were

---

121 *Albert and Le Compte v Belgium* (1983) 5 EHRR 533.

122 (2002) 34 EHRR 19.

123 *Pretto v Italy* (1983) No 7984/77, judgment of 8 December 1983.

124 *Pretto v Italy,* No 7984/77, judgment of 8 December 1983 at para 26.

125 *Sutter v Switzerland* 6 EHRR 272, judgment of 2 February 1984.

126 *Axen v Federal Republic of Germany* (1984) 6 EHRR 195.

127 *Werner v Austria* No 21835/93, judgement of 24 November 1997.

128 *Szucs v Austria* (1997) 26 EHRR 310.

the full texts of their judgments openly available to the public in their registries, and access was limited to those with a "legitimate interest". Here, the ECtHR found that there had been a violation of Art 6 in that the access to the judicial pronouncements had not been sufficiently widely available.

The ECtHR also found a violation in *Campbell and Fell v United Kingdom*,[129] where, in prison disciplinary hearings, the Board of Visitors did not pronounce its judgment publicly and took no other actions to make any decision public.

A "Reasonable Time"

This concept[130] has been decided by the ECtHR as being necessary in order to "... protect all parties to court proceedings... against excessive procedural delays".[131] In actuality, what it does is more to incentivise against undue delay. The "clock" starts in terms of what might constitute a reasonable time when the person is charged with a criminal offence, which is logical.[132] However, in civil cases there is no such definitive point, so the time usually commences from the date of the initiation of court proceedings. In either situation the determination of the "clock" stopping is when the case is finally decided; the ECtHR will then look at any application to see if the particular case has taken longer than a reasonable time to have been concluded. In neither civil nor criminal cases is there an absolute time limit, and the issues are always determined by the particular facts of the case in point. **[6–52]**

The complexity of the case will be determined by a number of elements; questions of fact as well as legal issues,[133] the nature of the facts that are to be established,[134] together with the number of accused persons and/or witnesses,[135] or even whether there may be international aspects.[136] Plainly, the more complex the case, the longer the proceedings may be seen as reasonable, so, for example, in the complex case of *Boddaert v Belgium*[137] six years and three months was not considered unreasonable by the ECtHR. **[6–53]**

Nevertheless, even in very complex cases, unreasonable delays can be found, so that in the case of *Ferantelli and Santangelo v Italy*,[138] which concerned not only a complex murder trial, but also had the additional issues of dealing with juveniles, the ECtHR felt, even so, that 16 years was unreasonable as a time scale. **[6–54]**

---

129 (1984) 7 EHRR 165.

130 This is also considered by Art 5(3), which stipulates that "Everyone arrested or detained ... shall be brought promptly before a judge or other officer authorised by law to exercise judicial power and shall be entitled to trial within a reasonable time or to release pending trial."

131 *Strogmuller v Austria* (1969) 1 EHRR 155.

132 Since criminal proceedings potentially impact more seriously on the person of the applicant, they will usually be considered more urgently, particularly where pre-trial detention is concerned.

133 *Katte Klitsche de la Grange v Italy*, (1994) 19 EHRR 368.

134 *Triggiani v Italy*, (1991) ECHR 20, No 13509/87.

135 *Angelucci v Italy*, No 12666/87, judgment of 19 February 1991; *Andreucci v Italy*, No 12955/87, judgment of 27 February 1992.

136 *Manzoni v Italy*, No 19218/91, judgment of 1 July 1997.

137 No 12919/87 (1992). The case was particularly complex since it concerned a difficult murder enquiry and the parallel progression of two cases.

138 [1996] 23 EHRR 288.

Plainly, if it is the applicant who has caused some delay, this will obviously weaken the strength of his or her complaint, but this should not be confused with the concept that an applicant has made full use of all procedures in pursuing his or her case; indeed, an applicant is not required to co-operate actively in expediting the proceedings which might lead to his or her own conviction.[139] The ECtHR stated in *Unión Alimentaria Sanders SA v Spain* that the applicant's duty is only to " ... show diligence in carrying out the procedural steps relevant to him, to refrain from using delaying tactics and to avail himself of the scope afforded by domestic law for shortening the proceedings".[140]

[6–55] Delays which are attributable to the State may be taken into account when determining whenever there has been compliance with the reasonable time guarantee, and the State will be held responsible for delays caused by all its administrative or judicial authorities. When dealing with cases concerning length of proceedings, the ECtHR has also had regard to the point that domestic courts are under a duty to deal properly with the cases before them.

The ECtHR held in the case of *Zimmerman and Steiner v Switzerland* that contracting States have a duty to " ... organise their legal systems so as to allow the courts to comply with the requirements of Article 6 (1) including that of trial within a reasonable time".[141] This means that there is a clear duty on domestic courts to ensure that all those who play a role in the proceedings do their utmost to avoid any unnecessary delay.

Independent and Impartial Tribunal

[6–56] There is a close interrelationship between these two aspects of the Art 6 guarantee, since any tribunal not independent of the executive power[142] of the State is likely to be in breach of the impartiality requirement when the State is involved in the action.[143] In the case of *Zand v Austria*, the ECtHR stated:

> "It is the object and purpose of the clause in Article 6 (1) requiring that the courts shall be 'established by law' that the judicial organisation in a democratic society must not depend on the discretion of the Executive, but that it should be regulated by law emanating from Parliament. However, this does not mean that delegated legislation is as such unacceptable in matters concerning the judicial organisation. Article 6 (1) does not require the legislature to regulate each and every detail in this field by formal Act of Parliament, if the legislature establishes at least the organisational frame-work for the judicial organisation."[144]

---

[139] *Eckle v FRG* (1983) 5 EHRR 1 at para 82

[140] No 11681/85 1989 at para 35

[141] *Zimmerman and Steiner v Switzerland* (1983) 6 EHRR 17 at para 29. Where the reason for a delay was a long-term backlog of work in the State's court system, there was a violation of the reasonable time guarantee in Art 6 as the State had not taken adequate measures to cope with the situation. It is unlikely that a violation would be found where the backlog is only temporary and/or exceptional and the State has taken the necessary remedial action reasonably promptly. Once again, we look to proportionality.

[142] The tribunal must be independent of both the executive and the parties: *Ringeisen v Austria*, (1979–80) 1 EHRR 455.

[143] See *Cooper v UK* (2003) 39 EHRR 171.

[144] *Zand v Austria* (1978) 15 DR 70 at para 69.

The test employed to decide if there is a breach is not only subjective, where there is proof of bias, but also objective where there may be seen to be doubt that the requirement has been met. Taking these together, independence can be considered in terms of the manner of appointment of tribunal members, the duration of their office, the ability to withstand outside pressures and, lastly, whether the body presents an appearance of independence.[145]

Taking these indicators in turn, the presence of judicial or legally-qualified members in a tribunal will be taken to be a sign of its independence.[146]

In the second place, if the members of a tribunal are appointed for fixed terms of reasonable length, then this will also be an indicator of independence, so that in the case of *Le Compte v Belgium,*[147] the provision of a fixed six-year term fulfilled this requirement. More contentiously, in *Campbell and Fell*[148] the Prison Board of Visitors' members were appointed for only three years, but, although this was considered by the ECtHR to be somewhat short, it was acknowledged that, since the posts were unpaid and it was difficult to get adequately-qualified members, it did not constitute a violation of Art 6. **[6–57]**

However, the objective "appearance of independence" test was considered to have been breached in the case of *Findlay.*[149] The case concerned an Army court martial where the convening officer decided what charges were brought, appointed the members of the court martial (who were of inferior rank to himself, and under his direct command in some cases), confirmed the court martial sentence, and, indeed, was empowered to vary it. Finally he had the power to dissolve the whole process. Perhaps unsurprisingly, there were considered to be doubts as to the appearance of the independence and impartiality of the process as a whole.

This was also seen in *Piersack v Belgium,* in which the trial judge had previously been employed as head of the prosecution department which had investigated and instigated the case originally. Although there was no indication of bias on the part of the judge, the ECtHR still held that there had been a breach of this objective test, saying that if: **[6–58]**

> " ... an individual, after holding in the public prosecutor's department an office whose nature is such that he may have to deal with a given matter in the course of his duties,

---

[145] E.g. *Campbell and Fell v United Kingdom* (1984) 7 EHRR 165, *Findlay v United Kingdom* (1997) 24 EHRR 221 in terms of independence, and on the requirement of impartiality, *McGonnell v UK* (2000) *Times*, 22nd February 2000. *Re: Pinochet (No 2)* [2000] 1 AC 119. Tribunal was defined in the above terms in *Belilos v Switzerland* (1988) 10 EHRR 466 at para 64.

[146] Members of a tribunal appointed by the executive will not in itself violate the ECHR: *Campbell and Fell v United Kingdom* (1984) 7 EHRR 165. To establish a violation of Art 6, the applicant would need to show that the practice as a whole was unsatisfactory, or that the establishment of the particular tribunal was influenced by motives suggesting an attempt to achieve a particular outcome: *Zand v Austria* (1978) 15 DR 70.

[147] *Albert and Le Compte v Belgium* (1983) 5 EHRR 533.

[148] *Campbell and Fell v United Kingdom* (1984) 7 EHRR 165.

[149] *Findlay v United Kingdom* (1997) 24 EHRR 221.

> subsequently sits in the same case as a judge, the public are entitled to fear that he does not offer sufficient guarantees of impartiality".[150]

The ECtHR went on to say that:

> " ... whilst impartiality normally denotes absence of prejudice or bias, its existence or otherwise can, notably under Article 6 (1) of the Convention, be tested in various ways. A distinction can be drawn in this context between a subjective approach, that is endeavouring to ascertain the personal conviction of a given judge in a given case, and an objective approach, that is, determining whether he offered guarantees sufficient to exclude any legitimate doubt in this respect".[151]

[6–59] There may also be bias on the part of other members of the court, but, where a domestic court has properly considered an allegation of bias and concluded that the trial was conducted fairly, the ECtHR will generally be unwilling to question the decision. To illustrate this we can contrast the cases of *Gregory v United Kingdom*[152] and *Sander v United Kingdom.*[153]

In the case of *Gregory* a note was passed to the judge from the jury stating: "Jury showing racial overtones. 1 member to be excused." The judge subsequently released the note to both the prosecution and the defence, and warned the jury to try the case according to the evidence and to put aside any prejudices. The ECtHR held that this action had been sufficient to discharge the onus of Art 6. It also considered it significant that the defence counsel had not pressed for discharge of the jury or questioned them in open court as to whether they were capable of returning a verdict on the evidence alone. The trial judge had acted clearly and decisively.

[6–60] In the later case of *Sander*, however, where there was a similar allegation of racism, the ECtHR considered that the judge's response to the allegation had been inadequate and that therefore a violation of Art 6 had occurred. Although the defence applied for a retrial, the judge asked the jury to consider their position overnight, and was told the next day in a letter that a juror who had made racist jokes apologised and claimed not to be racially biased.

The ECtHR stated that:

> " ... the judge should have reacted in a more robust manner than merely seeking vague assurances that jurors could set aside their prejudices and try the case solely on the evidence. By failing to do so, the judge did not provide sufficient guarantees to exclude any objectively justified or legitimate doubts as to the impartiality of the court. It follows that the court that condemned the applicant was not impartial from an objective point of view".[154]

---

150 *Piersack v Belgium* (1982) 5 EHRR 169 at para 30. See also *De Cubber v Belgium* (1984) 7 EHRR 236 and *Thorgeir Thorgeirson v Iceland* (1992) 14 EHRR 843, where the judge took over the prosecution role during the trial.

151 *Piersack v Belgium* (1982) 5 EHRR 169 at para 30.

152 *Gregory v United Kingdom* (1997) 25 EHRR 577.

153 *Sander v United Kingdom* (2001) 31 EHRR 44.

154 *ibid* at para 29.

Gregory was distinguished as there had been an allegation of racism but no admission, and the complaint had been imprecise. It is interesting to note that in the case of *Gregory* the vote was eight to one, whilst in *Sander* it was four to three.

Presumption of Innocence

Article 6(2) guarantees the presumption of innocence, and is independent of the other Art 6 guarantees, which means that there may well be a breach of this particular paragraph without necessarily breaching the rest of Art 6.[155] It extends to those who are concerned only with criminal offences, but only once they have actually been charged,[156] and has no application to procedures within a criminal investigation, such as blood, urine or breath testing, medical examinations or orders to produce documentation. It was stated in the case of *Barberá, Messegué and Jabardo v Spain* that the presumption of innocence: **[6–61]**

> " … requires, inter alia, that when carrying out their duties, the members of a court should not start with the preconceived idea that the accused has committed the offence charged; the burden of proof is on the prosecution, and any doubt should benefit the accused".[157]

This does not suggest a ban on proceedings or regulations which transfer the burden of proof to the accused to establish his or her defence, if the overall burden of establishing guilt remains with the prosecution. Nor does Art 6(2) necessarily prohibit presumptions of law or fact. The reality is that any rule which purports to shift the burden of proof,[158] or which applies any presumption against the accused, must be within " … reasonable limits which take into account the importance of what is at stake and maintain the rights of the defence".[159] In other words, we are once again looking at reasonableness and proportionality. **[6–62]**

There is an argument here concerning the presumption of innocence and the freedom from self-incrimination, so that a domestic law requirement on a driver to say who had been driving a car during the commission of a driving offence was compatible with Art 6.[160] It fulfilled a public objective of keeping drunk drivers off the roads, and could not lead to a charge without other evidence being adduced of an offence. The obverse, inferences drawn from silence, was examined in the case of *Murray (John) v United Kingdom*,[161] where the applicant refused to explain his presence at the scene of a crime or to give evidence in court. The ECtHR considered that, given the weight of additional evidence, the inference of guilt drawn by the trial jury was "a matter **[6–63]**

---

155 *I and C v Switzerland*, No 10107/82, (1985) 48 DR 35

156 *Adolf v Austria* (1982) 4 EHRR 313.

157 (1989) 11 EHRR 360 at para 77.

158 Note *Lingens and Leitgens v Austria*, No 8803/79, (1983) 26 DR 171, where the burden of proof in criminal defamation cases to show that the statement is true does not contravene Art 6(2).

159 *Salabiaku v France* (1988) 13 EHRR 379 at para 28.

160 *Brown v Stott (Procurator Fiscal)* [2003] 1 AC 681.

161 *Murray (John) v United Kingdom* (1994) 22 EHRR 29.

of common sense and cannot be regarded as unfair or unreasonable in the circumstances." In addition, it did not have "the effect of shifting the burden of proof from the prosecution to the defence so as to infringe the principle of the presumption of innocence".[162]

[6–64] Nor does Art 6(2) contravene the principle of strict liability offences, which may be seen in the case of *Salabiaku v France*[163] which concerned the strict liability offence of drug smuggling, but the applicant contended that he had no knowledge of the drugs which were found in his luggage; meaning that the *actus reus* of smuggling was presumed from the fact of possession. The ECtHR held that a rebuttable presumption was not inconsistent with Art 6(2), the more so as there was an unused defence which may have shown it as being impossible to have known the contents of the luggage. Other rebuttable presumptions which have been held as consistent with the Art 6(2) requirement are that someone living with a prostitute could be assumed to be living off her earnings,[164] that a dog was dangerous by reason of its breed[165] and that a company director could be guilty of an offence committed by the company.[166] Article 6(3), which also applies only to criminal offences, sets out the rights of the defendant, namely, to be informed promptly of the nature and cause of the accusation against him,[167] to have adequate time and facilities for the preparation of a defence,[168] to defend himself in person or through legal assistance,[169] to examine witnesses against him and to obtain examination of witnesses on his behalf under the same conditions as witnesses against him,[170] and to have the assistance of an interpreter if he cannot understand or speak the language used in court.[171]

Article 6(3)(a)

[6–65] This sub-paragraph has similar wording to that in Art 5(2), which concerns persons detained pending trial, but the purpose of the two are very different, as Art 5(2) is for the aid of those challenging their imprisonment, and Art 6(3)(a) is concerned with the defendant challenging the accusation. This provision is linked to the information that

---

162 *ibid* at para 54.

163 *Salabiaku v France* (1988) 13 EHRR 379.

164 *X v UK*, No 5124/71, (1972) 42 CD 135.

165 *Bullock v United Kingdom* (1996) 21 EHRR 85.

166 *G v Malta*, No 16641/90 (1991) DA.

167 *Brozicek v Italy* (1989) 12 EHRR 371 and *Kamasinski v Austria* (1991) 13 EHRR 36.

168 *Can v Austria* (1985) 8 EHRR 14 at para 53 (Series A, No 96) and *Hadjianastassiou v Greece* (1996) 16 EHRR 219. The right of an accused to communicate with his or her lawyer has been recognised in a number of cases, e.g. *Campbell and Fell v UK* (1984) 7 EHRR 165.

169 *Pakelli v FRG* (1983) 6 EHRR 1, *Poitrimol v France* (1993) 18 EHRR 130.

170 Art 6(c)(d) provides for the right of an accused "to examine or have examined witnesses against him and to obtain the attendance and examination of witnesses on his behalf under the same conditions as witnesses against him." Note: this is not an absolute right (see, e.g. *Bricmont v Belgium* (1990) 12 EHRR 217. On the issue of anonymity in respect of witnesses, see, e.g. *Doorson v Netherlands* (1996) 22 EHRR 330.

171 *Kamasinski v Austria* (1991) 13 EHRR 36.

is required to be given to the accused at the time of the charge.[172] In *Mattocia v Italy*[173] the accused was given insufficient information about the time and place of the offence he was alleged to have committed, which the ECtHR ruled was part of the "material facts" which formed the basis of the allegation. Whilst the level of detail of information must, of necessity, vary from case to case, the accused:

> " ... must at any rate be provided with sufficient information as is necessary to understand fully the extent of the charges against him with a view to preparing an adequate defence".[174]

Although there are no formal requirements imposed on the method of giving information about the charge by Art 6(3)(a), this would usually be in writing, but if it is given orally,[175] then it must be comprehensible to the accused.[176] **[6–66]**

In the case of *Brozicek v Italy*,[177] where the accused was German, and made clear his difficulties with the Italian language to the domestic court, the ECtHR held that the Italian authorities had the responsibility to get the information translated unless they had reasonable grounds for believing that he could understand. This holds true for the applicant *or* his lawyer,[178] and the cost of such translation must be met by the State.[179]

Article 6(3)(b)

The definition of "adequate time and facilities for preparation of his defence" can be seen in the case of *Can v Austria*, where it was held that the accused must have " ... the opportunity to organise his defence in an appropriate way and without restriction as to the possibility to put all relevant defence arguments before the trial court, and thus to influence the proceedings".[180] Like Art 6(1), the "clock" on reasonable time will run from the moment a suspect is subject to the criminal charge, and will depend very much on the particular facts of the case and particularly the complexity. A principal issue is that the defence lawyer must have sufficient time to allow proper preparation of the case.[181] **[6–67]**

---

172 In the jurisprudence of the ECtHR the term "charge" is an autonomous concept which applies irrespective of the definition of a "charge" in domestic law. In the case of *Deweer v Belgium* (6903/75) (1980) ECHR 1 the ECtHR stated that the word "charge" should be given a substantive rather than a formal meaning, and it would look behind the appearances and investigate the realities of the procedure in question.

173 *Mattocia v Italy* (2000) 36 EHRR 825.

174 *ibid* at para 59. See also *Brozicek v Italy* (1989) 12 EHRR 371.

175 It may be sufficient to give this information during the questioning sessions immediately following arrest: *Kamasinski v Austria* (1989) 13 EHRR 36.

176 If posted, proof of delivery is required, and in the case of the accused having mental difficulties, then appropriate action must be taken to ensure understanding of the accusation: *Vaudelle v France* (2001) 37 EHRR 397.

177 *Brozicek v Italy* (1989) 12 EHRR 371.

178 *X v Austria*, No 6185/73 (1975) 2 DR 68.

179 Under Art 6(3)(e).

180 *Can v Austria* (1985) 8 EHRR 14 at para 53 (Series A, No 96).

181 *Ocalan v Turkey* (2005) 41 EHRR 45, where two weeks to prepare a 17,000-page file was found to be insufficient time in the Grand Chamber's judgment. However, in *X and Y v Austria*, No 7909/77, (1978) 15 DR 160, 17 days was considered "adequate" in a trial for misappropriation.

This principle implies a presumption that the accused's lawyer has unrestricted and confidential access to any client held in pre-trial detention in order to discuss all elements of the case. The right of the accused to communicate freely with his or her lawyer in the preparation of his or her defence may be considered as essential to the concept of a fair trial.[182] Where the accused, or his or her lawyers, allege that adequate facilities[183] have not been provided in order to prepare a defence, then the judge has the responsibility to decide whether or not the trial can go ahead without violating Art 6(3)(b).

[6–68] There may be justified restrictions, for instance, in the detention of those classified as exceptionally dangerous prisoners or persons charged with particularly serious terrorist offences. In one instance, the restriction was that the applicants were unable to receive legal visits for three weeks, and only able to correspond with their lawyers under judicial supervision during that period.[184] Once the legal visits had been authorised they were not monitored, and the Commission held that overall this was proportionate and reasonable in the circumstances.

[6–69] Facilities could also include access to documentation and evidence, and the Commission held in the case of *Jespers v Belgium* that:

> " ... the 'facilities' which everyone charged with a criminal offence should enjoy include the opportunity to acquaint himself, for the purposes of preparing his defence, with the results of investigations carried out throughout the proceedings. Furthermore, the Commission has already recognised that although a right of access to the prosecution file is not expressly guaranteed by the Convention, such a right can be inferred from Article 6, paragraph 3.b ... It matters little, moreover, by whom and when the investigations are ordered or under whose authority they are carried out ... In short, Article 6, paragraph 3.b, recognises the right of the accused to have at his disposal, for the purposes of exonerating himself or of obtaining a reduction in his sentence, all relevant elements that have been or could be collected by the competent authorities".[185]

The Commission added that this right was restricted to those facilities which assist or may assist in defence, and limitations on the disclosure of evidence to the applicant have been found acceptable where there is a sound reason in the interests of justice, even though the evidence was, arguably, of some significance to the defence.[186]

[6–70] In *Rowe and Davis v United Kingdom*[187] and *Fitt v United Kingdom*[188] the ECtHR looked at procedures for withholding evidence on public interest grounds and found that there would be compliance with Art 6 if the trial judge could see the evidence and decide whether or not to disclose this to the defence. This all comes back to the concept of an "equality of arms" between the prosecution and the defence. In addition, in terms of any appeal hearing subsequent to the trial, this equality will be maintained,

---

182 *Campbell and Fell v United Kingdom* (1984) 7 EHRR 165.
183 *Ocalan v Turkey* (2005) 41 EHRR 45.
184 *Kröcher and Möller v Switzerland*, No 8463/78, (1981) 26 DR 24.
185 *Jespers v Belgium*, No 8403/7827, (1981) 27 DR 61.
186 *Kurup v Denmark*, No 11219/63, (1968) 12 YB 438. In this case, to protect the identity of an informer.
187 *Rowe and Davis v United Kingdom* (2000) 30 EHRR 1.
188 *Fitt v United Kingdom* (2000) 30 EHRR 480.

although, for practical purposes, there will usually be a shorter time limit for compliance during the appeal process compared with that of the original trial.

Article 6(3)(c)

This really leads on from the above section, and the equality of arms consideration that both prosecution and defence should have no particular advantage, thereby ensuring fairness of trial. Although a person usually has the right to represent him- or herself, the ECtHR has held that this is not an absolute right. In the case of *Croissant v Germany*[189] it held that the requirement that a defendant be assisted by a lawyer at the domestic court proceedings was not incompatible with Art 6(3)(c). In contrast, in the case of *Brandstetter v Austria*[190] the ECtHR said that, although there was no finding of a violation of Art 6(3)(c), on the facts: [6–71]

> " ... the position might be different if it were established that, as a consequence of national law or practice in this respect being unduly severe, the risk of subsequent prosecution is such that the defendant is genuinely inhibited from freely exercising (his rights of defence)".[191]

However, a defence will usually mean the services of a lawyer and this may mean State-funded legal aid, since the State cannot require a person charged with a criminal offence to appear without representation.[192] In *Poitrimol* it was stated:

> "Although not absolute, the right of everyone charged with a criminal offence to be effectively defended by a lawyer, assigned officially if need be, is one of the fundamental features of a fair trial".[193]

If it is found that the accused has the right to free legal assistance, this must be practical and effective rather than merely theoretical and illusory, and is relevant throughout the trial and pre-trial process. In *Öcalan v Turkey,*[194] there was held to be a violation where the interrogation by various State functionaries carried on over seven days without the accused being allowed access to his lawyer. In the case of *Murray (John) v United Kingdom,*[195] where the terrorist suspect was detained under legislation allowing him no legal access for 48 hours, the ECtHR also found a violation. The reasoning included the fact that he had refused to answer any questions during that time, and adverse inferences could be drawn by the domestic court from that fact. The concept of "fairness", it held, was that to: [6–72]

> " ... deny access to a lawyer for the first forty-eight hours of police questioning, in a situation where the rights of the defence may well be irretrievably prejudiced, is - whatever the justification for such denial - incompatible with the rights of the accused under Article 6".[196]

---

[189] *Croissant v Germany* (1993) 16 EHRR 135.
[190] *Brandstetter v Austria* (1991) 15 EHRR 378.
[191] *ibid* at para 51.
[192] *Pakelli v FRG* (1983) 6 EHRR 1.
[193] *Poitrimol v France* (1993) 18 EHRR 130 at para 34.
[194] *Ocalan v Turkey* (2005) 41 EHRR 45.
[195] *Murray (John) v United Kingdom* (1994) 22 EHRR 29.
[196] *ibid* at para 63.

Article 6(3)(d)

[6–73] This provision does not give an accused an absolute right to call witnesses, nor does it confer a right to force the domestic courts to hear a particular witness. In order to bring an action, the applicant must therefore establish that the failure to hear a particular witness prejudiced his or her case.

It does not generally apply at the pre-trial stage, so, for instance, witnesses being questioned by the police cannot be questioned by the suspect. The domestic law of a State will have individual criteria for the admission of witnesses and the competent authorities can usually refuse to call a witness if it appears that their evidence will not be relevant. In addition, States often have rules which excuse some witnesses, such as family members, from giving evidence. This type of provision is manifestly not incompatible with Art 6(1) and 6(3)(d), as seen in the case of *Unterpertinger*,[197] where the ECtHR noted that the domestic court did not treat the statements by the applicant's former wife and step-daughter as items of information, but rather as proof of the truth of the accusations made by the women at the time. Since the applicant's conviction was based mainly on this evidence, the rights of the defence had not been sufficiently safeguarded in this instance.

[6–74] The majority of the cases in this area concern witnesses who are unable to be questioned for various reasons, some to safeguard witnesses against reprisals,[198] to protect police operational methods, such as informers,[199] or so that sex crime victims do not have to face their accused abuser.[200] In addition, there is an issue where a witness has simply disappeared,[201] fallen ill[202] or died.[203]

[6–75] In *Kostovski v Netherlands*[204] the ECtHR found a breach where a conviction was based to a decisive extent on the statements of two anonymous witnesses who gave evidence in the absence of the accused. This was based on the fact that their evidence was considered "decisive", but the ECtHR has not been entirely clear in its language about where the line should lie. It is accepted that the defence should have the opportunity to examine witnesses where the evidence forms the "main"[205] or "only"[206] basis for the conviction, but the right has also found to be engaged where the evidence only "played a part" in the conviction.[207]

197 *Unterpertinger v Austria* (1986) 13 EHRR 175, *Asch v Austria* (1991) 15 EHRR 597, the latter extending the group to include an unmarried partner.
198 *Van Mechelen v Netherlands* (1997) 25 EHRR 647.
199 *Lüdi v Switzerland* (1992) 15 EHRR 173, *Van Mechelen v Netherlands* (1997) 25 EHRR 647.
200 *SN v Sweden* (2002) 39 EHRR 304.
201 *Verdam v Netherlands* (1999) 28 EHRR CD 61.
202 *Bricmont v Belgium* (1990) 12 EHRR 217, *Kennedy v United Kingdom* (1998) 27 EHRR CD 266.
203 *Ferrantelli and Santangelo v Italy* (1996) 23 EHRR 288.
204 *Kostovski v Netherlands* (1989) 22 EHRR 330.
205 *Unterpertinger v Austria* (1986) 13 EHRR 175.
206 *Asch v Austria* (1991) 15 EHRR 597.
207 *Lüdi v Switzerland* (1992) 15 EHRR 173.

In the case of *Doorson v Netherlands*[208] the ECtHR explicitly took into account the interests of witnesses in its decision making, acknowledging the potential danger to witnesses who testify in criminal cases and the difficulties the State faces in securing that testimony: **[6–76]**

> "It is true that Article 6 does not explicitly require the interests of witnesses in general, and those of victims called upon to testify in particular, to be taken into consideration. However, their life, liberty or security of person may be at stake, as may interests coming generally within the ambit of Article 8 of the Convention. Such interests of witnesses and victims are in principle protected by other, substantive provisions of the Convention, which imply that Contracting States should organise their criminal proceedings in such a way that those interests are not unjustifiably imperilled. Against this background, principles of fair trial also require that in appropriate cases the interests of the defence are balanced against those of witnesses or victims called upon to testify".[209]

The case concerned the conviction of the applicant for a drug charge, based primarily on the evidence of two anonymous witnesses whose identities were known to the judge and who had been questioned at the appeals stage by the applicant's counsel, though not by the applicant, and a statement made to police by a witness who later disappeared (though with no suggestion of foul play) and so did not testify at trial. Finally, a statement made to police by a witness who then recanted the statement at the trial was also considered.

This obviously raised some questions for the ECtHR, but it considered that the use of anonymous witness statements at trial was not incompatible with the ECHR in all circumstances. The problems for the defence had been counterbalanced by the procedures followed by the judicial authorities,[210] and had been sufficient to enable the defence to challenge the witness evidence. In this instance, the domestic court had treated the witness evidence with the necessary circumspection and there had been, therefore, no violation of Art 6(3)(d). **[6–77]**

The *Doorson* case is significant in that it found that a defendant's right under Art 6(3)(d) could be limited by consideration of the interests of witnesses and potential victims. In the case of *SN v Sweden* the applicant was not given the chance to question a 10-year-old boy, whose statements relating to alleged sexual abuse by his teacher, were "virtually the sole evidence on which the courts' findings of guilt were based".[211] The boy was interviewed twice by police, the first being recorded on videotape and the second, five months later, on audiotape. The applicant's counsel consented to not being present during the latter interview, but did consult with the police as to the nature of questions that were to be put to the boy by the specially trained police unit involved. **[6–78]**

---

208 *Doorson v Netherlands* (1996) 22 EHRR 330.

209 *ibid* at para 70.

210 It was felt that the court of appeal's decision to preserve the anonymity of witnesses had been correctly motivated by the need to protect them from the risk of reprisals. The defence counsel had been able to question the witnesses, and the witnesses had identified the applicant from a photograph which he had acknowledged to be of himself.

211 *SN v Sweden* (2002) 39 EHRR 304 at para 46.

[6–79] The ECtHR was concerned with the "special features" of sexual offence proceedings, particularly the trauma which may have been involved for the child, and the potential issues under Art 8 of the ECHR. In its decision, the ECtHR held that there was no violation, finding it crucial that the applicant's lawyer had been involved in the line of questioning, and that this was sufficient to enable a challenge to the witness. In addition, the taped evidence played in court was sufficient to enable the applicant to challenge the statements and the witness's credibility.

It seems clear that the case law under Art 6(3)(d) is very dependent on the particular facts of the case before the ECtHR, and as it stated in the case of *Van Mechelen*:

> "Having regard to the place that the right to a fair administration of justice holds in a democratic society, any measures restricting the right of the defence should be strictly necessary. If a less restrictive measure can suffice then that measure should be applied".[212]

Article 6(3)(e)

[6–80] It has been seen above that the full participation of an accused person in his or her trial is the essence of the Art 6 guarantees, and Art 6(3)(e) follows this in that the accused is entitled to the State-funded assistance of an interpreter if he or she cannot understand or speak the language which is used in a particular court.[213] Whereas the right to State-funded legal assistance under Art 6(3)(c) is usually subject to a means test, the right to free interpretation applies to everyone charged with a criminal offence.

In *Luedicke, Belkacem and Koç v Federal Republic of Germany*[214] the ECtHR found that the provision prohibits absolutely a defendant being ordered to pay the costs of an interpreter, Art 6(3)(e) being " ... neither a conditional remission, nor a temporary exemption, nor a suspension, but a once and for all exemption or exoneration".[215] The ECtHR further stated that this principle covered " ... those documents or statements in the proceedings instituted against him which is necessary for him to understand in order to have the benefit of a fair trial".[216]

[6–81] This was refined somewhat in *Kamasinski v Austria*[217] with a more restrictive approach, holding that, although Art 6(3)(e) applied to documentary material disclosed before trial, it did not require written translations of all such documentation, merely the relevant pieces.[218] It should be noted that in this particular case, the defence counsel was competent in the applicant's mother tongue.

---

212 *Van Mechelen v Netherlands* (1997) 25 EHRR 647 at para 58.

213 The right to an interpreter will also extend to an accused suffering from deafness where the normal method of communication is by sign language.

214 *Luedicke, Belkacem and Koç v Federal Republic of Germany* (1978) 2 EHRR 149.

215 *ibid* at para 42.

216 *ibid* at para 48.

217 *Kamasinski v Austria* (1989) 13 EHRR 36.

218 The assistance " ... should be such as to enable the defendant to have knowledge of the case against him and to defend himself, notably by being able to put before the court his version of the events": *Kamasinski v Austria* (1989) 13 EHRR 36 at para 74.

It is also clear that the interpretation must be of sufficient quality to be "practical and effective":

> " . . . the competent authorities' obligation is not limited to the mere appointment of an interpreter but if they are put on notice in the particular circumstances, may also extend to exercising a degree of subsequent control over the adequacy of the interpretation provided".[219]

In the case of *Cuscani v United Kingdom*[220] the applicant, an Italian resident for some years in the UK, was denied official court interpretation following direct communication between the legal aid barrister, without recourse to his client, and the judge. Mr Cuscani therefore had to rely on his brother's "untested language skills". Once it had been established that interpretation was required it was unlikely that informal and unprofessional assistance would be sufficient, and on these grounds the ECtHR found a breach of the Article. [6–82]

2. Legitimate Justifications for Interference with the Right

In the drafting of Art 6 of the ECHR the nature of the right is inextricably concerned with the limitations on that right which can be clearly seen in its structure. This is in contrast to Articles such as Arts 8 and 10 where the guarantees are contained in one section and the limitations on those guarantees are contained in a second section. In this particular chapter, therefore, the entirety of the Article has been considered as a cohesive structure and the limitations have been included where they are most relevant for clarity of understanding. [6–83]

3. *Nullem Crimen Sine Lege*

Article 7 of the ECHR states: [6–84]

> "1. No one shall be held guilty of any criminal offence on account of any act or omission which did not constitute a criminal offence under national or international law at the time when it was committed. Nor shall a heavier penalty be imposed than the one that was applicable at the time the criminal offence was committed.
> 2. This article shall not prejudice the trial and punishment of any person for any act or omission which, at the time when it was committed, was criminal according to the general principles of law recognised by civilised nations."

Article 7 of the ECHR incorporates the *nullum crimen sine lege* principle. Article 7 creates a non-derogable prohibition on the retrospective application of the criminal law. Within the case law of the ECtHR, "lawfulness" in the sense of the ECHR has been adjudged as containing three overall aspects, those of accessibility, foreseeability and protection against arbitrary actions of States and State authorities. Article 7 applies these norms to a specific context, criminal law, in three principles: first, that the

---

219 *ibid* at para 74.

220 *Cuscani v United Kingdom* (2002) 36 EHRR 11.

law should have been in place when the offence was committed;[221] secondly, that the court should not sentence with any more rigour at a later date than when the offence was committed; and thirdly, that the law in any event should be both accessible and precise.

Post Facto Offences

[6–85] Taking the first of these aspects of Art 7, it would seem at face value to be a straightforward concept, but the common law must always have an aspect of flexibility whereby it is able to take into account the changing values and mores of society. The tension between the two aspects of certainty and flexibility within the law is resolved by the tenet that if the development of the law is foreseeable, then it will automatically be regarded as being fair and will not conflict with Art 7. This may be seen in the case of *Kokkinakis v Greece*[222] where the body of Greek law concerning proselytism, the ECtHR considered, was accessible to Mr Kokkinakis, had he researched sufficiently.[223] However, this clarity may be compared with the cases of *Hashman and Harrup v United Kingdom*,[224] where the court order of *contra bonos mores* ("against good morals"; roughly, "to be of good behaviour") was considered to be inexact and unclear to those on whom the penalty was imposed.

[6–86] The concept of "law" being foreseeable, whilst obviously applying to legislation and judicial law, also applies to what might be termed "State practice", where it is inconsistent with the existing State legislation or judicial body of law and is also inconsistent with the human rights which might be expected to have respect from the State. The applicants in the cases of *Streletz, Kessler and Krenz v Germany*[225] had been convicted of intentional homicide, as indirect participants, in connection with the killings of those who had attempted to cross the border between the German Democratic Republic (GDR) and the Federal Republic of Germany (FRG). The applicants, who had previously held senior positions in the GDR Government, could therefore be presumed to have been fully cognisant of both the applicable domestic law, and, indeed, specifically concerned with its implementation. The applicants had been convicted by virtue of their participation in the decision-making processes at senior levels of the GDR Government in the institution of the border policing policy calling for the use of lethal force against anyone attempting to cross the border. The ECtHR found that the domestic law in force in the GDR at the material time clearly identified

---

[221] It follows that one must have notice of a prohibited form of conduct in order to be held responsible for its infringement, which means in effect that the law must not be secret, and protects an individual from being convicted for a criminal offence which did not exist in law at the time the act was committed. This reflects the principle that only the law can define a crime and prescribe a penalty (*nullum crimen, nulla peona sine lege*).

[222] *Kokkinakis v Greece* (1993) 17 EHRR 397.

[223] The ECtHR held that the requirement that an offence be clearly defined by law "is satisfied where the individual can know from the wording of the relevant provision and, if need be, with the assistance of the courts' interpretation of it, what acts and omissions will make him liable": *Kokkinakis v Greece* (1993) 17 EHRR 397 at para 52.

[224] *Hashman and Harrup v United Kingdom* (2000) 30 EHRR 241.

[225] (2001) 33 EHRR 751.

the criminal offences, holding that in this case the relevant law was clear and identifiable. The criminal convictions of the applicants did not, therefore, contravene Art 7(1).[226]

Where the issue is not the actuality of the law, but a change in the interpretation of the law, the ECtHR has taken an approach that the development of rules of criminal liability through judicial interpretation may constitute such notice. Once again, the development in question must be consistent with the essence of the offence and could reasonably be foreseen.[227] As an example, one can consider *SW and CR v United Kingdom*[228] concerning the issue of forced sexual intercourse of one's wife, which, in the UK, had long been accepted as not being tantamount to rape. However, in 1995, the House of Lords held that this no longer applied. The ECtHR confirmed this to be the case,[229] with no violation of Art 7, since the constituent elements of rape had not changed and, given the progressive social developments in the 20th Century, the change in interpretation was foreseeable. **[6–87]**

Post Facto Penalties

The second element of Art 7(1) is that of the imposition of heavier penalties than were in force at the time of the commission of the crime. In order to examine this, it is necessary to consider what constitutes a penalty within the meaning of Art 7(1). This may be illustrated by considering the case of *Welch v UK*,[230] where the applicant committed a drugs offence in 1986 and was convicted in 1988. His sentence included a confiscation order for £59,000 pursuant to provisions in the Drug Trafficking Offences Act 1986, which came into force in 1987. If this sum was not forthcoming, the applicant faced another two years in prison for default. The question, therefore, was whether this was a "penalty", further to the original conviction, which the ECtHR considered to be the case, taking into account that the measure seemed to be punitive as well as preventative.[231] **[6–88]**

It seems that the ECtHR is prepared to consider a broad-based definition of a penalty in the sense of Art 7, the essential feature seeming to be that it should cover a detriment to the individual by the State from the time of the offence. Violations of this provision **[6–89]**

---

[226] One can compare the reasoning with that in the related case of *K-HW v Germany* (2001) 36 EHRR 1081, where the border guard was convicted of homicide "following orders", and no Art 7 breach was found.

[227] *Jorgic v Germany*, No 74613/01 2007.

[228] *SW and CR v United Kingdom* (1995) 21 EHRR 363.

[229] "The abandonment of the unacceptable idea of a husband being immune against prosecution for rape of his wife was in conformity not only with a civilised concept of marriage but also, and above all, with the fundamental objectives of the Convention, the very essence of which is respect for human dignity and human freedom." *SW and CR v United Kingdom* (1995) 21 EHRR 363 at para 42.

[230] *Welch v UK* (1995) 20 EHRR 247.

[231] One might consider the cases of *Dhoest v Belgium* (1991) 13 EHRR 802, where incarceration in a mental institution was for a therapeutic rather than a punitive purpose, and did not engage Art 7, and the requirement of a convicted sex offender signing a police register, which is, again, not punitive, but aimed at the prevention of re-offending: *Ibbotson v UK* [1999] Crim LR 153 and *Adamson v United Kingdom*, No 42293/98 1999.

have been found, however, where more severe penalties have been imposed on individuals convicted of criminal offences than were applicable at the time the offences were committed,[232] or where there has been no legal penalty for the offence[233] (in this instance, the wrong sentencing rules were applied, to the detriment of the accused). However, in the case of *Achour v France*,[234] the ECtHR held that a French law increasing the sentence for recidivists, enacted after the commission of the first offence, but before the second, did not engage Art 7 since it applied with effect from its entry into force. There was a difference between the taking of past events into consideration, and retrospective application of the law. The sentence imposed on the applicant had been applicable at the time he committed the second offence, the consequence of his crime was accessible and foreseeable as to its sentencing effect, and was, therefore, a legal penalty.

Article 7(2)

[6–90] Article 7(2) is concerned with whether a criminal act follows general guidelines recognised as conforming to the notion of " ... general principles of law recognised by civilised nations".[235] This is necessary within human rights discourse in that it may be clearly shown that legislation may be morally repugnant even while conforming to the legitimacy of the individual State, for instance, the racial purity laws of Nazi Germany. The exception created by Art 7(2) has the effect of allowing national and international legislation to be enacted to punish war crimes, such as torture and genocide, at a time subsequent to their commission. The logic behind this is that they would have been criminal according to the standards of their time, so that in the case of *Kononov v Latvia*, the ECtHR stated that:

> "... the laws and customs of war constituted particular and detailed regulations fixing the parameters of criminal conduct in a time of war, primarily addressed to armed forces and, especially, commanders ... Even the most cursory reflection by Mr Kononov, would have indicated that the acts, flagrantly unlawful ill-treatment and killing, had risked not only being counter to the laws and customs of war as understood at that time but also constituting war crimes for which, as commander, he could be held individually and criminally accountable.
>
> As to the applicant's submission that it had been politically unforeseeable that he would be prosecuted, the Court recalled its prior jurisprudence to the effect that it was legitimate and foreseeable for a successor State to bring criminal proceedings against persons who had committed crimes under a former regime. Successor courts could not be criticised for applying and interpreting the legal provisions in force at the relevant time during the former regime, in the light of the principles governing a State subject to the rule of law and having regard to the core principles (such as the right to life) on which the European Convention system is built. Those principles were found to be applicable to a change of

---

[232] *Ecer and Zeyrek v Turkey* (2001) 35 EHRR 672.

[233] *Gabarri Moreno v Spain* (2003) 39 EHRR 885.

[234] *Achour v France* (2007) 45 EHRR 2. In 1984 the applicant was found guilty of drug trafficking. In 1994 a new law came into force permitting an increased penalty for a person convicted of a serious offence who had previously been convicted of a serious offence, even if the previous offence pre-dated 1994. In 1995 the applicant was convicted of possessing drugs and was sentenced to an increased penalty in light of his previous conviction.

[235] Taken from Art 38, Statute of the International Court of Justice.

> regime of the nature which took place in Latvia following the Declarations of Independence of 1990 and 1991".[236]

The ECtHR accordingly found that Art 7 had not been violated.

Legitimate Justifications for Interference with the Right

It is clear that the guarantee of the right is seen as being of fundamental importance, in that a State cannot derogate from it, even in times of conflict or emergency.[237] Where it has been seen as violating the effective right to *nullum crimen, nulla peona sine lege* is when the State has not fulfilled the correct criteria for enforcing the law as it stands, whether judicial or legislative. The State must, therefore, be very certain that it is behaving in a way which is compliant with domestic law, and that the law making and subsequent interpretation must be both logical and foreseeable as to consequence. **[6–91]**

C. CFR

Article 47 deals with the right to an effective remedy and to a fair trial: **[6–92]**

> "Everyone whose rights and freedoms guaranteed by the law of the Union are violated has the right to an effective remedy before a tribunal in compliance with the conditions laid down in this Article.
>
> Everyone is entitled to a fair and public hearing within a reasonable time by an independent and impartial tribunal previously established by law. Everyone shall have the possibility of being advised, defended and represented.
>
> Legal aid shall be made available to those who lack sufficient resources in so far as such aid is necessary to ensure effective access to justice."

The first paragraph of this provision corresponds with Art 13 of the ECHR (which concerns the right to an effective remedy before a national authority). However, the protection afforded by the Union framework is more expansive than that offered by its ECHR counterpart because it guarantees a right to an effective hearing before a court, not just an authority. In the case of *Johnston* the European Court of Justice (ECJ) held that this is a principle of Union law.[238] The second paragraph of Art 47 corresponds with Art 6(1) of the ECHR discussed above,[239] while the third paragraph essentially reiterates the principle from the ECtHR in *Airey*.[240]

---

[236] *Kononov v Latvia*, No 36376/04 2010. Para 238–240. This was a Grand Chamber judgment, stemming from Red Army activity against alleged Partisans in Second World War Latvia.

[237] See Art 15 ECHR.

[238] *Johnston v Chief Constable of the Royal Ulster Constabulary*, Case 222/84, [1986] ECR 1651.

[239] Art 6(1) of the ECHR states: "In the determination of his civil rights and obligations or of any criminal charge against him, everyone is entitled to a fair and public hearing within a reasonable time by an independent and impartial tribunal established by law. Judgment shall be pronounced publicly but the press and public may be excluded from all or part of the trial in the interests of morals, public order or national security in a democratic society, where the interests of juveniles or the protection of the private life of the parties so require, or to the extent strictly necessary in the opinion of the court in special circumstances where publicity would prejudice the interests of justice."

[240] *Airey v Ireland* (1979) 2 EHRR 305 at para 11.

[6–93] Article 48 concerns the presumption of innocence and the right of defence and reflects Art 6(2) and Art 6(3) of the ECHR. In line with Art 52(3) of the CFR, this right has the same meaning and scope as the right guaranteed by the ECHR.

> "48.1. Everyone who has been charged shall be presumed innocent until proved guilty according to law.
>
> 48.2. Respect for the rights of the defence of anyone who has been charged shall be guaranteed."

[6–94] Article 49(1) and Art 49(2) focus on principles of legality and proportionality of criminal offences and penalties and reflect Art 7 of the ECHR. In line with Art 52(3) of the CFR, the Charter right has the same meaning as the ECHR right. Article 49(3)'s proportionality principle is enshrined in the common constitutional traditions of the Member States and has also been recognised in the case law of the ECJ.[241]

> "1. No one shall be held guilty of any criminal offence on account of any act or omission which did not constitute a criminal offence under national law or international law at the time when it was committed. Nor shall a heavier penalty be imposed than that which was applicable at the time the criminal offence was committed. If, subsequent to the commission of a criminal offence, the law provides for a lighter penalty, that shall be applicable.
> 2. This Article shall not prejudice the trial and punishment of any person for any act or omission which, at the time when it was committed, was criminal according to the general principles recognised by the community of nations.
> 3. The severity of penalties must not be disproportionate to the criminal offence."

Article 50 incorporates the principle of double jeopardy or *non bis in idem*. This states:

> "No one shall be liable to be tried or punished again in criminal proceedings for an offence for which he or she has already been finally acquitted or convicted within the Union in accordance with the law."

[6–95] This provision corresponds with Art 4 of Protocol No 7 to ECHR and the *non bis in idem* principle has also been upheld in case law of the ECJ.[242] In line with Art 50, the *non bis in idem* principle applies not only within the jurisdiction of one State but also between the jurisdictions of several Member States.[243]

---

241 Explanation of the Praesidium of the Convention which drafted the charter—available at: http://infoportal.fra.europa.eu/InfoPortal/infobaseShowContent.do?btnCat_257&btnCountryBread_169, last accessed 21 June 2012.

242 See, for example, Cases 18/65 and 35/65, *Gutmann v Commission* [1966] ECR 103. With regard to the principle of double jeopardy in Ireland, see *People (DPP) v O'Shea* [1982] IR 384.

243 Explanation of the Praesidium of the Convention which drafted the charter—available at: http://infoportal.fra.europa.eu/InfoPortal/infobaseShowContent.do?btnCat_321&btnCountryBread_169, last accessed 21 June 2012.

D. International and Regional Laws

At an international level, the right to equality before the law "requires all individuals to have equal access to the courts and to be viewed in law in a non-discriminatory manner, especially with respect to the judicial determination of their rights and duties".[244] Smith comments that, as part of the right, the right to a fair trial "is one of the most inventively elaborated and dynamically interpreted rights today, it is 'judge made law' in the true sense of the word, constantly developing".[245] **[6–96]**

The right to a fair trial and the right to fair procedures have been incorporated into both the Universal Declaration of Human Rights (UDHR) and the ICCPR. The UDHR contains various references to issues concerning the right to a fair trial, but the main provision dealing with this issue is Art 10, which states:

> "Everyone is entitled in full equality to a fair and public hearing by an independent and impartial tribunal, in the determination of his rights and obligations and of any criminal charge against him".[246]

The ICCPR deals with the right to a fair trial in Arts 14 and 15. Article 14 states: **[6–97]**

> "1. All persons shall be equal before the courts and tribunals. In the determination of any criminal charge against him, or of his rights and obligations in a suit at law, everyone shall be entitled to a fair and public hearing by a competent, independent and impartial tribunal established by law. The press and the public may be excluded from all or part of a trial for reasons of morals, public order (ordre public) or national security in a democratic society, or when the interest of the private lives of the parties so requires, or to the extent strictly necessary in the opinion of the court in special circumstances where publicity would prejudice the interests of justice; but any judgement rendered in a criminal case or in a suit at law shall be made public except where the interest of juvenile persons otherwise requires or the proceedings concern matrimonial disputes or the guardianship of children.
> 2. Everyone charged with a criminal offence shall have the right to be presumed innocent until proved guilty according to law.
> 3. In the determination of any criminal charge against him, everyone shall be entitled to the following minimum guarantees, in full equality: (a) To be informed promptly and in detail in a language which he understands of the nature and cause of the charge against him; (b) To have adequate time and facilities for the preparation of his defence and to communicate with counsel of his own choosing; (c) To be tried without undue delay; (d) To be tried in his presence, and to defend himself in person or through legal assistance of

---

[244] R Smith, *Textbook on International Human Rights* (5th ed, Oxford University Press, Oxford, 2012) p 264.

[245] *ibid*, p 265.

[246] See also Arts 6, 7, 8 and Art 11, which states: "(1) Everyone charged with a penal offence has the right to be presumed innocent until proved guilty according to law in a public trial at which he has had all the guarantees necessary for his defence. (2) No one shall be held guilty of any penal offence on account of any act or omission which did not constitute a penal offence, under national or international law, at the time when it was committed. Nor shall a heavier penalty be imposed than the one that was applicable at the time the penal offence was committed." See D Weissbrot and M Hallendorf, "Travaux préparatoires of the fair trial provisions: Articles 8-11 of the Universal Declaration of Human Rights" (1999) 21 HRQ 1061.

> his own choosing; to be informed, if he does not have legal assistance, of this right; and to have legal assistance assigned to him, in any case where the interests of justice so require, and without payment by him in any such case if he does not have sufficient means to pay for it; (e) To examine, or have examined, the witnesses against him and to obtain the attendance and examination of witnesses on his behalf under the same conditions as witnesses against him; (f) To have the free assistance of an interpreter if he cannot understand or speak the language used in court; (g) Not to be compelled to testify against himself or to confess guilt.
> 4. In the case of juvenile persons, the procedure shall be such as will take account of their age and the desirability of promoting their rehabilitation.
> 5. Everyone convicted of a crime shall have the right to his conviction and sentence being reviewed by a higher tribunal according to law.
> 6. When a person has by a final decision been convicted of a criminal offence and when subsequently his conviction has been reversed or he has been pardoned on the ground that a new or newly discovered fact shows conclusively that there has been a miscarriage of justice, the person who has suffered punishment as a result of such conviction shall be compensated according to law, unless it is proved that the non-disclosure of the unknown fact in time is wholly or partly attributable to him.
> 7. No one shall be liable to be tried or punished again for an offence for which he has already been finally convicted or acquitted in accordance with the law and penal procedure of each country."

[6–98] Article 15 then incorporates the *nullum crimen sine lege* principle, seen above in the discussion on Irish law and on Art 7 of the ECHR.

At a regional level, the right to a fair trial is provided for in Arts 3, 7 and 26 of the African Charter on Human and Peoples' Rights, Arts 3, 8, 9 and 10 of the American Convention on Human Rights and Art 13 of the Arab Charter on Human Rights.

Conclusion

[6–99] As can be seen from the above discussion, the right to a fair trial is one of the most frequently adjudicated rights in the ECHR. The incorporation of the ECHR into Irish law in 2003 has allowed a more expansive and insightful analysis of the right guaranteed under Art 38.1 by the Irish Courts. O'Donnell assessed the relationship between the Irish constitutional guarantee and the ECHR provision, stating:

> "Looking at the specific features provided for by Article 6 it is possible to find in the Irish Constitution counterparts with a high degree of similarity."[247]

The common factor between the ECHR and the Irish Constitution is clearly that of the rule of law. However, while the Irish constitutional provision on the right to a fair trial is short and circumscribed, the Irish courts have succeeded in extrapolating various ancillary rights from the text, bringing it closer in spirit to the vastly more expansive text and jurisprudence of the ECHR.

---

[247] D O' Donnell, "A Comparison of Article 6 of European Convention on Human Rights and the Due Process Requirements of The Constitution of Ireland", 4(2) JSIJ (2004), pp 41–42.

CHAPTER 7
The Right to Privacy

Introduction

The right to privacy is a multi-faceted right, covering different areas of an individual's life, including decision-making, privacy of the person and his or her space, and privacy of information. Craig identified a number of varying reasons why the right to privacy should be, and is, protected, including the right of the individual to be let alone, the right for a person's activities not to be interfered with, the right to autonomy, the right to creativity, the right to mental health and the right to intimacy.[1] Delany and Carolan comment that the right to privacy is a "comparatively recent notion".[2] This right is, however, becoming more important across legal systems, with, technological advancements, enhanced communications systems, security threats, etc, increasingly facilitating and demanding access to people's private lives. With increased opportunities for invasion of privacy comes the need for greater protection of the right to privacy. Despite its modernity, the right to privacy is protected in various international and regional human rights instruments and "has received widespread recognition as a constitutional value",[3] in various States, including Ireland. While the Irish Constitution does not explicitly protect the right to privacy, the right has been found to fall within the "personal rights of the citizen" which find protection in Art 40.3.1°. As with other rights, the protection afforded to the right to privacy has expanded since the incorporation of the European Convention on Human Rights (ECHR) into domestic law by means of the ECHR Act 2003, with Art 8 of the ECHR protecting respect for private life. The first part of this chapter focuses on how the Irish Constitution protects the right to privacy, while the second explores Art 8 of the ECHR. The protection of the right to privacy under EU and international legal regimes is then examined. **[7–01]**

1 See J Craig, "Invasion of Privacy and Charter Values" (1997) 42 McGill LJ 355.
2 H Delany and E Carolan, *The Right to Privacy* (Thomson Round Hall, Dublin, 2008), p 33.
3 *ibid.*

A. Irish Constitution

[7–02] The right to privacy is an unenumerated right under the Irish Constitution and is protected under Art 40.3.1°:

> "The State guarantees in its laws to respect, and, as far as practicable, by its laws to defend and vindicate the personal rights of the citizen."

The right to privacy was first considered by the Irish courts in the case of *McGee v AG*[4] when the Supreme Court considered the constitutionality of s 17(3) of the Criminal Law Amendment Act 1935, which prohibited the importation of contraceptives into the State. The court found that this provision was unconstitutional, but the reason for the decision differed between the judges. While Walsh J held that the provision infringed Art 41 of the Constitution because it interfered with the privacy of a husband and wife, three members of the majority found that the provision was unconstitutional as a result of the protection afforded by Art 40.3 and held that the right to privacy, in marital relationships, was an unenumerated right. Budd J stated:

> "Whilst the 'personal rights' are not described specifically, it is scarcely to be doubted in our society that the right to privacy is universally recognised and accepted with possibly the rarest of exceptions, and that the matter of marital relationship must rank as one of the most important of matters in the realm of privacy".[5]

[7–03] The right to privacy in *McGee* was limited to a right to marital privacy. However, a general right to privacy was also held to exist under Art 40.3 of the Constitution in the case of *Norris v AG.*[6] The plaintiff had claimed that ss 61 and 62 of the Offences Against the Person Act 1861 and s 11 of the Criminal Law (Amendment) Act 1885, which effectively criminalised homosexual acts,[7] were unconstitutional, interfered with his private life and infringed his right to privacy. While his claim was dismissed, O'Higgins CJ stated that a right to privacy or to be let alone was not absolute and stated that the State had an interest "in the general moral wellbeing of the community" and was "entitled, where it was practicable to do so, to discourage conduct which is

---

[4] *McGee v AG* [1973] IR 284.

[5] *ibid* at 322.

[6] *Norris v AG* [1984] IR 36. Other cases which confirm the status of the right to privacy as an unenumerated right are: *Foy v An t-Ard Chláraitheoir* [2002] IEHC 116; *Re a Ward of Court (No 2)* [1996] 2 IR 79 and *Desmond v Glackin (No 2)* [1993] 3 IR 67.

[7] s 61 of the Act of 1861 concerned the offence of buggery committed with a person or an animal, and set a maximum penalty of penal servitude for life. s 62 of the Act dealt with associated offences, e.g. attempts and assaults for the purpose of committing buggery. The penalty for this was a maximum of two years' imprisonment. Both sections were repealed in 1993 save insofar as they apply to animals. s 11 of the Act of 1885 provided: "Any male person who, in public or private, commits, or is a party to the commission of, or procures or attempts to procure the commission by any male person of, any act of gross indecency with another male person, shall be guilty of a misdemeanor, and being convicted thereof shall be liable at the discretion of the court to be imprisoned for any term not exceeding two years, with or without hard labour." While not expressly criminalising homosexual behaviour, the effect of these provisions taken together was to criminalise sexual acts between males. s 11 of 1885 Act was repealed in full in 1993.

morally wrong and harmful to a way of life and to values which the State wishes to protect".[8] Dissenting, Henchy J stated:

> "That a right of privacy inheres in each citizen by virtue of his human personality, and that such is constitutionally guaranteed as one of the unspecified personal rights comprehended by Article 40, s. 3 are propositions that are well attested by previous decisions of this Court".[9]

1. Nature of the Right

Source and Scope of the Right

The difficulty in comprehending the nature and extent of the right to privacy as enshrined in the Constitution was highlighted by the Supreme Court in *Norris.* Henchy J acknowledged the recognition of the right to marital privacy in *McGee* but then went on to state: **[7–04]**

> "There are many other aspects of the right to privacy, some yet to be given judicial recognition. It is unnecessary for the purpose of this case to explore them".[10]

More discussion was afforded to the nature of the right in the case of *Kennedy v Ireland*[11] which centred on the issue of the tapping of journalists' phones. Hamilton P stated that the "right to privacy is not in issue, the issue is the extent of that right or the extent of the right to be let alone".[12] He then linked the right to privacy with the democratic nature of the State, commenting that although the right is not explicitly protected under the Constitution it is "one of the fundamental personal rights of the citizen which flow from the Christian and democratic nature of the State" and "[t]he nature of the right to privacy must be such as to ensure the dignity and freedom of an individual in the type of society envisaged by the Constitution, namely, a sovereign, independent and democratic society".[13] The right to privacy has also been linked with the concept of autonomy in the sense that it is "necessary for the expression of an individual personality".[14]

Analysing the interpretation given to the right to privacy in these cases, it is clear that the Irish judiciary has been willing to find quite an expansive basis for this right, including the democratic nature of the State, dignity[15] and autonomy, meaning that it can be engaged in various spheres of an individual's life at different levels.[16] **[7–05]**

---

[8] *Norris v AG* [1984] IR 36 at 64.
[9] *ibid* at 71.
[10] *ibid* at 72.
[11] *Kennedy v Ireland* [1987] IR 587.
[12] *ibid* at 592.
[13] *ibid* at 593.
[14] *Norris v AG* [1984] IR 36 at 72.
[15] See E J Bloustein, "Privacy as an aspect of human dignity" (1964) 39 NYU L Rev 962.
[16] Delany and Carolan comment that "[t]he right to privacy is protected because it secures the citizen's dignity and autonomy as a socially-situated individual. This implies that privacy rights can potentially be engaged in a wide variety of social situations." H Delany and E Carolan, *supra* n 2, p 38.

The Elements of the Right

[7–06] In Ireland, the right to privacy was applied at a very limited, personal level in the case of *McGee*, but subsequent cases facilitated the expansion of the right to privacy into other realms of the individual's life.[17] These include various aspects of one's personal and business life and privacy with regard to information. Delany and Carolan refer to these different elements as "dimensions of privacy" and categorise them as decisional privacy, spatial privacy and informational privacy.[18]

Decision Making

[7–07] The decisional dimension of privacy "denotes the ability of the individual to make his own choices without the involvement of external agencies".[19] Irish courts have dealt with this element of the right to privacy on a number of occasions, and have generally referred to it as the right to be let alone.[20] This is evident in the cases of *McGee* and *Norris* which both questioned the constitutionality of legislation which interfered with their right to make decisions about an individual's private life. The issue of decision making as an element of privacy was discussed by Hamilton CJ in the case of *Re a Ward of Court (No 2)*, who stated that the "loss by an individual of his or her mental capacity does not result in any diminution of his or her personal rights recognised by the Constitution, including the right to life, the right to bodily integrity, the right to privacy, including self-determination, and the right to refuse medical care or treatment".[21] Agreeing with this sentiment Denham J stated:

> "Part of the right to privacy is the giving or refusing of consent to medical treatment. Merely because medical treatment becomes necessary to sustain life does not mean that the right to privacy is lost, neither is the right lost by a person becoming insentient. Nor is the right lost if a person becomes insentient and needs medical treatment to sustain life and is cared for by people who can and wish to continue taking care of the person. Simply it means that the right may be exercised by a different process. The individual retains their personal rights".[22]

Denham J went on to state: "A constituent of the right of privacy is the right to die naturally, with dignity and with minimum suffering".[23]

Privacy of Person and Personal Space

[7–08] Spatial privacy refers to the right of the individual not to be encroached upon in certain locations where privacy would be expected, the most obvious being the home. The concept also includes the right of the individual to protection of his or her "zone of personal space",[24] which encompasses protection against surveillance.

---

[17] Gallagher comments that the "notion of privacy is potentially a broad one into which different senses of privacy are conflated" – P Gallagher, "Tribunals and the Erosion of the Right to Privacy" (1999) 4(9) *Bar Review* 406, p 407.

[18] See H Delany and E Carolan, *supra* n 2, pp 20–22. See also P Gallagher, *supra* n.17.

[19] H Delany and E Carolan, *supra* n 2, p 38.

[20] See, for example, *Kennedy v Ireland* [1987] IR 587 at 592.

[21] *Re a Ward of Court (No 2)* [1996] 2 IR 79 at 126.

[22] *ibid* at 163.

[23] *ibid.*

[24] H Delany and E Carolan, *supra* n 2, p 48.

The spatial dimension of privacy covers interference with a person's body or activities. A quite recent interesting case with regard to privacy of the body is the case of *Sinnott v The Nationalist and Leinster Times Ltd*,[25] where Budd J held that the publication of a photograph of the plaintiff playing Gaelic football, in which his genitalia could be seen, constituted a breach of his constitutional right to privacy. While Mr Sinnott was playing football in a public place, the court still found that his right to privacy was breached. This seems to be an expansion of the right to privacy by the Irish courts, to cover photographs or "unlawful exposure"[26] of the body. This can be contrasted with a previous case of *Murray v Falcon Holidays*[27] where the plaintiff unsuccessfully sued when a photograph which had been taken of her while on holidays was used by the defendants in one of their promotional brochures.

The issue of surveillance has been discussed in the Irish courts with regard to the right to privacy. The seminal case on this matter is *Kennedy v Ireland*[28] which focused on the unlawful interception of communication. It was held that the tapping of journalists' phones amounted to a breach of their right to privacy. Hamilton P stated: **[7–09]**

> "The dignity and freedom of an individual in a democratic society cannot be ensured if his communications of a private nature, be they written or telephonic, are deliberately, consciously, and unjustifiably intruded upon and interfered with".[29]

Following on from the decision in *Kennedy*, two pieces of legislation were enacted in this area, namely, the Postal and Telecommunications Services Act 1993[30] and the Interception of Postal Packets and Telecommunications Messages (Regulation) Act 1993.[31] In October 2001, the Taoiseach publicly apologised to three journalists whose phones were tapped by government agencies during the 1980s, for "the inappropriate invasion of their privacy and interference by the State with their role as journalists".[32]

In *Kane v Governor of Mountjoy Prison*[33] the applicant complained that surveillance by Gardaí of his movements breached his right to privacy. Finlay J commented that overt surveillance was "capable of gravely affecting the peace of mind and public reputation of any individual"[34] and therefore required justification with regard to the circumstances of the case, which, he found was present in this case. **[7–10]**

---

[25] *Sinnott v The Nationalist and Leinster Times Limited* (Unreported, High Court, 30 July 2008), *The Irish Times*, 31 July 2008.
[26] H Delany and E Carolan, *supra* n 2, p 46.
[27] *Murray v Falcon Holidays* (Unreported, Circuit Court), *The Irish Times*, 8 April 2004 and 7 May 2005.
[28] *Kennedy v Ireland* [1987] IR 587.
[29] *ibid* at 593.
[30] s 98 of this Act criminalises the interception of the content of communications.
[31] The lawful interception of communications by State authorities is regulated under this Act. See M Collins, "Telephone Tapping and the Law in Ireland" (1993) 3 (1)ICLJ 31.
[32] "Apology for Phone Tapping," *The Irish Times*, 26 October 2001.
[33] *Kane v Governor of Mountjoy Prison* [1988] IR 757.
[34] *ibid* at 769.

This issue of surveillance was also discussed in *X v Flynn*[35] which centred on a rape victim who successfully applied for an injunction prohibiting journalists from watching her movements, besetting her and harassing her.

[7–11] This area of law is now regulated by the Criminal Justice (Surveillance) Act 2009, which allows surveillance to be carried out by members of An Garda Síochána, members of the Defence Forces and officers of the Revenue Commissioners.

Spatial privacy also relates to the protection of particular locale in which a person would generally be expected to find privacy. The right to privacy in the home overlaps with the inviolability of the dwelling place which is provided for in Art 40.5 of the Constitution.[36] However, the relationship between the Art 40.5 protection and the more general right to privacy protection under Art 40.3.1° has not been discussed by the courts in any great depth. The case of *Hanahoe v Hussey*[37] established that the right to privacy extends from protection of privacy in the home to the individual's place of business. That case concerned a search of a solicitor's office by Gardaí. News of the search had been leaked and when the Gardaí turned up to the office to carry out the search members of the media were present. The solicitors then claimed that their right to privacy had been breached, a claim with which the court agreed, having regard to the European Court of Human Rights (ECtHR) case of *Niemietz v Germany.*[38] In the case of *Cogley v RTÉ*[39] it was held that the secret filming of an individual's workplace also amounted to a breach of the right to privacy.

[7–12] The spatial dimension of the right to privacy has also been found to extend to medical institutions, hotels and other locations[40] in various jurisdictions. The extension of the right to privacy to such locations may find favour in Irish courts in the future. However, it seems that there must be a significant link between the individual and the protected locale. In this regard, Delany and Carolan state that "[a]lthough the home is generally regarded as the central core of the right to territorial privacy, claims may potentially be made in respect of any area to which the individual might withdraw in expectation of private refuge".[41]

Privacy of Information

[7–13] The third area covered by the right to privacy concerns the dissemination of private information, generally by the media. This aspect of the right to privacy has not attracted much litigation of note in Ireland to date. However, the cases of *Hanahoe v Hussey,*[42] discussed above, and *Gray v Minister for Justice, Equality and Law Reform*[43] illuminate this area of law to a certain extent. In *Gray*, members of An Garda Síochána

[35] *X v Flynn* (Unreported, High Court, 19 May 1994).
[36] See *DPP v McCreesh* [1992] 2 IR 239 and *Simple Imports Ltd v Revenue Commissioners* [2000] 2 IR 243.
[37] *Hanahoe v Hussey* [1998] 3 IR 69.
[38] *Niemietz v Germany* (1993) 16 EHRR 97.
[39] *Cogley v RTÉ* [2005] 4 IR 79.
[40] See H Delany and E Carolan, *supra* n 2, pp 46–48.
[41] *ibid*, p 46.
[42] *Hanahoe v Hussey* [1998] 3 IR 69.
[43] *Gray v Minister for Justice, Equality and Law Reform* [2007] IEHC 52.

had disclosed to the media that a convicted rapist had been released from prison and was living in a certain household. Members of the household complained that they had been subjected to harassment and intimidation as a result of this disclosure. The court accepted that their right to privacy was infringed.

Data Protection

The Office of the Data Protection Commissioner was established under the Data Protection Act 1988. The legislation was updated by the Data Protection (Amendment) Act 2003, which implements the provisions of Directive 95/46/EC. The main thrust of the Acts is that individuals should be able to control how data relating to them is used. The Data Protection Commissioner, an independent Government appointee, has the responsibility for upholding those rights of individuals which are laid out in the Acts. The majority of law in relation to data protection emanates from the EU, and is referred to in the EU section below. [7–14]

The Extent of the Right to Privacy

Whilst the early discussion of the right to privacy in the Irish Constitution focused on the right to privacy as a personal right, more recent cases have questioned the extension of the right to business affairs. This issue was discussed in the case of *Haughey v Moriarty* where Hamilton CJ stated that "[f]or the purposes of this case, and not so holding, the Court is prepared to accept that the constitutional right to privacy extends to the privacy and confidentiality of a citizen's banking records and transactions".[44] [7–15]

This issue was revisited in the case of *Caldwell v Mahon*[45] where the court discussed whether the right to privacy extended to business affairs Hanna J stated:

> "Does, therefore, a right to privacy exist at all in connection with the applicant's business affairs? I am reluctant to hold that no such right exists. In truth, I see no logical reason why it should not. This question, I feel, merits far more debate than the context of this case permitted. Notwithstanding this, I am satisfied to proceed on the basis that the right to privacy does extend to business affairs. It seems to me, however, that such right can only exist at the outer reaches of and the furthest remove from the core personal right to privacy".[46]

In this regard, Hanna J affirmed the statement of Ackerman J in the South African Constitutional Court in the case of *Bernstein v Bester*: [7–16]

> "A very high level of protection is given to the individual's intimate personal sphere of life and the maintenance of its basic preconditions and there is a final untouchable sphere of human freedom that is beyond interference from any public authority. So much so that, in regard to this most intimate core of privacy, no justifiable limitation thereof can take place. But this most intimate core is narrowly construed. This inviolable core is left behind once an individual enters into relationships with persons outside this closest intimate sphere; the individual's activities then acquire a social dimension and the right to privacy in this context becomes subject to limitation".[47]

---

[44] [1999] 3 IR 1 at 58.
[45] *Caldwell v Mahon* [2007] 3 IR 542.
[46] *ibid* at 548.
[47] *Bernstein v Bester* [1996] 4 BCLR (South Africa) 449.

2. Legitimate Justifications for Interference with the Right

[7–17] In the case of *Kennedy v Ireland*, Hamilton P discussed the limitations which could be legitimately placed on the right to privacy, stating that "its exercise may be restricted by the constitutional rights of others, by the requirements of the common good and is subject to the requirements of public order and morality".[48]

Denham J also discussed the nature of the legitimate interferences with the right to privacy in *Re a Ward of Court (No 2)*, commenting that "[t]he right to privacy is not absolute. It has to be balanced against the State's duty to protect and vindicate life".[49] She then quoted from the US case of *Re Quinlan* that " ... the individual's right to privacy grows as the degree of bodily invasion increases".[50]

It is clear, therefore, that the right to privacy is limited in the interest of the common good, for reasons of public order and morality and when balanced against others' rights.

Common Good

[7–18] One of the most significant cases which highlights how the right to privacy can be legitimately interfered with for the reason of the common good is *Haughey v Moriarty*, which concerned resolutions of the Oireachtas which established Tribunals of Inquiry. Hamilton CJ stated:

> "The exigencies of the common good require that matters considered by both Houses of the Oireachtas to be of urgent public importance be inquired into, particularly when such inquiries are necessary to preserve the purity and integrity of our public life without which a successful democracy is impossible."[51]

The case of *Foy v An t-Ard Chláraitheoir (No 2)*[52] has significant importance in human rights law in Ireland, as it led to the first declaration of incompatibility with the ECHR. Constitutional rights such as the right to privacy and the right to marry were discussed, together with the necessity to limit these rights for the common good/good of society.

[7–19] Dr Lydia Foy (*Foy v An t-Ard Chláraitheoir (No 1) and (No 2)*)[53] was a transgender woman who underwent gender reassignment surgery in 1992 and subsequently applied for a new birth certificate which recorded her acquired female gender and to change her name from Donal Mark to Lydia Annice in 1993. The General Register Office

---

48 *Kennedy v Ireland* [1987] IR 587 at 592.

49 *Re a Ward of Court (No 2)* [1996] 2 IR 79 at 163.

50 *Re Quinlan* (1976) 355 A 2d 647.

51 *Haughey v Moriarty* [1999] 3 IR 59.

52 *Foy v An t-Ard Chláraitheoir (No 2)* [2007] IEHC 470. The second declaration of incompatibility with the ECHR came in the case of *Donegan v Dublin City Council* [2012] IESC 18, where the Supreme Court held that s 62 Housing Act 1966, which allowed a local authority to secure a court order for possession of a council house without an independent inquiry, was incompatible with Art 8 ECHR, regarding the right to respect for private and family life.

53 *Foy v An t-Ard Chláraitheoir* [2002] IEHC 116 and *Foy v An t-Ard Chláraitheoir* [2007] IEHC 470.

refused to issue a new birth certificate with a changed gender and name. She took a case against the Registrar General and the Attorney General, seeking judicial review of the decision not to issue an amended birth certificate. If the Registrar General was not allowed to amend the Register of Births and issue a new certificate, then she claimed that the Registration of Births and Deaths (Ireland) Act 1863, as amended, and the 1880 Regulations made thereunder, which set out the duties of the Registrar, were unconstitutional insofar as they did not allow for a correction to be made to the original birth certificate and thereby violated her constitutional rights to dignity and privacy and the right to marry. Various experts gave evidence on the issue of gender identity during the case but eventually McKechnie J held that biological factors determine sex, and as such, Dr Foy was determined correctly to be male at birth. He also held that the Registrar General did not have the authority to amend birth certificates to reflect a change in gender. He then held that, while Irish law created some inconvenience for transgender people, Dr Foy's constitutional rights had not been violated. With regard to the right to privacy, McKechnie J stated:

> "On the constitutional issue the existence of the rights to dignity, to privacy and equality has been acknowledged. It is said that such rights are not absolute and must be considered in the context of the rights of others, including family members, the general public and society itself. Whilst it is recognised that this may cause some inconvenience to a transsexual, nonetheless the State by its positive acts, has arrived at a situation where a fair balance now exists between the rights of persons like the applicant and the rights of others and society who would be affected by any such change".[54]

He then called on the Government to review the legislative framework with regard to transgender people. McKechnie J's judgment preceeded the ECtHR's *Goodwin*[55] decision by two days. The ECtHR case focused on similar facts as *Foy* but the ECtHR focused on Art 8 of the ECHR dealing with private life, and stated that the right included the right for each person to establish details of his or her own identity as a human. *Foy (No 2)* was heard by McKechnie J again in the High Court in 2007, by which time the ECHR had been incorporated into Irish law, and various courts in other jurisdictions had dealt favourably with cases concerning transgender people. McKechnie J placed considerable weight on the ECtHR jurisprudence, stating that "the decision in Goodwin changed dramatically and irreversibly the position of transsexuals under the Convention".[56] McKechnie J did not accept that Dr Foy's constitutional rights had been violated but held that because Irish legislation prevented the legal recognition of transgender persons, it was incompatible with the ECHR. He therefore granted the first declaration of incompatibility with the ECHR made under s 5 of the ECHR Act 2003. The State appealed the decision in February 2008 but dropped the appeal again in June 2010. An Advisory Group was set up by the Government to review the legal framework with regard to transgender people and reported in June 2011.[57] It recommended that the legal framework be amended to **[7–20]**

[54] *Foy v An t-Ard Chláraitheoir* [2002] IEHC 116 at 91.

[55] *Goodwin v UK* (2002) 35 EHRR 18.

[56] *Foy v An t-Ard Chláraitheoir* [2007] IEHC 470 at 84.

[57] Department of Social Protection, *Report of the Gender Recognition Advisory Group*, 15 June 2011, available at: http://www.welfare.ie/EN/Policy/Legislation/Pages/gragreportjune11.aspx, last accessed 21 June 2012.

allow for recognition of transgender people and to allow their right to marry in their acquired gender. However, the recommendations of this Report have yet to be implemented.[58]

Public Order and Morality[59]

[7–21] The issue of interference with the right to privacy on the grounds of public order and morality has not been considered in much depth by the Irish courts, although it has been referred to at a superficial level in a number of cases. In *Norris v Attorney General*, for example, O'Higgins CJ stated that the State had "an interest in the general moral wellbeing of the community" and could, therefore, "discourage conduct which is morally wrong and harmful to a way of life and to values which the State wishes to protect".[60]

Activities by State agents, such as investigations into, and surveillance of, individuals and situations deemed to be a threat to public order and morality, can be regarded as legitimate interferences with the right to privacy. In the case of *Trent v Garda Commissioner*[61] it was held that inquiries made by the Garda Síochána Complaints Board into the plaintiff's life were legitimate interferences with his right to privacy.[62]

[7–22] For many years, surveillance by Government agencies in Ireland was unregulated.[63] As mentioned above, surveillance is now regulated by legislation in the form of the Criminal Justice (Surveillance) Act 2009, which deals with surveillance by members of An Garda Síochána, members of the Defence Forces and officers of the Revenue Commissioners. The Act empowers nominees,[64] generally with authorisation from a

---

[58] See report of former Council of Europe Commissioner for Human Rights, Thomas Hammarberg, *Report by the Commissioner for Human Rights on his visit to Ireland 26–30 November 2007*, Comm DH (2008), Strasbourg, 30 April 2008.

[59] See TJ McIntyre, "Criminal Justice (Surveillance) Act 2009" (2009) *Irish Current Law Statutes Annotated* 15 and A Gillespie, "Covert Surveillance, Human Rights and the Law" (2009) 19 ICLJ 71.

[60] *Norris v AG* [1984] IR 36 at 64.

[61] *Trent v Garda Commissioner* [1999] IEHC 84.

[62] See also, *Barry v Medical Council* [1998] 3 IR 368.

[63] See Law Reform Commission Reports which criticise lack of regulation: Law Reform Commission, *Consultation Paper on Privacy: Surveillance and the Interception of Communications* (1996); and Law Reform Commission, *Report on Privacy: Surveillance and the Interception of Communications* (1998).

[64] s 4 states: "(1) A superior officer of the Garda Síochána may apply to a judge for an authorisation where he or she has reasonable grounds for believing that—(*a*) as part of an operation or investigation being conducted by the Garda Síochána concerning an arrestable offence, the surveillance being sought to be authorised is necessary for the purposes of obtaining information as to whether the offence has been committed or as to the circumstances relating to the commission of the offence, or obtaining evidence for the purposes of proceedings in relation to the offence, (*b*) the surveillance being sought to be authorised is necessary for the purpose of preventing the commission of arrestable offences, or (*c*) the surveillance being sought to be authorised is necessary for the purpose of maintaining the security of the State. (2) A superior officer of the Defence Forces may apply to a judge for an authorisation where he or she has reasonable grounds for believing that the surveillance being sought to be authorised is necessary for the purpose of maintaining the security of the State. (3) A superior officer of the Revenue

District Court Judge, to carry out surveillance, using certain specified devices,[65] on suspected criminals, and allows for information obtained through the surveillance operation to be admitted in court.[66] The legislation is limited in its scope and still leaves a number of surveillance activities unregulated, e.g. those not carried out by a Garda, a member of the Defence Forces or an officer of the Revenue Commissioners.

Other Constitutional Rights

An individual's right to privacy must be balanced with the constitutional rights of others, e.g. the administration of justice[67] and the right to freedom of expression.[68] In the case of *Roe v Blood Transfusion Service Board*, for example, Laffoy J refused to make an order allowing the plaintiff, who claimed she was infected with Hepatitis C from her treatment with contaminated blood products, to take proceedings under the fictitious name of Bridget Roe. Laffoy J stated: **[7–23]**

> "[T]he public disclosure of the true identities of parties to civil litigation is essential if justice is to be administered in public. In a situation in which the true identity of a plaintiff in a civil action is known to the parties to the action and to the court but is concealed from the public, members of the general public cannot see for themselves that justice is done".[69]

B. ECHR

Article 8 ECHR: **[7–24]**

> "1. Everyone has a right to respect for his private and family life, his home and his correspondence.
> 2. There shall be no interference by a public authority with the exercise of this right except such as is in accordance with the law and is necessary in a democratic society in the interests of national security, public safety or the economic well-being of the country, for the prevention of disorder or crime, for the protection of health or morals or for the protection of the rights and freedoms of others."

1. Nature of the Right

Article 8 is unique within the ECHR Articles in that it does not consider a single protected action, such as the right to life or freedom of expression, but rather, a bundle of **[7–25]**

Commissioners may apply to a judge for an authorisation where he or she has reasonable grounds for believing that—(*a*) as part of an operation or investigation being conducted by the Revenue Commissioners concerning a revenue offence, the surveillance being sought to be authorised is necessary for the purpose of obtaining information as to whether the offence has been committed or as to the circumstances relating to the commission of the offence, or obtaining evidence for the purpose of proceedings in relation to the offence, or (*b*) the surveillance being sought to be authorised is necessary for the purpose of preventing the commission of revenue offences …"

65 s 1 of the Criminal Justice (Surveillance) Act 2009.

66 s 14 of the Criminal Justice (Surveillance) Act 2009.

67 See *Re Ansbacher (Cayman) Ltd* [2002] 2 IR 517.

68 *M v Drury* [1994] 2 IR 8.

69 *Roe v Blood Transfusion Service Board* [1996] 3 IR 67 at 71.

four associated areas, and speaks of having "respect" for them.[70] The wording, therefore, is strongly suggestive of the giving of some margin of appreciation to the individual State.

The scope of Art 8 has developed in a rather broad way in all four areas of private life, family life, home and correspondence, and has, therefore, been widely interpreted to include perhaps the most obvious sort of State interference by means of police or security service surveillance, phone tapping, mail interception, etc. However, it has also developed a more nuanced body of case law concerning respect for personal dignity and autonomy with which the State must not interfere and which, further, it is obliged to facilitate.

[7–26] The scope of the Article has been used broadly by the ECtHR, in that the four interests of Art 8(1) are relatively autonomous, but without defining exactly the limits of meaning contained within each one. This means that the limits are not, therefore, constrained by a particular national interpretation. The usual approach of the ECtHR is to apply Art 8(1) to the particular case facts, but in certain cases it has also melded the various aspects of Art 8(1) into a whole, perhaps in order to avoid this definition of individuality.[71] Of course, this also allows the case law to develop through the "living instrument" concept in order to allow for, and to take consideration of, social and technical developments, especially information and surveillance technology.

Definition

[7–27] The concept of privacy is so difficult to define in this celebrity, information-addicted age that it may even be disadvantageous for a State to define it too closely. It can be argued that the four areas covered by Art 8(1) are quite distinct, but also that there is an overlap in the practical use of Art 8(1) as regards home, family life and correspondence; in terms of "privacy", this is a wider term, and has been interpreted, to a certain extent, with a view to the margin of appreciation of the individual State.

There are two obligations within this right to respect for privacy; the State has both a positive[72] and a negative[73] obligation, the latter being rather more engaged, indeed, so far engaged as to be the subject of State argument that it is the sole obligation.[74] The suggestion here was that a State should only give consideration to its own interference with the protected right by a public body. This narrow interpretation was addressed and dismissed by the ECtHR when it stated that Art 8 gave:

[70] Although Art 2 of Protocol 1 requires the State to "... respect the right of parents to ensure ... education and teaching in conformity with their own religious and philosophical convictions", which is plainly somewhat analogous to the scope of Art 8.

[71] *Klass v FRG* (1978) 2EHRR 214, *Kopp v Switzerland* (1998) 27 EHRR 91, where telephone conversations were considered part of private life, family life and correspondence.

[72] *McGinley and Egan v UK* (1998) 27 EHRR 1, where the applicant was a victim of State inaction, in this instance the lack of effective procedures for the dissemination of relevant information.

[73] That the State should refrain from interference with the life of a citizen; *Gul v Switzerland* (1996) 22 EHRR 93.

[74] For example, *Lingens v Austria* (1986) 8 EHRR 407.

> "... obligations (which) may involve the adoption of measures designed to secure respect for private life even in the sphere of the relations of individuals between themselves".[75]

Gender

In relation to gender, the ECtHR originally considered[76] that the disadvantage to applicants of a State refusal to retrospectively alter their birth certificates was outweighed by the need of the State to keep a reasonably uncomplicated system of registration, and, on the balance of convenience, that it was not in the public interest to have, essentially, self-certification of gender identity confirmed by the State. Further,[77] that the right to marry under UK law (marriage could only be between two persons of the opposite sex) did not conflict with the Art 12 right as regard transsexuals. This stance was modified a little in the case of *B v France*,[78] but remained much the same, insofar as other cases suggested that in such a complex area of moral, scientific and social argument, there was a great deal of scope for individual States to legislate as they saw fit.[79] There was no particular obligation for any contracting State to recognise an Art 8(1) right with regard to a transsexual's right to full legal and/or social status, especially in terms of the right to marry, and no need, as the ECtHR saw it, for a unified approach. [7–28]

However, this changed with the case of *Goodwin v UK*,[80] in which the ECtHR considered that the margin of appreciation had narrowed for the State, in that there was now perceived to be: " ... the unsatisfactory situation in which post-operative transsexuals live in an intermediate zone as not quite one gender or another ...",[81] and that this was "no longer sustainable". In respect of *Rees*[82] and *Cossey*,[83] the ECtHR also noted that there was no evidence adduced as to the detrimental impact on the public interest of changing the registration of birth certificates, and that whilst this interest may well be valid, it was no longer to be considered a complete barrier for the applicants. [7–29]

Sex Life and Privacy

The issue of gender leads naturally on to the issue of a private sex life, and *Dudgeon v UK*[84] laid out clearly that Art 8(1) applied to this aspect of privacy, in that one's sex life is one of the more intimate areas of private life and therefore guaranteed by the ECHR. This suggests, in turn, that any interference must be comprehensively justified, which is usually argued on the grounds of the Art 8(2) areas of health and/or morals. [7–30]

---

[75] *X and Y v Netherlands* (1985) 8 EHRR 235 at para 23.
[76] *Rees v UK* (1986) 9 EHRR 56.
[77] *Cossey v UK* (1990) 13 EHRR 622.
[78] (1992) 16 EHRR 1.
[79] *Sheffield and Horsham v UK* (1998) 27 EHRR 163, *X, Y and Z v UK* (1997) 24 EHRR 143.
[80] (2002) 35 EHRR 18.
[81] *ibid* at para 90.
[82] *Rees v UK* (1986) 9 EHRR 56.
[83] *Cossey v UK* (1990) 13 EHRR 622.
[84] (1982) 4 EHRR 149.

An example of this is the case of *Laskey, Jaggard and Brown v UK.*[85] The case[86] concerned the consensual activities of a group of sado-masochistic homosexual men over a 10-year period, where there was no apparent coercion, nor was any hospitalisation required for any of the injuries inflicted for pleasure. The activities took place in a private home and had been videotaped, but the videotape was not intended to be seen by anyone outside the group. The men intended that their activities were, and should remain, within the private sphere. The argument brought before the ECtHR by three of the men concerned their right to privacy under Art 8. The ECtHR found that, even though a number of men were involved and the proceedings videotaped, the right to privacy had been infringed. The question then became one of whether the interference was justified in a democratic society, and the ECtHR found that it was. Since the harm involved genital injury or torture, it was, therefore, serious harm, and the State should have the right to legislate for the level of harm to which a person may consent, thereby overriding the issue of the level of private morality. Given the reduced charges and sentences imposed, and considering the full details of the acts, the ECtHR judged that the State response had been both necessary and proportionate.

[7–31] *Laskey* was followed in *KA and AD v Belgium*[87] where the facts were similar in that there had been adjudged actual bodily harm in sado-masochistic acts, together with filming. Here, the ECtHR found that the severity and relative danger of some of the acts justified State measures against the applicants as necessary and proportionate.[88]

[7–32] It is worth noting, nevertheless, that *Laskey* was distinguished in *ADT v UK.*[89] This concerned a UK law defining the number of men who could legitimately have homosexual sex as a group. The court duly considered that there had been interference with Art 8(1), but in the particular case, there was no justification to stop groups of men behaving in an illegal way. The activities were restricted solely to a close group of friends, and, therefore, the margin of appreciation must be seen to be narrow and so the prosecution could not be justified.

[7–33] In principle, then, the ECtHR reiterated that the private sexual life of the individual should not be the concern of the State as regards consenting adults.

[7–34] Although Art 8(1) has been interpreted broadly, it is nevertheless necessary to point out that the right to respect for privacy *per se* is not protected, only the right to respect for a private life. In practical terms, however, this interpretation has tended to extend the meaning of "private life" so far that it is sometimes difficult to define the exact borders between it and "privacy". In the case of *Niemietz v Germany*[90] the ECtHR

---

[85] (1997) 24 EHRR 39.

[86] Originally stemming from *R. v Brown* [1994] 1 AC 212, where the defendants were found guilty of the statutory offences of wounding and causing actual bodily harm. Their defence, rejected by the House of Lords, was consent, as the court found that this would only operate as a defence where the public interest was concerned.

[87] *KA and AD v Belgium* (Nos 42758/98 and 45558/99), unreported, 17 February 2005.

[88] A factor in this judgment may have been that the applicants had not honoured the use of a "safe word" used by the Masochists to stop their actions.

[89] (2001) 31 EHRR 33.

[90] (1993) 16 EHRR 97.

found that the definition must include the right to both establish and develop relationships with other people, who may initially be outside the sphere of an "inner circle" private life, expanding the concept of having one's own space. That these relationships extended into the workplace was established by the case of *Halford v UK*.[91] In the instance of secret surveillance, there was clear law that the surveillance was a violation of private life, shown, for example, in the successive cases of *Klass v FRG*,[92] *Malone v UK*[93] and *Khan v UK*,[94] but *Halford* established a right to a private telephone conversation whilst on work premises.

In the case of *Peck v United Kingdom*,[95] where the attempted suicide of the applicant was caught on CCTV and subsequently released, without either obtaining consent or anonymising him, the ECtHR found a significant breach of Art 8.

State Information on the Individual

With the ever-increasing use of surveillance and technology, the ability of the State to gather and store personal information has led to a certain amount of legal consideration concerning the extent to which the State should be able to access the personal information and images of a citizen without the consent of that citizen. These questions will invariably concern the compatibility of the domestic law with Art 8. Generally speaking, the State has two agencies collecting and collating information, the Police, whose information will be seen as being concerned primarily with the prevention and detection of crime, and the security services, whose remit covers threats to national security, either within or without the particular State. In the latter case, by the nature of the process, there are unlikely to be opportunities for the examination of the intelligence or the gathering process. [7–35]

However, there are a few cases where this has been considered by the ECtHR, such as *McVeigh v United Kingdom,*[96] where the applicants were questioned, searched, fingerprinted and photographed under anti-terrorism legislation.[97] The retention of records, they argued, constituted a violation of their right to a private life. However, the Commission held that the information was relevant for intelligence purposes, and the wider social need to fight terrorism outweighed what could be considered as minor infringements of the applicants' rights. [7–36]

Likewise, in *Murray v United Kingdom*[98] the recording of the applicant's personal details and photographing of him when he was arrested was considered to be within the [7–37]

---

[91] (1997 24 EHRR 523.

[92] (1978) 2 EHRR 214.

[93] (1984) 7 EHRR 14.

[94] (2001) 31 EHRR 45.

[95] *Peck v United Kingdom* (2003) 36 EHRR 719. The applicant had not at that stage been charged with or convicted of any offence, whilst the TV broadcast where the footage appeared was about crime prevention, and the media coverage was therefore a serious breach of his private life.

[96] *McVeigh v United Kingdom* (1981) 5 EHRR 71. However, it was also found that prohibiting detainees from notifying their wives of their whereabouts while they were held and questioned for 45 hours, in the absence of any danger that accomplices would be warned, was a breach.

[97] Prevention of Terrorism (Supplemental Temporary Provisions) Order 1976.

[98] *Murray v United Kingdom* (1994) 19 EHRR 191.

remit of the State for the purpose of investigating terrorism, as none of the personal details recorded actually appeared irrelevant in relation to the arrest and interrogation procedures.

Given these cases, the suggestion is that the ECtHR will afford a wide margin of appreciation to the State when the issue of terrorism is raised in relation to Art 8, and that the wider safety of the public will be a large determinant factor.

[7–38] Photography is widely used by police forces, but whether the taking of photographs by the police amounts to an intrusion into an individual's private life will depend to a large extent on whether it related to private matters or public incidents, and whether the material thus obtained was envisaged for a limited use or was to be made available in some form to the general public.

The case of *Friedl v Austria*[99] concerned the taking of pictures of the applicant, among others, during a legitimate demonstration. The State claimed that it wished to retain these images for future recognition, and, allegedly, to facilitate ensuing investigation proceedings for any offences relating to the demonstration. The State claim was that this did not breach any Art 8 rights, the argument being that the police had merely been recording incidents related to a public incident, in a public place, in which the applicant was voluntarily taking part. This, they contended, meant that there had been no intrusion into the "inner circle" of the applicant's private life. This inner circle is something about which the ECtHR has been very much concerned, and can be seen with respect to the Press. This did not breach Art 8 rights, the argument being that the police had merely been recording incidents related to a public incident, in a public place, in which the applicant was voluntarily taking part. So there was no intrusion into the "inner circle" of the applicant's private life. This inner circle analogy is something about which the ECtHR has been very keen, and can also be seen in decisions relating to the press and media.

[7–39] Information which the police can legitimately keep will be the records of past offences together with information obtained in investigations where no prosecution was able to be brought at that time. This latter type of information will be engaged where organised crime or terrorism are the targets of the investigation, and retention of information is therefore permissible; this plainly overlaps with the requirements of the security services.

Human Rights and Environment

[7–40] Whilst not an obvious area for discussion, human rights and protection of the environment are related in fundamental ways. Environmental degradation can undermine human rights (the right to life, Art 2, for example, can be threatened by air or water pollution). On the other hand, environmental protection may be aided by freedom of expression (Art 10) by providing and publicising information on environmental threats.

[7–41] However, and despite this interrelationship between human rights and environmental protection, there is ample debate as to the existence of, and very little textual

[99] *Friedl v Austria* (1995) 21 EHRR 83. See also *X v UK*, No 5877/72, 12 October 1973.

recognition of, a human right to a healthy environment. It is not mentioned as such in the Universal Declaration of Human Rights 1948, or in either the International Covenant on Civil and Political Rights 1966 (ICCPR) or the International Covenant on Economic, Social and Cultural Rights 1966 (ICESCR). However, Principle 1 of the Stockholm Declaration on the Environment 1972 recognises that:

> "Man has the fundamental right to freedom, equality and adequate conditions of life, in an environment of a quality that permits a life of dignity and well-being, and he bears a solemn responsibility to protect and improve the environment for present and future generations. In this respect, policies promoting or perpetuating apartheid, racial segregation, discrimination, colonial and other forms of oppression and foreign domination stand condemned and must be eliminated."

In addition, Principle 1 of the Rio Declaration on Environment and Development 1992 states that "[h]uman beings are at the centre of concerns for sustainable development. They are entitled to a healthy and productive life in harmony with nature."

Unfortunately, despite worthy aims, these instruments are non-binding for their signatories. Although the African Charter on Human and Peoples' Rights 1981,[100] and the American Convention on Human Rights[101] do recognise environmental issues, the ECHR is silent on this, and the Council of Europe failed to adopt a draft Protocol on Environmental rights in the 1970s. However, without fully recognising a right to a healthy environment, the jurisprudence of the ECtHR has grown to provide some level of environmental rights protection, mainly through Art 8 claims, and State interferences with property rights in order to protect the environment have generally been seen as justified by the ECtHR.[102] **[7–42]**

As an example, toxic fumes emanating from a factory could prevent individuals from enjoying their private life. In such a case, an environmental nuisance could thus give rise to a breach of Art 8 claim. The evolution of Strasbourg's case law can be seen through successive cases such as *X and Y v FRG,*[103] where the Commission declared the application of members of an environmental organisation (contesting the use of marshlands for military purposes), inadmissible on the ground that the ECHR does not recognise a right to nature preservation. In *Powell and Rayner v UK*[104] the Art 8 claim, related to aircraft noise at Heathrow Airport, failed in view of the wide margin of appreciation granted to contracting States in balancing the right to private life with the economic wellbeing of the country. **[7–43]**

---

[100] African Charter on Human and Peoples' Rights 1981, Art 24: "All peoples shall have the right to a general satisfactory environment favourable to their development."

[101] American Convention on Human Rights' San Salvador Protocol of 1988, Art 11: "1. Everyone shall have the right to live in a healthy environment and to have access to basic public services. 2. The States Parties shall promote the protection, preservation, and improvement of the environment."

[102] *Buckley v UK* (1997) 23 EHRR 482; *Chapman v UK* (2001) 33 EHRR 399.

[103] *X and Y v Federal Republic of Germany* (1976) 15 DR 161.

[104] *Powell and Rayner v UK* (1990) 12 EHRR 355, (1990) ECHR Ser A No 172.

Guerra v Italy[105] confirmed the finding in *Lopez-Ostra*,[106] and clarified that Art 8 imposed positive obligations on the State to ensure effective respect for private and family life. However, in *Hatton v UK* the previous line of jurisprudence was at first confirmed by the Chamber in its 2001 decision,[107] where the conclusion was that the UK failed to strike a fair balance between the community's interests and the applicants' right to private life. However, this was later overturned by the Grand Chamber in its 2003 decision, with the ECtHR reaffirming that "there is no explicit right under the Convention to a clean and quiet environment".[108] In conclusion, it would seem that whilst the case law relating to Art 8 does not appear to allow the reading of a definitive right to a clean environment into the Article, it clearly recognises some level of environmental protection.

Freedom of the Press v Private Life

[7–44] This argument, the tension between the requirements of Arts 8 and 10, has been highlighted most recently with the "super-injunctions" argument, whereby the UK courts have installed injunctions forbidding all mention of newspaper stories involving celebrities, and even forbidding disclosure of the injunction itself. This led to parliamentary privilege being used to name certain parties who had obtained these injunctions, and to the widespread use of Twitter being similarly utilised. This may lead to the question of whether the ECHR is able to control the blogosphere adequately, when considering modern technological communication in terms of these two Articles.

[7–45] In *Von Hannover v Germany,*[109] the ECtHR held that the protection of speech in public matters should be upheld only insofar as it contributes to the democratic debate, and that although the applicant was a public figure, she also had a right to a private life. The direction seen in the UK cases of *Campbell v MGN*[110] and *Murray v Big Pictures*[111] suggests a higher protection of privacy for public figures, but in certain circumstances only, where there could be seen to be a legitimate expectation of privacy (for instance, with children).

[7–46] In *Mosley v News Group Newspapers,*[112] the UK courts applied a stricter test of public interest, much more in line with *Von Hannover*. But when Mosley attempted to suggest that freedom of the press be more effectively curtailed by requiring editors to agree all stories with the parties involved, the ECtHR rejected his arguments.[113] It considered that a general requirement of prior notification risked having a negative effect on

---

105 (1998) 26 EHRR 357] No 14967/89, 19 February 1998.

106 *Lopez-Ostra v Spain*, 1995) 20 EHRR 277, 20 EHHR, Ser A, 1994 at para 51 "severe environmental pollution may affect individuals' well-being and prevent them from enjoying their homes in such a way as to affect their private and family life adversely."

107 No 36022/97 (2002) 34 EHRR 1 concerning, like *Powell and Rayner v UK* (1990) 12 EHRR 355, (1990) ECHR Ser A No 172, aircraft noise pollution near Heathrow Airport.

108 Grand Chamber in *Hatton v UK* (2003) 37 EHRR 28. Later restated in the case of *Fadeyeva v Russia*, (2007) 45 EHRR 10 No 55723/00, 30 November 2005.

109 *Von Hannover v Germany* (2006) 43 EHRR 7.

110 *Campbell v MGN* [2005] 1 WLR 3394.

111 *Murray v Big Pictures* [2008] 3 WLR 1360.

112 *Mosley v News Group Newspapers* [2008] EWHC 687 (QB).

113 *Mosley v UK*, No 48009/08, 10 May 2011.

investigative journalism, and that there should be considered a margin of appreciation for each contracting State in terms of redress and for the protection of privacy, and that for the information to be revealed, it must be of "public interest" and not just of "interest to the public".

2. Legitimate Justifications for Interference with the Right

Article 8 is a qualified right, which means that for an Art 8 claim to be successful, there should be an interference with Art 8(1) attributable to the State and this interference should not be justified on one of the grounds listed in Art 8(2). [7–47]

For an Art 8 breach to arise it thus must be shown:

- first, that the issue at stake comes within the scope of Art 8, i.e. can it come under one of the four headings, or a combination of them?;
- secondly, that the State has either interfered directly with Art 8(1), or failed to take appropriate measures (a positive duty) to guarantee the right to private life; and
- thirdly, that this interference/failure to act is not in accordance with law, necessary in a democratic society, and justified on one of the grounds listed in Art 8(2), i.e. in the interests of national security, public safety or the economic well-being of the country, for the prevention of disorder or crime, for the protection of health or morals or for the protection of the rights and freedoms of others.

It is always for the applicant to show that there has been an interference with the right to respect for privacy,[114] and it is therefore sometimes necessary to show that the applicant is a "victim", and therefore that there has been the likelihood of a violation.[115]

If the State has been found to have interfered with the Art 8 right, then the ECtHR will have to consider whether the interference has been "in accordance with the law" and whether it is "necessary in a democratic society". Article 8(2) provides a list where the interference may be justified,[116] and there is a great deal of scope for the State to offer justifying reasons, including, it should be noted, that of the "economic well-being of the country". [7–48]

[114] *Campbell and Fell v United Kingdom* (1984) 7 EHRR 165.

[115] *Klass v FRG* (1978) 2 EHRR 214. The activity of covert phone tapping was difficult to prove by its very nature, but with the applicant as a victim, the ECtHR could then see that: "In the mere existence of the legislation itself there is involved, for all those to whom the legislation could be applied, a menace of surveillance ..." (at para 41).

[116] It is interesting to note that the ECtHR values legal process highly, and in the case of *Niemietz v Germany* (1993) 16 EHRR 97, the search of a lawyer's office was not justified, since " ... where a lawyer is involved, an encroachment on professional secrecy may have repercussions on the proper administration of justice and hence on the rights guaranteed by Article 6 of the Convention" (at para 37).

The State must also show that the interference has an objective, and, hence, that there is a pressing need for that objective and for the necessary interference with the right.

C. CFR

[7–49] Article 7:

> "Everyone has the right to respect for his or her private and family life, home and communications."

Article 8:

> "1. Everyone has the right to the protection of personal data concerning him or her.
> 2. Such data must be processed fairly for specified purposes and on the basis of the consent of the person concerned or some other legitimate basis laid down by law. Everyone has the right of access to data which has been collected concerning him or her, and the right to have it rectified.
> 3. Compliance with these rules shall be subject to control by an independent authority."

[7–50] Article 7 corresponds with Art 8 of the ECHR and focuses generally on the autonomous aspect of privacy.[117] The word "correspondence" in the ECHR was substituted by the word "communications" in the CFR in order to take account of technological advancements.[118] In accordance with Art 52(3) of the CFR, the meaning and scope of the Art 7 protection are the same as those of the corresponding Article of the ECHR.

There has been limited case law before the European Court of Justice (ECJ) on the issue of privacy; however, the European Court of Justice has held that the respect for a private life under Art 8 of the ECHR includes a right not to disclose information regarding the state of one's health.[119]

The EU has adopted various legislative measures in the realm of privacy, particularly with regard to privacy of communications, including Regulation (EC) No 1211/2009 of the European Parliament and of the Council establishing the Body of European Regulators for Electronic Communications (BEREC) and the Office. This Body is tasked with contributing to the "development and better functioning of the internal market for electronic communications networks and services, by aiming to ensure a consistent application of the EU regulatory framework for electronic communica-

[117] See M Eriksson, "Article 7: Respect for Family and Private Life" in *Commentary by the EU Network of Independent Experts on Fundamental Rights*, June 2006, pp 78–89, available at: http://infoportal.fra.europa.eu/InfoPortal/infobaseShowContent.do?btnCat_300&btnCountryBread_169, last accessed 21 June 2012.

[118] Explanation of the Praesidium of the Convention which drafted the Charter of Fundamental Rights of the European Union – see http://infoportal.fra.europa.eu/InfoPortal/infobaseShowContent.do?btnCat_231&btnCountryBread_169. Treaty establishing a Constitution for Europe – Final Act – Declaration concerning the explanations relating to the Charter of Fundamental Rights [2004] OJ C310/424.

[119] Case C-404/92 P, *X v Commission of the European Communities* [1994] ECR I-4737.

tions".[120] In addition, Directives have been adopted with regard to the interception of telecommunications.[121]

Article 8 of the CFR is a new departure in the human rights framework as the protection of personal data has not been recognised as a specific right in other human rights instruments, with such issues usually falling within the ambit of a general privacy-protection provision. Given the development of new information and communications technologies which facilitate automatic processing of personal data and the retention of personal data by various governmental agencies for various reasons, including to combat terrorism, the need for regulation of this area is obvious. Article 8 builds on the Convention for the Protection of Individuals with regard to Automatic Processing of Data (1991), which has been ratified by all EU member states, and its Additional Protocol regarding Supervisory Authorities and Transborder Dataflow (2001). The instrument does not define "personal data" but a definition is provided in Directive 95/46/EC which states that personal data means: **[7–51]**

> "any information relating to an identified or identifiable natural person ('data subject'); an identifiable person is one who can be identified, directly or indirectly, in particular by reference to an identification number or to one or more factors specific to his physical, physiological, mental, cultural or social identity".[122]

Whilst there has been little case law of the European Court of Justice on the scope of data protection, the Court has held that the inclusion of information about public body employee salaries in an annual report constitutes the processing of personal data.[123] While Art 8 seeks to protect personal data against interference by EU institutions and bodies and Member States when they implement EU law, the ECJ also dealt with the protection of personal data in relations between individuals. In *Lindqvist*[124] the ECJ held that a person who identified people on an internet page by using names or other means did, in fact, process data within the meaning of Art 3(1) of Directive 95/46/EC. **[7–52]**

[120] Art 1 of Regulation (EC) No 1211/2009 of the European Parliament and of the Council of 25 November 2009 establishing the Body of European Regulators for Electronic Communications (BEREC) and the Office [2009] OJ L337/1.

[121] Directive 2002/58/EC of the European Parliament and of the Council of 12 July 2002 concerning the processing of personal data and the protection of privacy in the electronic communications sector [2002] OJ L201/37, amended by Directive 2006/24/EC of the European Parliament and of the Council and Directive 2009/136/EC of the European Parliament and of the Council.

[122] Art 2(a) of Directive 95/46/EC of the European Parliament and of the Council of 24 October 1995 on the protection of individuals with regard to the processing of personal data and on the free movement of such data [1995] OJ L281/31.

[123] Cases C-465/00, C-138/01 and C-139/01, Österreichischer Rundfunl [2003] ECR I-4989. See also Case C-404/92, *X v Commission*; Case C-274/99 P *Connolly v Commission* [2001] ECR I-1611; Case C-275/06 *Promusicae* [2008] ECR I-271; Case 553/07, *College van burgemeester en wethouders van Rotterdam v Rijkeboer* and Case C-73/07 *Satakunnan Markkinapörssi and Satamedia* [2008] ECR I-0000; Case C-73/07, *Tietosuojavaltuutettu v Satakunnan Markkinapörssi Oy.*

[124] Case C-101/01, *Bodil Lindqvist* [2003] ECR I-12971.

The European Data Protection Supervisor is the authority responsible for monitoring the application of data protection requirements by EU institutions and bodies.[125]

D. International and Regional Laws

[7–53] The right to privacy is protected in a number of universal and regional human rights instruments, including in Art 12 of the Universal Declaration of Human Rights. This states:

> "No one shall be subjected to arbitrary interference with his privacy, family, home or correspondence, nor to attacks upon his honour and reputation. Everyone has the right to the protection of the law against such interference or attacks."

This is elaborated on in Art 17 of the ICCPR, which states:

> "1. No one shall be subjected to arbitrary or unlawful interference with his privacy, family, home or correspondence, nor to unlawful attacks on his honour and reputation. 2. Everyone has the right to the protection of the law against such interference or attacks."

[7–54] General Comment 16 (1988) of the Human Rights Committee, *The Right to Respect of Privacy, Family, Home and Correspondence, and Protection of Honour and Reputation,* clarifies the meaning of Art 17 ICCPR:

> "The gathering and holding of personal information on computers, data banks and other devices, whether by public authorities or private individuals or bodies, must be regulated by law. Effective measures have to be taken by States to ensure that information concerning a person's private life does not reach the hands of persons who are not authorized by law to receive, process and use it, and is never used for purposes incompatible with the Covenant. In order to have the most effective protection of his private life, every individual should have the right to ascertain in an intelligible form, whether, and if so, what personal data is stored in automatic data files, and for what purposes. Every individual should also be able to ascertain which public authorities or private individuals or bodies control or may control their files. If such files contain incorrect personal data or have been collected or processed contrary to the provisions of the law, every individual should have the right to request rectification or elimination."

[7–55] The right to privacy is also provided for in Art 14 of the International Convention on the Protection of the Rights of All Migrant Workers and Members of Their

---

125 Data protection is also dealt with in Art 16 of the Treaty on the Functioning of the European Union (TFEU). This states: "1. Everyone has the right to the protection of personal data concerning them. 2. The European Parliament and the Council, acting in accordance with the ordinary legislative procedure, shall lay down the rules relating to the protection of individuals with regard to the processing of personal data by Union institutions, bodies, offices and agencies, and by the Member States when carrying out activities which fall within the scope of Union law, and the rules relating to the free movement of such data. Compliance with these rules shall be subject to the control of independent authorities. The rules adopted on the basis of this Article shall be without prejudice to the specific rules laid down in Article 39 of the Treaty on European Union ..."

Families,[126] Arts 22[127] and 23[128] of the Convention on the Rights of Persons with Disabilities and Art 16 of the Convention on the Rights of the Child.[129]

At a regional level, the right to privacy is protected by Art 11 of the American Convention on Human Rights[130] and Art 21 of the Arab Charter on Human

126 This provision states: "No migrant worker or member of his or her family shall be subjected to arbitrary or unlawful interference with his or her privacy, family, correspondence or other communications, or to unlawful attacks on his or her honour and reputation. Each migrant worker and member of his or her family shall have the right to the protection of the law against such interference or attacks."

127 This provision states: "1. No person with disabilities, regardless of place of residence or living arrangements, shall be subjected to arbitrary or unlawful interference with his or her privacy, family, or correspondence or other types of communication or to unlawful attacks on his or her honour and reputation. Persons with disabilities have the right to the protection of the law against such interference or attacks. 2. States Parties shall protect the privacy of personal, health and rehabilitation information of persons with disabilities on an equal basis with others."

128 This provision states: "1. States Parties shall take effective and appropriate measures to eliminate discrimination against persons with disabilities in all matters relating to marriage, family, parenthood and relationships, on an equal basis with others, so as to ensure that: (a) The right of all persons with disabilities who are of marriageable age to marry and to found a family on the basis of free and full consent of the intending spouses is recognized; (b) The rights of persons with disabilities to decide freely and responsibly on the number and spacing of their children and to have access to age-appropriate information, reproductive and family planning education are recognized, and the means necessary to enable them to exercise these rights are provided; (c) Persons with disabilities, including children, retain their fertility on an equal basis with others. 2. States Parties shall ensure the rights and responsibilities of persons with disabilities, with regard to guardianship, wardship, trusteeship, adoption of children or similar institutions, where these concepts exist in national legislation; in all cases the best interests of the child shall be paramount. States Parties shall render appropriate assistance to persons with disabilities in the performance of their child-rearing responsibilities. 3. States Parties shall ensure that children with disabilities have equal rights with respect to family life. With a view to realizing these rights, and to prevent concealment, abandonment, neglect and segregation of children with disabilities, States Parties shall undertake to provide early and comprehensive information, services and support to children with disabilities and their families. 4. States Parties shall ensure that a child shall not be separated from his or her parents against their will, except when competent authorities subject to judicial review determine, in accordance with applicable law and procedures, that such separation is necessary for the best interests of the child. In no case shall a child be separated from parents on the basis of a disability of either the child or one or both of the parents. 5. States Parties shall, where the immediate family is unable to care for a child with disabilities, undertake every effort to provide alternative care within the wider family, and failing that, within the community in a family setting."

129 This provision states: "1. No child shall be subjected to arbitrary or unlawful interference with his or her privacy, family, or correspondence, nor to unlawful attacks on his or her honour and reputation. 2. The child has the right to the protection of the law against such interference or attacks."

130 This provision states: "1. Everyone has the right to have his honor respected and his dignity recognized. 2. No one may be the object of arbitrary or abusive interference with his private life, his family, his home, or his correspondence, or of unlawful attacks on his honor or reputation. 3. Everyone has the right to the protection of the law against such interference or attacks."

Rights.[131] Interestingly, this right is not included in the African Charter on Human and Peoples' Rights.[132]

Conclusion

[7–56] The right to privacy is a complex and multi-layered area of litigation within the ECtHR, and the concentration on "respect for" rather than simply a "right" means that a considerable margin of appreciation is possible between contracting States, particularly in the contentious areas of sexuality and interpersonal relationships.

[7–57] It is clear that the "living instrument" doctrine is very much in the contemplation of the ECtHR, and so the expansion of the right to, for example, environmental issues and those more contentious gender issues which could never have been contemplated by the ECHR drafters shows the underlying ability of the ECtHR and the ECHR to be relevant to a modern society. It is also obvious that the interpretation of the right to privacy by the ECtHR has facilitated the expansion of the right in Ireland in various ways. This is clearly apparent in the decision in the *Foy*[133] case, discussed above.

---

131 This provision states: "1. No one shall be subjected to arbitrary or unlawful interference with regard to his privacy, family, home or correspondence, nor to unlawful attacks on his honour or his reputation. 2. Everyone has the right to the protection of the law against such interference or attacks."

132 For a critique of the African Charter, see C Heyns, "The African Regional Human Rights System: The African Charter" (2003/4) 108 Penn State LR 679.

133 *Foy v An t-Ard Chláraitheoir* [2002] IEHC 116 and *Foy v An t-Ard Chláraitheoir* [2007] IEHC 470.

CHAPTER 8
The Rights of the Family

Introduction

Both nationally and internationally, the rights of the family are promoted and guaranteed by numerous instruments. The family is regarded as the principle unit of society, and various aspects of family life, including marriage and children, are widely protected. This chapter analyses the meaning of "family" under the Irish Constitution and the nature of the constitutional protections guaranteed to the family. It then proceeds to discuss the protection of family life under the European Convention on Human Rights (ECHR) and under EU law, before concluding with a discussion of the protection of the family and family life under international human rights law. **[8–01]**

A. Irish Constitution

Article 41.1.1°: **[8–02]**

> "The State recognises the Family as the natural primary and fundamental unit group of Society, and as a moral institution possessing inalienable and imprescriptible rights, antecedent and superior to all positive law."

Article 41.1.2°:

> "The State, therefore, guarantees to protect the Family in its constitution and authority, as the necessary basis of social order and as indispensable to the welfare of the Nation and the State."

Article 41 guarantees rights to the family and also imposes obligations on the State to protect the family and the institution of marriage. Article 41.1.1° recognises that a number of undefined rights accrue to the family and Art 41.1.2° proceeds to guarantee the protection of these rights. The nature, scope and limitation of the protections guaranteed to the family have been interpreted and clarified in case law. The remainder of Art 41 considers the issues of the place of the woman in the home and the dissolution of marriage. Article 41 is also closely linked with Art 42, which addresses education, as the family is also defined as "the primary and natural educator of the child".[1] However, the right to education in general, and the right to education in the context of the family, will be addressed in Chapter 15. It should also be noted that additional constitutional rights, set out in Art 40.3, also attach to family members. However, the focus of the first part of this discussion is on Art 41.1.

1. Nature of the Right

[8–03] The language of Art 41 clearly indicates that the rights of the family have been influenced by a natural law philosophy, as it describes the family as "a moral institution possessing inalienable and imprescriptible rights, antecedent and superior to all positive law".[2] Whyte has underlined how such rights were influenced by the Catholic Church ethos[3] and the Constitutional Review Group has stated:

> "Article 41 was a novel provision in 1937. The Constitution of 1922 contained no provision relating to family and marriage. It is generally considered that Articles 41 and 42 were heavily influenced by Roman Catholic teaching and Papal encyclicals. They were clearly drafted with only one family in mind, namely, the family based on marriage".[4]

The Meaning of "Family" in Art 41.1.2°

[8–04] Despite the fact that the Constitution guarantees to protect "the family" in Art 41.1.2°, it fails to define what is meant by the family. However, the Supreme Court has clarified the meaning of the family for constitutional purposes in a number of cases, including *State (Nicolaou) v An Bord Uchtála*,[5] *G v An Bord Uchtála*[6] and *WO'R v EH (Guardianship)*.[7] In these cases the Supreme Court restricted the meaning of the family

---

1 Art 42.1.

2 Art 41.1.1°

3 See JH Whyte, *Church and State in Modern Ireland* (2nd ed, Gill and Macmillan, Dublin, 1980), pp 52 and 377. Also see WR Duncan, "Supporting the Institution of Marriage in Ireland" (1978) XIII Irish Jurist 215.

4 *Report of the Constitution Review Group* (Stationery Office, Dublin, 1996), p 296.

5 [1966] IR 567.

6 [1980] IR 32.

7 [1966] 2 IR 248.

to a family based on marriage.[8] The court held in *Murray v Ireland*[9] that a family can consist of a married couple with children, and a married couple without children.[10] The family, however, does not include an unmarried cohabiting couple and their children. Rather, such a *de facto* family is protected under Art 40.3 of the Constitution,[11] rather than under Art 41.1.2°.

In certain cases, families not based on marriage may be treated in the same way as a family based on marriage,[12] e.g. the Civil Partnership and Certain Rights and Obligations of Cohabitants Act 2010 deals with the rights and obligations of same-sex and opposite-sex couples who have been cohabiting but have not married.

This distinction between families based on marriage and families not based on marriage was addressed in the Report of the Constitution Review Group in 1996. The Group did not recommend that a change be made to the Constitution to extend protection and rights to *de facto* families. The Group felt that such a move would create an amount of uncertainty. The Group did, however, recommend that the guarantee to protect the family based on marriage would be complemented by a general guarantee to ensure respect for family life, regardless of marriage.[13] **[8–05]**

The Scope of Art 41.1.2°

While the Constitution guarantees the protection of the family, it does not state from whom or what this protection is necessary. This issue has been clarified to an extent through case law. In *L v L*[14] the Supreme Court was of the opinion that such protection may be warranted against the State itself, e.g. if new legislation is enacted which would interfere with the family in some way. This was further highlighted when the constitutionality of the Matrimonial Home Bill 1993 was tested in the Supreme Court. Finlay CJ held that the Bill was unconstitutional based on its incompatibility with Art 41 as the provisions of the Bill did not constitute "reasonably proportionate intervention by the State with the rights of the family"[15] and constituted "a failure by the State to protect the authority of the family".[16] **[8–06]**

---

[8] See J Ennis, "Marriage: Redefined and Realigned with *Bunreacht na hÉireann*" (2010) 1(2) IJLS 29.

[9] [1985] IR 532.

[10] In *Murphy v AG* [1982] IR 241 at 286, Kenny J defined "marriage" as a "permanent, indissoluble union of man and woman". In *CT v DT* [2003] 1 ILRM 321 at 374, Murray J gave an updated definition, taking into consideration the legality of divorce. He stated: "Of course society, as always, evolves and continues to evolve and there are a far greater number of committed partnerships established outside marriage than was heretofore the case. Nonetheless, marriage itself remains a solemn contract of partnership entered into between man and woman with a special status recognised by the Constitution. It is one which is entered into in principle for life. It is not entered into for a determinate period".

[11] *G v An Bord Uchtála* [1980] IR 32.

[12] See J Eardly, "The Constitution And Marriage - The Scope Of Protection" (2006) 24 ILT 167.

[13] *Report of the Constitution Review Group*, *supra* n 4, pp 321–323.

[14] [1992] 2 IR 77.

[15] *In re Article 26 and the Matrimonial Home Bill 1993* [1994] 1 IR 305 at 326.

[16] *ibid.*

[8–07] Casey states that Art 41.1.2° "is not to be interpreted as creating a constitutional shield for crimes committed within the family".[17] This principle is illustrated in the case of *People (DPP) v T.*[18] In this case a father had been found guilty of committing sexual offences against his daughter and his wife had been a witness for the prosecution. On appeal, the father claimed that the wife's evidence was invalid at common law under the rule that one spouse was not a competent witness against the other. Counsel for the father claimed that this common law rule was complemented by the constitutional protection of the family in Art 41. The court rejected this argument, however, on the grounds that whilst Art 41 protected the family as a unit, each member of the family also benefitted from personal constitutional rights. In the present case, the child's right to bodily integrity trumped the rights of the family as a unit.

[8–08] It was held in the case of *PH v John Murphy and Sons Ltd*[19] that the protection afforded by Art 41.1.2° to the family extended to protection against legislation and deliberate acts of State organs and/or officials which impaired its "constitution and authority".[20] However, it did not extend to cover negligent acts of State officials, even if they resulted in the destruction of the "constitution and authority"[21] of the family. Costello J gave the example of the killing of parents by the negligent driving of a State-owned vehicle, with the children consequently being placed in different foster homes. He stated:

> "It must be remembered that the court is construing a constitutional document whose primary purpose in the field of fundamental rights is to protect them from unjust laws enacted by the legislature and from arbitrary acts committed by State officials. It would require very clear words to construe the State's constitutional obligations (as distinct from its common law obligations) as including a duty to ensure that its officials would not drive carelessly. I do not think that the words employed in Article 41 are apt to do so, and the State's guarantee of protection does not, in my judgment, include a guarantee that its officials will drive State vehicles without negligence".[22]

Therefore, while the protection offered by Art 41.1.2° is limited to deliberate and not negligent acts, a remedy for such negligent acts still exists at common law. Casey highlights the reluctance of Costello J to extend the constitutional protection to negligent acts, and states:

> " ... the courts, though accepting that the Constitution creates rights of action against private persons for breach of constitutionally protected rights, have generally been reluctant to move beyond the established categories of the law of torts".[23]

[17] J Casey, *Constitutional Law in Ireland* (3rd ed, Thomson Round Hall, Dublin 2000), p 617.
[18] Unreported, Court of Criminal Appeal, 27 July 1988.
[19] [1987] 2 1 IR 621.
[20] Art 41.1.2°.
[21] *ibid.*
[22] [1987] 1 IR 621 at 626–627.
[23] J Casey, *supra* n 17, p 617.

2. Legitimate Justifications for Interference with the Right

While the Constitution can protect the family from unreasonable interference by the State, the guarantee in Art 41.1.2° has been interpreted as a qualified guarantee. In *Murray v Ireland*, Costello J stated: [8–09]

> " ... the exercise by the Family of its imprescriptible and inalienable right to integrity as a unit group, can be severely and violently restricted by the State when, for example, its laws permits a father to be banned from a family home or allow for the imprisonment of both parents".[24]

A number of limitations to Art 41.1.2° have been interpreted in case law concerning inter-State families and non-nationals.[25] For example, in the case of *Abdelkefi v Minister for Justice*[26] it was held that Art 41.1.2° does not guarantee a non-national spouse or parent the right to enter or reside in Ireland. Further case law also illustrates that the protections espoused in Art 41.1.2° do not preclude an non-national spouse or parent from deportation.[27] However, such actions are unlikely, as shown in the case of *Fajujonu v Minister for Justice.*[28] The plaintiffs were a married foreign couple along with their child who was born in Ireland. The parents had two younger children, also born in Ireland. Under the Aliens Act 1935 and subsequent regulations the couple required the permission of the Minister for Justice to remain in the State. They did not have such permission. When the prospective employer of the father sought a work permit for him from the Department of Labour, their situation was noted by the Department of Justice. Whilst the Minister for Justice did not make a deportation order against the father, he requested that he make arrangements to leave the State. The parents and their child then challenged the request under Art 41. The Supreme Court emphasised the rights of the Irish-born children as part of a family unit. Finlay CJ stated:

> " ... where, as occurs in this case, an alien has in fact resided for an appreciable time in the State and has become a member of a family unit within the State containing children who are citizens, there can be no question but that those children, as citizens, have got a constitutional right to the company, care and parentage of their parents within a family unit. I am also satisfied that *prima facie* and subject to the exigencies of the common good that that is a right which these citizens would be entitled to exercise within the State".[29]

While deportation was not precluded under Art 41, the Minister for Justice would only resort to such measures in extreme circumstances "if, after due and proper consideration ... he is satisfied that the interests of the common good and the protection of the State and its society justifies an interference with what is clearly a [8–10]

---

24 [1985] IR 532 at 538.

25 See E Whelan, "The Right to Family Life v Immigration Control: The Application of Article 8 of the European Convention on Human Rights in Ireland" (2006) 6(1) HLJ 93.

26 [1984] ILRM 138.

27 See *Pok Sun Shum v Ireland* [1986] ILRM 593 and *Osheku v Ireland* [1986] IR 733.

28 [1990] 2 IR 151.

29 *ibid* at 164.

constitutional right".[30] Walsh J continued in the same vein and stated that the Minster would only issue a deportation order if he was satisfied:

> "[t]hat the interests of the common good of the people of Ireland and of the protection of the State and its society are so predominant and so overwhelming in the circumstances of the case, that an action which can have the effect of breaking up this family is not so disproportionate to the aim sought to be achieved as to be unsustainable".[31]

[8–11] Deportation was also the subject of the *Adeoye* case.[32] Mr Adeoye was a Nigerian national. He arrived in Ireland in 2009 and unsuccessfully applied for asylum. A deportation order was made in 2010. He failed to report to the Garda National Immigration Bureau but was arrested in January 2011 and deported the following month. He, his wife (an Irish citizen) and his daughter (an Irish citizen) applied to the court for judicial review of the Minister's decision not to set aside the deportation order pursuant to s 3(11) of the Immigration Act 1999. Mrs Adeoye also had another daughter from a previous relationship and said Mr Adeoye was the only father she ever knew. The High Court took into consideration a number of factors when deciding whether the deportation breached the right to a family life. It considered the costs associated with Mrs Adeoye and her children travelling to visit Mr Adeoye in Nigeria, the difficulties with obtaining visas, the difficulties in meeting in third countries, the financial situation of Mrs Adeoye, etc. Hogan J stated:

> " . . . as things stand, it is not clear to me how this couple could ever realistically have any real interpersonal contact or how their marriage could actually survive what may amount to a permanent separation. It is sobering to reflect that the couple's daughter – who was admittedly born several months after the Minister's decision – might never actually get to see her father during her childhood".[33]

Hogan J went on to quash the Minister's decision not to set aside the deportation order, stating, "[t]he essential point here is that the Constitution protects the fundamentals of marriage and it insists that the State respects the essence of that relationship".[34]

3. The Place of the Woman in the Home

[8–12] Article 41.2.1°:

> "In particular, the State recognises that by her life within the home, woman gives to the State a support without which the common good cannot be achieved."

Article 41.2.2°:

> "The State shall, therefore, endeavour to ensure that mothers shall not be obliged by economic necessity to engage in labour to the neglect of their duties in the home."

---

[30] *ibid* at 162.
[31] *ibid* at 166.
[32] *Adeoye v Minister for Justice, Equality and Law Reform, Ireland and the Attorney General*, [2011] IEHC 397.
[33] *ibid* at 10.
[34] *ibid* at 11.

These provisions are some of the most controversial in the Constitution and have been hotly debated in recent times.[35] An interesting question is whether these provisions provide women with any tangible constitutional rights? The Constitutional Review Group considered this and commented that "[n]otwithstanding its terms, it has not been of any particular assistance even to women working exclusively within the home".[36] Case law elucidating these provisions is quite scarce, but the cases that do deal with them seem to indicate that no concrete rights accrue to women as a result of their place within the home. In the case of *L v L*,[37] mentioned above, a woman, whose marriage had broken down after almost 20 years, and who had worked exclusively within the home during her marriage, sought a judicial separation. She, along with one of her sons, lived in the family home, for which her husband had paid and in whom the legal title to the home was vested. The wife claimed a beneficial interest in the property. The High Court found, even though she had made no monetary contribution to the home, that she had a number of rights, deriving from Art 41. The High Court found that the wife was entitled to a 50 per cent beneficial ownership in the property. Barr J stated:

> "In my view the judiciary has a positive obligation to interpret and develop the law in a way which is in harmony with the philosophy of Article 41 as to the status of women in the home. It is also in harmony with that philosophy to regard marriage as an equal partnership in which a woman who elects to adopt the full-time role of wife and mother in the home may be obliged to make a sacrifice, both economic and emotional, in doing so. In return for that voluntary sacrifice, which the Constitution recognises as being in the interest of the common good, she should receive some reasonable economic security within the marriage. That concept can be achieved, at least in part, by recognising that as her role as full-time wife and mother precludes her from contributing, directly or indirectly, in money or money's worth from independent employment or avocation towards the acquisition by her husband of the family home and contents, her work as home-maker and in caring for the family should be taken into account in calculating her contribution towards that acquisition – particularly as such work is of real monetary value".[38]

However, this decision was reversed on appeal. In the Supreme Court, McCarthy J stated that "[i]t would be making a quantum leap in constitutional law to hold that by her life within the home the mother acquired a beneficial interest in it".[39] The circumstances of this case would now be covered by legislation in the form of the Judicial Separation and Family Law Reform Act 1989 and the Family Law (Divorce) Act 1996. The issue of rights accruing to women under Art 41 has not been clarified any further through case law and as stated by Casey, Art 41.2.2° "is of little practical utility".[40] The Constitutional Review Group recommended replacing Art 41.2.1° and Art 41.2.2° with the following unitary provision: "The State recognises that home and **[8–13]**

[35] See *Report of the Constitution Review Group*, *supra* n 4, p 333 – the report states: "Article 41.2 assigns to women a domestic role as wives and mothers. It is a dated provision much criticised in recent years".

[36] *ibid.*

[37] [1992] 2 IR 77.

[38] *ibid* at 98–99.

[39] *ibid* at 111.

[40] J Casey, *supra* n 17, p 627.

family life gives to society a support without which the common good cannot be achieved. The State shall endeavour to support persons caring for others within the home".[41]

4. The Protection of the Institution of Marriage

[8–14] Article 41.3.1°:

> "The State pledges itself to guard with special care the institution of Marriage, on which the Family is founded, and to protect it against attack."

The rationale for the constitutional protection of the institution of marriage as set out in Art 41.3.1° was highlighted in the case of *TF v Ireland*,[42] where Hamilton CJ stated:

> "It is because of its close connection with the family that the institution of marriage receives the pledge of the State to guard it with special care and protect it against attack. It is clear, accordingly, that this pledge is given in recognition of the contribution made by the institution of marriage to the welfare of the nation and the State, and the pledge must be seen in this light. It is not concerned solely with marriage itself, or with the spouses in a marriage, but also with the common good".[43]

It follows that people who are married are granted rights by virtue of their marriage, just as members of a family are granted rights by virtue of their membership of a family. The types of "marital rights" covered by Art 41.3.1° were discussed in the case of *Murray v Ireland*,[44] with Finlay CJ stating:

> " … the fact that the Constitution so clearly protects the institution of marriage necessarily involves a constitutional protection of certain marital rights. They include the right of cohabitation; the right to take responsibility for and actively participate in the education of any children born of the marriage; the right to beget children or further children of the marriage; and the right to privacy within the marriage: privacy of communication and of association".[45]

[8–15] Additional "marital rights" were discussed in further case law. A number of cases highlighted that the constitutional guarantee to guard the institution of marriage against attack meant that the State could not financially penalise a married couple or treat them less favourably than a non-married couple.[46] For example, the issue of tax in relation to a married couple was discussed in the case of *Murphy v AG*.[47] In this case the Supreme Court held that to impose a heavier tax on a working married couple than on a cohabiting married couple infringed the Art 41.3.1° guarantee. Later cases, such

[41] *Report of the Constitution Review Group*, *supra* n 4, pp 333–334.
[42] [1995] 1 IR 321.
[43] *ibid* at 372.
[44] [1991] ILRM 465.
[45] *ibid* at 472.
[46] This is now updated with the Civil Partnership and Certain Rights and Obligations of Cohabitants Act 2010.
[47] [1982] IR 241.

as *Muckley v Ireland*[48] and *Hyland v Minister for Social Welfare*[49] confirmed this principle. The case of *Greene v Minister for Agriculture*[50] dealt with the issue of a subsidy scheme for farmers which took into consideration additional income of married couples, but not of unmarried couples. Murphy J stated:

> " . . . the imposition of a scheme by the State or any of its agents on married couples living together which is substantially different from one placed on unmarried couples living together is in breach of the pledge by the State to guard with special care the institution of marriage and to protect it from attack".[51]

The payment of children's allowance to single parents does not, however, infringe Art 41.3.1°. The case of *MacMathúna v AG*[52] held that such financial support was child-centred and, therefore, was not an attack on the institution of marriage.

5. Civil Partnership

A large number of statutory bodies and non-governmental organisations have presented reports and recommendations on the issues of same-sex marriage and civil partnership over the last decade,[53] which pushed for a change in legislation. **[8–16]**

In 2004 the Civil Registration Act was passed which prohibits same-sex marriage, as an "impediment to marriage" exists if "both parties are of the same sex".[54] The same year, the case of Katherine Zappone and Ann Louise Gilligan[55] came before the High Court. The couple had married in Vancouver, Canada in 2003 and they sought to have this marriage recognised for the purposes of filing joint tax returns in Ireland. The case was heard in 2006, and it was held that marriage under the Irish Constitution was always meant to comprise a marriage between a man and a woman. The court did recognise the significant difficulties faced by same-sex couples as a result of the legislation then in force and stated:

> "It is to be hoped that the legislative changes to ameliorate these difficulties will not be long in coming. Ultimately, it is for the legislature to determine the extent to which such changes should be made".[56]

The case was appealed in February 2007 but will not be heard as the applicants have issued fresh proceedings challenging the constitutionality of the Civil Registration Act

[48] [1985] IR 472.
[49] [1989] IR 624.
[50] [1990] 2 IR 17.
[51] *ibid* at 26.
[52] [1995] 1 IR 484.
[53] See, e.g. the Equality Authority's *Report on Same-Sex Couples* of 2001, and on *LGB Equality* of 2007, the Irish Commission on Human Rights' *Report on* De facto *Couples* of 2006; and the Irish Council for Civil Liberties' *Initiatives on Relationships Equality* of 2005. See also, the Law Reform Commission's *Recommendations on Rights and Duties of Cohabitants* (LRC 82-2006).
[54] s 2 of the Civil Registration Act 2004.
[55] See J Mee, "Marriage, Civil Partnership and the Prohibited Degrees of Relationship" (2009) 27 ILT 259; DP Boyle, "Increased Rights for Same-Sex Couples and Cohabitants" (2011) 29 ILT 55 and J Ennis, "Marriage: Redefined and Realigned with *Bunreacht na hÉireann*" (2010) 1(2) IJLS 29.
[56] *Zappone and Gilligan v Revenue Commissioners* [2008] 2 IR 417 at 513.

2004 and the Civil Partnership and Certain Rights and Obligations of Cohabitants Act 2011.

[8–17] The law on civil partnership was significantly amended in 2010, with the enactment of the Civil Partnership and Certain Rights and Obligations of Cohabitants Act, which came into force on 1 January 2011. This Act grants certain rights and places certain obligations on same-sex couples that are similar to the rights granted to, and obligations placed on, married couples. In addition, the legislation grants certain rights to long-term cohabiting couples (same-sex and opposite-sex) who have not married. Following on from this piece of legislation, the first civil partnership was registered in Ireland on 7 February 2011. The Act provides for parity of treatment between married couples, civil partners and cohabiting couples in terms of tax and social welfare. With regard to tax, the Finance (No 3) Act 2011 was amended in 2011 to take account of civil partnership, while the social welfare law had already been amended in 2010.

The Act has been criticised by some for allowing the retention of significant differences in treatment between cases of civil marriage and civil partnership.[57]

6. Divorce

[8–18] Divorce was not legal under the 1937 Constitution until it was amended following a referendum in 1996. Prior to the amendment in 1996, Art 41.3.2° stated: "No law shall be enacted providing for the grant of a dissolution of marriage." After the referendum, this statement was deleted completely and replaced with the following:

> "A Court designated by law may grant a dissolution of marriage where, but only where, it is satisfied that
>
> i. at the date of the institution of the proceedings, the spouses have lived apart from one another for a period of, or periods amounting to, at least four years during the five years,
>
> ii. there is no reasonable prospect of a reconciliation between the spouses,
>
> iii. such provision as the Court considers proper having regard to the circumstances exists or will be made for the spouses, any children of either or both of them and any other person prescribed by law, and
>
> iv. any further conditions prescribed by law are complied with."

[8–19] It is clear, therefore, that while the amendment removed the prohibition on divorce, it placed a number of restrictions on the granting of such. The constitutional provisions on divorce are fleshed out in the Family Law (Divorce) Act 1996 (as amended).[58] This piece of legislation clarifies, and expands on, a number of issues emanating from the

---

[57] See Marriage Equality, *Missing Pieces. A comparison of the rights and responsibilities gained from civil partnership compared to the rights and responsibilities gained through civil marriage in Ireland* (2011).

[58] See A Shatter, *Family Law in the Republic of Ireland* (4th ed, Butterworths, Dublin, 1997), pp 369–398; and J Casey, *supra* n 17, p 627.

constitutional provision. Section 10 clarifies that once a divorce decree is granted the individuals are free to marry again.

Foreign Divorce

Article 41.3.3°: **[8–20]**

> "No person whose marriage has been dissolved under the civil law of any other State but is a subsisting valid marriage under the law for the time being in force within the jurisdiction of the Government and Parliament established by this Constitution shall be capable of contracting a valid marriage within that jurisdiction during the lifetime of the other party to the marriage so dissolved."

This provision was interpreted in the case of *Mayo-Perrott v Mayo-Perrott*,[59] in which the Supreme Court held that it did not prohibit the recognition of foreign divorce decrees. Kingsmill Moore J stated that at the time the Constitution was enacted, "a divorce effected by a foreign court of persons domiciled within its jurisdiction was regarded as valid in our jurisdiction".[60]

7. Guardianship, Custody and Adoption

None of these issues are dealt with in the Constitution, but are all regulated by legislation. The Guardianship of Infants Act 1964 provides that both the mother and father of an infant are joint guardians.[61] This situation was construed as being a "statutory expression of the rights already guaranteed by the Constitution"[62] in the case of *B v B*.[63] Custody is also dealt with in s 10(2) of the Guardianship of Infants Act 1964. This provision states that a child's parents are *prima facie* entitled to custody of this child, which, according to Henchy J in *G v An Bord Uchtála,*[64] is consistent with the constitutional provisions on the family. However, as noted by Casey, "whether this is simply a rule of prudence or the expression of a *right* is unclear".[65] A court may, however, grant custody to non-parents in certain circumstances.[66] Any court decisions regarding children must be made with the child's welfare as the "first and paramount consideration".[67] "Welfare" is defined in the Guardianship of Infants Act 1964 as comprising "the religious and moral, intellectual, physical and social welfare of the infant".[68] One of the most controversial aspects of the legislation is s 11(4) which provides that in the case of unmarried parents the mother is assumed to be the **[8–21]**

---

59 [1958] IR 336.
60 *ibid* at 346. See also *Bank of Ireland v Caffin* [1971] IR 123; *Gaffney v Gaffney* [1975] IR 133 and *T v T* [1983] IR 29.
61 s 6(1). s 3 defines an infant as anyone under the age of 21, but this has been amended by the Age of Majority Act 1985, which reduces this age to 18.
62 J Casey, *supra* n 17, p 628.
63 [1975] IR 54.
64 [1980] IR 32 at 85.
65 J Casey, *supra* n 17, p 629.
66 See s 11 of the Guardianship of Infants Act 1964 as amended by ss 6 and 9, Age of Majority Act 1985, s 13 Status of Children Act 1987, s 40 Judicial Separation and Family Law Reform Act 1989 and ss 8 and 9 Children Act 1987.
67 s 3 of the Guardianship of Infants Act 1964.
68 s 2 of the Guardianship of Infants Act 1964.

guardian and the father must make an application for guardianship. This is deemed to be the case for all unmarried parents, even if the father's name is on the birth certificate. This leads to a situation in which unmarried parents must either decide to make a statutory declaration that they wish to be joint guardians.[69] If the unmarried parents have more than one child, a statutory declaration has to be made in respect of each child. If the mother refuses to make this statutory declaration, the father can apply to the court to the appointed as a joint guardian under s 11. An unmarried father can lose guardianship rights if it is determined that this is in the best interests of the child. An unmarried mother can never lose guardianship of her child. If the parents of a child marry after the child is born, then the father automatically becomes a joint guardian of the child. In relation to same-sex couples, there is no legislation in place to allow a partner of a same-sex relationship to apply for guardianship of the child. These provisions, both in relation in unmarried couples and same-sex couples, have been heavily criticized as being discriminatory. There is certainly an equality argument that could be made under the Constitution but it is likely that the limitations on that right coupled with the position of the family based on marriage would act so as to prevent the success of any such argument.

[8–22] The Constitution does not deal explicitly with adoption[70]; rather it is regulated by legislation. Prior to the enactment of the Adoption Act 1952, official adoptions did not exist. The Adoption Act 1952 did not require the consent of the natural father for the making of an adoption order,[71] and a natural father had no way of blocking such an order. In the case of *State (Nicolaou) v An Bord Uchtála*[72] the Supreme Court found that this did not infringe the equality guarantee enshrined in Art 40.1 or the unenumerated rights guarantee of Art 40.3, as these were natural, personal rights and the non-married father of a child did not have any natural rights to the child. However, the situation of unmarried fathers has improved, following the case of *Keegan v Ireland*[73] before the European Court of Human Rights (ECtHR). In this case an unmarried couple, who had been cohabiting, had a child. Before the child was born, the relationship broke down and the cohabitation ceased. The father saw the child when she was one-day old, but he was stopped from seeing her again. The mother informed the father that she had placed the child for adoption when she was one-month old. The father then began Circuit Court proceedings in an attempt to gain guardianship of the child which would have given him the right to object to the making of an adoption order. He also sought custody of the child. The Circuit Court duly appointed the father as guardian and also granted him custody of the child. This decision was appealed by the mother and by the prospective adopters. Barron J in the High Court submitted a number of questions regarding guardianship legislation for determination to the Supreme Court. In *JK v VW*[74] the Supreme Court held that

[69] SI No 5 of 1998 Guardianship of Children (Statutory Declaration) Regulations 1998.
[70] See C Noctor, "Adoption, Consent and the Constitution" (1996) 3(1) DULJ 50.
[71] s 14(1) of the Adoption Act 1952.
[72] [1966] IR 567.
[73] (1984) 18 EHRR 342.
[74] [1990] 2 IR 437.

guardianship legislation granted an unmarried father a right to apply to be appointed as guardian, which did not necessarily translate into a right to be appointed guardian and the court also held that the natural father had no constitutional right to be appointed as guardian. Rather, the court must regard the welfare of the child as the first and paramount consideration. Finlay CJ stated:

> "The blood link between the infant and the father and the possibility for the infant to have the benefit of the guardianship by and the society of its father is one of many factors which may be viewed by the court as relevant to its welfare.
>
> In a case such as the present case where the applicant for appointment as a guardian is linked to the application for a present order of custody, regard should not be had to the objective of satisfying the wishes and desires of the father to be involved in the guardianship of and to enjoy the society of his child unless the courts has first concluded that the quality of welfare which would probably be achieved for the infant by its present custody, which is with the prospective adoptive parent, as compared with the quality of welfare which would probably be achieved by custody with the father, is not to an important extent better".[75]

Some controversy has arisen in recent years as unmarried couples and same-sex couples are not allowed to adopt in Ireland. Only married couples, the mother, father or relative of the child or a single person who satisfies the Adoption Authority that it is desirable and in the best interests of the child.[76] This situation is clearly discriminatory. The House of Lords was recently faced with the question of whether this prohibition on unmarried couples in Northern Ireland from adopting was compatible with the European Convention on Human Rights.[77] The majority of the Law Lords agreed that this prohibition was in fact discriminatory and was incompatible with both Arts 8 and 14 of the Convention. In finding that discrimination had occurred, the House of Lords had to decide whether the discrimination could be justified in the circumstances. There are two potential justifications for this. Firstly, the protection of the traditional family based on marriage is an obvious justification. Secondly, the protection of the best interests of the child must also be considered. However, the House of Lords held that drawing a line excluding unmarried couples from adoption was irrational and contradicts the notion that the court should consider on a subjective basis whether adoption by a particular person is in the best interests of the child. The House of Lords also rejected the notion that the best interests of the child should be balanced against the interests of the community as a whole. Lord Hoffmann held that while

> "it is one thing to say, in general terms, married couples are more likely to be suitable adoptive parents than unmarried ones...[I]t is altogether another to say that one may rationally assume that no unmarried couple can be suitable adoptive parents".

Therefore, the discrimination could not be justified and was contrary to Art 14 of the ECHR. As a result of this decision and a failure on the part of the responsible authorities in the North to amend the existing laws, the Northern Ireland Human Rights Commission launched legal proceedings against the Northern Ireland Executive

---

[75] *ibid* at 447.

[76] s 33 Adoption Act 2010.

[77] *In Re P and Others (AP) Appellants (Northern Ireland)* [2008] UKHL 38.

in a bid to bring about legislative change in the North. The lessons from the Northern Ireland suggest that the position in Ireland is becoming untenable. Firstly, the best interests of the child may not be fully realised under the current legislation. The legislation provides for an anomalous situation in which an individual in a stable non-marital relationship is eligible to adopt a child but a couple in a stable non-marital relationship are not considered so eligible. Baroness Hale in the House of Lords held that the choice is between giving a child one new legal parent or giving them two and the best interests of the child is surely better protected by granting the child the right to two legal parents. Secondly, family life has altered dramatically in Ireland and as noted by the All Party Oireachtas Committee on the Constitution 1996, there is little evidence to support the continuous discrimination against unmarried couples in the adoption context.[78]

[8–23] Barron J then refused the plaintiff the relief sought and subsequently an adoption order was made. The plaintiff then brought a case against the State to the ECtHR. In *Keegan v Ireland*[79] the ECtHR held that the plaintiff's rights under Art 8 and Art 6(1) of the ECHR had been violated. The ECtHR held that Art 8's guarantee to protect family rights was not restricted to families based on marriage. Following on from *Keegan* the Adoption Act 1998 required that an unmarried father be consulted with regard to adoption (s 7). Adoption in Ireland is now regulated by the Adoption Act 2010, which introduces a new regulatory framework for adoption and highlights the best interests of the child principle. The Act only allows children to be adopted from States that have ratified the Hague Convention on Protection of Children and Co-Operation in Respect of Intercountry Adoption 1993 (s 9). The Adoption Authority of Ireland (s 94) was set up under the Act and replaced the Adoption Board. While the adoption framework is strengthened by this Act, the rights of unmarried fathers with regard to adoption are still much weaker than the rights of mothers. A non-married father's consent is still not required for an adoption order to be made, unless he has been appointed as the child's guardian. The Act does, however, reinforce the requirement to notify the father of adoption proceedings (s 16). It remains the case that for children born outside of marriage in Ireland, only the mother has automatic rights to guardianship.

8. The Rights of the Child

[8–24] In recent years, children's rights have been to the fore of public debate and there have been a number of proposals for the inclusion of children's rights in the Constitution.[80] The UN Committee on the Rights of the Child also recommended that Ireland accord the "best interests of the child" principle constitutional status in 2006.[81] The Joint Committee on the Constitutional Amendment on Children has recommended the

---

78 See further E Dewhurst, "Adoption and Unmarried Couples" (2008) (Aug/Sept) ILSG 16.

79 (1994) 18 EHRR 342.

80 See S Conneely, "Children's Rights in Constitutional Law" (2003) (6)3 IJFL 2; C McLoone, "Children's Rights within the Constitution and the proposed Constitutional Referendum" (2009) 12(3) IJFL 72; A Parkes, "Children Should Be Seen and Not Heard? A Reflection on the Proposed Constitutional Amendment" (2008)11(3) IJFL 58; and F Martin, "Key Roles of the Ombudsman for Children in Ireland: Promotion of Rights and Investigation of Grievances" (2004) 26 DULJ 56.

81 UN Committee on the Rights of the Child Concluding Observations on Ireland, 29 September 2006, CRC/C/IRL/Co/2.

inclusion of a constitutional provision to ensure better protection of the rights of the child in a number of fields, including guardianship, adoption, custody, care and upbringing.[82] The current Programme for Government prioritises such a referendum and the commitment to such a referendum was included in the 2011 State report to the Human Rights Council of the UN.[83]

9. The Right to Marry and Found a Family

Kenny J held that the right to marry was one of the citizen's personal rights in *Ryan v Attorney General*.[84] However, this is not an absolute right and the State can place limitations on it, e.g. age limits and prohibition of marriage between certain relatives. The right to found a family was also found to fall under this category of rights by Costello J in *Murray v Attorney General*.[85] In this case a husband and wife who had been sentenced to life imprisonment for capital murder wished to start a family and claimed that their right to beget children was constitutionally protected. This right, they claimed, was being infringed, as although they were allowed to meet, all meetings were supervised and they were prohibited from engaging in intimate marital relations. However, the judge balanced their right to beget children with the State's power to restrict their liberty and stated that prisoners could exercise such rights only when it did not place unreasonable demands on the prison system. Given that such a right would extend to all married prisoners, the judge held that to facilitate all married prisoners' right to beget children would place an unreasonable demand on prisons. This decision was upheld in the Supreme Court.[86] The right to same-sex couples to marry has also been at the forefront of the right to marry debate in Ireland. Although same-sex couples have the right to civil partnership under the Civil Partnership legislation, this does not have the same legal status as marriage. As a result there is currently a challenge set to be heard in the High Court on this very question of right of same-sex couples to marry. This case will involve very interesting questions relating to the right to equality, the definition of marriage and the balancing of constitutional rights in Ireland. **[8–25]**

B. ECHR

Article 8: **[8–26]**

> "1. Everyone has the right to respect for his private and family life, his home and his correspondence.
>
> 2. There shall be no interference by a public authority with the exercise of this right except such as is in accordance with the law and is necessary in a democratic society in the interests of national security, public safety or the economic well-being of the country, for the prevention of disorder or crimes, for the protection of health or morals, or for the protection of the rights and freedoms of others."

---

[82] Joint Committee on the Constitutional Amendment on Children, *Proposal for a constitutional amendment to strengthen children's rights*, Final Report, February 2010.

[83] National report submitted in accordance with para 15(a) of the annex to Human Rights Council resolution 5/1/A/HRC/WG.6/12/IRL/1.

[84] *Ryan v Attorney General* [1965] IR 294.

[85] *Murray v Attorney General* [1985] IR 532.

[86] [1991] ILRM 465.

1. Nature of the Right

[8–27] In addition to respect for family life, Art 8 seeks to protect three other interlinking rights, namely, respect for private life, respect for home and respect for correspondence. Harris *et al* comment that the ECtHR "has taken a flexible approach to the definition of the individual interests protected, with the result that the provision continues to broaden in scope".[87] This chapter will, however, focus only on respect for family life, and the right to private life is dealt with in Chapter 7. It is important to note the difference between the Irish constitutional and ECHR approach to the family. While the Constitution protects various rights which accrue to members of the family, the ECHR protects the respect for a family life. The ECHR also protects the right to marry and found a family under Art 12.

This respect for family life is ensured, under Art 8(2), which places an obligation on contracting States not to interfere arbitrarily with a person's family life. The ECtHR has also stated that there may "in addition be positive obligations inherent in 'effective' respect for family life"[88] in Art 8(1) which would require contracting States to take action in certain circumstances in order to ensure the respect for family life.

The Meaning of "Family Life" under the ECHR

[8–28] We saw that "family" has a particular meaning under Bunreacht na hÉireann, which is restricted to the family based on marriage. The meaning of "family" under the ECHR is quite different and the "elaboration of the idea of 'family life' is one of the best examples of the way the Commission and Court have interpreted the Convention to take account of social changes".[89] Indeed, two of the major cases in relation to the meaning of "family", were taken against Ireland before the ECtHR, *Johnston v Ireland*[90] and *Keegan v Ireland*.[91] In the case of *Johnston v Ireland*[92] the Irish interpretation of the family, limited to a family based on marriage, was rejected. Indeed, the ECtHR has gone even further to include within the meaning of the family, potential family arrangements.[93] For example, in the case of *Wakefield v UK*[94] the Commission found that the relationship between a fiancé and fiancée could be regarded as family life. A situation of informal relationships, where a couple are not married or even engaged can also be regarded as constituting family life, if it is a stable, long-term relationship.[95] Harris *et al* comment that the ECtHR "has taken into account increasingly the substance and reality of relationships, acknowledging developments in social practices and the law in European states".[96]

---

87 DJ Harris *et al*, *Law of the European Convention on Human Rights* (2nd ed, Oxford University Press, Oxford, 2009), p 361.
88 *Kroon v Netherlands* (1995) 19 EHRR 263 at para 31.
89 Harris *et al*, *supra* n 87, p 371.
90 *Johnston v Ireland* (1987) 9 EHRR 203.
91 *Keegan v Ireland* (1994) 18 EHRR 342.
92 *Johnston v Ireland* (1987) 9 EHRR 203. See also *Marckx v Belgium* (1979–80) 2 EHRR 330.
93 *Keegan v Ireland* (1994) 18 EHRR 342.
94 *Wakefield v UK*, No 15817/89, 1 October 1990, 66 DR 251 at para 255.
95 *Berrehab v Netherlands* (1989) 11 EHRR 322 at para 21.
96 Harris *et al*, *supra* n 87, p 372.

The Meaning of "Respect" under the ECHR

The ECtHR stated, in the case of *X and Y v Netherlands*, that Art 8: [8–29]

> " ... does not merely compel the state to abstain from ... interference: in addition to this primarily negative undertaking, there may be positive obligations inherent in an effective respect for private and family life".[97]

This existence of positive obligations inherent in Art 8 is supported by the ECtHR's comments in *Marckx v Belgium*,[98] and in *Airey v Ireland*.[99] The nature and extent of such positive obligations is, however, uncertain. In the case of *Abdulaziz, Cabales and Balkandali v UK*[100] the ECtHR stated:

> " ... especially as far as those positive obligations are concerned, the notion of 'respect' is not clear-cut: having regard to the diversity of practices followed and the situations obtaining in the Contracting states, the notion's requirements will vary considerably from case to case".[101]

In order to ensure respect "regard must be had to the fair balance that has to be struck between the competing interests of the individual and the community as a whole".[102] Whether a contracting State's obligations to ensure respect are negative or positive, it retains a certain margin of appreciation, which is very important in the context of Art 8, given the sensitive areas it seeks to protect. [8–30]

Children and Family Life

The ECtHR stated in the case of *Berrehab v Netherlands* that in the case of a child of married parents, "from the moment of the child's birth and by the very fact of it, there exists between him and his parents a bond amounting to 'family life'".[103] When a child is born to unmarried, but cohabiting, parents the ECtHR has found that this relationship would also benefit from the protection of Art 8.[104] It was established in the case of *Marckx v Belgium*[105] that the relationship between an unmarried mother and her child constituted a family relationship for the purposes of Art 8. The situation differs, however, in the case of an unmarried father and his child. In such situations, the ECtHR has considered the type and nature of relationship between the father and the child, rather than automatically recognising it as falling within the remit of Art 8.[106] In general, the ECtHR will only refrain from categorising the relationship between a father and child as family life in exceptional circumstances.[107] [8–31]

---

[97] *X and Y v Netherlands* (1986) 8 EHRR 235 at para 23. See also the case of *Johnston v Ireland* (1987) 9 EHRR 203 at para 55 PC.
[98] *Marckx v Belgium* (1979–80) 2 EHRR 330.
[99] *Airey v Ireland* (1979–80) 2 EHRR 305.
[100] *Abdulaziz, Cabales and Balkandali v UK* (1985) 7 EHRR 471.
[101] *ibid* at para 67.
[102] *Hokkanen v Finland* (1994) 19 EHRR 139.
[103] *Berrehab v Netherlands* (1988) 11 EHRR 322 at para 21.
[104] *Johnston v Ireland* (1987) 9 EHRR 203 at para 75 PC.
[105] *Marckx v Belgium* (1979–80) 2 EHRR 330.
[106] See, for example, *Boughanemi v France* (1996) 22 EHRR 228 at para 35.
[107] See *Ahmut v Netherlands* (1996) 24 EHRR 62 at para 60.

A genetic link is not a prerequisite for a finding of the existence of family life. In the case of *X, Y and Z v UK*,[108] the ECtHR held that the family situation that existed between a transsexual male and the child which was born to his wife by artificial insemination of donor sperm came within the remit of Art 8.

[8–32] The ECtHR has yet to determine whether a same-sex relationship constitutes family life for the purposes of Art 8.[109] The Commission, however, found that a stable relationship between two women and the child born to one of the women by means of donor insemination fell under the rubric of private life, rather than family life.[110] However, following on from the approach taken in the case of *X, Y and Z v UK*, disregarding the need for a genetic link, the ECtHR could extend the scope of Art 8 to same-sex couples and their children.[111]

The ECtHR has found that family life does not only exist between couples and parents and children, but also between siblings,[112] an uncle and nephew,[113] and grandparents and grandchildren.[114] However, the level of respect a contracting State may be required to give for a family may decrease, depending on the remoteness of the relationship between the members.[115] In each case the ECtHR will take cognisance of the nature of the relationship.

Adoption

[8–33] Article 8 does not mention adoption and the ECtHR has held that the ECHR does not include the right to adopt a child.[116] The ECtHR has placed particular importance on the best interests of the child in cases concerning adoption, stating that adoption means "providing a child with a family, not a family with a child".[117] The adoption of a child negates the existence of one family life and the creation of a new family life between a child and its adoptive parents.[118] A fostering arrangement may give rise to the existence of family life, but this will depend on the circumstances of the fostering arrangement.[119] However, the placement of a child in care does not negate the existence of family life.[120]

---

[108] (1997) 24 EHRR 143 at para 37.

[109] See *Rees v UK* (1986) 9 EHRR 961, confirmed in *Cossey v UK* (1990) 13 EHRR 622, but reversed by *Goodwin v UK* (2002) 35 EHRR 447. Same-sex marriage is not yet recognised under Art 12, but three Council of Europe States allow it and 16 States have civil partnerships laws.

[110] *S v UK*, No 11716/85, 14 May 1986, (1986) 47 DR 274.

[111] See *Evans v United Kingdom* (2008) 46 EHRR 34 regarding *in vitro* fertilisation.

[112] *Moustaquim v Belgium* A 193 (1993) 13 EHRR 802 at para 56. See also *Olsson v Sweden No. 1* A 130 (1988) 11 EHRR 259 at para 81 PC.

[113] *Boyle v UK* A 282-B (1994) 19 EHRR 1

[114] *Marckx v Belgium* (1979–80) 2 EHRR 330 at para 45 PC. See also *Price v UK*, No 12402/86, 14 July 1988, (1988) 55 DR 224 at 237.

[115] See Harris *et al*, *supra* n 87, p 374.

[116] *Fretté v France* (2004) 38 EHRR 438. This case related to a rejection of an adoption application on the basis of sexual orientation. The complaint was made under Art 14 in conjunction with Art 8.

[117] *ibid* at para 42.

[118] *X v France*, No 9993/82, 5 October 1982, (1982) 31 DR 241.

[119] *Gaskin v UK* (1989) 12 EHRR 36 at para 49.

[120] *W v UK* A 121 (1987) 10 EHRR 29 at para 59. See also the case of *Olsson v Sweden (No 1)* (1988) 11 EHRR 259 at para 59.

The Protection of Marriage under the ECHR

While marriage is not a pre-requisite for the ECHR protection of respect for family life, the majority of situations which fall under Art 8 involve a formal marriage and, in general, formal marriage situations "are accompanied by enough of substance for them to be regarded as constituting family life".[121] Certain "sham marriages", e.g. A marriage entered into in order to gain a visa or obtain nationality, would probably not fall within the remit of Art 8.[122] Foreign marriages recognised by national law should fall under the protection of Art 8, which is most relevant in the case of polygamous marriages.[123] [8–34]

Divorce

The ECHR does not contain any provision regarding divorce,[124] "though the effective enjoyment of family life may require that the state establish procedures which may result in the termination of some obligations of family life in certain circumstances".[125] In the case of *Airey v Ireland*[126] the ECtHR found that such procedures came in the form of judicial separation, whereby a wife was no longer forced to cohabit with an abusive husband. [8–35]

While family life can be terminated between a couple upon divorce,[127] a child-parent relationship can remain after the divorce of the parents. In the case of *Berrehab v Netherlands*,[128] the ECtHR held that the family life between a father and daughter survived the divorce between the father and mother. While the mother had custody of the child, the father maintained a good relationship with her, which the State was bound to respect under Art 8.

2. Legitimate Justifications for Interference with the Right

A contracting State can legitimately interfere with respect for family life in certain situations. These are set out in Art 8(2). State interference will be legitimate: [8–36]

- if it is in accordance with the law;
- if it has a legitimate aim, e.g. if it is in the interests of national security, etc; and
- if it is necessary in a democratic society.

The burden is on the applicant to establish the fact of interference.

---

121 Harris *et al*, *supra* n 87, p 372.

122 See *Benes v Austria*, No 18643/91, 6 January 1992, (1992) 72 DR 271.

123 See *Alam and Khan v UK*, No 2991/66, 1 January 1967, (1967) 10 YB 478 and *A and A v Netherlands*, No 14501/89, 6 January 1992, (1992) 72 DR 118 at 121–123.

124 This was a deliberate omission, and discussed in *Johnston v Ireland* (1987) 9 EHRR 203. Even as a living instrument the Strasbourg institutions could not add a right which was absent in the *travaux préparatoires.*

125 Harris *et al*, *supra* n 87, p 372.

126 *Airey v Ireland* (1979) 2 EHRR 305.

127 See *Berrehab v Netherlands* (1989) 11 EHRR 322.

128 *ibid.*

In Accordance with the Law

[8–37] In order for State interference with the right to respect for family life to be legitimate, it must be in accordance with the law, i.e. it must have a legal basis. In addition, the law "must be clear and precise, and it must contain a measure of protection against arbitrariness by public authorities".[129] The concept of "law" in this regard was discussed by the ECtHR in *Olsson v Sweden (No 1)*.[130] The ECtHR examined a Swedish law which allowed for children to be taken into care on a number of quite vague grounds, including "lack of care" and "any other condition in the home". While the ECtHR acknowledged the general nature of these provisions, it accepted them as "law" for the purposes of Art 8. The difficulty in formulating a formal test for "law" has been highlighted by Harris *et al*, who state: "[the] question cannot be resolved in the abstract but must take into account the nature of the applicant's right and the precise reasons for which the state seeks to interfere with it".[131]

Legitimate Aim

[8–38] The State has to set out the aim of the interference with a person's Art 8 rights. In general, contracting States have been able to prove before the ECtHR that their reason for interference was, in fact, legitimate. In relation to respect for family life, the ECtHR accepted parents' family lives could be legitimately interfered with by being separated from their children, because the separation was in the best interests of others.[132] In addition, in the case of *Andersson (M and R) v Sweden*[133] the ECtHR held that children's right to family life could be legitimately interfered with by separating them from their parents in the interest of protecting their health and morals.

Necessary in a Democratic Society

[8–39] It is up to the State to indicate why it has interfered in the right to respect for private life. The issue of necessity was discussed in the case of *Handyside v UK*, in which it was stated:

> "The Court notes ... that, while the adjective 'necessary' ... is not synonymous with 'indispensable', neither has it the flexibility of such expressions as 'admissible', 'ordinary', 'useful', 'reasonable' or 'desirable'".[134]

In the case of *Olsson v Sweden*, the ECtHR stated:

> "According to the Court's established case-law, the notion of necessity implies that an interference corresponds to a pressing social need and, in particular, that it is proportionate to the legitimate aim pursued".[135]

---

[129] Harris *et al*, *supra* n 87, p 400.
[130] *Olsson v Sweden (No 1)* (1988) 11 EHRR 259.
[131] Harris *et al*, *supra* n 87, p 406.
[132] *Olsson v Sweden (No 1)* (1988) 11 EHRR 259.
[133] *Andersson (M and R) v Sweden* (1992) 14 EHRR 615.
[134] *Handyside v UK* (1979–80) 1 EHRR 737 at para 48.
[135] *Olsson v Sweden (No 1)* (1988) 11 EHRR 259 at para 67.

The concept of a democratic society was considered in the case of *Dudgeon v UK*, where the ECtHR noted that two of the characteristics of such a society were tolerance and broad-mindedness.[136]

The recent case of *Emre v Switzerland*[137] also deals with the issue of what is necessary in a democratic society. Mr Emre was a national of Turkey who had settled in Switzerland with his parents in 1986. He was convicted of a number of offences between 1994 and 2000 and consequently the Neuchâtel Canton Aliens Office ordered his deportation in 2003 for an indefinite period, a decision which was later upheld by the Federal Court. Mr Emre applied to the ECtHR in 2004, claiming that the deportation for an indefinite period was a breach of Art 8, which was accepted by the ECtHR. Mr Emre then applied to the Federal Court in 2009 seeking a revision of the original judgment. The Court agreed to this and limited his exclusion from Switzerland to a period of 10 years. The same year Mr Emre married a German national and obtained a German residence permit. He then applied to have the deportation order lifted as he wished to settle in Switzerland but was unsuccessful. The ECtHR confirmed that the deportation order had been in accordance with the law and pursued a legitimate aim (in this case, the prevention of crime). However the ECtHR decided that the State had not struck a fair balance between his right to a family life and the public interest. The ECtHR held that the 10-year prohibition on entering Switzerland was not necessary in a democratic society. It held that the Federal Court, in order to implement the previous decision of the ECtHR, should have lifted the deportation order against Mr Emre with immediate effect. The ECtHR therefore decided that there had been a violation of Art 8 taken in conjunction with Art 46 (binding force and execution of judgments). **[8–40]**

3. The Right to Marry and Found a Family

Article 12: **[8–41]**

> "Men and women of marriageable age have the right to marry and to found a family, according to the national laws governing the exercise of this right."

This provision is not subject to the same limitations as Art 8. Rather, the provision is only limited to the extent that it applies to men and women getting married "according to the national laws governing this right." According to Jacobs, White and Ovey:

> "[t]he correct view ... is that Article 12 imposes an obligation to recognise, both in principle and in practice, the right to marry and to found a family. This obligation implies that the restrictions placed on these rights by national law must be imposed for a legitimate purpose ... and must not go beyond a reasonable limit to attain that purpose".[138]

Such a restriction would be a law prohibiting incest.

---

136 *Dudgeon v UK* (1981) 4 EHRR 149 at para 53.

137 *Emre v Switzerland (No 2)*, No 5056/10, 11 October 2011.

138 Jacobs, White and Ovey, *The European Convention on Human Rights* (5th ed, Oxford University Press, Oxford, 2010), p 353.

[8–42] The ECtHR has accepted that marriage confers a special status on those who enter into it[139] and so has dismissed a number of discrimination claims made by unmarried couples which raised interesting issues of entitlement to tax relief, benefits, etc.[140]

The ECtHR has also upheld the right of a prisoner to marry in a jail,[141] and in the case of *Dickson v UK*[142] the ECtHR dealt with the issue of the right of prisoners to found a family. A life-sentence prisoner met and married his wife while both of them were serving prison terms. Prison authorities and the Home Office refused his request for facilities to artificially inseminate his wife during his continued custody. He claimed the prison service's response to his requests deprived him of his right to found a family as his wife would be at least 51 years old by the time he was released. He appealed to the ECtHR unsuccessfully initially, but this was overturned by the Grand Chamber.

A UK law which prohibited the marriage between a father-in-law and daughter-in-law where neither of the parties' spouses had died was tested in the case of *B and L v United Kingdom*.[143] While the purpose of the UK law had been to protect the integrity of the family, the ECtHR held that this law was in violation of Art 12.[144]

[8–43] In the recent case of *Schalk and Kopf v Austria*,[145] the ECtHR found that the State had not breached Art 12 by not allowing a same-sex couple to marry. A minority of the judges were of the opinion that the State had violated Art 14, taken in conjunction with Art 8, and that Austria had an obligation to introduce a registered partnership law. The ECtHR referred to Art 9 of the Charter of Fundamental Rights (CFR), discussed below, and emphasised that this instrument did not refer to a right to marry between a man and a woman. Hodson comments that "this judgment undoubtedly heralds the somewhat faltering start of a more robust engagement by the Court with the increasingly pressing issue of same-sex relationships".[146]

4. Equality between Spouses

[8–44] Article 5 of Protocol 7 deals with the issue of equality between spouses. This provision states:

> "Spouses shall enjoy equality of rights and responsibilities of a private law character between them, and in their relations with their children, as to marriage, during marriage and in the event of its dissolution. This article shall not prevent States from taking such measures as are necessary in the interests of the children."

The rights which fall under this provision are only in the area of private law and therefore areas such as social welfare, tax, criminal law, etc are not affected.[147]

---

139 *Shackell v UK*, No 45851/99, 27 April 2000.
140 *Burden v UK* (2008) 47 EHRR 857.
141 *Hamer v UK* (1982) 4 EHRR 139.
142 (2008) 46 EHRR 41.
143 *B and L v United Kingdom* (2006) 42 EHRR 195.
144 There had actually been proposals in the UK to amend this law before the ECtHR heard the case.
145 *Schalk and Kopf v Austria* (2011) 53 EHRR 20.
146 L Hodson, "A Marriage by any other Name?" (2011) 11(1) HRLR 1.
147 See Explanatory Memorandum to Protocol 7, Council of Europe Document H(84)5.

C. CFR

Article 7: [8–45]

> "Everyone has the right to respect for his or her private and family life, home and communications."

Article 7 of the CFR seeks to protect the right to respect for family life.[148] Similar to Art 8 of the ECHR, Art 7 also seeks to protect respect for private life, home life and correspondence/communications. The CFR also contains provisions on the right to marry and on economic and social rights.

Article 9:

> "The right to marry and the right to found a family shall be guaranteed in accordance with the national laws governing the exercise of these rights."

Article 33:

> "1. The family shall enjoy legal, economic and social protection.
>
> 2. To reconcile family and professional life, everyone shall have the right to protection from dismissal for a reason connected with maternity and the right to paid maternity leave and to parental leave following the birth or adoption of a child."

All of these provisions of the CFR are to be interpreted in light of the ECHR provisions on the right to respect for family life.[149] It should be noted, however, that before the adoption of the CFR the concept of the family[150] had been dealt with under secondary legislation with regard to the free movement of persons[151] which focuses on the family as one based on marriage and/or biological link. The European Court of Justice (ECJ) had built up a significant body of case law in relation to family issues before the adoption of the CFR. This case law dealt with issues such as the status of divorced and separated people and cohabitants. In relation to the first issue, in earlier cases the ECJ had been quite inconsistent in its approach to the question of the impact of marriage breakdown on spousal rights under EU law.[152] On the other hand, the ECJ [8–46]

---

[148] See C McGlynn, "Families and the European Union Charter of Fundamental Rights: progressive change or entrenching the status quo?" (2001) 26 ELRev 582.

[149] Art 52(3) of the CFR.

[150] See H Stalford, "Concepts of Family Under EU Law – Lessons from the ECHR" (2002) 16 IJLPF 410 at 412.

[151] See, for example, Article 10 of Regulation (EEC) No 1612/68 of the Council of 15 October 1968 on freedom of movement for workers within the Community [1968] OJ Special Edn, No I.257/2, p 476, which defined a family as including the worker's "spouse and their dependants who are under the age of 21 or who are dependants as well as dependent relatives in the ascending line of the worker and his spouse". . This has since been repealed by Article 41 of Regulation 492/2011 OJ 2011, Vol 54, L 141, p 1.

[152] See H Stalford, *supra* n 150 at 416. See Case 267/83, *Diatta v Land Berlin* [1986] 2 CMLR 164, Case C-370/90, *R. v IAT and Singh, Ex p Secretary of State for the Home Department* [1992] ECR 1-1265 and *R. v Secretary of State for the Home Department, Ex p Sandhu* [1982] CMLR 553.

clearly excluded cohabitants from the definition of the family in the case of *Reed*,[153] where an unemployed Briton was prohibited from cohabiting with her British partner, a migrant worker, in the Netherlands. The jurisprudence of the ECJ was seen to be more restrictive in its interpretation of "family" and family rights than the ECtHR.[154] However, as Stalford points out, "[r]ecent years have seen the European institutions adopting a much more responsive, purposive approach to the regulation"[155] of family life, again, as a result of promoting worker mobility as well as under equal opportunities legislation.

[8–47] Since the adoption of the CFR, Art 7 is to be interpreted in light of the ECHR provisions on the right to respect for family life.[156] The right to respect for family life was recognised by the ECJ in the *Carpenter* case[157] as one of the general principles of EU law. In interpreting this right, the ECJ referred to both Art 8 of the ECHR and the case law of the ECtHR. Other Court of Justice cases also referred in depth to the ECHR when dealing with the rights of the family.[158]

D. International and Regional Laws

[8–48] Numerous regional and international instruments seek to protect the family and family life.[159] The most fundamental of these is the Universal Declaration of Human Rights 1948, which in Art 16 identifies the family as "the natural and fundamental group unit of society and is entitled to protection by society and the State".[160] Martin comments that "[t]his phrase is repeated regularly in other international instruments almost as a mantra".[161] Article 23(1) of the International Covenant on Civil and Political Rights 1966 (ICCPR) echoes the language of Art 41 of Bunreacht na hÉireann with regard to the description of the family. This provision states:

> "1. The family is the natural and fundamental group unit of society and is entitled to protection by society and the State.

---

153 Case 59/85, *Netherlands State v Reed* [1989] 2 CMLR 448. See K Lundström, "Family life and the freedom of movements of workers in the European Union" (1996) 10 IJLPF 250.

154 See, in general, H Stalford, *supra* n 150.

155 H Stalford, *supra* n 150 at 413.

156 Art 52(3) of the CFR.

157 Case C-60/00, *Carpenter v Secretary of State for the Home Department* [2002] ECR I-6279 at para 41. The ECtHR composed a number of criteria which should be considered in relation to the deportation of a third-country national and its impact on the right to a family life (the *Boultif* criteria) – *Boultif v Switzerland* (2001) 33 EHRR 50 at para 48.

158 See, for example, Case C-109/01, *Secretary of State for the Home Department v Akrich* [2003] ECR I-9607 and Case C-127/08, *Metok v Minister for Justice, Equality and Law Reform* [2008] ECR I-06241. An important recent case before the Court of Justice which dealt to a certain extent with the right to a family life is the case of *Zambrano* (Case C-34/09), Opinion of 30 September 2010 and judgment of 8 March 2011. This case concerned the residence rights of third-country national parents of two minors who were born in Belgium. The parents had not been deported earlier due to a civil war in their home state of Colombia. While the Advocate General focused on the right to respect for a family life, the Court of Justice chose to focus on Art 20 of the Treaty on the Functioning of the European Union (TFEU) on citizenship.

159 See F Martin, "The Changing Face of Family Law in Ireland" (2005) 5(1) JSIJ 16 at 24–26.

160 Universal Declaration of Human Rights 1948, Art 16.

161 F Martin, *supra* n 159 at 24.

> 2. The right of men and women of marriageable age to marry and to found a family shall be recognized.
> 3. No marriage shall be entered into without the free and full consent of the intending spouses.
> 4. States Parties to the present Covenant shall take appropriate steps to ensure equality of rights and responsibilities of spouses as to marriage, during marriage and at its dissolution. In the case of dissolution, provision shall be made for the necessary protection of any children."

Article 10 of the International Covenant on Economic, Social, and Cultural Rights 1966 (ICESCR) reiterates some basic rights concerning family life and then goes on to establish further rights of pregnant mothers to maternity leave and social security.[162] Economic and social rights are also dealt with at a regional level in the European Social Charter, which states: **[8–49]**

> "With a view to ensuring the necessary conditions for the full development of the family, which is a fundamental unit of society, the Contracting Parties undertake to promote the economic, legal and social protection of family life by such means as social and family benefits, fiscal arrangements, provisions of family housing, benefits for this newly married, and other important means".[163]

At an international level, numerous other instruments deal with different aspects of family life, including adoption,[164] minimum age and consent for marriage,[165] the rights of the child,[166] and the protection of migrant workers.[167] At a regional level, family rights are dealt with in Art 18 of the African Charter on Human and Peoples' Rights 1981, Art 17 of the American Convention on Human Rights 1969 and Art 21 of the Arab Charter on Human Rights 2004.[168] **[8–50]**

Conclusion

One of the main difficulties in promoting and protecting the rights of the family is identifying who is a member of that group because "'[t]he Family' might appear easy to recognise, but may not be susceptible to a definition that meets with universal **[8–51]**

---

[162] Art 10 of the ICESCR.

[163] Art 16 of the European Social Charter, adopted in 1961 and revised in 1996.

[164] See, for example, Declaration on Social and Legal Principles relating to the Protection and Welfare of Children, with special reference to Foster Placement and Adoption Nationally and Internationally, adopted by General Assembly resolution 41/85 of 3 December 1986.

[165] See, for example, Convention on Consent to Marriage, Minimum Age for Marriage and Registration of Marriages, 521 UNTS 231 and Recommendation on Consent to Marriage, Minimum Age for Marriage and Registration of Marriages, General Assembly resolution 2018 (XX), 20 UN GAOR Supp (No 14) at 36, UN Doc A/60141 (1965).

[166] Adopted and opened for signature, ratification and accession by General Assembly resolution 44/25 of 20 November 1989.

[167] See, for example, International Convention on the Protection of the Rights of All Migrant Workers and Members of Their Families, adopted by General Assembly resolution 45/158 of 18 December 1990.

[168] Arab Charter on Human Rights 2004. Art 21 is similar to Art 8 of the ECHR. It states: "No one shall be subjected to arbitrary or unlawful interference with regard to his privacy, family, home or correspondence, nor to unlawful attacks on his honour or his reputation."

acceptance legally or socially, no matter what culture is involved".[169] The interpretation of Art 41 of the Irish Constitution proffered to date by Irish courts has been restrictive, being limited to the family based on marriage.[170] Martin comments that:

> "[g]lobally and nationally, the socio-legal boundaries and parameters of Family Law are being pushed out further and further not only from an international, or indeed a European Union, perspective, but also as a result of progressive domestic judicial jurisprudence which has sometimes been ahead of the Irish Legislature in terms of defining the nature and scope of legal principles in the area".[171]

[169] F Martin, *supra* n 159 at 18. See also G Shannon, "The Internationalisation of Irish Family Law" (2005) 5(1) JSIJ 42.
[170] See M Ní Shúilleabháin, "Accommodating Cultural Diversity under Irish Family Law" (2002) 24 DULJ 175.
[171] F Martin, *supra* n 159 at 17–18.

CHAPTER 9
The Right to Property

Introduction

The right to property receives significant protection at an Irish, European and international level and has been the subject of a high level of litigation given that it is of great import not only to individuals but also to corporate entities.[1] The protection of the right at the Irish level is very similar to the protection at the Council of Europe and European Union levels. For example, comparable definitions of property, what constitutes an interference with property and what constitute legitimate justifications for interference with property which can be seen throughout the case law. **[9–01]**

This chapter will elucidate the general principles governing the protection of property in Ireland through an examination of the constitutional principles, the regional developments and the international protection of this right.

A. Irish Constitutional Protection

Article 40.3.2°: **[9–02]**

> "2° The State shall, in particular, by its laws protect as best it may from unjust attack and, in the case of injustice done, vindicate the life, person, good name, and property rights of every citizen."

[1] For interesting discussions on the right to property see: FS Hoffman, "The Right to Property" (1909) Int J of Ethics 477; INS Nireekshak, "The Right to Property: Above All?" (1971) 6(34) Econ and Pol Weekly 3167; S Khandekar, "Women's Right to Property" (1995) 30(24) Econ and Pol Weekly 1402; M Nakamura, "Economic Activities and the Right to Property" (1990) 53(2) Law & Contemp Probs 1; C Rotherham, "Judicial Discretion and the Right to Property", (1998) 57(3) CLJ 630.

Article 43:

> "1. 1° The State acknowledges that man, in virtue of his rational being, has the natural right, antecedent to positive law, to the private ownership of external goods.
>
> 2° The State accordingly guarantees to pass no law attempting to abolish the right of private ownership or the general right to transfer, bequeath, and inherit property.
>
> 2. 1° The State recognises, however, that the exercise of the rights mentioned in the foregoing provisions of this Article ought, in civil society, to be regulated by the principles of social justice.
>
> 2° The State, accordingly, may as occasion requires delimit by law the exercise of the said rights with a view to reconciling their exercise with the exigencies of the common good."

[9–03] The right to property,[2] has double protection under the Constitution in both Art 40.3.2° and in Art 43. The State has clear positive and negative obligations both to protect property rights against attack and ensure vindication. Yet the right is not an absolute one and there are some limitations in the interests of social justice and the common good. The precise nature of the relationship between these two Articles of the Constitution is unclear and in "hardly any branch of constitutional law has judicial opinion shown so much fluctuation".[3] This section of the chapter will attempt to clarify this relationship and elucidate the general principles of property rights in Ireland.[4]

1. Nature of the Right

The Relationship between Article 40.3.2° and Article 43

[9–04] One of the most important issues to deal with in relation to this right is the relationship between Art 40.3.2° and Art 43, how these Articles interact in the development of property rights and what this interaction means for individuals seeking to rely upon the property right provisions of the Constitution. Are there separate bundles of rights under each Article or are they to be read as one? The case law in relation to this issue has been confused but it would appear that, in recent years at least, a clearer consensus is emerging.

---

[2] *Re Article 26 and the Health (Amendment) (No 2) Bill 2004* [2005] 1 IR 105 at 202. See further, O Doyle, *Constitutional Law: Text, Cases and Materials* (Clarus Press, Dublin, 2008) at 135 who notes that "[t]he protection of private property is seen as central to the functioning of a liberal democratic society as it gives individuals a stake in the world and the space within which to develop their life plans reasonably free from state instruction".

[3] J Casey, *Constitutional Law in Ireland* (3rd ed, Round Hall Sweet & Maxwell, Dublin, 2000) at 662.

[4] For a history of the development of property rights in the Irish constitution see R Walsh, "Private Property Rights in the Drafting of the Irish Constitution: A Communitarian Compromise" (2011) 18(1) DULJ 86. See Also J O'Reilly, "Constitutional Implications of recent decisions affecting Property Rights" (1983) ILT 63.

In one of the first cases to discuss this issue in detail, *Buckley and Others (Sinn Féin) v Attorney General and Another,*[5] the Supreme Court interpreted Art 43 without any reference to Art 40.3.2°, as a right which protected not only against the abolition of private property (which is clear from the express wording of Art 43) but also the protection of individual property rights. In response to an argument that what the exigencies of the common good required was a matter for the legislature and was not reviewable by the courts, the Supreme Court held legislative action was at all times reviewable by the courts, the Supreme Court held such action was at all times reviewable by the courts on the grounds that (a) the Oireachtas was forbidden to enact legislation that was in any way repugnant to the Constitution (Art 15.4), (b), the courts had the ultimate jurisdiction to determine whether this was in fact the case (Art 34.3.2° and Art 34.4.4°) and (c), Art 43, unlike Art 45, was justiciable.[6] In this case, the Supreme Court was presented with a challenge to the Sinn Féin Funds Act 1947 which required the payment of the funds of the organisation to a Board who would make charitable payments from these funds. The Supreme Court held that as the Act purported to remove all rights relating to the property from the plaintiffs (the Sinn Féin party) and as there was no conflict with the exigencies of the common good, the Act was considered unconstitutional. Doyle commends the decision for identifying that citizens have individual property rights which are protected by the Constitution and rejecting the contention that the scope of the exception in Art 43 was purely a matter for the Oireachtas.[7] Any other result may have led to the Oireachtas excluding "itself from all future assessment of whether private property rights had been breached".[8] **[9–05]**

However, this very strict protection of property rights appears to have been tempered somewhat in the case of *Foley v Irish Land Commission and the Attorney General,*[9] where the court considered a provision of the Land Act 1946 which essentially provided for forfeiture by a landowner of property in a case where they failed to meet certain terms, such as, dwelling on the property. Considering the decision in *Buckley,*[10] and the strict interpretation of the property guarantee, it would be appropriate to conclude that the court would have decided that as this was, similar to *Buckley,*[11] involving a complete deprivation of a property right, that this was inconsistent with the constitutional guarantee. However, O'Byrne J clearly emphasised that: **[9–06]**

> " ... not all limitations placed by the Oireachtas on private property ... is repugnant to the Constitution and, accordingly, void. If this argument be sound, the Constitution has certainly placed serious fetters upon the Legislature in dealing with property rights and the Court is not prepared to accept such a far-reaching proposition".[12]

The court held that as the Land Commission had no beneficial interest in the matter, the work of the Land Commission was of great "social and public import" and was

5 *Buckley and Others (Sinn Féin) v Attorney General and Another* [1950] IR 67.
6 J Casey, *supra* n 3 at p 664.
7 O Doyle, *supra* n 2 at p 138.
8 *ibid.*
9 *Foley v Irish Land Commission and the Attorney General* [1952] IR 118.
10 *Buckley and Others (Sinn Féin) v Attorney General and Another* [1950] IR 67.
11 *ibid.*
12 *Foley v Irish Land Commission and the Attorney General* [1952] IR 118 at 153 (*per* O' Byrne J).

"necessary or desirable for carrying out more effectually the policy of the Land Acts, that is, to further the common good", the Act was "not unconstitutional by reason of the provisions of Article 43".[13]

[9–07] This line of reasoning was continued in the case of *Attorney General v Southern Industrial Trust*[14], which involved the seizure of an illegally exported car by the custom authorities which the defendant had purchased without knowledge of the illegality. This case, Casey argues, "represents the court's least happy foray into the constitutional field" of property rights.[15] Similar to the decision in *Foley*, Lavery J in the Supreme Court, held that the provisions of the Customs (Temporary Provisions) Act 1945 were constitutional on the grounds that there were many statutes providing for the forfeiture and seizure of goods[16] which could be considered valid in accordance with the exigencies of the common good and principles of social justice. While the decision seems reasonable, the more interesting aspect of the judgment is the representation by Lavery J of the nature of Art 43. While, similar to the decisions in *Buckley*[17] and *Foley*,[18] he accepted that the courts had the jurisdiction to review legislation which was potentially in conflict with Art 43, the judgment "conveyed the impression that such claims were unlikely to succeed".[19] He also made an interesting reference to the relationship between Art 40.3.2° and Art 43 holding that property rights were properly found in Art 43 and that the rights to be found in Art 40.3.2° were, in fact, the same as those to be found in Art 43.

[9–08] Thankfully, these comments, and the clear conflict between this case and the previous jurisprudence, was specifically addressed by Kenny J in the case of *Central Dublin Development Association v Attorney General,*[20] beginning, as Casey describes, "a line of judicial reasoning following *Buckley* and rejecting *Southern Industrial Trust".*[21] Kenny J emphasised that the right to property is a personal right, a natural right to:

> " . . . individual or private ownership of worldly wealth" and that the "State cannot pass any law which abolishes all the bundle of rights called ownership or the general right to transfer, bequeath and inherit property".

However, the right is not absolute and must be:

> " . . . regulated by the principles of social justice and the State accordingly, may by law restrict their exercise with a view to reconciling this with the exigencies of the common good".

---

[13] *ibid* at pp 131–132 (*per* Dixon J).

[14] *Attorney General v Southern Industrial Trust* [1961] 109 ILTR 161.

[15] J Casey, *supra* n 3 at p 666. It is interesting thatrofessors W Murphy and Tanenhaus in Comparative Constitutional Law: Cases and Commentaries (New York, 1977) state that Lavery J "came to believe that the two sides, in their desire for a test case, had falsely stated the facts and resfused to allow barristers to cite the case".

[16] *Attorney General v Southern Industrial Trust* [1961] 109 ILTR 161 at 177 (*per* Lavery J).

[17] *Buckley and Others (Sinn Féin) v Attorney General and Another* [1950] IR 67.

[18] *Foley v Irish Land Commission and the Attorney General* [1952] IR 118.

[19] J Casey, *supra* n 3 at p 667.

[20] *Central Dublin Development Association v Attorney General* (1975) 109 ILTR 69.

[21] J Casey, *supra* n 3 at p 667.

Kenny J held that the courts have a duty to essentially determine whether this restriction is proportionate by inquiring: "whether the restriction is in accordance with the principles of social justice and whether the legislation is necessary to reconcile this exercise with the demands of the common good" and that "an abolition or restriction of rights without compensation will make the Act which does this invalid if it is an unjust attack on property rights".[22]

Since the decision in *Central Dublin Development Association v Attorney General,*[23] the courts have generally accepted that Art 40.3.2° and Art 43 must be read in conjunction with one another. In *Blake v The Attorney General*[24] O'Higgins CJ explained that Art 43: **[9–09]**

> " ... prohibits the abolition of private property as an institution, but at the same time permits, in particular circumstances, the regulation of the exercise of that right and of the general right to transfer, bequeath and inherit property. In short, it is an Article directed to the State and to its attitude to these rights, which are declared to be antecedent to positive law. It does not deal with a citizen's right to a particular item of property, such as a controlled premises".

Equally, Art 40 provides that the "State is bound, in its laws, to respect and as far as practicable to defend and vindicate the personal rights of citizens". O'Higgins CJ concluded that there:

> " ... exists, therefore, a double protection for the property rights of a citizen. As far as he is concerned, the State cannot abolish or attempt to abolish the right of private ownership as an institution or the general right to transfer, bequeath and inherit property. In addition, he has the further protection under Article 40 as to the exercise by him of his own property rights in particular items of property."[25]

Therefore, this has led to a position whereby Art 40.3.2° and Art 43 must now be considered as being read together. This leads to a number of important conclusions. In the case of *Dreher v Irish Land Commission*[26] it was held this close relationship means that: **[9–10]**

> " ... any State action that is authorised by Art 43 of the Constitution and conforms to that Article cannot by definition be unjust for the purpose of Article 40.3.2°".[27]

This statement was followed in several later cases, including *O'Callaghan v Commissioners of Public Works*[28] and *Madigan v Attorney General.*[29] The Supreme Court in

---

22 *Central Dublin Development Association v Attorney General* (1975) 109 ILTR 69 at 86 (*per* Kenny J.).

23 *ibid.*

24 *Blake v The Attorney General* [1982] IR 117 at 135 (*per* O'Higgins CJ).

25 *ibid* at 135 (per O'Higgins CJ). See also the supporting statement of Keane J in *I O'T v B* [1998] 2 IR 321 to the effect that in relation to individual applicants the protection which such citizens enjoy against unjust attacks on their property rights is derived from Art 40, under the heading "Personal Rights", and not from Art 43, which prohibits the abolition of the right of private ownership as an institution.

26 *Dreher v Irish Land Commission* [1984] ILRM 94.

27 *ibid* at 96 (*per* Walsh J).

28 *O'Callaghan v Commissioners of Public Works* [1985] ILRM 364.

29 *Madigan v Attorney General* [1986] ILRM 136 at 161.

Re Article 26 and the Health (Amendment) (No 2) Bill 2004[30] confirmed that this "remains a correct statement of the close relationship between the two Articles"[31] and Hogan and Whyte have concluded that "when considering constitutional protection of property rights, these Articles mutually inform each other."[32]

[9–11] The confusion surrounding the relationship between these two Articles has thankfully been clarified in recent years. However, it is unsurprising that the Constitutional Review Group sought the deletion and restatement of the property guarantee.[33] The current state of the law would appear to be that in determining whether any piece of legislation is repugnant to the property protections in the Constitution the courts will generally adopt the following approach:

> "firstly, to examine the nature of the property rights at issue; secondly, to consider whether the [Bill/Act] consists of a regulation of those rights in accordance with principles of social justice and whether the [Bill/Act] is required so as to delimit those rights in accordance with the exigencies of the common good; thirdly, in the light of its conclusions on these issues, to consider whether the [Bill/Act] constitutes an unjust attack on those property rights"[34].

The Nature of the Property Right at Issue

[9–12] Whether a property right exists, in the first instance, will depend on whether it can be defined as "property" within the meaning of Arts 40.3.2° and 43. It has been confirmed by the courts that both immoveable (including land[35]) and moveable assets[36] (including money,[37] vehicles and shares,[38] contractual rights[39] and rights

---

30 *Re Article 26 and the Health (Amendment) (No 2) Bill 2004* [2005] 1 IR 105.

31 *ibid* at 199.

32 G Hogan and G Whyte, *Kelly: The Irish Constitution* (4th ed, Butterworths, Dublin 2003) at pp 1978–1993.

33 *Constitution Review Group Report* (Stationery Office, Dublin, 1996) at pp 366–367. Art 40.3.2° and Art 43 should be deleted and replaced by a statement to the effect that "property rights, since they carry with them duties and responsibilities may be subject to legal restrictions conditions and formalities provided that they are duly required in the public interest and accord with the principles of social justice".

34 *Re Article 26 and the Health (Amendment) (No 2) Bill 2004* [2005] 1 IR 105 at 201.

35 *Attorney General v Southern Industrial Trust* [1961] 109 ILTR 161 (per Lavery J). See also *Central Dublin Development Association v Attorney General* (1975) 109 ILTR 69 (and to rights related to the ownership of land) See O Doyle, *supra* n 2 at p 141 and J Casey, *supra* n 3 at p 680.

36 *Lawlor v Minister for Agriculture* [1990] 1 IR 356 (per Murphy J) at 374. Intellectual property rights are also protected: See *Phonographic Performance (Ireland) Ltd. v Cody* [1998] 4 IR 504. Right to earn a livelihood can be considered to be a property right (*Re Article 26 and the Employment Equality Bill 1996* [1997] 2 IR 321) as can mutually contractual obligations in *Chestvale Properties v Glackin* [1992] ILRM 221.

37 *Buckley and Others (Sinn Féin) v Attorney General and Another* [1950] IR 67.

38 *In the Matter of Eylewood Limited and Ors* [2010] 3 JIC 0502 at 48 (even if these shares are worthless). It also includes the right of the guarantor to be indemnified by the company—at 82 (*per* Finlay Geoghegan J).

39 *Foley v Irish Land Commission and the Attorney General* [1952] IR 118 at 131 (*per* Dixon J). See also *PMPA v Attorney General* (1983) IR 339 at 359 (*per* O Higgins CJ) where it has been held that property rights include contractual rights. In *Condon v Minister for Labour* (No 2) (unreported High Court, 11 June, 1980) McWilliam J said: "As to section 3 of Article 40, accepting that the

arising from land ownership[40]) can be defined as property for the purposes of the constitutional guarantee.[41]

Cause of Action

However, a very specific issue has arisen before the Irish courts as to whether a cause of action can be considered to be "property" for the purposes of the property guarantee[42] or whether this could more properly be considered to be an unenumerated right to litigate protected by Art 40.3. In the earlier cases of *Foley v Irish Land Commission*[43] and *Attorney General v Southern Industrial Trust Ltd*,[44] it was held that the property rights guaranteed by Art 40.3.2°: **[9–13]**

> " ... are not rights over particular items of property but are the property rights guaranteed by Article 43, namely, the natural right to the private ownership of external goods and the general right to transfer, bequeath and inherit property. To divest a citizen of the ownership of a particular item of property in certain circumstances was held to be permissible under Article 43.2, of the Constitution".[45]

This would appear to preclude a determination that a right to a cause of action is included within the property guarantee. However, in the later cases of *O'Brien v Keogh*[46] and *O'Brien Manufacturing Engineering Co Ltd*[47] the Supreme Court held that a right to litigate a particular claim was a property right. This discrepancy in the case law was highlighted by the Supreme Court in the case of *Moynihan v Greensmyth.*[48] However, the court did not consider the question as the parties had conceded that a cause of action could be a property right under the Constitution and the Supreme Court felt constrained to decide the appeal on the basis of this concession. However, it emphasised that in doing so, "it does not necessarily accept that those concessions or assumptions are well founded".[49] The discrepancy was again highlighted by the Supreme Court in *Tuohy v Courtney.*[50] However, instead of attempting to reconcile the argument,[51] the court instead held that there was no material difference in protecting the right as an unenumerated one under Art 40.3 or as a property right. The

right to enter into contracts which are within the law and the right to enforce such contracts are personal rights and that a right under a contract is a property right so as to be protected by the provisions of the Article. I would refer to the judgment of O'Higgins, CJ, in *Moynihan v Greensmyth* (1977) IR 55". See also the right to hold a market (*DPP (Long) v McDonald* [1983] ILRM 223).

40 See for example the statutory right to renewal of a tenancy which might be protected under Arts 40.3.2° and 43: *Shanley v Commissioners of Public Works* (High Court, Carroll J, 31 October 1991).

41 G Hogan and G Whyte, *supra* n 32 at 1062.

42 *O'Brien v Manufacturing Engineering Co Ltd* [1973] 1 IR 334 at 367 (*per* Walsh J).

43 *Foley v Irish Land Commission* [1952] IR 118.

44 *Attorney General v Southern Industrial Trust Ltd.* (1957) 94 ILTR 161.

45 *Moynihan v Greensmyth* [1977] IR 55 at 71 (*per* O Higgins CJ).

46 *O'Brien v Keogh* [1972] IR 144.

47 *O'Brien Manufacturing Engineering Co. Ltd* [1973] IR 334.

48 *Moynihan v Greensmyth* [1977] IR 55.

49 *ibid* at 71 (*per* O'Higgins CJ).

50 *Tuohy v Courtney* [1994] 3 IR 1.

51 *ibid* at 46 (*per* Finlay CJ).

court considered, similar to Hogan and Whyte, that the question "may well indeed be ... academic"[52].

Economic Rights

[9–14] Another issue that has arisen for consideration is whether licences, planning permission and other "economic rights created by law"[53] can constitute property for the purposes of the constitutional guarantee. While the courts' response "has not been a model of clarity",[54] the general view would appear to be that economic rights which are created by law (enacted or delegated):

> " ... are subject to the conditions created by law and to an implied condition that the law may change those conditions. Changes brought about by law may enhance the value of those property rights ... or they may diminish them.... But an amendment of the law which by changing the conditions under which a licence is held, reduces the commercial value of the licence cannot be regarded as an attack on the property right in the licence — it is the consequence of the implied condition which is an inherent part of the property right in the licence".[55]

So while there is a property right in the licence, as it is created by law, it can also be legitimately restricted by law.

A useful example is the case of *Hempenstall v Minister for the Environment*[56] where the plaintiff argued that the changes to taxi regulations would:

> " ... have 'an immediate and devastating effect' on their taxi-cab licences ... [and] ... that the effect [would] be 'to effectively decimate the value of being a taxi-cab' 'licencee' ".[57]

[9–15] Costello J held that as this was a licence created by law, it was subject to the conditions that the law imposed on it which may change from time to time. While these changes might enhance or diminish the right, "this would not as a matter of law amount, in my opinion, to an attack on the applicants' property rights".[58] Costello J did not just restrict this principle to licences. He went on to hold that in most cases:

> " ... a change in the law which has the effect of reducing property values cannot in itself amount to an infringement of constitutionally protected property rights. There are many instances in which legal changes may adversely affect property values (for example, new zoning regulations in the planning code and new legislation relating to the issue of intoxicating liquor licences) and such changes cannot be impugned as being constitutionally invalid unless some invalidity can be shown to exist apart from the resulting property value diminution".[59]

---

52 *ibid* at 47 (*per* Finlay CJ). See also GW Hogan and GF Whyte, *supra* n 32 at 1064. In *Re Article 26 and the Health (Amendment) (No. 2) Bill 2004* [2005] 1 IR 105 a chose in action (i.e. the right of patients to recover unlawful nursing home charges) was considered a property right.

53 O Doyle, *supra* n 2 at p 141.

54 *ibid* at p 142.

55 *Hempenstall v Minister for the Environment* [1994] 2 IR 21 at 28 (*per* Costello J).

56 *ibid.*

57 *ibid* at 26 (*per* Costello J).

58 *ibid* at 28 (*per* Costello J).

59 *ibid* at 28–29 (*per* Costello J).

This would now appear to be the accepted line of reasoning in relation to economic rights created by law. In the case of *Gorman v Minister for the Environment*[60] Carney J in the High Court held that even though there is a property right in a licence which is capable of being recognised by law,[61] the nature of the property right enjoyed by holders of licences, although valuable, is "a right which is subject to an important qualification in that the licence is at all times subject to the conditions created by law".[62]

An example of a right which would not be considered to be protected by the guarantee is a quota, such as a milk quota, as a quota cannot be considered to be a licence or a permit "which may enhance the value of property which they own or occupy".[63] In relation to this link to enhancing the value of property, Keane J held that: [9–16]

> " . . . the fact that the right in question may effectively be disposed for cash does not mean that it is a property right. A person who is standing in a queue to buy a particular commodity and gives up his place to someone else for cash would not appear to be doing anything unlawful, but he is most assuredly not disposing of a property right, merely his right to occupy that particular place on public or private land at that particular time. Nor do I find that any assistance is to be derived from comparisons with patents, trademarks or copyright rights, which under our legal system are nowadays generically described as 'intellectual property rights'.
>
> Systems of law in developed societies invariably protect those who produce such intangible assets in the expectation of reward by creating a discrete structure of legal protection, embodied in our case in the relevant statutes. They are not remotely comparable in my view to the opportunities for profit presented by a regulatory scheme designed for the benefit of subsidised producers".[64]

Inheritance

Another issue that has arisen is whether an inheritance is a property right which is protected by the property guarantee and, if so, what is the extent of this protection. A useful example is the case of *O'B v S*[65] where the Supreme Court examined a case in which the natural child of her father and her mother, who were not married to each other, argued that the definition of "issue" in ss 67 and 69 of the Succession Act 1965, which appeared to include only legitimate issue, was invalid having regard to the provisions of the Constitution. Therefore the Supreme Court had to decide whether the Act did in fact discriminate between legitimate and illegitimate children and whether this statutory discrimination between legitimate and illegitimate issue was constitutional. Having decided that the Act did not apply to illegitimate children, the Supreme Court then went on to consider whether Art 43.2 confers a "constitutional right to intestate succession".[66] The Supreme Court concluded that it could not be stated: [9–17]

---

60 *Gorman v Minister for the Environment* [2001] 2 IR 414.

61 *ibid* at 426 (*per* Carney J).

62 *ibid* at 428 (*per* Carney J).

63 *Maher v Minister for Agriculture* [2001] 3 JIC 3003.

64 *ibid* (per Keane J).

65 *O'B v S* [1984] 1 IR 316 (*per* Walsh J). See case analysis in P O' Connor "The Succession Rights of Illegitimate Children" (1984) 2 ILT 63.

66 *ibid* at 330 (*per* Walsh J).

> "... as a matter of natural right that the children of a person who died intestate were necessarily entitled to succeed at the expense of their mother, the intestate's wife, or that she had any natural right to succeed on intestacy to the detriment of her children. Succession on intestacy does not depend on any act of the deceased property owner, unless the omission to make a will can be deemed to be an act of positive intention ... It appears to the Court that the phrase 'and inherit property' [in Article 43.2] must necessarily be related to the exercise of the power to transfer property by bequest and that what the State has guaranteed in that Article is to pass no law attempting to abolish the general right to inherit property so bequeathed".[67]

Therefore, there could be no constitutional right to succeed on intestacy. In relation to whether such a right could exist independently under Art 40.3.2°, the Supreme Court held that as there was no such right to intestate succession under Art 43, there was also no such right under Art 40.3.2°.[68]

[9–18] In this case the court was effectively stating that there is a right to inherit, but this only arises where this is clearly the intention of the testator. So in the case of intestacy, unless the omission to make a will was a conscious decision of the testator, no such right could arise. So in the case of *I O'T v B*[69] while Keane J held that the property rights of the applicants protected under Art 40.3 included the "right to ... inherit property"[70] and that the State is, accordingly, obliged to protect from unjust attack and vindicate the right of the applicants to inherit property", this could only arise "where, under the laws for the time being in force, they enjoy such a right in respect of specific property".[71]

Intellectual Property Rights

[9–19] While there is no express protection for intellectual property rights, it is generally accepted that they are included for protection within the constitutional guarantee.[72] They are also protected by secondary legislation such as the Trade Marks Act 1996, Patents Act 1992, the Copyright and Related Acts 2000 and the Industrial Design Act 2002.

Who Can Invoke the Property Guarantee?

[9–20] While it is axiomatic that individuals can invoke the property guarantee, there has been some discussion in the courts as to whether a legal body, such as a company, could invoke Art 43. The original position was that only natural persons could invoke property rights.[73] However, the decision in *Iarnród Éireann v Ireland*[74] confirmed that

---

67 *ibid.*

68 *ibid* at 330–331 (*per* Walsh J).

69 *I O'T v B* [1998] 2 IR 321.

70 *ibid* at 375 (*per* Keane J).

71 *ibid.* See also the observations of Walsh J in *OB v S* [1984] IR 316.

72 See for further information on the constitutional aspect of this topic: R Kennedy, "Was it author's rights all the time? Copyright as a constitutional right in Ireland" (2011) 18(1) DULJ 253; P Coughlan, "Compulsory Licences of copyright in Sound Recording" (1992) 10 ILT 180.

73 *PMPA v Attorney General* [1983] IR 339.

74 *Iarnród Éireann v Ireland* [1996] 3 IR 321.

companies, as legal persons, could hold constitutionally protected rights to property and could invoke these rights before the courts.[75]

2. Legitimate Interference with the Right to Property

Both Art 40.3.2° and Art 43 prohibit interferences with property rights. However, both Articles also make it clear that these rights are not absolute and interferences can be justified in certain circumstances. In this regard, Art 40.3.2° refers to "unjust attacks" on property rights implying that certain interferences may, in fact, be "just". Article 43 refers to the right of the State to delimit the right where social justice or the exigencies of the common good so require. Therefore, while there may be certain interferences with the right, these interferences may in certain circumstances be legitimate. The key question that the courts generally ask is whether the "challenged provision is an unjust attack on property rights".[76] **[9–21]**

Examining whether the challenged provision is an unjust attack will require an analysis of whether the provision is unjust in the sense of being retrospective, lacking fair procedures, being unreasonable and irrational, discriminatory, lacking proportionality and, in some cases, lacking compensation.[77] In conducting this analysis, the courts will have to determine what social justice and the common good require in the circumstances.[78]

The case of *Shirley v O'Gorman*[79] is illustrative of manner in which the courts define social justice and the common good. This case involved a statutory scheme under which the defendant (leasehold owner) had been found entitled to acquire a fee simple interest in a business premises. Peart J held that: **[9–22]**

> " ... social justice in the context of property rights means that there ought to be at least a fair, as opposed to equal, distribution of property amongst all members of the society, so that justice is achieved. In a democratic society, and one in which an open market operates, one could never achieve a situation where all citizens enjoyed ownership in the property of the State to an exactly equal degree. There will always be those who have more than others. In an extreme example, where the vast majority of property in the State was permitted by the laws of the State to remain in the ownership of a small group at the top of the tree so to speak, it could be seen as a justifiable interference with the property rights of those in such a protected and privileged position that they be required to make a share of that wealth available for the many at the middle or bottom of the tree, albeit on the basis of purchase or compensation. The passing of laws to facilitate the ownership in property being thus enjoyed by a greater number of persons in society would constitute the pursuit of a principle of social justice."

However, in implementing this principle, Peart J noted that the court would have to distinguish between the "objective of the legislation and the effect which its implementation may have in some instances". So for example, in the present case, the transfer of property was not being made to a person at the middle or bottom of the

---

[75] *ibid* at 365.
[76] J Casey, *supra* n 3 at p 669.
[77] GW Hogan and GF Whyte, *supra* n 32 at p 2004.
[78] J Casey, *supra* n 3 at p 663.
[79] *Shirley v O'Gorman* [2006] 1 JIC 3017.

tree but to a prosperous business entity. However, Peart J held that even though the legislation might lead to one case of an undeserving tenant acquiring the fee simple, "it does not detract from the objective of the legislation itself, which provides a scheme of wide and general application".[80]

[9–23] In relation to the proportionality test, the courts generally apply the proportionality test set out by Keane J in the case of *Iarnród Éireann v Ireland*[81] to the effect the interference with the property right must be rationally connected to the objective and not be arbitrary, unfair or based on irrational considerations, must impair the right as little as possible and be such that their effects on rights are proportional to the objective sought to be achieved.[82] This case involved a challenge to a provision of the Civil Liability Act 1961 which provided that where two defendants are held concurrently liable in a negligence claim, the plaintiff can enforce the full sum against either one regardless of the level of fault of the defendants. The defendant can then claim against the other defendant for the proportion of the award for which the other defendant is liable. The plaintiff in this case was injured when a train collided with a herd of cattle at a crossing owned and herded by the other defendant, a farmer. The plaintiff, a passenger on the train, sued both the farmer (who was found 70% liable) and Iarnród Éireann (who was found 30% liable). As the farmer could not make any significant contribution to the plaintiff, the liability for the entire amount fell on Iarnród Éireann who claimed that this was an unconstitutional breach of their property rights. The Supreme Court held that in legislating in this manner the State was attempting to balance the constitutional rights and that the Act was therefore justified. To decide any other way "would have been to exonerate . . . the blameworthy at the expense of the blameless".[83]

[9–24] Another useful example is the examination of the affordable and social housing schemes is the Art 26 reference of *Part V of the Planning and Development Bill 1999*.[84] The Supreme Court held that the Bill, which provided for planning authorities to require developers to provide up to 20 percent of the land in a development at agricultural use value rather than market value for the purposes of social and affordable housing, was proportionate. The Supreme Court held that the scheme passed both the rationality aspect of the test—the scheme was connected to an objective of sufficient importance to warrant interference with a constitutionally protected right given the serious social problems which they are designed to meet and related to concerns which in a free and democratic society should be regarded as pressing and substantial— and the impairment test—the scheme impaired the right as little as possible. Therefore, the scheme was proportionate to the aim sought to be achieved.

Doyle has commented that "it remains difficult to predict with confidence how the courts will react to particular restrictions of property rights"[85] as this is dealt with on a

---

[80] *ibid.*

[81] *Iarnród Éireann v Ireland* [1996] 3 IR 321

[82] *ibid* at 361–362.

[83] *Iarnród Éireann v Ireland* [1996] 3 IR 321 at 368.

[84] *Re Article 26 and Part V of the Planning and Development Bill 1999* [2000] 3 IR 321.

[85] O Doyle, *supra* n 2 at p 149. See also J Casey, *supra* n 3 at p 669.

case-by-case basis. However, there are certain trends which can be observed and which will be utilised here to explain how the courts react to certain interferences with property rights.[86] These trends can generally be divided into two separate factors identified by Casey: the nature of the interference and the presence or absence of compensation.[87]

The Nature of the Interference

Where the interference is in the nature of a physical intrusion on property rights, this will normally be "viewed less indulgently"[88] than a restraint upon the user of a property right reflecting the jurisprudence of the European Convention on Human Rights (ECHR). This can be seen in a number of clear examples which will now be examined. **[9–25]**

Control of Use

(i) Interferences Caused by Regulation of an Industry

Where the interference in question is for the purpose of regulating a particular industry, the courts give the legislature a lot of leeway in determining what is in the common good and are loath to impose their own views on the matter, as long as such provisions are considered proportionate in all the circumstances. In the case of *McDonald v Bord na gCon*[89] the Supreme Court had to consider whether s 47 of the Greyhound Industry Act 1958 which empowered Bord na gCon, with the consent of the Irish Coursing Club, by order to exclude a person from (*a*) being on any greyhound race track, (*b*) being at any authorised coursing meeting and (*c*) being at any public sale of greyhounds. The plaintiff brought a greyhound to a greyhound race track in Cork for the purpose of running the greyhound in a heat for the Cork Grand National, which was being run that evening. On production of the identity card issued in respect of the greyhound, it was noticed by an official at the track that certain figures, on the card had been altered, and did not correspond with figures appearing on the race card on sale to the public at the meeting. As a result, the dog was not allowed to run in the heat for which it had been entered. A letter was written to the plaintiff, on behalf of the Control Committee, requesting him to attend an inquiry at which the Control Committee intended to investigate the changing of the entries on the identity card. The plaintiff attended the inquiry and later he was informed, that the Control Committee had decided to recommend to the Board that an exclusion order should be made against him under the provisions of s 47 of the Greyhound Industry Act, 1958. After some further correspondence the Board, on the 14 February, 1961, made an exclusion order against the plaintiff. Walsh J for the Supreme Court, after a detailed examination of the legislation, decided that as the purpose of the Act was to "develop, improve and regulate an industry"[90] such legislation was, therefore, in the interests of the common good. **[9–26]**

---

[86] The chapter will utilize the helpful trends identified by O Doyle in Chapter 4 as well as some other trends noticed by the authors in examining the cases. See O Doyle, *supra* n 2 at p 149.
[87] J Casey, *supra* n 3 at p 669.
[88] *ibid.*
[89] *McDonald v Bord na gCon* [1965] IR 237.
[90] *ibid* at 239 (*per* Walsh J).

[9–27] Another useful example is the case of *PMPS Ltd v Attorney General*.[91] The plaintiff carried on an insurance and banking business, which included taking deposits, which over the years developed to a point where the banking aspect of the business was a considerable part of the business. In enacting legislation to control banking and the taking of deposits, which had not previously applied to the plaintiffs, the plaintiffs submitted that, if the effect of this legislation was to interfere with the banking business of the PMPS to the extent of wholly eliminating it, without any compensation, this amounted to an unjust attack on their property rights. They asserted that this was the reality of what the legislation implied in so far as the Society was concerned. However, the Supreme Court did not accept these submissions. There was no expropriation of either the business or the property rights of the plaintiffs and the Supreme Court described the legislation as merely a "regulation and control of the range of business which the Society may lawfully transact".[92] Also the Supreme Court held that the regulation was "reasonable, and was in accordance with the public interest and with the requirements of the common good".[93] Therefore, it could not be regarded as an unjust attack on property rights.

(ii) Interferences Caused by Regulating Land Use and Ownership

[9–28] Regulations concerning the use of land, particularly planning permission and compulsory purchase, have been the subject of many cases before the courts reflecting, what Doyle views as a, "concern on the part of the courts for the rights of landowners".[94] These regulations can come in many forms from planning permission to caps on rental income. It would appear that the courts will scrutinise closely the potential social justifications that might be put forward to justify such interferences.

[9–29] In the case of *Blake v Attorney General,*[95] the plaintiff, a land owner, challenged a cap placed by the State under the Rent Restrictions Acts on rents in certain controlled dwellings in order to provide cheaper accommodation for certain low-income tenants. The plaintiff argued that the selection of certain controlled dwellings was arbitrary and conducted irrespective of the means of either the tenant or the landlord. Also the plaintiff contended that the measure was unlimited in duration and was not associated with any particular emergency. The Supreme Court agreed with the plaintiff and held that the cap had been introduced:

> " . . . without compensation and without regard of the financial capacity or the financial needs of either group, in legislation which provides no limitation on the period of restriction, gives no opportunity for review and allows no modification of the operation of the restriction".[96]

It was, however, held to be disproportionate in the circumstances. Interestingly, in response to this case, the Oireachtas introduced the Housing (Private Rented Dwellings) Bill 1981 in order to assist tenants "who in many cases are elderly or

---

[91] *PMPS Ltd v Attorney General* [1983] IR 339.
[92] *ibid* at pp 360–361 (*per* O'Higgins CJ).
[93] *ibid* at 361 (*per* O'Higgins CJ).
[94] O Doyle, *supra* n 2 at p 149.
[95] *Blake v Attorney General* [1982] IR 117.
[96] *ibid* at pp 139–140 (*per* O'Higgins CJ).

among the poorer sections of the community" and who "would be faced with major increases in rents and for demands by their landlords for possession of the dwelling"[97] which was also referred to the Supreme Court.[98] This Bill was also found to be unconstitutional although the Supreme Court specifically indicated some sympathy for undue hardship of tenants. There was recognition that the Oireachtas was obliged to assist these tenants but that this could not be achieved by either the old Rent Restrictions Acts or the new Bill. Casey comments that rarely "has the legislature's range of policy options been so narrowed by judicial decision".[99] The situation was resolved by introducing a subsidy scheme via the social welfare system for tenants.[100]

In a series of cases on planning permission, the Supreme Court has held that although the requirement to get planning permission is an "encroachment on property rights",[101] such an encroachment is in the common good and is necessitated as such. In the case of *Pine Valley Developments v Minister for the Environment,*[102] a grant of outline planning permission was received from the Minister in relation to lands which were subsequently sold to the plaintiff. However, the County Council then refused to grant full planning permission in the terms of the outline permission. The plaintiff claimed that this constituted a breach of their property rights on the basis that it had paid a development price for the land which was now reduced. Finlay CJ, in the Supreme Court, held that the plaintiff's rights had not been infringed. The interesting aspect of this judgment is the statement of the court in relation to the issue of planning permission. The Supreme Court held that planning permission, far from diminishing the value of the land, had increased the value of the land and the plaintiff's rights. The Minister's decision to grant outline planning permission: [9–30]

> " . . . was not intended as any form of delimination or invasion of the rights of the owner of those lands but rather was intended as an enlargement and enhancement of those rights. The purchase of land for development purposes is manifestly a major example of a speculative commercial enterprise. Changes in market values or economic forces, changes in decisions of planning authorities and the rescission of them and many other factors may make the land more or less valuable in the hands of its purchasers".[103]

This would appear to contradict the view of planning permission as an encroachment of rights in *FPH Properties.*[104] However, thankfully, some clarity has been brought to the law by the consideration of *Part V of the Planning and Development Bill 1999*[105] where the Supreme Court assessed the constitutionality of the affordable and social housing schemes. The Supreme Court examined the history of planning legislation and noted that it has been a feature of Irish law for many years, adding that: [9–31]

---

[97] Dáil Éireann (Volume 331—9 December 1981) Housing (Private Rented Dwellings) Bill, 1981: Second Stage at 1374.
[98] *Re Article 26 and the Housing (Private Rented Dwellings) Bill 1981* [1983] IR 181.
[99] J Casey, *supra* n 3 at p 670.
[100] Housing (Private Rented Dwellings) Act 1982 s 23 (as amended).
[101] *State (FPH Properties SA) v An Bord Pleanála* [1987] IR 698 at 710 (*per* McCarthy J).
[102] *Pine Valley Developments v Minister for the Environment* [1987] IR 23.
[103] *ibid* at pp 45–46 (*per* Lardner J).
[104] *State (FPH Properties SA) v An Bord Pleanála* [1987] IR 698.
[105] *Re Article 26 and Part V of the Planning and Development Bill 1999* [2000] 3 IR 321.

> "... [e]very person who acquires or inherits land takes it subject to any restrictions which the general law of planning imposes on the use of the property in the public interest".[106]

The Supreme Court accepted that in certain cases a refusal of planning permission will depreciate the value in the open market of the land but noted conversely that "where the person obtains a permission for a particular development the value of the land in the open market may be enhanced".[107] In this case, the owner:

> "... may be required to cede some part of the enhanced value of land deriving both from its zoning for residential purposes and the grant of permission in order to meet what is considered by the Oireachtas to be a desirable social objective, namely the provision of affordable housing and housing for persons in the special categories and of integrated housing".[108]

The Supreme Court was contented that the scheme was rationally connected to a scheme of sufficient importance to warrant interference with property rights and was proportionate in the circumstances of the case.

Therefore, the general view of the courts relating to planning permission would appear to be that planning permission is not a limitation, but rather an enhancement of rights and that, therefore, limitations imposed by planning permission are not an unjust attack on property rights.

(iii) Interferences with Pursuing a Cause of Action

[9–32] While it is still uncertain whether a cause of action is a property right for the purposes of the constitutional guarantee, there have been a number of cases where a restriction on pursuing a cause of action, most notably by statutory limitation periods, have been considered by the courts. The argument of the plaintiffs in such cases is that the Statute of Limitations places a time limit on their right to pursue a cause of action (a property right). Where they do not take action within this time limit, they are then statute barred from taking their cause of action, effectively interfering with their property rights.

[9–33] The case of *O'Brien v Manufacturing Engineering Co Ltd*[109] is illustrative of this point. The plaintiff suffered injuries at work and received a payment of compensation from his employer under the Workman's Compensation Act 1934 and then instituted proceedings for damages based on the negligence of the employer, 26 months after the date of the accident. According to the Act, s 60(6) provided the acceptance by a workman of payments made in accordance with the Act of 1934 should not prevent the workman from maintaining an action at common law provided that the action was instituted within 12 months from the date of the accident or, if there were substantial grounds for not having brought such action within that period, within 24 months from the date of the accident. The plaintiff, who was statute barred, contended that this provision was inconsistent with his property rights under the Constitution. In the High Court, Pringle J considered that this provision was not an unjust attack on property

[106] *ibid* at 353.
[107] *ibid.*
[108] *ibid* at 354.
[109] *O'Brien v Manufacturing Engineering Co Ltd* [1973] I IR 118.

rights "as the section actually gave the plaintiff a property right which he would not otherwise have had, that is to say, the right on certain conditions to "have his cake and eat it" by accepting compensation under the Workmen's Compensation Act and then bringing an action for damages at common law". The Supreme Court agreed with the High Court and considered that the limitation period was not "of such unreasonably short duration having regard to the relatively weak position of a workman *vis-à-vis* his employer".[110]

Another example is the case of *Moynihan v Greensmyth*[111] in which the plaintiff was a passenger in a car that was involved in an accident caused by the negligence of the driver of the car, who was killed in the accident. The defendant, the personal representative of the deceased driver, argued that the plaintiff's claims were statute barred as the plaintiff had not commenced proceedings within two years of the death of the defendant as required by s 9 of the Civil Liability Act 1961. The Supreme Court, in accepting that a cause of action could be a property right for the purposes of this case, held that s 9 of the Act was designed to avoid excessive delays in the administration of estates during which "severe hardship might be caused and injustice done to innocent people"[112]. If they extended the time in cases of incapacity (in this case as the plaintiff was only 16 at the time the cause of action accrued) "the danger of stale claims being brought would be very real and could constitute a serious threat to the rights of beneficiaries of the estate of a deceased".[113] The Supreme Court considered that the legislature in balancing conflicting claims had made a fair compromise between protecting the right of the plaintiff to pursue a cause of action and the right of beneficiaries not to be subject to stale claims many years after the death of the defendant. **[9–34]**

The reasoning of the courts towards limitation periods is perhaps best described by the Supreme Court in *Tuohy v Courtney*[114] where it was held that while limitation periods were an interference with the right to litigate, this was not an unjust attack. There were three distinct reasons why such provisions were reasonable. The purpose of such legislation is first to protect defendants against stale claims and avoid the injustices which might occur to them were they asked to defend themselves from claims which were not notified to them within a reasonable time.[115] **[9–35]**

Secondly:

> "... they are designed to promote as far as possible expeditious trials of action so that a court may have before it, as the material upon which it must make its decision, oral evidence which has the accuracy of recent recollection and documentary proof which is complete, features which must make a major contribution to the correctness and justice of the decision arrived at".[116]

---

[110] *ibid* at 367 (*per* Walsh J).
[111] *Moynihan v Greensmyth* [1977] IR 55.
[112] *ibid* at 72 (*per* O' Higgins CJ).
[113] *ibid.*
[114] *Tuohy v Courtney* [1994] 3 IR 1.
[115] *ibid* at 48 (*per* Finlay CJ).
[116] *ibid* at 48 (*per* Finlay CJ).

[9–36] Thirdly, they are designed to promote as far as possible and proper a certainty of finality in potential claims which will permit individuals to arrange their affairs whether on a domestic, commercial or professional level in reliance to the maximum extent possible upon the absence of unknown or unexpected liabilities.

This view of limitations on pursuing causes of action has been approved by the courts in *Iarnród Éireann v Ireland*[117] and *White v Dublin City Council.*[118] Therefore, it would appear the statutory limitation periods which are of a reasonable length would be considered compatible with the constitutional guarantees in Arts 40 and 43.

(iv) Interferences Through Taxation

[9–37] The decisions of the courts relating to matters of taxation would appear to suggest that the courts are generally slow to intervene in taxation measures and will only be challenged where they are indisputably capricious in operation, having no relation to a person's ability to pay the levy imposed.[119] A good example of such a case is that of *Brennan v Attorney General*[120] where a system of levying rates on agricultural land based on a valuation mechanism which was over a century old was challenged by a group of farmers. The Supreme Court agreed that the system imposed an unfair burden on occupiers of poorer land. The Supreme Court noted that where "injustice becomes obvious the State had a duty to take action which it had failed to do in this case".[121] In continuing to use the same system without revision or review, the State:

> " ... failed to protect the property rights of those adversely affected by the system from future unjust attack. In the assessment of a tax, such as a county rate, reasonable uniformity of valuation appears essential to justice. If such reasonable uniformity is lacking the inevitable result will be that some ratepayer is required to pay more than his fair share ought to be. This necessarily involves an attack upon his property rights which by definition becomes unjust. The plaintiffs have established such injustice in this particular case".[122]

[9–38] However, outside of these very obvious cases of injustice, the courts generally tend not to interfere in matters of taxation. Of current interest is the challenge to the property tax in the case of *Madigan v Attorney General.*[123] The property tax was to be imposed upon all houses with a market value of over £65,000, provided the family income exceeded £20,000. The plaintiff challenged the tax on the grounds that it was an unjust attack on property rights. The Supreme Court held that this was not an unjust attack on property rights. The Government and the Oireachtas had specific roles in the determination of taxation policy and that a tax measure did necessarily interfere with the property rights of affected citizens. However, this interference was in accordance with social justice and required by the exigencies of the common good and so could not be considered to be an unjust attack on property rights.

117 *Iarnród Éireann v Ireland* [1996] 3 IR 321.
118 *White v Dublin City Council* [2004] 1 IR 545.
119 O Doyle, *supra* n 2 at pp 156–158.
120 *Brennan v Attorney General* [1985] ILRM 355.
121 *ibid* at 365 (*per* O'Higgins CJ).
122 *ibid* at 365 (*per* O' Higgins CJ).
123 *Madigan v Attorney General* [1986] ILRM 136.

Deprivation of Property

(i) Compulsory Purchase

Compulsory purchase has also been the subject of many cases before the courts. The courts generally protect the power of the state to compulsorily purchase land by insisting on the provision of compensation. In one of the earliest cases on this issue, *Fisher v Irish Land Commission*[124] the plaintiff challenged the Land Act 1939 on separation of powers grounds but conceded that the Constitution did not prevent the legislature from compulsorily expropriating land for public purposes. Casey notes that it would appear that the Supreme Court "regarded this concession as rightly made, and in no subsequent case has an attempt been made to establish the converse position"[125]. So for example, in *O'Brien v Bord na Móna*[126] the plaintiff, although challenging the compulsory purchase on other grounds, did not argue that it was prohibited by the constitutional protections on the grounds of property. [9–39]

There have been statements to the effect that compulsory purchase admittedly "amounts to a severe interference with constitutionally protected property rights".[127] However, this was specifically addressed by the Supreme Court in the case of *Clinton v An Bord Pleanála*[128] where Geoghegan J held: [9–40]

> "It is axiomatic that the making and confirming of a compulsory purchase order to acquire a person's land entails an invasion of his constitutionally protected property right. The power conferred on an administrative body such as a local authority or An Bord Pleanála to compulsorily acquire land must be exercised in accordance with the requirements of the Constitution, including respecting the property rights of the affected landowner ... Any decisions of such bodies are subject to judicial review. It would insufficiently protect constitutional rights if the court, hearing the judicial review application, merely had to be satisfied that the decision was not irrational or was not contrary to fundamental reason and common sense ... The acquiring authority must be satisfied that the acquisition of the property is clearly justified by the exigencies of the common good".[129]

In this regard it was held to be in the interests of the common good that sites which were derelict, neglected or contained unsightly structures be compulsorily acquired.[130] Therefore, it would appear that there is a general acceptance that compulsory purchase is justified by the exigencies of the common good and it would therefore be immune from constitutional challenge, other than on grounds that the rules of constitutional justice were not followed or that it was not required by the exigencies of the common good.

[124] *Fisher v Irish Land Commission* [1948] IR 3.
[125] J Casey, *supra* n 3 at p 663.
[126] *O'Brien v Bord na Móna* [1983] IR 255.
[127] *Egan v An Bord Pleanála* [2011] 2 JIC 1002 at 6.2.
[128] *Clinton v An Bord Pleanála (No 2)* [2007] 4 IR 701.
[129] *Egan v An Bord Pleanála* [2011] 2 JIC 1002 at 6.32.
[130] *ibid.*

(ii) Interferences by Retrospectively Altering Property Rights

[9–41] In general, the courts are very sceptical of any rules and provisions which try to alter retrospectively the property rights of individuals. The seminal case in this area is the case of *Re Article 26 and the Health (Amendment) Bill 2004*.[131] In this case, the court examined the constitutionality of proposed legislation which retrospectively altered a property right. It had emerged in 2004 that elderly people had been unlawfully charged for nursing home care since the 1970's. The Oireachtas, in order to prevent multiple claims, tried to retrospectively remove the right to claim for restitution. The Supreme Court held that in cases, such as the present one, where the abrogation of a property right is concerned, a very strict test will be applied. A justification based on the interests of the common good or on general public policy involving matters of finance alone would not be acceptable unless it was an "objective imperative for the purpose of avoiding an extreme financial crisis or a fundamental disequilibrium in public finances".[132] Therefore, the Bill was considered to be unconstitutional.

(iii) Interferences by Unequal Distribution of Costs

[9–42] The Supreme Court has held that interferences with property rights that involve an unequal distribution of costs between different sections of the community will be subject to strict scrutiny. In the case of *Re Article 26 and the Employment Equality Bill 1996*[133] the Supreme Court was tasked with considering the constitutionality of the Employment Equality Bill and, in particular for the purposes of this chapter, the provision relating to disabled persons in employment. This provision required employers to put in place special treatment and facilities for disabled persons to ensure their successful integration in the workplace unless to do so would place undue hardship on the employer. The Supreme Court considered that such provisions did interfere with the property rights of employers but that this was introduced with a view to:

> " ... reconciling the exercise of the rights in question with a specific aspect of the common good, i.e. the promotion of equality in the workplace between the disabled and their more fortunate fellow citizens".[134]

[9–43] The Supreme Court considered it just that society should bear the cost of this "laudable aim"[135] just as it was fair that businesses should all bear the cost of health and safety legislation, environmental protections and planning restrictions relating to ensuring accessibility in buildings. These were all considered part of the "industrialist's costs of production".[136] However, the provision of the Bill, "attempts to transfer the cost of solving one of society's problems on to a particular group"[137] requiring an employer to:

---

131 *Re Article 26 and the Health (Amendment) (No 2) Bill 2004* [2005] 1 IR 105. See also E O'Dell and G Whyte "Is this a country for old men and women? In Re Article 26 and the Health(Amendment) No. 2 Bill 2004 (2005)" 12(1) DULJ 368.

132 *Re Article 26 and the Health (Amendment) (No 2) Bill 2004* [2005] 1 IR 105 at 132.

133 *Re Article 26 and the Employment Equality Bill 1996* [1997] 2 IR 321.

134 *ibid* at 336.

135 *ibid* at 337.

136 *ibid.*

137 *ibid.*

> "... bear the cost of all special treatment and facilities which the disabled person may require to carry out the work unless the cost of the provision of such treatment or facilities would give rise to 'undue hardship' to the employer".[138]

More problematic for the Supreme Court was the fact that the Bill was drafted too broadly and did not exempt small firms or firms with a limited number of employees and had a very broad definition of "disability". Therefore, it was considered to be unconstitutional.

While this case would appear to stand for a general trend that the court will generally not agree with the imposition of costs on one sector of the community, there are certain aspects of the judgment that do not support this principle. For example, the Supreme Court seemed to accept the "polluter pays principle" and the idea that employers should bear the cost of health and safety regulations and accessibility requirements for disabled persons. All of these would appear to impose high cost on all employers and would, after this decision, appear to be constitutional despite the fact that they are imposed on all employers (one sector of the community) regardless of their size. However, the requirement to provide special accommodation for disabled employees was considered unconstitutional. It is hard to reconcile this decision with these other issues that the Supreme Court appeared to find constitutional in this case.[139] Perhaps the decision can be explained by examining the effect of imposing this provision on employers. The Supreme Court did make reference to the wide definition of disability and how employers would have difficultly calculating the cost of implementing this provision. This is certainly different to health and safety regulations and pollution costs as these costs are generally applied throughout the business and the cost of doing so is generally calculable in advance. Equally, the Supreme Court had concerns about the section which provided that if the provision of special treatment and facilities would cause undue hardship to the financial circumstances of the employer, the employer would have to disclose this financial information to a third party to justify the non-provision of special treatment. Perhaps it was these practical issues that influenced the decision of the court to refuse to impose the cost of this social justice policy on specific members of the community. **[9–44]**

Another good example of this principle relating to the sharing of cost is the case of *BUPA Ireland Ltd v Health Insurance Authorities*[140] in which the State introduced a risk equalisation scheme in the health insurance sector in which BUPA (a health insurance provider) had to pay VHI (another health insurance provider) a sum of money to equalise an inherent unfairness in the market place. This situation had arisen as a result of a new community rating scheme which provided that all insured persons would have to pay the same health insurance premiums regardless of age, gender or health profile. This impacted less directly on BUPA who had a lot of young clients as it was new to the marketplace. However, VHI, as it was the oldest health insurance provider in the State, had an older clientele and as such was facing larger costs as a result of the community rating scheme. The risk equalisation scheme attempted to remedy this problem by seeking cash transfers from insurers with lower risk members **[9–45]**

[138] *ibid* at 337–338.

[139] O Doyle, *supra* n 2 at p 160.

[140] *BUPA Ireland Ltd v Health Insurance Authorities* [2005] IEHC 291.

to insurers with higher risk members. While the community rating scheme was struck down on other grounds (notably that it was held to be *ultra vires* the power of the Minister for Health and Children), the statements by the McKechnie J in the High Court are illuminating. He considered that even though the risk equalisation scheme was a clear interference with property rights, this was justified by reference to the common good (the need to ensure affordable health insurance coverage among all ages) and the pressing and substantial need for such equality in the health insurance industry. Therefore, the High Court certainly considered that imposing the cost on one sector of society was necessary to ensure an equitable health insurance system.

(iv) Interferences in Times of Economic Crisis

[9–46] The unprecedented economic crisis which struck Ireland in recent years has been found to constitute a legitimate justification for certain attacks on property rights of citizens. The introduction of the National Assets Management Agency (NAMA) and reductions in funding in the health, education and other public sectors has led to interesting litigation concerning the balance between the protection of property rights and the exigencies of the common good in times of economic crisis.

The role of the National Asset Management Agency and its impact on property rights was addressed in the case of *Dellway Investments Limited and Others National Management Asset Agency.*[141] The Supreme Court considered a constitutional challenge to a provision of the National Management Asset Agency Act 2009 (s 69) by a property developer who disputed the acquisitions of his assets (substantial loans) by NAMA having regard to the impact of the section on his property rights. The appellants contended that the meaning given to an "eligible bank asset" provided for in s 69 of the Act of 2009 was so broad and the discretion of NAMA so untrammelled that it constituted an unjust attack on the property rights of the appellants. The Supreme Court held that the Oireachtas was entitled as a matter of policy to include in the Act a very broad definition of "eligible bank asset" and there were sufficient safeguards in the Act to protect against unwarranted interference such as the fact that the relevant bank had to decide to opt to participate in the statutory scheme and an "eligible bank asset" was not acquired by NAMA by reason of the fact alone of its eligibility but only if NAMA concluded that its acquisition was necessary. In these circumstances and with these safeguards in place, the provisions of s 69 could not be considered to be an unjust attack on the property rights of the appellants.

[9–47] One of the most interesting cases in recent years relating to the issue of property rights and the impact of the economic crisis is the case of *Haire v Minister for Health and Children.*[142] The plaintiffs were pharmacists who engaged in the provision of medicines to eligible members of the public under a contract agreed with the Health Service Executive. That contract allowed the Minister after consultation with a pharmacist's representative body, to approve or direct the rates to be paid in return for the provision

[141] *Dellway Investments Limited and Others v National Management Asset Agency* [2011] 4 JIC 1202.

[142] *Haire v Minister for Health and Children* [2009] IEHC 562.

of services under the contract. In response to the economic crisis and the deterioration of the public finances, the Government introduced the Financial Emergency Measures in the Public Interest Act 2009 and the corresponding Health Professionals (Reduction of Payments to Community Pharmacist Contractors) Regulations 2009 which allowed for the reduction of rates paid to the pharmacists. The plaintiffs challenged the provisions of both the Act and the Regulations on the grounds that they unjustly interfered with their property rights. In particular, they argued that their contractual property rights which they enjoyed under their contract had been infringed in an arbitrary, capricious and discriminatory manner. It was held by McMahon J in the High Court that the constitutional property rights relied on were contractual rights and were no more or no less than those they enjoyed under the contract. As the Minister was entitled to vary the rates under the contract, the varying of those rates pursuant to a statutory power did not infringe any constitutional right of the plaintiffs.[143] Equally, the reduction of the rates in question did not constitute an unjust attack on the plaintiffs' property rights. The Act of 2009 was a measured, proportionate and carefully drawn response to an unprecedented economic crisis and had a number of significant safeguards contained in it.[144]

The Presence or Absence of Compensation

The second issue that arises in the majority of cases under Art 40.3.2° and Art 43 is the issue of compensation.[145] The provision or non-provision of compensation for an interference with a property right may be determinative of whether the interference is compatible with the constitutional guarantee. The general rule is that where an interference with a property right is not compensated for, the provision will more than likely be found to be unconstitutional. Conversely, the payment of compensation may legitimate an interference with a property right. However, there are exceptions to this rule and compensation is not always a requirement.[146] **[9–48]**

The general rule, that compensation is required and should be at a level equivalent to full market value, is illustrated by the case of *DPP (Long) v McDonald*[147] where a byelaw which interfered with the operation of a fair was considered to be constitutional as long as the operation of the byelaw did not put the fair out of business, and even then only if compensation was paid for the interference. The Supreme Court has held in both *Re Article 26 and the Planning and Development Bill 1999*[148] and *Re Article 26 and the Health (Amendment) (No 2) Bill 2004*[149] that: **[9–49]**

[143] *Blake v The Attorney General* [1982] IR 117; *Condon v Minister for Labour (No 2)* (Unreported, High Court, McWilliam J, 11 June, 1980); *Hempenstall v Minister for the Environment* [1994] 2 IR 20 and *Shanley v Commissioners for Public Works in Ireland* [1992] 2 IR 477; See also *Irish Pharmaceutical Union v Minister for Health* [2007] IEHC 222, (Unreported, High Court, Clarke J, 29 June, 2007).

[144] *Moynihan v Greensmyth* [1977] IR 55; *Hamilton v Hamilton* [1982] IR 466 and *The Health (Amendment) (No 2) Bill 2004* [2005] IESC 7, [2005] 1 IR 105.

[145] S Dodd, "Notices preventing compensation" (2005) 12(4) IPELJ 156.

[146] J Casey, *supra* n 3 at 669.

[147] *DPP (Long) v McDonald* (1983) ILRM 223.

[148] *Re Article 26 and the Planning and Development Bill 1999* [2000] 2 IR 321.

[149] *Re Article 26 and the Health (Amendment) (No 2) Bill 2004* [2005] 1 IR 105.

> " ... there can be no doubt that a person who is compulsorily deprived of his or her property in the interests of the common good should normally be fully compensated at a level equivalent to at least the market value of the acquired property".[150]

The Supreme Court in *Re Article 26 and the Health (Amendment) (No 2) Bill 2004*[151] held that:

> " ... it is clear that where an Act of the Oireachtas interferes with a property right, the presence or absence of compensation is generally a material consideration when deciding whether that interference is justified pursuant to Article 43 or whether it constitutes an 'unjust attack' on those rights. In practice, substantial encroachment on rights, without compensation, will rarely be justified."[152]

[9–50] Exceptions to the general rule appear to involve cases in which (1) the interference with the property is limited or (2) where there are clear public policy justifications for the non-payment of compensation. An example of the first is the case of *O'Callaghan v Commissioners of Public Works*[153] in which the absence of any provision for compensation for the making of a preservation order in respect of a public monument on the plaintiff's lands did not render the legislation repugnant to the Constitution. O'Higgins CJ, held that that, "the [preservation] order does not deprive the owner of his ownership nor of his rights to use the monument in any manner not inconsistent with its preservation". At the time of the purchase of the property, the plaintiff was aware of the limitation. This was a legitimate "requirement of what should be regarded as the common duty of all citizens".[154] Therefore, as this was a limited interference with the property rights of the plaintiff, compensation was not necessarily payable.

[9–51] It is difficult to reconcile this case with that of *Electricity Supply Board v Gormley*[155] where the plaintiff challenged the right of the ESB to carry out works on her lands without the payment of some form of compensation. Similar to the *O'Callaghan* decision, the Supreme Court held that there are "particular cases" where the requirements of social justice or the common good do not require the payment of compensation.[156] In this case these included the "social benefits of electricity and its contribution to the economic welfare of the State".[157] However, in this case, it was held that the principles of social justice did not require that the plaintiff be denied compensation. This would initially appear at odds with the decision in *O'Callaghan* as both are cases in which there was minimal interference with property rights yet the courts came to different conclusions on the issue. Perhaps the *Gorman* case can be distinguished on the grounds that the legislation under which the order for the works

---

150 *ibid* at 352 (*per* Keane CJ).
151 *ibid.*
152 *ibid* at 352 (*per* Keane CJ).
153 *O'Callaghan v Commissioners of Public Works* [1985] ILRM 364.
154 *ibid* at pp 367–368 (*per* O'Higgins CJ).
155 *Electricity Supply Board v Gormley* [1985] 1 IR 129 (*per* Finlay CJ).
156 *ibid* at 150 (*per* Finlay CJ). See also in *Dreher v Irish Land Commission* [1984] ILRM 94 (*per* Walsh J).
157 *ibid* at 150 (*per* Finlay CJ).

was made also provided for a right to an *ex gratia* payment of compensation to be determined by the ESB, whereas in the *O'Callaghan* case no such right was available in the legislation. In the *Gorman* case, the Supreme Court placed a great deal of emphasis on the fact that the legislation lacked "the essential ingredient of the ultimate right to have the amount assessed by an independent arbiter or tribunal".[158] Therefore, the relevant provision of the Electricity (Supply) Act 1927, as amended, was unconstitutional. The decision illustrates that although compensation is not always required, the cases in which it is not required are extremely rare.

An example of the second type of case in which there is a public interest in the non-payment of compensation is the case of *Gilligan v Criminal Assets Bureau*[159]. In that case, the Supreme Court considered a challenge to the Proceeds of Crime Act 1996 which empowered the High Court to make interim and interlocutory orders freezing property which was alleged to be directly or indirectly related to the proceeds of crime and for the eventual disposal and sale of the property (the proceeds of which would go to the Exchequer) without compensation. While this constituted a clear interference with property rights without compensation, McGuinness J held that the State had a legitimate interest in the forfeiture of the proceeds of crime.[160] Adequate safeguards were contained in the legislation. For example, the respondent could intervene at any time and show good title to the property, at which point the property would be promptly returned and the State may be ordered to pay compensation to the individual involved. Similarly, the State in obtaining the freezing orders must present to the court evidence that the property in question is the proceeds of crime and that the respondent has no good title to it. The exigencies of the common good included measures designed to prevent the accumulation and use of assets which derived either directly or indirectly from criminal activities. The right to private property could not hold a place so high in the hierarchy of rights that it protects the position of illegally acquired assets.[161] This was a proportionate response by the legislature to the threat to society "posed by an entirely new type of professional criminal".[162] **[9–52]**

B. Protection under the European Convention on Human Rights

Article 1 Protocol 1(P1-1): **[9–53]**

> "Every natural or legal person is entitled to the peaceful enjoyment of his possessions. No one shall be deprived of his possessions except in the public interest and subject to the conditions provided for by law and by the general principles of international law.
>
> The preceding provisions shall not, however, in any way impair the right of a State to enforce such laws as it deems necessary to control the use of property in accordance with the general interest or to secure the payment of taxes or other contributions or penalties."

---

158 *ibid* at pp 150–151 (*per* Finlay CJ).
159 *Gilligan v Criminal Assets Bureau* [1998] 3 IR 185.
160 *ibid* at 237 (*per* McGuinness J).
161 *ibid.*
162 *ibid.*

1. Nature of the Right

Who is the Subject of the Right?

[9–54] P1-1 applies expressly to every natural and legal person. It is also important for the purposes of this Article that the applicant be the victim of the interference. So if the applicant is a company, then the company must have suffered some loss as a corporation.[163] If it is the rights of the shareholders that have been affected, then they are the proper applicants under P1-1. Harris points to a variety of cases in which in certain cases the separate legal personality of a corporation was set aside in order to ascertain the real "victim" of the interference.[164] However, this only occurs in very exceptional cases.

[9–55] A useful example of this is the case of *Khamidov v Russia*[165] in which the applicant and his brother (as co-owners) set up a limited liability company, Nedra, in order to run a bakery business. This business leased (from the applicant and his family who owned the land) a large estate of land and buildings in order to run the company but the applicant was excluded from the land after Russian police units took over the estate in order to run a counter-terrorism operation against the Chechen rebels. One of the initial questions for consideration by the ECtHR was the standing of the applicant to lodge an application in his own name rather than on behalf of the company as it was the company which had formal assignment under lease of the land and the property.[166] This case is useful in that it clearly reveals the thinking of the court in relation to this difficult question.

[9–56] The court reiterated its position that the general rule is that where acts and omissions affect a company, "the application should be brought by that company. Disregarding a company's legal personality as regards the question of being a "victim" will be justified only in exceptional circumstances".[167] The court did note that a company which has a sole owner can also be a "victim", "because in the case of a sole owner there is no risk of differences of opinion among shareholders or between shareholders and a board of directors as to the reality of infringement of Convention rights or to the most

[163] See the interesting contribution of A Austin, "Commerce and the European Convention on Human Rights" (2004) 11(9) CLP 223.

[164] D Harris *et al*, *Law of the European Convention on Human Rights* (Oxford University Press, Oxford, 2008) at 665. D Harris *et al* refer to the cases of *Olczak v Poland* (Application No 30417/96), *Pine Valley Developments v Ireland* (Application No 12742/87), *Ankarcrona v Sweden* (Application No 35178/97); *Eugenia Michaelidou Developments Ltd and Michael Tymvios v Turkey* (Application No 16163/90); *Agrotexim v Greece* (Application No 14807/89); *Lebedev v Russia* (Application No 4493/04); *TW Computeranimation GMbH v Austria* (Application No 53818/00); *Bayramov v Azerbaijan* (Application No 23055/03); *Druzstevni Zalonzna Pria v Czech Republic* (Application No 72034/01).

[165] *Khamidov v Russia* (No 72118/01).

[166] *ibid* at 121.

[167] *ibid* at 122. See also *Capital Bank AD v Bulgaria* (Application No 49429/99); *Camberrow MM5 AD v Bulgaria* (Application No 50357/99); *GJ v Luxembourg*, (Application No 21156/93) at 23; and *Agrotexim and Others v Greece*, (judgment of 24 October 1995, Series A no 330) at 66.

appropriate way of reacting to such an infringement".[168] This implies that the court will be more willing to set aside corporate personality in cases where there is only one sole owner of a company as in such cases it is easy to tie the decision making of the company to the owner of the company. Where there are multiple owners (as in this case), the situation would appear to be more complicated and the court would only pierce the corporate veil to identify the owners in exceptional circumstances. In this case the ECtHR found that such exceptional circumstances did exist because there were only two co-owners, these co-owners were brothers carrying on a family business through the company and it could be said that they had a "direct personal interest in the subject-matter of the present complaint".[169] In addition, the other co-owner clearly supported the application by the applicant as he had issued the applicant "with a general power of attorney confirming the applicant's right to represent him should it be necessary" and they did "not appear to have competing interests which could create difficulties"[170]. In the circumstances, the Court held that the applicant was a victim for the purposes of the claim and an infringement of P1-1 was also found in relation to the occupation and damage caused to the property of the applicant.

The Definition of "Possession"

The concept of "possession" is one of the most contentious issues regularly before the court. There are some general principles which can be drawn from the case law which can provide assistance in determining whether the interference complained of falls within P1-1. **[9–57]**

One of the most important rules is that the concept of "possession" has "an autonomous meaning" which is independent of what is classified as a possession within domestic law.[171] This means that although something might be considered to be property for the purposes of the Irish Constitutional protection, this may not be the case at the ECtHR level. Conversely, what may not be considered to be property at an Irish level, may well fall within the definition of "possessions" under the ECtHR. The ECtHR reserves the right to determine in each case, whether the interference complained of falls within the definition of possession.[172] A useful example of this principle is the case of *Tre Traktorer Aktiebolag v Sweden*[173] in which the applicant tried to claim that a liquor licence was a possession for the purposes of P1-1. The ECtHR held that even though the liquor licence conferred no right in national law, it could still be a "possession" for the purposes of the convention. In particular, the ECtHR noted that the licence was essential to the successful conduct of the business and its withdrawal would have adverse effects on the economic value of the business.[174]

---

[168] *ibid* at 123. See also *Ankarcrona v Sweden* (Application No 35178/97); *Dyrwold v Sweden*, (Application No 12259/86); *Nosov v Russia* (Application No 30877/02).

[169] *ibid* at 125.

[170] *ibid.*

[171] *Iatridis v Greece* (Application No 31107/96) at 54; *Beyeler v Italy* (Application No 33202/96) at 100; and *Broniowski v Poland* (Application No 31443/96) at 129; *Anheuser-Busch Inc v Portugal* (Application No 73049/01) at 63.

[172] See Case of the *Former King of Greece v Greece* (Application No 25701/94) at 60 and *Beyeler v Italy* (Application No 33202/96) at 100.

[173] *Tre Traktorer Aktiebolag v Sweden* (1989) 33 EHRR 309.

[174] See also the discussion in D Harris *et al*, *supra* n 164 at pp 658–659.

[9–58] The definition of "possession" is very broad and would appear to cover a wide variety of immoveable (or physical) assets[175] and moveable assets such as company shares[176] and intellectual property.[177] It includes contractual rights[178] such as leases[179] and judgment debts.[180] The concept of possession also covers certain rights and interests constituting assets[181] such as a cause of action unconditionally vested.[182] Harris contends that the essential characteristic tying all of these disparate interests together is the concept of the "acquired economic value of the individual interest".[183]

The ECHR also impliedly protects intellectual property which is supported by a host of secondary Council of Europe measures in the area including the European Convention relating to the Formalities Required for Patent Application (1953), the European Convention on the International Classification of Patents for Invention (1954), the Convention on the Unification of Certain Points of Substantive Law on Patents for Invention (1963) and the European Convention relating to Questions on Copyright Law and Neighbouring Rights in the Framework of Trans-frontier Broadcasting by Satellite (1994).

[9–59] Another important principle is that property rights can be lost in certain circumstances including (1) if it has long been impossible to exercise the right effectively, and (2) if the claim is made conditional upon the fulfilment of certain criteria such as "time limits, place of residence, nationality or proof of location of the property".[184] Cases in the former category have arisen as a result of the fall of the former Communist regimes in Eastern and Central Europe and in the reunification of Germany. A useful example is the case of *Von Maltzan v Germany*[185] where the law following the reunification of Germany expressly excluded the restitution of land expropriated between 1945 and 1949. The court restated the general principles relating to the definition of possession and then held that "the hope of recognition of a property right which it has been

[175] *Öneryildiz v Turkey* (Application No 48939/99) at 124. See also *Wiggins v UK* (Application No 7457/76) which referred to moveable and immoveable property.
[176] *Bramelid and Malmstrom v Sweden* (Application No 8588–89/79); *Sovtransavto Holding v Ukraine* (Application No 48553/99). D Harris *et al*, *supra* n 164 at pp 656.
[177] *Anheuser-Busch Inc v Portugal* (Application No 73049/01); *Smith-Kline and French Laboratories v Netherlands* (Application No 12633/ 87) (patent); *Lenzing AG v United Kingdom* (Application No 38817/97) (patent); *Anheuser-Busch Inc v Portugal* (Application No 73049/01) (trademark); *Aral, Tekin and Aral v Turkey* (Application No 24563/94) (copyright); *Melnychuk v Ukraine* (Application No 28743/03) (copyright). See also D Harris *et al*, *supra* n 164 at pp 656.
[178] *A, B and Company SA v FRG* (Application No 7742/76); *Association of General Practitioners v Denmark* (Application No 12947/87); *Gasus Dosier and Fordertechnik GmbH v Netherlands* (1995) 20 EHRR 403.
[179] D Harris *et al*, *supra* n 164 at pp 656 and see also *Mellacher v Austria* (1989) 12 EHRR 391; *JLS v Spain* (Application No 41917/98).
[180] *ibid*. See also *Stran Greek Refineries and Stratis Andreadis v Greece* (1994) 19 EHRR 293 and *Burdov v Russia* (2002) 38 EHRR 639.
[181] See *Iatridis v Greece* (Application No 31107/96) at 54 and *Beyeler v Italy* (Application No 33202/96) at 100.
[182] See *Kopecky v Slovakia* (Application No 44912/98).
[183] D Harris *et al*, *supra* n 164 at 657.
[184] *ibid* at 661.
[185] *Von Maltzan v Germany* [2005] 42 EHRR SE 11.

impossible to exercise effectively cannot be considered a "possession" within the meaning of P1-1, nor can a conditional claim which lapses as a result of the non-fulfillment of the condition".[186]

Legitimate Expectation

The concept of possession is not limited to "existing possessions" but is also capable of applying to claims, "in respect of which the applicant can argue that he has at least a reasonable and "legitimate expectation" of obtaining effective enjoyment of a property right".[187] In the case of *Kopecky v Slovenia,*[188] the applicant's father had been convicted of keeping, contrary to regulations then in force, gold and silver coins of numismatic value. Years later, the conviction was quashed and the applicant sought the restitution of his father's coins. The ECtHR had to consider whether the claim constituted an "asset" for the purposes of P1-1. The court had to consider in this context whether the applicant had a "legitimate expectation" of obtaining effective enjoyment of the coins.[189] The court highlighted the different forms of legitimate expectation that might exist and give rise to a claim under P1-1. **[9–60]**

The first notion of "legitimate expectation" was examined by the ECtHR in the case of *Pine Valley Developments Ltd and Others v Ireland.*[190] In this, and in subsequent cases, the ECtHR has held that the persons concerned:

> " ... were entitled to rely on the fact that the legal act on the basis of which they had incurred financial obligations would not be retrospectively invalidated to their detriment. In this class of case, the legitimate expectation is thus based on a reasonably justified reliance on a legal act which has a sound legal basis and which bears on property rights."[191]

Secondly, another form of legitimate expectation might be the expectation of a claim for damages arising under domestic law as in the case of *Pressos Compania Naviera SA and Others v Belgium.*[192] This form of "legitimate expectation" is not attached to a **[9–61]**

---

186 *ibid* at 74. See also *Prince Hans-Adam II of Liechtenstein v Germany* (Application No 42527/98) at 82-83 and *Gratzinger and Gratzingerova v the Czech Republic* (Application No 39794/98) at 69.

187 See, for example, *Prince Hans-Adam II of Liechtenstein v Germany* (Application No 42527/98) at 83; *Öneryildiz v Turkey* (Application No 48939/99) at 124.

188 *Kopecky v Slovenia (Application No 44912/98).*

189 *ibid* at 42.

190 *Pine Valley Developments Ltd and Others v Ireland* (judgment of 29 November 1991, Series A No 222) at 51. In that case, the court found that a "legitimate expectation" arose when outline planning permission had been granted, in reliance on which the applicant companies had purchased land with a view to its development. The planning permission, which could not be revoked by the planning authority, was "a component part of the applicant companies' property". See also the case of *Stretch v the United Kingdom*, (Application No 44277/98) at 35.

191 *ibid* at 47.

192 *Pressos Compania Naviera SA and Others v Belgium* (judgment of 20 November 1995, Series A No 332) at 31. The case concerned claims for damages arising out of accidents to shipping allegedly caused by the negligence of Belgian pilots. Under the domestic rules of tort, such claims came into existence as soon as the damage occurred. The court classified the claims as "assets" attracting the protection of P1-1.

property right, as it had been in the *Pine Valley Developments* case, but was implicit that no such expectation could come into play in the absence of an "asset" falling within P1-1. Therefore, in the *Pressos* case it was not:

> " . . . in itself constitutive of a proprietary interest; it related to the way in which the claim qualifying as an 'asset' would be treated under domestic law and in particular to reliance on the fact that the established case-law of the national courts would continue to be applied in respect of damage which had already occurred".[193]

[9–62] Thirdly, in order for "legitimate expectation" to be found, the applicants must have a "currently enforceable claim that was sufficiently established".[194] The ECtHR has held that there is a difference between a "mere hope of restitution" and "legitimate expectation" which "must be of a nature more concrete than a mere hope and be based on a legal provision or a legal act such as a judicial decision".[195] Similarly, where the applicant does not meet the national rules for claiming restitution then this will also preclude a determination that the applicant has a "legitimate expectation" under the ECHR.[196] The ECtHR in *Kopecky* appeared to distinguish these latter cases on the grounds that they were not really legitimate expectation claims at all, rather they were cases relating to whether the applicant had a claim amounting to an asset for the purposes of P1-1. In such cases, it would only amount to an asset where there was sufficient basis for it in national law.[197] Legitimate expectation would only arise where a proprietary interest of the applicant has suffered as a result of his reliance on a specific legal act.[198] In the case of *Kopecky,* the court held that it was neither a legitimate expectation nor a claim amounting to an asset as he had not satisfied the conditions required at national law.

Welfare Benefits

[9–63] The question of whether social welfare benefits fall within the concept of "possession" has been the subject matter of a number of cases before the court. There is a line of case law which holds that a welfare benefit derived under national law, even one which is non-contributory, may constitute a possession for the purposes of P1-1.[199] The applicant must first demonstrate that he has a legal right to a benefit under national law and that he fulfils all the criteria for receiving that benefit.

Positive and Negative Obligations

[9–64] The court has repeatedly held that P1-1 also establishes some positive obligations. The state not only has a negative obligation not to interfere with the right but it also has a positive obligation in certain cases to protect the right to property. A useful example is

[193] *ibid* at 48.
[194] *ibid* at 49.
[195] *ibid.* See also see also *Gratzinger and Gratzingerova v Czech Republic* (Application No 39794/98) at 73.
[196] *ibid* at 50.
[197] *ibid* at 52.
[198] *ibid* at 53.
[199] See *Gaygusuz v Austria* (Application No 17371/90) at 41; *Buchen v the Czech Republic*, (Application No 36541/97) at 46; or even more recently, *KouaPoirrez v France*, (Application No 40892/98) at 42.

the case of *Öneryildiz v Turkey*[200] which concerned a methane explosion in a rubbish tip which resulted in the deaths of 39 people and the destruction of 10 homes in the surrounding illegal settlement. The Government had been warned of the danger by an expert report which also made recommendations to deal with the issue but the Government failed to follow these recommendations or inform the inhabitants in the surrounding area of the danger. The ECtHR held that the State has both a negative duty not to interfere with property rights but also has a positive duty to protect property rights which had not been conducted in this case.[201] The ECtHR held that the genuine, effective exercise of the right protected by P1-1 did not depend merely on the State's duty not to interfere, but might require positive measures of protection, particularly where there was a direct link between the measures an applicant might legitimately expect from the authorities and his effective enjoyment of his possessions.

Such obligations might also arise in cases involving actions by private parties, where there are certain public interest considerations involved. In the case of *Broniowski v Poland*[202] the court held that positive obligations under P1-1 might require the State to take the measures necessary to protect property rights.

An important question for consideration is the manner in which these positive obligations are to be analysed. The court has admitted that the boundaries between the State's positive and negative obligations under P1-1 do not lend themselves to precise definition. However, it has clarified that the principles applied to both positive and negative obligations are similar. In both contexts, the ECtHR has held that regard must be had to the fair balance to be struck between the competing interests of the individual and of the community as a whole. In both contexts the State enjoys a certain margin of appreciation in determining the steps to be taken to ensure compliance with the Convention.[203] **[9–65]**

The nature and extent of the State's positive obligations will vary depending on the circumstances of each case.[204] The case of *Öneryıldız* resulted from obvious negligence on the part of the State and in that case the State was found to have breached its positive obligation to the applicant. The State is not obliged to act to prevent loss as a result of market forces,[205] economic reform,[206] or to protect against the effects of inflation.[207] Equally, where the case "concerns ordinary economic relations between private parties such positive obligations are much more limited".[208] That does not mean that the State does not have any obligation in cases involving litigation between **[9–66]**

200 *Öneryildiz v Turkey* (Application No 48939/99).

201 *ibid* at 134.

202 *Broniowski v Poland* (Application No 31443/96) at 143.

203 See *Hatton and Others v the United Kingdom* (Application No 36022/97) at 98 and the Grand Chamber judgment in *Broniowski v Poland* (Application No 31443/96) at 144.

204 *Kotov v Russia* (Application No 54522/00) at 111.

205 D Harris *et al*, *supra* n 164 at p 665.

206 *Gayduk v Ukraine* (Application No 45526/99).

207 *X v FRG* (Application No 8724/79).

208 *Kotov v Russia* (Application No 54522/00) at 111.

private entities.[209] On the contrary, States may be required to take measures to protect private property, even in situations involving private entities.[210] In the case of *Blumberga v Latvia*[211] the Court held:

> "When an interference with the right to peaceful enjoyment of possessions is perpetrated by a private individual, a positive obligation arises for the State to ensure in its domestic legal system that property rights are sufficiently protected by law and that adequate remedies are provided whereby the victim of an interference can seek to vindicate his rights, including, where appropriate, by claiming damages in respect of any loss sustained".

[9–67] The measures that a State may be required to take to ensure compliance with their positive obligations may be categorised as either preventative measures or remedial measures.[212] Examples of preventative obligations in the *Öneryıldız* case included the obligation to follow and implement the recommendations of the expert group or to warn the settlers about the dangers. Examples of remedial measures would include "an appropriate legal mechanism allowing the aggrieved party to assert its rights effectively",[213] compensation or expeditious processes. Although P1-1 contains no explicit procedural requirements, the existence of procedural positive obligations under this provision has been recognised by the Court in cases involving State authorities[214] and in cases between private parties only.[215] In the case of *Kotov v Russia*,[216] a case between private individuals, the court held that States were under an obligation to:

> " ... afford judicial procedures that offered the necessary procedural guarantees and therefore enabled the domestic courts and tribunals to adjudicate effectively and fairly any disputes between private persons".[217]

[9–68] *Kotov v Russia* involved insolvency proceedings between private entities. The applicant had suffered significant losses as a result of the liquidator's deliberate and unlawful actions. While the State was not directly responsible for the debts of private companies or the faults of their managers or liquidators, it was part of the States' duties under P1-1 to:

---

209 *Sovtransavto Holding v Ukraine* (Application No 48553/99) at 96 and *Kotov v Russia* (Application No 54522/00) at 112.

210 *Kotov v Russia* (Application No 54522/00) at 112. See also *Fuklev v Ukraine* (Application No 26772/95) at 89-91; *Kesyan v Russia* (Application No 36496/02) at 79–80; see also *Kin-Stib and Majkić v Serbia*, (Application No 12312/05) at 84; *Marcić and Others v Serbia*, (Application No 17556/05) at 56; *Matheus v France*, (Application No 62740/00) at 68 et seq.

211 *Blumberga v Latvia* (Application No 70930/01) at 67.

212 *Kotov v Russia* (Application No 54522/00) at 113.

213 *ibid* at 114.

214 See *Jokela v Finland*, (Application No 28856/95) at 45; *Zehentner v Austria*, (Application No 20082/02) at 73.

215 *Kotov v Russia* (Application No 54522/00) at 114.

216 *ibid.*

217 *ibid* at 114. See also *Sovtransavto Holdingv Ukraine* (Application No 48553/99) at 96; see also *Anheuser-Busch Inc v Portugal* (Application No 73049/01) at 83 and *Freitag v Germany*, (Application No 71440/01) at 54.

> " . . . at least set up a minimum legislative framework including a proper forum allowing persons who find themselves in a position such as the applicant to assert their rights effectively and have them enforced. Indeed, by failing to do so a State would seriously fall short of its obligation to protect the rule of law and prevent arbitrariness."[218]

In this case the court held that the State had complied with its positive obligations in this regard.

Interference with the Right

Article 1 provides for protection of the peaceful enjoyment of possessions. This has been defined by Harris as the right "to have, to use, to repair, to dispose of, to pledge, to lend, even to destroy one's own possessions".[219] Any interference with the exercise of this right could amount to an infringement of P1-1. There are numerous different ways in which an interference may occur. P1-1 expressly recognises certain interferences such as the deprivation of property or the control of the use of the property. However, the Article has not been confined to these types of interferences and various interferences, unrelated to deprivation or control of use, have been found to be an infringement of the Article.[220] For example, interferences have been found to occur in cases where there has been an imposition of financial liability[221] or where the State is responsible for a diminution of the economic value of a property.[222] The court will normally rule out that an interference relating to deprivation or control of use has occurred before it will consider an interference with peaceful enjoyment of property. The Court has reiterated that P1-1 comprises three distinct rules: **[9–69]**

> "The first rule, set out in the first sentence of the first paragraph, is of a general nature and enunciates the principle of peaceful enjoyment of property (P1-1-1). The second rule, contained in the second sentence of the same paragraph, covers deprivation of possessions and makes it subject to certain conditions (P1-1-2). The third rule, stated in the second paragraph, recognises that Contracting States are entitled, among other things, to control the use of property in accordance with the general interest (P1-2). The three rules are not "distinct" in the sense of being unconnected: the second and third rules are concerned with particular instances of interference with the right to peaceful enjoyment of property and should therefore be construed in the light of the general principle enunciated in the first rule. Both forms of interference defined must comply with the principle of lawfulness and pursue a legitimate aim by means reasonably proportionate to the aim sought to be realised".[223]

The determination as to whether the interference falls within one of these three rules will also determine the rules governing potential justification of the rule (see below). This section will examine some of the cases where interferences may be held to occur under the three headings: (1) interference by deprivation of possessions, (2) interference by control of use of possessions and (3) interference with peaceful enjoyment of possessions,

---

218 *ibid* at 117.

219 D Harris *et al*, *supra* n 164 at p 662.

220 *Sporrong and Lonnroth v Sweden* (Application No 7151/75; 7152/75).

221 *X v Netherlands* (Application No 2248/64).

222 *Krickl v Austria* (Application No 21752/93).

223 See *Jokela v Finland*, (Application No 28856/95) at 44 and 48.

Interference by Deprivation of Property (P1-1-2)

[9–70] A deprivation of property will occur where "all the legal rights of the owner are extinguished by operation of law or by the exercise of a legal power to the same effect".[224] Examples of deprivation of property include the physical taking or transfer of ownership of the property of the applicant. A useful example of this is the case of *James and Others v United Kingdom*[225] in which the applicants claimed and the ECtHR agreed that the compulsory transfer of their property under the Leasehold Reform Act 1967, as amended, which provided that leasehold tenants could compulsorily acquire the freehold interest in long lease properties gave rise to a deprivation of property within the meaning of P1-1 (but did not give rise to an infringement as it was considered that there were social benefits to the legislation).

[9–71] The determination that there has been a deprivation of property will not always be as clear as an expropriation of property. A deprivation might occur where the State interferes with the enjoyment of the property without divesting the owner of the title to the property. In such cases, the court has held that it is necessary not only to consider whether there has been a formal taking or expropriation of property but to look behind the appearances and investigate the realities of the situation complained of. Since the Convention is intended to guarantee rights that are "practical and effective", it has to be ascertained whether the situation amounted to a *de facto* expropriation.[226] A useful example of this is the case of *Elia Srl v Italy*[227] where the applicant company submitted that its land had been the subject of a *de facto* expropriation as a result of the combined effects of the prohibitions on building by the local town council, which had made the land worthless and impossible to dispose of.[228] The ECtHR noted that the measures imposed by the council did not entail a formal deprivation of possessions since the applicant company's right of property "remained intact from a legal standpoint".[229] In the absence of this transfer of property, the court must look behind the appearances and investigate the realities of the situation.[230] The court noted that all the effects complained of by the applicant company stemmed from its reduced ability to dispose of the property resulting from restrictions on the right of property and from the consequences of those restrictions on the value of the land. However, the court held that "although the right in question lost some of its substance, it did not disappear. The effects of the measures involved are not such that they can be regarded as a deprivation of possessions. The court observes in this connection that the applicant company was not denied access to its land and did not lose control of it and that, although it became more difficult to sell the land, that possibility in principle subsisted."[231] Therefore, there was no *de facto* deprivation within the meaning of P1-1. The court instead held that it was an interference with the enjoyment of property and

224 D Harris *et al*, *supra* n 164 at p 677.

225 (1986) 8 EHRR 123.

226 See the judgment of *Sporrong and Lönnroth v Sweden* (Application No 7151/75; 7152/75) at 63 and the *Vasilescu v Romania* judgment (Application No 27053/95) at 51.

227 *Elia Srl v Italy* (Application No 37710/97).

228 *ibid* at 53.

229 *ibid* at 54.

230 *ibid* at 55.

231 *ibid* at 56. See also see *Loizidou v Turkey* (Application No 15318/89) at 63, and *Sporrong and Lönnroth v Sweden* (Application No 7151/75; 7152/75) at 63.

fell to be dealt with under the first sentence of paragraph one of the Article. It is clear that proving a *de facto* interference will be difficult but access to and control of land would be important determining factors in this regard.

While a *de jure* deprivation of property is easily identifiable, cases of *de facto* deprivation are not so clear. This is evidenced by the case of *Brumarescu v Romania*[232] where the applicant's parents had built a house in the 1930s in Bucharest. The parents leased the ground floor to two brothers. In 1950, the State took possession of the house under a decree on nationalisation. However, they were allowed to live in one of the flats as tenants of the State. In 1973, the State sold the ground floor flat to the two brothers living there and this was inherited by the family of these two brothers. The Court of First Instance, whose decision was final and irrevocable, held that the decree of nationalisation of the parents' house had been a mistake and that the house should be returned to the applicant. The mayor of Budapest and the company managing State-owned housing were ordered to return the house to the applicant. This return was prevented after a case was taken to the Supreme Court by the family of the two brothers who had inherited the ground floor flat where the decision of the Court of First Instance was quashed. The ECtHR held that: **[9–72]**

> " ... the effect of the judgment of the Supreme Court of Justice was to deprive the applicant of all the fruits of the final judgment in his favour ... In consequence of the judgment of the Supreme Court of Justice, the applicant was accordingly deprived of the rights of ownership of the house which had been vested in him by virtue of the final judgment in his favour. In particular, he was no longer able to sell, devise, donate or otherwise dispose of the property. In these circumstances, the Court finds that the effect of the judgment of the Supreme Court of Justice was to deprive the applicant of his possessions within the meaning of the second sentence of the first paragraph of P1-1."

In this case, as the Supreme Court of Romania judgment effectively removed a right of ownership, the ECtHR essentially held that this was a *de facto* and a *de jure* expropriation by the State which fell to be considered as a deprivation of property.

Interference by Control of Use of Possessions (P1-2)

The control of the use of possessions can also amount to an interference according to paragraph 2 of P1-1. What will amount to a control of use will depend on the circumstances of each case to be determined by the ECtHR on a case by case basis. Some examples include cases which appear at first glance to be a loss of ownership but in fact are held to be cases involving a control of use. In *AGOSI,*[233] the forfeiture of the applicant father's gold coins was considered to be a control of use. Similarly in the case of *Air Canada,*[234] the forfeiture of aircraft which had been employed for the import of prohibited drugs was considered to be a control of use and not a deprivation. In the seminal case of *JA Pye (Oxford) Ltd and JA Pye (Oxford) Land Ltd v The United* **[9–73]**

---

[232] *Brumarescu v Romania* (Application No 28342/95).

[233] *AGOSI v United Kingdom* (Application No 9118/80) at 51.

[234] *Air Canada v the United Kingdom* (Application No 18465/91) at 34; see also *C.M. v France* (Application No 28078/95).

Kingdom[235] the common law rules of adverse possession which allowed land to be transferred to a squatter once a certain period of possession of the land adverse to the owner was established was not a deprivation of property but merely a control of use. The Court held that the applicant companies had not lost their land because of a legislative provision which permitted the State to transfer ownership in certain cases or because of a social policy of a transfer of ownership (which would constitute a deprivation of possessions) but rather "as the result of the operation of the generally applicable rules on limitation periods for actions for recovery of land".[236] The statutory provisions which resulted in the loss of beneficial ownership were not intended to deprive paper owners of their ownership, but rather to regulate questions of title in a system in which, historically, 12 years' adverse possession was sufficient to extinguish the former owner's right to re-enter or to recover possession, and the new title depended on the principle that unchallenged lengthy possession gave a title. The provisions of the 1925 and 1980 Acts which were applied to the applicant companies were part of the general land law, and were concerned to regulate, amongst other things, limitation periods in the context of the use and ownership of land as between individuals. The applicant companies were therefore affected, not by a "deprivation of possessions" within the meaning of the second sentence of the first paragraph of Art 1, but rather by a "control of use" of land within the meaning of the second paragraph of the provision".[237]

Interference with Peaceful Enjoyment of Possessions (P1-1-1)

[9–74] The seminal case in the area, and the origin of the principle that P1-1 does not just protect interferences amounting to deprivation and the control of use, is that of *Sporrong and Lonnroth v Sweden*[238]. In that case, property belonging to the applicants was tied up for over 20 years on an unexecuted expropriation permit which was issued by the city of Stockholm for the purposes of redevelopment. The owners during this time were prohibited from construction and development on the site. The applicants claimed that this was an interference with their property rights. The applicants claimed that although they were not formally deprived of their possessions:[239]

> "... the permits and prohibitions at issue subjected the enjoyment and power to dispose of their properties to limitations that were excessive and did not give rise to any compensation".[240]

The court accepted that in practice the expropriation permits "affected the very substance of ownership ... The applicants' right of property thus became precarious and defeasible"[241]. It amounted to an interference with their peaceful enjoyment of their possessions.

---

235 *JA Pye (Oxford) Ltd and JA Pye (Oxford) Land Ltd v The United Kingdom (Application No 44302/02)*.
236 *ibid* at 65.
237 *ibid.*
238 *Sporrong and Lonnroth v Sweden* (Application No 7151/75; 7152/75).
239 *ibid* at 58.
240 *ibid.*
241 *Sporrong and Lonnroth v Sweden* (Application No 7151/75; 7152/75) at 60.

Another type of interference that may amount to a peaceful enjoyment of possession is that related to access to possessions. An interesting case in this area is the case of *Loizidou v Turkey*[242]. In that case, the applicant, a Greek-Cypriot national, who owned property in the Turkish area of Cyprus claimed that she had been denied access to her property by the Turkish forces and because of this continuous denial of access had effectively lost all control over, "as well as all possibilities to use, to sell, to bequeath, to mortgage, to develop and to enjoy her land".[243] The court held that this continuous denial must be regarded as an interference with her rights. While it did not amount to a deprivation or a control of use of property, it did fall within the meaning of the first sentence of P1-1 in that it amounted to an interference with the peaceful enjoyment of possessions. The court held that "hindrance can amount to a violation of the Convention just like a legal impediment".[244] The decision would appear to be a sound one in that just because the property is in another State to which the applicant has no access, does not mean that they lose all right to their property.[245] **[9–75]**

Interferences with an individual's professional life may also constitute an interference with the peaceful enjoyment of possessions. In the case of *Malik v UK*[246] the court considered the suspension of a doctor from a list of doctors who could provide medical services to public patients The court, in examining other similar case law, held that in cases "involving professional practices, the court has taken the view that a restriction on applicants' right to practice the profession concerned, such as a refusal to register an applicant on a professional list, significantly affected the conditions of their professional activities and reduced the scope of those activities. Where, as a consequence of the restrictions, the applicant's income and the value of his clientele and, more generally, his business, fell, the court has held that there was interference with the right to peaceful enjoyment of possessions".[247] Similarly, the court has held, in cases concerning the granting of licenses or permits to carry out a business, that the revocation or withdrawal of such permits or licenses interferes with the right to the peaceful enjoyment of possessions.[248] However, in the case of *Malik*, the court did not consider that the applicant's rights had been interfered with as there were payments made to him during the period of suspension, there was no concrete evidence that his patient numbers actually fell, and that even if this had happened he failed to demonstrate that such reduction had any direct impact on him or on his financial situation.[249] **[9–76]**

[242] *Loizidou v Turkey* (Application No 15318/89).

[243] *ibid* at 58.

[244] *ibid* at 63.

[245] Similar cases include: *Cyprus v Turkey* (Application No 25781/94); *Eugena Mihaelidou Developments Ltd. and Michael Tymvios v Turkey* (Application No 16163/90.); *Demades v Turkey* (Application No 16219/90).

[246] *Malik v UK* (Application No 23780/08).

[247] *ibid* at 90. See also *Van Marle v Neherlands* (Application No 8543/79) at 42.

[248] *ibid* at 91. See also *Fredin v Sweden (No 1)*, (Application No 12033/86) (exploitation permit for a gravel pit); and *TreTraktörer AB v Sweden*, (1991) 13 EHRR 309 (concerning a licence to serve alcoholic beverages in a restaurant); *Rosenzweig and Bonded Warehouses Ltd v Poland*, (Application No 51728/99), (a licence to run a bonded warehouse); *Bimer SA v Moldova*, (Application No 15084/03); and *Megadat.com SRL v Moldova*, (Application No 21151/04).

[249] *ibid* at 106–109.

[9–77] Other cases of reliance on an interference with peaceful enjoyment of possessions occur where the situation is so complex, that definite interference in the form of a deprivation or control of use is not easily relied upon. A useful example of this is the case of *Beyeler v Italy*[250] where a right of pre-emption under contract was held null and void under a national law. The court did not consider it necessary to rule on whether this was a deprivation under Article 1. The court held that:

> " ... the complexity of the factual and legal position prevents its being classified in a precise category ... Moreover, the situation envisaged in the second sentence of the first paragraph of Article 1 is only a particular instance of interference with the right to peaceful enjoyment of property as guaranteed by the general rule set forth in the first sentence. The Court therefore considers that it should examine the situation complained of in the light of that general rule".[251]

This then freed the court from a determination as to whether the domestic authorities had been correct in their decision on the nature of the applicant's proprietary interest under national law.

2. Legitimate Justifications for Interference with the Right

[9–78] While there are three very distinct forms of interference and technically three distinct forms of justification, based on the wording of P1-1, the court has held that:

> " ... the three rules within that Article are not distinct or watertight in the sense of being unconnected and that the principles governing the question of justification are substantially the same, involving as they do the legitimacy of the aim of any interference, as well as its proportionality and the preservation of a fair balance".[252]

Also there is a fundamental requirement that the interference must in all cases be lawful. This section will, instead of addressing the types of interferences and their justifications in turn, will address the four conditions for justification identified by the court: lawfulness, a legitimate aim, proportionality and the fair balance test. Examples of interferences of each kind will be utilized in each section to demonstrate its application to each interference. This chapter will then turn to the issue of compensation and its impact on the decision of justification.

Lawfulness

[9–79] In order for an interference to be justified, it must first be lawful. If an interference is unlawful, it will automatically be incompatible with the Convention without need for further consideration. This is inherent in P1-1 which makes express reference for the need for interferences to be "subject to the conditions provided for by law" and for control of property to be conducted through the enforcement of "laws". More specifically, the court has held that the rule of law, one of the fundamental principles of

---

250 *Beyeler v Italy* (Application No 33202/96).
251 *ibid* at 106.
252 *JA Pye (Oxford) Ltd and JA Pye (Oxford) Land Ltd v The United Kingdom* (Application No 44302/02) at 62.

a democratic society, is inherent in all the Articles of the Convention.[253] Harris has commented that the requirement for lawfulness means that "the state must have a basis in national law for its interference and that the law concerned must be accessible, precise and foreseeable".[254] In relation to this latter aspect of accessibility, where the applicant is a private citizen, the awareness of the law and the ability to seek that information will be relevant to the court's assessment. However, where the applicant is, for example, a company, the court will place a higher level of knowledge on this entity as it had the means to seek expert advice on the matter.

In the case of *Fredin v Sweden (No 1)*[255] the court had to examine a control of the use of possessions of the applicants arising from the revocation by the State of a permit to exploit gravel on their property. An important aspect of the case was whether the interference was lawful. The applicants contended that the legal provisions underlying the impugned measure were not sufficiently foreseeable as to their effects or certain for the purposes of the Convention. The court reiterated that its power to review compliance with domestic law was limited[256] but held that the evidence available did not show that the revocation decision was contrary to Swedish law. With respect to foreseeability, the court found that the relevant provisions of the statute indicated the scope and manner of exercise of the discretion conferred on the authorities with sufficient precision, having regard to the subject matter, to meet the requirements of the Convention.[257] The provision of the statute responsible for the interference was therefore lawful. **[9–80]**

The court has limited power to review the compliance of a particular interference with domestic law,[258] especially if there is nothing from which it can conclude that the authorities applied the legal provisions in question manifestly erroneously or so as to reach arbitrary conclusions.[259] However, in order to be considered lawful the law upon which the interference is based should be in accordance with the domestic law of the contracting State, including the relevant provisions of its Constitution.[260] The case of *Mago and Others* (involving a deprivation of possessions) highlights the importance of compatibility of the interference with domestic law and the compatibility of the interfering provision with constitutional principles in that State. In *Mago and Others v* **[9–81]**

[253] *Iatridis v Greece* (Application No 31107/96) at 58; *Amuur v France* (Application No 19776/92) at 50.

[254] D Harris *et al*, *supra* n 164 at p 670 referring to cases *Spacek SRO v Czech Republic* (Application No 26449/95), *Cabonara and Venura v Italy* (Application No 24638/94); *Beyeler v Italy* (Application No 33202/96). See also *Beyeler v Italy* (Application No 33202/96) at 109; *Hentrich v France* (Application No 13616/88) at 42; and *Lithgow and Others v United Kingdom* (Application No 9006/80) at 110.

[255] *Fredin v Sweden (No 1)* (Application No 12033/86).

[256] *ibid* at 50; see also *Håkansson and Sturesson v Sweden* (Application No 11855/85) at 47.

[257] *ibid*. See also *Lithgow and Others v United Kingdom* (Application No 9006/80) at 110, and *Eriksson v Sweden* (Application No 11373/85) at 59.

[258] *Beyeler v Italy* (Application No 33202/96) at 108; *Håkansson and Sturesson v Sweden* (Application No 11855/85) at 47.

[259] *ibid*. See also *Tre Traktorer Aktiebolag v Sweden* (1989) 33 EHRR 309.

[260] *King of Greece and Others*, (Application No 25701/94) at 78 and 82.

Bosnia and Herzegovina[261]the law which cancelled the occupancy rights of the applicants was a statute (the Restitution of Flats Act 1998), the relevant provision of which (s 3(a)) the Constitutional Court had considered in accordance with the constitution. Therefore, the Court held that it was clearly provided for by law within the meaning of P1-1.

[9–82] An interesting issue is that related to an interference caused by deprivation of possessions. In the second sentence of P1-1, it states that no one shall be deprived of his possession except in the public interest and subject to the conditions provided for by law and by the general principles of international law. International law has specific rules in relation to expropriation of the property of non-nationals and the impact of compensation on the determination. However, of more immediate concern is the import that should be afforded to this term in the context of an interference caused by a deprivation of possessions. Harris has noted that there are two possible interpretations to be placed on this term.[262] First, the reference should only be interpreted as benefiting non-national property holders. Secondly, the reference should be interpreted as applying to both nationals and non-nationals. The Court in the case of *James v United Kingdom*[263] seemed to prefer the first interpretation and held that the inclusion of the reference can be seen to serve at least two purposes.

> "Firstly, it enables non-nationals to resort directly to the machinery of the Convention to enforce their rights on the basis of the relevant principles of international law, whereas otherwise they would have to seek recourse to diplomatic channels or to other available means of dispute settlement to do so. Secondly, the reference ensures that the position of non-nationals is safeguarded, in that it excludes any possible argument that the entry into force of Protocol No 1 (P1) has led to a diminution of their rights. In this connection, it is also noteworthy that Article 1 (P1-1) expressly provides that deprivation of property must be effected 'in the public interest': since such a requirement has always been included amongst the general principles of international law, this express provision would itself have been superfluous if Article 1 (P1-1) had had the effect of rendering those principles applicable to nationals as well as to non-nationals."[264]

Legitimate Aim

[9–83] Regardless of whether the interference is held to be a deprivation, a control of use or an interference with peaceful enjoyment of possessions, where the interference does not pursue a legitimate aim, it will be held to be incompatible with the Convention. The requirement is implicit in the "public interest" and "general interest" statements in relation to deprivations and control of use in P1-1 and has been read into the justification process for interferences with peaceful enjoyment of possessions.[265]

It is for the State to prove that the interference constituted a legitimate aim in the circumstances of the case. The court has held that measures taken in pursuance of EU

---

[261] *Mago and Others v Bosnia and Herzegovina* (Applications Nos 12959/05, 19724/05, 47860/06, 8367/08, 9872/09 and 11706/09).

[262] D Harris *et al*, *supra* n 164 at 679.

[263] *James v United Kingdom* (Application No 8793/79).

[264] *ibid* at 62.

[265] *Beyeler v Italy* (Application No 33202/96).

law[266] and measures for the implementation of economic and social policy[267] are all capable of constituting legitimate aims. Harris has commented that the standard of proof is relatively low and "it is difficult to imagine circumstances in which the Court would dispute the purpose alleged by the Government".[268]

Some examples of the application of this test will now be examined. The case of *Mago and Others v Bosnia and Herzegovina*[269] is illustrative of the approach of the court in cases of deprivation of property. In this case, the applicants, had their occupancy rights of their pre-war flats in Sarejevo and Mostar cancelled which prevented them returning to their flats. The court accepted that a public interest aim such as a "policy calculated to enhance social justice within the community" would be a legitimate aim within the meaning of P1-1. The court also clarified that an aim may be in the public interest "even if the community at large has no direct use or enjoyment of the property taken".[270] **[9–84]**

In the area of control of use, the State has a wider discretion in relation to the aims that it seeks to pursue in the general interest.[271] Harris comments that States can effect control by "requiring positive action by individuals as well as by imposing restrictions on their activities".[272] Cases have included controls relating to planning, environmental, social, health and safety and customs restrictions as well as limitation periods for litigation, inheritance laws, rent controls and the regulation of professions or businesses. Restrictions on the use of intellectual property would also be included in these restrictions. One of the most seminal cases in the area of control of use of the case of *JA Pye (Oxford) Ltd and JA Pye (Oxford) Land Ltd v The United Kingdom*. This case arose out of a dispute over the ownership of 23 hectares of agricultural land in Berkshire. The disputing parties were two companies JA Pye (Oxford) Ltd. and JA Pye (Oxford) Land Ltd., the owners of the land and their neighbours, Mr. And Mrs. Graham, who had been in possession of the property for over 12 years. The Grahams had occupied the land under a grazing agreement until 31 December 1983, after which their permission to continue farming on the land had been withdrawn. The Grahams continued in occupation and in 1997 sought to register a caution in the Land Registry against the owner's title on the grounds that they had obtained title to the property by virtue of the doctrine of adverse possession. The applicant companies sought the possession of the land. The Grand Chamber held that the doctrine of adverse possession was a control of use of the land (see above) and had a legitimate aim. The **[9–85]**

[266] *Dangeville v France* (Application No 36677/97) and *Bosphorus Airway v Ireland* (Application No 45036/98). See also D Harris *et al*, *supra* n 164 at p 668.

[267] The burden in such cases will shift to the applicant to show that the State's reliance on this legitimate economic or social aim is "manifestly without reasonable foundation" See D Harris *et al*, *supra* n 164 at p 668 and cases *Broniowski v Poland* (Application No 31443/96); *James v United Kingdom* (Application No 8793/79); *Jahn v Germany* (Application No 46720/99) and *JA Pye (Oxford) Ltd and JA Pye (Oxford) Land Ltd v The United Kingdom* (Application No 44302/02).

[268] D Harris *et al*, *supra* n 164 at p 668.

[269] *Mago and Others v Bosnia and Herzegovina* (Applications Nos 12959/05, 19724/05, 47860/06, 8367/08, 9872/09 and 11706/09).

[270] *ibid* at 99. (See *James and Others v the United Kingdom* (Application No 8793/79 at 45–48).

[271] D Harris *et al*, *supra* n 164 at p 686.

[272] *ibid* at 687.

court considered that statutory limitation periods are compatible with the Convention having several important purposes "namely to ensure legal certainty and finality, protect potential defendants from stale claims which might be difficult to counter and prevent the injustice which might arise if courts were required to decide upon events which took place in the distant past on the basis of evidence which might have become unreliable and incomplete because of the passage of time".[273] Therefore, the Grand Chamber held that the existence of a 12-year limitation period for actions for recovery of land was a legitimate aim in the general interest.[274] The Grand Chamber then went on to consider the extinguishment of title after the 12-year limitation period. It held that States are entitled to a wide margin of appreciation in implementing social and economic policy and the Court would respect the legislature's judgment as to what was in the public interest as long as such a policy was not manifestly without reasonable foundation.[275] The Grand Chamber determined that "it must be open to the legislature to attach more weight to lengthy, unchallenged possession than to the formal fact of registration",[276] even in the case of registered land. Such a policy was not manifestly without reasonable foundation.

[9–86] Another interesting issue in relation to interferences caused by a control of use is the fact that Art 1 para 2 allows:

> " ... a practically unlimited power to a state 'to enforce such laws as it deems necessary ... to secure the payment of taxes or other contributions or penalties' ".[277]

In determining the "fair balance" test in this context the court will examine whether significant procedural guarantees are in place to establish the liability of the applicant. If this is the case then generally, the court will not interfere in the level, means of assessment or enforcement of the tax. A useful example is the case of *The National and Provincial Building Society, The Leeds Permanent Building Society and the Yorkshire Building Society v The United Kingdom*[278] where the ECtHR held that in determining the fair balance in a case involving taxation measures:

> " ... it is recognised that a contracting State, not least when framing and implementing policies in the area of taxation, enjoys a wide margin of appreciation and the Court will respect the legislature's assessment in such matters unless it is devoid of reasonable foundation".[279]

In this case, the court did not consider that the aim of the measure was "without reasonable foundation having regard to the public-interest considerations which underpinned the proposal" which included an:

---

[273] *JA Pye (Oxford) Ltd and JA Pye (Oxford) Land Ltd v The United Kingdom* (Application No 44302/02) at 68.
[274] *ibid* at 70.
[275] *ibid* at 68. See also *Zvolský and Zvolská v the Czech Republic*, (Application No 46129/99) at 67.
[276] *ibid* at 74.
[277] D Harris *et al*, *supra* n 164 at p 692.
[278] *The National and Provincial Building Society, The Leeds Permanent Building Society and the Yorkshire Building Society v The United Kingdom* (Application No 21319/93).
[279] *ibid* at 80.

> "... obvious and compelling public interest to ensure that private entities do not enjoy the benefit of a windfall in a changeover to a new tax-payment regime and do not deny the Exchequer revenue simply on account of inadvertent defects in the enabling tax legislation".[280]

The court considered that the actions taken by the respondent State did not upset the balance which must be struck between the protection of the applicant societies' rights to restitution and the public interest in securing the payment of taxes.

A useful example of a case involving an interference with peaceful enjoyment of possessions is the case of *Sporrong and Lonnroth v Sweden*[281] in which the property of the applicants was tied up for a number of years by long-term unexpected expropriation permits during which time the applicants were limited in their use and enjoyment of the properties. In that case, the court accepted that "town-planning policy" could be a legitimate aim within the meaning of P1-1.[282] [9–87]

Fair Balance Test / Proportionality

This test requires the court to assess whether "a fair balance was struck between the demands of the general interest of the community and the requirements of the protection of the individual's fundamental rights".[283] The ECtHR appears to give a very wide discretion to States in determining what amounts to a general interest of the community and does not subject that determination to serious scrutiny.[284] [9–88]

One of the seminal cases in this area is that of *Sporrong and Lonnroth v Sweden*[285] in which the expropriation permits held on the applicants' property were never enforced for a number of years during which time the applicants could not deal with their property. The court had to consider whether a fair balance was struck between the demands of the general interest of the community and the requirements of the protection of the individual's fundamental rights.[286] The court reiterated that the search for this balance is inherent in the whole of the Convention and is also reflected in the structure of P1-1. The State had argued that the legitimate aim sought to be achieved was that of "town-planning" and the court recognised that in an:

> "... area as complex and difficult as that of the development of large cities, the contracting States should enjoy a wide margin of appreciation in order to implement their town-planning policy."[287]

However, there were a number of the features of the law that suggested that a fair balance between this aim and that of the rights of the applicant had not been met. One such feature was the inflexibility of the law[288] which did not provide for a modification [9–89]

---

280 *ibid.*
281 *Sporrong and Lonnroth v Sweden* (Application No 7151/75).
282 *ibid* at 69.
283 *ibid.*
284 D Harris *et al*, *supra* n 164 at p 667.
285 *Sporrong and Lonnroth v Sweden* (Application No 7151/75).
286 *ibid* at 69.
287 *ibid.*
288 *ibid* at 70.

provision leaving the applicants in "complete uncertainty as to the fate of their properties".[289] This could have been achieved by the inclusion of a provision for:

> " ... re-assessing, at reasonable intervals during the lengthy periods for which each of the permits was granted and maintained in force, the interests of the City and the interests of the owners".[290]

This clearly indicates that a lack of flexibility and opportunity for review of a law will be a relevant consideration in determining whether a fair balance has been struck. Similarly, the additional problem of the prohibitions on construction "accentuated even further the prejudicial effects of the length of the validity of the permits".[291] The combination of the measures:

> " ... created a situation which upset the fair balance which should be struck between the protection of the right of property and the requirements of the general interest: the Sporrong Estate and Mrs. Lönnroth bore an individual and excessive burden which could have been tendered legitimate only if they had had the possibility of seeking a reduction of the time-limits or of claiming compensation".[292]

Therefore the court found a violation of P1-1 in this case.

[9–90] This test has also been employed in the context of cases dealing with deprivations and cases dealing with control of use. In those cases, the court often refers to the fair balance test and then goes on to see if there is a legitimate aim and whether this aim is proportionate to the aim sought to be achieved. The proportionality element of the case law is essentially the same as the fair balance test and has been applied in many cases.

[9–91] For example, in the case of *Former King of Greece and others v Greece,*[293] the court had to consider the proportionality of a measure which deprived the applicants of certain estates of land in Greece. The legitimate aim put forward by Greece was the protection of the forests and archeological sites in Greece and the preservation of the constitutional status of the republic. The court in determining the proportionality of the measure made reference to the need to strike a:

> " ... fair balance between the demands of the general interest of the community and the requirements of the protection of the individual's fundamental rights".[294]

In determining this balance the court had to decide whether there was a reasonable relationship of proportionality between the means employed and the aim sought to be realised by any measure depriving a person of his possessions.[295] Of particular concern in this case was the lack of compensation. The court has held that the:

---

[289] *ibid.*
[290] *ibid.*
[291] *ibid* at 72.
[292] *ibid* at 73.
[293] *Former King of Greece v Greece* (Application No 25701/94)
[294] *ibid* at 89.
[295] *ibid.* See also *Pressos Compania Naviera SA and Others v Belgium* (Application No 17849/91) at 38).

> " ... taking of property without payment of an amount reasonably related to its value will normally constitute a disproportionate interference and a total lack of compensation can be considered justifiable under Article 1 of Protocol No. 1 only in exceptional circumstances".[296]

This reference to compensation was also relevant in the *Sporrong and Lonnroth v Sweden* decision. In that case the lack of compensation did not make the taking of the applicants' property wrongful.[297] However, there was no convincing explanation as to why the Greek authorities failed to award compensation to the applicants. This lack of any compensation: [9–92]

> " ... for the deprivation of the applicants' property upsets, to the detriment of the applicants, the fair balance between the protection of property and the requirements of public interest".[298]

Therefore the court held that a violation of P1-1 had occurred.

Similarly in cases relating to the control of use, the fair balance proportionality test is central to the determination as to whether an interference is compatible with the Convention. Once again in the seminal case of *Pye*, the Grand Chamber also had to determine whether a fair balance had been struck between the demands of the general interest and the interest of the individuals concerned. There were four significant issues for consideration by the Grand Chamber; the length of the limitation period, the absence of compensation, the absence of procedural protection and finally, the windfall that would be visited upon the new owner. First, the court held that the limitation period and the rule which extinguished the title did little more than regularise the positions of the parties to the dispute, namely to confirm that the person who has acquired title by 12 years' adverse possession is the owner. Indeed, this reflected the aim of the land registration legislation. The Grand Chamber was of the opinion that very little action on the part of the applicant companies could have stopped the time from running and would have meant that the possession by the squatters would no longer have been adverse. Secondly, in relation to the issue of compensation, the Grand Chamber was of the opinion that: [9–93]

> "... a requirement for compensation would sit uneasily alongside the very concept of limitation periods, whose aim is to further legal certainty by preventing a party from pursuing an action after a certain date".[299]

It noted further that the Land Registration Act 2002 in the United Kingdom did not provide for compensation to be payable by the new owner of registered land on expiry of the limitation period. Thirdly, the Grand Chamber considered that the applicant companies were not totally without procedural protection. It was at all times open to them to remedy the position by bringing a court action for re-possession of land. Such an action would have stopped time running. Even after the expiry of the limitation period, it was open to them to argue that the occupiers had not been in adverse possession as defined by domestic law. Finally, the Grand Chamber felt that the [9–94]

---

296 *ibid* at 90. See also *Holy Monasteries v Greece* (Application No 13092/87) at 71)

297 *ibid*. See also *Papamichalopoulos and Others v Greece* (Application No 14556/89) at 36.

298 *ibid* at 93.

299 *Pye* at 79.

possibility of the adverse possessor being able to receive a windfall profit did not affect the overall assessment of the proportionality of the legislation. If limitation periods are to fulfil their purpose, they must apply regardless of the size of the claim. The value of the land could not therefore be of any consequence to the outcome of the case.

The Impact of Compensation

[9–95] It can be seen, particularly in the assessment of fair balance or proportionality, that the issue of compensation is often determinative or, at least very relevant, to the determination as to whether the interfering measure strikes a fair or proportionate balance between the public interest and the rights of the applicant. Two major issues have arisen in the courts case law: (a) the impact of a lack of compensation and (b) the impact of less than full compensation.

Lack of Compensation

[9–96] There appears to be two general rules relating to a lack of compensation in the case law. Where there is a deprivation of possessions, failure to provide compensation will normally result in a decision that there has been an infringement of the property right and a total lack of compensation could only be justified in very exceptional circumstances.[300] However, in cases of control of use or interferences with peaceful enjoyment of possessions, the lack of compensation is a factor to be taken into consideration in determining whether a fair balance has been achieved but is not of itself sufficient to constitute a violation of P1-1[301].

[9–97] An example of a case involving a total deprivation of possessions and a lack of compensation is the case of *Jahn and Others v Germany*[302] which involved the obligation on the owners of the property to reassign their property to the tax authorities without compensation as a result of German reunification. The court noted that this case involved a deprivation of possessions and that there was no compensation. The general rule was that this would constitute an infringement of P1-1 unless there were exceptional circumstances in this case justifying the lack of compensation. The court reiterated that the State had a wide margin of appreciation when passing laws in the context of a change of political and economic regime.[303] The court considered that there were a number of decisive factors in the case but most particularly the social justice element to the legislation concerned and that in the circumstances the court concluded that in the unique context of German reunification, the lack of any compensation did not upset the "fair balance" that had to be struck between the protection of property and the requirements of the general interest.[304] Therefore there was no violation of P1-1.

---

[300] *Jahn v Germany* (Application No 46720/99) at 94; *Holy Monasteries v Greece* (Application No 13092/87) at 71; *Zvolský and Zvolská v The Czech Republic*, (Application No 46129/99) at 70).

[301] *Anonymos Touristiki Etairia Xenodocheia Kritis v Greece,* (Application No 35332/05) at 45; *Brosset-Triboulet and Others v France* (Application No 34078/02) at 94.

[302] *Jahn and Others v Germany* (Applications Nos 46720/99, 72203/01 and 72552/01).

[303] *ibid* at 113, *Kopecký v Slovakia* (Application No 44912/98) at 35; *Zvolský and Zvolská v The Czech Republic*, (Application No 46129/99) at 67-68 and 72; *Von Maltzan and Others v Germany* (Application Nos 71916/01, 71917/01 and 10260/02) at 77 and 111-12.

[304] *ibid* at 117.

A case involving a control of use (the principles of which would also apply in the context of interferences with the peaceful enjoyment of possessions) is the case of *Pye v United Kingdom*, involving a challenge to the concept of adverse possession which the Grand Chamber had classified as a control of use of possessions. One particular area of challenge was the fact that there was no compensation payable and the applicants argued that this amounted to an infringement of P1-1. The court considered the concept of compensation in a case concerning a control of use and concluded that in the cases in which a situation was analysed as a control of use, even though the applicant had lost possessions[305] no mention was made of a right to compensation. This was only something to be considered as to whether a fair balance had been struck. The Court then noted that a requirement of compensation for the situation brought about by a party failing to observe a limitation period would sit uneasily alongside the very concept of limitation periods, whose aim is to further legal certainty by preventing a party from pursuing an action after a certain date.[306] Therefore a fair balance had been struck and there was no violation of P1-1 in the circumstances. **[9–98]**

Less than Full Compensation

While a total lack of compensation will engender the specific rules outlined above, the rules relating to less than full compensation are somewhat different. In these circumstances, there is no real distinction between cases involving deprivations, control of use or an interference with peaceful enjoyment of possessions, other than the fact that cases involving deprivations are always give more scrutiny. However, there are some general rules in this regard. **[9–99]**

Normally, compensation should be reasonably related to the value of the property concerned. However, in some exceptional cases, legitimate objectives of "public interest" may call for reimbursement of less than the full market value.[307] In the case of *James and Others,*[308] the issue was whether, in the context of leasehold-reform legislation, the conditions empowering long-term leasehold tenants to acquire their property struck a fair balance. The court held that as this occurred in the context of social and economic reform in which the burden borne by the freeholders was not unreasonable, the compensation was adequate even though the amounts received by the interested parties were less than the full market value of the property. In *Lithgow and Others,*[309] the court examined an issue relating to the nationalisation of companies engaged in the aircraft and shipbuilding industries, as part of the economic, social and political programme, which was intended to provide a sounder organisational and economic footing and bring to the authorities a greater degree of public control and accountability. The Court held that, in this context, the arrangements for compensating the shareholders concerned were fair and not unreasonable as compared with the **[9–100]**

---

[305] *AGOSI v United Kingdom* (Application No 9118/80) at 51 and *Air Canada v the United Kingdom* (Application No 18465/91) at 34.

[306] *Jahn and Others v Germany* (Applications Nos 46720/99, 72203/01 and 72552/01) at 117.

[307] *Holy Monasteries v Greece* (Application No 13092/87) at 71; *Lithgow and Others v United Kingdom* (Application No 9006/80) at 121; *James v United Kingdom* (Application No 8793/79) at 54.

[308] (1986) 8 EHRR 123.

[309] *Lithgow and Others v United Kingdom* (Application No 9006/80).

full value of the shares. The Court has also held that less than full compensation may also be necessary where property is taken for the purposes of "such fundamental changes of a country's constitutional system as the transition from monarchy to republic".[310] The State also has a wide margin of appreciation when enacting laws in the context of a change of political and economic regime.[311] The Court has reaffirmed this principle in *Broniowski*[312] (in the context of the country's transition towards a democratic regime). The Court has also reiterated these principles in "the exceptional context of German reunification".[313]

[9–101] In the case of *Scordino v Italy (No 1)*[314] the Court observed that the compensation awarded to the applicants was calculated on the basis of the criteria laid down in law. It noted that these criteria provided for compensation that was far lower than the market value of the property in question and was also subject to taxation.[315] As the case was one of direct expropriation, and was not carried out as part of a process of economic, social or political reform nor linked to any other specific circumstances, the Court could not discern any legitimate objective "in the public interest" capable of justifying less than reimbursement of the market value.[316] Consequently, the court held that there had been a violation of P1-1.

C. CFR

[9–102] Article 17 CFR states:

> "1. Everyone has the right to own, use, dispose of and bequeath his or her lawfully acquired possessions. No one may be deprived of his or her possessions, except in the public interest and in the cases and under the conditions provided for by law, subject to fair compensation being paid in good time for their loss. The use of property may be regulated by law in so far as is necessary for the general interest.
>
> 2. Intellectual property shall be protected"

The right to property under the CFR is protected under Art 17. The wording of Art 17 bears close resemblance to P1-1 of the ECHR in that it prohibits interferences in the form of an interference with the peaceful enjoyment of possessions, deprivation or control of use. The right is not absolute and the conditions for justifying an interference are similar to those under the ECHR including a requirement of lawfulness, a requirement of legitimate aim and proportionality.

[9–103] Unusually, there is a distinct reference to compensation which is not available under the ECHR or the Irish Constitution. This would imply that a complete absence of compensation in the CFR context would amount to an infringement with Art 17.

---

310 *Former King of Greece v Greece* (Application No 25701/94) at 87.
311 *Kopecký v Slovakia* (Application No 44912/98) at 35.
312 *Broniowski v Poland* (Application No 31443/96) at 185.
313 *Von Maltzan and Others v Germany* (Application Nos 71916/01, 71917/01 and 10260/02) at 77 and 111–12; *Jahn v Germany* (Application No 46720/99).
314 *Scordino v Italy (No 1) (*Application No 36813/97).
315 *ibid* at 100–101.
316 *ibid* at 102.

However, there is no requirement that the compensation be equivalent to full market value. The only requirement is that this compensation is fair and paid in good time.

This section will examine the cases where the right to property has been considered in the European Union context and will elucidate the principles governing this area of EU law. Of further significant note is the express reference to intellectual property rights which while not expressly recognised in the ECHR or the Irish Constitutional context have been impliedly held to be covered by the property guarantees. The express reference in the context of the CFR highlights the significant importance of these rights in the EU context.

1. Nature of the Right

The right to property (even prior to the CFR and Art 17) forms part of the general principles of community law.[317] As is the case in the context of the ECHR, the right under EU law is not absolute and any restriction or interference must be viewed in light of its social function: **[9–104]**

> " ... provided that any restrictions in fact correspond to objectives of general interest pursued by the Community and do not constitute in relation to the aim pursued a disproportionate and intolerable interference, impairing the very substance of the rights guaranteed"[318]

This is essentially a fair balance test that is commonly applied in the ECHR context.

In determining the nature, extent and scope of the right to property, the Court of Justice of the European Union (CJEU) has drawn inspiration from the constitutional traditions common to the Member States and from the guidelines supplied by international treaties for the protection of human rights on which the Member States have collaborated or to which they are signatories.[319] The ECHR has special significance in that respect.[320] For example, in determining whether there has been an interference with the right to property, the CJEU essentially follows the same line of **[9–105]**

---

[317] The first case where this was impliedly recognised was the case of C 4-73 *Nold, Kohlen- und Baustoffgroßhandlung v Commission of the European Communities* (1974) ECR 491. It was first expressly recognised in the case of Case 44/79, *Liselotte Hauer v Land Rheinland Pfalz* [1979] ECR 3727 at 17. See also Joined Cases C-453/03, C-11/04, C-12/04 and C-194/04 *ABNA and Others* [2005] ECR I-10423 at 87; Case T-113/96 *Dubois et Fils v Council and Commission* [1998] ECR II-125, at 73).

[318] Joined Cases C-453/03, C-11/04, C-12/04 and C-194/04 *ABNA and Others* [2005] ECR I-10423 at 87; C–155/04 *Alliance for Natural Health and Others* [2005] ECR I-6451 at 126; Case 5/88 *Wadxmfv Bundesamt ßir Ernährung und Forstwirtschaft* [1989] ECR 2609 at 18; Case C–22/94 *Irish Farmers Association and Others v Minister for Agriculture, Food and Forestry, Ireland and the Attorney General* at 27; Case C–280/93 *Germany* v *Council* [1994] ECR I-4973 at 78; Case C–368/96 *The Queen v The Licensing Authority established by the Medicines Act 1968 (acting by The Medicines Control Agency), ex parte Generics (UK) Ltd, The Wellcome Foundation Ltd and Glaxo Operations UK Ltd and Others* [1998] ECR I-07967 at 79; Case C–200/96 *Metronome Musik* [1998] ECR I-1953 at 21 and Case 265/87 *Schräder v Hauptzollamt Gronau* [1989] ECR 2237 at 15.

[319] Case 44/79, *Liselotte Hauer v Land Rheinland Pfalz* [1979] ECR 3727 at 15.

[320] Case C–274/99 P *Connolly v Commission* [2001] ECR I-1611 at 37, and Case C–94/00 *Roquette Frères* [2002] ECR I-9011 at 25.

reasoning as the ECtHR. In this regard a useful example is the case of *Friuli-Venezia*[321] in which the CJEU held that in order to determine the scope of the fundamental right to property, a general principle of Community law, account must be taken of P1-1. The CJEU went on to examine whether the interference was a deprivation, a control of use or an interference with the peaceful enjoyment of possessions (and decided that in this case it amounted to a control of use) despite the fact that this form of wording does not appear in the EU context. This utilisation of the same procedures as is used in the context of the ECHR is not surprising considering the strong link between the CFR and the ECHR and the similarity in the wording of the two documents. Therefore the principles governing the ECHR will also apply in this context.

What is Property?

[9–106] What constitutes "property" for the purposes of EU law has rarely been considered by the CJEU but a wide variety of things have been held to fall within the definition of property. It certainly includes all immovable and moveable[322] assets, as well as intellectual property rights. It would include things such as "planning permission, unenforced expropriation orders and prohibition on construction, the economic interests arising from a licence to sell alcohol, a permit for gravel extraction, hunting rights over land, shares, patents, an enforceable debt, and legal claims for compensation and restitution of assets".[323] Article 17 would have a very similar interpretation to the definition of property that currently exists under the ECHR jurisprudence. One of the few judgments to consider this issue was that of The Queen, on the application of: *Swedish Match AB, Swedish Match UK Ltd v Secretary of State for Health,*[324] concerning the prohibition on the marketing of tobacco products for oral use.[325] In that case the economic operators involved attempted to argue that their right to property had been infringed by the Directive. In this case the court held that the operators' right to property was not engaged as:

> " . . . no economic operator can claim a right to property in a market share . . . since such a market share constitutes only a momentary economic position exposed to the risks of changing circumstances".[326]

The court went on to say that an economic operator could also not claim an acquired right or a legitimate expectation:

---

[321] Case C-347/03 *Regione Friuli-Venezia Giulia* [2005] ECR I-3785 21.

[322] Case T-195/00 *Travelex Global and Financial Services and Interpayment Services v Commission* [2003] ECR II-1677 at 140.

[323] Fundamental Rights Agency, *Commentary on the Charter of Fundamental Rights: Article 17 Right to Property* (Vienna: Fundamental Rights Agency) at 165.

[324] Case C–210/03 *Swedish Match AB, Swedish Match UK Ltd v Secretary of State for Health* [2004] ECR I-11893.

[325] Art 8, Directive 2001/37 of the European Parliament and of the Council of 5 June 2001 on the approximation of the laws, regulations and administrative provisions of the Member States concerning the manufacture, presentation and sale of tobacco products.

[326] Case C–210/03 *Swedish Match AB, Swedish Match UK Ltd v Secretary of State for Health* [2004] ECR I-11893 at 73. See also Case C-280/93 *Germany v Council* [1994] ECR I-4973 at 79 and Case C-122/95 *Germany v Council* [1998] ECR I-973 at 77.

> " . . . that an existing situation which is capable of being altered by decisions taken by the Community institutions within the limits of their discretionary power will be maintained".[327]

This is also the case where the existing situation has to be altered in order to comply with the obligations arising from international agreements concluded by the Community.[328] Similarly, the CJEU has held that the guarantees accorded by the right to property cannot be extended to protect mere commercial interests or opportunities, the uncertainties of which are part of the very essence of economic activity.[329] **[9–107]**

Article 17 also expressly protects intellectual property, a right which is merely implied in the ECHR and Irish contexts. Secondary legislation has been developed at an EU level to protect various aspects of intellectual property.[330]

Procedural Fairness

The protection of procedural rights in the process of interfering with a right to property is considered very significant by the court and a lack of respect for procedural rights can lead to a finding of an infringement of the right to property. In the case of *Omar Mohammed Othman v Council of the European Union and Commission of the European Communities*[331] arising from restrictive measures taken by regulation against persons associated with Osama bin Laden, the Al-Qaeda network and the Taliban including the freezing of funds, the court placed significant emphasis on the lack of procedural fairness in the impugned Regulation. In particular, the CJEU noted that the Regulation[332] was adopted without furnishing any guarantee enabling the complainant to put his case to the competent authorities in a situation in which the restriction on his property rights must have been significant. This was exacerbated by the general application of the measures and the actual continuation of the measures.[333] **[9–108]**

[327] *ibid* at 73. See also Case 52/81 *Faust v Commission* [1982] ECR 3745 atgraph 27; Case C-350/88 *Delacre and Others* v *Commission* [1990] ECR I-395 at 33 and 34, and Case C–280/93 *Germany v Council* [1994] ECR I-4973 at 89.

[328] Case C-295/03 P *Alessandrini Srl, established in Treviso (Italy), Anello Gino di Anello Luigi & C. Snc, established in Brescia (Italy), ArpigiSpA, established in Padua (Italy), BestfruitSrl, established in Milan (Italy), Co-FruttaSpA, established in Padua, Co-Frutta Soc. coop. arl, established in Padua, Dal Bello SifeSrl, established in Padua, FrigofruttaSrl, established in Palermo (Italy), GarlettiSnc, established in Bergamo (Italy), London Fruit Ltd, established in London (United Kingdom), v Commission of the European Communities* [2005] ECR I-5673.

[329] Case 4/73 *Nold v Commission* [1974] ECR 491 at 14. See also C–120/06 P and C–121/06 P *FIAMM v Council of the European Union and Commission of the European Communities* [2008] ECR I-6513 at 185.

[330] Directive 91/250/EEC on legal protection of software; Directive 92/100/EEC on lend and lease of certain rights in the field of intellectual property; Directive 93/83/EEC concerning harmonization of certain rules relating to satellite and cable broadcasting; Directive 93/98/EEC on harmonization of copyright and neighbouring rights; Directive 96/9 on legal protection of databases; and Directive 89/104/EEC on trademarks.

[331] Case T-318/01 *Othman v Council* [2009] OJ C180.

[332] Council Regulation (EC) No 881/2002 of 27 May 2002 imposing certain specific restrictive measures directed against certain persons and entities associated with Osama bin Laden, the Al-Qaeda network and the Taliban.

[333] Case T-318/01 *Othman v Council* [2009] OJ C180 at 91.

Therefore, this constituted an unjustified restriction on his right to property.[334] Consequently, the contested Regulation, in so far as it concerned the applicant was annulled.

2. Legitimate Interferences with the Right

[9–109] In determining whether there has been an infringement of the right to property, the CJEU has adopted the same procedures as apply in the context of the ECHR. Thus it has been held that in order to be justified, an interference must comply with the principle of lawfulness and pursue a legitimate aim by means reasonably proportionate to that aim.[335] This is essentially the same as the fair balance test under the ECHR, P1-1.

Lawfulness

[9–110] As regards lawfulness, the CJEU adopts the same tests as apply in the ECHR context, in that the law must be sufficiently clear, precise and accessible. In the *Alessandrini* case,[336] the CJEU referred to an exchange of letters on the subject annexed to the EC-Hungary Agreement on Wines which expressly imposed the interference and Decision 93/724 which approved the act on behalf of the Community. This was sufficiently clear and precise to constitute a "lawful" interference. This particular issue rarely arises in the EU context mainly as the challenges are to regulations, directives, decisions or recommendations which would all be considered to be "lawful" within this context. However, in some cases where there is a dispute or reference relating to a national implementing measure, this issue may become more relevant.

Legitimate Interest

[9–111] The CJEU has given Member States a very wide discretion in relation to the general public interest or legitimate aim that they are pursuing and the CJEU generally accepts the aims raised by Member States without further inquiry. Some examples of legitimate aims that have been raised by Member States and accepted by the CJEU include the need to provide consumers with clear and accurate information on certain products,[337] the need to protect producers on their territory against distortions of competition,[338]

---

[334] *ibid* at 92.

[335] See *Jokela v Finland (*judgment of 21 May 2002, *Reports of Judgments and Decisions* 2002-IV, at 48. See Case C-295/03 P *Alessandrini Srl, established in Treviso (Italy), Anello Gino di Anello Luigi & C. Snc, established in Brescia (Italy), ArpigiSpA, established in Padua (Italy), BestfruitSrl, established in Milan (Italy), Co-FruttaSpA, established in Padua, Co-Frutta Soc. coop. arl, established in Padua, Dal Bello SifeSrl, established in Padua, FrigofruttaSrl, established in Palermo (Italy), GarlettiSnc, established in Bergamo (Italy), London Fruit Ltd, established in London (United Kingdom) v Commission of the European Communities* [2005] ECR I-5673 at 125.

[336] Case C-295/03, *Alessandrini Srl and others v European Commission.*

[337] Case C–295/03 P *Alessandrini Srl, established in Treviso (Italy), Anello Gino di Anello Luigi & C. Snc, established in Brescia (Italy), ArpigiSpA, established in Padua (Italy), BestfruitSrl, established in Milan (Italy), Co-FruttaSpA, established in Padua, Co-Frutta Soc. coop. arl, established in Padua, Dal Bello SifeSrl, established in Padua, FrigofruttaSrl, established in Palermo (Italy), GarlettiSnc, established in Bergamo (Italy), London Fruit Ltd, established in London (United Kingdom) v Commission of the European Communities* [2005] ECR I-5673 at 127.

[338] *ibid* at 128.

the need to maintain international peace and security,[339] the need to avoid repetition of tests on human and animals unless absolutely necessary,[340] the need to protect the economic and social situation of the inland waterways,[341] and the need to protect public health.[342]

Proportionality/Fair Balance Test

The concept of proportionality involves a balancing of this general interest and the property rights of the applicant. In a tobacco advertising case,[343] on the validity and interpretation of Directive 2001/37/EC of the European Parliament and of the Council of 5 June 2001 on the approximation of the laws, regulations and administrative provisions of the Member States concerning the manufacture, presentation and sale of tobacco products, the national court asked whether the Directive was invalid in whole or in part by reason *inter alia* of infringement of the fundamental right to property. The claimants maintained that Arts 5 and 7 of the Directive infringed the fundamental right to property, which provides that use of a trademark in the course of trade is not to be unjustifiably encumbered by special requirements such as its use in a manner detrimental to its capability to distinguish the goods or services of one undertaking from those of other undertakings. **[9–112]**

They claimed that the very large size of the new health warnings required by Art 5 of the Directive constituted a serious infringement of their intellectual property rights. Those warnings would dominate the overall appearance of tobacco product packaging and curtail or prevent the use of their trademarks by the manufacturers of those products. In accepting that the protection of public health was a legitimate aim, the court then had to consider whether the Directive balanced this general interest fairly with the property rights of the applicant. The court noted that the only effect produced by Art 5 of the Directive was to restrict the right of manufacturers of tobacco products to use the space on some sides of cigarette packets to show their trademarks, "without prejudicing the substance of their trademark rights, the purpose being to ensure a high level of health protection"[344]. In light of this, Art 5 constituted a proportionate restriction on the right to property compatible with the protection afforded that right by Community law. **[9–113]**

In relation to Art 7 of the Directive, which provided that certain descriptors could not be used in the packaging of tobacco products, the court acknowledged that Art 7 entailed some prohibition but held that this was only in relation to the packaging of tobacco products and on using a trademark incorporating one of the descriptors referred to in that provision. The court was placated by the fact that a manufacturer of tobacco products could continue, notwithstanding the removal of that description **[9–114]**

---

[339] Case T-390/08 *Bank Melli Iran v Council* [2009] ECR II-3967 at 111.

[340] Case C–368/96, *Generics (UK) and others*, [1998] ECR I-7967 at 83.

[341] C–204/94 *Faroe Seafood and Others* [1996] ECR I-2465 at 71.

[342] Case C–293/97, *Standley* (1999) ECR I-2603 at 55. See also Case C-491/01, *BAT and Imperial Tobacco* [2002] ECR I-11458 at 150; Case C-210/03 *Swedish Match AB, Swedish Match UK Ltd v Secretary of State for Health* [2004] ECR I-11893 at 74.

[343] Case C–491/01, *BAT and Imperial Tobacco* [2002] ECR I-11458.

[344] Case C–491/01, *BAT and Imperial Tobacco* [2002] ECR I-11458 at 150.

from the packaging, to distinguish its product by using other distinctive signs. In addition, the Directive provided for a sufficient period of time between its adoption and the entry into force of the prohibition under Art 7[345] in order for the business to make any alterations necessary. Therefore, Art 7 was not a disproportionate or intolerable interference impairing the very substance of the right.

3. The Impact of Compensation

[9–115] While Art 17 of the CFR provides for a right to fair compensation within a reasonable period of time, prior to this provision, the rules relating to compensation essentially followed the ECHR decisions on this point. Compensation is only available where loss is suffered as a result of a loss of a property right. This was a central issue in the case of the *Irish Farmers Association and Others v Minister for Agriculture, Food and Forestry, Ireland and the Attorney General.*[346] In that case the plaintiffs argued that the reduction in their milk quotas without compensation amounted to an infringement of their property rights. The CJEU held that the reduction in the milk quota did not interfere with the actual substance of their right to property in that the Irish producers were still able to continue to pursue their trade or profession as milk producers. Therefore, no compensation would have been payable as this did not amount to an infringement of a property right.

[9–116] The question that will arise under Art 17 is the issue of what amounts to fair compensation. Will this be equate with the "full market value" of the property, or will be CJEU be persuaded by the decisions of the ECtHR in this context relating to paying a lesser sum in exceptional cases? The decision of the CJEU in *Booker Aquaculture Ltd*[347] is illuminating in this regard. In that case the Court examined a case of fish owners, whose fish were destroyed without compensation pursuant to Directive 93/53 where there was an outbreak of a particular disease in the fish stock. The applicants submitted that the issue of compensation was an important consideration in the determination as to whether the legislation in issue struck a fair balance between the general interest and the private rights of the fish owners. The applicants agreed that there was a general interest in the destruction of the fish but that the complete absence of compensation for persons affected by national measures implementing the directive infringed the principle of proportionality.[348] The Scottish Ministers, the UK, French, Italian, Netherlands and Norwegian Governments as well as the Council and the Commission contented that there was no general principle of community law requiring the payment of compensation in such circumstances and that the absence of compensation was compatible with the case law of the ECHR. The CJEU held that the objective of the Directive was to contribute to the completion of the internal market in aquaculture animals and products and forms part of a regime intended to introduce minimum Community measures for the control of certain fish diseases.[349]

345 *ibid* at 152.

346 Case C–22/94 *Irish Farmers Associationand Others v Minister for Agriculture, Food and Forestry, Irelandand the Attorney General* at 27.

347 Joined Cases C-20/00 and C-64/00 *Booker Aquaculture and Another v The Scottish Ministers* [2003] ECR I-7411

348 *ibid* at 50.

349 *ibid* at 78.

In assessing proportionality, the court noted that the:

> " ... measures are urgent and are intended to guarantee that effective action is implemented as soon as the presence of a disease is confirmed and to eliminate any risk of the spread or survival of the pathogen".[350]

The measures, the CJEU held, did not deprive the owners of the use of their fish farms and enabled them to carry on their activities there.[351] Further, the immediate destruction and slaughter of all the fish enabled owners to restock the affected farms as soon as possible.[352] The owners of such business are aware that it carries commercial risks. For example, the CJEU noted that the farmers can expect "that a fish disease may break out at any moment and cause them loss. Such risk is inherent in the business of raising and selling livestock and is the consequence of a natural occurrence".[353] The CJEU also noted that fish which show clinical signs of disease have no marketable value. Even though some of the fish slaughtered were healthy, of commercial size and could have been marketed or processed for human consumption: [9–117]

> " ... any loss eventually suffered by farmers by reason of the immediate slaughter ... arises from the fact that they have been unable to choose the most advantageous time for their sale. In fact, because of the risk of their presenting clinical signs of disease in future, it is impossible to determine a more advantageous time for their sale. So far as all other types of fish are concerned, it is not possible to establish whether they have any marketable value either, because of the risk that in the future they will develop clinical signs of disease".[354]

Therefore, the lack of compensation was not a disproportionate and intolerable interference impairing the very substance of the right.

Whether this decision would now be possible under the CFR given the express right to fair compensation contained in Art 17 is worth considering. Perhaps the CJEU would determine that this was not a deprivation or control of use of property and thus hold that no compensation would be payable. If, however, they were to determine otherwise, some measure of compensation would be payable. What would amount to fair in the circumstances might be a small token amount considering the decision of the CJEU in this case. [9–118]

D. International and Regional Laws

The right to property is also protected at an international level.[355] Article 17 of the Universal Declaration on Human Rights (UDHR) protects the peaceful enjoyment of [9–119]

350 *ibid* at 79.
351 *ibid* at 80.
352 *ibid* at 81.
353 *ibid* at 83.
354 *ibid* at 84.
355 See J Mchangama, "The Right to Property in Global Human Rights Law" *Cato Policy Report*, May/June 2011 available at http://www.cato.org/pubs/policy_report/v33n3/cprv33n3-1.html, last accessed 31 August 2012.

property and provides special protection against the arbitrary deprivation of property. This was a very controversial provision during the drafting of the UDHR considering the varying political ideologies surrounding property rights prevailing at the time. This is further reflected in a complete absence of any protection for the right to property in either the International Covenant on Civil and Political Rights (ICCPR) of the International Covenant on Economic, Social and Cultural Rights (ICESCR). Although there is some limited protection of intellectual property rights in Art 15 of the ICESCR.

Specific protection for the property of minority groups is provided for in many of the conventions. So, for example, Art 5 of UN Convention on the Elimination of Racial Discrimination (CERD) also protects the right to property and in particular has issued a General Recommendation in relation to the right to property and refugees and displaced persons. The Committee on the Elimination of Racial Discrimination noted all refugees and displaced persons have, "after their return to their homes of origin, the right to have restored to them property of which they were deprived in the course of the conflict and to be compensated appropriately for any such property that cannot be restored to them"[356]. Art 15 of the UN Convention on the Rights of Migrant Workers and Members of their Families (CRMW) and Art 12 of the UN Convention on the Rights of Persons with Disabilities (CRPD) also protect the right to property of migrants and disabled persons respectively.

Some limited protection of the right to property is also to be found in Arts 15 and 16 of the UN Convention on the Elimination of Discrimination Against Women (CEDAW). Art 15 provides for equality between men and women before the law and, particularly, in regards to the administration of property. The Committee on the Elimination of Discrimination Against Women has repeatedly emphasized the importance of legal autonomy for women so that she can hold property in her own name[357] without which her ability to provide for herself and her dependent's is limited. Similarly, the Committee on the Elimination of Discrimination Against Women has also highlighted in Article 16(1)(h) of CEDAW the importance of the right of a woman to "own, manage, enjoy and dispose of property" as "central to a woman's right to enjoy financial independence, and in many countries will be critical to her ability to earn a livelihood and to provide adequate housing and nutrition for herself and for her family".[358]

[9–120] At a regional level, the right to property is protected by Art 21 of the American Convention on Human Rights, Art 14 of the African Charter on Human and Peoples Rights and Art 31 of the Arab Charter on Human Rights.

[356] Committee on the Elimination of Racial Discrimination, *General Recommendation No 22: Article 5 and refugees and displaced persons : 24.08.1996.*

[357] Committee on the Elimination of Discrimination Against Women, General Recommendation No 21 (13th session, 1994) at 7.

[358] *ibid*

Conclusion

[9–121]

> "In essence . . . the jurisprudence of the Irish courts invites close comparisons with that of their European counterparts in Luxembourg and Strasbourg, even if, as we have seen, judges employing similar methodologies and reasoning techniques sometimes arrive at very different conclusions"[359].

The protection of the right to property at the three levels is very comparable. This can be first identified in the definition of property that has been adopted at an Irish, Council of Europe and EU level. While there are some small differentials (particularly in relation to causes of action as property rights), generally what is considered property at a national level, is considered property at a regional level and vice versa. The same can be said for the definition of what constitutes an interference with the right to property. While not expressly stated, the issues which have constituted interferences at a national level can be easily compared with those that have been identified under the ECHR, most notably a control of use and a deprivation. In the EU context, the CJEU has expressly recognised the definition of interferences that has been developed by the ECtHR. This can also be seen in justification stage where the Irish courts have developed a proportionality test which is very similar to the fair balance test adopted by the ECtHR and the EU. Finally, in relation to the issue of compensation, while the Irish and ECHR protections seem to be similar, the express recognition of a right to fair compensation at an EU level singles this particular level of protection out for special note. There has not yet been a case in the area of property rights which deals with this express reference to compensation but it will be interesting to see whether the CJEU will follow the reasoning of the ECtHR in this regard or whether it will chart its own unique path in this area.

[359] G Hogan, "The Constitution, Property Rights and Proportionality" (1997) 32(1) Ir Jur 373 at 389.

CHAPTER 10
Freedom of Expression

Introduction

The freedom of expression[1] is acknowledged in almost all domestic and all regional and international systems as a basic human requirement and as a cornerstone of a democratic society.[2] It is an essential element of the rule of law, as freedom of expression allows individuals to participate in political and social debate.[3] The right to freely express oneself is also a vital aspect of human dignity and self-fulfillment.[4] The importance of this right was highlighted in the 1789 Declaration of the Rights of Man and the Citizen as "[t]he free communication of thoughts and opinions is one of the **[10–01]**

[1] The freedom of expression and the freedom of speech are sometimes used interchangeably in the literature and in legal frameworks—see M Forde, *Constitutional Law* (2nd ed, First Law, Dublin, 2004), p 533. As the Irish Constitution refers specifically to the freedom of expression, this chapter focuses on this concept.

[2] For a discussion of the comparative protection of expression, see T Daly, "Strengthening Irish Democracy: A Proposal to Restore Free Speech to Article 40.6.1°(i) of the Constitution" (2009) 16(1) DULJ 228.

[3] The Constitutional Review Group described the freedom of speech and expression as follows: "Indeed, the right of free speech and of expression is one which is guaranteed in virtually every constitution and relevant international human rights instrument. The right of free speech is generally considered to be a key fundamental right and, in this respect, the language of the German Constitutional Court in its celebrated decision in the *Luth* case 7 Berf GE 198 (1958) cannot be improved upon: 'The basic right to freedom of opinion is the most immediate expression of the human personality in society and, as such, is one of the noblest of human rights ... It is absolutely basic to a liberal-democratic order because it alone makes possible the constant intellectual exchange and the contest among opinions that form the lifeblood of such an order; it is the matrix, the indispensable condition of nearly every other form of freedom.'" – *Report of the Constitutional Review Group* (Stationery Office, Dublin, 1996), p 268.

[4] See M Forde, *supra* n 1, p 533. See also K Boyle, "Freedom of Expression and Democracy" in *Human Rights: A European Perspective* (L Heffernan ed, Round Hall Press, Dublin, 1994), p 211.

most precious rights of man".[5] While, generally, this right has been associated with the freedom of the press or free speech, it can also encompass issues such as language choice and communication in non-verbal forms.[6] In the Irish context, freedom of expression is guaranteed, subject to certain limitations, under Art 40.6.1°(i) of the Constitution. This chapter reviews the domestic law with regard to freedom of expression before looking at this right in a European Convention on Human Rights (ECHR) and Charter of Fundamental Rights (CFR) context and at its protection under international human rights law.

A. Irish Constitution

[10–02] Article 40.6.1°(i):

> "The State guarantees liberty for the exercise ... subject to public order and morality of ... the right of the citizens to express freely their convictions and opinions. The education of public opinion being, however, a matter of such grave import to the common good, the State shall endeavour to ensure that organs of public opinion, such as the radio, the press, the cinema, while preserving their rightful liberty of expression, including criticism of Government policy, shall not be used to undermine public order or morality or the authority of the State. The publication or utterance of blasphemous, seditious, or indecent matter is an offence which shall be punishable in accordance with law."

The freedom of expression resides alongside the guarantees for freedom of assembly and association in Art 40.6 of the Constitution and all guarantees relating to these rights are subject to public order and morality considerations. This chapter focuses on the freedom of expression and the connected right of freedom to communicate, while freedom of assembly and association are dealt with elsewhere in this book (Chapters 12 and 13). While the freedom of expression can be seen to have a dual function, (1) ensuring the freedom to voice opinions on politics and society, and (2) as a protection of human dignity, Doyle states that "political justification for free expression is, in the Irish context, the most compelling".[7]

[10–03] While, as stated above, freedom of expression is generally regarded as a necessary component of a democratic society and is extensively protected in domestic legal systems the world over, the Irish constitutional protection of the rights has been labeled "the Achilles' heel of Ireland's democratic system".[8] The constitutional protection of the freedom of expression is generally criticised as being inadequate,[9] being "weak and heavily circumscribed",[10] and does not compare well with other domestic protections

---

[5] Art 11, Declaration of the Rights of Man and the Citizen 1789.

[6] The European Court of Human Rights (ECtHR) has, for example, provided a very expansive interpretation of the right to freedom of expression enshrined in Art 10 which has been held to include forms of dress, musical performances, etc.

[7] O Doyle, *Constitutional Law: Text, Cases and Materials* (Clarus Press, Dublin, 2008), p 195.

[8] T Daly, *supra* n 2, at 228.

[9] McGonagle has stated: "A guarantee of freedom of expression may have been enshrined in the ... Constitution of 1937 but its formulation was so qualified and ambivalent as to leave expression and information issues virtually untouched and unlitigated for several decades to come" – M McGonagle, "Freedom of Expression and Information" in IrHRYb (G Quinn ed, Round Hall Sweet & Maxwell, Dublin, 1995), p 130.

[10] *Constitutional Review Group Report*, *supra* n 3, p 291.

of the freedom of expression or, indeed, international standards.[11] Coupled with, or perhaps, because of, the weak protection proffered by Art 40.6.1°(i), there has been a lack of litigation on this issue,[12] leading Hogan to comment that the right to freedom of expression has "remained stubbornly underdeveloped and under-litigated"[13] until recently. This led the Constitutional Review Group to comment in 1996:

> "Indeed, unlike other areas of the personal rights provisions, the relative paucity of the case law in this area is such that not much would be lost if Article 40.6.1°.i were to be replaced".[14]

Given the considerable criticism of the provision and the lack of engagement with it by the judiciary, it is unsurprising that there have been recommendations that it be amended and replaced with a provision similar to Art 10 of the ECHR, which has fewer limitations than the constitutional provision, and affords a higher level of protection to the freedom of expression.[15] **[10–04]**

Indeed, there has been an increase in litigation on the freedom of expression since the enactment of the European Convention on Human Rights Act 2003, leading Daly to comment:

> "While the past decade has seen the Irish courts' frosty attitude to free speech thaw considerably, greater protection of the right has been achieved, not by interpreting Article 40.6.1°(i) more generously, but by sidelining it altogether. Rather than directly addressing the difficulties posed by the constitutional text and case law, the courts appear to have begun circumventing them in free speech cases by reference to Article 10 ECHR, on the basis of the *European Convention on Human Rights Act 2003* which incorporated the Convention into Irish law".[16]

The expansion of the right to freedom of expression by the Irish courts in recent times is evidenced in the 2007 decision of *Dillon v DPP*,[17] in which the High Court struck down s 3 of the Vagrancy (Ireland) Act 1847. One of the grounds for this removal was that a prohibition on begging was seen as an interference with the right to freedom of expression and to communicate. De Valera J referred to the conclusion by Barrington J in the case of *Murphy v Independent Radio and Television Commission*[18] that the right to communicate pursuant to Art 40.3, and the right of freedom of expression pursuant to Art 40.6.1°, accepts the right of the citizen to express his or her needs "by words and **[10–05]**

---

[11] See T Daly, *supra* n 2.

[12] Daly comments that there has been "a lack of judicial commitment to free speech" and an "absence of any coherent judicial philosophy regarding free speech" — T Daly, *supra* n 2 at p 228.

[13] G Hogan, "Historical origins of Article 40.6.1°" in *The Irish Constitution: Governance and Values* (E Carolan and O Doyle eds, Thomson Round Hall, Dublin, 2008), at p 71

[14] *Constitutional Review Group Report*, *supra* n 3, p 269.

[15] *ibid*, pp 269–270.

[16] T Daly, *supra* n 2 at p 237. Daly also states: "In the decade since 2000, the dominant approach of the courts to free speech has been much more protective, according the right significant weight and scrutinising restrictions on its exercise with greater intensity and depth."

[17] *Dillon v DPP* [2007] IEHC 480.

[18] *Murphy v Independent Radio and Television Commission* [1999] 1 IR 12.

gestures as well as by rational discourse".[19] De Valera J proceeded to state that "in applying this dictum to begging as already defined, the Act clearly offends against freedom of expression as provided for in Article 40.6.1 of the Constitution".[20]

1. Nature of the Right

The Relationship between the Freedom of Expression and the Right to Communicate

[10–06] The scope of the constitutional protection of expression[21] guaranteed in Art 40.6.1°(i) is somewhat unclear. This provision does not explicitly mention the right to actually communicate or disseminate thoughts, opinions or ideas to the wider public. Nor is the right to communicate afforded specific protection elsewhere in the Constitution. In order for the freedom of expression to be actually realised, however, the right to communicate what one wants to express is vital. The Irish courts have, therefore, recognised an unenumerated right to communicate and have also attempted to find a "home" for this unenumerated right within the Constitution. A review of the case law illustrates that the relationship between the freedom of expression and the right to communicate that which one wants to express is growing closer.

[10–07] The High Court first held that an unenumerated right to communicate existed under the constitution in *Attorney General v Paperlink Ltd*, where Costello J stated:

> " . . . it seems to me that as the act of communication is the exercise of such a basic human faculty that a right to communicate must inhere in the citizen by virtue of his human personality and must be guaranteed by the Constitution . . .The exercise of the right can take many forms and the right to express freely convictions and opinions is expressly provided for in Article 40.6.1°. But the activity which the defendants say is inhibited in this case is that of communication by letter and as this act may involve the communication of information and not merely the expression of convictions and opinions I do not think that the constitutional provision dealing with the right to express convictions and opinions is the source of the citizen's right to communicate. I conclude that the very general and basic human right to communicate . . . must be one of those personal unspecified rights of the citizen protected by Article 40.3.1°".[22]

The separation of the right to communicate from the right to freedom of expression is very unusual when compared to other domestic and international provisions on the topic of freedom of expression, which normally view the freedom of expression as encompassing the right to communicate, or indeed the right to communicate as a prerequisite for the freedom of expression to be adequately realised. The divorce of these two rights is perhaps indicative of a lack of judicial scrutiny as regards the nature and interdependence of these rights. In the later case of *Brandon Books*,[23] however, the

[19] See *Dillon v DPP* [2007] IEHC 480 at 17.

[20] *ibid.*

[21] Forde states, regarding the term "expression": "[i]t has an obvious core meaning but does it, or can it in certain circumstances, embrace gestures and indeed demonstrative action?" M Forde, *supra* n 1, p 533.

[22] *AG v Paperlink Ltd* [1984] ILRM 373.

[23] *AG for England and Wales v Brandon Book Publishers Ltd* [1986] 1 IR 597.

High Court held that Art 40.6.1°(i) included a constitutional right to publish, which marked something of a reunion of the right to communication and freedom of expression.

The relationship between expression and communication was addressed again in the case of *Oblique Ltd v Promise Production Company* [1994] 1 ILRM 74. Keane J stated: **[10–08]**

> "Article 40.6.1° is concerned not with the dissemination of factual information, but the rights of the citizen, in formulating or publishing convictions or opinions, or conveying an opinion; and the rights of all citizens, including conveying information, arises in our law, not under Article 40.6.1° but under Article 40.3.1°".[24]

However, in the later case of *Irish Times Ltd v Ireland*[25] the Supreme Court took a more holistic view of these issues, taking cognisance of the more expansive ECHR protection of the freedom of expression. Barrington J stated:

> "Article 40.6.1(i) is unique in conferring liberties and rights upon the 'organs of public opinion' . . . These rights must include the right to report the news as well as the right to comment on it. A constitutional right which protected the right to comment on the news but not the right to report it would appear to me to be a nonsense. It therefore appears to me that the right of the citizens 'to express freely their convictions and opinions' guaranteed by Article 40 of the Constitution is a right to communicate facts as well as a right to consent to comment on them. It appears to me also that when the European Convention on Human Rights states that the right to freedom of expression is to include 'freedom. . .to receive and impart information' it is merely making explicit something which is already implicit in Article 40.6.1 of our Constitution".[26]

The relationship between expression and communication was revisited by the Supreme Court in *Mahon v Post Publications Ltd*[27] in 2007, when Fennelly J stated: **[10–09]**

> "Clearly, the Constitution, unequivocally guarantees both the right to express convictions and opinions and the right to communicate facts or information. These rights are inseparable. It matters little, at least for present purposes, which Article of the Constitution expresses the guarantee. The right of a free press to communicate information without let or restraint is intrinsic to a free and democratic society".[28]

The current situation seems to be that the protection of the freedom of expression under Art 40.6.1°(i) includes an implicit right to receive and impart information, as formulated under Art 10 of the ECHR. This right exists alongside the unenumerated right to communicate which is housed in Art 40.3.1°.

---

24 *Oblique Ltd v Promise Production Company* [1994] 1 ILRM 74 at 6.

25 *Irish Times Ltd v Ireland* [1998] 1 IR 539.

26 *ibid* at 404–405. This interpretation was affirmed by the Supreme Court again in *Murphy v Independent Radio and Television Commission* [1999] 1 IR 12 at 24–25.

27 *Mahon v Post Publications Ltd* [2007] 3 IR 338.

28 *ibid* at 377.

The Scope of the Right to Freedom of Expression

[10–10] From the wording of Art 40.6.1°, it is clear that political speech is protected. Doyle states: "The reference to 'criticism of Government policy', if nothing else, implies that speech linked to the political process is protected by the Article".[29]

[10–11] However, the Irish courts have expanded the interpretation of the provision to include all speech in the public domain. This is clear from the case of *Murphy v IRTC*.[30] In this case the applicant argued that s 10(3) of the Radio and Television Act 1988 was unconstitutional. This provision prohibits the broadcast of any advertisement "which is directed towards any religious or political end or which has any relation to an industrial dispute.". The Independent Radio and Television Commission (IRTC) had relied on this provision to prevent a radio station from broadcasting an advertisement regarding a presentation of the evidence of the resurrection of Christ. Barrington J stated:

> "The Court agrees ... that the learned trial judge was perhaps unduly restrictive in denying to the applicant any right to rely on Article 40.6.1° because he was not attempting to influence public opinion. The Court doubts if the guarantee of freedom of expression contained in Article 40.6.1° is confined to those who wish to influence public opinion. A politician who addresses the nation over the airwaves is clearly attempting to influence public opinion. But an advertisement, though apparently directed at an individual consumer, may also be intended to influence consumers greatly".[31]

Thus, the freedom of expression covers instances of political, religious and also more general speech. The issue of commercial speech has not really received much attention in Ireland, but as the ECHR and EU increasingly seek to provide some level of protection to commercial speech,[32] it is probable that this trend will be accepted by Irish courts in the future.[33]

[10–12] In *Attorney General (SPUC) v Open Door Counselling*,[34] and affirmed in *SPUC Grogan (No 5)*,[35] concerning the provision of information on abortion, the Supreme Court noted the place of the freedom of expression in the hierarchy of constitutional rights, stating that "no right could constitutionally arise to obtain information the purpose of which was to defeat the constitutional rights of the child".[36]

---

29 O Doyle, *supra* n 7, p 197.

30 *Murphy v IRTC* [1999] 1 IR 12. See also *Colgan v IRTC* [2000] 2 IR 490.

31 *Murphy v IRTC* [1999] 1 IR 12 at 25.

32 See CR Munro, "The Value of Commercial Speech" (2003) 62(1) CamLJ 134.

33 See O Doyle, *supra* n 7, p 197.

34 *Attorney General (Society for the Protection of Unborn Children) v Open Door Counselling and Well Woman Clinic* [1988] IR 593.

35 *SPUC v Grogan (No 5)* [1998] 4 IR 343.

36 *AG (SPUC) v Open Door Counselling* [1988] IR 593 at 625. Daly comments in relation to this hierarchy of rights: "Free speech concerns were jettisoned through a rather crude application of the hierarchy of rights doctrine, simplistically categorising the right to life of the unborn as the superior right and focusing exclusively on its vindication" – T Daly, *supra* n 2 at 238.

The nature of the right to freedom of expression was also discussed in the case of *Mahon v Post Publications Ltd*[37] where Fennelly J stated that the right "extends the same protection to worthless, prurient and meretricious publication as it does to worthy, serious and socially valuable works".[38]

To Whom does the Right Apply?

It is clear from the wording of Art 40.6.1°(i) that both citizens (and perhaps non-citizens)[39] and controllers of organs of public opinion, including the radio, press and cinema, can benefit from the protection of the provision. The list is not exhaustive, however, and it seems unquestionable that newer media, including the internet, would also fall within the protective remit of Art 40.6.1°(i).[40] **[10–13]**

2. Legitimate Justifications for Interference with the Right

The freedom of expression is clearly not an unlimited right, and indeed, the legitimate justifications for interference with the right are many and varied.[41] It is important to note that in *Murphy v IRTC*[42] in 1999, the Supreme Court held that a proportionality test should be applied to all restrictions of free expression.[43] **[10–14]**

Public Order, Morality and the Authority of the State

The Constitution allows for interferences with the right to freedom of expression on the grounds of "public order or morality or the authority of the State".[44] The scope of these legitimate interferences has been elucidated in case law, e.g. the case of *State (Lynch) v Cooney.*[45] This case, which was the first freedom of expression case to come before the courts, focused on former s 31 of the Broadcasting Act 1960 which sought to protect the authority of the State by prohibiting broadcasts of certain organisations which had, it was felt, an intention to undermine the authority of the State. The constitutionality of this section was at question.[46] This provision empowered the Minister for Posts and Telegraphs to direct the national broadcaster, Raidió Teilifís Éireann (RTÉ) to refrain from broadcasting certain matters if he was of the opinion that the information would undermine the authority of the State.[47] The Minister had **[10–15]**

---

[37] *Mahon v Post Publications Ltd* [2007] 3 IR 388.

[38] *ibid* at 375.

[39] See the debate on the application of constitutional rights to non-citizens in the Introduction to this book.

[40] See O Doyle, *supra* n 7, p 198.

[41] Doyle comments that "the courts have generally – though not universally – been fairly tolerant of restrictions on free expression" – O Doyle, *supra* n 7, p 199.

[42] *Murphy v IRTC* [1999] 1 IR 12 at 26.

[43] With regard to the proportionality test, see B Foley, "The Proportionality Test: Present problems" (2008) 1 JSIJ 67.

[44] Art 40.6.1°(i) of the Constitution.

[45] *State (Lynch) v Cooney* [1982] IR 337.

[46] s 31(1) of the Broadcasting Authority Act 1960 was amended by s 3 of the Broadcasting Act 2001 and the Act was repealed in 2009.

[47] Former s 31(1) stated that the Minister for Justice "may by order direct the Authority to refrain from broadcasting the matter or any matter of the particular class, and the Authority shall comply with the Order."

made an order under s 31 of the 1960 Act directing RTÉ to refrain from broadcasting any matter on behalf of, or which invited the support of, Sinn Féin, even if the matter was not a political broadcast.[48]

[10–16] In the High Court, O'Hanlon J found that s 31 infringed Art 40.6.1°(i). O'Hanlon J had interpreted s 31 to mean that where the Minister held a *bona fide* opinion that a matter would undermine the authority of the State if broadcast, the reason for his opinion could not be reviewed by the High Court. The Supreme Court, however, held that the basis of the Minister's opinion could be reviewed by the courts, given the presumption of constitutionality. Therefore, the applicant's right to freedom of expression had not been unduly infringed. With regard to Art 40.6.1°(i), the court stated:

> "This provision enables the State, in certain instances, to control ... rights and freedoms. The basis for any attempt at control must be, according to the Constitution, the overriding considerations of public order and morality. The constitutional provision in question refers to organs of public opinion and these must be held to include television as well as radio. It places upon the State the obligation to ensure that these organs of public opinion shall not be used to undermine public order or public morality or the authority of the State. It follows that the use of such organs of opinion for the purpose of securing or advocating support for organisations which seek by violence to overthrow the State or its institutions is a use which is prohibited by the Constitution. Therefore, it is clearly the duty of the State to intervene to prevent broadcasts on radio or television which are aimed at such a result or which in any way would be likely to have the effect of promoting or inciting to crime or endangering the authority of the State".[49]

[10–17] The court then went on to provide guidelines as to the extent of the legality of interferences with the right to freedom of expression on public order and morality grounds. It continued:

> "These, however, are objective determinations and obviously the fundamental rights of citizens to express freely their convictions and opinions cannot be curtailed or prevented

---

[48] This Order, which remained in force until 1994, stated:
"2. Radio Telefís Éireann [*sic*] is hereby directed to refrain from broadcasting any matter which is—
(1) an interview, or report of an interview, with a spokesman or with spokesmen for any one or more of the following organisations, namely, (a) the organisation styling itself the Irish Republican Army (also the I.R.A. and Óglaig na hÉireann), (b) the organisation styling itself Sinn Féin, (c) the organisation styling itself Republican Sinn Féin, (d) the organisation styling itself the Ulster Defence Association, (e) the organisation styling itself the Irish National Liberation Army (also the I.N.L.A.), (f) any organisation which in Northern Ireland is a proscribed organisation for the purposes of section 21 of the Act of the British Parliament entitled the Northern Ireland (Emergency Provisions) Act, 1978,
(2) a broadcast, whether purporting to be a political party broadcast or not, made by, or on behalf of, or advocating, offering or inviting support for, the organisation styling itself Sinn Féin or the organisation styling itself Republican Sinn Féin.
(3) a broadcast by any person or persons representing, or purporting to represent, the organisation styling itself Sinn Féin or the organisation styling itself Republican Sinn Féin." SI No 13 of 1987. With regard to the interpretation of this instrument, see *O'Toole v RTÉ (No 2)* [1993] ILRM 458.

[49] *State (Lynch) v Cooney* [1982] IR 337 at 361.

> on any irrational or capricious ground. It must be presumed that when the Oireachtas conferred these powers on the Minister it intended that they be exercised only in conformity with the Constitution".[50]

Limitations on the freedom of expression with regard to the authority of the State are also allowed under the Official Secrets Act 1963. Part 2 of that Act prohibits the publication of any matter which is classified as secret or confidential. Section 4(1) states:

> "[a] person shall not communicate any official information to any other person unless he is duly authorised to do so in the course of and in accordance with his duties as the holder of a public office or when it is his duty in the interest of the State to communicate it."

Part 3 of the 1963 Act prohibits the communication of military and Garda information and "any other matter whatsoever information as to which would or might be prejudicial to the safety or preservation of the State".[51]

Limitations on the freedom of expression for the protection of the State are also laid out in Part 2 of the Offences Against the State Act 1939 which prohibits the dissemination of documents which are treasonable, seditious or incriminating. These are documents which emanate from any organisation which is proscribed under Part 3 of that Act.

Publication of Court Proceedings

In *Cullen v Toibín*[52] the Supreme Court lifted an injunction on the publication of an article in a newspaper concerning a case that was due to be heard before the Court of Criminal Appeal, stating that "freedom of the press and of communication which is guaranteed in the Constitution cannot be lightly curtailed".[53] Similarly, in *Irish Times v Ireland*[54] the Supreme Court struck down restrictions placed on the contemporaneous coverage of a criminal trial by the Circuit Court. The decision focused mainly on Art 34.1 of the Constitution which requires that justice be administered in public, but also focused on Art 40.6.1°(i), with Barrington J commenting: **[10–18]**

> "The freedom of expression guaranteed by Article 40.6.1° of the Constitution includes criticism of government policy. *A fortiori* it includes criticism of other aspects of State activity including the working of the courts".[55]

In *Independent Newspapers of Ireland Ltd v Judge Anderson*[56] the High Court dealt with another case regarding restrictions on the publication of information on trials, holding that a restrictive order could only be made when it was necessary to ensure a fair trial. Clarke J commented: **[10–19]**

> "If any restrictive order is justified under *Irish Times Limited* principles then, in order to amount to a justified interference with Article 34.1, such an order must, in my view,

---

[50] *ibid.*
[51] s 9 of the Official Secrets Act 1963.
[52] *Cullen v Toibín* [1984] ILRM 577.
[53] *ibid* at 582.
[54] *Irish Times v Ireland* [1998] 1 IR 359.
[55] *ibid* at 406.
[56] *Independent Newspapers of Ireland Ltd v Judge Anderson* [2006] 3 IR 341.

> comply with principles analogous to those which have been developed under the doctrine of proportionality. Such an order should, therefore:
> i. be designed only to restrict the publication of material which, it is adjudged, would cause serious prejudice leading to a real risk to a fair trial; and
> ii. should do so in a manner which interferes as little as possible with the entitlement to report fully on all aspects of the administration of justice; and
> iii. should do so in a way which is proportionate".[57]

Publication of Personal and Confidential Information / Prior Restraint Orders

[10–20] In general, the Irish Courts have been reluctant to allow the right to freedom of expression to be trumped for reasons pertaining to the publication of personal or confidential information. In the case of *M v Drury*[58] the High Court refused to grant an order to restrain the publication of an article in relation to the applicant's married and family life, particularly facts relating to her relationship with a member of the clergy. O'Hanlon stated:

> "In the present case the court is asked to intervene to restrain the publication of material, the truth of which has not as yet been disputed, in order to save from the distress that such publication is sure to cause, the children of the marriage who are all minors. This would represent a new departure in our law, for which, in my opinion, no precedent has been shown, and for which I can find no basis in the Irish Constitution, having regard, in particular, to the strongly-expressed guarantees in favour of freedom of expression in that document".[59]

In *Foley v Sunday Independent Ltd*[60] the High Court refused to grant an injunction to stop the publication of an article in the *Sunday Independent* which would identify the plaintiff as a police informant, which, he claimed, would risk his constitutional right to bodily integrity.

[10–21] In *Mahon v Post Publications*[61] the Supreme Court refused an application by the Mahon Tribunal to stop the publication of confidential information being distributed to witnesses before the public hearings of the Tribunal, based on the right to freedom of expression. In its decision the court referred extensively to the ECHR freedom of expression regime.

Another case dealing with the freedom of expression and the Mahon Tribunal is the 2009 case of *Mahon v Keena*,[62] where the Supreme Court quashed a High Court order which required journalists to reveal their sources for an article concerning the Mahon Tribunal. The court, once again, depended heavily on previous decisions on the freedom of expression of the ECtHR, especially the 1996 case of *Goodwin v UK* which will be discussed in more depth later in this chapter,[63] referring only cursorily to Irish constitutional protection of the freedom of expression.[64]

---

57 *ibid.*
58 *M v Drury* [1994] 2 IR 8.
59 *ibid* at 17.
60 *Foley v Sunday Independent Ltd* [2005] 1 IR 88.
61 *Mahon v Post Publications* [2007] 3 IR 338.
62 *Mahon v Keena* [2010] 1 IR 336.
63 *Goodwin v The United Kingdom* (1996) 22 EHRR 12.
64 See T Daly, *supra* n 2 at 242.

When assessing the limits of the freedom of expression and communication, the courts have conceded that these rights can be limited by confidentiality interests (*Oblique Financial Services Ltd v The Promise Production Co Ltd*[65]), but they have also found that confidentiality must be weighed against the public interest in the publication of the information (*National Irish Bank v RTÉ*[66]).

Defamation

Irish defamation law was recently amended[67] with the enactment of the Defamation Act 2009 (the 2009 Act),[68] which repealed the Defamation Act 1961. The 2009 Act defines defamation in the following terms in s 6: **[10–22]**

> "(1) The tort of libel and the tort of slander—
> (*a*) shall cease to be so described, and
> (*b*) shall, instead, be collectively described, and are referred to in this Act, as the 'tort of defamation'.
> (2) The tort of defamation consists of the publication, by any means, of a defamatory statement concerning a person to one or more than one person (other than the first-mentioned person), and 'defamation' shall be construed accordingly.
> (3) A defamatory statement concerns a person if it could reasonably be understood as referring to him or her.
> (4) There shall be no publication for the purposes of the tort of defamation if the defamatory statement concerned is published to the person to whom it relates and to a person other than the person to whom it relates in circumstances where—
> (*a*) it was not intended that the statement would be published to the second-mentioned person, and
> (*b*) it was not reasonably foreseeable that publication of the statement to the first-mentioned person would result in its being published to the second-mentioned person.
> (5) The tort of defamation is actionable without proof of special damage."

Schedule 2 of the 2009 Act contains the "Minimum Requirements in Relation to Press Council" which states that one of the objectives of the Press Council is to ensure "the protection of freedom of expression of the press",[69] but the 2009 Act does not refer to freedom of expression in any other place. Section 33 of the 2009 Act allows the court to make interim, interlocutory or permanent orders prohibiting the publication or further publication of the defamatory statement. However, as with the cases concerning prior restraint orders discussed above, any such orders granted will be considered in light of the ECHR and its strong freedom of expression protection. Even before the enactment of the 2009 Act, the courts had been influenced by Art 10 of the ECHR in defamation cases. In *Hunter v Duckworth*,[70] Ó Caoimh J stated: **[10–23]**

> "I am satisfied that no essential difference exists between the provisions of the Convention and the provisions of Article 40.6.1° of the Constitution. What is relevant

[65] *Oblique Financial Services Ltd v The Promise Production Co Ltd* [1994] 1 ILRM 74.
[66] *National Irish Bank v RTÉ* [1998] 2 IR 465.
[67] See TJ O'Dowd, "Ireland's New Defamation Act" (2009) 1(2) JMediaL 173.
[68] Defamation Act 2009, Act No 31 of 2009.
[69] Sch 2, para 2(a) of the Defamation Act 2009.
[70] *Hunter v Duckworth* [2003] IEHC 81.

is how they should be interpreted. It is clear that the Convention does not provide as such for the protection of one's reputation. However, Article 10 recognises that the protection given to freedom of expression may be curtailed and may be subject to restrictions as are prescribed by law and as are necessary in a democratic society for a variety of interests including the protection of the reputation or rights of others. It is, however, necessary, to assess whether the common law of defamation as traditionally interpreted in this jurisdiction meets the requirements of the Constitution. In interpreting the Constitution this Court can have regard to the interpretation of the Convention insofar as it indicates how Article 40.6.1° may be interpreted".[71]

Blasphemy[72]

[10–24] The final paragraph of Art 40.6.1°(i) states that the "publication or utterance of blasphemous, seditious, or indecent matter is an offence which shall be punishable in accordance with law".[73] Irish censorship laws also prohibit the publication of blasphemous material.[74] Doyle comments that "[a]s this regime was dismantled, it seemed that the constitutional offence of blasphemy would come into sharper focus".[75] The issue of blasphemy is a contentious one, with many questioning the need for retention of the reference to blasphemy in the Constitution. The Law Reform Commission's 1991 Consultation Paper stated that "there is no place for the offence of blasphemous libel in a society which respects freedom of speech"[76] and the Constitutional Law Review Group stated in 1996 that the "retention of the present constitutional offence of blasphemy is not appropriate".[77]

[10–25] The seminal case on this issue is *Corway v Independent Newspapers (Ireland) Ltd*[78] which discussed the meaning of blasphemy. The applicant had sought leave, pursuant to s 8 of the Defamation Act 1961, of the High Court to institute proceedings concerning an allegedly blasphemous cartoon which was published in connection with an article on the divorce referendum by Independent Newspapers (Ireland) Ltd. Leave was refused and the applicant appealed to the Supreme Court. The cartoon portrayed a caricature of a rotund priest holding a host in one hand and a chalice in the other. The cartoon depicted him offering the host to three figures, portraying three politicians, Mr Prionsias de Rossa, Mr Ruairí Quinn and Mr John Bruton who are turned away from the priest and appear to be waving goodbye. Above the cartoon were printed the words "Hello progress - bye bye Father" followed by a question mark.[79] The applicant claimed that the cartoon was calculated to insult the feelings and religious beliefs of the newspaper readers. Barrington J, speaking for the Supreme Court, discussed the meaning of blasphemy. He commented that blasphemy is not

---

[71] *ibid.*

[72] See Law Reform Commission, *Consultation Paper on the Crime of Libel* (August 1991), pp 63–92. See also P O'Higgins, "Blasphemy in Irish Law" (1960) 23(2) MLR 151.

[73] These concepts are not dealt with specifically within Art 10 of the ECHR, but have still been litigated as part of a general freedom of expression.

[74] See, for example, s 7(2) of the Censorship of Films Act 1923.

[75] O Doyle, *supra* n 7, p 205.

[76] Law Reform Commission, *Consultation Paper on the Crime of Libel* (August 1991), p 231.

[77] *Constitutional Review Group Report*, *supra* n 3, p 274.

[78] *Corway v Independent Newspapers (Ireland) Ltd* [1999] 4 IR 484.

[79] This seemed to reference a phrase used during the referendum campaign by some of the campaigners against divorce, i.e. "Hello divorce—bye bye daddy".

defined in the Constitution or in an Act of the Oireachtas and then turned to the definition of the concept in Murdoch's Dictionary:

> "The crime which consists of indecent and offensive attacks on Christianity, or the Scriptures, or sacred persons or objects calculated to outrage the feelings of the community. The Constitution declares that the publication or utterance of blasphemous matter is an offence which shall be punishable in accordance with law... The mere denial of Christian teaching is not sufficient to constitute the offence".[80]

Barrington J then went on to comment:

> "There is no doubt that the crime of blasphemy exists as an offence in Irish Law because the Constitution says so. It says that the publication or utterance of blasphemous matter *'is an offence which shall be punishable in accordance with the law'.* Yet the researches of the Law Reform Commission would appear to indicate that the framers of the Constitution did not intend to create a new offence. This may explain why there is no statutory definition of blasphemy. The Censorship of Films Act, 1923 s. 7(2) and s. 13(1) of the Defamation Act, 1961 assume that the crime exists without defining it. It would appear that the legislature has not adverted to the problem of adapting the common law crime of blasphemy to the circumstances of a modern State which embraces citizens of many different religions and which guarantees freedom of conscience and a free profession and practice of religion".[81]

He went on to conclude that given the uncertainty of the law on blasphemy the Court "could not see its way to authorising the institution of a criminal prosecution for blasphemy against the Respondents".[82] This judgment was criticised by Cox, who stated: **[10–26]**

> "It may well be that blasphemy as a crime should not exist at Irish law, being an unwarranted restriction on the right to freedom of expression . . . This, however, is not the point. The people endorsed a constitution that *did* require that blasphemy be a crime. The Courts, as guardians of the Constitution are bound to enforce the terms of that constitution without fear or favour and in a spirit of political and social independence. The failure of the Supreme Court to do so in *Corway*, on the grounds that a constitutional term was of uncertain definition, was passive judicial activism in stark form and amounted to a subtle yet telling attack on the grounding principles of constitutional democracy".[83]

Following on from the lack of definition in *Corway*, and in spite of the comments of the Law Reform Commission in 1991 that "there is no place for the offence of blasphemous libel in a society which respects freedom of speech",[84] the Defamation **[10–27]**

---

[80] H Murdoch, *Murdoch's Dictionary of Irish Law* (Topaz Publications, Dublin, 1988), quoted in *Corway v Independent Newspapers (Ireland) Ltd* [1999] 4 IR 484 at 11.

[81] *Corway v Independent Newspapers (Ireland) Ltd* [1999] 4 IR 484 at 36.

[82] *ibid* at 38.

[83] N Cox, "Constitutional Law-Constitutional Interpretation-Passive Judicial Activism-Constitutional Crime of Blasphemy" (2000) 22 DULJ 21.

[84] Law Reform Commission, *Consultation Paper on the Crime of Libel* (August 1991), p 231. The Law Reform Commission felt that the Prohibition of Incitement to Hatred Act 1989 sufficed to protect religious belief in this matter.

Act 2009[85] was enacted. The 2009 Act abolished the common law offence of sedition (s 35) but an offence of blasphemy (and an interesting definition of blasphemy) was added to the statute books (s 36).[86]

B. ECHR

[10–28] Article 10:

> "(1)Everyone has the right to freedom of expression. This right shall include freedom to hold opinions and to receive and impart information and ideas without interference by public authority and regardless of frontiers. This Article shall not prevent States from requiring the licensing of broadcasting, television or cinema enterprises.
>
> (2) The exercise of these freedoms, since it carries with it duties and responsibilities, may be subject to such formalities, conditions, restrictions or penalties as are prescribed by law and are necessary in a democratic society, in the interests of national security, territorial integrity or public safety, for the prevention of disorder or crime, for the protection of health or morals, for the protection of the reputation or rights of others, for preventing the disclosure of information received in confidence, or for maintaining the authority and impartiality of the judiciary."

1. Nature of the Right

[10–29] This freedom has been described as the "essential foundation of a democratic society".[87] Autonomy is a key feature of the theory of liberal democracy. Without the free flow of ideas it can be argued that self-fulfilment and real participation in democracy is impossible, and Art 10 is therefore concerned with the right of an individual citizen to be free from unreasonable restrictions on his or her freedom of expression by the State.[88] As with all qualified rights, any restriction which the State seeks to justify must be proportionate, necessary, prescribed by law and refer to one of the legitimate aims outlined in the Article itself.

---

[85] Act No 31 of 2009.

[86] s 36 states: "(1) A person who publishes or utters blasphemous matter shall be guilty of an offence and shall be liable upon conviction on indictment to a fine not exceeding €25,000. (2) For the purposes of this section, a person publishes or utters blasphemous matter if— (a) he or she publishes or utters matter that is grossly abusive or insulting in relation to matters held sacred by any religion, thereby causing outrage among a substantial number of the adherents of that religion, and (b) he or she intends, by the publication or utterance of the matter concerned, to cause such outrage. (3) It shall be a defence to proceedings for an offence under this section for the defendant to prove that a reasonable person would find genuine literary, artistic, political, scientific, or academic value in the matter to which the offence relates. (4) In this section 'religion' does not include an organisation or cult—(a) the principal object of which is the making of profit, or (b) that employs oppressive psychological manipulation—(i) of its followers, or (ii) for the purpose of gaining new followers."

[87] UN Human Rights Council, Resolution 7/36.

[88] It is possible to discern a sort of hierarchy of speech within the overarching term. Political discourse would be at the top of the pyramid, gossip and indecent material at the base. See, e.g. *Sunday Times v UK* (1979) 2 EHRR 245 and *Von Hannover v Germany* (2005) 43 EHRR 1. See also the comments of Lady Hale in *Jameel v Wall St Journal* [2006] UKHL 44.

The main areas of significance in the use of Art 10 have been those of public interest speech[89] and the freedom of the Press,[90] usually clashing with Art 8 rather than any other provision. However, it has also been defined as covering a variety of different methods of expression – artistic production (painting, sculpture, drama, film, photography) and public protest, and covers, most importantly, not only the right to impart information, but also to receive it. Its particular importance was acknowledged in the drafting of s 12 of the UK Human Rights Act 1998,[91] and it is the only ECHR right that explicitly carries with it responsibilities and it can be legitimately restricted by the State on a whole range of grounds.[92]

Parameters of Protection

Article 10 protects both positive and negative rights. An example of a negative right is the right to remain silent and not to incriminate oneself. This is protected by Art 10 and there is a general rule that one should be presumed innocent until proven guilty.[93] However, even this negative right is not absolute.[94] An illustration of this is the case of *Brown v Stott (Procurator Fiscal),*[95] where the need to find out the driver of a car who had committed an offence was for the general good of society.[96] **[10–30]**

In addition, it is clear that the ECtHR will carefully consider whether the use of Art 10 is applicable where the State has other authority collateral to it, as in the cases of *Glasenapp*[97] and *Kosiek,*[98] where the applicants wished to join the German civil service, which takes significant notice of an applicant's political leaning. In this instance the ECtHR found that access had been limited not by political views, but by qualification, thereby putting the issue outside the remit of Art 10. This may be contrasted with the cases of *Otto v Germany*[99] and *Vogt v Germany,*[100] where political views were again an issue, but the applicants were already employed, and the ECtHR considered that the

---

89 *Sunday Times v UK* (1979) 2 EHRR 245.

90 *Lingens v Austria* (1986) 8 EHRR 407, *Jersild v Denmark* (1994) 19 EHRR 1.

91 "(4) The court must have particular regard to the importance of the Convention right to freedom of expression and, where the proceedings relate to material which the respondent claims, or which appears to the court, to be journalistic, literary or artistic material (or to conduct connected with such material), to—

(a) the extent to which—

  (i) the material has, or is about to, become available to the public; or

  (ii) it is, or would be, in the public interest for the material to be published;

(b) any relevant privacy code."

92 For example, English legislation and common law restrict what can be said about terrorism, court proceedings, someone else's reputation, race, religion, secrets (official and private) obscene or indecent materials.

93 This compliments Art 6.

94 *Funke v France* (1993)16 EHRR 297, *K v Austria* (1993) No 16002/90, judgment of June 6[1] 1993 at para 46.

95 [2001] 2 All ER 97.

96 Confirmed by the ECtHR in *O'Halloran and Francis v UK* (2005) 46 EHRR 21.

97 *Glasenapp v FRG* (1986) 9 EHRR 25.

98 *Kosiek v FRG* (1986) 9 EHRR 328.

99 No 27574/02, 24 November 2005.

100 (1995) 21 EHRR 205.

main issue was not employment opportunity, but an interference with freedom of expression, and therefore within the material scope of Art 10.

[10–31] Interestingly, Art 10 also requires a degree of horizontal application in that a State has a positive obligation to ensure that citizens can use the right of expression in terms of effective communication.[101] Although the ECtHR has declined to offer definitive guidance on the extent to which the horizontal effect of the ECHR may be relied upon,[102] it can be seen from a number of cases that there does exist a positive obligation on the State in certain situations. This, however, varies depending on "... considerations of distributive justice and the equitable allocation of resources required for different administrative tasks ...",[103] and the fact that " ... regard must be had to the fair balance that has to be struck between the general interest of the community and the interests of the individual".[104]

[10–32] In this last case, the ECtHR emphasised its view of the importance of Art 10 in terms of a private person exercising violence or the threat of violence in order to subdue the free speech of another, in this case the Press. It should be noted that the newspaper in question was not a State entity, but was failed by the State in that its repeated requests for protection were not given sufficient weight or acted upon by the Turkish Government. Similarly, in *Fuentes Bobo v Spain,*[105] where a public criticism of a radio station led to the lawful dismissal of a broadcaster, the ECtHR decided that the Spanish Government had failed in its duty to safeguard freedom of expression from threats. This case can be compared with the earlier case of *Rommelfanger v FRG,*[106] where the stance of the Catholic Church with respect to abortion was brought into question by a doctor employed by a Catholic hospital. In this instance, the right of the employer to dismiss the doctor was upheld as the positive obligation on the State did not go beyond what was a reasonable compulsion on the doctor to agree with the Church's doctrine on such a fundamental Catholic issue.

Total Freedom?

[10–33] One might consider that freedom of expression gives a right to information, and Art 10(1) does indeed include "freedom ... to receive ... information", but it is clear from the ECtHR that this does not include a general right.[107] Those cases where the right was denied generally concern the right of a citizen to access information held by the government, with the telling comment that:

> "Article 10 does not, in circumstances such as those of the present case, confer on the individual a right of access to a register containing information on his personal position,

[101] A Clapham, *Human Rights in the Private Sphere* (Clarendon Press, Oxford, 1993), p 231.
[102] *VGT Verein gegen Tierfabriken v Switzerland* (2001) EHRR 159.
[103] *Appleby v UK* (2003) 37 EHRR 38 at para 40.
[104] *Ozgur Gundem v Turkey* (2001) 31 EHRR 49 at para 43.
[105] *Fuentes Bobo v Spain* (2001) 31 EHRR 50 No 39293/98.
[106] No 12242/86, judgment of 6 September 1989.
[107] *Leander v Sweden* (1987) 9 EHRR 433, *Gaskin v UK* (1989) 12 EHRR 36.

> nor does it embody an obligation on the Government to impart such information to the individual".[108]

Even given the qualification of the first sentence, it is clear that the ECtHR has taken a specific view on the right of access to government data. Whilst there was an interpretation of the European Commission of Human Rights in *Guerra v Italy*[109] which gave residents at risk of potential health hazards the right to information from their local authority, the ECtHR continued with a more limited viewpoint.[110] The present stance may be taken from *Sirbu v Moldova*:

> "[t]he negative state duty of freedom to receive information ... basically prohibits a government from restricting a person from receiving information that others wish or may be willing to impart to him ... (and) ... cannot be construed as imposing on a State, in circumstances such as those of the present case, positive obligations to disclose to the public any secret documents or information concerning its military, intelligence service or police".[111]

Press and Political Freedom of Expression

There is an inevitable overlap between the Press and the political sphere, and the ECtHR has frequently emphasised[112] the central role it considered that the reporting of political speech and personnel had as being vital in a functioning democracy: [10–34]

> "Freedom of the press ... affords the public one of the best means of discovering and forming an opinion of the ideas and attitudes of political leaders. More generally, freedom of political debate is at the very core of the concept of a democratic society which prevails throughout the Convention".[113]

This suggests that any argument restricting press censorship will be more difficult for the State to justify, with the ECtHR referring to the press as having the "vital role" of "public watchdog".[114] The obverse is also true, that political representatives should have a degree of privileged protection, given the public interest of having informed debate.[115]

To this end, the ECtHR has introduced interpretive tools such as "chilling effect" and "less restrictive alternative", so that in the case of *Lombardo*,[116] even a relatively low level of damages awarded against local councillors for their criticism of local authority would be considered to have a "chilling effect" on their right to free speech and the [10–35]

---

108 *Leander v Sweden* (1987) 9 EHRR 433 at para 74.
109 (1998) 26 EHRR 357 at para 43.
110 *Guerra v Italy* (1998) 26 EHRR 357 at para 53.
111 *Sirbu v Moldova*, Nos. 73562/01, 73565/01, 73712/01, 73744/01, 73972/01 and 73973/01, 15 June 2004 at para 18.
112 For example, *Mathieu-Mohin and Clerfayt v Belgium* (1987) 10 EHRR 1, *Bowman v UK* (1998) 26 EHRR 1, *Sener v Turkey* (2003) 37 EHRR 34 No 26680/95 at para 40, *Lombardo v Malta* (1999) 48 EHRR 23 No. 7333/06.
113 *Lingens v Austria* (1986) 8 EHRR 40 at para 42.
114 *Observer and Guardian v UK* (1991) 14 EHRR 153 at para 59 (The "Spycatcher" Case).
115 *Lombardo v Malta* (1999) 48 EHRR 23 No 7333/06 para 53.
116 *Lombardo v Malta* (1999) 48 EHRR 23 No 7333/06.

true democratic process. This also has a counterpart in the higher legislative field, so that parliamentarians can effectively pursue their debates,[117] and that an individual might fully contribute with the interest of the whole body politic in mind.

[10–36] With regard to the election process itself, as demonstrated in the case of *Bowman v UK*,[118] the ECtHR will also take a wide view of any restriction of free speech on those making their opinions known. In this case, Bowman, a prominent anti-abortionist, had her organisation distribute 1.5 million leaflets during the 1992 Parliamentary elections, stating the particular view of each candidate on abortion, thereby violating a 1983 Statute which prohibited any individual not running for office from spending more than £5 "... with a view to promoting or procuring the election of a candidate".[119]

[10–37] Whilst the Statute specifically made an exception for the media, and had a legitimate aim in securing equality between the candidates,[120] it had still to fulfil the requirement of Art 10(2), in that the restriction on freedom of expression had to be one which was "necessary in a democratic society". The restriction was found to be disproportionate since it "...operated for all practical purposes as a total barrier to (the applicant's) publishing information with a view to influencing the voters".[121] Although the ECtHR, in Grand Chamber, acknowledged that the restriction was only applicable during an election, it also felt that distribution at times other than at elections would not have served the same purpose, and that the cost to Bowman of standing for election would not have been realistic, given the cost and likely forfeit of deposit. Since neither press comment on politicians nor political advertising by the main parties had any particular restrictions placed upon them during elections, it was the right of Ms Bowman to publish information which was of relevance to political debate.[122]

[10–38] The seminal case on press freedom is probably *Sunday Times v UK*,[123] in which the ECtHR emphasised that the *Handyside* principles[124] were of especial importance as regards freedom of the Press. The result of the ruling is that account must now be taken of the amount of public interest in the case, since this is what will determine the level of interference which may be exercised on that freedom, as demonstrated by the case of *Observer and Guardian v UK*,[125] so that, whilst restraint is not prohibited as such by Art 10, the dangers of such action, particularly on the Press, would require the exercise of enhanced scrutiny. Certainly in cases such as *Castells v Spain*,[126] it is clear that this

---

[117] *Cordova v Italy* (2003) 40 EHRR 974.
[118] (1998) 26 EHRR 1.
[119] s 75 of the Representation of the People Act 1983.
[120] That of preventing wealthy third parties from campaigning for or against a particular candidate.
[121] *Bowman v United Kingdom* (1998) 26 EHRR 1 at para 47.
[122] It should be noted that in *Janowski v Poland* (1999) 29 EHRR 705, the insulting of civil servants was not a violation of an Art 10 right, in that they did not, in this instance, " ... form part of an open discussion of matters of public concern."
[123] (1979) 2 EHRR 245.
[124] Namely, that freedom of expression constitutes one of the essential foundations of a democratic society, and forms one of the basic conditions for both its progress and that of the development of every man.
[125] (1991) 14 EHRR 153.
[126] (1992) 14 EHRR 445.

scrutiny is expected to be exercised not only by public and legislative bodies, but, in turn, by the public in the form of public opinion, informed by a free Press. Nor should there be unreasonable obstructions to that reporting function, so that the conviction and fining of a journalist on the grounds of criminal defamation was disproportionate, in that the subject he was investigating, that of police brutality, was one of legitimate public concern.[127] Nor can there be unreasonable restrictions on access to reportage. In the case of *Gsell v Switzerland*,[128] concerning State interference with the reporting of a protest, the State view that there was a clear and present danger was outweighed by a lack of need for the emergency provision banning reportage and the total lack of evidence that the applicant would cause any disturbance.

2. Legitimate Justifications for Interference with the Right

In general, the ECtHR gives contracting States a wide margin of appreciation when it comes to policing the sort of moral or religious expression they allow, suggesting that what may be acceptable on the streets or in the Press of a liberal country may legitimately be prohibited in a neighbouring State. The ECtHR, however, takes a much narrower view on restrictions to political expression since such State censorship plainly strikes at the heart of democratic values. The ECtHR has consistently maintained that any State interference with Art 10 rights must be justified by "imperative necessities", stating that: **[10–39]**

> "The Court's supervisory functions oblige it to pay the utmost attention to the principles characterising a 'democratic society'. Freedom of expression constitutes one of the essential foundations of such a society, one of the basic conditions for its progress and for the development of every man. [Article 10(2)] is applicable not only to 'information' or 'ideas' that are favourably received or regarded as inoffensive or as a matter of indifference, but also to those that offend, shock or disturb the state or any sector of the population".[129]

The ECtHR has also commented that in its decision making there must be seen to be "...pluralism, tolerance and broadmindedness without which there is no 'democratic society'".[130]

This means, amongst other things, that every "formality", "condition", "restriction" or "penalty" imposed in this sphere must be proportionate to the legitimate aim pursued.[131]

Confidential Sources

In order to pursue investigative journalism in the public interest, it is essential that journalists can insist on source confidentiality, even though the State will often wish to **[10–40]**

---

[127] *Thorgeirson v Iceland* (1992) 14 EHRR 843.
[128] No 12675/05, 8 October 2009.
[129] *Handyside v UK* (1979–80) 1 EHRR 737 at para 49. This might look at first as though claiming freedom of expression might be a trump card – but it is not. See, e.g. *Re W (Children)* [2005] EWHC 1564 (Fam).
[130] *Vereingung Demokrtatischer Soldaten Osterrichs and Gubi v Austria* (1994) 20 EHRR 56 at para 36.
[131] *Handyside v UK* (1979–80) 1 EHRR 737 at para 49.

find out the identity of the person who has divulged what is, usually, highly confidential information.[132] Once again, one can easily discern the "chilling effect" that enforced source disclosure would have on reportage, but it is also necessary for compromise where there can be seen to be other issues at stake, hence, the ECtHR has consistently given a narrow margin of appreciation to contracting States.[133] In addition the ECtHR has made the point that " ... protection of journalistic sources is one of the basic conditions for press freedom, as is reflected in the laws and the professional codes of conduct in a number of Contracting States".[134]

[10–41] It is necessary, therefore, to consider the balance found by the ECtHR in the protection of journalistic sources against the wider public interest. In the case of *Goodwin,*[135] the applicant, who was a trainee journalist with "The Engineer" magazine, received phone information regarding the financial status of a company. Although the source wished to remain anonymous, the information appeared to come from a confidential corporate plan, one copy of which had gone missing. The company subsequently obtained an order preventing the applicant from disclosing the confidential information and, under s 10 of the UK Contempt of Court Act 1981, required the applicant to divulge the identity of his source. Goodwin appealed unsuccessfully to the UK Court of Appeal and House of Lords, refusing to disclose his source, and was subsequently fined £5,000.

[10–42] The ECtHR, if it was to uphold an interference with freedom of expression, must have found that it was "prescribed by law", hence, s 10 of the Contempt of Court Act 1981 must have fulfilled the requirements of precision and foreseeability of precision and foreseeability, and this it duly found. However, publication of the confidential information was already prohibited by an injunction, and therefore the order for disclosure of the source was not necessary, and thus in breach of Art 10. It was made clear that the company had legitimate reasons for disclosure, namely to prevent further dissemination of the confidential information (other than by publication) and to take action against the source, who was presumed to be an employee. The ECtHR held, however, that these reasons had to be subservient to the public interest of a free press in a democratic society.

[10–43] However, in the need for prevention of disorder or crime, the ECtHR may have to consider a different viewpoint, as illustrated by the case of *Nordisk Film and TV A/S v Denmark*,[136] where an undercover journalist infiltrated a paedophile association in order to make a documentary. The police, investigating serious child abuse, obtained an order for the company to produce unedited covert footage and the reporter's notes. The issue turned, for the ECtHR, on defining a source. Since those who were

[132] See: H Fenwick and G Phillipson, *Media Freedom Under the Human Rights Act* (Oxford University Press, Oxford, 2006), chapter 9.

[133] *Sanoma Utigevers BV v Netherlands* (2010) 51 EHRR 31, where the ECtHR insisted that there should be independent legal assessment of safeguards in order to assess whether the interests of criminal investigation can override public interest, particularly that of the protection of journalistic sources.

[134] *Goodwin v the United Kingdom* (1996) 22 EHRR 123 at para 39.

[135] *Goodwin v the United Kingdom* (1996) 22 EHRR 123.

[136] No 40485/02, 8 December 2005.

inadvertently participating in the documentary could not knowingly have consented to being sources, they could not be considered to be in danger of the "chilling effect" doctrine on future participation. This being the case, there could not be an issue with their freedom of expression, and so only the reporter had the putative right under Art 10. Since the ECtHR was asking the company not for sources, but for its own research material, then the proportionality of the interference was deemed to be justified.

If the identification of an individual is involved, then the ECtHR will usually start at a presumption that the interference is not justified. When an article was published concerning a government minister and a tax scandal, the journalist found himself the subject of a surprise raid under very wide-ranging search warrants. The evident aim of this was not the uncovering of evidence *per se*, but the identification of individuals who had informed the journalist, presumably breaching confidence.[137] **[10–44]**

Plainly, the ECtHR considers that the public interest in freedom of expression must override that of source identification unless there is a compelling reason for it to be otherwise, and the State should take that into account when considering such an interference with the right.

Defamation

There is an inevitable overlap between Arts 8 and 10, and this is clearly seen in the area of defamation, where a person's right to protection of his or her privacy and family from untrue statements which may be damaging must be balanced against freedom of expression and press freedom. This can be seen clearly in the UK case of *Campbell v Mirror Group Newspapers Ltd*[138] where the paper had published stories about celebrity model, Naomi Campbell, relating to her attendance at Narcotics Anonymous meetings, although she had previously stated publicly that she did not take drugs. The House of Lords held that the publication of the fact that Ms Campbell was seeking treatment was necessary to set the record straight given her previous statements, but the additional information, including the photographs, was an unjustified intrusion into her private life. Balancing the competing interests, in this particular case, the right to privacy under Art 8 outweighed freedom of expression under Art 10.[139] **[10–45]**

It is worth noting that Art 10(2) specifically allows for restriction on the grounds of protection for the rights or *reputations* of others.

Obviously, this provision makes it plain that the law of defamation in any particular contracting State is not generally incompatible with reasonable restriction on free speech, but that the law should have sufficient clarity to be able to fit within the **[10–46]**

[137] *Roemen and Schmit v Luxembourg*, No 51772/99, 25 February 2003. Also *Ernst v Belgium* (2003) 37 EHRR 724.

[138] [2005] 1 WLR 3394.

[139] *Douglas v Hello! Magazine (No 3)* [2005] 3 WLR 881. The phrase in s 12(4) of the Human Rights Act 1998 to "have particular regard" for Art 10 ECHR rights was taken to mean having equal regard for the limitations to the right contained in the second paragraph of Art 10, which included "the rights and reputations of others"; in other words, the court must have equal regard for Art 8 rights.

requirement of being "prescribed by law". So whilst there is a wide margin of appreciation of the needs of the State,[140] the basic requirement of the ECtHR is that any legal requirement must be proportionate and must not have any effect of unnecessary restriction on free speech.

[10–47] There is a widespread supposition that public figures, by their very nature, must expect a degree of scrutiny, and particularly when the public figure is a politician; by undertaking a political role, he or she opens him- or herself up knowingly for examination[141] and must, therefore, expect to show a greater degree of tolerance to criticism.[142] The reverse also holds, that on retirement from public life, the figure reverts to the status of a private citizen, with commensurately less tolerance to criticism[143] and a greater expectation of respect for his or her privacy.

[10–48] The ECtHR has considered the matter of defamation in terms of value judgments and factual assertions, the latter being more concerned with evidentiary proof than the former, but there is often no clear line of distinction,[144] and so requires careful individual examination in each case. If the statement of fact is not proven to be true, then there is defamation, but the ECtHR has taken care to focus on specific points when considering whether they fall into a particular category.[145]

In Lingens,[146] where the criminal defamation conviction was held to be disproportionate, the relevant comments were, taken in an overall context of political debate on Fascism, more offensive than defamatory. *Oberschlick (No 2)*[147] followed this reasoning by stating that the description of a leading politician as "an idiot" was not defamatory on the grounds that it was an opinion (and therefore a value judgment not requiring the same evidential burden as a factual statement), and hence, was protected under Art 10.

[10–49] In considering the need for proof, a journalist would be required to produce *prima facie* evidence,[148] and it is clear that "[it is] not in principle incompatible with Article 10 to place on a defendant in libel proceedings the onus of proving to the civil standard the truth of defamatory statements".[149] However, in the case where the statements may contain false assertions, the ECtHR may also consider the motivation of the individual as to publication. In the case of *Salov v Ukraine*,[150] a presidential candidate was convicted of falsehood when a limited number of "forged" newspapers suggested that the late president had died of an alcoholic disease and that he had a "criminal

---

140 See, for example, *Tolstoy Miloslavsky v UK* (1995) 20 EHRR 442.
141 *Lingens v Austria* (1986) 8 EHRR 407.
142 *Oberschlick v Austria* (1995) 19 EHRR 389, *Oberschlick v Austria (No 2)* (1998) 25 EHRR 357.
143 *Tammer v Estonia* (2001) 37 EHRR 857.
144 *Krone Verlag nGmbH and Co KG and MEDIAPRINT Zeitungs –und Zeitschriftenverlag GmbH and Co KG v Austria*, No 42429/98, 20 March 2003.
145 *Tolstoy Miloslavsky v UK* (1995) 20 EHRR 442.
146 *Lingens v Austria* (1986) 8 EHRR 407.
147 *Oberschlick v Austria (No. 2)* (1997) 25 EHRR 357.
148 *McVicar v UK* (2002) 35 EHRR 566.
149 *Steele and Morris v UK* (2005) 41 EHRR 403.
150 (2007) 45 EHRR 51 No 65518/01, 6 September 2005.

entourage" which had staged a *coup d'etat*. However, the ECtHR found there was no evidence that the applicant had intended to deceive voters and he had not personally produced the information, whether true or untrue. In contrast, the case of *Perna v Italy*[151] concerned a public prosecutor, suggested by a journalist to have abused his authority in bringing proceedings against a political figure, Mr Andreotti, for aiding and abetting the mafia. The suggestion was that the prosecutor, Mr Caselli, was acting from a political motive. The ECtHR found that these were factual assertions, and, since the journalist could not adduce any evidence for them ever having occurred, there was clear evidence of defamation.

C. CFR

The freedom of expression is protected under Art 11 of the CFR.[152] This states: **[10–50]**

> "1. Everyone has the right to freedom of expression. This right shall include freedom to hold opinions and to receive and impart information and ideas without interference by public authority and regardless of frontiers.
>
> 2. The freedom and pluralism of the media shall be respected."

Paragraph 1 of Art 11 is very similar to the protection afforded to the right to freedom of expression under Art 10 of the ECHR, and in line with Art 52(3) of the CFR, the meaning and scope of this right are the same as those guaranteed by the ECHR. In addition, the limitations which can legitimately be imposed on the right may not exceed those set out in Art 10(2) of the ECHR. However, this is without prejudice to any limitations which EU law may impose on Member States in relation to licensing arrangements provided for in Art 10(1) of the ECHR.

Paragraph 2 focuses on the freedom of the media and is based on Council Directive 89/552/EEC,[153] the Protocol on the System of Public Broadcasting in the Member States[154] and on case law of European Court of Justice (ECJ) (now the Court of Justice), including *Stichting Collectieve Antennevoorziening Gouda*.[155]

Given the nature of the EU, the main focus of the right to freedom of expression is in the area of commercial activity and the ECJ dealt with numerous cases concerning this **[10–51]**

---

151 (2003) 36 EHRR 944.

152 The explanation of the Praesidium with regard to the interpretation of this provision is discussed below, see: http://infoportal.fra.europa.eu/InfoPortal/infobaseShowContent.do?btnCat_300&btnCountryBread_169, last accessed 21 June 2012.

153 Council Directive 89/552/EEC of 3 October 1989 on the coordination of certain provisions laid down by Law, Regulation or Administrative Action in Member States concerning the pursuit of television broadcasting activities [1989] OJ L298/23. This Directive was repealed by Art 34 of Directive 2010/13/EU.

154 *Protocol on the system of public broadcasting in the Member States*, Protocol annexed to the Treaty of Amsterdam amending the Treaty of the European Union, the Treaties establishing the European Communities and certain related acts (Treaty of Amsterdam. See D Ward, "State aid or band aid? An evaluation of the European Commission's approach to public service broadcasting" (2003) 25 MedCulSoc 233.

155 Case C-288/89, [1991] ECR I-4007.

aspect of the right to freedom of expression in the past.[156] One of the most controversial cases was that of *Grogan v Ireland*,[157] which subsequently came before the ECtHR.[158] The case concerned the distribution in Ireland by student unions of information on abortion services in the United Kingdom. The abortion services constituted a service within the meaning of Art 60 EEC Treaty, but the Court's decision focused on the tenuous link between the student unions and the service providers and the ECJ held that the Irish Government's restriction on freedom of expression did not fall for consideration under Art 59 of the EEC Treaty.

D. International and Regional Laws

[10–52] The importance of the freedom of expression was highlighted very early on in the international human rights framework of the UN. Indeed, at the very first session of the UN General Assembly in 1946, Resolution 59(I) was adopted, stating "Freedom of information is a fundamental human right and... the touchstone of all the freedoms to which the United Nations is consecrated."

Article 19 of the Universal Declaration of Human Rights[159] states:

> "Everyone has the right to freedom of opinion and expression; this right includes freedom to hold opinions without interference and to seek, receive and impart information and ideas through and media and regardless of frontiers."

[10–53] Smith comments that the "drafters of the United Nations Declaration envisaged freedom of expression as a means of securing the full exchange of information intra- and internationally".[160] This was followed and expanded by Art 19 of the International Covenant on Civil and Political Rights (ICCPR)[161] which states:

> "1. Everyone shall have the right to hold opinions without interference.
> 2. Everyone shall have the right to freedom of expression; this right shall include freedom to seek, receive and impart information and ideas of all kinds, regardless of frontiers, either orally, in writing or in print, in the form of art, or through any other media of his choice.
> 3. The exercise of the rights provided for in paragraph 2 of this article carries with it special duties and responsibilities. It may therefore be subject to certain restrictions, but these shall only be such as are provided by law and are necessary:
> (a) For respect of the rights or reputations of others;

[156] For an analysis of the main cases concerning freedom of expression before the ECJ, see G Halami, "Article 11: Freedom of Expression" in *Commentary by the EU Network of Independent Experts on Fundamental Rights* (June 2006), pp 115–123, available at: http://infoportal.fra.europa.eu/InfoPortal/infobaseShowContent.do?btnCat_300&btnCountryBread_169, last accessed 21 June 2012.

[157] Case C-159/90, *The Society for the Protection of Unborn Children Ireland Ltd* [1991] ECR I-4685 (judgment of 4 October 1991).

[158] *Open Door Counselling and Dublin Well Women v* (1993) 15 EHRR 244.

[159] Universal Declaration on Human Rights 1948.

[160] R Smith, *Textbook on International Human Rights Law* (5th ed, Oxford University Press, Oxford, 2012), p 303.

[161] International Covenant on Civil and Political Rights 1966.

(b) For the protection of national security or of public order (ordre public), or of public health or morals".[162]

Article 20 then prohibits any war propaganda and the advocacy of national, racial or religious hatred constituting incitement to discrimination, hostility or violence. Cases before the Human Rights Committee have illustrated the expansive interpretation given to the meaning of "expression" in the international human rights framework, which include the waving of protest banners, artistic expression, etc.[163] **[10–54]**

At a regional level, the right to freedom of expression is protected under Art 13 of the American Convention on Human Rights,[164] Art 9 of the African Charter on Human and Peoples' Rights,[165] and Art 32 of the Arab Charter on Human Rights.[166]

Conclusion

While the right to freedom of expression under the Irish Constitution initially received little attention, since the incorporation of the ECHR into Irish law, the nature of the right to freedom of expression has been increasingly debated in Irish courts. The **[10–55]**

---

[162] In relation to the limitations on Art 19 of the ICCPR, see the case of *Faurisson v France* (CCPR/C/58/D/550/1993). Mr Faurisson had stated that Nazi Concentration camps did not contain gas chambers. The Human Rights Committee found that limitations on his freedom of expression were necessary under Art 19(3).

[163] See the case of *Kivenmaa v Finland* (CCPR/C/50/D/412/1990).

[164] This provision states: "1. Everyone has the right to freedom of thought and expression. This right includes freedom to seek, receive, and impart information and ideas of all kinds, regardless of frontiers, either orally, in writing, in print, in the form of art, or through any other medium of one's choice. 2. The exercise of the right provided for in the foregoing paragraph shall not be subject to prior censorship but shall be subject to subsequent imposition of liability, which shall be expressly established by law to the extent necessary to ensure: a. respect for the rights or reputations of others; or b. the protection of national security, public order, or public health or morals. 3. The right of expression may not be restricted by indirect methods or means, such as the abuse of government or private controls over newsprint, radio broadcasting frequencies, or equipment used in the dissemination of information, or by any other means tending to impede the communication and circulation of ideas and opinions. 4. Notwithstanding the provisions of paragraph 2 above, public entertainments may be subject by law to prior censorship for the sole purpose of regulating access to them for the moral protection of childhood and adolescence. 5. Any propaganda for war and any advocacy of national, racial, or religious hatred that constitute incitements to lawless violence or to any other similar action against any person or group of persons on any grounds including those of race, color, religion, language, or national origin shall be considered as offenses punishable by law."

[165] This provision states: "1. Every individual shall have the right to receive information. 2. Every individual shall have the right to express and disseminate his opinions within the law."

[166] This provision states: "1. The present Charter guarantees the right to information and to freedom of opinion and expression, as well as the right to seek, receive and impart information and ideas through any medium, regardless of geographical boundaries. 2. Such rights and freedoms shall be exercised in conformity with the fundamental values of society and shall be subject only to such limitations as are required to ensure respect for the rights or reputation of others or the protection of national security, public order and public health or morals."

influence of the ECHR on the interpretation of this right is nowhere clearer than in the case of *Mahon v Keena*[167] where the Supreme Court relied almost completely on the ECHR provision and ECtHR case law with regard to the right to freedom of expression, rather than on Art 40.6.1°(i) of the Constitution. Indeed, Daly comments that "[i]n *Keena*, Article 40.6.1°(i) almost disappears completely".[168] Daly goes on to comment that: "Irish democracy has long waited for its final cornerstone, free speech, to be built. It is unfortunate, then, that this cornerstone is being constructed by marginalising the very instrument, Bunreacht na hÉireann, on which our democratic State is founded". Given the international acceptance of the right to freedom of expression as a basic requirement of a democratic society and its prevalence in international and regional instruments, it is suggested that additional scrutiny of the nature of limitations of the Irish constitutional provision is needed, perhaps with a view to amendment, in order to ensure stronger protection for this basic right.

---

167 *Mahon v Keena* [2010] 1 IR 336.
168 T Daly, *supra* n 2 at 242.

CHAPTER 11
The Right to Freedom of Religion

Introduction

Religion or belief is an essential aspect of the human personality and as such receives express protection under the Irish Constitution, the European Convention on Human Rights (ECHR) and the Charter of Fundamental Rights (CFR). The concept of freedom of religion covers a wide variety of issues from non-discrimination on grounds of religion, to freedom of thought, conscience and religion and the freedom to manifest one's religion. These rights are protected to various extents at national and regional level and are subject to specific limitations in certain contexts. However, what ties all the provisions together is an absolute protection of the right to freely choose a belief or non-belief. This chapter will elucidate the principles of the freedom of religion at a national, regional and international level. **[11–01]**

A. Irish Constitutional Protection

[11–02]

> "1. The State acknowledges that the homage of public worship is due to Almighty God. It shall hold His Name in reverence, and shall respect and honour religion.
>
> 2. 1° Freedom of conscience and the free profession and practice of religion are, subject to public order and morality, guaranteed to every citizen.
>
> 2° The State guarantees not to endow any religion.
>
> 3° The State shall not impose any disabilities or make any discrimination on the ground of religious profession, belief or status.
>
> 4° Legislation providing State aid for schools shall not discriminate between schools under the management of different religious denominations, nor be such as to affect

> prejudicially the right of any child to attend a school receiving public money without attending religious instruction at that school.
>
> 5° Every religious denomination shall have the right to manage its own affairs, own, acquire and administer property, movable and immovable, and maintain institutions for religious or charitable purposes.
>
> 6° The property of any religious denomination or any educational institution shall not be diverted save for necessary works of public utility and on payment of compensation"

1. Nature of the Right

[11–03] Unlike other rights in the Irish Constitution, which are generally grouped together in an Article of the Constitution, the protection of the freedom of religion is guaranteed by Art 44 exclusively, signalling "its importance in Irish society".[1] The dominance of the Roman Catholic Church in Irish society and its influence on the drafters of the Constitution is certainly reflected in this Article. The religious guarantee of Art 44 has rarely reached the courts and there are only a few decisions analysing the nature and scope of the provision. Casey comments that whenever this issue has come before the courts:

> " ... its central concern has been the influence of the majority Roman Catholic Church on certain issues of public policy—censorship of publications, education and, especially, family matters being among them".[2]

This chapter will elucidate those principles that are readily discernible from the case law on the constitutional guarantee.

What is a "Religion" for the Purposes of Article 44?

[11–04] While the definition of "religion" has never been considered by the Irish courts as a distinct issue in a case, there have been some judicial statements on the issue. It has been stated, *obiter*, that Art 44 protects "traditional and popular religions and religious denominations"[3] such as Roman Catholicism, the Church of Ireland and the Presbyterian Church and is not restricted to the Christian religion "but extended to other religious denominations".[4] In *Re Article 26 and the Employment Equality Bill 1996*[5] the Supreme Court, *obiter*, in determining the meaning of "religious denomination" for the purposes of Art 44.2.5°, held that a clearer picture of what is meant by this term could be drawn from the provisions of the old Art 44.1.2° which was deleted by the fifth amendment to the Constitution in 1972. This article referred expressly to the special position of the Holy Catholic Apostolic and Roman Church as Guardian of the faith professed by the majority of the citizens. Equally, the old Art 44.1.3° (also deleted in 1972) provided for recognition of the Church of Ireland, the Presbyterian Church, the Methodist Church, the Religious Society of Friends, as well as the Jewish

---

1 J Casey, *Constitutional Law in Ireland* (3rd ed, Round Hall Sweet & Maxwell, Dublin, 2000) at p 685.

2 *ibid* at 687.

3 *Temple Street v D and Another* [2011] IEHC 1 at para 27 (*per* Hogan J).

4 See *McGee v Attorney General* [1974] IR 284 at 317 (*per* Walsh J).

5 *Re Article 26 and the Employment Equality Bill 1996* [1996] 2 IR 321.

congregations and "the other religious denominations existing in Ireland at the date of the coming into operation of this Constitution".[6]

However, Art 44 also protects "minority religions and religious denominations whose tenets are regarded by many as unconventional". In this respect in the case of *Temple Street v D and Another,*[7] Hogan J held that Jehovah's Witnesses would fall into this latter category and were therefore protected under Art 44.[8] This wide definition of religion would appear to be based on the idea that it is not for the State to determine which religions are orthodox and which are not or to be the arbiter of religious truth.[9]

Some direction on the definition of religion might also be gleaned from the Defamation Act 2009 which introduced an offence of blasphemy.[10] In this regard, the definition of religion is not elucidated in the legislation. However, the definition of what does not constitute a religion is included. The Act provides that the term "religion" for the purposes of the blasphemy law, does not include an "organisation or cult (a) the principle object of which is the making of profit, or (b) that employs oppressive psychological manipulation—(i) of its followers, or (ii) for the purpose of gaining new followers".[11] **[11–05]**

What is Protected by Article 44?

Article 44 protects a wide variety of issues relating to religion including respect and honour for religion (Art 44.1), freedom of conscience and free profession and practice of religion (Art 44.2.1°), a prohibition on endowment of religion (Art 44.2.2°), protection against religious discrimination (Art 44.2.3°), protection against discrimination in the provision of State-aid to schools and the right of a child not to attend religious instruction in a school receiving public money (Art 44.2.4°), the right of religious denominations to certain property rights (Art 44.2.5°) and the protection of the property of religious denominations and educational institutions from diversion of their property (Art 44.2.6°). **[11–06]**

Article 44.1 (Respect and Honour for Religion)

This provision of Art 44 is reminiscent of the terms of the Preamble and is explicable when one considers the historical context in which the Constitution was drafted. The influence of the Roman Catholic Church at the time of drafting the Constitution was paramount and this provision reflects the important place that religion held in society at the time. Despite its obvious historical significance, the legal implication of this provision is not very clear and has not been considered by the courts. Some references **[11–07]**

---

6 See the old Art 44.1.3°, as deleted by the Fifth Amendment to the Constitution, 1972.

7 *Temple Street v D and Another* [2011] IEHC 1. See further RB Flowers "Freedom of Religion versus Civil Authority in Matters of Health" (1979) 446 Annals Amer Acad Pol & Soc Sc 149; MR Brown, "The Psychedelic Perspective: The Freedom of Religion Defense" (1983) 11(2) Am Indian LR 125; R Heywood "Parents and medical professionals: conflict, cooperation, and best interests" (2012) 20(1) MedLR 29.

8 *Temple Street v D and Another* [2011] IEHC 1 at para 28 (*per* Hogan J).

9 See the case of *West Virginia Board of Education v Barnette* (1943) 319 US 624. See in the Irish context, *Corway v Independent Newspapers* (1999) 7 JIC 3006.

10 s 36, Defamation Act 2009.

11 s 36(4), Defamation Act 2009.

have been made to it *obiter* in certain judgments, such as in the case of *Quinn's Supermarket Ltd v Attorney General*[12] where Walsh J noted that the "Constitution reflects a firm conviction that we are a religious people" but more importantly indicated that Art 44.1 does "not confine the benefit of that acknowledgement to members of the Christian faith".[13] Therefore, despite the very obvious references to the Roman Catholic faith, Art 44.1 provides for respect and honour for all religions.

Article 44.2.1° (Freedom of Conscience, Free Profession and Practice of Religion)

[11–08] Article 44.2.1° protects against interferences with freedom of conscience, free profession and the free practice of religion. These interferences can arise through State action or through the action of private parties.[14] However, these rights are not absolute and are subject to limitations on the grounds of public order and morality. The case law to date has focussed most specifically on the protection of freedom of profession and practice of religion and few cases have centred on the issue of freedom of conscience, an issue that has received more significant attention under the ECHR (see below).

Freedom of Conscience

[11–09] Some references to the nature and scope of Art 44.2.1° can be found in the case of *McGee v Attorney General.*[15] The case highlights the remit of freedom of conscience as protected under Art 44.2.1°. This case involved a 27-year old mother of four who was informed by her medical advisor that another pregnancy would carry serious risks and would put her life at risk due to certain medical complications. She decided, with her husband, to import contraceptive jelly from the UK which was confiscated by the Customs Authorities as it was contrary to s 17 of the Criminal Law (Amendment) Act 1935 which made it a criminal offence to import contraceptives into Ireland. Mrs McGee argued that this was contrary, inter alia, to her social conscience which was protected by Art 44.2.1°. The Supreme Court held that as the whole context of Art 44 was related to religion, the protection of freedom of conscience was not a "constitutional guarantee of a right to live in accordance with one's conscience subject to public order and morality. What the Article guarantees is the right not to be compelled or coerced into living in a way which is contrary to one's conscience and, in the context of the Article, that means contrary to one's conscience so far as the exercise, practice or profession of religion is concerned".[16] Therefore, Art 44.2.1° does

---

[12] *Quinn's Supermarket Ltd v Attorney General* [1972] IR 1 at p 23 (*per* Walsh J).

[13] *ibid.*

[14] See J Casey, *supra* n 1 at p 695 who cites the Employment Equality Act 1998 (as amended by the Equality Act 2010) and its prohibition on religious discrimination (s 6 as amended) as an example of the fact that the State has the power to restrict private citizens from infringing on the principles of Art 44. See also the discussion in the US context in Case Note "Freedom of Religion as Basis for Access to Private Apartment Buildings" (1948) 48(7) CLR 1105. See also the restriction on landlords: R Cannon"The Bigoted Landlord: A Re-Examination of Schlegel v Corcoran and Gross [1942] IR 19" (2005) 12(1) DULJ 248.

[15] *McGee v Attorney General* [1974] IR 284 at pp 316–317 (*per* Walsh J).

[16] *ibid.*

not protect social conscience, as claimed by Mrs McGee in this case, but protects religious conscience.

This certainly raises the issue of conscientious objectors in a military or employment context. This debate has arisen in Ireland recently in the context of civil partnership. In the debates surrounding the promulgation of the Civil Partnership and Certain Rights and Obligations of Cohabitants Act 2010, it was argued that an exemption should be included for registrars who had a conscientious objection to performing civil ceremonies.[17] While it was eventually decided that no such exemption would be allowed, the constitutional compatibility of this provision with Art 44 is worth considering. It is arguable that the provisions of the Act, in not allowing an exemption, are compatible with the Constitution despite the strong protections inherent in Art 44. First, from the decision in *McGee*, it would appear clear that only if this objection were found to be a conscientious objection based on a religious ground would it fall to be protected under Art 44. Secondly, even if such an objection had a religious basis, there is also an issue as to whether the courts would draw a distinction between working life and private life. The court in *McGee* clearly held that a person had right not to be compelled or coerced into "living" in a way which was contrary to one's conscience. While Art 44 might protect the right of an individual to practice his or her religious conscience in their private life, this might not extend to working life, particularly where the work involved is of a public nature and paid for from public funds. Finally, the protected right is subject to certain limitations based on public order and morality. **[11–10]**

Freedom of Profession and Practice of Religion

The nature and scope of the protection of the profession and practice of religion and the manner in which it can be interfered with can be seen in the case of *Quinn's Supermarket Ltd v Attorney General*.[18] In this case, the court had to assess the compatibility of a Ministerial Order of 1948 made under the Shops (Hours of Closing) Act 1938. This Act provided that butcher shops were restricted to certain hours of business but that kosher shops were exempt from these regulations. The plaintiff was prosecuted when he opened his store (a non-kosher shop) in defiance of these regulations. The plaintiff argued that this was discrimination on grounds of religion based on Art 44.2.3°. Walsh J agreed that this amounted to discrimination on grounds of religion under Art 44.2.3° but held that if the order did not exist, the right of members of the Jewish faith to practice and profess their religion would be interfered with in contravention of Art 44.2.1°. The Supreme Court made some interesting statements in relation to Art 44.2.1° and in relation to what might constitute an interference with such a right. **[11–11]**

First, the court held that the overall purpose of Art 44 was to guarantee free practice of religion. Secondly, in certain circumstances, this would require the State to make legislative distinctions (such as the exemption of kosher shops from legislation) to achieve this free practice and profession of religion. Thirdly, this is subject to public **[11–12]**

[17] See as a useful US comparison on this point Case Note "Freedom of Religion. Exemption of Conscientious Objectors from Military Service" (1943) 43(1) CLR 112.

[18] *Quinn's Supermarket Ltd v Attorney General* [1972] IR 1.

order and morality. In this case, the court held that as the measure was disproportionate, it was contrary to Art 44.2.3°.

Article 44.2.2 (No Endowment of Religion)

[11–13] This particularly direct provision of Art 44.2.2° provides that the State shall not endow any religion.[19] The courts have held that the term "endow" refers to the "vesting of property or income in a religion as such in perpetual or quasi-perpetual form"[20] and the "selection of a favoured State religion for which permanent financial provision is made out of taxation or otherwise".[21] Any action of this type is therefore constitutionally prohibited. The Supreme Court has also held that concurrent endowment, that is the vesting of property or income in all religions concurrently, is also prohibited by Art 44.2.2°.[22]

[11–14] Some conflict has arisen in this context in relation to the provision of public funds to religious orders that are running hospitals. Does this constitute an unconstitutional endowment of property or income on a religion? There appears to be no clear consensus on this point. While there is some merit in the view that this action is not unconstitutional as the prohibition in Art 44.2.2° applies only in relation to endowments for an exclusively religious purpose, there is also merit in the argument that such hospitals are run in a manner which is religious (so for example certain treatments or procedures may not be carried out in such hospitals where such treatments or procedures are contrary to the rules of the religion concerned) and so the provision of public funds is therefore endowing a particular religion.

[11–15] Similar arguments can be made in relation to the public funding of certain denominational schools in Ireland. This was considered in the case of *Campaign to Separate Church and State v Minister for Education*[23] where the plaintiff argued that the public funding of school chaplains was a violation of Art 44.2.2°. The Supreme Court dismissed the claim. The Supreme Court considered that the provision of public funds to schools had a long tradition in Ireland and that had become a "central feature of the Irish schools system".[24] There was also explicit reference to the State-aid of schools in Art 44.2.4° which was clearly contemplated by the framers of the Constitution. In this regard, the Supreme Court held that the payment of monies to a denominational school for educational purposes is not an endowment of religion.[25]

---

19 See as an interesting US comparison "Use of Taxation and Licensing in the Suppression of Freedom of Religion and the Press" (1942) 52(1) YLJ 168.

20 *Campaign to Separate Church and State v Minister for Education* [1998] 2 ILRM 81 at 88 (*per* Keane J).

21 *Re Article 26 and the Employment Equality Bill 1996* [1996] 2 IR 321 at 354.

22 *supra* n 20.

23 *ibid.*

24 *ibid.*

25 *ibid.* See also *Re Article 26 and the Employment Equality Bill 1996* [1996] 2 IR 321 at 354.

This prohibition on endowment of religion has also been interpreted as including an implicit prohibition on the establishment of a religion in the State.[26] In the case of *Campaign to Separate Church and State v Minister for Education*[27] the court held that:

> "[w]hile there was no express provision in the Constitution prohibiting the establishment ... of a church by law, it is obvious that any such law would be impossible to reconcile with the prohibition of religious discrimination in Art 44.2.3°".[28]

It was argued in the case of *McNally and Reilly v Attorney General*[29] that the law (s 99 of the Charities Act 2009) which made it an offence to sell Mass cards which were not the subject of an arrangement with a bishop or order of priests of the Roman Catholic Church, was contrary to Art 44 on the grounds that it amounted to a quasi-establishment of a religion.[30] The High Court disagreed that this amounted to quasi-establishment. MacMenamin J held that the State: **[11–16]**

> " ... need not always be entirely neutral and these are matters in which it may engage to the limited degree permissible, provided such process does not discriminate or impose a religious disability".[31]

Article 44.2.3° (Non-Discrimination on Grounds of Religion)

In a manner comparable with many constitutions, regional and international agreements, the Irish Constitution protects individuals from the imposition of disabilities and from discrimination on the grounds of religious profession, belief or status. There are a number of interesting questions that arise in relation to the definition, scope and extent of this provision which have been considered by the Irish courts and it is one of the most utilised of the protections inherent in Art 44. **[11–17]**

What Does Discrimination Mean?

The definition of discrimination would appear to refer specifically to the creation of "distinctions", "differences" or "to distinguish" between persons or bodies on grounds of religious profession, belief or status.[32] It would appear to cover instances of both direct and indirect discrimination.[33] One of the seminal cases in this area is the case of *Quinn's Supermarket Ltd v Attorney General*[34] concerning the exemption of kosher butcher stores from the closing times imposed on other butchers. In defining discrimination, Walsh J **[11–18]**

---

[26] See in the US context: C Siler, "The Establishment Clause: Teaching First Amendment Rights Using Primary Sources" (1990) 5(1) OAH Magazine of History 35. See also for a more general discussion: WG Katz, "Freedom of Religion and State Neutrality" (1953) 20(3) UCLR 426; A Zimmermann and LD Weinberger "Secularization by law? The establishment clauses and religion in the public square in Australia and the United States" (2012) 10(1) IJCL 208.

[27] *Campaign to Separate Church and State v Minister for Education* [1998] 2 ILRM 81.

[28] *ibid* at 88 (*per* Keane J).

[29] *McNally and Reilly v Attorney General* [2009] IEHC 573.

[30] See E Daly, "Regulating Religious Function: The Strange Case of Mass Cards" (2010) 9(1) HLJ 55.

[31] *McNally and Reilly v Attorney General* [2009] IEHC 573 at para 172 (*per* Macmenamin J).

[32] See *Quinn's Supermarket Ltd v Attorney General* [1972] IR 1 at 16 (*per* Walsh J).

[33] J Casey, *supra* n 1 at p 698.

[34] *Quinn's Supermarket Ltd v Attorney General* [1972] IR 1.

held that to discriminate is "to create a difference between persons or bodies or to distinguish between them".[35] In this case, the legislation exempting the kosher shops from the regulations was discriminatory and even though it was necessary to ensure the free practice of religion, was disproportionate in the circumstances.

[11–19] A useful example of such an interference is the case of *Mulloy v Minister for Education*[36] in which the plaintiff, a teacher and a priest, challenged certain regulations made by the Minister which provided that teachers who had spent time teaching in certain developing countries could count that service for salary increment and pension purposes when they returned home to Ireland. However, these regulations only applied to lay teachers. The court held that this scheme made a clear distinction between lay teachers and teachers who were members of a religious order. This amounted to discrimination on grounds of religious status and could not be justified as it was not necessary to implement the constitutional right to practice religion.[37] Walsh J held that if this distinction were constitutionally permissible "it would enable the State to prefer religious to lay people, or vice-versa, in a matter which is in no way concerned with the safeguarding or maintenance of the constitutional right to free practice of religion or freedom of conscious or of profession of religion".[38]

[11–20] The protection in Art 44 protects against both positive and negative discrimination. In the case of *McNally and Reilly v Attorney General*[39] which concerned a law (s 99 of the Charities Act 2009) which made it an offence to sell Mass cards which were not the subject of an arrangement with a bishop or order of priests of the Roman Catholic Church, the issue of religious discrimination contrary to Art 44.2.3° arose. MacMenamin J in the High Court considered the concepts of both preferential or detrimental discrimination. While most discrimination is negative in that it causes some loss or "disability" to the plaintiff on religious grounds, "it is not necessary to establish a constitutional religious detriment".[40] In this case, the plaintiff argued that the law created a preferential discrimination in favour of the Roman Catholic Church. The High Court, in this case, held that any question of preferential treatment must be seen against the background of Art 44.2.5° pertaining to denominational autonomy and free practice guarantee in Art 44.1. MacMenamin J held that there are occasions in which the State may recognise and buttress the tenets of a particular religion, insofar as it does not in any way impinge on the beliefs of other denominations or citizens.[41] However, the limited support in this case for the Roman Catholic Church:

> " ... does not constitute any prejudicial State intrusion or discrimination where the status of a priest or an organised religion is advanced justifiably over a lay person or a business".[42]

---

[35] *ibid* at 16 (*per* Walsh J).
[36] *Mulloy v Minister for Education* [1975] IR 88.
[37] *ibid* at 96 (*per* Walsh J).
[38] *ibid.*
[39] *McNally and Reilly v Attorney General* [2009] IEHC 573.
[40] *ibid* at para 160 (*per* MacMenamin J).
[41] *ibid* at para 165 (*per* MacMenamin J).
[42] *ibid* at para 166 (*per* MacMenamin J).

All that was required here was simple evidential proof from a Bishop or an order of priests. There are many laws which require similar proofs from religious bodies such as marriage laws and private statutes regulating hospitals.

What are the Covered Grounds of Discrimination?

The Constitution clearly states that discrimination on grounds of religious profession, belief or status is prohibited. In the *Mulloy*[43] case, the Supreme Court clarified the meaning of these terms. The Supreme Court held that "profession" refers to the particular faith professed by an individual, "belief" refers to their particular beliefs and includes non-belief, and "status" refers to a person's rank or position in a given religion.[44] In the case of *Mulloy,*[45] it was the status ground, that is, the fact that Father Mulloy was a priest that constituted the grounds of discrimination. Therefore, the provision can be considered to be very broad in that it covers various aspects of the practice of religion from the non-believer to the member of the religious orders. **[11–21]**

Another illuminating example is the case of *M v An Bord Uchtála*[46] in which the plaintiffs, a married couple, sought to adopt the child of the wife who was born outside of wedlock. However, s 12 of the Adoption Act 1952 provided that an adoption order could only be made if the adoptive parents were of the same religion as the child's parents or, if the child was born outside of wedlock, its mother. The Adoption Board refused to make the order on the basis that the mother's husband was of a different religion. The plaintiffs argued that this was discrimination by the State on the grounds of religious profession and belief. The court held that s 12 was unconstitutional on the grounds that it precluded a couple from different religions from adopting a child and was in breach of Art 44.2.3°. **[11–22]**

To Whom Does the Guarantee Apply?

The wording of Art 44.2.3° is particularly clear. It refers expressly to the actions of the State. Therefore the State cannot discriminate on grounds of religion. While, private parties are not prohibited from discriminating on grounds of religion under the Constitution, legislation places many restrictions in this area for employers and the providers of goods and services.[47] Just because a private entity receives public funds does not make it an entity or agent of the State for the purposes of Art 44.2.3°. Therefore, in the case of *McGrath and Ó Ruairc v Trustees of the College of Maynooth*[48] the fact that Maynooth University was receiving funds from the Higher Education Authority did not mean that it was a State entity. To read the constitutional guarantee in this way would be an unwarranted extension of the plain words of the Constitution. **[11–23]**

---

43 *Mulloy v Minister for Education* [1975] IR 88.

44 *ibid* at 91 (per Butler J). See also Walsh J at 96. See also the discussion in the US context in Case Note "Freedom of Religion, the Atheist, and the Torcaso Case" (1961) 47(2) VLR 315.

45 *ibid.*

46 *M v An Bord Uchtála* [1975] IR 81.

47 See the Employment Equality Acts 1998–2004 and the Equal Status Acts 2000–2004.

48 *McGrath and Ó Ruairc v Trustees of the College of Maynooth* [1979] ILRM 166.

Article 44.2.4° (State-aid for Schools and the Right of the Child to Opt Out of Religious Instruction)

[11–24] This unusual provision clearly protects the historical relationship between denominational schools and the State. The provision makes it clear that the State cannot discriminate in the provision of funding to denominational schools, a clear exception to the non-endowment principle established in Art 44.2.2°. Equally, the provision makes it clear that the child has a right (one of the only express references in the Constitution to the rights of the child) to opt out of religious instruction in a publically funded school.

[11–25] While these provisions may appear to be rather benign, there has been some debate in relation to the right of the child to opt out of religious instruction and the integrated curriculum established by the Department of Education in 1971 which encouraged the integration of secular and religious education.[49] Casey argues that this makes opting out impossible[50] and it certainly raises the possibility of a "conflict of rights" between the right to opt out of religious instruction and the right of denominational schools to provide an integrated curriculum and other measures to preserve the religious ethos of the school.[51] The Constitutional Review Group[52] argue that publically funded denominational schools should provide for separate secular and religious instruction and Casey comments that there should be a reversion to the pre-1971 situation in which the provision of religious instruction was timetabled separately to other subjects so that students could opt out if they were of an alternative faith. This issue has particular significance in primary schools where there is no separate timetabling of classes.

[11–26] However, another line of argument is identifiable in the Supreme Court in *Campaign to Separate Church and State v Minister for Education,*[53] where Barrington J made an important distinction between religious education and religious instruction. Barrington J held that "a child who attends a school run by a religious denomination different from his own may have a constitutional right not to attend religious instruction at the school but the Constitution cannot protect him from being influenced, to some degree, by the religious "ethos" of the school. A religious denomination is not obliged to change the general atmosphere of its school merely to accommodate a child of a different religious persuasion who wishes to attend that school".[54] While this view has been questioned by some academics who argue that it might not be so easy to distinguish religious education and religious instruction in this way,[55] it is arguable that

[49] See G Whyte, "Education and the Constitution: Convergence of Paradigm and Praxis" (1990) 25(1) Ir Jur 69.
[50] J Casey, *supra* n 1 at p 701.
[51] *Constitution Review Group Report* (Stationery Office, Dublin, 1996) at p 386.
[52] See R Barrett, "Church and State in Light of the Report of the Irish Constitution Review Group" (1998) 5(1) DULJ 51.
[53] *Campaign to Separate Church and State v Minister for Education* [1998] 2 ILRM 81.
[54] *ibid* at 357–358 (*per* Barrington J).
[55] O Doyle, *Constitutional Law: Text, Cases and Materials* (Clarus Press, Dublin, 2008) at p 302.

the decision of Barrington J in this case is an eminently sensible one that balances the right of the child and the rights of the school in a fair and just manner.[56]

Article 44.2.5° (Property Rights of Religious Denominations)

Article 44.2.5° provides that religious denominations shall have the right to manage their own affairs, own, acquire and administer property, moveable and immovable, and maintain institutions for religious and charitable purposes. This provides a clear autonomy for religious institutions to manage their own affairs without State interference in relation to doctrine, worship and ordination.[57] In *Re Article 26 and the Employment Equality Bill 1996,*[58] the Supreme Court shed some light on this particular provision. In particular, it noted that Art 44.2.5° includes the right to control religious, educational or medical institutions either directly or indirectly (e.g. though a board of trustees or guardians).[59] **[11–27]**

While again this may seem to be a very obvious addition, considering the religious influence in the drafting of the Constitution, this particular provision has led to modern developments such as a limitation on the right to equality on grounds of religion in employment in the Employment Equality Act 1998. Section 37(1) of this Act provides that a religious, educational or medical institution which is under the direction or control of a body established for religious purposes or whose objectives include the provision of services in an environment which promotes certain religious values shall not be taken to discriminate against a person if (a) it gives more favourable treatment, on the religion ground, to an employee or a prospective employee over that person where it is reasonable to do so in order to maintain the religious ethos of the institution, or (b) it takes action which is reasonably necessary to prevent an employee or a prospective employee from undermining the religious ethos of the institution. This provision clearly undermines the protection against discrimination on grounds of religion and would appear to ratify the decision in *Flynn v Power*[60] in which a female teacher, who had a relationship with a married man and had a child out of wedlock was dismissed on the grounds that she openly rejected the norms of behaviour and the ideas which the school promoted. The High Court held that as the school was a religious one, the respondents were entitled to conclude that "her conduct was capable of damaging their efforts to foster in the pupils norms of behaviour and religious tenets which the school had been established to promote"[61] and therefore her dismissal was not unfair.[62] **[11–28]**

Section 37(1) was considered in the Art 26 reference to the Supreme Court of the *Employment Equality Bill 1996*.[63] The court referred to its previous case law relating to **[11–29]**

[56] See for an interesting comparison with the US on the issue of science instruction: Case Note "Freedom of Religion and Science Instruction in Public Schools" (1978) 87(3) YLJ 515.

[57] J Casey, *supra* n 1 at p 702.

[58] *Re Article 26 and the Employment Equality Bill 1996* [1997] 2 IR 321.

[59] *ibid* at 354.

[60] *Flynn v Power* [1985] IR 648.

[61] J Casey, *supra* n 1 at p 704.

[62] See G Whyte, "Protecting Religious Ethos in Employment Law: A Clash of Cultures" (2005) 12(1) DULJ 169.

[63] *Re Article 26 and the Employment Equality Bill 1996* [1997] 2 IR 321.

discrimination and held that a discrimination could be justified as long as it has as its aim the free practice and profession of religion. An interesting argument in the case related to whether the definition of "ethos" in s 37(1) was to be considered to be an objective (from the view of the court) or subjective (from the view of the religious order) one.[64] The Supreme Court held that the term "ethos" was to be interpreted in a subjective manner and that "each religious denomination should be respected when it says what its ethos is".[65] The role of the court will be to determine whether the measures taken to meet this ethos are reasonable or reasonably necessary in the circumstances. Casey argues that the effect of s 37(1) is to give the principle of church autonomy primacy over other constitutional values.[66] Schools, hospitals and other institutions run by religious orders are given a specific exception to the non-discrimination principle that is not available to other employers and this will apply regardless of the fact that they are in receipt of State funds.

[11–30] Another illuminating example in relation to the autonomy of religious orders is the case of *McGrath and Ó Ruairc v Trustees of the College of Maynooth*.[67] In this case the court had to consider whether the statutes of the College of Maynooth (Ireland's national seminary and pontifical university) which authorised the dismissal of Mr McGrath and Mr Ó Ruairc were constitutional with regard to Art 44.4.3°. The statutes provided that as Mr McGrath, who was at the time a priest, did not wear his clerical dress in College and had, without the required permission, published writing prejudicial to ecclesiastical authority and that as Mr O'Ruairc had been laicised and continued to teach in the seminary, they had committed infringements and could be dismissed. The plaintiffs argued that these Statutes violated their right to non-discrimination on religious grounds in that a lay person was treated differently from a priest, imposing greater obligations on priests and particularly in light of the fact that the character of Maynooth had changed in that Maynooth was now a State university as it received funds from the Higher Education Authority. The Supreme Court rejected this argument on the basis of Art 44.2.5°. The court held that Maynooth was still a seminary and was thus a religious institution within the meaning of Art 44.2.5° which had specific autonomy to manage its own affairs.

Article 44.2.6° (Diversion of Property of any Religious Denomination)

[11–31] This particular section makes provision for the payment of compensation in the case of the diversion of the property of any religious denomination. It also provides that no such diversion should occur unless it is necessary for works of public utility. There has only been one very recent case dealing specifically with this issue. It is an illuminating decision highlighting some the main questions inherent in Art 44.6.2° as helpfully elucidated by Casey.[68]

64 *ibid* at 350–352.
65 *ibid* at 359.
66 J Casey, *supra* n 1 at p 703.
67 *McGrath and Ó Ruairc v Trustees of the College of Maynooth* [1979] ILRM 166.
68 J Casey, *supra* n 1 at p 706.

What does "Property of Any Religious Denomination Mean"?

A plain reading of this term would suggest that it refers to any of the property of any religious denomination. While there are some questions over property held on trust for certain purposes, Casey has suggested that this term should be defined as referring to "property which, directly or indirectly, comes under the aegis of a religious denomination"[69]. In the case of *Sister Mary Christian and Others v Dublin City Council*[70] the High Court accepted that the land owned by the religious order involved which had been zoned in the Dublin Development Plan in a manner claimed to be unlawful by the religious order, was property within the meaning of Art 44.2.6°. The treatment of Art 44.2.6° in the case appeared to view property as defined for the purposes of the property rights guarantee and property for the purposes of Art 44.2.6° as being interchangeable. Therefore, perhaps the definition of property in Art 44.2.6° is in fact the same as that defined for the purposes of the property rights guarantee. **[11–32]**

What does "Proprty of Any Religious Denomination Mean"?

While academics have described the use of the term "divert" variously as "odd", and of merely historical interest and clearly conveying the idea of "taking or acquisition",[71] the only decision shedding any light on this issue is that of *Sister Mary Christian and Others v Dublin City Council.*[72] **[11–33]**

In that case Clarke J considered the term "divert" and asked whether it was "merely an antiquated form of a description for something in the nature of compulsory acquisition?" or could "properly be said to have been diverted by some lesser form of interference?"[73] In the case at hand, the plaintiffs argued that the extent of the interference with their ability to use their lands brought about by the zoning in the development plan, amounted to such a "significant restriction on their ability to use the lands in question in a beneficial way such as to render it a 'diversion' of the lands in question".[74] Clarke J held that if this was the case and zoning did amount to a diversion, then it would be impermissible having regard to the terms of Art 44.2.6°. On the facts, Clarke J did not find it necessary to reach a definitive conclusion on whether there may be measures "short of the full transfer of ownership of all interests in land or property away from a religious or educational institution" that might amount to a diversion for the purposes of Art 44.2.6°.[75] However, he did consider that some form of *de facto*, as opposed to *de jure* deprivation, might amount to a diversion. In this regard, he held that it was likely that "a requirement without compensation to enter into a form of lease which would give the right to occupy institutional property to some third party even though not removing full ownership would amount to a 'diversion'."[76] However, on the facts, it did not consider that a restrictive form of zoning that was otherwise "justified and proportionate",[77] could amount to a diversion for the purposes **[11–34]**

---

[69] *ibid* at p 707.

[70] *Sister Mary Christian and Others v Dublin City Council* [2012] IEHC 163.

[71] J Casey, *supra* n 1 at p 707.

[72] *Sister Mary Christian and Others v Dublin City Council* [2012] IEHC 163.

[73] *ibid* at para 12.21 (*per* Clarke J).

[74] *ibid* at para 12.22 (*per* Clarke J).

[75] *ibid* at para 12.23 (*per* Clarke J).

[76] *ibid* at para 12.23 (*per* Clarke J).

[77] *ibid* at para 12.24 (*per* Clarke J).

of Art 44.2.6°. He based this decision on three factors. First, the lands in question still remained fully owned by the institution. Secondly, the lands could still be used for their existing purposes "be it school, hospital or the like"[78]. Thirdly, where it becomes necessary to develop the lands further for those institutional purposes, or for some limited form of non-institutional purpose, "permission can be obtained".[79] In conclusion, the zoning, while restrictive, fell "far short of any type of transfer of the benefit of ownership of lands which might be regarded as a 'diversion' for the purposes of Art. 44.2.6°".

Therefore, it is clear that a *de jure* taking or acquisition would be a diversion within the meaning of Art 44.2.6°. It is also clear that a *de facto* taking might also amount to a diversion as long as it completely deprives the owner of any use or enjoyment of the property.

What Does "Necessary Works of Public Utility" Mean?

[11–35] The term "necessary works of public utility" has been described as a term "bristling with difficulties".[80] "Public utility" could cover everything from roads and railways to drainage, lighting, water and power. However, the term "necessary" would appear to refer to some type of proportionality test relating to the necessity to deprive the institution of their property to carry out these "public works".

What is the Definition of "Educational Institution"?

[11–36] The term "educational institution" can be read in two ways. First, it could be considered to refer to any educational institution regardless of the religious or non-religious nature of the institution. Secondly, it could be read in light of Art 44 and refer only to "religious educational institutions".[81] There have been no judicial decisions on this point so it is difficult to say which the courts would prefer although the situation of the phrase in Art 44, instead of in Art 42 dealing with education, would appear to lend support to the latter interpretation.

2. Legitimate Interferences with the Rights

[11–37] As there are various different justifications related to each right, the rights and their limitations will be considered in turn, followed by a consideration of the principle of proportionality which applies in relation to each right.

Article 44.2.1°: Freedom of Conscience, Practice and Profession of Religion

[11–38] Article 44.2.1° provides that the freedom of conscience, practice and profession of religion are subject to limitations in the interests of public order and morality. This is also subject to a proportionality test which will be considered below. Crimes such as bigamy, human sacrifice, child labour and manslaughter on the grounds of religious motivation, while all associated with religious practices, can be prohibited on the grounds of public order and morality. Casey has commented that the "range of situations where an asserted religious belief may conflict with legal provisions seems

[78] *ibid.*
[79] *ibid.*
[80] J Casey, *supra* n 1 at p 707.
[81] *ibid* at p 708.

virtually limitless".[82] However, in most cases, it is likely that the combination of the presumption of constitutionality and a wide reading of the definition of public order and morality "would suffice to validate the impugned legislation"[83].

A useful example is the case of *Murphy v Independent Radio and Television Commission*[84] relating to s 10(3) of the Radio and Television Act 1988 which provided that no advertisement shall be broadcast which is directed towards any religious end. The Supreme Court in this case held that this was a restriction on the freedom to profess religion. However, this freedom was subject to limitations in the interests of the common good. Applying the proportionality test, Barrington J held that the ban was "rationally connected to the objective of the legislation" and was not "arbitrary, unfair or based on irrational considerations".[85]

Article 44.2.3°: Discrimination on Grounds of Religion

The courts have held that discrimination on grounds of religion is not always constitutionally invalid. Certain distinctions are necessary to achieve the overriding objective of Art 44, which has been held to be the free practice of religion.[86] [11–39]

Proportionality[87]

In all cases, the courts must assess whether the restriction or interference is proportionate in all the circumstances of the case. In the case of *Quinn's Supermarket Ltd v Attorney General*, the Supreme Court held that the interference (legislation which applied to butcher shops but not to kosher butcher shops) was discriminatory but had been necessary to achieve the free practice and profession of religion for people of the Jewish faith. However, in the circumstances, the Supreme Court held that the restriction was disproportionate. The court held that there was no evidence that the free practice of Jewish religion would be hampered in any way by the application of the fixed hours to the kosher meat shops. The Supreme Court did consider that discrimination for the purposes of opening on Saturdays would be constitutional but the terms of the regulations were not capable of being modified by deletion to confine it to Saturdays (the regulations provided an exemption for everyday). Therefore the regulation was invalid as it was disproportionate to the aim sought to be achieved.[88] [11–40]

Another useful example is the case of *Murphy v Independent Radio and Television Commission*[89] in which the plaintiff wished to advertise their seminar about the resurrection of Christ on 98FM. While the radio station had no issue with this, the Independent Radio and Television Commission (a statutory body to regulate this industry) refused them permission to do this on the grounds that it was prohibited by s 10(3) of the Radio and Television Act 1988 which provides that no advertisement [11–41]

---

82 J Casey, *supra* n 1 at p 693.
83 *ibid.*
84 *Murphy v Independent Radio and Television Commission* [1998] 2 ILRM 360.
85 *ibid* at p 374 (*per* Barrington J).
86 *Quinn's Supermarket Ltd v Attorney General* [1972] IR 1.
87 See Lord Hoffmann, "A Sense of Proportion" (1997) 32(1) Ir Jur 49.
88 *Quinn's Supermarket Ltd v Attorney General* [1972] IR 1 at 27 (*per* Walsh J).
89 *Murphy v Independent Radio and Television Commission* [1998] 2 ILRM 360.

shall be broadcast which is directed, *inter alia*, towards any religious or political end. The plaintiff argued that this provision constituted discrimination on grounds of religion as prohibited by Art 44.2.3°. The Supreme Court dismissed the appeal on the grounds that there was no discrimination in this case as the prohibition was directed at material of a particular class and that "[a]ll people in the same position are treated equally". However, there was a limitation on the freedom of the individual to profess and practice religion under Art 44.2.1°. The Supreme Court held that such a right was not unlimited and the court had to consider whether this interference was proportionate in the circumstances. In order to determine this the court applied the test outlined in *Heaney v Ireland*[90] which provides that the means chosen must be (a) rationally connected to the objective and not be arbitrary, unfair or based on irrational considerations; (b) impair the right as little as possible, and (c) be such that their effects on rights are proportionate to the objective. In this case, the Supreme Court held that the limitation placed on the constitutional right was "minimalist"[91] and "very slight".[92] The applicant could advance his views in speech or by writing or by holding assemblies or associating with persons of like mind to himself.

> "He has no lesser right than any other citizen to appear on radio or television. The only restriction placed on his activities is that he cannot advance his views by a paid advertisement on radio or television"[93].

[11–42] Counsel for the applicant argued that a more proportionate measure might have been to have a selective administrative system whereby inoffensive religious advertising would be permitted. However, the court held that the Oireachtas may have thought that this would be inappropriate as it would "involve agents of the State in deciding which advertisements, in this sensitive area would be likely to cause offence and which not".[94] In any case, the Supreme Court was of the view that once the Oireachtas had respected the principle of proportionality, it was not for the court to "interfere simply because it might have made a different decision".[95] This would appear to indicate that as long as the decision of the State meets the proportionality test, the courts will be loath to interfere.

B. Protection under the European Convention on Human Rights

[11–43] Article 9:

> (1) Everyone has the right to freedom of thought, conscience and religion; this right includes freedom to change his religion or belief, and freedom, either alone or in community with others and in public or private, to manifest his religion or belief, in worship, teaching, practice and observance.

---

[90] *Heaney v Ireland* [1994] 3 IR 593 at 607 (*per* Costello J).

[91] *Murphy v Independent Radio and Television Commission* [1998] 2 ILRM 360 and [1999] 1 IR 12 at 26 (*per* Barrington J).

[92] *ibid* at 27 (*per* Barrington J).

[93] *ibid* at 26 (*per* Barrington J).

[94] *ibid* at 27 (*per* Barrington J).

[95] *ibid.*

(2) Freedom to manifest one's religion or beliefs shall be subject only to such limitations as are prescribed by law and are necessary in a democratic society in the interests of public safety, for the protection of public order, health or morals, or the protection of the rights and freedoms of others.

1. The Nature of the Right

This Article is concerned with the protection for an individual's belief, not necessarily his/her religion or faith, as it equally protects a non-belief, and the jurisprudence mainly considers the right to manifest such beliefs.[96] The case law therefore suggests that the State may have the negative duty to desist from interfering with thought, conscience and religion, but also that there is a positive obligation to protect the right. **[11–44]**

The case law is of relatively recent vintage, stemming, in terms of detailed analysis, from the case of *Kokkinakis v Greece*, where the ECtHR considered:

> "It is, in its religious dimension, one of the vital elements that go to make up the identity of believers and their conception of life, but it is also a precious asset for atheists, agnostics, sceptics and the unconcerned."[97]

The Scope of the Right

This case has, therefore, given a broad latitude to the question of religion,[98] and, with the expansion of the number of ECHR signatory States, has led to a commensurate widening of the bodies considered under the Article. One would expect the main world faiths of Christianity,[99] Islam,[100] Buddhism,[101] Judaism,[102] Hinduism[103] and Sikhism[104] to have been represented, but in addition, the scope has been extended to Jehovah's Witnesses,[105] and the Church of Scientology.[106] **[11–45]**

The court has made it clear that "belief" cannot be equated with "opinion", so that while some philosophical beliefs have been given a degree of protection[107], the court has made it clear on a number of occasions that "... not all opinions or convictions constitute beliefs in the sense protected by Art 9(1) of the Convention."[108] This was in

---

[96] N Bratza "The 'precious asset': freedom of religion under the European Convention on Human Rights" (2012) 14(2) Ecc LJ 256.

[97] *Kokkinakis v Greece* (1993) 17 EHRR 397 at para 31.

[98] The ECtHR has, so far, declined to give a definitive definition of a "religion".

[99] *Stedman v UK* (1997) 23 EHRR 168.

[100] *X v UK* (1981) No 8160/78 22 DR 27.

[101] *X v UK* (1975) No 5442/72 1 DR 41.

[102] *D v France* (1983) No 10180/82 35 DR 1993.

[103] *ISKON v UK* (1994) No 20490/92 18 EHRR CD 133.

[104] *X v UK (1982)* No 8231/78 28 DR 5.

[105] *Manoussakis v Greece* (1996) 23 EHRR 387.

[106] *Church of Scientology Moscow v Russia* (2007) 46 EHRR 304. See para 64, where Art 11 was read in the light of Art 9. Also see *The Moscow Branch of the Salvation Army v Russia* [2006] ECHR 72881/01 at paras 74 and 75. See "*The Moscow Branch of the Salvation Army v Russia*" (2006–2007) 17(1) HRCD 53–56.

[107] For example, pacifism, *Arrowsmith v UK* (1978) No 7050/75 19 DR 5, veganism, *H v UK* (1993) 16 EHRR 44, and opposition to abortion in *Knudsen v Norway* (1985) No 11045/84 42 DR 247.

[108] *Pretty v UK* (2002) 35 EHRR 1 at para 82.

the context of the right to assisted suicide being a belief[109], but idealistic[110] aims, or those lacking coherence[111] have also been refused by the court. However, a guideline as to the general judicial mindset may be taken from the comment in *Campbell and Cosens v United Kingdom* that a belief should "... attain a certain level of cogency, seriousness, cohesion and importance"[112], relating to a "...weighty and substantial aspect of human life and behaviour" and, having been found to do so, to then be considered worthy of protection under the ECHR principles.

[11–46] This width of application can be further illustrated within the ECHR since Art 9 is closely formulated, both in the drafting and its interpretation, to freedom of expression under Art 10 and to the right of association under Art 11. In addition, it should be noted that Art 2 Protocol 1[113] concerns religious beliefs in the context of education, and Art 14 makes explicit reference to religious belief as one of the grounds on which discrimination should be prevented:

> "The enjoyment of the rights and freedoms set forth in this Convention shall be secured without discrimination on any ground such as sex, race, colour, language, religion, political or other opinion, national or social origin, association with a national minority, property, birth or other status".

Although the prohibition of discrimination found in Art 14 is limited, since it applies only to "the rights and freedoms set forth" in the ECHR, Protocol 12[114] establishes a more universal prohibition of discrimination in that:

> "... the enjoyment of any right set forth by law shall be secured without discrimination on any ground such as sex, race, colour, language, religion, political or other opinion, national or social origin, association with a national minority, property, birth or other status".

Conscientious Objection

[11–47] There is no specific right to conscientious objection contained within Art 9, which may be particularly relevant in States where military conscription is the norm, although it has been found that a State may choose to substitute a non-military service as an alternative to conscription,[115] without engaging Art 4 ECHR (freedom from slavery,

---

[109] Although the court also considered that this came more under the concept of personal autonomy, and was, therefore more appropriately addressed under Art 8 ECHR. *Pretty v UK* (2002) 35 EHRR 1 at para 82.

[110] *Vereininging Rechtwinkels Utrecht v Netherlands* (1986) 46 DR 200.

[111] *X v FRG (*1978) No 8741/79 24 DR 137.

[112] *Campbell and Cosens v United Kingdom* (1982) 4 EHRR 29 at para 36, though this was in the context of Art 2, Protocol 1.

[113] Art 2 Protocol 1 ECHR: "No person shall be denied the right to education. In the exercise of any functions which it assumes in relation to education and to teaching, the State shall respect the right of parents to ensure such education and teaching in conformity with their own religious and philosophical convictions."

[114] Which has been signed by Ireland, but not yet ratified.

[115] *Grandrath v FRG* (1996) No 2299/64 10 YB 626. A contracting State could decide whether or not to grant a right to recognise conscientious objectors. If such a right was granted, objectors could then be required to perform civilian service as a substitute without any right to be exempted. See also the 1977 Commission decision of *X v Germany* No 7705/76.

servitude or forced or compulsory labour). However, in the recent case of *Bayatyan v Armenia*,[116] concerning Mr Bayatyan's conviction for draft evasion, though leaving open the question of whether the conviction was lawful, the ECtHR considered that since the majority of Council of Europe Member States, including Armenia, had already recognised, both in law and practice, the right to conscientious objection, Art 9 should no longer be read in conjunction with Art 4. It stated that:

> "In this respect, the Court notes that Art 9 does not explicitly refer to a right to conscientious objection. However, it considers that opposition to military service, where it is motivated by a serious and insurmountable conflict between the obligation to serve in the army and a person's conscience or his deeply and genuinely held religious or other beliefs, constitutes a conviction or belief of sufficient cogency, seriousness, cohesion and importance to attract the guarantees of Art 9 (see, *mutatis mutandis, Campbell and Cosans v the United Kingdom*, 25 February 1982, § 36, Series A no. 48, and, by contrast, *Pretty v the United Kingdom*, no. 2346/02, § 82, ECHR 2002 III). Whether and to what extent objection to military service falls within the ambit of that provision must be assessed in the light of the particular circumstances of the case".[117]

Manifestation of Belief

Finally, the drafting of Art 9 means that there are very distinct differences in the internal phrasing, so that the "right to freedom of thought, conscience and religion" is followed by the right to "change his religion or belief"; omitting thought and conscience. This distinction may seem to be relatively unimportant, but when one considers Art 9(2) "freedom to manifest one's religion or beliefs", then it seems clear that the manifestation of religion or belief is protected,[118] whereas manifestations of thought and conscience are not.[119] The obvious corollary to this concept is the suggestion that one may manifest or express one's religion or belief (subject to Art 9(2)), but not actually manifest or "actualise" thought or conscience under Art 9[120]. These aspects are referred to as the internal and external dimensions of Art 9 (the *forum internum*[121] and *forum externum*) and it is the external dimension which most exercises the ECtHR jurisprudence. In its most simplified form, one might say that the gist of the case law from Art 9 is that one can believe whatever one wishes, but may not necessarily manifest those beliefs, and this may require the Court to define the *forum internum* in a narrow channel. **[11–48]**

---

116 *Bayatyan v Armenia* (2006) No 23459/03 Grand Chamber Judgment, 7 July 2011.

117 *ibid* at para 110

118 The implication from this being that freedom of thought, conscience and religion not involving manifestation of belief cannot be subject to State interference, but since this would involve a State interfering with thought processes, this may be something of an Orwellian situation.

119 Which suggests that these may be considered under Art 10 (the "freedom to hold opinions"), with the reservations given by Art 10(2).

120 See M Evans *Religious Liberty and International Law in Europe* (Cambridge University Press, Cambridge, 1997) at p 285.

121 *Van den Dungen v Netherlands* (1995) No 22838/93 DR80 at para 147.

In the case of *Buscarini and others v San Marino*,[122] for example, the applicants, who had been elected to the San Marino Parliament, were required to take an oath[123] on the Bible as a condition of their appointment to office. This, the applicants argued, meant that this *de facto* required the swearing of allegiance to a particular religion, which they were not prepared to do, whilst the government responded with the argument that the oath was more of historical and social than religious significance.

[11–49] The ECtHR, however, agreed with the initial Commission decision that it "would be contradictory to make the exercise of a mandate intended to represent different views of society within Parliament subject to a prior declaration of commitment to a particular set of beliefs", and that the imposition of the requirement could not be deemed to be "necessary in a democratic society".[124] This, rather neatly, made it unnecessary for the court to consider an examination of the *forum internum.*

In terms of the issue of the expulsion of non-nationals to States where there may be the possibility of religious persecution, this has, likewise, been considered narrowly, with the court overtly stating that they will not impose "... an obligation on contracting States effectively to act as indirect guarantors of freedom of worship for the rest of the world".[125]

Church and State

[11–50] The relationship between a Church and the State in which it operates is, essentially, one of neutrality:

> "... the believer's right to freedom of religion encompasses the expectation that the community will be able to function peacefully free from arbitrary State intervention".[126]

This can include participation in the appointment of religious leaders by the State, so that in the case of *Hasan and Chuash v Bulgaria*, senior Muslim clerics were put into place by the State over leaders those preferred by members of the community. The objective of the government was, in fact, to avoid conflict within the Muslim community, but the ECtHR considered that:

> "... the role of the authorities in such circumstances is not to remove the cause of tension by eliminating pluralism, but to ensure that the competing groups tolerate each other".[127]

[11–51] The court must also remain neutral and fair in terms of its recognition of faiths recognised within the State,[128] and also as regards permission to use premises as places of worship (e.g. planning permits, building regulations).[129] Although most educational

[122] *Buscarini and others v San Marino* (1999) 30 ECHR 208.
[123] ("I ... swear on the Holy Gospels ever to be faithful to and obey the Constitution of the Republic ...").
[124] *Buscarini and others v San Marino* (1999) 30 ECHR 208 at para 39.
[125] *Z and T v UK* (2006) No 27034/05. In this context, it is worth noting that Art 3 may well be considered as an alternative route of action.
[126] *Hasan and Chuash v Bulgaria* (2000) 34 ECHR 1339 at para 78.
[127] *Serif v Greece* (1999) 31 EHRR 561.
[128] *Metropolitan Church of Bessarabia v Moldova* (2001) 35 EHRR 306.
[129] *Manoussakis v Greece* (1996) 23 EHRR 387.

issues are decided under Art 2, Protocol 1 (as above) it is clear that the State has a responsibility to ensure that "... information or knowledge included in the curriculum is conveyed in an objective, critical and objective manner".[130] This leads to the positive protections that a State must give to the communal aspect of religious worship,[131] and to the protection of groups from harassment or attacks due to faith.[132]

Manifestation of Belief

Whilst Art 9(1) clearly protects the right to " ... manifest his religion or belief ...", this manifestation must be part of " ... worship, teaching, practice and observance." The ECtHR has ruled that, when discussing "practice", this "... does not cover each act which is motivated or influenced by a religion or belief".[133] What this means is, in essence, that the manifestation of the practice should be integral to the manifestation of the faith so that, in this instance, the theory of pacifism would probably be protected, but distributing pacifist leaflets was not held to be the "practice" of pacifism. We are therefore looking to the regulation of the nature of a manifestation, not to the regulation of its motivation, which would, obviously, be more problematic. The obvious problem with this is the danger that the court will be, in effect, deciding on what is "reasonable" for adherents of a faith to believe,[134] and this can be considered in light of *Leyla Şahin v Turkey*.[135] The wearing of an Islamic headscarf was upheld by the ECtHR as a manifestation of faith, in that it "... constituted an interference with the applicant's right to manifest her religion", but the Court made the point that its finding was "... without deciding whether such decisions are in every case taken to fulfil a religious duty".[136] **[11–52]**

The case suggests that the ECtHR may be prepared to take a position where a widely held religious manifestation may be presumed to fall within Art 9(1) in regard to "worship, teaching, practice and observance".

Although there have been interesting and contradictory cases (such as *Ivanova v Bulgaria*[137] and *Thlimmenos v Greece*[138]) the ECtHR position on religious manifestation or display in the workplace seems to indicate that there will be no action permissible under Art 9 if the applicant has voluntarily accepted a job which has some restrictions on **[11–53]**

---

130 *Folgero v Norway* (2007) 26 EHRR 1147 at para 84.

131 *Cyprus v Turkey* (2001) 35 EHRR 731.

132 *97 Members of the Gldani Congregation of Jehovah's Witnesses and 4 Others v Georgia* (2007) 46 EHRR 613.

133 *Arrowsmith v UK* (1978) No 7050/75 19 RR 5 at para 19. See also the later cases of *Metropolitan Church of Bessarabia v Moldova* (2001) 35 EHRR 306 and *Hasan and Chuash v Bulgaria* (2000) 34 ECHR 1339.

134 See e.g. *Valsamis v Greece* (1996) 24 EHRR 294 and *Efstratriou v Greece* (1996) 24 EHRR 298.

135 *Leyla Şahin v Turkey* (2005) 44 EHRR 99.

136 *ibid* at para 78.

137 *Ivanova v Bulgaria* (2007) No52435/99. Where an evangelical Christian lost her job, but, unlike Stedman, consideration of the issue of her resigning was not addressed by the court. See also "*Ivanova v Bugaria*" (2006–2007) 17(4) HRCD pp 771–774.

138 *Thlimmenos v Greece* (2000) 31 EHRR 411. The court found an Art 14 ECHR discrimination issue.

their religious manifestation. In the case of *Stedman v UK*,[139] which concerned a Christian unwilling to work on a Sunday, the court held that she was free to resign her position if she found it too conflicting, and similarly in *Ahmad v UK*,[140] the applicant "... remained free to resign if and when he found that his teaching obligations conflicted with his religious duties".[141] Even when a minister has a doctrinal dispute with his religious organisation, he is considered free to resign from the Church.[142] There has been some criticism of ECtHR that this narrow interpretation displays a lack of understanding of employment pressures "in the real world" and makes the court "... slow in giving acknowledgement to the complete range of manifestations of religion or belief".[143]

2. Legitimate Justifications for Interference with the Right

Prescribed by Law

[11–54] Although Art 9(1) has total protection for the *forum internum*, the restriction of manifestation of the right, *forum externum*, can be justified under Art 9(2) if "... prescribed by law and ... necessary in a democratic society." The first part has been considered in case law under other articles, most particularly *Sunday Times v UK*[144] where the phrase "prescribed by law" has been taken as meaning "adequately accessible" and "... formulated with sufficient precision to enable the citizen to regulate his conduct."[145] In terms of Art 9, it was further defined by the ECtHR:

> "The interference with the internal organisation of the Muslim community and the applicants' freedom of religion was not 'prescribed by law' in that it was arbitrary and was based on legal provisions which allowed an unfettered discretion to the executive and did not meet the required standards of clarity and foreseeability".[146]

This was followed by other cases involving official church recognition by the State,[147] a condemned prisoner's access to a priest,[148] and disrupting a meeting of Jehovah's Witnesses.[149]

As regards what might be considered as "a legitimate aim", the State has a range of possible grounds for interference; "in the interests of public safety, for the protection of public order, health or morals, or the protection of the rights and freedoms of others." The most often used of these, perhaps unsurprisingly, has been the public order

---

139 *Stedman v UK* (1997) 23 EHRR 168.

140 *Ahmad v UK* (1991) 4 EHRR 126.

141 *ibid* at 135.

142 *Knudsen v Norway* (1985) No 11045/84 42 DR 247.

143 PM Taylor, *Freedom of Religion: UN and European Human Rights Law and Practice*, (Cambridge University Press, Cambridge, 2005) at p 234.

144 *Sunday Times v UK* (1979) 2 EHRR 245.

145 *ibid* at para 49.

146 *Hasan and Chuash v Bulgaria* (2000) 34 ECHR 1339 at para 86.

147 *Biserica Adevărat Ortodoxă din Moldova v Moldova* (2007) No 184/02 and *Mitropolia Basarabieişi Exarhatul Plaiurilorv Moldova* (2001) No 45701/99. See "Mitropolia Basarabieişi Exarhatul Plaiurilorv Moldova" (2001) 12(3) HRCD 441–442.

148 *Poltoratskiiy v Ukraine* (2003) 39 EHRR 916.

149 *Kuznetsov and others v Russia* (2007) No 184/02. See *Kuznetsov and others v Russia* (2006–2007) 17(3) HRCD 465–468.

argument, covering events as diverse as from access to a Druid ceremony[150] to a protest against alcohol and pornography.[151] The health aspect has covered prisoners being required to keep cells clean[152] and the wearing of motorcycle helmets.[153]

Necessary in a Democratic Society

In respect of whether actions are "necessary in a democratic society", the ECtHR found that this had not been proven in the case of *The Supreme Holy Council of the Muslim Community v Bulgaria*[154]: [11–55]

> "The Court reiterates that the autonomous existence of religious communities is indispensable for pluralism in a democratic society. While it may be necessary for the State to take action to reconcile the interests of the various religions and religious groups that coexist in a democratic society, the State has a duty to remain neutral and impartial in exercising its regulatory power and in its relations with the various religions, denominations and beliefs. What is at stake here is the preservation of pluralism and the proper functioning of democracy, one of the principal characteristics of which is the possibility it offers of resolving a country's problems through dialogue, even when interfering in internal disputes between adherents of a religious community they are irksome.
>
> In the present case, the relevant law and practice and the authorities' actions ... had the effect of compelling the divided community to have a single leadership against the will of one of the two rival leaderships. As a result, one of the groups of leaders was favoured and the other excluded and deprived of the possibility of continuing to manage autonomously the affairs and assets of that part of the community which supported it. ... The Government have not stated why in the present case their aim to restore legality and remedy injustices could not be achieved by other means, without compelling the divided community under a single leadership".[155]

In short, the measures had not been needed, and were, in any event, unsuccessful, so the State had, in this instance, exceeded its authority in terms of the margin of appreciation.[156]

Rights and Freedoms of Others

The last interference, that of the "rights and freedoms of others" has proven controversial, and had led to narrow interpretation by the court. This can be seen most easily in the area of religious dress, and the case of *Leyla Şahin v Turkey*[157] which has already been mentioned above. This followed *Dahlab v Switzerland,*[158] where the [11–56]

[150] *Chappell v UK* (1987) 53 DR 241.
[151] *Håkenssen v Sweden* (1983) 5 EHRR 297.
[152] *X u UK* (1982) No 8231/78 28 DR 5.
[153] *X v UK* (1978) No 7992/77 14 DR 234.
[154] *The Supreme Holy Council of the Muslim Community v Bulgaria* (2004) No 39023/97.
[155] *ibid* at para 73.
[156] See also *Agga v Greece (No 2)* (2002) Nos 50776/99, 52912/99 and *Serif v Greece* (1999) 31 EHRR 561 (above).
[157] *Leyla Şahin v Turkey* (2005) 44 EHRR 99.
[158] *Dahlab v Switzerland* (2001) No 42393/98. See *Dahlab v Switzerland* (2001) 12(1) HRCD 141–142.

court found that the banning of wearing the Islamic veil was justified as the State had the legitimate aim of preserving religious neutrality within a multi-faith society.

However, it should be noted that the decision in *Şahin* was not universally well received, particularly in the academic world, since the reasons for the decision were felt to be outside the remit of the court, and were paternalistic, showing:

> "Inadequate application of the margin of appreciation doctrine; narrow interpretation of the freedom of religion; imposition of 'fundamental secularism'; adverse implications of Muslim women's right to education; and promotion of the image of Islam as a threat to democracy".[159]

Proselytism

[11–57] In the area of proselytism, the question of necessity in a democratic society has been raised. The cases of *Kokkinakis* and *Larissis* demonstrate that even though the aim of anti-proselytism laws may be legitimate, it may not succeed as being necessary. So, in the former case, the court held that there was a difference between "true evangelism" and "improper proselytism",[160] with the first being quite legitimate but the second, being a "corruption or deformation" of evangelism and therefore unacceptable. The reasoning for this was that this could:

> " ... take the form of activities offering material or social advantage with a view to gaining new members for a Church or exerting improper pressure on people in distress or in need; it may even entail the use of violence or brainwashing; more generally, it is not compatible with respect for the freedom of thought, conscience and religion of others".[161]

The contrasting case of *Larissis*[162] concerned the conviction of Pentecostal Air Force senior officers for the proselytism of three men under their command. The court held that military hierarchical structures differed from civilian life in that junior members could more easily feel under pressure, and even feel harassed by senior officers.

[11–58] It was, therefore, justified that the officers should have been convicted since the relevant domestic law had been designed to protect individual servicemen from any ideological or religious coercion:

> "The Court observes that it is well established that the Convention appliesin principle to members of the armed forces as well as to civilians. Nevertheless, when interpreting and applying its rules in cases such as the present, it is necessary to bear in mind the particular characteristics of military life and its effects on the situation of individual members of the armed forces.... In this respect, the Court notes that the hierarchical structures which are a feature of life in the armed forces may colour every aspect of the relations between military personnel, making it difficult for a subordinate to rebuff the approaches of an

---

[159] A Vakulenko, "'Islamic Headscarves' and the European Convention on Human Rights: an Intersectional Perspective" (2007) 16(2) S&LS 190.

[160] It should be noted that the Council of Europe, in the Parliamentary Assembly Recommendation 1492 (1999), called for State domestic action on " ... illegal practices carried out in the name of groups of a religious, esoteric or spiritual nature."

[161] *Kokkinakis v Greece* (1993) 17 EHRR 397 at para 169.

[162] *Larissis v Greece* (1998) 27 EHRR 329.

> individual of superior rank or to withdraw from a conversation initiated by him. Thus, what would in the civilian world be seen as an innocuous exchange of ideas which the recipient is free to accept or reject, may, within the confines of military life, be viewed as a form of harassment or the application of undue pressure in abuse of power. It must be emphasised that note very discussion about religion or other sensitive matters between individuals of unequal rank will fall within this category. Nonetheless, where the circumstances so require, States may be justified in taking special measures to protect the rights and freedoms of subordinate members of the armed forces".[163]

The aim of pluralism in Art 9 is seen as central by ECtHR:

> " ... the autonomous existence of religious communities is indispensable for pluralism in a democratic society. ... What is at stake here is the preservation of pluralism and the proper functioning of democracy, one of the principal characteristics of which is the possibility it offers of resolving a country's problems through dialogue, even when they are irksome".[164]

Therefore, the protection of individual belief should promote mutual respect for and tolerance of others' beliefs, suggesting that State authorities have a positive duty to ensure that any right under Art 9 is effective. This concept of pluralism also means that those holding particular religious views must "... tolerate and accept the denial by others of their religious beliefs and even the propagation by others of doctrines hostile to their faith".[165] **[11–59]**

There has been criticism of ECtHR for a lack of consistency in its jurisprudence, and for sometimes failing to address philosophical or religious obligations fully, while also being criticised for taking a paternalistic viewpoint. Overall, the court has tended towards a conservative approach, but with the increasingly diverse nature of multi-faith Europe, it is submitted that this is likely to see some change in emphasis in the future.

C. CFR

Article 10: **[11–60]**

> "1. Everyone has the right to freedom of thought, conscience and religion. This right includes freedom to change religion or belief and freedom, either alone or in community with others and in public or in private, to manifest religion or belief, in worship, teaching, practice and observance.
>
> 2. The right to conscientious objection is recognised in accordance with the national laws governing the exercise of this right."

1. Nature of the Right

The right to freedom of religion utilises essentially the same language that can be seen in Art 9 of the ECHR and based on the very few judgments relating to this issue at an **[11–61]**

---

[163] *ibid* at para 59.
[164] *The Supreme Holy Council of the Muslim Community v Bulgaria* (2004) No 39023/97 at para 93.
[165] *Otto-Preminger-Institut v Austria* (1994) No 13470/87ECHR 26 at para 47.

EU level, the jurisprudence of the ECtHR is entirely relevant in the determination of the scope and nature of Art 10 CFR.[166] This was expressly recognised by Advocate General Bot in *Federal Republic of Germany v Y, Z.*[167] Of significant interest is the express reference to conscientious objection, something which is not expressly stated in the Irish Constitution or the ECHR. The express reference in the context of the CFR implies a certain significance should be attached to this particular aspect of freedom of thought, conscience and religion.

What is Religion for the Purposes of Article 10?

[11–62] While there are no judgments or secondary legislation on this point, the opinion of Advocate General Bot in *Federal Republic of Germany v Y, Z*[168] is illuminating in this regard. He defines religion in the broadest possible terms covering "theistic, non-thestic and atheistic beliefs, and not only traditional religions, such as Catholicism or Islam, but also more recent or minority religions".[169]

What is Protected by Article 10?

[11–63] While clearly the right of conscientious objection is protected expressly, the question of what other rights are protected within the wide scope of freedom of religion should be examined. There are many aspects to freedom of religion which are protected under Art 9 and are equally protected in the EU context. There is a freedom to have a religion, to have none or to change faith which appears to enjoy "absolute protection".[170] There is also a freedom to manifest one's faith, "alone or in common, in private or in public, by worship, teaching, practice or the performance of rituals"[171]. This aspect of the right is not absolute and is subject to the same limitations expressed in Art 9(2) of the ECHR. Freedom from discrimination on the grounds of religion would also fall within this category of rights.

[11–64] One of the only judgments of the CJEU relating to freedom of religion and discrimination on grounds of religion is the case of *Prais v Council of the European Communities*[172] in which the applicant's request to take the open Council competition tests for the position of a linguistic expert at a later date, was rejected by the defendant. The applicant sought annulment of this decision on the grounds that her request to sit the test at a later date was based on her religious beliefs. The date fixed by the defendant was the first day of the Jewish feast of Shavout, during which it is not permitted to travel or to write. The applicant claimed that this amounted to religious discrimination contrary to the fundamental rights of the individual. She also claimed

---

[166] GM Golding, "Human Rights in the European Communities – Religious Freedom" (1982) 17(1) Ir Jur 127.

[167] Case C–71/11 and C–99/11 *Federal Republic of Germany v Y, Z* (Judgment is still pending) opinion of Advocate General Bot at para 32.

[168] *ibid.*

[169] *ibid* at para 34.

[170] *ibid* at paras 34–35.

[171] *ibid* at para 36. See P Lerner and AM Rabello, "The Prohibition of Ritual Slaughtering (Kosher, Shechita and Halal) and Freedom of Religion of Minorities" (2006/2007) 22(7) J of L & Rel. 1.

[172] Case 130/75, *Prais v Council of the European Communities.*

that Art 27 of the staff regulations should be interpreted in a manner that the defendant should be able to arrange the test date so as to enable every candidate to take part in the tests, whatever his religious circumstances.[173] The defendant did not deny that Art 27 should be read to require non-discrimination on grounds of religion and did not deny that the right of freedom of religion forms part of the fundamental rights recognised in community law.

However, the defendant did not think that either of these rights should afford the plaintiff the relief which she claimed.[174] This would involved an "elaborate administrative machinery" as the definition of religion in Art 27 of the staff regulations applied to all creeds and so it would be necessary to ascertain the details of all the religions practiced in all Member States before setting a date for the test.[175] It was necessary, for fairness and equality, to have the tests on the same day for every candidate and so the right to free profession of religion had to be balanced against this necessity.[176] If the applicant had informed the authority in time, suitable dates could have been arranged but as this did not occur, the authority was not in a position to change the date once it was fixed and the other candidates had been informed. As the defendant had not been so informed in this case, it was entitled to refuse to change the date in this case.[177] This is the very first reference to religious discrimination in the context of the EU. What is interesting about the decision is that even at this early stage, the CJEU recognised the fundamental importance of freedom of religion as a principle of community law. This right included a right to freedom from discrimination on grounds of religion. [11–65]

The freedom from discrimination on grounds of religion is protected not only by the Charter but also by secondary legislation in the employment context. Council Directive 2000/78/EC of 27 November 2000[178] establishing a general framework for equal treatment in employment and occupation protects against both direct and indirect discrimination on grounds of religion. Direct discrimination is taken to occur where one person is treated less favourably that another is, has been or would be treated in a comparable situation, on grounds of religion or belief.[179] Indirect discrimination is taken to occur where an apparently neutral provision, criterion or practice would put persons having a particular religion or belief at a particular disadvantage compared with other persons unless (i) that provision, criterion or practice is objectively justified by a legitimate aim and the means of achieving that aim are appropriate and necessary. Therefore, in the context of direct discrimination on grounds of religion or belief there is no justification but in the context of indirect discrimination the employer can argue that the discrimination is justified by a [11–66]

173 Case 130/75, *Prais v Council of the European Communities* at paras 7–9.
174 *ibid* at para 10.
175 *ibid* at para 11.
176 *ibid* at para 15.
177 *ibid* at para 19.
178 Official Journal L 303, 02/12/2000 P 0016–0022.
179 Art 1(2)(a), Directive 2000/78/EC of 27 November 2000 establishing a general framework for equal treatment in employment and occupation protects against both direct and indirect discrimination on grounds of religion

legitimate aim which is proportionate in the circumstances. There have been no cases on the religion ground based on the Directive to date therefore what would constitute a legitimate justification in the context of religion or belief is still unclear.

2. Justifications for Interference with the Right

[11–67] It is clear from the early decision in *Prais* that proportionality plays a significant role in the determination of claims relating to discrimination and freedom to practice religion. This was confirmed in the opinion of Advocate General Bot in *Federal Republic of Germany v Y, Z*[180] which concerned a reference from the Bundesverwaltungsgericht in Germany relating to two Pakistani nationals, Y and Z, who were seeking refugee status on the grounds of religious persecution. The two nationals were active members of the Ahmadiyya community which is an Islamic reformist movement, whose religious activities are severely restricted by the Pakistani Penal Code. Y and Z were not able to profess their faith publically without being convicted of blasphemy, which is punishable by imprisonment or even the death penalty. What is interesting about the opinion of Advocate General Bot in this case is the fact that he makes some general statements about the nature, scope and limitations on freedom of religion in answering the questions posed by the national court. In particular, he noted that the freedom of religion is not an absolute right and that it is subject to limitations which are necessary to the equilibrium of life. Equally, Directive 2000/78/EC which protects against discrimination in the employment context provides for indirect discrimination to be legitimated in certain circumstances as long as the proportionality requirement is met.

[11–68] Other justifications for interference with the right can be identified in Directive 2000/78/EC which provides for an exception from discrimination on grounds of religion in employment. This provides that in the case of occupational activities within churches and other public or private organisations the ethos of which is based on religion or belief, a difference of treatment based on a person's religion or belief shall not constitute discrimination where, by reason of the nature of these activities or of the context in which they are carried out, a person's religion or belief constitute a genuine, legitimate and justified occupational requirement, having regard to the organisation's ethos.[181] Therefore, the Directive does not prejudice the right of churches and other public or private organisations, the ethos of which is based on religion or belief, to require individuals working for them to act in good faith and with loyalty to the organisation's ethos. This provision is reminiscent of s 37(1) of the Employment Equality Act 1998 in Ireland and provides for a similar subjective test as to the ethos of the organisation. The only role for the courts in such circumstances is to assess the reasonableness of the measures taken by the organisation in the pursuance of this role. This provision was clearly a compromise provision to certain States with strong religious affinities. However, it constitutes a specific form of legitimate interference with the general right to non-discrimination on grounds of religion or belief.

---

[180] Case C–71/11 and C–99/11 *Federal Republic of Germany v Y, Z* (Judgment is still pending) opinion of Advocate General Bot.

[181] Art 4(2), Directive 2000/78/EC of 27 November 2000 establishing a general framework for equal treatment in employment and occupation protects against both direct and indirect discrimination on grounds of religion.

D. International and Regional Laws

The right to freedom of religion is also protected at an international level[182] and can be divided into two separate rights: equality on grounds of religion and the freedom of religion.[183] [11–69]

Non-discrimination on grounds of religion is protected by virtue of Art 2 of the UDHR and Art 2 of the CCPR. Art 2 of the CESCR and the CRC and Arts 1 and 7 of the CRMW also make provision for protection against discrimination on grounds of religion.

Freedom of religion is protected by Art 18 UCHR and the CCPR which is defined as including the right:

> " ... to change his religion or belief, and freedom, either alone or in community with others and in public or private, to manifest his religion or belief in teaching, practice, worship and observance".

Similarly, Arts 24 and 27 of CCPR extends this right to children and minorities respectively. More specifically, Art 18 of the CCPR protects the right to freedom of religion which is defined, similarly to the UDHR, as including rights "to have or to adopt a religion or belief of his choice, and freedom, either individually or in community with others and in public or private, to manifest his religion or belief in worship, observance, practice and teaching". However, Art 18(2) also protects against coercion which would impair the freedom to have or to adopt a religion or belief of one's choice which is phrased as an absolute right echoing the situation in Ireland, the ECHR and in the EU. Freedom to manifest one's religion or belief is not absolute and the CCPR makes provision for limitations on this aspect of the right "as are prescribed by law and are necessary to protect public safety, order, health, or morals or the fundamental rights and freedoms of others".[184] Similar provisions can be found in Art 18 of the CRC. Freedom of religion is also protected by Art 5(d)(vii) of CERD, Art 18 of CRC and Art 12 of CRMW. Interestingly, there is no mention of freedom of religion in the CESCR, CEDAW, CAT or in the CRPD. [11–70]

Regional protection can be found in Art 12 of the American Convention on Human Rights, Art 30 of the Arab Charter of Human Rights and Art 8 of the African Charter on Human and Peoples' Rights.

182 B Dickson, "The United Nations and Freedom of Religion" (1995) 44(2) ICLQ 327.

183 For a general overview of international protections see J A Coons, "Freedom of Religion: A World Report by Kevin Boyle, Juliet Sheen" (2001) 49(1) AJCL 161. For a general overview of regional protection in the United States see J J Rosenbaum, "Religion, Democracy and Human Rights" (2003) 16 HHRJ 179 and in South Africa see N Smith, "Freedom of Religion in the Constitutional Court" (2001) 118(1) SALJ 1. For a discussion on China see L Junning, "Freedom of Religion: The Primary Human Right: The World Does Not Belong to Caesar" (2010) 6(2) Ch Law & Rel Mon 41; Sudan: A M Tier, "Freedom of Religion under the Sudan Constitution and Laws" (1982) 26(2) J of AL 133; A J Nieuwenhuis, "State and religion, a multidimensional relationship: some comparative law remarks" (2012) 10(1) IJCL 153.

184 Art 18(3), CCPR.

Conclusion

[11–71] One of the first questions to consider in determining a claim in relation to the freedom of religion to is decide whether a particular belief falls within the definition of religion as defined at a national and regional level. What is interesting is that the definition of religion at both these levels is incredibly broad and covers a wide range of majority as well as minority religions. Similarly, the protection of the right at a national and regional level is comparable with non-discrimination and the protection of the freedom to practice and profess a faith all given express protection under the relevant instruments. There are certain limitations on these rights. In Ireland, for example, the principle of non-discrimination can be justifiably interfered with in order to protect the right to profess a religion. At a regional level, indirect discrimination in the employment context can be justified by reference to a legitimate aim which is proportionate. Equally, there are limitations in the interest of the common good (in the Irish context) and for the protection of the public interest in the freedom to manifest one's religion. However, all of these limitations are subject to the common protection of the doctrine of proportionality thus shielding the right from excessive interferences.

CHAPTER 12
The Right to Peaceful Assembly

Introduction

The right to gather and assemble peacefully as a group, whether for the purpose of protest or for the purpose of a meeting or attending a concert, has long been recognised as a fundamental human right.[1] The right is a positive one and imposes obligations on the State to ensure that people have the right to assemble peacefully. However, this right is not absolute and is subject to certain limitations. This chapter will describe and analyse the constitutional protection of the right to peaceful assembly, followed by an analysis of the European Convention on Human Rights (ECHR) and under the Charter of Fundamental Rights (CFR). The final section of the chapter will provide an overview of the protection of the right under international human rights law. **[12–01]**

A. Irish Constitutional Protection

Article 40.6.1°ii: **[12–02]**

> "[The State guarantees liberty for the exercise, subject to public order and morality, of]... the right of the citizens to assemble peaceably and without arms. Provision may be made by law to prevent or control meetings which are determined in accordance with law to be calculated to cause a breach of the peace or to be a danger or nuisance to the general public and to prevent or control meetings in the vicinity of either House of the Oireachtas."

Article 40.6.2°:

> "Laws regulating the manner in which the right of ... free assembly may be exercised shall contain no political, religious or class discrimination."

1 Recognition at an international level can be identified in the Universal Declaration of Human Rights 1948, Art 20.

[12–03] The right to freedom of assembly in Ireland is protected by Art 40.6.1°ii which provides, subject to certain limitations, the right of citizens to assemble peacefully and unarmed without any political, religious or class discrimination. While the actual content and scope of the Article has never been considered by the courts,[2] the extensive limitations[3] permitted by the Constitution on grounds of public order, morality and the control of certain meetings have received much greater attention.

1. Nature of the Right

[12–04] The exact scope of the protection guaranteed under Art 40.6.1°ii has never been considered by the Irish courts. However, the following principles can be gleaned from the constitutional guarantee and the limited jurisprudence:

Purpose of the Assembly

[12–05] The main scope of the protection suggests that persons are entitled to assemble peacefully for the purpose of protest or a meeting, subject to certain limitations. It would appear that the constitutional guarantee as set out in Art 40.6.1°ii is not just a negative right but also imposes a positive obligation on the State to ensure that persons have the right to exercise free assembly effectively.

Assembly must be Peaceful

[12–06] In the first instance, the Constitution specifically provides that the "bearing of arms" is not protected. Even if this was not mentioned in the Constitution itself, the bearing of arms would automatically negate the "peaceful" element of the assembly and would not be covered by the protection of the Article. In the case of *People (DPP) v Kehoe,*[4] a large crowd of protesters proceeded towards the British Embassy in Dublin in protest at the conditions and events occurring at the H-Block Prison in Northern Ireland. The protest became violent when police erected barriers to prevent the protesters from approaching the Embassy. In an appeal against conviction for obstruction of government,[5] McCarthy J made a rare passing reference to Art 40.6.1°ii. He noted that a "very large proportion of those taking part in the march were there for the purpose of exercising their constitutional right to express peacefully their social and political opinion",[6] but the very fact that certain marchers were carrying offensive implements and weapons negated the "peaceful" element of the assembly.

---

[2] Hogan and Whyte (G Hogan and G Whyte, *J.M. Kelly: The Irish Constitution* (4th ed, Butterworths, Dublin, 2003), p 1780) note that the right to freedom of assembly has been mentioned in two cases but not addressed specifically. See *Brendan Dunne Ltd v Fitzpatrick* [1958] IR 29; *People (DPP) v Kehoe* [1983] IR 136, considered below.

[3] Hogan and Whyte have commented that some of the restrictions are so extensive that there are "legitimate concerns about the extent to which the Constitution may effectively protect the right to assemble in certain situations." *ibid*, p 1780.

[4] [1983] IR 136.

[5] Contrary to s 7 of the Offences Against the State Act 1939, as amended by s 2 of the Criminal Law Act 1976 and s 18 of the Criminal Justice (Amendment) Act 2009.

[6] *supra* n 4 at 139 (*per* McCarthy J).

Secondly, any breach of the "peaceful" element of the assembly would not benefit from the protection of the Constitution. In the case of *Brendan Dunne v Fitzpatrick,*[7] involving a trade dispute, Budd J held that "if citizens in the course of an assembly commit a breach of the peace or some other breach of the law, they thereby disturb public order and their actions are not protected by the Constitution in respect of the breach of the law committed".[8]

Interference with the Right

While there is no specific jurisprudence on this point directly, the prevention, dispersal or interference with a peaceful assembly would constitute an interference under Irish law. Similarly, failure to grant a licence or other authorisation for an assembly could constitute an interference with the right. **[12–07]**

2. Legitimate Justifications for Interference with the Right

The right to free and peaceful assembly is not an absolute right and even if there is an interference with the right to assembly, there may still be a legitimate justification for such interference under the Constitution. Provision is made in Art 40.6.1°ii for limitations based on public order, public morality and the control of certain meetings which are determined, in accordance with law, to be calculated to cause a breach of the peace or to be a danger or nuisance to the general public or are in the vicinity of either House of the Oireachtas. **[12–08]**

Limitations in the Interests of Private Rights

Protection of private property against trespass: while there is a right to assemble on private property, for example to attend a concert or a festival, this right is subject to the consent of the owner to the assembly. If the owner does not consent to the assembly, then it will be considered a trespass and is unlawful.[9] Where the property is publically owned, other considerations, such as liabilities in tort, will apply.[10] **[12–09]**

Limitations in the Interests of Public Utility

Protection of highways against obstruction: the common law restricts the use of highways to activities for which they were constructed, i.e. passage and re-passage. Therefore, the assembly of persons on a highway is considered an obstruction and contrary to common law. **[12–10]**

However, a line of case law has developed which suggests that the highway can be utilised for other "reasonable" uses.[11] What is considered "reasonable" usage is a

[7] [1958] IR 29.
[8] *ibid* at 35 (*per* Budd J).
[9] See Criminal Justice (Public Order) Act 1994 (Pt 2A), as inserted by the Housing (Miscellaneous Provisions) Act 2002 (s 24). See G Hogan and G Whyte, *supra* n 2, p 1781 and J Casey, *Constitutional Law in Ireland* (3rd ed, Round Hall Sweet & Maxwell, Dublin, 2000), p 587.
[10] Hogan and Whyte note that, even on public property, an assembly might amount to a nuisance to nearby occupiers. *supra* n 2, p 1781.
[11] *Ferguson v O' Gorman* [1937] IR 620.

matter for determination by the courts on the facts of each individual case.[12] In the case of *Lowdens v Keaveney*,[13] the court held that in determining the reasonableness of an obstruction regard should be had to the occasion and duration of the use, the place and the hour. The court gave as an example the holding of a public funeral of a Minister which might occasion persons to assemble on the street to express their condolences. Common sense and grace would suggest that this would not be a criminal offence.[14] Another factor which has been considered important in determining reasonableness, is whether the obstruction is stationary (often considered unreasonable) or in a procession (considered reasonable in some cases).[15] If the obstruction is considered unreasonable, it is contrary to common law and is considered a nuisance.[16]

[12–11] One issue that has arisen is the potential criminal liability that may arise for obstruction of the highway and whether public order is a sufficient justification for such an interference with the right to free assembly under the Constitution.[17] The Criminal Justice (Public Order) Act 1994[18] provides that any person who without lawful authority or reasonable excuse, wilfully prevents or interrupts the free passage of any person or vehicle in any public place is guilty of an offence. This constitutes an interference with the right to assemble on a highway which can only be justified by reference to the public order exception under the Constitution. Any challenge to this provision based on Art 40.6.1°ii would be met by arguments that the legislation is proportionate, as first, it does provide that the interruption must be without lawful authority or reasonable excuse, and secondly, it must be wilful. This statutory provision has not, to date, received any judicial consideration as to its compatibility with Art 40.6.1°ii. However, these provisions would appear to strike a fair balance between the protection of public order and the right of persons to peaceful assembly.

In a similar vein, the Road Traffic Act 1961 provides that a person shall be liable to an offence if he or she commits any act (whether by commission or omission) which

---

[12] The Constitution Review Group has recommended that this right to assemble on a public roadway for stationary meetings should be left for consideration by the courts on a case-by-case basis. Constitution Review Group, *Report of the Constitution Review Group* (Stationery Office, Dublin, 1996), p 306.

[13] [1903] 2 IR 82. This case involved a band playing on a street who were requested to cease playing and who, on continuing to play, caused an inevitable obstruction due to the number of people following the band down the street.

[14] *ibid* at 87.

[15] J Casey is of the view that the case law would suggest that the courts take a more favourable view at common law to processions on the highway rather than stationary meetings. J Casey, *supra* n 9, p 588. J Casey refers to Professor Williams who has pointed out that this more favourable approach to processions is outmoded and that the same standard of reasonableness should apply in both circumstances. D Williams, *Keeping the Peace* (Hutchinson, London, 1967), p 216 in J Casey, *supra* n 9, p 588. This latter interpretation would also appear to be more in line with the jurisprudence emanating from the European Court of Human Rights (ECtHR).

[16] *R v Clarke (No 2)* [1964] 2 QB 315. This case followed the case of *Lowdens v Keaveney supra* n 13 and agreed that the test to be applied in such cases is whether or not the use of the highway is reasonable in all the circumstances.

[17] J Casey, *supra* n 9, p 588.

[18] s 9, as amended by s 22 and Sch 2 of the Intoxicating Liquor Act 2008 and s 3 of the Criminal Justice (Public Order) Act 2003.

causes, or is likely to cause, traffic through any public place to be obstructed unless he or she had lawful authority for the act complained of or that it was due to an unavoidable accident.[19]

Limitations in the Interest of Peace and Order

Protection of society against riot and disorder: legislation[20] is in place to criminalise the offences of "riot"[21] and "violent disorder".[22] These offences effectively criminalise assemblies where such assemblies are characterised by riot or violent disorder and would appear to be compatible with the public order justification explicit in Art 40.6.1°ii. The Public Meeting Act 1908 also provides that any person who acts in a disorderly manner at a lawful public meeting is guilty of an offence[23] and the Ecclesiastical Courts Jurisdiction Act 1860[24] provides that it is an offence to commit riotous, violent or indecent behaviour in places of worship. **[12–12]**

Protection of society against breach of the peace: the Garda Síochána also have a wide-ranging power under common law[25] to disperse an assembly where they fear that a breach of the peace *may* occur.[26] In the case of *Humphries v Connor*,[27] the court held that a police officer was justified in removing an emblem from a person which might provoke a breach of the peace, despite the fact that the wearing of the emblem in itself was perfectly lawful. This particular common law power has not been utilised in

[19] s 98 of the Road Traffic Act 1961.
[20] Criminal Justice (Public Order) Act 1994.
[21] s 14 of the Criminal Justice (Public Order) Act 1994. Riot shall be committed where 12 or more persons who are present together at any place (whether public or private) use or threaten to use unlawful violence for a common purpose and the conduct of these persons, taken together, is such as would cause a person of reasonable firmness present at a place to fear for his or her own or another person's personal safety (s 14(1)(a) and (b) of the Criminal Justice (Public Order) Act 1994). It is immaterial whether the 12 or more persons threaten to use unlawful violence simultaneously; the common conduct can be inferred from conduct and no person of reasonable firmness need actually be present at the place (s 14(2) of the Criminal Justice (Public Order) Act 1994). The crime carries penalties on indictment of a fine or a term of imprisonment not exceeding 10 years (s 14(3) of the Criminal Justice (Public Order) Act 1994).
[22] s 15 of the Criminal Justice (Public Order) Act 1994. In relation to the offence of violent disorder, once again the law punishes the assembly of three or more persons present together at any place where they use or threaten the use of unlawful violence and the conduct of these persons, taken together, is such as would cause a person of reasonable firmness present at that place to fear for his or her or another person's safety (s 15(1)(a) and (b) of the Criminal Justice (Public Order) Act 1994). A person shall not be convicted unless he or she intends to use or threatens to use violence or is aware that his or her conduct may be violent or threaten violence (s 15(3) of the Criminal Justice (Public Order) Act 1994). Similar penalties as attach to the offence of riot apply (s 15(4) of the Criminal Justice (Public Order) Act 1994).
[23] s 1 of the Public Meeting Act 1908, as amended by s 3 and Sch 1 of the Electoral Act 1963.
[24] s 2 of the Ecclesiastical Courts Jurisdiction Act 1860.
[25] The seminal case in this area is *Humphries v Connor* (1864) 17 ICLR 1, where it was held that the police had a duty to preserve the peace and prevent a breach of the peace and that any act necessary to achieve this aim was lawful.
[26] J Casey is of the view that this is "possibly still good law", *supra* n 9, p 591.
[27] *supra* n 25.

Ireland for a number of years, but in the absence of any decisions to the contrary, the power still remains in force in Ireland.

[12–13] The main issue surrounding this power is in what circumstances the Garda Síochána will have the authority to disperse an assembly. The line of cases in this area suggests that the Garda Síochána do not have to wait until a breach of the peace has occurred but that they have a "paramount duty ... to preserve the breach of the peace unbroken"...by whatever means are available for the purpose.[28] The courts have continued to uphold this common law power – a power which in effect, "subordinates the claims of individual liberty to consideration of the public good".[29] Maddox argues that the decision in *Humphries v Connor* was an "eminently sensible position which allows, on a rare occasion, public utility to override the exercise of lawful rights",[30] and that the exception is a relatively limited one. Any other construction of the rule could lead to a dangerous precedent "where the law of the land" would be circumvented by "the law of the mob supreme".[31]

[12–14] Another issue that has arisen in relation to this common law power of dispersal, is the degree of force that can be used to disperse an assembly. In the seminal case of *Lynch v Fitzgerald*,[32] a youth was killed by a bullet fired by a police officer who was trying to repress an attempt by the youth and others to disrupt a cattle sale. The disruptors were armed with sticks and had broken the police cordon. The youth had followed the disruptors along with a few other onlookers. The police re-established the cordon and trapped the disruptors and the youth. The police then fired on the disruptors killing the youth. The court held that only moderate force should be used to disperse an assembly and that it should be proportionate according to the circumstances of the case and to the end sought to be achieved.[33] The use of firearms by the Garda Síochána should be used only in extreme cases and only then as a "last resort to preserve life".[34]

The lack of any statutory provisions in the area and the lack of recent consideration by the courts "leaves a considerable discretion to the police",[35] and Casey has called for this common law power to be put on a statutory footing. The Constitution Review Group recommended that "because there is some risk that this aspect of Article 40.6.1°.ii might be interpreted as enabling the authorities to curtail the right of free speech and assembly simply because the sensibilities of the others might be offended", the Article should be amended.[36]

28 *O' Kelly v Harvey* (1883) 14 LR Ir 105 at 109 (*per* Law C).
29 *Coyne v Tweedy* [1898] 2 IR 167 at 171 (*per* Sir P O' Brien LCJ).
30 N Maddox, "Regulating Peaceable Assembly under Irish Law — Some Comparative Guidance for Local Authorities" (2005) 23 ILT 10.
31 *supra* n 25 at 9 (*per* Fitzgerald J).
32 [1932] IR 382.
33 J Casey, *supra* n 9, p 592.
34 *supra* n 32 at 405 (*per* Hanna J).
35 J Casey, *supra* n 9, p 592.
36 Constitution Review Group, *supra* n 12, p 286.

Protection of society against a breach of the peace by binding over: the Courts (Supplemental Provisions) Act 1961 provides for the jurisdiction of the courts to make an order binding a person to the peace or to good behaviour and requiring him or her to enter into a recognisance in that behalf.[37] This provision was challenged in the case of *Gregory v Judge Windle*[38] on the grounds that the power to bind a person over constituted preventative justice and punished conduct "which has yet to occur and which may not occur,"[39] a method of guarding "against future lawlessness".[40] However, O' Hanlon J held that the power is a "beneficial and necessary jurisdiction, which, if exercised prudently and with discretion, does not give rise to any conflict with the constitutional guarantee of personal liberty".[41] However, this may now have to be reconsidered in light of the decision of the ECtHR in the case of *Hashman and Harrup v The United Kingdom*[42] where the power of magistrates to bind over persons for breach of the peace was found to be contrary to Art 10 of the ECHR.[43] Academic discourse in the United Kingdom and in the United States has considered that "the procedure is obviously vulnerable to a variety of constitutional objections as a denial of due process of law or 'natural justice' and an abridgment of the right to freedom of speech".[44] **[12–15]**

Meetings

Meetings, and thus the assembly of persons for a specific purpose, can be limited in accordance with law as detailed below[45]: **[12–16]**

Meetings by, or for, unlawful organisations: it is unlawful to hold a public meeting which is held, or purports to be held, by or on behalf of or by arrangement or in concert with an unlawful organisation[46] or for the purpose of aiding, abetting, or encouraging an unlawful organisation or of advocating the support of an unlawful organisation.[47] Where an officer of the Garda Síochána, not below the rank of chief superintendent, is of the opinion that the holding of a particular public meeting would be a contravention of this provision of the Offences Against the State Act 1939, the officer can by notice or by publication to the person concerned in the holding or organisation of the meeting, prohibit the holding of such meeting, and thereupon the holding of such meeting shall become and be unlawful.[48]

---

[37] s 54 of the Courts (Supplemental Provisions) Act 1961.
[38] [1994] 3 IR 616.
[39] *ibid* at 617.
[40] *R (Orr) v Londonderry JJ* (1891) 28 LR Ir 481.
[41] *supra* n 38 at 622.
[42] [2000] 30 EHRR 241.
[43] See Chapter 10 on Freedom of Expression for more information.
[44] DG Barnum, "Freedom of Assembly and the Hostile Audience in Anglo-American Law" (1981) 29(1) AJCL 59 at 67. *Cf* AD Grunis, "Binding Over to Keep the Peace and Be of Good Behaviour in England and Canada" (1976) PL 16 at 17.
[45] See G Hogan and G Whyte, *supra* n 2, pp 1780–1792.
[46] s 27(1) of the Offences Against the State Act 1939.
[47] *ibid.*
[48] s 27(2) of the Offences Against the State Act 1939.

There is a right to appeal such a notice to the High Court and the High Court, if it so thinks proper, can annul the notice.[49] If a person proceeds to hold, organise or take part in such a meeting, he or she shall be guilty of an offence under the 1939 Act.[50]

The term "public meeting"[51] refers not only to a stationary meeting of persons but also to a procession and includes meetings held in a public place, on unenclosed land, in a building or on enclosed land to which the public are admitted, whether with or without payment.

[12–17] Meetings which constitute an interference with justice: any meeting, procession or demonstration in public that constitutes an interference with the course of justice shall be considered an offence.[52] What constitutes an interference with the course of justice is defined in broad terms and includes where the meeting is:

> "intended, or is of such character as to be likely, directly or indirectly to influence any court, person or authority concerned with the institution, conduct or defence of any civil or criminal proceedings (including a party or witness) as to whether or how the proceedings should be instituted, conducted, continued or defended or as to what should be their outcome".[53]

Meetings held in the vicinity of the Oireachtas: there is no automatic prohibition on holding any public meeting or procession within one half-mile from any building in which both Houses or either House of the Oireachtas are or is sitting or are or is about to sit.[54] However, the Offences Against the State Act 1939 provides that if an officer of the Garda Síochána, not below the rank of chief superintendent, has, by notice, prohibited the holding of such a meeting or procession[55] or has called on such persons to disperse,[56] the holding of such a meeting or procession will constitute an offence.[57]

[12–18] Whether this provision is compatible with the constitutional right to free assembly is questionable, given the broad discretion granted to the Garda Síochána. While there is a specific reference in the Constitution to the control of meetings within the vicinity of

---

49 s 27(3) of the Offences Against the State Act 1939.

50 s 27(4) of the Offences Against State Act 1939, as amended by s 2(7) of the Criminal Law Act 1976. A person guilty of such offence is liable on summary conviction to a fine not exceeding £500 (€634.86), or, at the discretion of the court, to imprisonment for a term not exceeding 12 months or to both such fine and imprisonment.

51 s 27(5) of the Offences Against the State Act 1939.

52 s 4(1)(a) of the Offences Against the State (Amendment) Act 1972. A person found guilty of this offence shall be liable on summary conviction to a fine not exceeding £200 (€253.95) or, at the discretion of the court, to imprisonment for a term not exceeding 12 months or to both (s 4(2)(a) of the Offences Against the State (Amendment) Act 1972), or on indictment to a fine not exceeding £1000 (€1269.73) or to imprisonment for a term not exceeding five years or both (s 4(2)(b) of the Offences Against the State (Amendment) Act 1972).

53 s 4(1)(b) of the Offences Against the State (Amendment) Act 1972.

54 s 28(1) of the Offences Against the State Act 1939.

55 s 28(1)(a) of the Offences Against the State Act 1939.

56 s 28(1)(b) of the Offences Against the State Act 1939.

57 s 28(2) of the Offences Against the State Act 1939. Contravention of this section shall make the person liable on summary conviction to a fine not exceeding £50 (€63.49) or, at the discretion of the court, to a term of imprisonment not exceeding three months or both.

the Houses of the Oireachtas, this could not have been meant to provide for a broad discretionary power, with no appeal mechanism, to be vested in the Gárda Síochána. Casey comments that, in theory, a challenge based on s 28 could be made by judicial review. However, even with this possibility, the potential for unjustifiable interference with free assembly is real. Casey refers to the US Supreme Court decision in *Cox v Louisiana*[58] where Goldberg J held that it is:

> "unconstitutional to enable a public official to determine which expressions of view will be permitted and which will not or to engage in invidious discrimination among persons or groups either by use of a statute providing a system of broad discretionary licensing power or, as in this case, the equivalent of such a system by selective enforcement of an extremely broad prohibitory statute".[59]

While this issue has never been considered in the Irish courts, Casey does advocate that the provision be repealed.[60] The Report of the Committee to Review the Offences Against the State Acts 1939-1998[61] also agreed that the provision was likely to be unconstitutional on the ground that it was "impermissibly overboard".[62]

Meetings which distribute certain materials: the Criminal Justice (Public Order) Act 1994 provides that it is an offence[63] for any person in a public place to "distribute or display any writing, sign or visual representation which is threatening, abusive, insulting or obscene with intent to provoke a breach of the peace or being reckless as to whether a breach of the peace may be occasioned".[64]

Meetings considered to be loitering: the Criminal Justice (Public Order) Act 1994 also **[12–19]** provides that where a member of the Garda Síochána finds a person in a public place and suspects, with reasonable cause, that such person without lawful authority or reasonable excuse is acting in a manner which consists of loitering in a public place in circumstances (which may include the company of other persons) that give rise to a reasonable apprehension for the safety of persons or the safety of property or for the maintenance of the public peace, the member may direct the person so suspected to desist from acting in such a manner and leave immediately the vicinity of the place concerned in a peaceable or orderly manner.[65]

While the penalty on summary conviction for this offence is normally a fine not exceeding €1000 or a term of imprisonment not exceeding three months,[66] there is power in the Criminal Justice Act 2006 to make "a restriction on movement order", as

---

[58] (1965) 379 US 536 referred to in Casey, *supra* n 9, p 590.
[59] (1965) 379 US 536 at 557-558 (*per* Goldberg J).
[60] J Casey, *supra* n 9, p 590.
[61] (Government Publications, Dublin, 2002), paras 6.137 – 6.139.
[62] G Hogan and G Whyte, *supra* n 2, p 1783.
[63] s 7(2) of the Criminal Justice (Public Order) Act 1994, as amended by the Intoxicating Liquor Act 2008, s 22 and Sch 2. It provides that a person will be liable on summary conviction to a fine not exceeding €1000 or a term of imprisonment not exceeding three months or both.
[64] s 7(1) of the Criminal Justice (Public Order) Act 1994.
[65] s 8(1)(b) of the Criminal Justice (Public Order) Act 1994.
[66] s 8(3) of the Criminal Justice (Public Order) Act 1994, as amended by s 22 and Sch 2 of the Intoxicating Liquor Act 2008.

an alternative to the term of imprisonment.[67] The court may, to the extent that it thinks fit, restrict the movement of the offender by requiring the offender to be or not to be in certain specified places[68] for not more than six months.[69] The offender must also keep the peace and be of good behaviour during this time.[70] This could have the potential to interfere with the right of the offender to assemble in a certain place or to take part in certain meetings. While the Oireachtas has been careful to specify the restrictions in these circumstances, the Constitution Review Group Report was of the view that "the powers in question are too broad and far-reaching".[71]

Picketing

[12–20] Picketing can be defined as "the application of moral pressure by several persons maintaining a conspicuous presence in the vicinity of a particular premises".[72] There are circumstances where picketing may constitute an offence at common law such as nuisance or trespass or may be contrary to statute in cases where the picketing amounts to the offence of "watching and besetting". [73] Therefore, all pickets will be considered unlawful unless they are conducted in accordance with s 14 of the Industrial Relations Act 1990 and do not constitute an obstruction. However, Casey would suggest that there is a potential for unjustifiable discrimination against persons who are involved in a trade dispute and those who want to gather in a peaceful manner to picket premises on other grounds.[74]

Non-Discrimination

[12–21] The Constitution provides that the exercise of the right to free assembly shall be limited only by legislation which does not contain political, religious or other class discrimination.[75] While this has never been judicially considered in the Irish courts in the context of free assembly, it does provide for a measure of review of any limitations which might infringe the constitutional guarantee of equality.

B. Protection under the European Convention on Human Rights

[12–22] Article 11:

> "1. Everyone has the right to freedom of peaceful assembly and to freedom of association with others, including the right to form and to join trade unions for the protection of his interests.
> 2. No restrictions shall be placed on the exercise of these rights other than such as are prescribed by law and are necessary in a democratic society in the interests of national security or public safety, for the prevention of disorder or crime, for the protection of health or morals or for the protection of the rights and freedoms of others. This article

[67] s 101(1) of the Criminal Justice Act 2006.
[68] s 101(2)(a) and (b) of the Criminal Justice Act 2006.
[69] s 101(3) of the Criminal Justice Act 2006.
[70] *ibid.*
[71] Constitution Review Group, *supra* n 12, p 306.
[72] *supra* n 2, p 1786.
[73] s 9(1)(d) of the Non-Fatal Offences Against the Person Act 1997.
[74] J Casey, *supra* n 9, p 596.
[75] Art 40.6.2°.

shall not prevent the imposition of lawful restrictions on the exercise of these rights by members of the armed forces, of the police or of the administration of the State."

1. Nature of the Right

The right to freely assemble peacefully applies to both public and private meetings on public thoroughfares whether the assembly is static (demonstration) or moving (processing) [76] The ECtHR has clarified that the right to peaceful assembly imposes both positive and negative obligations on the contracting State.[77] States are not only required to ensure that there is no interference with the right (negative obligation) but are also tasked with ensuring that people can exercise their right effectively (positive obligation). The ECtHR has held that "genuine, effective freedom of peaceful assembly cannot ... be reduced to a mere duty on the part of the State not to interfere: a purely negative conception would not be compatible with the object and purpose of Article 11".[78] This positive obligation is of even greater importance to persons "holding unpopular views or belonging to minorities, because they are more vulnerable to victimisation".[79] [12–23]

An example of the positive obligation on States imposed by Art 11 is evident in one of the seminal cases on the issue of free, peaceful assembly before the ECtHR, the case of *Plattform "Ärzte Für Das Leben" v Austria*, involving a demonstration by doctors against abortion.[80] This demonstration was disrupted by counter-demonstrations, despite the presence of a large police contingent.[81] The ECtHR held that participants at a demonstration must "be able to hold the demonstration without having to fear that they will be subjected to physical violence by their opponents"[82] because of the potential deterrent effect this would have on people with common ideas or interests. [12–24]

Interference with the Right

There have been a number of interesting cases before the ECtHR in relation to what constitutes an interference with the right to peaceful assembly. [12–25]

Prior authorisation: one particular issue that has arisen is the requirement in many States, that those persons seeking to assemble gain prior authorisation from the authorities. Prior notification requirements or authorisation requirements "would not normally encroach upon the essence" of the right to free assembly.[83] Such notifications serve to balance the rights of those seeking to assemble and the rights and freedoms of others and also to prevent disorder and crime.[84] However, in certain special cases,

[76] *Sergey Kuznetsov v Russia* (Application No 10877/04) at para 35.
[77] *Plattform "Ärzte Für Das Leben" v Austria* (1991) 13 EHRR 204.
[78] *ibid* at para 32. See also *Bączkowski v Poland* (Application No 1543/06) at para 64.
[79] *Bączkowski v Poland, ibid.* The ECtHR ultimately held that the interference was not justified as it was not prescribed by law. See also *Saya v Turkey* (Application No 4327/02) at para 44.
[80] *supra* n 77. In this case, the ECtHR held that there had been no violation as the State, through the large contingent of police officers, had done enough to attempt to secure the right to peaceful assembly for the applicants.
[81] *supra* n 77 at para 8.
[82] *supra* n 77 at para 32.
[83] *Éva Molnár v Hungary* (Application No 10346/05) at para 35.
[84] *ibid* at para 37.

namely if an immediate response to a current event, for example a political event,[85] is warranted in the form of a public demonstration, there may not be time to make a notification or seek an authorisation. In such cases, the ECtHR has held that dispersing the spontaneous demonstration "solely because of the absence of the requisite prior notice, without any illegal conduct by the participants, may amount to a disproportionate restriction on the freedom of assembly".[86] In *Bączkowski v Poland*, the applicants wished to hold a meeting to alert public opinion to issues of discrimination against minorities.[87] The applicants were ultimately refused authorisation to assemble on the grounds that the demonstration would potentially cause traffic chaos and that there may be potential counter-demonstrations. The applicants appealed the decisions and were successful. However, the decisions of the appeals bodies were delayed and issued after the date upon which the marches were held. The ECtHR noted that the applicants had taken a risk in holding the marches given that official bans were in force. Refusals to give authorisation:

> "could have had a chilling effect on the applicants and other participants in the assemblies. It could also have discouraged other persons from participating in the assemblies on the grounds that they did not have official authorisation and that, therefore, no official protection against possible hostile counter-demonstrators would be ensured by the authorities".[88]

This refusal and delay in the appeals process constituted an interference with the right to free assembly.

Penalties for mere assembly: the ECtHR has held that convicting a person for taking part in an assembly which is not illegal, unauthorised or obstructing traffic amounts to an interference with the right to assemble peacefully.[89] Sanctions and penalties for breaching the procedure for organising and holding a public assembly have also been held to amount to interference.[90]

[12–26] Unjustifiable dispersal: dispersing a group of marchers, without legitimate justification, who are authorised to assemble also constitutes an interference with the freedom to assemble peacefully.[91] In the case of *Saya v Turkey*,[92] a group of individuals, who had received prior authorisation to hold a May Day march, were stopped by the police and when they continued to march, the police again intervened and injured some of the members of the group. The ECtHR held that there had been an unjustifiable interference with the freedom to assemble peacefully as the group had received prior authorisation to march.

[85] *ibid* at para 36.
[86] *ibid.*
[87] *Bączkowski v Poland, supra* n 78 at para 7.
[88] *supra* n 78 at para 67.
[89] *Galstyan v Armenia* (Application No 26986/03) at para 101; *Ashughyan v Armenia* (Application No 33268/03) at para 77.
[90] *supra* n 76 at para 36.
[91] *Saya v Turkey, supra* n 79.
[92] *ibid.*

2. Legitimate Justifications for Interference with the Right

Under the ECHR, an interference will constitute a breach of Art 11 unless it is prescribed by law, pursues one of the legitimate aims of national security, public safety, the prevention of disorder or crime, the protection of health or morals or the protection of the rights and freedoms of others and is necessary in a democratic society for the achievement of those aims. **[12–27]**

Prescribed by law: the law must be formulated with sufficient precision to enable the citizen to "foresee, to a degree that is reasonable in the circumstances, the consequences which a given action may entail".[93] Public order offences, despite their broad definition, have been held to be compliant with this requirement.[94] In the case of *Galstyan v Armenia*,[95] the ECtHR considered the case of an applicant who was arrested for taking part in a Mother's Day protest which highlighted the policies and practices of the Government, particularly against women, on the grounds that he had engaged in anti-social behaviour and obstructed traffic. He argued that this was contrary to his right to assemble peacefully. The ECtHR held that there was an interference with the right to free assembly and went on to consider whether this interference could be justified. In relation to the requirement that the interference be prescribed by law, the ECtHR held that the applicant had been arrested under a piece of domestic law which prescribed a penalty for disturbing public order and peace of citizens which was formulated with sufficient precision to satisfy the requirements of Art 11.[96] **[12–28]**

Legitimate aims: the ECtHR has acknowledged that the prevention of public disorder[97]and protecting the rights of others, such as the right to freedom of movement and the orderly circulation of traffic[98] are all legitimate aims for interfering with an assembly. In *Galstyan v Armenia*,[99] the ECtHR also had to consider whether the public order offences had a legitimate aim. The ECtHR held that the law in question was designed for the "prevention of disorder" and therefore had a legitimate aim.[100]

Necessary in a democratic society: the expression "necessary in a democratic society" has been interpreted as implying that the interference should correspond to a "pressing social need" and should be proportionate to the aim sought to be achieved.[101] However, this is a very narrow test and the ECtHR reiterated in *Galstyan v Armenia*[102] **[12–29]**

---

93 *Galstyan v Armenia*, *supra* n 89 at para 106.

94 *ibid* at para 107; *Ashughyan v Armenia*, *supra* n 89 at para 81; *Saya v Turkey*, *supra* n 79 at para 42; *Patyi v Hungary* (Application No 5529/05) at para 31; *Éva Molnár v Hungary*, *supra* n 83 at para 23; *Sergey Kuznetsov v Russia*, *supra* n 76 at para 38.

95 *supra* n 89.

96 *ibid* at para 107.

97 *ibid* at para 110; *Ashughyan v Armenia*, *supra* n 89 at para 85; *Saya v Turkey*, *supra* n 79 at para 42.

98 *Patyi v Hungary* (Application No 5529/05) at paras 32-34; *Éva Molnár v Hungary*, *supra* n 83 at para 29; *Sergey Kuznetsov v Russia*, *supra* n 76 at para 38.

99 *Galstyan v Armenia*, *supra* n 89.

100 *ibid* at para 110.

101 *Patyi v Hungary*, *supra* n 98 at para 38.

102 *Galstyan v Armenia*, *supra* n 89.

that the right to peaceful assembly is subject to a number of exceptions which must be narrowly interpreted and the necessity for "any restrictions must be convincingly established".[103] In the case of *Galstyan v Armenia*,[104] the ECtHR concluded that the applicant was sanctioned "for the mere fact of being present and proactive at the demonstration in question, rather than for committing anything illegal, violent or obscene in the course of it".[105] The ECtHR held that:

> "the very essence of the right to freedom of peaceful assembly would be impaired, if the State was not to prohibit a demonstration but was then to impose sanctions, especially such severe ones, on its participants for the mere fact of attending it, without committing anything reprehensible".[106]

Therefore, the ECtHR held that the actions of the police in this case were not necessary in a democratic society and constituted an unjustifiable interference with Art 11.

Proportionality: in determining whether, on the facts, the decisions of the authorities are proportionate, the ECtHR has reiterated the need to strike a fair balance between the rights of those wishing to exercise the right to free assembly and the protection of the rights and freedoms of others.[107]

[12–30] Where an assembly is not peaceful, incites violence or is unauthorised, criminal sanctions are considered compatible with Art 11.[108] Where the assembly is of a "disorderly character", the dispersal of such an assembly could "not be said to be at variance with the object and purpose of Article 11".[109] However, the imposition of a sanction for participation in an assembly that has not been prohibited, so long as the person does not commit any reprehensible acts, is not acceptable under the ECHR.[110] Equally, the ECtHR has held that contracting States have to tolerate a certain level of disruption in order to allow persons the right to assemble peacefully. The ECtHR has held that:

> "any demonstration in a public place may cause a certain level of disruption to ordinary life, including disruption of traffic, and where demonstrators do not engage in acts of violence it is important for the public authorities to show a certain degree of tolerance towards peaceful gatherings".[111]

---

[103] *ibid* at para 114.

[104] *Galstyan v Armenia, supra* n 89.

[105] *ibid* at para 117.

[106] *ibid.*

[107] *Patyi v Hungary, supra* n 98 at para 42. In this case, the mechanical reliance of the authorities on the same reasons (fear of traffic chaos) was neither relevant nor sufficient to meet any pressing social need (at para 44).

[108] *Galstyan v Armenia, supra* n 89 at para 115. In this case, the ECtHR held that the applicant had been sanctioned for the mere fact of being present and proactive at a demonstration and, therefore, the interference with the right to free assembly was not necessary in a democratic society.

[109] *Éva Molnár v Hungary, supra* n 83 at para 41.

[110] *Galstyan v Armenia, supra* n 89 at para 115. See also *Ezelin v France* (Application No 11800/85).

[111] *Ashughyan v Armenia, supra* n 89 at para 90. In this case, the ECtHR held that the conviction of the applicant for "obstruction of street traffic" and "making a loud noise" was an interference with her right to free assembly which was not necessary in a democratic society as there were over 30,000 other protestors, the traffic had been suspended on account of the demonstration and the

In cases where there is a serious threat of counter-demonstrations, the ECtHR has allowed the domestic authorities a wide discretion in how they control such assemblies.[112] The mere existence of risk is insufficient for banning the event. The ECtHR has held that the authorities must produce concrete estimates of the potential scale of the demonstrations in order to evaluate the resources required to neutralise the situation.[113] Mere reliance on the potential for conflict without such assessment, "endorse[s] the intentions of persons or organisations that clearly and deliberately intended to disrupt a peaceful demonstration in breach of the law and public order".[114]

Margin of appreciation: in relation to the margin of appreciation given to States in such circumstances, the ECtHR has held that while there is a certain margin of appreciation given to contracting States, this is not unlimited.[115] The margin of appreciation was raised in the case of *Alekseyev v Russia*[116] where the Russian Government claimed that a demonstration on discrimination against homosexuals should be banned on principle as it was "incompatible with religious doctrine and the moral values of the majority". The ECtHR reiterated the very fundamental nature of the right and held that it would be "incompatible with the underlying values of the Convention if the exercise of Convention rights were made conditional on its being accepted by the majority".[117] [12–31]

C. CFR

Article 12 of the CFR: [12–32]

> "1. Everyone has the right to freedom of peaceful assembly and to freedom of association at all levels, in particular in political, trade union and civic matters, which implies the right of everyone to form and to join trade unions for the protection of his or her interests.
> 2. Political parties at Union level contribute to expressing the political will of the citizens of the Union."

Article 12 of the CFR provides for the protection of the right to peaceful assembly. This right is to be interpreted in light of Art 11 of the ECHR[118] and is subject to the same limitations as exist under the ECHR.

One of the major issues that has arisen at a European Union level is the extent to which fundamental rights, such as the right to peaceful assembly, is compatible with the four freedoms guaranteed by the Treaty on European Union (TEU).

---

police had made no attempt to move the demonstrators on account of traffic and there was no suggestion made that the loud noise made by the applicant involved any obscenity or incitement to violence. This led the ECtHR to the conclusion that the applicant had been sanctioned for the mere fact of being present and proactive at the demonstration, "rather than for committing anything illegal, violent or obscene in the course of it" (at para 92); *Saya v Turkey*, *supra* n 79 at para 46; *Patyi v Hungary*, *supra* n 98 at para 40.

[112] *Alekseyev v Russia* (Application Nos 4916/07, 25924/08 and 14599/09) at para 75.

[113] *ibid* at para 75.

[114] *ibid* at para 76.

[115] *Galstyan v Armenia*, *supra* n 89 at para 114.

[116] *supra* n 112 at para 78.

[117] *supra* n 112 at para 81.

[118] Art 52(3) of the CFR.

[12–33] In the seminal case of *Schmidberger*,[119] involving a group called the *Transitforum Austria Tirol*, an association to protect the biosphere in the Alpine region, notice was given to the local authorities in Innsbruck, in accordance with the law, that they were planning a demonstration on the Brenner motorway on a certain date for the duration of four hours resulting in the motorway being closed to all traffic during this time.[120] The demonstration was considered lawful and was allowed to go ahead.[121] *Schmidberger* was an international transport undertaking which operated six articulated heavy goods vehicles. It took legal action against Austria on the basis that five of its vehicles were unable to use the highway due to Austria's failure to ban the demonstration. *Schmidberger* argued that the failure on the part of the Austrian authorities to ban the demonstration and to intervene to prevent that trunk route from being closed amounted to a restriction of the free movement of goods.[122] One of the questions arising before the European Court of Justice (ECJ) was:

> "whether the principle of the free movement of goods ... requires a Member State to keep open major transit routes and whether that obligation takes precedence over fundamental rights such as the freedom of expression and the freedom of assembly guaranteed by Articles 10 and 11 of the ECHR".[123]

[12–34] The case essentially involved a balancing exercise between a fundamental right guaranteed by the ECHR and a fundamental freedom guaranteed by the TEU. The ECJ held that the failure to ban the demonstration did amount to a measure having equivalent effect to a quantitative restriction.[124] The ECJ held that the fact that the demonstration was in pursuit of environmental and public health objectives was not relevant to the determination and what was more relevant was the objective pursued by the authorities in making the decision to allow the demonstration.[125] In this case, the ECJ held that it was clear that the Austrian authorities were inspired by the fundamental rights of the demonstrators to free expression and assembly.[126] The protection of rights "is a legitimate interest which, in principle, justifies a restriction of the obligations imposed by Community law, even under a fundamental freedom".[127] The ECJ looked at the fact that the demonstration had been authorised by the authorities,[128] traffic was only obstructed on a single route, on a single occasion and the purpose was not to restrict the trade of goods of a particular type or from a particular source.[129] Also the ECJ referred to the actions taken by the authorities to ensure the demonstration passed off smoothly, alternative routes had been designated

119 Case C-112/00, *Schmidberger, Internationale Transporte and Planzüge v Republik Österreich* [2003] ECR I-5659.
120 *ibid* at para 10.
121 *ibid* at para 13.
122 *ibid* para 16.
123 *ibid* at para 20.
124 *ibid* at para 64.
125 *ibid* at para 68.
126 *ibid* at para 69.
127 *ibid* at para 74.
128 *ibid* at para 84.
129 *ibid* at para 85.

and security arrangements had been made for the site of the demonstration.[130] Therefore, the Austrian authorities "were entitled to consider that an outright ban on the demonstration would have constituted unacceptable interference with the fundamental right of the demonstrators to gather and express peacefully their opinion in public".[131] There were no less restrictive measures that could have been imposed in the circumstances and therefore the restriction on the free movement of goods was justified.[132]

Therefore, while the exercise of fundamental rights, such as the freedom to assemble peacefully, can be a legitimate justification for interference with a fundamental freedom under the TEU, the exercise must be balanced against the fundamental freedoms, such as the freedom to provide goods and services, and must be considered in accordance with the principle of proportionality.[133] Advocate General Trstenjak concluded that central to *Schmidberger* was the idea of "equal ranking for conflicting fundamental rights and fundamental freedoms which, ultimately, by an examination of the proportionality of the opposing restrictions in question, were brought fairly into balance".[134] **[12–35]**

D. International and Regional Laws

The right to free assembly is also protected by other regional human rights regimes and at an international level. **[12–36]**

International protections: the right to peaceful assembly is protected by Art 20 of the Universal Declaration of Human Rights, Art 21 of the International Covenant on Civil and Political Rights, Art 5(ix) of the International Convention on the Elimination of all forms of Racial Discrimination and Art 15 of the United Nations Convention on the Rights of the Child. However, the right is not absolute and is subject to certain limited exceptions.

Regional protections: regionally (other than Europe which is dealt with above), the right to peaceful assembly is protected under the following regional instruments:

a. Organisation of American States: Art 15 of the American Convention on Human Rights[135];

---

130 *ibid* at para 87.

131 *ibid* at para 89.

132 *ibid* at para 93.

133 Case C-438/05, *International Transport Workers' Federation and Finnish Seamen's Union v Viking Line ABP, OÜ Viking Line Eesti* at para 46; Case C-341-05, *Laval un Partneri Ltd v Svenska Byggnadsarbetareförbundet, Svenska Byggnadsarbetareförbundets avd. 1, Byggettan Svenska Elektrikerförbundet* at para 96.

134 Case C-271/08, *European Commission v Federal Republic of Germany* (opinion of Advocate General Trstenjak delivered on 14 April 2010) at para 196.

135 Art 15 states: "The right of peaceful assembly, without arms, is recognized. No restrictions may be placed on the exercise of this right other than those imposed in conformity with the law and necessary in a democratic society in the interest of national security, public safety or public order, or to protect public health or morals or the rights or freedom of others."

b. Organisation of African Unity: Art 11 of the African Charter on Human and Peoples' Rights[136]; and
c. League of Arab States: Art 28 of the Arab Charter on Human Rights.[137]

Conclusion

[12–37] The right to assemble peacefully is protected by the Constitution, the ECHR and the CFR and ensures that all persons may assemble peacefully in public and private places in a variety of forms and for a variety of purposes, as long as the assembly or the actions of its participants remain, at all times, lawful. Legitimate interferences for the protection of public order and, in certain cases, morality would appear to be commonplace under the Constitution, the ECHR and the CFR. However, the constitutional protection would appear to be substantially weaker than the protection offered by the regional instruments. This probably arises due to the very express limitations on meetings in the text of the Constitution, which place severe restrictions on the right. The very narrow margin of appreciation given to States, the influence of the doctrine of proportionality and the narrow interpretation of limitations on the right to peaceful assembly, all contribute to a more robust protection of the right at a regional level.

[136] Art 11 states: "Every individual shall have the right to assemble freely with others. The exercise of this right shall be subject only to necessary restrictions provided for by law in particular those enacted in the interest of national security, the safety, health, ethics and rights and freedoms of others."

[137] Art 28 states: "Citizens have the freedom of assembly and association in peaceful manner. No restrictions shall be imposed on either of these two freedoms except when it is necessary for national security, or public safety, or the protection of the rights and freedoms of others."

CHAPTER 13
The Right to Free Association

Introduction

The right to free association to form or join clubs, societies, political parties or trade unions is regarded as a fundamental weapon in the protection of democracy and is often closely linked with the right to free expression. The protection of the right at a national, regional and international level is legally well developed and specific bodies of law have grown up around freedom of association and its impact on political parties, trade unions and other associations. The right is not absolute and is subject to certain restrictions. However, these restrictions are generally strictly construed and are subjected to rigorous analysis through the operation of the proportionality test. Due to its link with free choice, expression and democracy, freedom of association has become one of the most protected rights at a national, regional and international level. This chapter will examine the evolution and development of the right at a national, regional and international level and will outline the similarities and the differences in protection across these three regimes. **[13–01]**

A. Irish Constitutional Protection

Article 40.6.1°iii: **[13–02]**

> "The State guarantees liberty for the exercise, subject to public order and morality, of . . . iii. The right of the citizens to form associations and unions. Laws, however, may be enacted for the regulation and control in the public interest of the exercise of the foregoing right."

Article 40.6.2°:

> "Laws regulating the manner in which the right of forming associations and unions and the right of free assembly may be exercised shall contain no political, religious or class discrimination".

[13–03] The right to freedom of association in Ireland is protected by Art 40.6.1°iii which provides, subject to certain limitations in the public interest, that citizens have a right to form associations and unions. This right is founded on the concepts of liberty and democracy. Freedom of association:

> " ... is a pre-existing natural right, inhering in human kind by virtue of its rational and social being and is essential to the exercise of various other rights such as the right to engage effectively in political speech, to organise for industrial purposes or otherwise, to take part in elections, or participate in sporting or cultural events, and many more".[1]

As there are different forms of associations with different restrictions and limitations, it is intended to deal with different types of associations separately.

1. Nature of the Right

[13–04] The right to freedom of association is not an absolute right and is subject to certain limitations based on public order, morality and the public interest.[2] While these limitations are expressly mentioned in the Irish Constitution, in general the legislature and the courts have been very slow to interfere with the right to free association and few restrictions actually exist.[3] The courts have emphasised the important link with liberty and have been clear to emphasise the freedom associated with the right. The courts have also recognized that a corollary of this right to freedom of association is a right to dissociation.[4]

Trade Unions

[13–05] The courts have often dealt with the freedom of association in the context of trade unions and some interesting decisions have emerged from the case law.

The Right to Join, Refuse to Join or Leave a Union

[13–06] It has been held that there is no constitutional right to join a particular union. There may be certain restrictions on joining a trade union that may prevent a person from joining that particular union but this is not in itself unconstitutional. In *Murphy v Stewart*,[5] the plaintiff was refused consent to leave one trade union (Union A) and so was prevented, by the rules of Union B, from joining Union B. The Supreme Court held that there is:

> " ... no constitutional right to join the union of one's choice. The constitutional guarantee is the guarantee to form associations or unions, but in ordinary circumstances before a person can join an existing union or association he must be entitled to do so either by law, or by the rules of that association or union, or by the consent of its members".[6]

---

1 *Equality Authority v Portmarnock Golf Club and Ors and Cuddy and Anor* [2009] IESC 73 (*per* Hardiman J) at Section G.

2 See T Caraway, "Freedom of Association: Battering Ram or Trojan Horse?" (2006) 13(2) RPE 210.

3 J Casey, *Constitutional Law in Ireland* (3rd ed, Round Hall, Dublin 2000) at p 597.

4 *Educational Company Ltd v Fitzpatrick (No 2)* (1961) IR 345 and *Meskell v CIE* (1973) IR 121.

5 [1973] IR 97.

6 *ibid* at 117–118 (*per* Walsh JJ).

This is a necessary corollary of the rule that a person should be free to dissociate (discussed above).

The courts have also held that a person cannot be compelled to join a trade union. In *Educational Company of Ireland v Fitzpatrick (No 2)*,[7] the defendants (members of a trade union) sought to compel the plaintiff (employer) to force non-trade union members to join their union. When the plaintiff refused to comply, the defendants picketed the plaintiff's premises, and the plaintiff sought an injunction to restrain the defendants. The Supreme Court held that the concept of freedom of association means that the:

> "... citizen is 'free' to form and ... join, such associations and unions, and if he is free to do so, that obviously does not mean that he must form or join associations and unions, but that he may if he so wills".[8]

The court therefore held that a person has a right to join any association and has a right not to join any association.

Also, it has been held that a person cannot have their choice of association limited in any way. In *National Union of Railwaymen and Others v Sullivan and Others*,[9] the Supreme Court had to consider a provision of the Trade Union Act 1941 which provided for the construction of a "Trade Union Tribunal" with power to designate certain unions in a workplace. The Supreme Court held that this provision was unconstitutional in that it:

> "... purports to limit the right of the citizen to join one or more prescribed association, i.e. the Union or Unions in respect of which a determination has been made. Any such limitation does undoubtedly deprive the citizen of a free choice of the persons with whom he shall associate".[10]

Closed Shops

The Constitution does not permit the operation of a closed shop which can be defined as a "system under which one's continued employment depends on remaining a member of a union".[11] It does not matter whether this system is enforced by the employer (e.g. by threatening to dismiss an employee if they do not join a particular union or making employment conditional upon joining a particular trade union) or the trade union themselves (e.g. picketing an employer to force non-union members to join a union was restrainable by injunction in the *Educational Co*[12] case). Equally, the legislature is also prevented by Art 40.6.1°.iii from legislating for the creation or operation of a closed shop.[13] **[13–07]**

---

7 [1961] IR 345. Followed in *Meskell v CIE* [1973] IR 121.
8 [1961] I IR 345 at 362 (*per* Budd JJ).
9 [1947] IR 77.
10 *ibid* at 99 (*per* Murnaghen JJ).
11 J Casey, *supra* n 3 at p 606.
12 [1961] IR 345.
13 *ibid.*

Fair Procedures in the Operation of Trade Unions

[13–08] Another interesting aspect of Art 40.6.1° is the right to fair procedures in the operational aspects of a trade union. In *Rodgers v ITGWU*,[14] the association, a trade union, held a meeting, advertised as a meeting for the purposes of a discussion on wages, when in fact a discussion on a retirement proposal was held. The plaintiff missed the meeting and the court had to consider whether there had been a breach of Art 40.6.1° in this context. The High Court[15] held that as there was a right to join or not join a trade union and that a necessary part of this right was the right to participate in the democratic process within the rules of that trade union, this right to participation should be protected. Although, it added that it was a matter for the union to decide how this should be carried out. Doyle criticises the case on the grounds that it recognises a right to join a union, which was expressly rejected in *Murphy v Stewart*.[16] Given that there is an absence of a right to join a union, Doyle comments that "it is difficult to derive a right to fair procedures from that source".[17] However, even if there is no right to join a union, once accepted into a union, it could be argued, as held in *Rodgers v ITGWU*, that fair and democratic procedures would be essential to the assurance of the constitutional right to association and without such a right, the right to free association, would be meaningless. This view is supported by the statement of Costello J in *Doyle v Croke*[18] who held that if the right to join a union was to be effective, it had to include a right to be protected from procedures that might be unfair to a particular member.

Recognition of Trade Unions

[13–09] There is no right to have a particular association recognised and this has been particularly controversial in the case of trade unions as employers cannot be compelled to recognise any trade union.[19] The Constitutional Review Group did not recommend that this right should be protected by the Constitution on the grounds that the right to freedom of association is "principally designed to regulate the relationship between the State and individuals" and "should not have horizontal effect" as it would be "contrary to the voluntary nature of industrial relations", it might damage foreign investment and it is a matter which is more properly disposed of through legislative means.[20]

Political Parties and Other Associations

[13–10] As in the case of trade unions, there is no right to join a political or other association. This line of reasoning has also been followed in relation to sports clubs where the

---

[14] [1978] ILRM 51. Followed in *Doyle v Croke* [1988] J JISLL 170.

[15] [1978] ILRM 51 (*per* Finlay P).

[16] [1973] IR 97.

[17] O Doyle, *Constitutional Law: Text, Cases and Materials* (Clarus Press, Dublin, 2008) at p 211.

[18] *supra* n 14.

[19] *Dublin College ASA v City of Dublin VEC*, High Court, 31 July 1981; *Abbott and Whelan v ITGWU* [1982] I JSILL 56; *Nolan Transport (Oaklands) Ltd v Halligan* [1995] ELR 1; and *Association of General Practitioners Ltd v Minister for Health* [1995] I IR 382.

[20] Constitution Review Group, *Report of the Constitution Review Group* (Stationery Office, Dublin, 1996) at p 293.

courts have held that there is no right to join a sports club.[21] In the case of *Equality Authority v Portmarnock Golf Club*,[22] the court had to consider whether s 8 of the Equal Status Act 2000 which provided that if a club was a discriminating club[23] it could have its license to sell intoxicating liquor removed, was compatible with Art 40.6.1°. The argument was that s 8 might be an unconstitutional coercion of the club's members to associate in a particular way. O'Higgins J held that this was not an interference with the right to freedom of association as it did not impact on the right of the members to associate with each other, to carry on the main activities of the club or the right to exclude women. It merely removed the club license, which was not a "primary or core activity of the Club". Doyle argues that the obiter comments of O'Higgins J in this case in relation to the withdrawal of a licence to sell alcohol, raises questions as to the dividing line between legitimate and illegitimate coercions and the comments of O'Higgins J would appear to suggest that this would depend on how closely it impacts on the core activities of the organisation.[24] Therefore, where the coercion interferes with the core activities of a particular association, this might be incompatible with Art 40.6.1°.

Interference with the Right

Any interference with the right to join, leave or participate in a trade union, political party or other association may be incompatible with Art 40.6.1°. In *Education Company of Ireland v Fitzpatrick (No 2)*,[25] the court specifically addressed the issue of what constituted an interference with the right to free association. While some interferences are obvious (preventing someone joining, participating in or leaving an association or coercing someone to join an association), the court addressed a situation where pressure is applied to certain individuals to coerce them into joining or leaving an association. Kingsmill Moore J defined coercion as: **[13–11]**

> "... forcing a person by action or threat of action to do or abstain from doing something which he is unwilling to do or abstain from doing, and which, but for such action or threats of action, he would not do or abstain from doing. Attempted coercion is the attempt (which may not be successful) by action or threat of action to produce a similar result".[26]

Kingsmill Moore J also made a distinction between legitimate (where, for example, a person who joins an association with extreme tenets become unpopular as a result) and illegitimate (where the legislature intervenes to authorise or facilitate coercion by

---

21 *O'Donohoe v O'Baroid* [1999] ICLY 873.

22 [2005] IEHC 235. For a discussion of this issue more generally see also Comments and Notes "Discrimination in Private Social Clubs: Freedom of Association and Right to Privacy" (1970) 6 Duke LJ 1181.

23 A discriminating club is defined by s 8(2) of the Equal Status Act 2000 which provides that a club shall be considered to be a discriminating club if it has any rule, policy or practice which discriminates against a member of an applicant for membership, or a person involved in its management discriminates against a member or an applicant for membership in relation to the affairs of the club.

24 O Doyle, *supra* n 17 p 212.

25 *supra* n 7.

26 *ibid* at 396.

attempting to legalise certain acts) coercion.[27] The campaign of picketing in this case constituted illegitimate pressure. Doyle has criticised this distinction as he believes the line is particularly difficult to draw and this would certainly appear to be true from the case law.[28]

2. Legitimate Justifications for Interference with the Right

[13–12] Interferences with the right to free association are permitted in certain cases where such interference is considered to be in the public interest or in the furtherance of another constitutional right. In this regard, a distinction has been drawn in the case law between the regulation of the exercise of the right (which may be permissible in certain circumstances) and the prohibition or control of the exercise of the right. The latter, being a denial of the right altogether, is not constitutionally permissible.[29]

[13–13] Therefore, as long as restrictions do not amount to a complete frustration of the right, they will generally be upheld by the courts. In *PMPS v Attorney General*,[30] the plaintiffs challenged s 5 of the Industrial and Provident Societies (Amendment) Act 1978 on the grounds that it did not allow the plaintiff members to hold or accept deposits for a period of five years after the enactment of the Act which the Society had been formed to do. The plaintiff argued that this amounted to a complete restriction on the right to freedom of association as it frustrated the purpose for which he and his associates joined together. However, the Supreme Court held that there was a distinction between a prohibition on association and a regulation of the exercise of association. The law in question merely regulated what the association could do and not whether they could associate or not and was justified in the public interest of regulating the banking sector. Similarly in *Aughey v Ireland*,[31] the Supreme Court held that a law, which provided that permission of the Garda Commissioner was required before a representative association for the purposes of controlling or influencing pay, pensions and conditions of service of the Gardaí could be set up, was not contrary to the Constitution. The court held that s 1 of the Garda Síochana Act 1977 was not a restriction on the freedom to associate completely but merely a regulation of the exercise of that right and this could be justified by reference to public interest concerns.

Legitimate Interferences in the Public Interest

Registration Requirements

[13–14] The only existing legislative restriction on the formation of certain associations is that, in certain circumstances, they must be registered. For example, the Electoral Act 1992 as amended[32] governs the registration of political parties and makes provision for an application to be made to the Registrar of Political Parties.[33] There are certain

---

[27] *ibid* at 396–397.
[28] J Casey, *supra* n 3 at pp 8–33.
[29] *NUR v Sullivan* [1947] IR 77 at 101–102 (*per* Murnaghan JJ); adopted in *PMPS v Attorney General* [1983] IR 339.
[30] [1983] IR 339.
[31] [1989] ILRM 87.
[32] Electoral (Amendment) Act 2001.
[33] s 25, Electoral Act 1992 as substituted by s 11, Electoral (Amendment) Act 2001.

requirements which must be met before the registration will be accepted which are laid out in s 25 (as amended).[34] These include evidence that the party is constituted for the purpose of contesting certain elections,[35] meets certain minimum membership requirements,[36] and has a written constitution or other such document governing its membership.[37] Once these requirements are met, the Registrar can only refuse to register the party if the name of the party is (a) identical to, or resembles, one already registered and which may be likely to mislead, confuse or deceive, (b) is more than six words long or (c) if the party is operating to a particular part of the State, does not indicate this in the name.[38] There is an appeal available from the decision of the Registrar.[39]

A challenge to registration requirements in the context of political parties was made in *Loftus v Attorney General*[40] which challenged the right of the Registrar of Political Parties under s 13(2) of the Electoral Act 1963, to register a party who in his opinion is a genuine political party organised to contest a general election. Parties who were already in the Dáil at the time of the election were automatically registered whereas other parties had to go through the Registrar. The plaintiff's party, "The Christian Democratic Party of Ireland" was refused registration. The Supreme Court rejected the argument that s 13(2) was contrary to Art 40.6.1°.iii on the grounds that it interfered with the right to freely associate. O'Higgins CJ held that it was in the public interest to regulate political parties in this manner as otherwise: **[13–15]**

> " ... genuine political action might be destroyed by a proliferation of bogus front organisations calling themselves political parties but with aims and objectives far removed from the political sphere".[41]

However, academics have criticised the decision for not granting the electorate any level of scrutiny to differentiate between legitimate and illegitimate parties themselves rather than leaving this to an unelected official to determine.[42]

Unlawful Organisations

Under Part III of the Offences Against the State Act 1939, unlawful organisations can be suppressed and their members can be liable to a criminal offence. The definition of an unlawful organisation is very broad and includes any organisation that: **[13–16]**

> " ... (a) engages in, promotes, encourages, or advocates the commission of treason or any activity of a treasonable nature, or (b) advocates, encourages, or attempts the procuring

[34] s 25 of the Electoral Act 1992 has been amended by ss 1, 11, 39 and 42 of the Electoral (Amendment) Act 2001 and by ss 1 and 81 of the Electoral Act 1997.

[35] s 25(4)(a), Electoral Act 1992 as substituted by s 11, Electoral (Amendment) Act 2001 provides that the party should be organised to contest a Dáil election, a European election, a local election or an election to Údarás na Gaeltachta.

[36] s 25(4)(b), Electoral Act 1992 as substituted by s 11, Electoral (Amendment) Act 2001.

[37] s 25(4)(c), Electoral Act 1992 as substituted by s 11, Electoral (Amendment) Act 2001.

[38] s 25(5), Electoral Act 1992 as substituted by s 11, Electoral (Amendment) Act 2001.

[39] s 25B(1), Electoral Act 1992 as substituted by s 11, Electoral (Amendment) Act 2001.

[40] [1979] IR 221.

[41] O Doyle, *supra* n 17 at p 242.

[42] *ibid* at pp 211–212

> by force, violence, or other unconstitutional means of an alteration of the Constitution, or (c) raises or maintains or attempts to raise or maintain a military or armed force in contravention of the Constitution or without constitutional authority, or (d) engages in, promotes, encourages, or advocates the commission of any criminal offence or the obstruction of or interference with the administration of justice or the enforcement of the law, or (e) engages in, promotes, encourages, or advocates the attainment of any particular object, lawful or unlawful, by violent, criminal, or other unlawful means, or (f) promotes, encourages, or advocates the non-payment of moneys payable to the Central Fund or any other public fund or the non-payment of local taxation"[43]

and any

> " ... terrorist group that engages in, promotes, encourages or advocates the commission, in or outside the State, of a terrorist activity".[44]

Such organisations can be suppressed,[45] the property of the organisation vested in the Minister for Justice[46] and members can be prosecuted.[47]

Trade Union Regulation

[13–17] Trade Unions are also restricted in their operation by the Trade Union Acts 1871–1990. The main restrictions involve restricting negotiating rights by legislating for unions to hold negotiation licences or to be classified as an excepted body within the terms of the legislation before they enter negotiations. Failure to do so is an offence under the relevant legislation.[48]

Legitimate Interferences Relating to Other Constitutional Rights

[13–18] It has also been held that freedom of association can only be exercised in so far as it does not interfere with the constitutional rights of others. Other rights are also consequent upon Art 40.6.1°.iii, such as the right to strike. This was recognised implicitly in *Education Company of Ireland v Fitzpatrick (No 2)*[49] but would clearly be a qualified right. For example, the right to strike may not be exercised in circumstances

[43] s 18, Offences Against the State Act 1939.
[44] s 5(1), Criminal Justice (Terrorist) Offences Act 2005.
[45] s 19, Offences Against the State Act 1939.
[46] s 22, Offences Against the State Act 1939 as amended by s 50, Criminal Justice (Terrorist) Offences Act 2005.
[47] s 21, Offences Against the State Act 1939 as amended by s 2, Offences Against the State (Amendment) Act 1972, ss 2 and 16, Criminal Law Act 1976 and ss 4, 6, 48 and 49 of the Criminal Justice (Terrorist) Offences Act 2005.
[48] s 6, Trade Union Act 1941 as amended. For more information see G Whyte, Industrial Relations and the Irish Constitution (1981) 16(1) Ir Jur 35; B Wilkinson, "Workers, Constitutions and the Irish Judiciary: A Jurisprudence of Labour Liberty?" (1989) 24(2) Ir Jur 198; N Howlin and R Fitzpatrick, "The Feasibility of Mandatory Trade Union Recognition in Ireland" (2007) 14(1) DULJ 178; M Doherty, "Union Sundown? The future of collective representation rights in Irish law" (2007) 4 (4) IELJ 96; J Casey, "Reform of Collective Bargaining Law: Some Constitutional Implications" (1972) 7(1) Ir Jur 1; R Craig, "Where the River Lagan flows — Is there a right?" (2008) 5(2) IELJ 63.
[49] *supra* n 7 at 397 (per Kingsmill Moore J).

where it clearly interferes with the rights of others as in the case of *Crowley v Ireland*.[50] In that case, the Irish National Teachers' Organisation (INTO) was in dispute with a school board of management over the appointment of a new principal. A strike ensued at the school and other INTO members in other schools in the area also refused to enrol the students affected in their schools. A number of parents, on behalf of their children, claimed that this interfered with the right of their children to free primary education as protected by Art 42.4 of the Constitution. McMahon J held that the exercise of the right to strike for the purpose of infringing the constitutional rights of others was an abuse of that right. The purpose of the strike had nothing to do with terms and conditions of employment but was solely carried out to exert pressure on the school management, by depriving children of their right to education.[51] Therefore, where the right to freely associate interferes with the constitutional rights of another, the courts will balance these rights and where it appears that the right to freely associate is being used in a manner specifically designed to deny another constitutional right, the court will legitimately restrict the right to free association in favour of the protection of another right.

3. Non-Discrimination

The Constitution provides that the exercise of the right to freedom of association shall be limited only by legislation which does not discriminate on political, religious or other grounds.[52] While this has never been judicially considered in the Irish courts in the context of freedom of association, it does provide for a measure of review of any limitations which might infringe the constitutional guarantee of equality. **[13–19]**

B. Protection under the European Convention on Human Rights

Article 11: **[13–20]**

(1) "Everyone has the right to freedom of peaceful assembly and to freedom of association with others, including the right to form and to join trade unions for the protection of his interests."

(2) "No restrictions shall be placed on the exercise of these rights other than such as are prescribed by law and are necessary in a democratic society in the interests of national security or public safety, for the prevention of disorder or crime, for the protection of health or morals or for the protection of the rights and freedoms of others. This article shall not prevent the imposition of lawful restrictions on the exercise of these rights by members of the armed forces, of the police or of the administration of the State."

1. Nature of the Right

Harris describes Art 11 and the protection of the freedom of association as embracing "a complex of ideas, not all of which are fully worked out in practice under the Convention" including trade union and association representation. Similar to the Irish constitutional position, there is no right to become a member of a particular **[13–21]**

---

[50] [1980] IR 102.
[51] J Casey, *supra* n 3 at p 611.
[52] Art 40.6.2°.

association[53] (as this would interfere with the rights of the other members to disassociate) or be compelled to join a particular association or be disadvantaged if he or she chooses not to do so.[54] Freedom of association is closely linked with freedom of assembly in the ECHR context as both are listed together under Art 11. This linkage is also evident in the case law as the cases often involve groups of individuals (potential associations) who have been involved in some form of demonstration (assembly). The case law is also linked by the interpretation of Art 11 given by the European Court of Human Rights (ECtHR). The ECtHR has imposed, in both contexts, negative obligations on states not to interfere with the rights but also positive obligations on states to protect the right against interference by the state and third parties.[55] One of the leading cases is *Plattform "Ärtze für das Leben" v Austria*[56] in which an association of doctors campaigning against abortion held two demonstrations in an effort to bring about reform of the law in Austria. These demonstrations were subsequently disrupted by counter-demonstrators despite the presence of a large contingent of police. The ECtHR held that freedom of association is closely linked with freedom of assembly in the ECHR context as both are listed together under Art 11. This linkage is also evident in the case law as the cases often involve groups of individuals (potential associations) who have been involved in some form of demonstration (assembly). The interpretation of the case law by the ECtHR has seen the imposition, in both terms of assembly and association, negative obligations on States not to interfere with the rights and also positive obligations on States to protect the right against interference by the state and third parties.[57]

> " ... genuine, effective freedom of peaceful assembly cannot, therefore, be reduced to a mere duty on the part of the State not to interfere: a purely negative conception would not be compatible with the object and purpose of Article 11 (art. 11). Like Article 8 (art. 8), Article 11 (art. 11) sometimes requires positive measures to be taken, even in the sphere of relations between individuals, if need be"[58].

In this instance the ECtHR found that the Austrian law was, in fact, sufficient to comply with the positive obligation on the State to protect associations and assemblies, and the ECtHR went on to state that the positive duty of States under Art 11 can be defined as a duty to "take reasonable and appropriate measures to enable lawful demonstrations to proceed peacefully".[59] The ECtHR noted, however, that a State

---

53 *Cheall v United Kingdom* [1985] 8 EHRR 74 at para 185.

54 *Young, James and Webster v United Kingdom* [1981] 4 EHRR 38 at para 55.

55 See JF Akandjii-Kombe, *Positive Obligations under the European Convention on Human Rights* (Strasbourg, Council of Europe, 2007) at 51. See also *Plattform "Arzte fur das Leben" v Austria* (1988) No 5/1987/128/179 and *Wilson & the National Union of Journalists and Others v The United Kingdom*, nos 30668/96, 30671/96 and 30678/96 at 41.

56 (1988) No 5/1987/128/179.

57 See JF Akandjii-Kombe, *Positive Obligations under the European Convention on Human Rights* (Strasbourg: Council of Europe, 2007) at 51. See also *Plattform "Arzte fur das Leben" v Austria* (1988) No 5/1987/128/179 and *Wilson & the National Union of Journalists and Others v. the United Kingdom*, Nos 30668/96, 30671/96 and 30678/96 at 41.

58 *ibid* at 32.

59 *ibid* at 34.

could not guarantee this absolutely and that States would have a wide discretion in the choice of the means to be used.[60] The court further emphasized that the obligation States enter into under Art 11 "is an obligation as to measures to be taken and not as to results to be achieved".[61]

In more recent cases, the ECtHR has also held that states have an "obligation of neutrality"[62] and an "obligation to carry out an effective investigation"[63] into breaches of Art 11 rights. In relation to the obligation of neutrality, it was held in the case of *Ouranio Toxo and others v Greece*[64] that it:

> "is incumbent upon public authorities to guarantee the proper functioning of an association or political party, even when they annoy or give offence to persons opposed to the lawful ideas or claims that they are seeking to promote. Their members must be able to hold meetings without having to fear that they will be subjected to physical violence by their opponents. Such a fear would be liable to deter other associations or political parties from openly expressing their opinions on highly controversial issues affecting the community".[65]

In the same case, the ECtHR held that States have an additional obligation "to take effective investigative measures" in cases where breaches of the rights to assembly and association have been alleged.[66]

What is an Association for the Purposes of the ECHR?

The definition of association under the European Convention on Human Rights (ECHR) is rather wide and very few associations have been excluded from the scope of Art 11. It includes groups of individuals set up for a particular purpose and operating on a stable basis. Naturally, this applies to political parties,[67] trade unions and other associations such as sports clubs and religious associations (see para 13-31 below). The definition of association is autonomous, meaning that just because such a grouping is not recognised by national law as an association, this does not prohibit it from protection under Art 11.[68] Some examples of exclusions from the scope of Art 11 include organisations that are public-law institutions "founded not by individuals but by the legislature" which "remain. ... integrated within the structures of the State", pursuing aims that are "in the general interest" as opposed to the interests of [13–22]

60 *ibid* at 34.
61 *ibid* at 34.
62 JF Akandjii-Kombe, *Positive Obligations under the European Convention on Human Rights* (Council of Europe, Strasbourg, 2007) at p 51.
63 *ibid.*
64 *Ouranio Toxo and others v Greece (*2005) Application No 74989/01.
65 *ibid* at 37.
66 *ibid* at 43. See also *Özgür Gündem v Turkey* (2000) Application No 23144/93 at 45.
67 *KPD v FRG* (Application No 250/57); *Refah Partisis v Turkey* [2003] 37 EHRR 1.
68 The concept of "association" under the ECHR is autonomous. See *Sigurjonsson v Iceland* (1993) 16 EHRR 462; *Chassagnou v France* (1999) 29 EHRR 61.

members.[69] As an example, the ECtHR has held that professional associations, such as Bar Associations, are not necessarily considered to fall within the scope of Art 11.[70]

What Constitutes an Interference with this Right?

[13–23] The court has held that a refusal to register associations, where registration is required, may amount to an interference with the right to freedom of association.[71] The possibility of requesting an authority to reconsider the decision taken by it does not as a rule constitute an effective remedy.[72] Also, an interference may occur in circumstances where individuals do not have the right to avail themselves of the power to form associations and have these associations recognised by the State. Harris notes that this does not mean that States have a positive obligation to provide for a legal framework for the recognition of all associations, but most States do have such frameworks in operation.[73] For example in the case of *Moscow Branch of Salvation Army v Russia*,[74] the ECtHR held that an interference had occurred in circumstances where the organisation had been registered under law but was refused re-registration when the law was changed as they did not meet the new requirements of the law. Similarly, a delay in the re-registration process can amount to an interference with Art 11.[75] Naturally, interference with the day to day operation of the essential activities of an association might also constitute an interference with Art 11.

2. Legitimate Justifications for Interference with the Right

[13–24] Under the Convention, an interference will constitute a breach of Art 11 unless it is prescribed by law, pursues one of the legitimate aims of national security, public safety, for the prevention of disorder or crime, for the protection of health or morals or for the protection of the rights and freedoms of others, and is necessary in a democratic society for the achievement of those aims.

---

69 *Le Compte, Van Leuven and Se Meyere v Belgium* [1981] 4 EHRR 1 paras 64–65.

70 See *Le Compte, Van Leuven and De Meyere v Belguim* (1981) 4 EHRR 1 at 64-65; *A v Spain* (1990) No 13570/88.

71 *Sidiropoulos and Others v Greece* (Application No 57/1997/841/1047); *APEH Üldözötteinek Szövetsége and Others v Hungary* (Application No 32367/96); *Gorzelik and Others v Poland* [GC] (Application No 44158/98) (see in this regard *Human Rights Case Digest* (2001) 12(4) at p 649.); *Partidul Comunistilor (Nepeceristi) and Ungureanu v Romania* (Application No 46626/99); *United Macedonian Organisation Ilinden and Others v Bulgaria (No 2)* (Application No 34960/04); *Tsonev v Bulgaria* (Application No 45963/99); *Moscow Branch of the Salvation Army v Russia* (Application No 72881/01); *Ramazanova and Others v Azerbaijan* (Application No 44363/02); *Zhechev v Bulgaria* (Application No 57045/00); *Bekir-Ousta and Others v Greece* (Application No 35151/05); and *Emin and Others v Greece* (Application No 34144/05).

72 *Granger v the United Kingdom* (Application No 11932/86); *Roseiro Bento v Portugal* (Application No 29288/02); *Stankov, Trayanov, Stoychev, the United Macedonian Organisation Ilinden, Mechkarov and Others v Bulgaria* (Application Nos 29221/95, 29222/95, 29223/95, 29225/95 and 29226/95); and *United Macedonian Organisation Ilinden and Others v Bulgaria (No 2) ibid.*

73 D Harris, M O' Boyle, C Warbrick, E Bates, C Buckley, *Law of the European Convention on Human Rights*, (2nd ed, Oxford University Press, Oxford, 2009) at p 535.

74 *supra* n 71.

75 *Ramazanova v Azerbaijan*, *supra* n 54. Here there was a delay of four years.

The manner in which the ECtHR will interpret legitimate interferences with Art 11 will depend to a large extent on the type of association that the Court is addressing.

Political Parties

In the context of political parties, the court interprets interferences with freedom of association very strictly in light of the importance of political parties to the democratic process and "only convincing and compelling reasons"[76] will justify restrictions on the freedom of association. In the earliest case on this issue, *United Communist Party of Turkey v Turkey*,[77] the political party ("United Communist Party of Turkey") was dissolved and a ban was placed on its founders from holding office in any new political party. The reason for the ban and the dissolution of the party was the fact that the party had expressly recognised in its literature the "Kurdish Nation" and this, Turkey argued, constituted a threat to the territorial integrity of Turkey. Having established that political parties fall within the remit of Art 11 and that this clearly constituted an interference with Art 11, the court went on to consider whether there was a legitimate justification for the interference. **[13–25]**

"Prescribed by Law"

The ECtHR has held that in order for an interference to be justified it must be prescribed by law.[78] In the case of *United Communist Party of Turkey v Turkey*, it was clear that the written law both dissolved and implemented bans on the members of the party and therefore there was no doubt that the interference was prescribed by law. **[13–26]**

"Legitimate Aim"

Secondly, the ECtHR has held that the State must have a legitimate aim when it is regulating political parties. The Turkish Government maintained in the case of *United Communist Party of Turkey v Turkey* that the interference "pursued a number of legitimate aims: ensuring national security, public safety and territorial integrity and protecting the rights and freedoms of others".[79] In that case the ECtHR agreed that due to the fact that there was a potential conflict between the aims of the party as expressed and with Turkish territorial integrity, the protection of national security was a legitimate aim in these circumstances.[80] **[13–27]**

"Necessary in a Democratic Society"

In *United Communist Party of Turkey v Turkey*, the ECtHR had to also consider whether the dissolution and subsequent ban was necessary in a democratic society. The ECtHR reiterated the close link between Art 11 and Art 10 which protects opinion and expressions[81] and held that such a link is even stronger in the case of political parties "in view of their essential role in ensuring pluralism and the proper functioning of **[13–28]**

---

[76] *Refah Partisis v Turkey*, *supra* n 67 at para 103 and *Gorzelik v Poland*, *supra* n 71 at para 94.
[77] [1998] 26 EHRR 121.
[78] *ibid* at para 38.
[79] *ibid* at para 39.
[80] *ibid* at para 41.
[81] *ibid* at para 42; *Young, James and Webster v United Kingdom*, *supra* n 54 at para 57; and *Vogt v Germany* (Application No 17851/91) at para 64.

democracy"[82] and the State is the "ultimate guarantor of the principle of pluralism".[83] The

> "only type of necessity capable of justifying an interference with any of those rights is, therefore, one which may claim to spring from "democratic society". Democracy thus appears to be the only political model contemplated by the Convention and, accordingly, the only one compatible with it".[84]

Exceptions to this rule must be construed strictly, "only convincing and compelling reasons can justify restrictions"[85] and State parties are given a "limited margin of appreciation".[86]

[13–29] In the instant case, the party had been dissolved on two main grounds: firstly, that it had the word "communist" in its name contrary to Turkish law and secondly, that the party supported separatism and the division of the Turkish State. In relation to the first argument, the ECtHR held that "a political party's choice of name cannot in principle justify a measure as dramatic as dissolution in the absence of other relevant and sufficient circumstances" and, particularly, in this case as the State had provided no concrete evidence that the party had a communist ideological background.[87] The ECtHR examined the documentation of the party and noted that it made no claim, "other than for recognition of their existence"[88] and held that:

> " ... there can be no justification for hindering a political group solely because it seeks to debate in public the situation of part of the State's population and to take part in the nation's political life in order to find, according to democratic rules, solutions capable of satisfying everyone concerned".[89]

While the ECtHR was aware that it could not be ruled out that the literature might not reflect the party's true intentions, this would have to be considered in light of the actions of the party and as it had been dissolved as soon as it had been formed, it did not have a chance to take any action, which amounted to penalisation for "conduct relating solely to the exercise of freedom of expression".[90] Therefore, the actions of the State were not necessary in a democratic society.

[13–30] The ECtHR has made it clear that in the context of political parties, the court will take a very strict approach to any deviations from Art 11, in view of the importance of Art 11 to the protection of democracy and freedom of expression. A similar decision was made in the case of *Socialist Party v Turkey*,[91] which also involved the dissolution of a

---

[82] *ibid* at para 42.
[83] *ibid* at para 44. In the *Informationsverein Lentia and Others v Austria* (Application Nos 13914/88; 15041/89; 15717/89; 15779/89; 17207/90) the ECtHR described the State as the ultimate guarantor of the principle of pluralism, at 38.
[84] *United Communist Party of Turkey v Turkey* [1998] 26 EHRR 121 at para 45.
[85] *ibid* at para 46.
[86] *ibid.*
[87] *ibid* at para 53.
[88] *ibid* at para 56.
[89] *ibid* at para 57.
[90] *ibid* at para 58.
[91] Application No 21237/93.

fledgling party. However, in the case of *Refah Partisis v Turkey,*[92] the ECtHR took the opposite view in a case involving the dissolution and ban of a large and well established political party. The ECtHR held that the party's objectives, combined with their actions, clearly established that the party was intent on removing secularism in Turkey. In this regard, the ECtHR laid out a three stage test to assess whether the actions of the State were necessitated by a pressing social need:

(i) whether there was plausible evidence that the risk to democracy, supposing it had been proved to exist, was sufficiently imminent:
(ii) whether the acts and speeches of the leaders and members of the political party concerned were imputable to the party as a whole; and
(iii) whether the acts or speeches imputable to the political party formed a whole which gave a clear picture of a model of society conceived and advocated by the party which was incompatible with the concept of a democratic society.[93]

In this case, the ECtHR held that: (i) the party had a real chance of seizing power and would implement its proposals on doing so; (ii) the acts were imputable to the party as a whole as the main party had not distanced themselves from the comments of the members involved; and (iii) the development of a plurality of legal systems "one of which would be religion based is a societal system that is incompatible with the Convention" and that a State was entitled to oppose "religious fundamentalism" when viewed from its own historical experience.[94] Therefore the court concluded that the dissolution of the party was not disproportionate.

Other Associations

Other associations, such as those formed for social, economic, political, cultural, religious purposes, etc, also fall within Art 11 on the grounds that such organisations are also important to the "proper functioning of democracy".[95] In these cases, the strict standard and limited margin of appreciation developed by the court in relation to political parties continues to apply, particularly where the case raises issues of political or religious affiliation.[96] **[13–31]**

In relation to religious associations, the ECtHR has held that the right to freedom of association must be read in conjunction with Art 9 (the freedom to manifest a religious belief). This raises specific issues relating to religious associations, which can be either discouraged or considered suspect by certain State authorities. Where a State attempts to recognize, and subsequently refuses to register a religious association, the State will have to have very weighty reasons for this non-recognition or registration. In the case of *Moscow Branch of the Salvation Army v Russia,*[97] the ECtHR had to consider whether a

[92] *supra* n 67.
[93] D Harris *et al*, *supra* n 73 at pp 529–530; *Refah Partisis v Turkey, supra* n 67 at para 104; and *Partidul Comunistilor (Neperceristi) and Ungureanu v Romania* [(2005] 44 EHRR 340 at para 48.,
[94] *supra* at para 124.
[95] *Sidiropoulos and Others, supra* n 67 at para 40; *Association of Citizens Radko and Paunkovski* (Application No 74651/01) at para 66; and *United Macedonian Organisation Ilinden and Others v Bulgaria (No 2)*, *supra* n 71 at para 33.
[96] *ibid.*
[97] (2006) 44 EHRR 912.

decision by Russian authorities to refuse to re-register the applicant's religious association, following changes to the law on registration of religious associations, amounted to a breach of Art 9 and Art 11 of the ECHR.

In emphasizing the link between Art 9 and 11 the ECtHR held that

> "while religious freedom is primarily a matter of individual conscience, it also implies, *inter alia*, 'freedom to manifest [one's] religion' alone and in private or in community with others, in public and within the circle of those whose faith one shares. Since religious communities traditionally exist in the form of organised structures, Article 9 must be interpreted in the light of Article 11 of the Convention, which safeguards associative life against unjustified State interference. Seen in that perspective, the right of believers to freedom of religion, which includes the right to manifest one's religion in community with others, encompasses the expectation that believers will be allowed to associate freely, without arbitrary State intervention. Indeed, the autonomous existence of religious communities is indispensable for pluralism in a democratic society and is thus an issue at the very heart of the protection which Article 9 affords".[98]

The ECtHR held in *Moscow Branch of the Salvation Army v Russia* that where a religious community had been operating as such for over seven years, the reasons for refusing registration would have to be "particularly weighty and compelling".[99] The ECtHR held that there had been a breach of Art 11 when read in light of Art 9 and of the positive duties of neutrality inherent in Art 11.

Another interesting case which highlights the inherent link between Art 9 and Art 11 involved the Church of Scientology. In the case of *Church of Scientology Moscow v Russia*[100] the ECtHR had to consider whether the refusal to register the Church of Scientology in Moscow as a religious association was in breach of Art 11. In light of the decision in *Moscow Branch of the Salvation Army v Russia*, the State would have to show weighty and compelling reasons to refuse to register the association. As Russia failed to do so in the case of *Church of Scientology v Russia*, the ECtHR held that there had been a breach of Art 11 when read in light of Art 9. In coming to this conclusion, the ECtHR held that the Church of Scientology was a "religious community" within the meaning of Art 9, that the refusal to recognise this community amounted to an interference with the rights to freedom of association under Art 11 and the freedom to manifest one's religion under Art 9 and that the right to freedom of religion under Art 9 encompassed a right to practice one's religion in the company of others without State interference. The court concluded that "in denying registration to the Church of Scientology of Moscow, the Moscow authorities did not act in good faith and neglected their duty of neutrality and impartiality vis-à-vis the applicant's religious community".[101]

The decisions of the ECtHR in these cases highlight the strong link between freedom of association under Art 11 and freedom of religion under Art 9. The ECtHR is of the view that Art 11 supports the full enjoyment of Art 9 and that the role of the State in relation to recognition of religious associations under Art 11 must be one of

---

98 *ibid* at 58.
99 *ibid* at 96.
100 (2007) ECHR 258.
101 *ibid* at para 97.

impartiality. Clearly, only weighty and compelling reasons will constitute a legitimate interference with the association rights of religious communities under Art 11.

A useful example of how the ECtHR deals with interferences in relation to associations other than religious ones is the case of *Gorselik v Poland*,[102] where the ECtHR had to consider the refusal of the Polish authorities to register an association called "Union of People of Silesian Nationality" on the grounds that the Silesian people were not an national minority (as claimed in the memorandum of association of the organisation) and any such designation would give the group rights under Polish electoral laws. Having established the application of, and interference with, Art 11 in this case, the ECtHR went on to consider whether there was a legitimate justification in these circumstances.

"Prescribed by Law"

The ECtHR has reiterated time and time again that the expression "prescribed by law" requires firstly that the impugned measure should have a basis in domestic law. It also refers to the quality of the law in question, requiring that it: **[13–33]**

> " ... be accessible to the persons concerned and formulated with sufficient precision to enable them—if need be, with appropriate advice—to foresee, to a degree that is reasonable in the circumstances, the consequences which a given action may entail and to regulate their conduct".[103]

In this case, the ECtHR was satisfied that the law was formulated with sufficient precision to enable the applicants to regulate their conduct.

"Legitimate Aim"

The ECtHR considered that the aim of preventing disorder, protecting the rights of others, including the possible abuse of electoral law and protecting the existing democratic institutions and procedures in Poland were sufficient aims in this case.[104] This suggests that the level of scrutiny given to legitimate aims, as provided by States, is limited at this stage of the inquiry. **[13–34]**

"Necessary in a Democratic Society"

The ECtHR has recognised that the fundamental importance of the right to free association and the "ability to establish a legal entity in order to act collectively in a field of mutual interest is one of the most important aspects of freedom of association"[105] and that any restrictions would be subject to rigorous supervision by the ECtHR.[106] It has noted that: **[13–35]**

> " ... although individual interests must on occasion be subordinated to those of a group, democracy does not simply mean that the views of the majority must always prevail: a

[102] *supra* n 71.

[103] *Gorselik v Poland, supra* n 71 at para 64.

[104] *ibid* at para 76.

[105] *ibid* at para 88; *Sidiropoulos and Others v Greece, supra* n 71 at para 40.

[106] *Gorselik v Poland, ibid* at para 88; *United Communist Party of Turkey and Others v Turkey, supra* n 77 at para 42 *et seq.*; *Socialist Party and Others v Turkey, supra* n 91 at para 41 *et seq*; and *Refah Partisis v Turkey, supra* n 67 para 86 *et seq.*

> balance must be achieved which ensures the fair and proper treatment of minorities and avoids any abuse of a dominant position".[107]

In the context of democracies, freedom of association can be particularly valuable as it helps to "express and promote its identity" which "may be instrumental in helping a minority to preserve and uphold its rights".[108]

[13–36] In the case of *Gorzelik v Poland*, however, "the risk that the association and its members might claim electoral privileges was inherent in any decision that allowed them to form the association"[109] and "the appropriate time for countering the risk of the perceived mischief, …was at the moment of registration of the association and not later."[110] Therefore, there was a pressing social need for taking the action stated. In relation to the proportionality of the action, the court determined that:

> " … the refusal was not a comprehensive, unconditional one directed against the cultural and practical objectives that the association wished to pursue, but was based solely on the mention, in the memorandum of association, of a specific appellation for the association. It was designed to counteract a particular, albeit only potential, abuse by the association of its status as conferred by registration. It by no means amounted to a denial of the distinctive ethnic and cultural identity of Silesians or to a disregard for the association's primary aim, which was to 'awaken and strengthen the national consciousness'".[111]

With this in mind, the measure was not disproportionate.

[13–37] This case is in direct contrast to the decision in *Siriropoulos v Greece*[112] in which the dissolution of an organisation purporting to preserve the tradition and culture of the Macedonian minority was considered to be disproportionate because there was no evidence that the organisation was set up with the intention of undermining Greece's territorial integrity and there was provision in the law to dissolve the association once registered if it pursued aims contrary to those contained in the memorandum of association or contrary to the law.[113]

[13–38] This would suggest that the court pays particular attention to the intention of the organisation and the measures in place to prevent that organisation from interfering with the democratic processes in the State. This decision can therefore be reconciled with *Gorselik v Poland* where there was a clear intention in the actions of the association to achieve rights for a minority group which was not so designated by national law and which would have stark implications for the electoral process. More recent cases have rejected arguments by States based on "alleged separatist ideas capable of arousing confrontational attitudes and based on historical interpretations

[107] *ibid* at para 90; *Young, James and Webster v The United Kingdom, supra* n 54 at para 63; and *Chassagnou and Others v France* (Application Nos 25088/94, 28331/95 and 28443/95).
[108] *ibid* at para 93.
[109] *ibid* at para 102.
[110] *ibid* at para 103.
[111] *ibid* at para 105.
[112] *ibid.*
[113] *Siriropoulos v Greece, supra* n 71 at paras 45-46.

considered absurd by the authorities and the majority of the population,"[114] arguments based on characterisations of the group's goals as political and capable of being pursued solely by a political party,[115] or problems with fulfilling certain minor aspects of the registration legislation,[116] unless the defect could be regarded as so significant as to preclude registration and impossible to cure in the course of the registration proceedings.[117] While States are entitled to require organisations seeking official registration to comply with reasonable legal formalities, that is always subject to the condition of proportionality.[118]

Trade Unions

Article 11 expressly recognises the right to form and join a trade union which implies naturally a freedom of choice in the formation and joining of a union.[119] Article 11 therefore covers a wide range of rights. It also includes a negative right not to join or to withdraw from a trade union (a right to dissociate).[120] **[13–39]**

Closed Shops

There is a right in the Convention not to be forced to join a trade union which is predicated on the importance attached to Arts 9 and 10 of the Convention.[121] This normally takes the form of a closed shop agreement whereby the individual is told that their employment is dependent upon them joining a trade union either prior to entering the job or while they are in the job.[122] The very first case dealing with a post-entry closed shop agreement was the case of *Young, James and Webster v United Kingdom*. In this case, the court accepted that not all compulsions to join a union would be an interference with Art 11 but held that where the compulsion "strikes at the very substance of the freedom guaranteed by Article 11", then this, in the absence of **[13–40]**

---

[114] *United Macedonian Organisation Ilinden and Others v Bulgaria (No 2), supra* n 71 at para 36;. *United Macedonian Organisation Ilinden – PIRIN and Others v Bulgaria* (Application No 59489/00) paras 58–62; *Etxeberria and Others v Spain* (Application Nos 35579/03, 35613/03, 35626/03 and 35634/03) at para 55.

[115] *ibid* at para 38; *United Macedonian Organisation Ilinden and Others v Bulgaria* (Application No 59491/00) at para 73; *Zhechev v Bulgaria* (Application No 57045/00) at paras 52–57.

[116] *ibid* at para 40.

[117] *ibid* at paras 65–69 and *Tsonev v Bulgaria* (Application No 45963/99) at paras 55 and 57.

[118] *Ertan and Others v Turkey* (Application No 57898/00); *Tebieti Mühafize Cemiyyeti and Israfilov v Azerbaijan* (Application No 37083/03) at para 72; *Hayvan Yetiştiricileri SendikasI v Turkey* (Application No 27798/08); and *Republican Party of Russia v Russia* (Application No 12976/07) at para 87.

[119] *Vördur Ólafsson v Iceland* (Application No 20161/06) at para 45; *Young, James and Webster, supra* at n 54 at para 52.

[120] *Gustaffson v Sweden* (Application No 15573/89) at para 45; *Sigurdur A. Sigurjónsson v Iceland* (Application No 16130/90) at para 35.

[121] *Vördur Ólafsson v Iceland, supra* n 119 at para 45; *Siguður A. Sigurjónsson, ibid* at paras 35–37; *Chassagnou and Others v France, supra* n 107 at para 103; *Young, James and Webster, supra* at n 51 at para 57; and *Sørensen and Rasmussen v Denmark* (Applications Nos 52562/99 and 52620/99) at para 54.

[122] *Sørensen and Rasmussen v Denmark, ibid* at para 56. See also F von Prondzynski, "Freedom of Association and the Closed Shop: The European Perspective" (1982) 41(2) CLJ 256.

some very strong justification, will amount to an interference with Art 11.[123] In this regard, the court has attached significance to "the notion of personal autonomy" as an essential corollary of the individual's freedom of choice implicit in Art 11.[124]

[13–41] In *Sorensen and Rasmussen v Denmark*,[125] the court had to consider a pre-entry closed shop agreement. In that case, the court had to decide whether such a compulsion struck at the very substance of the negative right to freedom of association (a right to dissociate) guaranteed by Art 11 of the Convention. First, the court reiterated that:

> " ... the fact that the applicants accepted membership of SID as one of the terms of employment does not significantly alter the element of compulsion inherent in having to join a trade union against their will. If they had refused they would not have been recruited".

In this context, the court accepted that individuals applying for employment often find themselves "in a vulnerable situation and are only too eager to comply with the terms of employment offered".[126] This compulsion did in fact strike at the very substance of freedom of association.[127] In considering whether a fair balance had been struck between the applicants' interests and the need to ensure that trade unions are able to strive for the protection of their members' interest, the court held that:

> "Where the domestic law of a Contracting State permits the conclusion of closed-shop agreements between unions and employers which run counter to the freedom of choice of the individual inherent in Article 11, the margin of appreciation must be considered reduced ... In assessing whether a Contracting State has remained within its margin of appreciation in tolerating the existence of closed-shop agreements, particular weight must be attached to the justifications advanced by the authorities for them and, in any given case, the extent to which they impinge on the rights and interests protected by Article 11. Account must also be taken of changing perceptions of the relevance of closed-shop agreements for securing the effective enjoyment of trade union freedom ..."[128]

and as there:

> " ... is little support in the Contracting States for the maintenance of closed-shop agreements and ... their use in the labour market is not an indispensable tool for the effective enjoyment of trade union freedoms ... "

the State had failed to protect the applicant's right to free association.[129]

---

[123] *Young, James and Webster*, *supra* n 54 at para 55; *Vördur Ólafsson v Iceland*, *supra* n 119 at para 45; *Gustafsson v Sweden*, *supra* n 120 at para 45; *Sigurður A. Sigurjónsson v Iceland*, *supra* n 120 at para 36; and *Sørensen and Rasmussen v Denmark*, *supra* n 121 at para 54.

[124] *Vördur Ólafsson v Iceland*, *supra* n 119 at para 46 and *Sørensen and Rasmussen v Denmark*, *supra* n 121 at para 54.

[125] *supra* n 121.

[126] *Sørensen and Rasmussen v Denmark*, *supra* n 121 at para 59.

[127] *ibid* at para 64.

[128] *ibid* at para 58.

[129] *supra* n 121 at para 76.

An interesting case involving a negative right not to join a union but unrelated to closed shop agreements is the case of *Vördur Ólafsson v Iceland.*[130] In that case, the applicant was under a statutory obligation to pay an industry fee to the Federation of Icelandic Industries (FII), an organisation of which he was not a member and to which his trade union was not affiliated. The ECtHR noted that the fee was "levied on a restricted group of persons and disbursed to a private law association for use by the association without any significant involvement or control by public authorities".[131] The civil or administrative sanction attached to the non-payment of the fee was considered as less serious than in other cases examined by the court where an applicant's refusal to join a union resulted in the loss of his employment or professional license and, in consequence, his means of livelihood,[132] although much less serious consequences have also been held to be incompatible with the Convention.[133] In this case, the fact that the applicant was obliged by statute financially to support a private law organisation that was not one of his own choosing and which advocated policies which the applicant deemed to be fundamentally contrary to his own political views and interests was an interference with Art 11[134] which could not be justified as it failed to pursue a legitimate aim.[135] The ECtHR has held that in the area of trade union freedom, the contracting States enjoy a wide margin of appreciation as to how the freedom of trade unions to protect the occupational interests of their members may be secured.[136] However, in this case as the national law defined the FII's role and duties in an open-ended manner and failed to set out specific obligations for the FII, "there was also a lack of transparency and accountability, *vis-à-vis* non-members such as the applicant, as to the use of the revenues from the Industry Charge".[137] The court held that there were no adequate safeguards in place to prevent "the disputed arrangement giving the FII a more favourable standing in its pursuit of the specific interests of its members and placing the applicant and other non-members like him at a disadvantage compared to them".[138] **[13–42]**

The Right of Trade Unions to Regulate their Own Affairs

Trade unions have always been recognised by the ECtHR as autonomous bodies free to regulate their own internal affairs and draw up their own rules.[139] However, naturally **[13–43]**

[130] *Vördur Ólafsson v Iceland, supra* n 119.
[131] *ibid* at para 49.
[132] *Young, James and Webster, supra* n 54 at para 55; *Sigurður A. Sigurjónsson v Iceland, supra* n 120 at paras 36–37.
[133] *Sørensen and Rasmussen v Denmark, supra* n 121 at para 61.
[134] *Vördur Ólafsson v Iceland, supra* n 119 at para 54; *Sørensen and Rasmussen, supra* n 121 at para 61; *Sigurður A. Sigurjónsson v Iceland, supra* n 120 at para 37; and *Young, James and Webster, supra* n 54 at para 57.
[135] *ibid* at para 73.
[136] *ibid* at para 75; *Swedish Engine Drivers' Union v Sweden* (Application No 5614/72) at para 39; *Gustaffson v Sweden, supra* n 120 at para 45; *Schettini and Others v Italy* (Application No 29529/95); *Wilson, National Union of Journalists and Others v the United Kingdom* (Application Nos 30668/96, 30671/96 and 30678/96) at para 44; and *Sørensen and Rasmussen v Denmark, supra* n 121 at para 58.
[137] *Vördur Ólafsson v Iceland, supra* n 119 at para 82.
[138] *ibid.*
[139] *Associated Society of Locomotive Engineers and Fireman v United Kingdom* [2007] 45 EHRR 793 at para 38.

the State is entitled to draw up certain rules and regulations affecting their operation in the public interest, mainly to prevent abuse of a dominant position in the labour market. However, the ECtHR views any interference in such cases very strictly. In the case of *Cheall v United Kingdom*[140] for example, a membership-protection agreement involving a number of unions, involved the applicant being expelled from his union at the request of his previous union who were both involved in this agreement. The European Commission on Human Rights held that while matters of admission to membership and expulsion were normally matters for the unions themselves, "nonetheless for a right to join a union to be effective the state must protect the individual against any abuse of a dominant position". Examples of such abuse included situations where "exclusion or expulsion was not in accordance with union rules or where the results were wholly arbitrary or where the consequences of exclusion or expulsion resulted in exceptional hardship such as job loss because of a closed shop".[141]

Trade Union Action Against Third Parties

[13–44] Trade unions often involve themselves in situations that involve third parties, for example when a union decides to picket an employer. A good example is the case of *Gustafsson v Sweden*.[142] In that case, the union picketed an employer who had not agreed to be bound by a collective bargaining agreement in his workplace causing considerable financial damage. The employer could have applied the collective agreement by becoming a member of one of the employer's associations concerned or negotiating a separate agreement with the union. The applicant declined to do either as he was opposed in principle to collective bargaining. He argued that the union picketing of his restaurant which caused him considerable financial damage and put pressure on him to join the employers association was in breach of his negative right not to join an association.[143] The court held that:

> "Article 11 does not secure any particular treatment of the trade unions, or their members, by the State, such as a right to conclude any given collective agreement, the words 'for the protection of [their] interests' in Article 11 para. 1 show that the Convention safeguards freedom to protect the occupational interests of trade-union members by trade-union action. In this respect the State has a choice as to the means to be used and the Court has recognised that the concluding of collective agreements may be one of these".[144]

In this regard, the contracting States should enjoy a wide margin of appreciation in their choice of the means to be employed. The court held that:

> " . . . the union action must have entailed a considerable pressure on the applicant to meet the union's demand that he accept to be bound by a collective agreement, either by joining an employers' association or by signing a substitute agreement".[145]

[140] Application No 10550/83.
[141] *Cheall v United Kingdom* at para 186.
[142] *supra* n 120.
[143] *Gustafsson v Sweden, supra* n 120 at para 44.
[144] *ibid* at para 45. See, *Swedish Engine Drivers' Union v Sweden, supra* n 137 at paras. 39–40.
[145] *Gustafsson v Sweden, supra* n 120 at 52.

However, only the first alternative involved membership of an association. The court went on to hold that:

> "It is true that, had the applicant opted for the second alternative, he might have had less opportunity to influence the contents of future collective agreements than as a member of an employers' association. On the other hand, a substitute agreement offered the advantage that it would have been possible to include in it individual clauses tailored to the special character of the applicant's business. In any event, it does not appear, nor has it been contended, that the applicant was compelled to opt for membership of an employers' association because of economic disadvantages attached to the substitute agreement".[146]

As the applicant's objection was essentially a political one, it did not impact on the enjoyment of the freedom of association.[147]

Right to Protect Members' Interests

Article 11 imposes a positive obligation on States to ensure that trade unions can function effectively and protect their members' interests. Any interference with their function which impacts on members may potentially be in breach of the Convention. The court protects the right of trade unions to be heard by the employer on behalf of its members,[148] the right to protect employees from financial incentives to renounce union membership,[149] the right to be given the legal authority to conduct collective bargaining,[150] the right to conduct collective bargaining and enter into collective agreements. It does not include a right to be consulted by the employer,[151] or an unfettered right to strike[152] or to recognition of a union.[153] Harris argues that the decisions of the ECtHR would appear to provide only the "barest minimum of protection for trade unions in the protection of their members' interests".[154] **[13–45]**

3. Restrictions on Public Service Employees

Finally, it should be noted that Art 11(2) restricts the operation of the provision in the case of members of the armed forces, of the police or of the administration of the State. In cases relating to this area, the ECtHR has applied the proportionality test as to whether restrictions are necessary in a democratic society. Relying on its case law relating to the freedom of association in general, the court has interpreted Art 11(2) by restricting State action to measures that are strictly construed and are justified by convincing and compelling reasons.[155] **[13–46]**

---

[146] *ibid.*
[147] *ibid.*
[148] *National Union of Belgian Police v Belgium* [1975] 1 EHRR 617 at para 39.
[149] *Wilson, National Union of Journalists and Others v United Kingdom, supra* n 137 at 47-48.
[150] *Demir and Baykara v Turkey* (Application No 34503/97) at para 151.
[151] *supra* n 148.
[152] *Schmidt and Dahlstrom v Sweden* [1976] I EHRR 632 at para 36; *Federation of Offshore Workers Trade Unions v Norway* (Application No 38190/97).
[153] *Wilson, National Union of Journalists and Others v United Kingdom, supra* n 137 at 47–48.
[154] D Harris *et al, supra* n 73 at p 545.
[155] *Haber Sen and Cinar v Turkey* [2006] 46 EHRR 374 at para 35.

C. CFR

[13–47] Article 12 CFR:

(1) "Everyone has the right to freedom of peaceful assembly and to freedom of association at all levels, in particular in political, trade union and civic matters, which implies the right of everyone to form and to join trade unions for the protection of his or her interests.
(2) Political parties at Union level contribute to expressing the political will of the citizens of the Union."

Article 12 of the Charter of Fundamental Rights (CFR) and Art 151 of the Treaty on the Functioning of the European Union (TFEU) provides for the protection of the right to freedom of association. This right is to be interpreted in light of Art 11 of the ECHR[156] and is subject to the same limitations as exist under the ECHR.

[13–48] One of the major issues that has arisen at a European Union (EU) level is the extent to which fundamental rights, such as the right to freedom of association, is compatible with the four freedoms guaranteed by the TEU. In this regard the court has held that:

> " ... the protection of fundamental rights is a legitimate interest which, in principle, justifies a restriction of the obligations imposed by Community law, even under a fundamental freedom guaranteed by the Treaty, such as the free movement of goods".[157]

Due to the operation of the CFR the determinations of the ECtHR are very influential on the decisions of the Court of Justice of the European Union (CJEU). Most of the decisions in the EU context have involved trade unions and collective bargaining agreements.[158]

1. Nature of the Right

[13–49] The CJEU has held that the freedom of association in EU law protects both the right to take collective action and the right to strike[159] as fundamental rights "which forms an integral part of the general principles of Community law the observance of which the Court ensures".[160] However the CJEU has stated that it is not an absolute right and can be subject to certain restrictions.[161]

---

[156] Art 52(3) CFR.

[157] Case C–438/05, *International Transport Workers' Federation and Finnish Seamen's Union v Viking Line ABP, OÜ Viking Line Eesti* at para 46; Case C–112/00 *Schmidberger, Internationale Transporte and Planzüge v Republik Österreich* at para 74; Case C–36/02 *Omega Spielhallen- und Automatenaufstellungs-GmbH v Oberbürgermeisterin der Bundesstadt Bonn* at para 35.

[158] C O'Mara, "European Developments – The Right to Strike and Collectively Bargain" (2010) 7(2) IELJ 62.

[159] *International Transport Workers' Federation and Finnish Seamen's Union v Viking Line ABP, OÜ Viking Line Eesti ibid* at para 43.

[160] *ibid* at para 44.

[161] See below for more details on restrictions to the right.

Freedom of association in EU law also comprises the right to join and the right not to join a trade union.[162] However, like the provisions of the Irish Constitution and the ECHR, it does not provide for an absolute right to join any union as this would interfere with the other members of the union's right to disassociate.[163]

2. Legitimate Justification for Interference with the Right

The CJEU has recognised that the right to freedom of association can be subject to certain restrictions and to the principles of proportionality.[164] **[13–50]**

One of the most significant cases which dealt with this difficult issue of the balancing of the four freedoms against the fundamental right to association is the case of *Lavel.*[165] In that case, Lavel posted approximately 35 workers (earning 40 percent less than their Swedish counterparts) to Sweden to work on building sites belonging to a subsidiary of Lavel incorporated in Sweden. Lavel faced trade union blockades when it refused to sign a collective agreement which would provide for more favourable conditions than that required by Swedish national law for its posted workers. The CJEU held that the trade union action constituted a restriction on the freedom to provide services which could only be justified if it pursued a legitimate objective compatible with the Treaty and was justified by overriding reasons of public interest. It also had to be proportionate.[166]

The CJEU considered that the right to take collective action:

> " ... for the protection of the workers of the host State against possible social dumping may constitute an overriding reason of public interest within the meaning of the case-law of the Court which, in principle, justifies a restriction of one of the fundamental freedoms guaranteed by the Treaty".[167]

It was claimed by the trade unions and the Swedish government and accepted in principle by the CJEU that the blockading action was aimed at the protection of **[13–51]**

[162] Case C–499/04 *Hans Werhof v Freeway Traffic Systems GmbH & Co. KG* at para 33; Case C-415/93 *Union Royale Belge des Sociétés de Football Association and Others v Bosman and Others at para* 79; Case C–274/99 *P Connolly v Commission.*

[163] Case C-1002/05 *ASLEF v United Kingdom*. See also C Barnard "A proportionate response to proportionality in the field of collective action" (2012) 37(2) ELR 117.

[164] *International Transport Workers' Federation and Finnish Seamen's Union v Viking Line ABP, OÜ Viking Line Eesti, supra*, n 158 at para 46; *Schmidberger, Internationale Transporte and Planzüge v Republik Österreich, supra* n 158 at para 77; and *Omega Spielhallen—und Automatenaufstellungs-GmbH v Oberbürgermeisterin der Bundesstadt Bonn, supra* n 158 at para 36.

[165] Case C–341/05 *Laval un Partneri Ltd v Svenska Byggnadsarbetareförbundet, Svenska Byggnadsarbetareförbundets avdelning 1, Byggettan and Svenska Elektrikerförbundet.*

[166] *Laval ibid* at para 101; Case C–398/95 *Syndesmos ton en Elladi Touristikon kai Taxidiotikon Grafeion v Ypourgos Ergasias* at para 21; Case C–451/03 *Servizi Ausiliari Dottori Commercialisti Srl v Giuseppe Calafior* at para 37; and Case C–94/04 *Federico Cipolla v Rosaria Fazari* at para 61.

[167] *Laval, supra* n 165 at para 102; Joined Cases C-369/96 and C-376/96 *Arblade and Others* at para 36; Case C-165/98 *Mazzoleni and ISA* at para 27; Joined Cases C-49/98, C-50/98, C-52/98 to C-54/98 and C-68/98 to C-71/98 *Finalarte and Others* at para 33; and *International Transport Workers' Federation and Finnish Seamen's Union v Viking Line ABP, OÜ Viking Line Eesti, supra* n 158 at para 77.

workers, one of the social aims of the Treaty. However, the CJEU noted that in reality, the compulsion imposed on Lavel to sign the collective agreement could not be justified by reference to the protection of workers.[168] As long as Lavel was complying with the minimum protection standards applicable within the host Member State, then this action would not be justified. As Sweden had no legal provision for the collective agreement to be incorporated into Swedish law, Lavel could not be held to be in contravention of minimum standards. The court held that industrial action could not be allowed where the negotiations on pay form part of a national context characterised by a lack of provisions, of any kind, which are sufficiently precise and accessible that they do not render it impossible or excessively difficult in practice for such an undertaking to determine the obligations with which it is required to comply as regards minimum pay.[169] To do otherwise would force an undertaking to surpass the minimum standards acknowledged within the posted workers' directive and, as a consequence, would make it less "attractive" for companies to provide such services outside their borders.

[13–52] Similarly, in November 2005, a case, *Viking Line ABP v FSU* (*Finnish Seaman's Union) and ITF*[170] (hereinafter referred to as the *Viking Line* case), was brought before the UK's Commercial Court by a Finnish shipping company, seeking an injunction against the actions of the Finnish Seaman's Union and the International Transport Workers Federation, who were threatening to picket and boycott their vessels docked in the United Kingdom.[171] The International Transport Workers' Federation ("ITF") had also tried to prevent negotiations between the ITF affiliated unions in Estonia and Viking Line. The unions were acting in defiance of the plans of the company to re-flag its vessel in Estonia and replace its existing crew, composed mostly of Finnish seafarers, with cheaper workers from Estonia. The unions were not opposed to the re-flagging *per se* but to the possibility of loss of employment for their members and a reduction in the terms and conditions of employment of the crew.[172] The main issue before the court was whether the actions of the unions were contrary to the community rules on free movement.

[13–53] Waller LJ in the Court of Appeal, unconvinced as to the merits of a strict application of the freedom of establishment rules in such a case, sought a reference to the CJEU citing 10 pertinent questions on various aspects of this case. He sought confirmation from the court as to the applicability of the freedom of establishment rules in this context and their compatibility with the principles of social policy outlined in Title XI of the EC Treaty. In the event that the CJEU held that the freedom of establishment rules were applicable, he also sought guidance from the court as to whether the case involved direct or indirect discrimination and whether or not these restrictions could be justified in the circumstances.

---

168 *Laval, supra* n 165 at para 108.
169 *ibid* at para 108; *Arblade and Others, supra* n 167 at para 43.
170 [2005] EWCA Civ 1299.
171 [2005] All ER 155.
172 *Viking Line ABP v FSU (Finnish Seaman's Union) and ITF, supra* n 170 at para 52.

In the *Viking Line*[173] case the CJEU was asked to consider whether the actions of trade unions in attempting to restrict a re-flagging of a vessel in an open registry and the consequent loss of employment and a reduction in terms and conditions of employment of seafarers, fall within the scope of the EC Treaty provisions on free movement or in the alternative whether such actions on the part of the trade unions or the State are in fact justified by reference to the objective principles of social policy as outlined in the Treaty provisions of Title XI.

On the 23 May 2007, Advocate General Maduro gave his opinion on the merits of this case.[174] Advocate General Maduro opined that the provisions on freedom of establishment and services are "by no means irreconcilable with the protection of fundamental rights or with the attainment of the Community's social policy objectives".[175] Neither right is absolute nor did either take precedence over the other. Both could co-exist within the confines of each other successfully. The CJEU agreed. The Court held, firstly, that collective action falls within the scope of Art 43 EC. While the right to take collective action, including the right to strike, is recognised as a fundamental right, the exercise of that right may nonetheless be subject to restrictions.[176] The court did not consider that it was an inherent part of such rights that the fundamental freedoms would be prejudiced to a certain degree.[177] The decision by the CJEU that the actions of the trade unions in this case fell within the principles of Art 43 EC meant that the actions of the trade unions would now have to be justified by reference to concepts such as public policy. **[13–54]**

In its judgment, the CJEU reiterated the fact that the freedom of establishment constitutes one of the fundamental principles of the Community. The principle applies both to ensuring that host Member States treat foreign nationals and companies equally to nationals of the Member States and to ensuring that the Member State of origin does not hinder the establishment in another Member State of one of its nationals or a company. Re-flagging a vessel constitutes an act of establishment as the "vessel serves as a vehicle for the pursuit of an economic activity that include fixed establishment in the State of registration".[178] The court concluded that the conditions laid down for the registration of vessels must not form an obstacle to the freedom of establishment.[179] The court held that the actions of the unions in this case had the effect of making less attractive, or even pointless, the exercise of the right to freedom of establishment of Viking, as their actions prevented both Viking and its subsidiaries from enjoying the same treatment[180] in the host Member State as other economic operators established in that State. The coordinated policies of the ITF were at least liable to restrict this right also.[181] Therefore, the court concluded that the collective **[13–55]**

173 *ibid*
174 *ibid*
175 *ibid* at para 23 (*per* Advocate General Maduro).
176 *ibid* at para 44.
177 *ibid* at para 52.
178 *ibid* at para 70.
179 *ibid* at para 71.
180 *ibid* at para 72.
181 *ibid* at para 73.

action in this case constituted a restriction on the freedom of establishment.[182] The court then moved straight to a consideration of whether the restriction on the freedom of establishment could be justified in this particular case. Ireland, Germany and Finland supported the contention of the ITF that the restrictions were justified since they were "necessary to ensure the protection of a fundamental right recognised under Community law and their objective is to protect the rights of workers, which constitutes an overriding reason of public interest".[183] The court held that since the Community had a social as well as an economic purpose, the rights to free movement must be balanced against the objectives pursued by social policy, which include, "improved living and working conditions"[184]. The court held that it was for the national court to determine whether the actions of the unions in this case concerned the protection of workers. The court gave guidance on how this could be examined. First, it held that the actions of the unions would not involve the protection of workers if it were established that the jobs or conditions of employment at issue were not jeopardised or under serious threat.[185] Secondly, if the undertaking given by the company was as binding as a collective agreement and if it was of a nature as to provide a guarantee to the workers that the statutory provisions would be complied with and the terms of the collective agreement would be maintained, the protection of workers would again not be in issue.[186] However, even if the national court determined that the jobs of such workers were under serious threat, it would still have to ascertain whether the collective action is suitable for ensuring the achievement of the objective pursued and does not go beyond what was necessary to attain that objective.[187]

[13–56] Once again, the CJEU gave guidance on what it considered objective and necessary in the circumstances. It held that collective action is "one of the main ways in which trade unions protect the interests of their members".[188] The national court must examine whether the unions had any other means at its disposal that were less restrictive of freedom of establishment and whether these means had been exhausted before the action was initiated. In relation to the actions of the ITF, the court held that to the extent that the policy:

> " . . . results in ship owners being prevented from registering their vessels in a State other than that of which the beneficial owners of those vessels are nationals, the restrictions on freedom of establishment resulting from such action cannot be objectively justified".[189]

This is due to the fact that the policy of solidarity action against flag of convenience vessels will operate regardless of whether there will be a harmful effect on the working conditions of employees.[190]

---

182 *ibid* at para 74.
183 *ibid* at para 76.
184 *ibid* at para 79.
185 *ibid* at para 81.
186 *ibid* at para 82.
187 *ibid* at para 85.
188 *ibid* at para 86.
189 *ibid* at para 88.
190 *ibid* at para 89.

This judgment effectively restricts the role of trade unions to actions that are for the protection of jobs or conditions of employment which are jeopardised or under threat and where no undertaking is available. Even then, the actions of unions must be objective and necessary in the circumstances. If the unions have less restrictive means at their disposal, they will be compelled to adopt these less restrictive means of collective action.

D. International and Regional Laws

The right to freedom of association is also protected by other regional human rights regimes and at an international level. **[13–57]**

International Protections

The right to freedom of association is protected by Art 20 of the Universal Declaration of Human Rights, which states: **[13–58]**

(1) Everyone has the right to freedom of peaceful assembly and association.
(2) No one may be compelled to belong to an association.

The right is also protected in other international instruments such as Art 22 of the International Covenant on Civil and Political Rights, Art 5(ix) of the Convention on the Elimination of All Forms of Racial Discrimination and Art 15 of the Convention on the Rights of the Child. However, the most important organisation dealing with the right to freely associate, and indeed, with labour standards in general, at an international level is the International Labour Organisation (ILO), which is an agency of the United Nations (UN). It adopted Convention 87 concerning Freedom of Association and Protection of the Right to Organise in 1948 and Convention 98 on the Right to Organise and Collective Bargaining in 1949. Ireland ratified both Conventions in 1955. Article 2 of Convention 87 declares that "Workers and employers, without distinction whatsoever, shall have the right to establish and, subject only to the rules of the organisation concerned, to join organisations of their own choosing without previous authorization". Regionally (other than Europe which is dealt with above), the right to peaceful association is protected by Art 16 of the American Convention on Human Rights,[191] Art 10 of the African Charter on Human and Peoples' Rights[192] and Art 28 Arab Charter on Human Rights.[193]

---

[191] Art 16 states: "1. Everyone has the right to associate freely for ideological, religious, political, economic, labor, social, cultural, sports, or other purposes. 2. The exercise of this right shall be subject only to such restrictions established by law as may be necessary in a democratic society, in the interest of national security, public safety or public order, or to protect public health or morals or the rights and freedoms of others. 3. The provisions of this article do not bar the imposition of legal restrictions, including even deprivation of the exercise of the right of association, on members of the armed forces and the police".

[192] Art 10 states: "1. Every individual shall have the right to free association provided that he abides by the law. 2. Subject to the obligation of solidarity provided for in 29 no one may be compelled to join an association".

[193] Art 28 states: "Citizens have the freedom of assembly and association in peaceful manner. No restrictions shall be imposed on either of these two freedoms except when it is necessary for national security, or public safety, or the protection of the rights and freedoms of others."

Conclusion

[13–60] The right to freedom of association is highly protected and highly developed and the legal and intellectual authorities are abundant. The right to free association includes at all levels a right to form and join an association and the right not to join an association. The right to join an association does not mean that one has an absolute right to join an association. If the individual is rejected from a particular association, then this does not interfere with their right to join a union, rather it protects the rights of the association members to disassociate themselves from the individual. Various rules and procedures exist for the protection of the right to freely associate in relation to political parties, trade unions and other associations but three important aspects remain the same. There must be an interference with the right to association, and this can take the form of a closed shop agreement or a delay in, or refusal to, register an association. Any interference must be justified by reference to a legitimate aim, often linked to public order, morality or national security and this interference must also be proportionate. The protection of the right is so strong at a variety of levels, that proving that any interference is justified is often extremely difficult. While the Irish constitutional jurisprudence and the ECHR jurisprudence has been highly developed, there is still some development left to emerge at an EU level which to date has been entirely focused on trade unions and their impact on the free movement principles.

CHAPTER 14
The Right to Earn a Livelihood

Introduction

The right to earn a livelihood is variously described as the right to work, the right to engage in work, the right to pursue an occupation or profession or the right to earn a living. While these terms are essentially interchangeable, the various levels of protection afforded to this right at national, regional and international levels reflects an uneasiness with the recognition and protection of this particular right. Central to this inconsistency in protection is the issue of first generation (civil and political) rights and second generation (economic, social and cultural rights). The right to earn a livelihood is often considered a second generation right and as such receives less protection than other rights.[1] However, there is a growing recognition that this right is central to the fulfilment of other civil and political rights and attempts to bring the right within the scope of first generation rights have been achieved by linking the right with property rights. This chapter will discuss the recognition, interpretation, and protection of the right at a national, regional and international level. **[14–01]**

A. Irish Constitutional Protection

Article 40.3: **[14–02]**

> "1° The State guarantees in its laws to respect, and, as far as practicable, by its laws to defend and vindicate the personal rights of the citizen"

[1] For more information on this topic see the interesting contribution of D Rossa Phelan, "The Concept of Social Rights" (1994) 1(1) DULJ 105; GW Hogan, "Unenumerated Personal Rights: Ryan's Case Re-evaluated" (1990) 25(1) IJ 95; R Walsh, "Private Property Rights in the Drafting of the Irish Constitution: A Communitarian Compromise" (2011) 18(1) DULJ 86; E Keane, "Socio-Economic Rights and National Law" (2008) 26 ILT 62.

One of the many unenumerated rights in the Irish Constitution, the right to earn a livelihood, has been the subject of numerous cases before the courts in Ireland. Despite this, however, the limits of the right have not been adequately delineated. This section attempts to highlight the main provisions of the rule in Irish law.

1. Nature of the Right

[14–03] The right to earn a livelihood has been held to be an unenumerated right under Art 40.3, derived from Art 45, which is headed "Directive Principles of Social Policy". Article 45 is specifically stated to be non-justiciable but Kenny J in *Murtagh Properties v Cleary*[2] clearly articulated that this does not mean that "the Courts may not take it into consideration when deciding whether a claimed constitutional right exists".[3] The right includes the right to "prepare for and follow a chosen career"[4] and to work and earn a livelihood.[5] It has also been held to derive "as one of the bundle of rights arising from the ownership of private property capable of being commercially used and so receives the protection of Article 40. 3.2".[6]

The nature of the right was discussed in the case of *Moyne v Londonderry Port and Harbour Commissioners*[7] where it was held that in order to succeed in an action relating to the right to earn a livelihood, it is not necessary that "the party responsible is the State or an organ or agent of the State" and that while Art 40.3.1°:

> " ... certainly imposes obligations and duties on the State ... it also recognises that the citizen enjoys personal rights. So, if within the State the exercise of any of their constitutionally protected rights is invalidly infringed (whether or not the wrongdoer is an agent of the State) a claim for damages may lie".[8]

[14–04] Therefore, any public or private party that interferes with the right to earn a livelihood could be held liable in damages for breach of this constitutional right. The application of the right to actions of private parties was copper-fastened in the case of *Parsons v Kavanagh*[9] where the plaintiff operated by statutory licence a passenger bus service between Clonmel and Dublin which was interfered with when a competing unlicensed operator started to provide a similar service at a lower price on the same route.

---

2 [1972] 1 IR.

3 *ibid.* This was also followed in *De Búrca v Attorney General* [1976] IR 38 (per Pringle J): "The personal rights of a citizen guaranteed by Article 40.3.1° are not limited to the elementary matters specified in s 2 of that Article since they include a right to have recourse to the High Court to defend and vindicate a legal claim (*Macauley v Minister for Posts and Telegraphs*) and the correlative right to defend oneself in criminal and civil proceedings: *In re Haughey.* These personal rights also include a right to bodily integrity (*Ryan v The Attorney General*) and the right to earn a livelihood: *Murtagh Properties v Cleary*".

4 *Landers v Attorney General* [1973] 109 ILTR 1 (*per* Finlay P).

5 *Murphy v Stewart* [1973] IR 97.

6 *Cafolla v O'Malley* [1985] IR 486 (*per* Costello JJ).

7 [1986] IR 229.

8 *ibid* at 315.

9 [1990] ILRM 560.

O'Hanlon J held that the right to earn a livelihood included a protection against unlawful activity which materially impairs that right.[10]

The right has not been interpreted as a positive one but rather, to date, has been viewed as a purely negative one. In *Shanley v Galway Corporation*[11] the Supreme Court noted that:

> " ... while the Constitution, by implication, and as an unspecified personal right, provides that the State shall "as best it may" protect the plaintiff's right to earn a livelihood as a personal right, it does not impose a positive duty either on the State or on any body such as a local authority to which the State may have delegated powers, to provide a livelihood for the plaintiff".

2. Interference with the Right

The right to earn a livelihood should not be unjustifiably interfered with. The constitutional protection of the right to earn a livelihood can be used to challenge "unreasonable restrictions on entry to a trade or profession"[12] or unreasonable restrictions on the carrying on of a trade or profession. A good example of this is the case of *Landers v Attorney General*[13] where the plaintiff's 8 year-old son, who had an exceptional singing voice, was restricted from singing after the plaintiff and the child's manager were both convicted under ss 2(b) and (c) of the Prevention of Cruelty to Children Act 1904 which placed restrictions on the location and times during which the child could perform. Finlay P acknowledged that there exists an unenumerated right "to prepare for and follow a chosen career" and that the statute was a restriction on this right. However, there were legitimate justifications, such as the protection of children, for the interference in this case.[14] **[14–05]**

A reduction in profit was also considered to be potentially an infringement on the right to earn a livelihood in *Cafolla v O'Malley.*[15] In that case, the court had to consider whether a provision (s 14) of the Gaming and Lotteries Act 1956 was constitutional. The applicant argued that as the Act limited the prize and stake that could be won or placed on a gaming machine, this limited the profit that was to be gained by him, the proprieter of an amusement arcade. Specifically, he argued that since the Act, licence fees and taxes had increased but the limits in the Act had remained the same. Both the High Court and the Supreme Court held that the Irish Constitution does not "guarantee ... to every citizen ... that he or she shall have the right to carry on business as an amusement caterer (or for that matter any other occupation or vocation)".[16] Costello J in the High Court considered that the: **[14–06]**

[10] *ibid* at 566. See also the case of *Lovett v Grogan* [1995] 3 IR 132 at 142, where this case was approved and applied.

[11] [1995] 1 IR 396 at 407 (*per* Finaly CJJ).

[12] J Casey, *Constitutional Law in Ireland* (3rd ed, Round Hall Sweet & Maxwell, Dublin, 2000) at p 405.

[13] *supra* n 4.

[14] See further discussion in the contribution of F Mannion, "The Player, Not the Play—The Relationship between Performers' Protection Legislation and Statutory Duties" (1992) 10 ILT 276.

[15] *supra* n 6.

[16] *ibid* (*per* Costello JJ).

> "... events which have happened combined with the continued operation of s 14 have not closed down the plaintiff's business and have not stopped him from exercising his right to earn a livelihood in his O'Connell Street premises. What has happened is that in real terms a greater restriction on his means of livelihood now exists than that imposed by (the admittedly severe but constitutionally valid) restrictions which existed in 1963".

While not explicitly stated, it would appear that both the High Court and, subsequently, the Supreme Court considered this to be an attack on the right to earn a livelihood, as both courts then went on to consider the legitimate justifications that might exist for such an attack and agreed that there were sufficient justifications in this case. However, this case should not be taken as evidence for the proposition that all reductions in profit will amount to an interference with the right to earn a livelihood.

[14–07] The courts have held that "the infliction of a pecuniary loss does not in itself establish that an infringement of the constitutionally protected right to earn a livelihood has taken place"[17] and the courts will look at all the circumstances of the case to see whether, in conjunction with other issues, pecuniary loss might be evidence that an interference has occurred. An interesting case relating to the attack on the right to earn a livelihood and a link to the issue of pecuniary loss, is the case of *Browne, Hopkins and Spicer v Attorney General.*[18] In that case, sales representatives complained that a tax which was imposed on their company cars was an infringement on their right to earn a livelihood. They claimed that the car was "a tool of his trade"[19] and to impose a tax on this was unconstitutional. The court, however, held that this was not an interference with the right to earn a livelihood. Murphy J in the High Court noted that the tax was not imposed on their business activities or on the car in the course of employment but was:

> "... expressed to tax a sum of money equal to the value of the benefit which the plaintiffs enjoy from a particular motor car being available to them for their private use. It is not the car that is taxed. It is not the business use that is taxed. It is not even the private use that is taxed. It is the availability for private use that is the subject-matter of the tax".[20]

[14–08] Therefore, the tax could not be an interference with the right to earn a livelihood. Interestingly, the plaintiffs argued that while theoretically this may be the case, in practice, it operated as to be, "wholly disproportionate to the value of the benefit received by them",[21] particularly where they may not use the car in a private capacity at all. However, Murphy J held that the tax was designed to tax, not the private use but the "availability for private use"[22] and if

> "... then availability is to be taxed there seems to be no compelling reason why the tax should be restricted to the value actually derived by the taxpayer from the object provided for his benefit. If a taxpayer does not for whatever reason, avail of a country residence or townhouse provided by his employer he may still be liable to tax on the expense incurred

---

[17] *Moyne v Londonderry Port and Harbour Commissioners, supra* n 7 at 317.
[18] [1989] IR 26; [1991] 1 IR 409.
[19] *ibid.*
[20] *ibid* at 65.
[21] *ibid* at 66.
[22] *ibid* at 68.

> by the employer in providing the accommodation. No doubt such tax is designed on the assumption, which is hardly unreasonable, that an employer will not provide or an employee accept a *damnosa hereditas*. The employer may provide a motor car but hardly a white elephant".[23]

Whether the existence of a monopoly interferes with the right to earn a livelihood is worth considering.[24] The case law to date has established that the courts will examine each situation very carefully on its facts, but that the State, certainly, has a legitimate interest in certain circumstances of operating a monopoly that the courts will endeavour to protect. Where the monopoly is operated by a non-State entity, the courts would appear to apply a very strict assessment of the impact of the monopoly on the right to earn a livelihood which will also require a high level of justification. In the case *Murphy v Stewart*,[25] Walsh J noted that if a trade union was abusing its monopoly, by preventing people from exercising the right to work, that this might amount to a breach of the constitutional guarantee. However, in the case of a State entity, as was examined in the case of *Attorney General v Paperlink*,[26] the Court will give more leeway to the State. The court held, in this case, that although the right arose from Art 45 and although Art 45: **[14–09]**

> " . . . demonstrated a view that the social order should not be based on a system in which all means of production were covered by the State, and a preference for one in which industry and commerce were mainly carried on by private citizens rather than State agencies . . . it did not follow that the Oireachtas could not legislate to establish trading corporations or public utilities, nor was it legitimate to infer that the State was called upon in legal proceedings to justify a State monopoly".[27]

3. Legitimate Justifications for Interference with the Right

The right to earn a livelihood is not absolute and is subject to certain restrictions. In the case of *Attorney General v Paperlink*,[28] the defendant sought to operate a postal service in Dublin but as there was a statutory monopoly on postal services, he was not entitled to do so and he argued that this was in breach of his right to earn a livelihood. The court held that while there was a right to earn a livelihood and that it had been interfered with in this case, the right was not absolute and there were certain legitimate justifications such as the common good which would justify an interference with the right to earn a livelihood. Certain restrictions are necessary. Griffith J in *Hand v Dublin Corporation*[29] noted that: **[14–10]**

> "The right to trade and earn a livelihood is not an unqualified right. In modern times there must be few professions, occupations, trades, or industrial or commercial undertakings which are not subject to what Costello J in *Attorney General v Paperlink Ltd.* [1984] I.L.R.M. 373 [at p 384] referred to as 'legitimate legal restraints'."[30]

---

[23] *ibid.*
[24] See L Flynn, "Locating the Missing Link: Postal Communication Monopolies in Irish and EC Law" (1992) 10 ILT 233.
[25] [1973] IR 97.
[26] [1984] ILRM 373.
[27] J Casey, *supra* n 12 at p 406.
[28] [1984] ILRM 373.
[29] [1991] 1 IR 409.
[30] *ibid* at 419.

[14–11] Another good example of a legitimate justification which provides some insight into the line of reasoning used by the courts in relation to this right is the case of *Cafolla v O'Malley*.[31] In that case, s 14 of the Gaming and Lotteries Act 1956, as amended, limited the maximum prizes that could be won in a slot machine. The plaintiff, who was the proprietor of an amusement hall which operated slot machines, was convicted of exceeding these limits and sought a declaration that s 14 was invalid, having regard to the right to earn a livelihood, particularly as the cost of living and cost of operating such machines had increased greatly since 1956 and, as such, was now infringing on his right to earn a livelihood as it was effectively reducing his profits. Costello J, in dismissing the claim in the High Court, recognised that a right to earn a livelihood was protected by Art 40.3.1° and that there was restriction on the right to earn a livelihood in this case. However, there were justifiable reasons for this restriction. The court held that it was for the plaintiff to show that there was no reasonable justification and the plaintiff had failed to show in this case that the common good did not require such restrictions.

[14–12] As to the types of justifications that might be available in such a case, it is worth considering the decision of both Costello J in the High Court and that of the Supreme Court in *Cafolla v O'Malley*. In the High Court, Costello J placed significant emphasis on the fact that the Act was not arbitrary but rather the Act had a "damaging effect on the profitability of the plaintiff's business". Examples of legitimate laws which "do not necessarily conflict with the Constitution" might include those that:

> " . . . prohibit fishermen from fishing at certain times and limit the nature and size of their catches, restrict the hours of trading in licensed premises, fix the price at which goods can be sold or services remunerated—all of which adversely affect the livelihood of those engaged in the activity concerned".

What the plaintiff had to show was that the:

> " . . . restrictions of which he complains are not reasonably required by the exigencies of the common good. If he cannot do this, then no injustice has been established because no injustice arises from a restriction so required".

As the plaintiff's claim was not that the law was unreasonable, but merely that it operated more restrictively in the current climate, the plaintiff failed to meet this exacting standard. Costello J held that it was not for the court to:

> " . . . decide what level of restrictions are reasonably necessary to curb gaming in licensed amusement halls; these are matters peculiarly within the jurisdiction and competence of the Oireachtas".

All the court is entitled to do is to consider "whether they are capable of being so justified". The Supreme Court upheld the decision of the High Court.

[14–13] Similarly in the case of *Hand v Dublin Corporation*,[32] where the plaintiffs claimed that the refusal to renew their licence to conduct a street trading business after they were

---

[31] [1985] IR 486.
[32] *supra* n 29.

charged with two or more offences under the Casual Trading Act 1980, was not in breach of their right to earn a livelihood. The Supreme Court noted that the right was not an unqualified one and that in considering the justification for an interference with such a right, the court had to balance the legitimate interests of the members of the public and those using the street and those carrying on business in the area and other casual street traders and it was open to the Oireachtas to provide for strict control and regulations having regard to the exigencies of the common good.[33] Another similar example is the case of *Shanley v Galway Corporation*[34] where a street food trader claimed that the new licensing provisions of Galway Corporation which meant that he could now only trade in two designated areas and in one of these areas food could not be served, infringed his right to earn a livelihood. However, the court once again referred to the common good as a legitimate justification in the circumstances.

The case of *Cox v Ireland*[35] is a good example of a case where an interference with a right was held to be unjustified. In that case, the plaintiff was a qualified vocational teacher and was arrested in November 1987, and charged before a Special Criminal Court with certain offences under the Firearms Acts 1925–1971, relating to the unlawful possession of three firearms and a quantity of ammunition which were scheduled offences under Part V of the Offences Against the State Act 1939. The plaintiff pleaded guilty and was sentenced to two years' imprisonment. While he was in jail, the school employed a substitute teacher in his place. Section 34(1)(3) and (5) of the Act of 1939 provided that: **[14–14]**

> "Whenever a person who is convicted by a Special Criminal Court of an offence which is, at the time of such conviction, a scheduled offence for the purposes of Part V of this Act, holds at the time of such conviction an office or employment remunerated out of the Central Fund or moneys provided by the Oireachtas or moneys raised by local taxation, or in or under or as a paid member of a board or body established by or under statutory authority, such person shall immediately on such conviction forfeit such office, employment, place, or emolument and the same shall forthwith become and be vacant".

The result of the Minister's enforcement of s 34 of the Act of 1939 was that the plaintiff's post at the School was vacated; that he was ineligible for re-employment at the school, or at any school funded by the State, for seven years from the date of his conviction; that his pension and other such rights and expectations have been forfeited and that he had lost his right to pay-related social insurance benefits for a like period. Barr J in the High Court noted that the provision did not apply to all crimes provided for in the same Act, or to crimes not tried in the Special Criminal Court, or to other persons not in the employ of the State, and there was nothing to suggest that it was imposed in the interest of the common good. "On the contrary its unreasonable, erratic operation is itself against the common good, which requires consistency and fairness in the application of the law".[36] The Supreme Court agreed that the provision was a **[14–15]**

---

33 *supra* n 29 at 420.
34 *supra* n 11.
35 [1992] 2 IR 504.
36 *ibid* at 513 (*per* Barr JJ)

"major inroad"[37] on the right to earn a livelihood as it limited not only his ability to continue in his pre-conviction employment but also his ability to take up alternative employment in the same field and operated as a "major curtailment of his earning capacity".[38] In examining whether this inroad was justified the Supreme Court noted that the State is entitled "for the protection of public peace and order, and for the maintenance and stability of its own authority"[39] to provide for penalties and forfeitures as a deterrent from criminal activity. However, in this case, the court held that the section was impermissibly wide and indiscriminate.

B. Protection under the European Convention on Human Rights

[14–16] Article 1 Protocol 1:

> "Every natural or legal person is entitled to the peaceful enjoyment of his possessions. No one shall be deprived of his possessions except in the public interest and subject to the conditions provided for by law and by the general principles of international law.
>
> The preceding provisions shall not, however, in any way impair the right of a State to enforce such laws as it deems necessary to control the use of property in accordance with the general interest or to secure the payment of taxes or other contributions or penalties."

1. Nature of the Right

[14–17] The right to earn a livelihood does not exist independently in the European Convention of Human Rights (ECHR). However, the European Court of Human Rights (ECtHR) has held that certain aspects of this right are protected by Art 1, Protocol 1. In relation to Art 1, Protocol 1, this protects the right to exercise a profession and not to have the peaceful enjoyment of this right interfered with, to be deprived of this right or to have the use of this right controlled.

[14–18] The right extends, not only to professional practices and existing business, but to legitimate expectations of business. In the case of *Oklešen v Slovenia*,[40] the ECtHR had to consider whether the provision of funeral services by licence was a possession within the meaning of Art 1, Protocol 1. In this instance the provision had been removed from the applicants by an effective State monopoly which had been granted to another private company.[41] The ECtHR reiterated that the concept of "possessions" in the first part of Art 1 of Protocol 1 has "an autonomous meaning which is not limited to ownership of physical goods and is independent from the formal classification in domestic law".[42] Accordingly, the ECtHR held that as well as physical goods, "certain rights and interests constituting assets may also be regarded as "property rights", and thus as "possessions" for the purposes of this provision".[43] It was held that the

---

37 *supra* n 35 at 522 (*per* Finlay CJ).
38 *supra* n 35 at 522 (*per* Finlay CJ).
39 *supra* n 35 at 522 (*per* Finlay CJ).
40 Application No 35264/04.
41 *Oklešen v Slovenia ibid* at para 53; *Kopecký v Slovakia* (Application No 44912/98 at para 40).
42 *ibid* at para 54.
43 *ibid.*

"applicability of Art 1 Protocol 1 therefore extends also to professional practices and their clientele, as these are entities of a certain worth that have in many respects the nature of private rights, and thus constitute assets".[44] The ECtHR went on to extend the concept by including protection not only of existing possessions, but also "assets, including claims, in respect of which the applicant can argue that he has at least a reasonable and 'legitimate expectation' of obtaining effective enjoyment of a property right".[45] In this case, the ECtHR held that the applicant had developed a significant level of goodwill in relation to funeral provision, such as preparation of bodies and transport of remains, during his seven years of providing this service. However, once the State designated it as a public utility and was legally entitled to entrust Komunala Novo Mesto (KMN) with this service provision, the question then arose as to whether the applicant could be expected to have a reasonable expectation of being able to continue in the provision of this service. The ECtHR held that he could not have had such a legitimate expectation as he had been aware for some years that the law was going to change, and it followed that the actions of both the State and KMN could not, therefore, constitute an interference with the applicants possessions.[46]

The application of Art 1 Protocol 1 to the practice of professions is also beyond doubt. A useful example is the case of *Malik v United Kingdom*[47] where the applicant, a general medical practitioner, had a contract with the National Health Service (NHS) to provide medical services to NHS patients registered with his medical practice. He could provide this service by treating the patients himself or employing another doctor to do so. He was also entitled to quarterly payments based on the number of patients registered with his practice. Following a monitoring visit, the applicant was advised that he was temporarily suspended pending a hearing to "to protect the interests of patients while a more detailed investigation into the issues of concern take place" as it was determined that he posed a serious risk to patients in his care. This suspension was due mainly to: **[14–19]**

> " ... inadequate disease registers and patient records; lack of clinical knowledge in relation to bipolar disorder, emergency contraception and smoking cessation; inadequate maternity services; lack of proper sterilising equipment and the discovery of a bottle of orange juice in a fridge containing flu vaccine; and inadequate arrangements for out-of-hours cover and opening hours".[48]

[44] *ibid*; See also *Van Marle and Others v the Netherlands*, (Application Nos 8543/79; 8674/79; 8675/79; 8685/79 at para 41); and *Buzescu v Romania* (Application No 61302/00 at para 81).

[45] *ibid* at para 55; See also *Prince Hans-Adam II of Liechtenstein v Germany* (Application No 42527/98 at para 83).

[46] *ibid* at para 62; See also *mutatis mutandis Öneryildiz v Turkey* (Application No 48939/99 at para 1216); and *Zhigalev v Russia* (Application No 54891/00 at paras 143 and 146).

[47] (Application No 23780/08).

[48] *ibid* at para 12; See also *Van Marle and Others v The Netherlands* (Application Nos 8543/79; 8674/79; 8675/79; 8685/79 at para 41). In another case involving an alleged interference with an applicant's medical practice, the Commission noted that the "vested interests" in the applicant's medical practice could be regarded as "possessions" (See *Karni v Sweden* (Application No 11540/85, Commission decision of 8 March 1988, Decisions and Reports 55 at p 157).

At a subsequent hearing, the applicant was suspended for six months. The applicant complained that this suspension amounted to an interference with his right to peaceful enjoyment of his possessions. The court held that:

> " ... property rights existed in cases concerning professional practices where by dint of their own work, the applicants concerned had built up a clientele. It explained that this clientele had, in many respects, the nature of a private right and constituted an asset and, hence, a possession within the meaning of the first sentence of Article 1".[49]

[14–20] However, in this case the court held that while goodwill may be an element in the valuation of a professional practice or business, future income is only a possession "once it has been earned, or an enforceable claim to it exists".[50] The court held in this case that as the doctor had been paid at a rate of 90 percent of his normal remuneration during his suspension, had failed to produce concrete evidence that there was a significant reduction in numbers as a consequence of his suspension or that this had any direct impact on him or on his financial situation and as the applicant was prevented from selling the goodwill in his practice and that any decrease in its marketable value was therefore of no consequence to him, there was no interference with his possessions under Art 1 Protocol 1.

This right has also been held to apply to lawyers and their practices. The ECtHR has explained that:

> " ... law practices and their clientele [are] entities of a certain worth that ha[ve] in many respects the nature of a private right and thus constitute [...] assets and therefore possessions within the meaning of the first sentence of Article 1".[51]

[14–21] Certain interferences with the right to practice a profession might involve an interference with the right to earn a livelihood. In a case involving the annulling of the registration of a Romanian lawyer which prevented him from practicing his profession, the ECtHR has held that this limitation on the ability of the lawyer to provide a full range of services, and the associated loss of income, was an unjustified interference with his property rights under Art 1, Protocol 1 of the ECHR.[52] In the case of *Malik v United Kingdom*, involving the suspension of a medical practitioner, the court held that a:

> " ... restriction on applicants' right to practise the profession concerned, such as a refusal to register an applicant on a professional list, significantly affected the conditions of their professional activities and reduced the scope of those activities. Where, as a consequence

---

[49] *Malik v United Kingdom, supra* n 47 at para 89.

[50] *ibid* at para 93; See also *Ian Edgar [Liverpool] Ltd v United Kingdom* (Application No 37683/97); and *Denimark Limited and Others v United Kingdom* (Application No 37660/97).

[51] *ibid* at para 89; See also *Olbertz v Germany* (Application No 37592/97); *Döring v Germany* (Application No 37595/97); and *Wendenburg v Germany* (Application No 71630/01)

[52] *Buzescu v Romania* (Application No 61302/00 at para 88).

> of the restrictions, the applicant's income and the value of his clientele and, more generally, his business, fell, the Court has held that there was interference with the right to peaceful enjoyment of possessions".[53]

Similarly, the revocation or withdrawal of a permit or licence to practice a profession or trade has been held to interfere with the right to the peaceful enjoyment of possessions and the economic interests connected with the underlying business.[54] In this regard, the court has held that where the maintenance of a license is one of the principle conditions for the carrying on of the business, and its withdrawal has had adverse effects on the goodwill and value of the business, this will constitute an interference with Art 1, Protocol 1.[55] Termination of a licence which is connected to the carrying on of a business may amount to an interference with the right to the peaceful enjoyment of possessions.[56]

2. Legitimate Justifications for Interference with the Right

Such interference can only be justified if, after the ECtHR is satisfied that it is lawful and not arbitrary, it has struck a fair balance between the general interests of the community and the requirements of the protection of the individual's fundamental rights.[57] In this regard, there must be a "reasonable relationship between the means employed and the aims pursued".[58] A good example of this occurring is the case of *Van Marle and Others v The Netherlands*,[59] where four accountants sought registration by the Board of Admission to the accountancy profession but were rejected on the grounds that their applications were unsatisfactory on certain points and did not show sufficient professional competence. The applicants alleged that as a result of this decision "their income and the value of the goodwill of their accountancy practices had diminished".[60] The ECtHR agreed that this was a property right within the meaning of Art 1, Protocol 1 as: [14–22]

> " ... by dint of their own work, the applicants had built up a clientèle; this had in many respects the nature of a private right and constituted an asset and, hence, a possession within the meaning of the first sentence of Article 1 Protocol 1".[61]

The refusal to register the applicants "radically affected the conditions of their professional activities and the scope of those activities was reduced. Their income fell, [14–23]

---

53 *Malik v United Kingdom, supra* n 47 at para 90; See also *Van Marle and Others v The Netherlands, supra* n 48 at para 42.

54 *ibid* at para 90: See also *Fredin v Sweden (No 1)* (Application No 12033/86 at para 40), in respect of an exploitation permit for a gravel pit; *Tre Traktörer AB v Sweden* (Application No 10873/84 at para 53), concerning a licence to serve alcoholic beverages in a restaurant; and *Rosenzweig and Bonded Warehouses Ltd v Poland* (Application No 51728/99 at para 49), which involved a licence to run a bonded warehouse.

55 *Tre Traktörer AB v Sweden ibid* at paras 43 and 53.

56 *Malik v United Kingdom, supra* n 47 para 92; See also *Bimer SA v Moldova* (Application No 15084/03 at para 49; and *Megadat.com SRL v Moldova* (Application No 21151/04) at para 63.

57 *Buzescu v Romania, supra* n 52 at para 89.

58 *ibid.*

59 *Van Marle and Others v The Netherlands, supra* n 48.

60 *ibid* at para 39.

61 *ibid* at para 41.

as did the value of their clientèle and, more generally, their business"[62] which amounted to an interference with this right. However, the court held that this interference was justified on the grounds that the law in the Netherlands was designed to promote the "general interest" of structuring a profession "that is important to the entire economic sector by providing the public with guarantees of the competence of those who carry on that profession",[63] that "a fair balance between the means used and the intended aim was at any rate ensured by transitional provisions enabling the former unqualified accountants to gain entry to the new profession on prescribed conditions".[64] Therefore, it was held that there was no breach of Art 1 Protocol 1.

C. CFR

[14–24] Article 15:

> "1. Everyone has the right to engage in work and to pursue a freely chosen or accepted occupation.
> 2. Every citizen of the Union has the freedom to seek employment, to work, to exercise the right of establishment and to provide services in any Member State.
> 3. Nationals of third countries who are authorised to work in the territories of the Member States are entitled to working conditions equivalent to those of citizens of the Union."

1. Nature of the Right

[14–25] Interestingly, the right to engage in work, as dealt with by the Court of Justice of the European Union (CJEU) has fundamentally been linked to property rights, as is the case with the ECHR and would appear to have a negative, as opposed to a positive, interpretation. While the right to engage in work as provided for in Art 15 has not been a central element in any cases before the ECJ to date, there have been some mentions of the right to engage in work in certain cases which are worth examining. For example, the court has indicated that the right to engage in work is, in fact, a general principle of community law.[65] However, no definition has been given as to the nature or content of the right or what might constitute an interference with such a right.

[14–26] What is interesting about the right to engage in work as protected by Art 15 is that there is a distinct linkage with the right to property (similar to the conception under the ECHR). For example in the case of *Syndicat des thoniers méditerranéens and Others v Commission*,[66] the applicants, who were sea-fisherman, sought compensation for the loss which they allegedly suffered as a result of the adoption of Commission Regulation (EC) No 530/2008[67] which prohibits fishing for Bluefin tuna in certain areas of the Atlantic Ocean and Mediterranean Sea by purse seiners flying flags of

---

62 *ibid* at para 42.
63 *ibid* at para 43.
64 *ibid.*
65 Case C—1/11 *Interseroh Scrap and Metals Trading GmbH v Sounderabfall-Management Gesellschaft Rheinland Pfalz mbH (SAM)* 29 March 2012.
66 Case T—574/08. The hearing took place in May 2012 and judgment is still pending.
67 Commission Regulation (EC) No 530/2008 of 12 June 2008 establishing emergency measures as regards purse seiners fishing for Bluefin tuna in the Atlantic Ocean, east of longitude 45°W, and in the Mediterranean Sea, *Official Journal*, L155, 12 June 2008 pp 0009–0010.

certain nationalities, including French flags. One of the arguments made by the applicants was that this Regulation breaches the right to engage in work and the right to property as guaranteed by the Charter of Fundamental Rights (CFR). While this case has not yet been heard it is interesting that that the applicants chose to link the right to engage in work with the right to property and provides some insight into the types of claims that might be based on this article and where interferences with this right might occur in European Union (EU) law.

Another example of the potential use of Art 15 is a reference in the opinion of Advocat-General Kokott in the case of *Pensionsversicherungsanstalt v Christine Kleist*[68] where Dr Kleist, who was employed as Chief Physician at the Austrian Pensionsversicherungsanstalt, was compulsorily retired at the age of 60 by her employer. The basis for this was a provision of a collective agreement under which doctors could be retired upon reaching the statutory normal pensionable age. Under Austrian law the normal pensionable age was at the time 65 for men and 60 for women. The question arose as to whether this constituted discrimination on the grounds of sex. While the CJEU did not deal with the question of the engagement of Art 15 in this case, Advocat-General Kokott in his opinion clearly envisaged that Art 15 might be engaged in a case of this sort and he commented that women are "adversely affected to a greater extent than their male colleagues in respect of their right to engage in work and pursue their occupation".[69] Therefore, Art 15 might be engaged and interfered with in cases where discrimination interferes with a certain person's right to engage in work and pursue their occupation. **[14–27]**

A very interesting use of Art 15 was made in the appeal[70] against the order of the General Court of the European Union in *Mauerhofer v Commission*[71] where the appellant alleged that the Commission had breached his fundamental right to engage in work as protected by Art 15, his right to enjoy the freedom to conduct a business under Art 16 and his right to property as recognized in the ECHR.[72] The case involved a dispute surrounding an administrative order issued by the Commission. The CJEU rejected the claim and did not deal with the issue of the breaches of Arts 15 and 16 and the ECHR on the grounds that the appeal could only deal with errors of law in the decision of the General Court, whereas the arguments of the appellant were attributable, not to the General Court, but to the Commission. However, once again this case gives some indication of the potential use of the right, its specific link to property rights and the potential interferences that might be considered by the CJEU. Equally, the right to engage in work has also been argued in a very recent case, *Fares Al-Chihabi v Council of the European Union*, where certain Council Regulations relating to restrictive measures in view of the situation in Syria,[73] allegedly interfere **[14–28]**

---

[68] Case C-356/09 *Pensionsversicherungsanstalt v Christine Kleist*.

[69] *Pensionsversicherungsanstalt v Christine Kleist, ibid* at para 51.

[70] Case C–433/10 P *Mauerhofer v Commission.*

[71] Case T-515/08.

[72] *Mauerhofer v Commission ibid* at para 97.

[73] Council Regulation (EU) No 878/2011 amending Regulation (EU) No 442/2011 concerning restrictive measures in view of the situation in Syria, *Official Journal*, L288, 02 September 2011 pp 0001–0005; Council Regulation (EU) No 1011/2011 amending Regulation (EU) No 442/2011 concerning restrictive measures in view of the situation in Syria, *Official Journal* L269 13 October

with the applicant's fundamental rights in an unjustified and disproportionate manner, in particular the right to engage in work and conduct a business. Once again this case has not yet been heard, but the references to the right indicate its growing significance in EU law and the variety of potential claims in which it might be utilised. It is also important to recognise here the overlap with the freedom to conduct a business protected by Art 16 CFR. The freedom to conduct a business has been held to constitute a particular expression of the freedom to pursue a trade or profession and has the status of a general principle of Community law.[74] However, the principle is not absolute[75] and restrictions may be imposed on the exercise of the freedom to pursue a trade or profession "provided that such restrictions in fact correspond to objectives of general interest pursued by the European Union and do not constitute in relation to the aim pursued a disproportionate and intolerable interference, impairing the very substance of the rights guaranteed".[76]

2. Legitimate Interferences with the Right

[14–29] While there have been very few mentions of what might legitimate an interference with a right, once again some information can be gleaned from the references made to the right by the CJEU. This has arisen most recently in relation to age discrimination and the issue of mandatory retirement. One particular example is the case of *Fuchs and Köhler*[77] which involved a case relating to the mandatory retirement of State prosecutors in Germany at the age of 65. In this case the CJEU held that States should read the prohibition against age discrimination in light of the right to engage in work[78] and that:

> " ... particular attention must be paid to the participation of older workers in the labour force and thus in economic, cultural and social life. Keeping older workers in the labour force promotes diversity in the workforce ... [and] ... contributes to the realising of their potential and to the quality of life of the workers concerned".[79]

2011 pp 0018–0020; Council Decision 2011/522/CFSP amending Decision 2011/273/CFSP concerning restrictive measures against Syria, *Official Journal* L228 02 September 2011 pp 0016–0018; Council Decision 2011/684/CFSP amending Decision 2011/273/CFSP concerning restrictive measures against Syria, *Official Journal* L269 pp 0033–0035; Council Regulation (EU) No 442/2011 concerning restrictive measures in view of the situation in Syria *Official Journal* L121 pp 0001–0010.

[74] See R Streinz,"EUV/EGV-Kommentar" (Munich 2003) at 2607, who argues that the Court has developed the freedom to pursue a trade or activity as a fundamental principle of Community law simply as the freedom to conduct a business. A similar view is taken by M Knecht in *EU Kommentar* (edited by J Schwarze) (Baden-Baden, Nomos, 2nd edition, 2009).

[75] See Case 4/73 *Nold v Commission* [1974] ECR 491 at 14; Case C-44/94 *Fishermen's Organisations and Others* [1995] ECR I-3115 at 55; Case C-200/96 *Metronome Musik* [1998] ECR I-1953 at 21; Joined Cases C-20/00 and C-64/00 *Booker Aquaculture and Hydro Seafood* [2003] ECR I-7411 at 68; and Joined Cases C-37/02 and C-38/02 *Di Lenardo and Dilexport* [2004] ECR I-6911 at 82.

[76] See the excellent discussion of Advocate General Trstenjak in Case C 316/09 *MSD Sharp & Dohme GmbH v Merckle GmbH* at 84.

[77] Case C-159/10 *Fuchs and Köhler v Land Hessen*

[78] *ibid* at para 62.

[79] *ibid* at para 63.

However, in considering this right, States had to strike a balance between the diverging interests of older workers and the importance of sharing work among the generations.[80] States may choose to prolong working life or provide for early retirement and it is for the State to "find the right balance between the different interests involved, while ensuring that they do not go beyond what is appropriate and necessary to achieve the legitimate aim pursued".[81] A number of important points can be obtained from the discussion of the right in this case. First, the right to engage in work can be engaged where there is a dismissal from employment. Secondly, such a right can be interfered with by such a dismissal or a removal of work. Finally, this right is not absolute and has to be balanced against the legitimate interests involved, which should be proportionate. [14–30]

Another interesting mention of the right arises in the case of *Interseroh Scrap and Metals Trading GmbH v Sounderabfall-Management Gesellschaft Rheinland Pfalz mbH (SAM)*[82] where the CJEU had to consider whether Art 18(4) of Regulation No 1013/2006[83] did not permit an intermediary dealer arranging a shipment of waste to avoid disclosing the name of the waste produced to the consignee of the shipment which had an impact on the right not to disclose business secrets. The CJEU examined Art 15(1), 16 and 17 of the CFR and held that both the right to property, the freedom to pursue a trade or business and the protection of business secrets are general principles of EU law.[84] However, the court held that: [14–31]

> " . . . even if the obligation to disclose the name of the waste producer to the consignee of a shipment of waste were to constitute a breach of the protection of the business secrets of intermediary dealers, that could not have the consequence of restricting the scope of a provision of secondary law that is clear and unconditional".[85]

Therefore, while these rights are significantly strong, they are not absolute and can be legitimated in certain circumstances.

D. International and Regional Laws

The right to engage in work and earn a livelihood is protected in a variety of international and regional documents. Article 23, Universal Declaration of Human Rights guarantees everyone "the right to work, to free employment, to just and favourable conditions of work and to protection against unemployment", Art 6, [14–32]

---

80 *ibid* at para 64.
81 *ibid* at para 65.
82 Case C-1/11 *Interseroh Scrap and Metals Trading GmbH v Sounderabfall-Management Gesellschaft Rheinland Pfalz mbH (SAM)*.
83 Regulation (EC) No 1013/2006 of the European Parliament and of the Council on Shipments of Waste, *Official Journal* L190 pp 001–0098.
84 *Interseroh Scrap and Metals Trading GmbH v Sounderabfall-Management Gesellschaft Rheinland Pfalz mbH (SAM), supra* n 65 at para 44; See also Case C–280/93 *Germany v Council* at para 78; Joined Cases C–20/00 and C-64/00 *Booker Aquacultur Ltd and Hydro Seafood GSP Ltd v The Scottish Ministers* at para 68; Joined Cases C–154/04 and C–155/04 *Alliance for Natural Health and Others* at para 126; and Joined Cases C–453/03, C–11/04, C–12/04 and C–194/04 *ABNA and Others* at para 87; and Case C–450/06 *Varec SA v Belgian State* at para 49.
85 *ibid.*

International Covenant on Economic Social and Cultural Rights protects "the right of everyone to the opportunity to gain his living by work" and Art 11 of the same Convenant protects the "right to earn an adequate standard of living". Article 5(1)(i) of the International Convention on the Elimination of all forms of Racial Discrimination provides for protection for the rights to work, to free choice of employment, to just and favourable conditions of work, to protection against unemployment, to equal pay for equal work and to just and favourable remuneration. Similarly, Art 11(1)(a) of the Convention on the Elimination of all forms of Discrimination Against Women recognises the right to work as an inalienable right of all human beings. People with disabilities are specifically protected by Art 27 of the United Nations Convention on the Rights of Persons with Disabilities which recognises the right of persons with disabilities to work, on an equal basis with others, including the opportunity to gain a living by work freely chosen or accepted in a labour market and a work environment that is open, inclusive and accessible to persons with disabilities.

[14–33] The guarantee of a right to earn a livelihood at an international level has been interpreted to imply three specific obligations. The obligation to respect the right (that States must not destroy a person's opportunity to earn his or her living), the obligation to protect the right (States must prevent this opportunity from being destroyed by third parties) and the obligation to fulfil the right (States must provide the opportunity to earn one's living to each person who currently does not have this opportunity).[86]

[14–34] At a regional level, some protections exist. However, as this is often considered a social and economic right, it is often omitted from major regional instruments. For example, the European Social Charter, Art 1 protects the right; however, this is not reflected in other regional instruments such as the American Convention on Human Rights. The right is protected by Art 15 of the African Charter on Human and Peoples' Rights[87] and by Art 34 of the Arab Charter on Human Rights. The right to work is given extensive positive protection in this latter convention. It is heralded as a natural right of every citizen. States: "shall endeavor to provide, to the extent possible, a job for the largest number of those willing to work, while ensuring production, the freedom to choose one's work and equality of opportunity without discrimination of any kind on grounds of race, colour, sex, religion, language, political opinion, membership in a union, national origin, social origin, disability or any other situation".

Conclusion

[14–35] The right to earn a livelihood is not expressly recognised in the Irish Constitution, nor does this right always find explicit protection at regional or international levels, although there are some recent exceptions. However, the right is considered to be an unenumerated right under Art 40.3 of the Constitution and one of the personal rights of the citizen. The ECHR does not expressly recognise such a right but it has been held

86 Circle of Rights, Economic, Social and Cultural Rights Activism, "The Human Right to Work". See http://www1.umnedu/humanrts/edumat/IHRIP/circle/modules/module10.htm#_edn4, last accessed 27 July 2012.

87 Art 15 states: "Every individual shall have the right to work under equitable and satisfactory conditions, and shall receive equal pay for equal work".

to be an implied right within the right to property which is protected by Art 1 Protocol 1 to the ECHR. For the first time, there is an express recognition of the right at an EU level under Art 15 of the CFR reflecting the express recognition of this right at an international level. While the jurisprudence of the CJEU is still at a very early stage, the indications would suggest that the broad interpretation of the right, as found in the ECHR and in the Irish Constitution, will predominate and that while certain legitimate interferences will be allowed, these will have to be proportionate in all the circumstances. The express recognition of the right at an EU level will have very positive implications for the development of the right at a national level and in the Council of Europe in future years.

CHAPTER 15
The Right to Education

Introduction

The right to education has been internationally recognised as a fundamental right since the adoption of the Universal Declaration on Human Rights (UDHR) in 1948 and has since been enshrined in various international, regional and domestic instruments. The importance of this right is clear, as it not only allows for personal development but also enables the individual to access information on how to implement and achieve other human rights. The right to education, one of the very few socio-economic rights protected by the Irish Constitution, is set out in Art 42.The constitutional protection of the right to education is the focus of the first part of this chapter. The second part discusses how the first Optional Protocol to the European Convention on Human Rights (ECHR) protects the right to education and the chapter concludes with a review of the protection of the right to education under the Charter of Fundamental Rights (CFR) framework and under international and regional human rights instruments. [15–01]

A. Irish Constitution

Article 42: [15–02]

> "1. The State acknowledges that the primary and natural educator of the child is the Family and guarantees to respect the inalienable right and duty of parents to provide, according to their means, for the religious and moral, intellectual, physical and social education of their children.
>
> 2. Parents shall be free to provide this education in their homes or in private schools or in schools recognised or established by the State.
>
> 3. 1° The State shall not oblige parents in violation of their conscience and lawful preference to send their children to schools established by the State, or to any particular type of school designated by the State.
> 2° The State shall, however, as guardian of the common good, require in view of actual conditions that the children receive a certain minimum education, moral, intellectual and social.

> 4. The State shall provide for free primary education and shall endeavour to supplement and give reasonable aid to private and corporate educational initiative, and, when the public good requires it, provide other educational facilities or institutions with due regard, however, for the rights of parents, especially in the matter of religious and moral formation.
>
> 5. In exceptional cases, where the parents for physical or moral reasons fail in their duty towards their children, the State as guardian of the common good, by appropriate means shall endeavour to supply the place of the parents, but always with due regard for the natural and imprescriptible rights of the child."

The right to education, as enshrined in Art 42, is very much connected to the provision on the rights of the family which precedes it in the text of the constitution. Rather than a general statement, protecting an individual's right to education, which can be seen, for example, in Art 26 of the UDHR, i.e. "Everyone has the right to education", the formulation of Art 42 is quite convoluted. It is not child-centred in that it does not emphasise the importance of education for the development of the child, and indeed, only requires that children receive a "certain minimum education".[1] Rather, the main aim of the article is to protect the role of the family as the primary and natural educator of the child, and to prevent the State from interfering with the family unit in this regard except in exceptional cases. Article 42 does also, however, obligate the State to provide for free primary education. Recent Irish case law illustrates the influence of international human rights instruments on the interpretation of the right to education, however. For example, in *D v Refugee Appeals Tribunal*[2] Hogan J held that the denial of the right to education amounted to persecution for the purposes of the Refugee Act 1996. In coming to this conclusion he made reference to the fundamental nature of the right to education as enshrined in various international and regional instruments, including the First Optional Protocol to the ECHR and the CFR.

1. Nature of the Right

[15–03] Article 42 has two main elements; protecting the primacy of the family unit in educating children and obliging the State to provide for free primary education. However, before these can be discussed in more detail, the first question which must be addressed, is what is meant by "education" in a constitutional context?

What is "Education"?

[15–04] Article 42 requires the State to provide for free primary education and does not provide any exceptions to this obligation. However, the provision does not require the State to provide for any form or level of education other than primary education, rather it requires the State to:

---

[1] Art 42.3.2°.

[2] [2011] IEHC 431. This case concerned a young Serbian boy who was of Ashkali/Roma ethnicity. His parents applied for asylum on his behalf on the basis that he would suffer persecution, in the form of being prevented from receiving a basic education as a result of discrimination, if he was returned to Serbia. The application for asylum was refused but leave was granted to appeal to the High Court.

> "... endeavour to supplement and give reasonable aid to private and corporate educational initiative, and, when the public good requires it, provide other educational facilities or institutions ...".[3]

This is, clearly, a very weak requirement. While the Irish Constitution obligates the State to provide for free primary education, it does not define the term "education", nor does it seek to explain the nature or extent of the education which the State must provide.

The nature of the educational experience that the State is required to provide for has been discussed in a number of cases which help to clarify the nature of the right to education in Irish law. This issue was first considered in the case of *Ryan v AG*[4] where counsel for Mrs Ryan contended that education had a very broad meaning and included the process of "rearing and nurturing'[5]. However, in the High Court Kenny J did not accept this interpretation of the term in the constitutional context, stating:

> "... it seems to me that the terms of the Article show that the word 'education' was not used in this wide sense in the Constitution. Section 1 of the Article recognises the 'right and duty of the parents to provide, according to their means, for the religious and moral, intellectual, physical and social education of their children,' but in section 2 it is provided that the parents are free to provide *this* education in their homes or in schools recognised or established by the State. The education referred to in section 1 must, therefore, be one that can be provided in schools and must, therefore, be one of a scholastic nature."[6]

In the Supreme Court Ó Dálaigh J agreed that the constitutional meaning of "education" **[15–05]** was not the broad process contended by Mrs Ryan, but defined the concept rather differently. He stated:

> "Education essentially is the teaching and training of a child to make the best possible use of his inherent and potential capacities, physical, mental and moral."[7]

However, it is clear that the interpretations of the term "education" in *Ryan* are quite limited and restricted. In later years, however, the Irish courts have attached a broader interpretation to the term "education" for the purposes of the constitution. This broadening has been influenced by developments in the United Nations (UN) and international human rights law.

In the case of *O'Donoghue v Minister for Health*[8] the applicant, who was physically and mentally disabled, sought an order from the State to provide him with free primary education on the basis of Art 42. He had been educated at home by his mother as there was no adequate place in the school system. The State contended that the applicant was uneducable for the purposes of Art 42. With regard to the meaning of education under the constitution, O'Hanlon J discussed the definitions afforded to the concept of education in *Ryan* and stated that the Supreme Court definition put forward by

---

3 Art 42.4.
4 [1965] 1 IR 294.
5 *ibid* at 309.
6 *ibid* at 310.
7 *ibid* at 350.
8 [1996] 2 IR 20.

Ó Dálaigh J was the more useful one. He also broadened out the definition of education, with reference to international human rights law.[9] He stated:

> "I conclude, having regard to what has gone before, that there is a constitutional obligation imposed on the State by the provisions of Article 42, s. 4 of the Constitution to provide for free basic elementary education of all children and that this involves giving each possible child such advice, instruction and teaching as will enable him or her to make the best possible use of his or her inherent and potential capacities, physical, mental and moral, however limited these capacities may be. Or, to borrow the language of the United Nations Convention and Resolution of the General Assembly – 'such education as will be conducive to the child's achieving the fullest possible social integration and individual development; such education as will enable the child to develop his or her capabilities and skills to the maximum and will hasten the process of social integration and reintegration'."[10]

O'Hanlon J then discussed the extension of the concept of education under Art 42 to special needs education, stating:

> "This process will work differently for each child, according to the child's own natural gifts, or lack thereof. In the case of the child who is deaf, dumb, blind, or otherwise physically or mentally handicapped, a completely different programme of education ought to be adopted and a completely different rate of progress has to be taken for granted, than would be regarded as appropriate for a child suffering from no such handicap ...".[11]

[15–06] Special needs education[12] is also regulated by the Education for Persons with Special Educational Needs Act 2004. This legislation provides that children are to be educated in an inclusive setting unless this would not be in the best interests of the child with special needs, or that it would impact on the effective provision of education for other children in mainstream education. This Act[13] provides that each child assessed with a special educational need should have a personal education plan.[14] This process is not in place yet but its implementation is being overseen by the National Council for Special Education (NCSE).[15]

[15–07] After the adoption of this piece of legislation the case of *O'Carolan v Minister for Education*[16] came before the High Court, where the level of education which the State is obligated to provide was discussed once again. The applicant, who was an autistic child, sought funding from the State for education in a centre in Wales because the school place offered to him in Dublin was not suitable for his needs. McMenamin J held that that relevant test in such cases was whether the education offered by the State was "appropriate", and concluded that, in this case, it was. This test seems to be at variance with earlier judgments, e.g. *O'Donoghue* which emphasise that education

---

[9] Para 3 UN Declaration on the Rights of Disabled Persons 1979.

[10] [1996] 2 IR 20 at 65.

[11] *ibid.*

[12] See M Smyth, "The Legislative and Policy Context of Special Educational Rights in Ireland", (2009) 27 ILT 221.

[13] For a discussion of this Act, see C O'Mahony, "Education for Persons with Special Educational Needs Act 2004—A New(ish) Beginning", (2004) 22 ILT 301.

[14] s 3, Education for Persons with Special Educational Needs Act 2004.

[15] http://www.ncse.ie, last accessed 28 June 2012.

[16] [2005] IEHC 296.

should allow a child to reach their potential, rather than just be "appropriate" for their needs.[17]

The Obligation of the State

Article 42 imposes various obligations on the State. First, Art 42.4 requires the State to "provide for" free primary education. This phrase was discussed in the case of *Crowley v Ireland*.[18] The Supreme Court clarified that the State is not under an obligation to provide free primary education itself, but rather to provide *for* such education. Kenny J stated: **[15–08]**

> " . . . the State is under no obligation to educate . . ." [and] " . . . the State is to provide the buildings, to pay the teachers who are under no contractual duty to it but to the manager or trustees, to provide means of transport to the schools if this is necessary to avoid hardship, and to prescribe minimum standards."[19]

In the case of *O'Shiel v Minister for Education*[20] the issue of the State's obligation in relation to funding schools was discussed. In this case the plaintiffs wanted to compel the State to fund a school which would be based on the Steiner philosophy. While the parents had a right to set up and run such a school at their own expense under Art 42.3.2° as it would meet the standard of a "certain minimum education", the Court held that the State was not under an obligation to fund such a school. Laffoy J stated:

> "In order to fulfil its constitutional obligation to provide for free primary education, in my view, the State must have regard to and must accommodate the expression of parental conscientious choice and lawful preference. However, this does not mean that the State must accede to an application for financial aid from any group of parents who are united in their choice of primary education which establishes that what is being provided by it is education, that it is being provided in a school and that it meets a standard of what can reasonably be defined as primary education, as the plaintiffs contended."[21]

Article 42 obligates the State not to require parents to send their children to schools established by the State if this is at variance with their "conscience and lawful preference". However, the State must ensure that children receive "a certain minimum education, moral, intellectual and social".[22] Under Art 42.3.2° the State can only interfere with this right to ensure that children receive a minimum standard of education. The meaning of "certain minimum standards" was discussed in *Re Article 26 and the School Attendance Bill 1942*[23] which examined the constitutionality of s 4 of the Bill. This provision empowered the Minister for Education to grant certificates to home educating parents which stated that their children were in receipt of suitable education. In defining the term "certain minimum standards" the court stated: **[15–09]**

---

17 See C O'Mahony, "The Right to Education and 'Constitutionally Appropriate' Provision", (2006) 28 DULJ 422.
18 [1980] IR 102.
19 *ibid* at 126.
20 [1999] 2 IR 321.
21 *ibid* at 347.
22 Art 42.3.2°.
23 [1943] IR 334.

> "... it seems to us that the State is free to act, so long as it does not require more than a 'certain minimum education' which expression, in the opinion of this Court, indicates a minimum standard of elementary education of general application."[24]

Thus, the court held that the powers granted to the Minister for Education were not in line with Art 42 as he or she could exercise these powers to require a higher level of education than the "certain minimum" level.

Article 42.5 is the most child-centred provision of Art 42 and places an obligation on the State "to supply the place of the parents" in exceptional circumstances where parents fail in their duty towards their children "but always with due regard for the natural and imprescriptible rights of the child". This provision is more concerned with the protection of children rather than their right to education. In *FN v Minister for Education*[25] the court interpreted Art 42.5 as providing a right for children to be cared for by the State.

To Whom does the Right Apply?

[15–10] In *Sinnott v Minister for Education*[26] the question of who can benefit from the right to education was addressed. Mr Sinnott, 23, was an autistic man who was seeking damages in the High Court for failure on the part of State to provide him with education under Art 42. In the past he had only received approximately two years worth of education from the State. He also sought injunctions with regard to his continuing right to education, as withdrawal of education services would result in a regression of his condition. In the High Court, he was awarded damages and an injunction which required the State to provide educational services to him for as long as they were reasonably required by him, which, because of the nature of his condition, meant that such services would be reasonably necessary for the rest of his life. The State appealed to the Supreme Court. The State did not contend that Mr Sinnott was not entitled to primary education under Art 42, but that the right to education in Art 42 ended when a person reached the age of 18. The Supreme Court agreed with this contention, despite the fact that no age limit is placed on the right in the text of the constitution. In coming to this conclusion, the court emphasised the primary role accorded to the family as the natural educator of the child. Denham J stated:

> "The essence of Article 42 is the concept of the family, and a child growing up in the heart of the family. Article 42 describes the situation of the education of a young person within the family unit, a young person who is growing and learning. It also makes provision for intervention for the common good to require that children receive a certain minimum education. A person who has achieved adulthood is no longer subject to parental authority or decisions such as are envisaged in Article 42."[27]

[15–11] The court rejected the contention of the plaintiff that the word "child" corresponded with "offspring", and interpreted the term to be "age-related". The court agreed with

---

[24] *ibid* at 345.
[25] [1995] 1 IR 409.
[26] [2001] 2 IR 545.
[27] *ibid* at 654.

the State that 18 was an appropriate cut-off point for the right to education. In interpreting Art 42, Denham J stated:

> "... on first impression it would appear that 14 is a more logical age than 18. However, the right to have free primary education provided is a fundamental and important right established by the Constitution. It is a right with which certain individuals or groups may encounter physical, mental or social difficulties in exercising. Therefore, the norm may not cover minorities. The right is given to all children. It is appropriate that the construction of the Article should ensure that all children may get the benefit of the right. Consequently, it is fitting that the age at which the right ceases to exist is when the person is no longer a child. Therefore it is reasonable to take the age at which society treats a young person as an adult as the age when the right ceases to exist. The State's case that the first plaintiff is recognised as an adult when he reaches 18 years of age is reasonable."[28]

Therefore, the right to a free primary education is limited to individuals under the age of 18 years.

The Primacy of the Family as Educator

Article 42 highlights the primary role of the family in the education of the child. First, it provides that the family "the primary and natural educator of the child"[29] and then it provides that the State should not: **[15–12]**

> "... oblige parents in violation of their conscience and lawful preference to send their children to schools established by the State, or to any particular type of school designated by the State".[30]

The primacy of the family in the education process was highlighted in *Sinnott*, where Denham J stated:

> "Article 42.4 is placed in an Article redolent of the family, where children are addressed as part of a family, where the primary educator is acknowledged as the family. It paints a picture of a family of two parents, mother and father, and children learning from their parents."[31]

However, as discussed above in relation to the case of *O'Shiel v Minister for Education*[32] the State is not under an obligation to provide funding for all schools which parents choose to set up.

2. Legitimate Justifications for Interference with the Right

The right to education under the constitution is not an unlimited right. It can be seen from the above discussion that the State is under an obligation to provide for free *primary* education only. The nature and extent of the concept of primary education has been clarified by means of case law, discussed above, e.g. in the case of *O'Donoghue v Minister for Health*.[33] This illustrates that the right to education, in the context of the **[15–13]**

---

[28] *ibid* at 654–655.
[29] Art 42.1.
[30] Art 42.3.1°.
[31] *Sinnott v Minister for Education* [2001] 2 IR 545 at 653.
[32] [1999] 2 IR 321.
[33] [1996] 2 IR 20.

constitution, is limited in a number of ways as regards level and standard. In the case of *Sinnott v Minister for Education*[34] the Supreme Court also confirmed that the right to free primary education is limited to those under the age of 18. An interesting issue is one related to compulsory attendance at school. While Art 42 is primarily concerned with the rights of parents, Art 42.3.2° provides that the State "shall, however, as guardian of the common good, require in view of actual conditions that the children receive a certain minimum education, moral, intellectual or social". The Education Welfare Act 2000, and in particular s 17, provides that the parents of a child (aged between six and 16 years) shall cause the child to attend a recognised school on each school day. There are some exceptions to this rule. So for example, a child may be registered or is in the process of being registered by the National Educational Welfare Board to receive education in a place other than in a recognized school, the child is temporarily attending a school outside the State and the parent of the child has notified the school in relation to this, the child is being educated outside the State or is in a programme of education prescribed by the Minister, or there is some other sufficient cause for the non-attendance. This legislation would appear to be constitutionally sound based on Art 42.3.2° and the obligation on the State to ensure a certain minimum level of education.

B. ECHR

[15–14] Protocol 1, Art 2:

> "No person shall be denied the right to education. In the exercise of any functions which it assumes in relation to education and to teaching, the State shall respect the right of parents to ensure such education and teaching in conformity with their own religious and philosophical convictions."

1. Nature of the Right

[15–15] Optional Protocol 1 of the ECHR contains three different rights which the original signatories could not agree to include in the convention itself, concerning property, education and elections. The right to education[35] is contained in Art 2 of this protocol, but it is by no means universally accepted, with a number of signatory States lodging reservations, including Ireland.[36]

The wording of the provision means that there is no obligation on a State to either provide a State run education, or to subsidise a privatised system, as these are considered to be at the discretion of a particular State. Where the State does have educational establishments, whether private or State run, then the State is concerned with any alleged denial of the right to education by those institutions.

---

[34] [2001] 2 IR 545.

[35] Which is a right residing primarily with the child. See *Campbell and Cosans v United Kingdom* (1982) 4 EHRR 293 para 40.

[36] "At the time of signing the (First) Protocol the Irish Delegate puts on record that, in the view of the Irish Government, Art 2 of the Protocol is not sufficiently explicit in ensuring to parents the right to provide education for their children in their homes or in schools of the parents' own choice, whether or not such schools are private schools or are schools recognised or established by the State." Deposited 25 February 1953.

This was seen in the seminal and still leading case in this area, the *Belgian Linguistic* case[37] where the court considered that: **[15–16]**

> "The negative formulation indicates, as confirmed by the preparatory work, that the contracting parties do not recognise such a right of education as would require them to establish at their own expense, or to subsidise, education of any particular type or at any particular level..."

The case concerned French-speaking residents of Belgium, who wanted their children to be educated in French. Dutch-speaking children in a particular French-speaking area were allowed to be educated in Dutch-speaking schools in a bilingual district outside the neighbourhood, but French-speaking children in an equivalent area could not attend the French-speaking schools in the same bilingual district and were compelled to attend their local Dutch-language schools.[38]

Article 2 can be seen to extend through the educational system up to higher education, since, although originally considered as merely applying to elementary education,[39] it has now been extended through the case of *Leyla Şahin v Turkey.*[40]

In the case of private education providers, the provision has no specific obligation on a State to have such establishments, rather the provision requires that the providers must have the freedom to establish them.[41] However, it is possible to suggest that the wording of the second sentence of this provision could entail the specific allowance by the State of a particular educational establishment in order to comply with the "religious and philosophical convictions" of parents. The word "education", as opposed to "teaching" is also not specifically addressed within the text of the provision,[42] but has been considered to be of wide interpretation:

> "... the education of children is the whole process whereby, in any society, adults endeavour to transmit their beliefs, culture and other values to the young, whereas teaching or instruction refers in particular to the transmission of knowledge and to intellectual development."[43]

It is also clear that the provisions of Art 2 are involved very much with substantive rights of private and family life, religion and expression contained in Arts 8, 9 and 10 ECHR, and are often considered in relation to the operation of Art 14 when discrimination is alleged in addition.

---

37 *Belgian Linguistic* Case (No 1) (1967), Series A, No 5 (1979–80) 1 EHRR 241 (No 2) (1968), Series A, No 6 (1979–80) 1 EHRR 252.

38 See also the similar *Cyprus v Turkey* (2001) 35 EHRR 731.

39 *Yanasik v Turkey* (1993) No 15424/89, 74 DR 14.

40 *Leyla Şahin v Turkey* (2005) 41 EHRR 109.

41 *Kjeldsen, Busk Madsen and Pedersen v* Denmark (1976) 1 EHRR 711.

42 For instance, Art 26(2) UNDHR declares that; "Education should be directed to the full development of the human personality and to the strengthening of respect for human rights and fundamental freedoms. It shall promote understanding, tolerance and friendship among all nations, racial or religious groups ...".

43 *Campbell and Cosens v United Kingdom* (1982) 4 EHRR 293 para 33.

2. Legitimate Justifications for Interference with the Right

[15–17] It is clear that the right is not in any sense absolute, but may be regulated by the State within a reasonable margin of appreciation. In considering restrictions on the right, therefore, the ECtHR will, as in other interpretive aspects, take into account whether they are " ... foreseeable for those concerned and pursue a legitimate aim", and " ... whether the means employed to realise the intended aim are reasonably proportionate to its attainment".[44]

[15–18] There have, therefore, been a number of occasions where restrictions on education have been upheld, such as in the area of home schooling[45] or the exclusion of a disruptive student.[46] In terms of clothing, the wearing of an Islamic headscarf was considered not to be an infringement of Art 2 when Leyla Şahin[47] was excluded from her examinations, and this case is also considered in the section on Art 9 (manifestation of religion or belief).

> "The right to education does not exclude recourse to disciplinary measures, including suspension or expulsion from an educational institution in order to ensure compliance with its internal rules."[48]

This was followed in the case of *Sulak v Turkey,*[49] where a university student was expelled for persistent cheating in examinations. This was considered perfectly acceptable in that any right to education was not absolute, but also included the right of educational institutions to compliance with any internal rules, including suspension or expulsion.

[15–19] However, in the case of *Timishev v Russia*[50] it was held that making a child's right to education conditional on the registration of their parents' residence was a breach of Art 2, having no legitimate aim (see 15-17). This was particularly so as the migrant card in question, which was necessary in State law as showing residential qualification, had been forcibly removed by State agencies. Likewise having no legal basis, as interpreted by the ECtHR, and also being an arbitrary decision for lack of evidence, was the decision in *Mursel Eren v Turkey.*[51] In this case a student's good results in an entrance examination were thought to be without explanation, and he was therefore refused a university place.

The ECtHR also held that the allocation of eighteen Roma children[52] to "special" schools for those deemed mentally deficient in the south-eastern Czech city of Ostrava was, in fact, a violation of both Art 2 of Protocol 1 and of Art 14 (indirect

---

[44] *Leyla Şahin v Turkey* (2005) 41 EHRR 109 para 154.

[45] *Konrad v Germany* (2006) No 35504/03, ECHR 2006-XIII, judgment of September 2006, *Leuffen v FRG* (1992) No 19844/92, judgment of 9 July 1992.

[46] *Kramelius v Sweden* (1996) No 21062/92, judgment, 17 January 1996, *Whitman v United Kingdom* (1989) No 13477/87, judgment 4 October 1989.

[47] *Leyla Şahin v Turkey* (2005) 41 EHRR 109.

[48] *ibid* at para 156.

[49] *Sulak v Turkey* No 24515/94, judgment of 17 January 1996.

[50] *Timishev v Russia* (2005) No 55762/00 44 EHRR 776.

[51] *Mursel Eren v Turkey* 44 EHRR 619.

[52] *D H v Czech Republic* (2006) No 57325/00, judgment 7 February 2006.

discrimination). The children, it was claimed, received a markedly inferior education, and that the segregation was based on their racial or ethnic identity rather than on their academic performance.

It is clear that Art 2 is meant to be read as a whole, but the second sentence specifically takes account of the religious and philosophical convictions of the parents. The State is enjoined to a positive obligation to "respect" these convictions, which means that it is not an absolute right on the part of the parents to have their wishes carried out with respect to their children's education. In other words, the parent cannot force the State to a course of action in line with the parents' particular views. The interpretation given by the ECtHR has been that "convictions" should be seen as " ... views that attain a certain level of cogency, seriousness, cohesion and importance",[53] and that reliance by parents on this *dicta* must be shown, therefore, to be very relevant to the instant case.[54] **[15–20]**

As far as the philosophical beliefs of parents are concerned, the ECtHR has suggested that the beliefs must have a valid basis, valid content,[55] must be definitively held, and must be the basis for their objection to the State action.[56]

In *Kjeldsen, Busk Madsen and Pedersen v* Denmark[57] the applicants were parents of children who were attending State primary schools,[58] in which the State had introduced compulsory sex education as part of the curriculum.[59] The applicants claimed that they wished to have their children exempted from this sex education, however, these requests were not met and, consequently, all of them withdrew their children from school. The ECtHR held that any teaching should respect parents' religious and moral convictions, but that Art 2 would be breached only if the teachers were advocating a particular type of sexual behaviour or set of morals rather than a generalised education as to sex. Since the parents still had the freedom to educate their children at home to instill their own particular religious convictions and beliefs the sex education provided by the schools was not a violation of Art 2. **[15–21]**

In the leading case of *Folgerø v Norway*[60] humanist parents objected to the effects of the Norwegian primary school curriculum being changed. What had been two separate subjects (Christianity and philosophy of life) were replaced by a single subject covering Christianity, religion and philosophy, known as KRL (kristendomskunnskap med religions- og livssynsorientering). Prior to this change, parents had been able to have their child exempted from Christianity lessons; however, it was only possible to request **[15–22]**

---

[53] *Campbell and Cosens v United Kingdom* (1982) 4 EHRR 293 para 36.

[54] *Hasan and Eylem Zengin v Turkey* (2007), No 1448/04 judgment of 9 October 2007. Held that the Alevi Islamic faith is a "religious conviction", and "certainly not a sect, nor a 'belief'".

[55] *Campbell and Cosens v United Kingdom* (1982) 4 EHRR 293.

[56] *Warwick v UK* (1986) No 9471/81, judgment of 18 July 1986.

[57] *Kjeldsen, Busk Madsen and Pedersen v Denmark* (1976) 1 EHRR 711.

[58] The Danish Constitution gives children free and compulsory education in State primary schools.

[59] There were included guidelines and safeguards against: a) showing pornography; b) teachers giving sex education to pupils when they were alone; c) giving information on methods of sexual intercourse; and d) using vulgar language while imparting sex education.

[60] *Folgerø and Others v Norway* (2007) No 15472/02, judgment 26 June 2007.

exemption from certain parts of KRL. Interestingly, the extent of the course, the ECtHR held, concentrated so much on Christianity that the *de facto* object of KRL was to give a Christian indoctrination to the upbringing of children, and so the need for "objective, critical and pluralistic" education had not been met.

[15–23] There is criticism of Art 2 Protocol 1 in that it does not guarantee a State-funded education system, although the existing systems in Europe are, of course, subject to the provision, so the criticism mainly concentrates not on the existence of the education, but the quality of it. Plainly this quality is dependent to a large extent on funding. It is arguable that this may be covered by the right to an "effective" education, but, so far, it is an issue which has not arisen before the ECtHR and given the present state of widespread economic hardship throughout Europe, as this passage is being written, it is possible that this may happen sooner rather than later.

C. CFR

[15–24] Article 14:

> "1. Everyone has the right to education and to have access to vocational and continuing training.
>
> 2. This right includes the possibility to receive free compulsory education.
>
> 3. The freedom to found educational establishments with due respect for democratic principles and the right of parents to ensure the education and teaching of their children in conformity with their religious, philosophical and pedagogical convictions shall be respected, in accordance with the national laws governing the exercise of such freedom and right."

This article is inspired by the common constitutional traditions of Member States and corresponds to Art 2 of Protocol 1 to the ECHR, as discussed previously. The CFR provisions have the same meaning and scope as the ECHR provisions in line with Art 52(3) of the CFR.[61] In addition, the CFR provision refers to vocational and continuing training, which is based on Art 10 of the European Social Charter.[62] Article 14 of the CFR also includes a provision on free compulsory education. This does not require that all establishments which provide education should do so free of charge, merely that each child should have the opportunity to attend an educational institution which does provide free education.

[15–25] Article 14(3) of the CFR should be read in conjunction with Art 16 relating to the freedom to conduct a business. The freedom of thought, conscience and religion, covered in Art 10 of the CFR should also be considered with regard to Art 14(3). The rights of the child are also protected in Art 24 of the CFR and the role of parents in a child's education enshrined in Art 14(3) is subject to the best interests of the child principle.

---

[61] See Explanations of the Praesidium of the Convention which drafted the Charter of Fundamental Rights of the European Union, available at: http://infoportal.fra.europa.eu/InfoPortal/infobaseShowContent.do?btnCat_182&btnCountryBread_169 (last accessed 28 June 2012).

[62] Revised European Social Charter 1996 ETS No 163.

The EU protects and promotes the right to education in various other ways apart from the CFR. For example, the right to education in a vocational context is also enshrined in the Community Charter of Fundamental Social Rights of Workers, adopted by the Heads of State of Government 1989. Paragraph 15 states:

> "Every worker of the European Community must be able to have access to vocational training and to receive such training throughout his working life. In the conditions governing access to such training there may be no discrimination of grounds of nationality
>
> The competent public authorities, undertakings or the social partners, each within their own sphere of competence, should set up continuing and permanent training systems enabling every person to undergo retraining, more especially through leave for training purposes, to improve his skills or to acquire new skills, particularly in the light of technological developments."

The EU Commission, especially through its Directorate-General Education and Culture facilitates co-operation between Member States in the fields of education and training.[63]

D. International and Regional Laws

The right to education has been included in numerous international and regional human rights instruments. Article 26 of the Universal Declaration of Human Rights (UDHR) provides that "Everyone has the right to education". This provision also discusses the nature of this right, focusing on how education can aid personal development and the international community by facilitating understanding of others. [15–26]

> "Education shall be directed to the full development of the human personality and to the strengthening of respect for human rights and fundamental freedoms. It shall promote understanding, tolerance and friendship among all nations, racial or religious groups, and shall further the activities of the United Nations for the maintenance of peace."

The importance of this right, and the rationale for including it in international human rights instruments is explained by Smith, who states that "the key to securing the universality of human rights lies in the right to education."[64]

The United Nations Economic, Scientific and Cultural Organisation (UNESCO) adopted the Convention against Discrimination in Education in 1960, building on the principle of non-discrimination and the right to education in the 1948 Declaration.

The right to education is also enshrined in Art 13 of the International Covenant of Economic, Social and Cultural Rights, Art 7 of the Convention on the Elimination of Racial Discrimination and Art 29 of the Convention on the Rights of the Child. The nature of the right has been further clarified by General Comment 1 of the Committee on the Rights of the Child, where education was identified as "an indispensable tool" in facilitating children: [15–27]

---

[63] See http://ec.europa.eu/education/external-relation-programmes/overview_en.htm, last accessed 28 June 2012.

[64] R Smith, *Textbook on International Human Rights* (5th ed, Oxford University Press, Oxford, 2012), p 329.

> " . . . to achieve in the course of his or her life a balanced, human rights-friendly response to the challenges that accompany a period of fundamental change driven by globalization, new technologies and related phenomenon."[65]

The right to education of people with disabilities is addressed in Art 24 of the UN Convention on People with Disabilities.[66] Article 24(1) provides that "States Parties recognize the right of persons with disabilities to education".

[15–28] In December 2011, the General Assembly of the United Nations (UN) adopted Declaration on Human Rights Education and Training which acknowledges:

> " . . . the fundamental importance of human rights education and training in contributing to the promotion, protection and effective realization of all human rights".[67]

At a regional level, the right to education is also protected under Art 13 of the Additional Protocol of 1988 to the American Convention on Human Rights 1969,[68] Art 25 of the African Charter of Human and Peoples' Rights 1981[69] and Art 41 of the Arab Charter of Human Rights 2004.[70]

---

[65] "The Aims of Education", General Comment 1 (2001) on the Convention on the Rights of the Child, CRC/GC/2001/1.

[66] UN Convention on the Rights of People with Disabilities 2006.

[67] UN Declaration on Human Rights Education and Training 2011, Preamble.

[68] Art 13 states: "1. Everyone has the right to education. 2. The States Parties to this Protocol agree that education should be directed towards the full development of the human personality and human dignity and should strengthen respect for human rights, ideological pluralism, fundamental freedoms, justice and peace. They further agree that education ought to enable everyone to participate effectively in a democratic and pluralistic society and achieve a decent existence and should foster understanding, tolerance and friendship among all nations and all racial, ethnic or religious groups and promote activities for the maintenance of peace. 3. The States Parties to this Protocol recognize that in order to achieve the full exercise of the right to education: a. Primary education should be compulsory and accessible to all without cost; b. Secondary education in its different forms, including technical and vocational secondary education, should be made generally available and accessible to all by every appropriate means, and in particular, by the progressive introduction of free education; c. Higher education should be made equally accessible to all, on the basis of individual capacity, by every appropriate means, and in particular, by the progressive introduction of free education; d. Basic education should be encouraged or intensified as far as possible for those persons who have not received or completed the whole cycle of primary instruction; e. Programs of special education should be established for the handicapped, so as to provide special instruction and training to persons with physical disabilities or mental deficiencies. 4. In conformity with the domestic legislation of the States Parties, parents should have the right to select the type of education to be given to their children, provided that it conforms to the principles set forth above. 5. Nothing in this Protocol shall be interpreted as a restriction of the freedom of individuals and entities to establish and direct educational institutions in accordance with the domestic legislation of the States Parties".

[69] Art 25 states: "States parties to the present Charter shall have the duty to promote and ensure through teaching, education and publication, the respect of the rights and freedoms contained in thepresent Charter and to see to it that these freedoms and rights as well as correspondingobligations and duties are understood."

[70] Art 41 states: "1. The eradication of illiteracy is a binding obligation upon the State and everyone has the right to education. 2. The States parties shall guarantee their citizens free education at least throughout the primary and basic levels. All forms and levels of primary

Conclusion

The importance of the right to education has been increasingly recognised in recent years in human rights discourse, at national and regional levels. The constitutional protection of the right to education is quite restrictive, and focuses on the rights of the family in educating the child rather than on the inherent right of a child to obtain an education and to develop his or her abilities and talents to the best of his or her potential. The right to education, being a socio-economic right, was originally omitted from the ECHR, which focused on civil and political rights. However, the increasing importance of the right was recognised by the inclusion of the right to education in the first Optional Protocol to the ECHR. The formulation of the right to education in this instrument differs from the Irish constitutional position, being more explicit in its protection of the right to education, although the provision is negatively phrased. The ECHR provision does, however, echo the Irish constitutional protection of the role of parents in the education of their children. The CFR has expanded the right to education to apply to vocational and continuing training. Such an expansion would be welcome in an Irish context. Irish law would also benefit from looking to the protection of the right to education enshrined in international human rights instruments, which offer a more explicit protection of the right and are more child-centred in their emphasis. **[15–29]**

---

education shall be compulsory and accessible to all without discrimination of any kind. 3. The States parties shall take appropriate measures in all domains to ensure partnership between men and women with a view to achieving national development goals. 4. The States parties shall guarantee to provide education directed to the full development of the human person and to strengthening respect for human rights and fundamental freedoms. 5. The States parties shall endeavour to incorporate the principles of human rights and fundamental freedoms into formal and informal education curricula and educational and training programmes. 6. The States parties shall guarantee the establishment of the mechanisms necessary to provide ongoing education for every citizen and shall develop national plans for adult education."

INDEX